ACCOUNTING PRINCIPLES

THIRD CANADIAN EDITION

ACCOUNTING PRINCIPLES

▶ **JERRY J. WEYGANDT** *Ph.D., C.P.A.*

Arthur Andersen Alumni Professor of Accounting
University of Wisconsin—Madison

▶ **DONALD E. KIESO** *Ph.D., C.P.A.*

KPMG Emeritus Professor of Accountancy
Northern Illinois University

▶ **PAUL D. KIMMEL** *Ph.D., C.P.A.*

University of Wisconsin—Milwaukee

▶ **BARBARA TRENHOLM** *M.B.A., F.C.A.*

University of New Brunswick—Fredericton

IN COLLABORATION WITH

▶ **VALERIE KINNEAR** *B.S.W., M.Sc. (Bus. Admin.), C.A*

Mount Royal College

John Wiley & Sons Canada, Ltd.

To our students — past, present, and future

National Library of Canadian Cataloguing in Publication Data

Jerry J. Weygandt
    Accounting principles

3rd Canadian ed.

Includes index.
ISBN 0-470-83375-0 (pt. 1)
ISBN 0-470-83376-9 (pt. 2)
ISBN 0-470-83378-5 (pt. 3)
ISBN 0-470-83438-2 (pt. 4)

    1. Accounting. I. Weygandt, Jerry J

HF5635.A3778 2003   657'.044   C2003-905260-5

Production Credits

Publisher: John Horne
Editorial Manager: Karen Staudinger
Publishing Services Director: Karen Bryan
Developmental Editor: Zoë Craig
Senior Marketing Manager: Janine Daoust
Manager, Business and Online Marketing: Carolyn J. Wells
New Media Editor: Elsa Passera
Editorial Assistant: Gail Brown
Design & Typesetting: Appleby Color Lab
Cover Design: Interrobang Graphic Design
CD Design & Programming: Ian Koo/Tia Seifert
Printing & Binding: Tri-Graphic Printing Limited

Printed and bound in Canada
10 9 8 7 6 5 4 3 2 1

John Wiley & Sons Canada, Ltd.
6045 Freemont Blvd.
Mississauga, Ontario L5R 4J3
Visit our website at: www.wiley.ca

Tejal Govande

Part One

Part Two

Part Three

Part Four

concepts for review >>

Before studying this chapter, you should understand or, if necessary, review:

a. The organization primarily responsible for setting accounting standards in Canada. (Ch. 1, p. 7)

b. The going concern assumption, the monetary unit assumption, the economic entity assumption, and the time period assumption. (Ch. 1, pp. 8–9 and Ch. 3, p. 101)

c. The cost principle, the revenue recognition principle, and the matching principle. (Ch. 1, p. 7 and Ch. 3, p. 101)

Corridor Pipeline a Lengthy Deal

Terasen Pipelines: www.terasenpipelines.com

FORT McMURRAY, Alta.—The Athabasca Oil Sands in Northern Alberta form the world's largest known hydrocarbon basin—77,000 square kilometres of sand, mineral rich clay, and water and bitumen, a type of thick crude oil. The region contains more than 5 billion barrels of mineable bitumen—more than twice the volume of conventional oil reserves left in Alberta.

In 1999, Shell Canada, along with Chevron Canada and Western Oil Sands Inc., launched the Athabasca Oil Sands Project, an undertaking that will see 1.65 billion barrels of bitumen extracted over the next 30 years. Key components of the project include the Muskeg River Mine, north of Fort McMurray, where bitumen is recovered through open-pit mining, and the Scotford upgrader, northeast of Edmonton, where the diluted bitumen is upgraded into a light synthetic crude oil.

The crucial link between the sites is the 493-kilometre Corridor pipeline, a dual pipeline system comprising a 12-inch line that carries diluent, or solvent, from Edmonton north to the mine and a 24-inch line that brings the diluted bitumen south to the upgrader, located near Shell's refinery. A section of the pipeline also transports supplemental feedstocks (diluted bitumen) and synthetic products between the upgrader and marketing terminals near Edmonton. From there, the synthetic oil is sent to refineries throughout North America to be converted into gasoline, diesel, jet fuel, and petrochemicals.

The Corridor pipeline was financed by Terasen Pipelines (Corridor) Inc., a wholly owned subsidiary of Terasen Inc. (formerly BC Gas). Costs, including engi-neering design, materials, financing charges, and tank fill and system start-up costs, reached $690 million.

Terasen Pipelines awarded a $70-million contract to construct the pipeline to Alberta-based Midwest Management Ltd., a subsidiary of the international engineering services firm AMEC. Midwest began the work in July 2000 and completed the project two years later, in August 2002. The system's pumping, metering, and storage facilities were built by Quebec-based SNC-Lavalin Inc. as part of a $100-million contract.

The Athabasca Oil Sands Project became fully operational in April 2003 and the following month the pipeline began carrying throughput at a rate of 72,000 cubic metres a day. While the system was constructed to serve the needs of Shell and its partners, it may eventually serve other shippers as well.

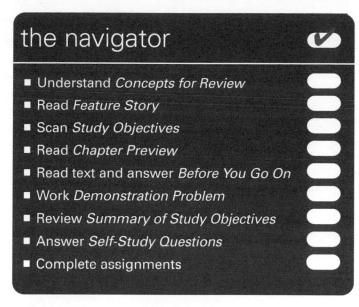

chapter 11

Accounting Principles

study objectives >>

the navigator

After studying this chapter, you should be able to:

1. Explain the meaning of generally accepted accounting principles and identify the key items of the conceptual framework.
2. Describe the basic objective of financial reporting.
3. Describe the qualitative characteristics of accounting information and apply them to the elements of financial statements.
4. Identify and apply the basic assumptions used by accountants.
5. Identify and apply the basic principles of accounting.
6. Identify and apply the constraints in accounting.
7. Explain the purpose of international accounting standards.

What you have learned up to this point in your accounting principles course is a process that leads to the preparation of a company's financial statements. These statements must effectively communicate financial information to users. In order to do so, generally accepted accounting principles must be respected. Otherwise, we would have to be familiar with every company's particular accounting and reporting practices in order to understand its financial statements. It would be difficult, if not impossible, to compare the financial results of different companies.

This chapter explores the conceptual framework used to develop generally accepted accounting principles. The chapter is organized as follows:

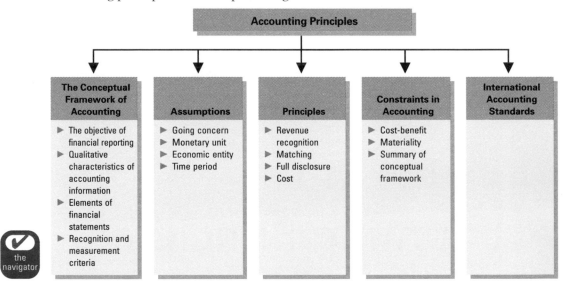

The Conceptual Framework of Accounting

study objective 1

Explain the meaning of generally accepted accounting principles and identify the key items of the conceptual framework.

The accounting profession has established a set of standards and rules that are recognized as a general guide for financial reporting. This recognized set of standards is called **generally accepted accounting principles (GAAP)**. "Generally accepted" means that these principles have substantial authoritative support through the Canadian and provincial business corporations acts and securities legislation. All companies whose shares or debt are publicly traded must follow GAAP. Most other companies also follow GAAP as it provides the most useful information.

GAAP is established by the CICA's Accounting Standards Board (AcSB). The Accounting Standards Oversight Council (AcSOC) oversees the activities of the AcSB and provides input. The AcSOC is composed of senior members from business, finance, government, universities, the accounting and legal professions, regulators, and the financial analyst community. These members have a broad perspective on the issues facing standard-setters.

A complete conceptual framework is published in the *CICA Handbook*, which outlines accounting and auditing recommendations and guidelines. Section 1000 of the handbook, "Financial Statements Concepts," presents the concepts that underlie the development and use of accounting principles. These concepts guide the choice of what to present in financial statements, decisions about alternative ways of reporting economic events, and the selection of appropriate ways of communicating such information. This

Helpful hint Accounting principles are affected by economic and political conditions, which change over time. As a result, accounting principles are not carved in stone, unlike the periodic table in chemistry or a formula in math.

increases the usefulness of financial statements. It also shows the limitations of accounting.

The conceptual framework is designed to:

1. Ensure that existing standards and practices are coherent and consistent
2. Provide a structure to permit a quick response to new issues
3. Increase the understandability, relevance, reliability, and comparability of financial reporting results

It is impossible to create accounting principles for all existing and future situations. Consequently, GAAP specifies a hierarchy of sources from which to seek guidance. In general, primary sources—such as those found in the *CICA Handbook*, in accounting guidelines, and in emerging issues abstracts—should be looked at first. These primary sources are listed, in descending order of authority, in Section 1100 of the handbook, "Generally Accepted Accounting Principles."

Where the primary sources of GAAP do not deal with a situation, the company should look to other sources—such as pronouncements of other accounting standard-setting bodies, research studies, and information found in accounting textbooks and journals. However, the overriding criterion is that any accounting principles applied using other sources must always be consistent with the primary sources of GAAP and the conceptual framework.

Professional judgement plays an especially important role in determining which accounting alternatives are consistent with GAAP and the conceptual framework. The Canadian philosophy with respect to setting standards is that it is impractical and impossible to specify a rule for every situation. Canadian standards—in contrast with standards in some other countries—are based on general principles rather than specific rules. Accountants can then use professional judgement, acquired through education and experience, in applying the conceptual framework to any situation.

The conceptual framework consists of four major sections:

1. The objective of financial reporting
2. The qualitative characteristics of accounting information
3. The elements of financial statements
4. Recognition and measurement criteria (assumptions, principles, and constraints)

We will discuss these sections in the following pages.

The Objective of Financial Reporting

Determining the objective of financial reporting requires answers to such basic questions as these: Who uses financial statements? Why? What information do the users need? How knowledgeable about business and accounting are financial statement users? How should financial information be reported so that it is best understood?

The primary objective of financial reporting is to provide useful information for decision-making. More specifically, the conceptual framework states that the objective of financial statements is to communicate information that is useful to investors, creditors, and other users in making resource allocation decisions and in assessing management stewardship.

In order to make resource allocation decisions (e.g., about investing or lending), users look for information in the financial statements about a company's ability to earn income and generate future cash flows. In order to assess management stewardship, users use the information in the financial statements to determine whether or not management acquired and used the company's resources in an optimal way. Consequently, financial statements must provide information about the following:

1. Economic resources (assets), obligations (liabilities), and equity
2. Changes in economic resources, obligations, and equity
3. Economic performance

study objective 2

Describe the basic objective of financial reporting.

The conceptual framework also describes the characteristics that make accounting information useful.

Qualitative Characteristics of Accounting Information

study objective 3

Describe the qualitative characteristics of accounting information and apply them to the elements of financial statements.

How does a company like The Forzani Group Ltd. decide how much financial information to disclose? In what format should its financial information be presented? How should assets, liabilities, revenues, and expenses be measured? In accordance with the objective of financial reporting, the primary criterion for judging such accounting choices is **decision usefulness**. The accounting practice selected should be the one that generates the most useful financial information for making a decision. To be useful, information should possess the following qualitative characteristics: understandability, relevance, reliability, and comparability.

Understandability

In order for the information provided in financial statements to be useful, it must be understandable to the users. Financial statements cannot realistically satisfy the varied needs of all users. Consequently, the objective of financial statements focuses primarily on the information needs of investors and creditors. Even within these two groups, users may vary widely in the types of decisions they make and in their level of interest in the information. At one extreme is a sophisticated creditor who carefully scrutinizes all aspects of the financial information. At the other extreme is an unsophisticated shareholder who may only scan the text and not study the numbers.

It is therefore necessary to establish a base level of **understandability** to assist both the preparer of financial information and its user. **The average user is assumed to have a reasonable understanding of accounting concepts and procedures, as well as of general business and economic conditions.** If this level of understanding does not exist, the user is expected to rely on professionals with appropriate expertise. By taking this course, you are well on your way to becoming an average user!

Relevance

Accounting information has **relevance** if it makes a difference in a decision. Relevant information has predictive or feedback value, or both. **Predictive value** helps users forecast future events. For example, when Forzani issues financial statements, the information in them is considered relevant because it provides a basis for predicting future earnings. **Feedback value** confirms or corrects prior expectations. When Forzani issues financial statements, it also confirms or corrects expectations about its financial health.

In addition, accounting information has relevance if it is **timely**. It must be available to decision-makers before it loses its ability to influence decisions. Many people believe that by the time annual financial statements are issued—sometimes up to six months after year end—the information has limited usefulness for decision-making. Timely *interim* financial reporting is essential to relevant decision-making.

Reliability

Accounting information has **reliability** if it is free of error and bias. In short, it can be depended on. To be reliable, accounting information must be **verifiable**: we must be able to prove that it is free of error and bias. It must also be a **faithful representation** of the economic substance, not just the form, of the transaction. To ensure reliability, external professional accountants audit financial statements. The Canadian Public Accountability Board further enhances reliability by providing independent oversight of the auditors of public companies.

Accounting information must also be **neutral**. It cannot be selected, prepared, or presented to favour one set of interested users over another. These three characteristics—verifiability, faithful representation, and neutrality—are often combined and called objectivity. Objectivity means that two individuals, each working independently, can review the same information and reach the same results or similar conclusions. Objectivity is affected by the use of **conservatism** in situations of uncertainty. **Conservatism** in accounting means that, when preparing financial statements, a company should choose the method that will be least likely to overstate assets and income. It does **not** mean, however, deliberately understating assets or income.

Comparability

Accounting information about a company is most useful when it can be compared with accounting information about other companies. Comparability results when different companies use the same accounting principles.

At one level, accounting principles are fairly comparable because they are based on generally accepted accounting principles. These principles, however, do allow for some variation. For example, there are a variety of ways to determine the cost of inventory. Often, these different cost flow assumptions result in different amounts of net income. As we will learn later in this chapter, the **full disclosure principle** makes comparisons of companies easier, as each company must disclose the accounting principles it uses. From the disclosures, the external user can determine whether the financial information is comparable.

Comparability is easier when accounting policies are used consistently. **Consistency** means that a company uses the same accounting principles from year to year. If a company selects FIFO as its inventory cost flow assumption in the first year of operations, it is expected to use FIFO in succeeding years. When financial information has been reported on a consistent basis, the financial statements permit meaningful analysis of trends within a company.

A company *can* change to a new accounting principle. Sometimes a change in accounting principle is mandated by the CICA, such as the implementation of the new standard on impairment of long-lived assets. At other times, it may be management's choice to change to a new accounting principle. To do so, management must prove that the new principle results in a reliable and more relevant financial presentation in the statements.

In the year in which a change in an accounting principle occurs, the change (and its impact) must be disclosed in the notes to the financial statements. This disclosure makes users of the financial statements aware of the lack of consistency. In addition, the past years of corporate performance must be presented as if the new accounting principle had been used in those years.

The qualitative characteristics of accounting information are summarized in Illustration 11-1.

Illustration 11-1 ◄

Qualitative characteristics of accounting information

Understandability	Relevance	Reliability	Comparability
1. Of accounting concepts and procedures.	1. Provides a basis for forecasts.	1. Is verifiable.	1. Different companies use similar accounting principles.
2. Of general business and economic conditions.	2. Confirms or corrects prior expectations.	2. Is a faithful representation.	2. A company uses the same accounting principles consistently from year to year.
	3. Is timely.	3. Is neutral.	
		4. Is conservative.	

Trade-Offs Between Qualitative Characteristics

Many accounting choices require trade-offs between qualitative characteristics. For example, there is often a trade-off between relevance and reliability. That is, there may be a trade-off between ensuring that financial information is produced on a timely basis and verifying the accuracy of the information included. In order to produce financial statements annually, estimates are required. These estimates reduce the accuracy of the information provided. However, if we were to wait until estimates were no longer necessary for things like uncollectible accounts, useful lives of property, plant, and equipment, and warranty recalls, the financial information would no longer be relevant. The conceptual framework does not always provide obvious solutions to accounting issues such as these. Rather, it enables professionals to judge the appropriate balance between these characteristics in a particular situation.

Elements of Financial Statements

An important part of the conceptual framework is a set of definitions that describe the basic terms used in accounting. This set of definitions is referred to as the **elements of financial statements**. They include such terms as assets, liabilities, equity, revenues, and expenses.

Because these elements are so important, they must be precisely defined and universally applied. Finding the appropriate definition for many of these elements is not easy. For example, should the value of a company's employees be reported as an asset on a balance sheet? Should the death of the company's president be reported as a loss? A good set of definitions should provide answers to these types of questions. Because you have already encountered most of these definitions in earlier chapters, they are not repeated here.

Recognition and Measurement Criteria

The objective of financial reporting, the qualitative characteristics of accounting information, and the elements of financial statements are very broad. Because accountants must solve practical problems, more detailed criteria are needed. **Recognition criteria help determine when items should be included or recognized in the financial statements. Measurement criteria outline how to measure or assign an amount to those items.** We classify these criteria as assumptions, principles, and constraints.

Assumptions provide a foundation for the accounting process. **Principles** indicate how economic events should be reported in the accounting process. **Constraints** allow a relaxation of the principles under certain circumstances. Illustration 11-2 outlines these recognition and measurement criteria (you know some of them from earlier chapters). They are discussed in more detail in the following sections.

Illustration 11-2 ▶

Recognition and
measurement criteria

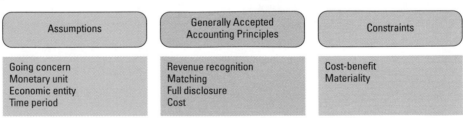

Assumptions	Generally Accepted Accounting Principles	Constraints
Going concern Monetary unit Economic entity Time period	Revenue recognition Matching Full disclosure Cost	Cost-benefit Materiality

BEFORE YOU GO ON . . .

►Review It

1. What are generally accepted accounting principles?
2. What is stated about generally accepted accounting principles in the Auditors' Report found in the financial statements of The Forzani Group Ltd.? The answer to this question is at the end of the chapter.
3. What is the basic objective of financial information?
4. What are the qualitative characteristics that make accounting information useful? Give an example of a trade-off between qualitative characteristics.

Related exercise material: BE11–1, BE11–2, BE11–3, BE11–4, BE11–5, and E11–1.

Assumptions

Assumptions provide a foundation for the accounting process. You already know the major assumptions from preceding chapters—the going concern, monetary unit, economic entity, and time period assumptions. We will review them here briefly.

study objective 4

Identify and apply the basic assumptions used by accountants

Going Concern Assumption

The **going concern assumption** assumes that the company will continue operating for the foreseeable future—that is, long enough to carry out its existing objectives. In spite of business failures, most companies have a fairly high continuance rate. The accounting implications of this assumption are critical. If a going concern assumption is not used, then assets such as buildings and equipment should be stated at their liquidation value (selling price less cost of disposal)—not at their historical cost. Amortization of these assets would not be needed. In each period, these assets would simply be reported at their anticipated liquidation value. Also, without this assumption, the current/long-term classification of assets and liabilities would not matter. Labeling anything as long-term would be difficult to justify.

Acceptance of the going concern assumption gives credibility to the cost principle. The only time the going concern assumption should not be applied is when liquidation appears likely. In that case, assets would be better stated at liquidation value than at cost.

ACCOUNTING IN ACTION ► Business Insight

On April 1, 2003, Air Canada filed for bankruptcy protection under the *Companies' Creditors Arrangement Act* (CCAA). Filing for protection under the CCAA gives companies time to reorganize their operations and hold talks with their major stakeholders—creditors, bondholders, unions, and suppliers. While CCAA protection is in place, creditors are prevented from taking any action against the airline. Financial statements issued by Air Canada while under CCAA were issued on a going concern, and not a liquidation, basis.

Air Canada said it planned on using US$700 million in special "debtor-in-possession" financing to keep operating while it restructured. "Air Canada is determined to do all in its power to restructure itself through this process and emerge as a world-class competitive and profitable airline," an airline affidavit filed with the Ontario Superior Court of Justice said.

Source: CBC News, *"Air Canada Granted Bankruptcy Protection,"* April 2, 2003.

Monetary Unit Assumption

The **monetary unit assumption** states that only transaction data that can be expressed in terms of money should be included in the accounting records. For example, the value of a company president would not be reported in a company's financial records because it cannot be expressed in dollars.

An important counterpart to the monetary unit assumption is the assumption that the unit of measure remains stable over time. That is, any effects of inflation (or deflation) are assumed to be minor and are therefore ignored.

Economic Entity Assumption

The **economic entity assumption** states that the activities of the entity must be kept separate and distinct from the activities of the shareholders (owners) and of all other economic entities. For example, it is assumed that the activities of Terasen Pipelines in our feature story can be distinguished from those of its parent company, Terasen Inc.

Time Period Assumption

The **time period assumption** states that the economic life of a business can be divided into artificial time periods. In other words, it is assumed that the activities of companies, such as Forzani or Terasen Pipelines, can be subdivided into months, quarters, or years for meaningful financial reporting purposes.

As discussed in Chapter 3, time periods of less than one year are called **interim** periods. Periods of one year are known as **fiscal** years or, if extending from January through December, **calendar** years. Public companies are required to present both quarterly (interim) and annual financial statements.

BEFORE YOU GO ON . . .

►Review It

1. What are the going concern assumption, the monetary unit assumption, the economic entity assumption, and the time period assumption?

Related exercise material: E11–2.

Principles

study objective 5

Identify and apply the basic principles of accounting.

From the fundamental assumptions of accounting described in the preceding section, the accounting profession has developed principles that dictate how economic events should be recorded and reported. In earlier chapters, we discussed the cost principle (Chapter 1) and the revenue recognition and matching principles (Chapter 3). We now examine a number of reporting issues related to these principles. In addition, another principle, the full disclosure principle, is discussed.

Revenue Recognition Principle

The **revenue recognition principle** says that revenue should be recognized in the accounting period in which it is earned. Applying this general principle can be difficult.

In Chapter 3, for example, we noted how difficult it was for Warner Bros. to estimate its *Harry Potter* revenues and match these revenues with expenses.

Another example is apparent in long-term construction projects. For example, Terasen Pipelines had the Corridor pipeline built over a two-year period, as discussed in our feature story. It incurred $690 million of costs paid to various companies between the years 2000 and 2002 to build the pipeline. However, no revenue was received until May 2003 when the pipeline began operating. In situations such as this, when should revenues be recorded and how should they be matched to expenses?

Revenue recognition guidelines help accountants determine when to recognize revenue. More specifically, revenue should be recognized when all of the guidelines below are met:

1. The production and/or sales effort is substantially complete.
2. Revenues can be objectively measured.
3. Collection is reasonably assured (an estimate can be made of amounts expected to be uncollectible).
4. Material expenses can be determined and matched.

Depending on the circumstances, the four criteria for revenue recognition can be satisfied at various points in time. These points range from at the point of sale to the later collection of cash. The most common points of revenue recognition are as follows:

1. At point of sale
2. During production
3. At completion of production
4. Upon collection of cash

ACCOUNTING IN ACTION ► Ethics Insight

There have been many high profile cases highlighting the improper application of the revenue recognition principle. These include the Livent, Enron, Lucent Technologies, Qwest Communications, Xerox, and AOL Time Warner cases, among others. Why did this happen? It happened because the revenue recognition principle has become increasingly difficult to apply as revenue-generating activities have become more innovative and complex. These activities include "swap" transactions, "bill and hold" sales arrangements, risk-sharing agreements, complex rights of return, price-protection guarantees, and post-sale maintenance contracts.

The revenue recognition principle has been pushed to its limits by the variety of possible interpretations of these activities. In addition, many companies felt pressure to report increasing income and deliberately advanced the reporting of revenue, or inflated revenue, to make their companies appear more profitable than they actually were.

Regulators and standard-setters now have this difficult topic at the top of their agendas.

Point of Sale

When a sale is involved, revenue is usually recognized at the **point of sale**. Consider a sale by Forzani. At the point of sale, the customer pays the cash and takes the merchandise. The company records the sale by debiting Cash and crediting Sales Revenue. If the sale were on account rather than for cash (assuming the company accepts credit sales, and the customer has a good credit rating), the company would record the sale by debiting Accounts Receivable and crediting Sales Revenue. This is the most common point of revenue recognition for goods and services. The product is complete and delivered, revenue can be objectively measured, collection has occurred or is reasonably assured, and expenses can be matched to the revenue.

Helpful hint Revenue should be recognized in the accounting period in which it is earned. This may not be the period in which the related cash is received. In a retail establishment, the point of sale is usually the critical point in the process of earning revenue.

During Production

Helpful hint Billing practices of professional accounting firms are another example of recognizing revenue during production. If a firm undertakes a job for a client that lasts for more than one month, the client is usually billed monthly for the hours of service provided and for any expenditures incurred to date.

In long-term construction contracts, revenue recognition is usually possible (and desirable) before the contract is completed. For example, assume that Warrior Construction Co. has a contract to build a dam for the Province of British Columbia for $400 million. Construction is estimated to take three years (starting early in 2004) at a cost of $360 million. If Warrior recognizes revenue only at the point of sale, it will report no revenues and no profit in the first two years. When completion and sale take place, in 2006, Warrior will report $400 million in revenues, costs of $360 million, and the entire profit of $40 million. Did Warrior really produce no revenues and earn no profit in 2004 and 2005? Obviously not. The earnings process is considered substantially completed at various stages. Therefore, revenue should be recognized as construction progresses during production.

The **percentage-of-completion method** recognizes revenue on a long-term project on the basis of reasonable estimates of the progress toward completion. First, progress toward completion is measured by comparing the costs incurred in a period to the total estimated costs for the entire project. Second, that percentage is multiplied by the total revenue for the project. The result is then recognized as revenue for the period. Third, the costs incurred in the current period are then subtracted from the revenue recognized during the current period to arrive at the gross profit. The formulas for this method are presented in Illustration 11-3.

Illustration 11-3 ▶

Formula to recognize revenue and gross profit—percentage-of-completion method

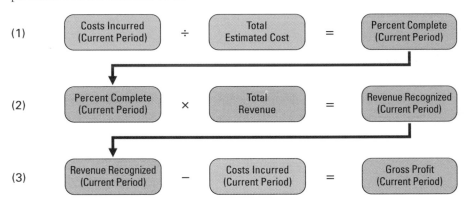

Let's look at an illustration of the percentage-of-completion method. Assume that Warrior Construction Co. has costs of $54 million in 2004, $180 million in 2005, and $126 million in 2006 on the dam project. The portion of the $400 million of revenue and gross profit recognized in each of the three years is shown below (all amounts are stated in millions):

Year	Costs Incurred (Current Period)	÷	Total Estimated Cost	=	Percent Complete (Current Period)	×	Total Revenue	=	Revenue Recognized (Current Period)	−	Costs Incurred (Current Period)	=	Gross Profit (Current Period)
2004	$ 54		$360		15%		$400		$ 60		$ 54		$ 6
2005	180		360		50%		400		200		180		20
2006	126		360		35%		400		140		126		14
Totals	$360								$400		$360		$40

In this example, the company's cost estimates were totally accurate. The costs incurred in the third year brought the total cost to $360 million—exactly what had been estimated. In reality, this does not always happen. Revisions of remaining estimates may be necessary as additional information becomes available.

When a revision of an estimate occurs, an additional step is added to the formula shown above in Illustration 11-3. Illustration 11-4 shows this new step (now step 3) and some minor adjustments to the wording of the formula as highlighted:

Illustration 11-4 ◄

Revising percentage-of-completion method

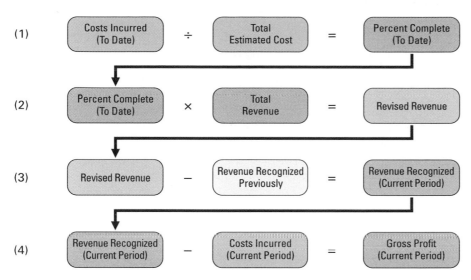

As is done when changing estimates of useful lives or residual values for amortization, the percentage-of-completion method data are only changed for current and future years, rather than retroactively. The percent complete is revised according to the new total estimated costs. A **cumulative percentage** is used, which is calculated by dividing the costs incurred to date by the revised total estimated cost. This formula is similar to the one shown in step 1 of Illustration 11-3, except that the costs incurred are cumulative (to date) rather than just for the current period.

Similar to step 2 of Illustration 11-3, this cumulative percentage is then multiplied by total revenue to determine the revised revenue amount. In a new step, not used when actual costs equal estimated costs, the revenue recognized previously is now deducted from the revised revenue. This has to be done in order to account for previously recorded amounts and "catch up" the difference in the estimate.

The remaining step (now step 4) is the same as step 3 demonstrated in Illustration 11-3, where actual costs are deducted from revenue to determine the amount of gross profit to recognize, as shown below.

To apply this formula for a change in estimate, assume the costs estimated to complete the dam project change partway through the three-year contract period for Warrier Construction Co. In 2005, the estimated total cost rises to $390 million, from its earlier estimate of $360 million. Actual costs incurred are $200 million in 2005 and $136 million in 2006.

The revised calculations for revenue, cost, and gross profit are shown below (all amounts in millions).

Year	Costs Incurred (To Date)	÷	Total Estimated Cost	=	Percent Complete (To Date)	×	Total Revenue	=	Revised Revenue	−	Revenue Recognized Previously	=	Revenue Recognized (Current Period)	−	Cost Incurred (Current Period)	=	Gross Profit (Current Period)
2004	$ 54		$360		15.0%		$400		$ 60.0		$ 0.0		$ 60.0		$ 54		$ 6.0
2005	254		390		65.1%		400		260.4		60.0		200.4		200		0.4
2006	390		390		100.0%		400		400.0		260.4		139.6		136		3.6
Totals													$400.0		$390		$10.0

The calculations for 2004 are unchanged from those shown on the previous page. However, because of the change in estimate in 2005, the revenue, cost, and gross profit change in 2005 and 2006. In 2005, the $254 million ($54 million in 2004 and $200 million in 2005) of actual costs incurred are shown on a cumulative basis. These costs are multiplied by the revised total estimated cost of $390 million in order to determine the percentage complete to date, 65.1%. This cumulative percentage is multiplied by total revenue to determine the revised revenue figure. This revenue amount, $260.4 million, includes the $60 million of revenue that was recognized in 2004. Therefore, the amount of revenue to be recognized in the current period is $200.4 million ($260.4 million − $60 million). The actual cost incurred for the period is then deducted from the revenue recognized in the same period to determine the gross profit.

In 2006, when the project is complete, costs incurred to date now total $390 million ($54 million in 2004, $200 million in 2005, and $136 million in 2006). One hundred percent of the contract revenue less any amounts recognized previously ($400 million − $260.4 million) is recognized in the current period. The actual cost incurred for the period is deducted from the revenue recognized in the same period to determine the gross profit.

The total contract revenue remains unchanged. However, the total cost rose from $360 million to $390 million after the change in estimate. Correspondingly, total gross profit fell from $40 million to $10 million because of the increased costs.

Sometimes there are cost overruns in the last year of a contract. In such cases, the remaining amount of revenue and cost are recognized in that year and the relevant percentage is ignored.

Use of the percentage-of-completion method involves some subjectivity. Errors are possible in determining the amount of revenue to be recognized and gross profit to be reported. But to wait until completion would seriously distort each period's financial statements. Naturally, **if it is not possible to obtain dependable estimates of costs and progress, then the revenue should be recognized at the completion of production** and not by the percentage-of-completion method.

Completion of Production

If Warrior Construction Co. were not able to estimate its costs with any degree of reliability, it would wait until the completion of production to recognize revenue. This is known as the **completed-contract method**. Revenue of $400 million, revised costs of $390 million, and a gross profit of $10 million would be reported at the completion of production in the year 2006. It is not until production is complete, in this case, that revenue, expenses, and gross profit can be reasonably determined.

Collection of Cash

Another basis for revenue recognition is the receipt of cash. The **cash basis** is generally used only when it is very difficult to determine the revenue amount at the time of a credit sale because collection is uncertain. The cash basis is sometimes used to account for instalment sales, which can have a greater risk of collectibility. Because of this, this revenue recognition approach is known as the **instalment method**.

Many consumer products are sold as an instalment sale, where customers make payments over an extended period of time. Cars, computers, home appliances, and furnishings are often sold on an instalment payment plan. If the company meets the revenue recognition guidelines (in particular, if it has a reasonable basis for estimating uncollectible accounts), it recognizes revenue from instalment sales at the point of sale.

Sometimes, however, ultimate collection of the sales price cannot be estimated reasonably. In these cases, companies use the instalment method, recognizing revenue when the cash is collected rather than at the point of sale.

Under the instalment method, each cash collection from a customer consists of (1) a partial recovery of the cost of the goods sold, and (2) partial gross profit from the sale. For example, if the gross profit margin on the sale is 40%, each subsequent receipt of cash consists of 60% recovery of the cost of goods sold and 40% gross profit. The formula to recognize gross profit is as follows:

Illustration 11-5 ◄

Gross profit formula—instalment method

```
┌─────────────────┐       ┌──────────────┐       ┌──────────────────┐
│ Cash Collections│   ×   │ Gross Profit │   =   │   Gross Profit   │
│  from Customers │       │    Margin    │       │    Recognized    │
│                 │       │              │       │  (Current Period)│
└─────────────────┘       └──────────────┘       └──────────────────┘
```

To illustrate, assume that in its first year of operations, a Saskatchewan farm machinery dealer has instalment sales of $600,000, for which collection is uncertain. Its cost of goods sold on these instalment sales is $420,000. Total gross profit is $180,000 ($600,000 − $420,000). The gross profit margin is 30% ($180,000 ÷ $600,000). The collections on the instalment sales are as follows: first year, $280,000 (down payment plus monthly payments); second year, $200,000; and third year, $120,000. The gross profit recognized is shown below (interest charges are ignored in this illustration):

Year	Cash Collections from Customers	×	Gross Profit Margin	=	Gross Profit Recognized
2003	$280,000		30%		$ 84,000
2004	200,000		30%		60,000
2005	120,000		30%		36,000
Totals	$600,000				$180,000

Under the instalment method of accounting, gross profit is recognized in the period the cash is collected in. As indicated earlier, the instalment method is used only when there is a risk of not collecting an account receivable. In this case, the sale itself is not sufficient evidence for revenue to be recognized.

Matching Principle (Expense Recognition)

The expression "Let the expense follow the revenue," shows that expense recognition is traditionally tied to revenue recognition. As you learned in Chapter 3, this practice is referred to as the **matching principle**. It says that expenses must be matched with revenues in the period in which efforts are made to generate revenues. Expenses are not necessarily recognized when cash is paid, or when the work is performed, or when the product is produced. They are recognized when the labour (service) or the product actually makes its contribution to revenue.

It is sometimes difficult to determine the accounting period in which the expense contributed to revenues. Several approaches have been developed for matching expenses and revenues on the income statement.

To understand these approaches, you first need to understand the nature of costs. Costs that will only generate revenues in the current accounting period are expensed immediately. It is not always possible to specifically associate costs with revenue generation. For example, it is impossible to match administrative salaries or interest costs with the revenue they help earn. These costs are expensed immediately during the period in which they are incurred. They are reported as operating expenses in the income statement and are called **expired costs**.

Costs that will generate revenues in future accounting periods are recognized as assets. Examples include merchandise inventory and prepaid expenses. These costs represent **unexpired costs**. Unexpired costs become expenses in two ways:

1. **Cost of goods sold.** Costs carried as merchandise inventory become expenses when the inventory is sold. They are expensed as cost of goods sold in the period when the sale occurs. There is therefore a direct matching of expenses with revenues.
2. **Operating expenses.** Other unexpired costs become operating expenses through use or consumption (as with store supplies), or through the passage of time (as with prepaid insurance). Operating expenses contribute to the revenues of the period, but their association with revenues is less direct than that of cost of goods sold.

► **Ethics note**

Many appear to do it, but few like to discuss it. It's earnings management. It's a clear violation of the revenue recognition and matching principles. Companies may time the sale of investments or the expensing of bad debts to accomplish earnings objectives. Prominent companies have been accused of matching one-time gains with one-time write-offs so that current-period earnings are not so high that they can't be surpassed in the next period.

These points about expense recognition are shown in Illustration 11-6.

Illustration 11-6 ▶

Expense recognition pattern

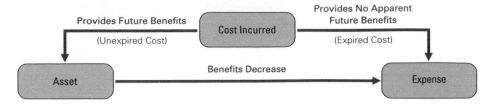

Full Disclosure Principle

The **full disclosure principle** requires companies to disclose circumstances and events which make a difference to financial statement users. Indeed, investors who lost money in Enron, WorldCom, and Global Crossing complained that the lack of full disclosure regarding some of the companies' transactions caused the financial statements to be misleading. Investors want to be made aware of events that can affect the financial health of a company.

The full disclosure principle is respected through two elements in the financial statements: the data they contain and the accompanying notes. The first note in most cases is a **summary of significant accounting policies**. The summary includes the methods used by the company when a choice is made between acceptable accounting principles. It presents, among others, the methods used for inventory costing and amortization. For example, The Forzani Group's first note in Appendix A at the end of this textbook discloses that the company has chosen the weighted average cost flow assumption and the declining-balance method of amortizing its building.

The information that is disclosed in the notes to the financial statements generally falls into three additional categories. These categories:

1. Provide supplementary detail or explanation (for example, a schedule of property, plant, and equipment)
2. Explain unrecorded transactions (for example, contingencies, commitments, subsequent events)
3. Supply new information (for example, information about related party transactions)

Deciding how much disclosure is enough can be difficult. Accountants could disclose every financial event that occurs and every contingency that exists. But the benefits of providing this additional information may be less than the cost of doing so. Determining where to draw the line on disclosure is not easy.

ACCOUNTING IN ACTION ▶ Business Insight

Companies preparing their annual reports are piling on the paper in order to ease Enron-type worries on the part of investors. In 2002, U.S.-based natural gas producer Williams Companies, Inc. turned out an eye-glazing annual report 1,234 pages long. Here in Canada, Nortel Networks Corporation added an extra two dozen pages to its annual report. Other companies have followed suit.

The trend to fuller disclosure has been a long time coming, observers say. But they caution that more paper does not necessarily mean more information that the average investor will understand. In addition, it is important to remember that annual reports are just one piece of the puzzle of information presented to decision-makers.

Source: Elizabeth Church, "No Item Too Small as Firms Cave to Enron Disclosure Craze," *The Globe and Mail,* April 1, 2002, B1.

Cost Principle

As you know, the **cost principle** requires assets to be recorded at cost. Cost is used because it is both relevant and reliable. Cost is **relevant** because it represents the price paid, the assets sacrificed, or the commitment made at the date of acquisition. Cost is **reliable** because it is objectively measurable, factual, and verifiable. It is the result of an exchange transaction. Cost is also the basis used in preparing financial statements.

The cost principle, however, has been criticized. One criticism is that it is irrelevant. After acquisition, the argument goes, cost is not equivalent to market value or current value. Despite the inevitability of changing prices due to inflation (or deflation), the accounting profession still follows the **monetary unit assumption** (referred to earlier in this chapter) in preparing financial statements. While admitting that some changes in prices do occur, the profession believes the unit of measure—the dollar—has remained sufficiently constant over time to provide meaningful financial information.

The basic principles of accounting are summarized in Illustration 11-7.

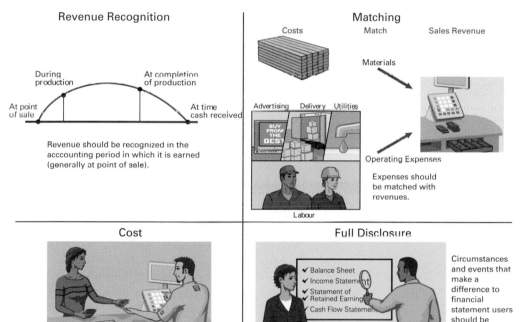

Illustration 11-7 ◄

Basic principles used in accounting

BEFORE YOU GO ON . . .

►Review It

1. What are the revenue recognition principle, the matching principle, the full disclosure principle, and the cost principle?
2. Identify the four points of revenue recognition. Provide an example of a company or product that would use each different point of revenue recognition.

Related exercise material: BE11–6, BE11–7, BE11–8, E11–3, E11–4, E11–5, and E11–6.

Constraints in Accounting

study objective 6

Identify and apply the constraints in accounting.

Constraints permit a company to modify generally accepted accounting principles without reducing the usefulness of the reported information. The constraints are cost-benefit and materiality considerations.

Cost-Benefit Constraint

The **cost-benefit** constraint ensures that the value of the information exceeds the cost of providing it. As we discussed earlier in this chapter, accountants could, in applying the full disclosure principle, disclose every financial event that occurs and every contingency that exists. However, providing additional information increases costs. The benefits of providing this information may be less than the costs in some cases.

Some believe that the benefit of applying GAAP to small businesses is not worth the cost. This has led to what is called the Big GAAP–Little GAAP controversy. Should there be one set of GAAP to which all businesses adhere, or should there be a different set for small businesses? The CICA is currently reviewing this matter, recognizing that the cost-benefit constraint can override the principle of one standard for all.

Materiality Constraint

Materiality relates to an item's impact on a firm's overall financial condition and operations. An item is material when it is likely to influence the decision of a reasonably careful investor or creditor. It is immaterial if its inclusion or omission has no impact on a decision-maker. In short, if the item does not make a difference in decision-making, GAAP does not have to be followed. To determine the materiality of an amount, the accountant usually compares it to such items as total assets, total liabilities, gross revenues, and cash and/or net income.

To illustrate how the materiality constraint is applied, assume that Yanik Co. purchases a number of low-cost pieces of office equipment, such as wastepaper baskets. Although the proper accounting would appear to be to amortize these wastepaper baskets over their useful lives, they are usually expensed immediately. This practice is justified because these costs are immaterial. Establishing amortization schedules for these assets is costly and time-consuming. It will not make a material difference in total assets and net income. Other applications of the materiality constraint are the nondisclosure of minor contingencies, and the expensing of any long-lived assets under a certain dollar amount.

Summary of Conceptual Framework

As we have seen, the conceptual framework for developing sound reporting practices starts with the objective for financial reporting. It continues with the description of qualities that make information useful. Elements of financial statements are then defined. Finally, more detailed recognition and measurement criteria are provided. These criteria take the form of assumptions, principles, and constraints. The conceptual framework is summarized in Illustration 11-8.

Illustration 11-8 ◄
Conceptual framework

International Accounting Standards

Foreigners buy Canadian grain, drink Canadian water, heat with Canadian fuels, celebrate Christmas with Canadian trees, eat Canadian potatoes, fly in Canadian planes, defend their countries with Canadian ships, listen to CBC radio, and guzzle Canadian beer. Canadians, in turn, drive Japanese and U.S. cars (often built with Canadian auto parts), wear Italian shoes and Scottish woollens, drink Brazilian coffee and Indian tea, eat Swiss chocolate bars while watching U.S. television, and sit on Danish furniture while heating with Arabian oil. The variety and volume of exported and imported goods indicates the extensive involvement of Canadian business in international trade. Almost 40% of all Canadian-made goods and services are sold as exports. For many Canadian companies, the world is their market.

In the global economy, many investment and credit decisions require the analysis of foreign financial statements. For example, one of The Forzani Group's top competitors is U.S.-based Foot Locker. Unfortunately, investors interested in investing in one of these two companies find comparing their financial statements challenging. Accounting standards can differ from country to country. This lack of uniformity results from differences in legal systems, processes for developing accounting standards, government requirements, and economic environments.

There is relief in sight for these differences, however, which is welcome news to investors and multinational corporations who operate in more than one country. Currently, such companies have to produce two or more sets of financial statements to meet the differing accounting requirements of the countries in which they operate. Swiss pharmaceutical giant Roche Group, which operates in more than 100 countries, estimates it could save $100 million annually if it only had to produce one set of financial statements.

Relief is coming thanks to the International Accounting Standards Board (IASB), which is heading the effort toward a worldwide convergence of accounting standards. **Convergence**, in this context, means that all standard-setters agree on a single answer. The words may not be the same, but the outcome will be. Following a country-specific standard will mean compliance with an international standard, and vice versa.

study objective 7

Explain the purpose of international accounting standards.

Most industrialized countries have already pledged to apply international accounting standards—at least for publicly listed companies—by the year 2007. Publicly traded companies in the European Union have committed to start using international accounting standards in 2005.

While no one questions the desirability of the world adhering to one set of accounting standards, some observers do question how realistic this deadline is. There are disagreements in some countries about some of the international accounting standards, such as those for financial instruments and fair value accounting. A significant number of countries believe that accounting standards should be used as tools to determine taxable income. Still other countries favour rule-based accounting standards, rather than principle-based accounting standards. Other concerns relate to the fact that the IASB has no enforcement power. Without an agreed-upon global means of enforcing international accounting standards, countries such as the U.S., whose Securities and Exchange Commission has significant enforcement power, are reluctant to sign on. There are also a myriad of other details that will take time to sort out. Still, the movement towards convergence is welcome and progress is under way.

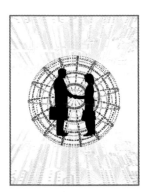

ACCOUNTING IN ACTION ▶ International Insight

According to the GAAP Convergence 2002 report, a report produced by the world's largest accounting firms, "significant progress is being made toward achieving the vision of a single worldwide language of financial reporting, notably for listed companies." Of the 59 countries surveyed, 95% say that they have adopted, or plan to adopt, international accounting standards. The convergence of worldwide accounting standards will make it easier for investors to compare opportunities and make informed decisions, and for companies to raise capital on world markets.

Source: GAAP Convergence 2002: A Survey of National Efforts to Promote and Achieve Convergence with International Financial Reporting Standards, International Forum on Accountancy Development.

BEFORE YOU GO ON . . .

▶Review It

1. What are the cost-benefit constraint and the materiality constraint?
2. What benefits will result from the international convergence of accounting standards?

Related exercise material: BE11–9, BE11–10, E11–7, E11–8, and E11–9.

Demonstration Problem 1

Additional Demonstration Problems

Wu Construction Company is under contract to build a condominium building at a contract price of $2 million. The building will take 18 months to complete, at an estimated cost of $1.4 million. Construction begins in November 2004 and is finished in April 2006. Actual construction costs incurred in each year are as follows: in 2004, $140,000; in 2005, $910,000; and in 2006, $350,000.

Instructions

Calculate the gross profit to be recognized in each year using the percentage-of-completion method.

Solution to Demonstration Problem 1

Year	Cost Incurred (Current Period)	÷	Total Estimated Cost	=	Percent Complete (Current Period)	×	Total Revenue (Current Period)	=	Revenue Recognized (Current Period)
2004	$ 140,000	÷	$1,400,000	=	10%	×	$2,000,000	=	$ 200,000
2005	910,000		1,400,000		65%		2,000,000		1,300,000
2006	350,000		1,400,000		25%		2,000,000		500,000
	$1,400,000								$2,000,000

Year	Revenue Recognized (Current Period)	−	Costs Incurred (Current Period)	=	Gross Profit (Current Period)
2004	$ 200,000	−	$ 140,000	=	$ 60,000
2005	1,300,000		910,000		390,000
2006	500,000		350,000		150,000
	$2,000,000		$1,400,000		$600,000

Action Plan

- The percentage-of-completion method recognizes revenue as construction occurs. It is viewed as a series of sales.
- Determine the percent complete by dividing costs incurred by total estimated costs.
- Multiply the percent complete by the contract price to find revenue to be recognized in the current period.
- Calculate gross profit: revenue recognized less actual costs incurred.

Demonstration Problem 2

The Wacky Web Company uses the instalment method to account for sales for which collection is uncertain. In 2004, its first year of operations, it has sales of uncertain collectibility of $900,000 with a cost of goods sold of $600,000. The cash collections on these sales are as follows: in 2004, $330,000; in 2005, $420,000; and in 2006, $150,000.

Instructions

Calculate the amount of gross profit to be recognized each year using the instalment method.

Solution to Demonstration Problem 2

Year	Cash Collections	×	Gross Profit Margin	=	Gross Profit Recognized
2004	$330,000	×	$33\frac{1}{3}\%$*	=	$110,000
2005	420,000		$33\frac{1}{3}\%$		140,000
2006	150,000		$33\frac{1}{3}\%$		50,000
	$900,000				$300,000

* $900,000 − $600,000 = $300,000 ÷ $900,000 = $33\frac{1}{3}\%$

Action Plan

- Use the instalment method when collection is uncertain.
- Calculate the gross profit margin: gross profit ÷ net sales.
- Recognize gross profit each period by multiplying cash collected by the gross profit margin.

the navigator

Summary of Study Objectives

1. *Explain the meaning of generally accepted accounting principles and identify the key items of the conceptual framework.* Generally accepted accounting principles are a set of rules and practices that is recognized as a general guide for financial reporting purposes. The key items of the conceptual framework are (1) the objective of financial reporting, (2) the qualitative characteristics of accounting information, (3) the elements of financial statements, and (4) recognition and measurement criteria (assumptions, principles, and constraints).

2. *Describe the basic objective of financial reporting.* The basic objective of financial reporting is to commu-nicate information that is useful to investors, creditors, and other users in making resource allocation decisions and in assessing management stewardship.

3. *Describe the qualitative characteristics of accounting information and apply them to the elements of financial statements.* To be judged useful, information should possess the following qualitative characteristics: understandability, relevance, reliability, and comparability. The elements of financial statements are a set of definitions that can be used to describe the basic terms used in accounting.

4. *Identify and apply the basic assumptions used by accountants.* The major assumptions are going concern, monetary unit, economic entity, and time period.

5. *Identify and apply the basic principles of accounting.* The major principles are revenue recognition, matching, full disclosure, and cost.

6. *Identify and apply the constraints in accounting.* The major constraints are the cost-benefit and materiality constraints.

7. *Explain the purpose of international accounting standards.* The International Accounting Standards Board is working to achieve uniformity in international accounting practices to simplify trade in world markets.

Glossary

Key Term Matching Activity

Comparability A quality that information is said to have if it can be compared to the accounting information of other companies because the companies all use the same accounting principles. (p. 533)

Completed-contract method A method in which revenue, expenses, and profit are recognized at the completion of production because revenues or costs cannot be reliably estimated. (p. 540)

Conceptual framework A coherent system of an interrelated objective, qualitative characteristics of accounting information, elements of financial statements, and recognition and measurement criteria that guides the development and application of accounting principles. (p. 531)

Conservatism Choice of an accounting method, when in doubt, that is least likely to overstate assets and net income. Conservatism modifies the reliability of accounting information. (p. 533)

Consistency Use of the same accounting principles from year to year. Consistency is a component of the comparability characteristic of accounting information. (p. 533)

Convergence Agreement amongst standard-setters on a single answer. Convergence means that a country's standard complies with an international standard, and vice versa. (p. 545)

Cost-benefit constraint The constraint that the costs of obtaining and providing information should not exceed the benefits gained. (p. 544).

Cost principle The accounting principle that requires assets to be recorded at their historical cost. (p. 543)

Economic entity assumption The accounting assumption that requires the activities of an economic entity to be kept separate from the activities of the shareholders (owners) and of all other entities. (p. 536)

Full disclosure principle The accounting principle that requires circumstances and events which make a difference to financial statement users to be disclosed. (p. 542)

Generally accepted accounting principles (GAAP) A set of rules and practices, having substantial authoritative support, that is recognized as a general guide for financial reporting purposes. (p. 530)

Going concern assumption The accounting assumption that the enterprise will continue operating for the foreseeable future. (p. 535)

Instalment method A method of recognizing revenue using the cash basis. Each cash collection consists of a partial recovery of cost of goods sold and partial gross profit from the sale. (p. 540)

Matching principle The accounting principle that says expenses should be matched with revenues in the period when efforts are made to generate those revenues. (p. 541)

Materiality constraint The constraint of determining whether an item is important enough to influence the decision of a reasonably careful investor or creditor. (p. 544)

Monetary unit assumption The accounting assumption that only transaction data expressed in monetary terms should be included in accounting records. Also assumes that the monetary unit (e.g., the dollar) is stable. (p. 536)

Objectivity A quality accounting information is said to have if two individuals working independently can review the information and reach the same results or similar conclusions. (p. 533)

Percentage-of-completion method A method of recognizing revenue on a long-term construction project. When costs can be reliably estimated, a portion of the total revenue can be recognized in each period by applying a percentage of completion. This percentage is determined by dividing the actual costs incurred during the period by the estimated costs for the entire project. (p. 538)

Point of sale The most common basis of revenue recognition, where revenue is recognized when goods or services are sold. Alternatives to this method are the percentage-of-completion, completed-contract, and instalment methods. (p. 537)

Relevance A quality that information is said to have if the information makes a difference in a decision. (p. 532)

Reliability A quality that information is said to have if the information can be verified as being free of error and bias. (p. 532)

Revenue recognition principle The accounting principle that says revenue should be recognized in the accounting period in which it is earned (generally at the point of sale). (p. 536)

Time period assumption The accounting assumption that says the economic life of a business can be divided into artificial time periods. (p. 536)

Understandability A quality that information in the financial statements is said to have if it is understandable to its users. (p. 532)

Self-Study Questions

Chapter 11 Self-Test

Answers are at the end of the chapter.

(SO 1) K **1.** Generally accepted accounting principles are:
- (a) a set of standards and rules that are recognized as a general guide for financial reporting.
- (b) established by the Canada Customs and Revenue Agency.
- (c) the guidelines used to resolve ethical dilemmas.
- (d) fundamental truths that can be derived from the laws of nature.

(SO 2) K **2.** Which of the following is not an objective of financial reporting?
- (a) To provide information that is useful in making resource allocation decisions
- (b) To provide information about economic resources, claims on those resources, and changes in them
- (c) To provide information that is useful in assessing management stewardship
- (d) To provide information about the market value of a business

(SO 3) K **3.** The primary criterion by which accounting information can be judged is:
- (a) consistency.
- (b) objectivity.
- (c) usefulness for decisions.
- (d) comparability.

(SO 3) K **4.** Verifiability is an ingredient of:

	Reliability	Relevance
(a)	Yes	Yes
(b)	No	No
(c)	Yes	No
(d)	No	Yes

(SO 5) AP **5.** Rioux Construction Company began a long-term construction contract on January 1, 2005. The contract is expected to be completed in 2006 at a total cost of $20 million. Rioux's revenue for the project is $23 million. Rioux incurred contract costs of $4 million in 2005. What gross profit should be recognized in 2005?
- (a) $600,000
- (c) $4.6 million
- (b) $3 million
- (d) $19 million

(SO 5) AP **6.** Glackin Company had instalment sales of $1 million in its first year of operations, whose collectibility is uncertain. The cost of goods sold on these instalment sales was $650,000. Glackin collected a total of $500,000 cash on the instalment sales. Using the instalment method, how much gross profit should be recognized in the first year?
- (a) $175,000
- (c) $350,000
- (b) $325,000
- (d) $500,000

(SO 5) K **7.** The full disclosure principle says that:
- (a) financial statements should disclose all assets at their cost.
- (b) financial statements should disclose only those events that can be measured in dollars.
- (c) financial statements should disclose all events and circumstances that would matter to users of financial statements.
- (d) financial statements should not be relied on unless an auditor has expressed an unqualified opinion on them.

(SO 4, 5, 6) K **8.** Valuing assets at their market value, rather than at their cost, is inconsistent with the:
- (a) time period assumption.
- (b) matching principle.
- (c) going concern assumption.
- (d) materiality constraint.

(SO 4, 5, 6) K **9.** The accounting term that refers to the tendency of accountants to favour understating assets and revenues in situations of uncertainty is known as:
- (a) the matching principle.
- (b) materiality.
- (c) conservatism.
- (d) the monetary unit assumption.

(SO 7) K **10.** The organization that issues international accounting standards is the:
- (a) Canadian Institute of Chartered Accountants.
- (b) International Accounting Standards Board.
- (c) Global Standards Agency.
- (d) Canadian Public Accountability Board.

Questions

(SO 1) K   1. (a) What are generally accepted accounting principles (GAAP)? (b) Explain the primary and secondary sources of GAAP.

(SO 1) C   2. Explain the role of professional judgement in financial accounting.

(SO 2) K   3. What is the basic objective of financial reporting?

(SO 3) C   4. Identify and explain the essential qualitative characteristics of accounting information.

(SO 3) C   5. Raynard Company substantially increased its net income in 2005 while keeping its inventory relatively the same. The president is very pleased with this. The chief accountant cautions him, however. She points out that since Raynard changed from the average cost to the FIFO cost flow assumption this year, there is a comparability problem. It will be difficult to determine whether the company's performance is better. Do you agree? Explain.

(SO 3) C   6. How is the concept of consistency related to the qualitative characteristic of comparability?

(SO 3) C   7. The type and amount of information included in financial reports results from a series of judgements about trade-offs. What are the objectives of these trade-offs?

(SO 3) C   8. How is the concept of objectivity related to the qualitative characteristic of reliability?

(SO 4) C   9. Why does it matter whether accountants assume an economic entity will remain a going concern? How does the going concern assumption support the use of the cost principle?

(SO 5) C   10. (a) When should revenue be recognized? (b) Why is the point of sale usually chosen as the date at which to recognize revenue?

(SO 5) C   11. (a) What are the advantages of using the percentage-of-completion method to recognize revenue? (b) When should a company use the completed-contract method instead of percentage-of-completion?

(SO 5) AP   12. Under what circumstances is it appropriate to wait until cash is collected to recognize revenue? Refer to the revenue recognition guidelines in your explanation.

(SO 5) C   13. Distinguish between expired costs and unexpired costs.

(SO 5) C   14. Where does the accountant disclose information about a company's financial position, operations, and cash flows?

(SO 5) C   15. Sue Leonard is the president of Better Books. She has no accounting background and cannot understand why market value is not used as the basis for accounting measurement and reporting. Explain what basis is used and why.

(SO 6) C   16. Describe the two constraints in the presentation of accounting information and provide an example of each.

(SO 6) C   17. The controller rounded all dollar figures in the company's financial statements to the nearest thousand dollars. "It's not important for our users to know how many pennies we spend," she said. Do you believe rounded financial figures can provide useful information for decision-making? Explain why or why not.

(SO 7) C   18. Your roommate believes that accounting standards are uniform throughout the world. Is your roommate correct? Explain.

(SO 7) C   19. How will the movement towards international convergence of accounting standards benefit multinational corporations and investors?

Brief Exercises

Identify items included in the conceptual framework.
(SO 1) K

BE11–1 Indicate which of the following items are included in the CICA's conceptual framework. (Write "Yes" or "No" beside each item in the list below.)

(a) The analysis of financial statement ratios
(b) The objective of financial reporting
(c) The qualitative characteristics of accounting information
(d) The elements of financial statements
(e) The rules for calculating taxable income
(f) The constraints on the application of generally accepted accounting principles
(g) The measurement of the market value of a business

Discuss accounting principles versus rules.
(SO 1) C

BE11–2 The failure of major corporations such as Enron and WorldCom has created considerable discussion on how detailed accounting principles should be. Some people argue that it is important to have a detailed set of accounting principles to cover every situation to ensure there are no more major corporate failures linked to accounting irregularities. Others argue that accounting principles should only apply broadly and that accountants should use their professional judgement in determining appropriate accounting principles for each specific situation. Discuss the advantages and disadvantages of each point of view.

BE11–3 Financial statements help users assess management stewardship, among other things. Some managers may be motivated to make accounting choices that improve the company's net income in order to improve their own performance bonus. Give an example of an accounting principle choice that management could use to (a) improve the company's net income, and (b) reduce the company's net income.

Discuss objective of financial reporting.
(SO 2) C

BE11–4 Presented below is a chart showing the qualitative characteristics of accounting information. Fill in the blanks from (a) to (f).

Identify qualitative characteristics of accounting information.
(SO 3) K

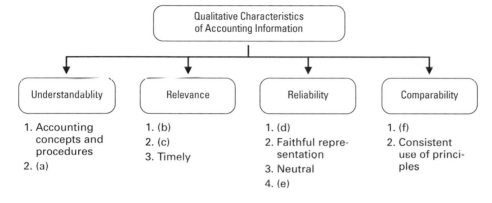

BE11–5 Presented below is a set of qualitative characteristics of accounting information:

Identify qualitative characteristics of accounting information.
(SO 3) K

1. Predictive value
2. Neutrality
3. Verifiability
4. Timeliness
5. Faithful representation

6. Comparability
7. Feedback value
8. Consistency
9. Conservatism
10. Understandability

Match these qualitative characteristics to the following statements, using numbers 1 to 10.

(a) _____ Accounting information is prepared based on the assumption that users have a reasonable understanding of accounting concepts and procedures, and general business and economic conditions.
(b) _____ Accounting information must be available to decision-makers before it loses its capacity to influence their decisions.
(c) _____ Accounting information provides a basis to evaluate a previously made decision.
(d) _____ Accounting information cannot be selected, prepared, or presented to favour one set of interested users over another.
(e) _____ Accounting information reports the economic substance, not the legal form, of the transaction.
(f) _____ Accounting information must be free of error and bias.
(g) _____ Accounting information about one company can be evaluated in relation to accounting information from another company.
(h) _____ Accounting information is prepared using the method that is least likely to overstate assets and net income when uncertainty exists.
(i) _____ Accounting information helps reduce uncertainty about the future.
(j) _____ Accounting information within a company is prepared using the same principles and methods from year to year.

BE11–6 Flin Flon Construction Company is under contract to build a commercial building at a price of $4.2 million. Construction begins in January 2004 and finishes in December 2006. Total estimated construction costs are $3 million. Actual construction costs incurred in each year are as follows: in 2004, $660,000; in 2005, $1.92 million; in 2006, $440,000. Calculate the revenue and gross profit to be recognized in each year, using the percentage-of-completion method.

Calculate revenue and gross profit—percentage-of-completion method.
(SO 5) AP

Calculate revenue and gross profit with change in estimate—percentage-of-completion method.
(SO 5) AP

BE11–7 Refer to the data presented in BE11–6. Assume that the estimated total costs rose from $3 million to $3.2 million in 2005. Actual costs incurred are $2.02 million in 2005 and $520,000 in 2006. Calculate the revenue and gross profit that should be recognized in 2005 and 2006.

Calculate gross profit—instalment method.
(SO 5) AP

BE11–8 Brassard Co. uses the instalment method to determine its net income. In 2004, its first year of operations, it had sales of uncertain collectibility of $800,000 and a cost of goods sold of $560,000. The collections on these sales were as follows: in 2004, $360,000; and in 2005, $440,000. Calculate the gross profit to be recognized for 2004 and 2005.

Identify assumption, principle, or constraint.
(SO 4, 5, 6) C

BE11–9 Presented below are accounting assumptions, principles, and constraints discussed in this chapter:

1. Economic entity assumption
2. Going concern assumption
3. Monetary unit assumption
4. Time period assumption
5. Cost principle
6. Matching principle
7. Full disclosure principle
8. Revenue recognition principle
9. Materiality constraint
10. Cost-benefit constraint

Instructions

Identify by number the accounting assumption, principle, or constraint that describes each situation below. Do not use a number more than once.

(a) _____ Is the rationale for why land is not reported at liquidation value. (Do not use the cost principle.)
(b) _____ Indicates that personal and business record-keeping should be separately maintained.
(c) _____ Ensures that all relevant financial information is reported.
(d) _____ Assumes that the dollar is the "measuring stick" for reporting financial performance.
(e) _____ Requires that GAAP be followed for all significant items.
(f) _____ Separates financial information into time periods for reporting purposes.
(g) _____ Requires recognition of expenses in the same period as related revenues.
(h) _____ Indicates that market value changes after a purchase are not recorded in the accounts.

Identify violation of principle or constraint.
(SO 5, 6) C

BE11–10 The Yoon Company uses the following accounting practices:

(a) Inventory is reported at cost when market value is lower.
(b) Revenue on instalment sales with uncertain collectibility is recognized at the time of sale.
(c) Small tools are recorded as long-lived assets and amortized.
(d) Paper clips expense appears on the income statement, at $10.
(e) Yoon currently records its accounting transactions and prepares its financial reports manually. The cost of implementing a new computerized accounting system to do these tasks is estimated to be $25,000. Annual savings are expected to be $10,000.
(f) Bad debt expense is recorded in the period when the account receivable is written off.

Indicate the accounting principle or constraint, if any, that has been violated by each practice.

Exercises

Identify elements of financial statements.
(SO 3) K

E11–1 Presented below are the basic elements of financial statements encountered in earlier chapters of the textbook:

1. Assets
2. Liabilities
3. Owners' Equity
4. Revenues
5. Expenses
6. Gains
7. Losses
8. Drawings

Instructions

Each statement below is an important aspect of an element's definition. Match the elements with the definitions. *Note*: More than one number can be placed in a blank. Each number may be used more than once or not at all.

(a) _____ Increases in assets or decreases in liabilities resulting from the primary business activities of the organization
(b) _____ Existing debts and obligations arising from past transactions
(c) _____ Changes to owners' equity caused by the company's peripheral activities

(d) _____ Resources owned by a business
(e) _____ Goods or services used in the process of earning revenue
(f) _____ Residual claim on total assets after deducting liabilities
(g) _____ The capacity to provide future benefits to the organization

E11–2 Skate Stop is owned by Marc Bélanger. It sells in-line skates and accessories. It shares space with another company, Ride Snowboards. Ride Snowboards is owned by Marc's wife, Lise Ert-Bélanger, who was an Olympic bronze medallist in snowboarding. Ride Snowboards sells snowboards and related accessories. The following transactions occurred during a recent year:

Apply economic entity assumption.
(SO 4) AP

(a) In January, Lise purchased fire and theft insurance for the year to cover the rented space and inventory. She paid for all the insurance since she had more cash than Marc.
(b) Marc paid the rent for the month of July since he had more cash that month than Lise.
(c) Marc recorded skate sales for the month of September.
(d) Lise purchased and paid for her winter inventory of snowboards in September.
(e) Marc and Lise had such a successful year that they went out to a fancy restaurant to celebrate. They charged the bill to Lise's company.
(f) Lise paid her annual membership fee to the local ski hill from company funds.
(g) Marc paid his annual membership fee to the curling club from company funds.

Instructions

Identify which of the above transactions should be recorded by Skate Stop, and which should be recorded by Ride Snowboards. State if the cost is a personal one, or if it relates to both companies and should be allocated to each of them.

E11–3 Consider the following transactions of Mitrovica Company for 2005:

Determine amount of revenue to be recognized.
(SO 5) AP

Interactive Homework

(a) Leased office space to Excel Supplies for a one-year period beginning September 1. The $24,000 of rent was paid in advance.
(b) Received a sales order for merchandise that cost $9,000. It was sold for $14,000 on December 28, 2005, to Warfield Company. The goods were shipped FOB destination on December 31. Warfield received them on January 3, 2006.
(c) Signed a long-term contract to construct a building at a total price of $1.6 million. The total estimated cost of construction is $1.2 million. During 2005, the company incurred $300,000 of costs and collected $330,000 in cash. The percentage-of-completion method is used to recognize revenue.
(d) Had merchandise inventory on hand at year end that amounted to $160,000. Mitrovica expects to sell the inventory in 2006 for $180,000.
(e) Issued a $6,000, six-month, 8% note receivable on September 1, interest payable at maturity.
(f) Sold merchandise that cost $30,000 for $50,000 on instalment contracts. The customers have signed contracts to pay $25,000 in 2006 and $25,000 in 2007.

Instructions

For each item above, indicate the amount of revenue Mitrovica should recognize for the year ended December 31, 2005. Explain.

E11–4 The following independent situations require professional judgement for determining when to recognize revenue from the transactions:

Identify point of revenue recognition.
(SO 5) C

(a) **Air Canada** sells you an advance purchase airline ticket in September for your flight home at Christmas.
(b) **Leon's Furniture** sells you a home theatre on a "no money down, no interest, and no payments for one year" promotional deal.
(c) The **Toronto Blue Jays** sell season tickets to games in the Skydome on-line. Fans can purchase the tickets at any time, although the season doesn't officially begin until April. It runs from April through October.
(d) The **RBC Financial Group** lends you money in August. The loan and the interest are repayable in full in November.
(e) In September, **Centennial College** collects tuition revenue for the term from new and returning students. The term runs from September through December.
(f) **Sears** sells you a sweater. In August, you placed the order using Sears' on-line catalogue. The sweater arrives in September and you charge it to your Sears credit card. You receive and pay the Sears bill in October.

Instructions

Identify when revenue should be recognized in each of the above situations.

E11–5 Shen Construction Company currently has one long-term construction project. The project has a contract price of $120 million with total estimated costs of $90 million. Shen uses the percentage-of-completion method. After two years of construction, the following costs have been accumulated:

Actual cost incurred, 2004	$30.0 million
Total estimated cost remaining after 2004	60.0 million
Actual cost incurred, 2005	49.5 million
Total estimated cost remaining after 2005	10.5 million

Instructions

(a) Determine the gross profit that should be recognized for each of the first two years of the construction contract, 2004 and 2005.

(b) How much gross profit will be recognized after 2005, assuming Shen's cost estimates are accurate?

(c) Assume instead that Shen revises the total estimated cost remaining after 2005 to $20.5 million instead of $10.5 million. Determine the amount of gross profit that should be recognized in 2005 and the amount that will be recognized after 2005 if there are no further revisions to the cost estimates.

E11–6 Blairmore Company sold equipment for $320,000 in 2004. Collections on the sale were as follows: in 2004, $70,000; in 2005, $190,000; and in 2006, $60,000. Blairmore's cost of goods sold is typically 65% of sales.

Instructions

(a) Determine Blairmore's gross profit for 2004, 2005, and 2006, assuming that Blairmore recognizes revenue under the instalment method.

(b) Determine Blairmore's gross profit for 2004, 2005, and 2006, assuming that Blairmore recognizes revenue using the point-of-sale basis.

E11–7 A number of reporting situations are described below:

(a) Tercek Company recognizes revenue during the production cycle. The price of the product, as well as the amount that can be sold, is not certain.

(b) In preparing its financial statements, Seco Company left out information about its cost flow assumption for inventories.

(c) Martinez Company amortizes patents over their legal life of 20 years as opposed to their economic life, which typically lasts from five to seven years.

(d) Ravine Hospital Supply Corporation reports only current assets and current liabilities on its balance sheet. Long-term assets and liabilities are reported as current. Liquidation of the company is unlikely.

(e) Barton Company reports its inventory on the balance sheet at its current market value of $100,000. The inventory has an original cost of $110,000.

(f) Bonilla Company is in its fifth year of operation and has yet to issue financial statements.

(g) Watts Company has inventory on hand that cost $400,000. Watts reports inventory on its balance sheet at its current market value of $425,000.

(h) Steph Wolfson, president of the Download Music Company, bought a computer for her personal use. She paid for the computer by using company funds and debited the computers account.

(i) Smith Company uses the FIFO cost flow assumption in 2003, changes to average cost in 2004, and returns to FIFO in 2005.

Instructions

For each of the above, list the assumption, principle, or constraint that has been violated, if any.

E11–8 Presented below are some business transactions that occur during 2005 for Ellis Co.:

1. Equipment worth $90,000 is acquired at a cost of $65,000 from a company that had water damage in a flood. The following entry is made:

Equipment	90,000	
Cash		65,000
Gain		25,000

2. The president of Ellis Co., Evan Ellis, purchases a truck for personal use and charges it to his expense account. The following entry is made:

Travel Expense	29,000	
Cash		29,000

3. An account receivable becomes a bad debt. The following entry is made:

Bad Debts Expense	15,000	
Accounts Receivable		15,000

4. Merchandise inventory with a cost of $222,000 is reported at its market value of $260,000. The following entry is made:

Merchandise Inventory	38,000	
Gain		38,000

5. An electric pencil sharpener costing $50 is being amortized over five years. The following entry is made:

Amortization Expense	10	
Accumulated Amortization —Pencil Sharpener		10

Instructions

In each of the situations above, identify the assumption, principle, or constraint that has been violated, if any. Review the appropriateness of the journal entries and give the correct journal entry, if one is needed.

E11–9 Presented below are the assumptions, principles, and constraints discussed in this chapter:

1. Economic entity assumption	6. Revenue recognition principle
2. Going concern assumption	7. Matching principle
3. Monetary unit assumption	8. Cost principle
4. Time period assumption	9. Materiality constraint
5. Full disclosure principle	10. Cost-benefit constraint

Identify assumption, principle, or constraint. (SO 4, 5, 6) C

Instructions

Identify by number the accounting assumption, principle, or constraint that describes each situation below. Do not use a number more than once.

(a) _____ Barb Denton runs her accounting practice out of her home. She separates her accounting practice records from her household accounts.
(b) _____ Companies prepare quarterly reports.
(c) _____ Revenue is sometimes recognized at various points of production.
(d) _____ The cost should not exceed the benefits.
(e) _____ Significant accounting policies are reported in the notes to the financial statements.
(f) _____ Assets are not stated at their liquidation values.
(g) _____ The effect of inflation for the current year is ignored in determining net income.
(h) _____ Dollar amounts on financial statements are often rounded to the nearest thousand.
(i) _____ Bad debts expense is recorded using the allowance method of accounting.
(j) _____ Land is recorded at its cost of $100,000 rather than at its market value of $150,000.

Problems: Set A

P11–1A Some companies have adopted a policy of recording substantial write-offs of goodwill. They claim the ongoing value of goodwill is difficult to measure and defend these write-offs as being a "conservative" accounting practice.

Comment on conservatism. (SO 3) C

Instructions

(a) Describe the current accounting requirements with respect to writing off goodwill.
(b) Explain the intent of conservatism.
(c) Does an overly aggressive write-off of goodwill fulfill the conservatism characteristic of accounting? Explain.

Comment on objective and qualitative characteristics of accounting information. (SO 3) C

P11–2A Yahoo! Inc. is the Internet's leading global consumer and business services company. The company was formed in January 1994 by two graduate students as a hobby and became a public company in April 1996. The company's shares peaked in value at US$237.50 per share in January 2000, and declined to a low of US$8 per share in September 2001. In September 2003, they were trading at approximately US$37 per share.

Instructions

(a) What is the objective of financial reporting? How does this objective meet or not meet Yahoo! Inc.'s investors' needs? How might the needs have changed after the company became publicly owned?

(b) Why would investors have paid as much as US$237 per share at the beginning of 2000 even though the accumulated losses of the company to December 1999 were almost US$26 million? And why were investors willing to pay only US$37 per share in September 2003 when the accumulated losses had been reduced to US$7.5 million by December 31, 2002? Include in your answer an assessment of the relevance and reliability of the information reported on Yahoo! Inc.'s financial statements.

Identify principle or assumption violated. Prepare correct entries. (SO 4, 5) AN

P11–3A Czyz and Ng are accountants at Kwick Kopy Printers. They are having disagreements concerning the following transactions that occurred during the year ended December 31, 2005:

1. Kwick Kopy bought equipment for $60,000, including installation costs. The equipment has a useful life of five years. Kwick Kopy amortizes equipment using the straight-line method. "Since the equipment as installed in our system cannot be removed without considerable damage, it will have no resale value. It should not be amortized but, instead, expensed immediately," argues Czyz.

2. Amortization for the year was $26,000. Since net income is expected to be low this year, Czyz suggests deferring amortization to a year when there is more net income.

3. Kwick Kopy purchased equipment at a fire sale for $18,000. The equipment would normally have cost $26,000. Czyz believes that the following entry should be made:

Equipment	26,000	
Cash		18,000
Gain on Purchase of Equipment		8,000

4. Czyz says that Kwick Kopy should carry its furnishings on the balance sheet at their liquidation value, which is $20,000 less than cost.

5. Kwick Kopy rented office space for one year, starting October 1, 2005. The total rent of $24,000 was paid in advance. Czyz believes that the following entry should be made on October 1:

Rent Expense	24,000	
Cash		24,000

The company's fiscal year ends on December 31.

6. Land that cost $41,000 was appraised at $49,000. Czyz suggests the following journal entry:

Land	8,000	
Gain on Appreciation of Land		8,000

7. On December 15, 2005, Kwick Kopy signed a contract with a customer to provide copying services for a six-month period at a rate of $1,000 per month starting January 1, 2006. The customer will pay on a monthly basis. Czyz argues that the contract should be recorded in December 2005 because the customer has always paid its bills on time in the past. The customer is legally obligated to pay the monthly amount because a contract has been signed. Czyz believes the following entry should be recorded:

Accounts Receivable	6,000	
Service Revenue		6,000

Ng disagrees with Czyz on each of the situations above.

Instructions

For each transaction, indicate why Ng disagrees. Identify the accounting principle or assumption that would be violated if Czyz's suggestions were used. Prepare the correct journal entry for each transaction, if any.

P11–4A Presented below are a number of business transactions that occurred during the current year for Durkovitch Company:

Prepare correct entries.
(SO 4, 5) AN

1. An order for $70,000 was received from a customer for products on hand. This order is to be shipped on January 9 next year. The following entry was made:

Accounts Receivable	70,000	
Sales		70,000

2. Because of a "flood sale," equipment worth $300,000 was acquired at a cost of $245,000. The following entry was made:

Equipment	300,000	
Cash		245,000
Gain on Purchase of Equipment		55,000

3. Because the general level of prices increased during the current year, Durkovitch determined that there was a $40,000 understatement of amortization expense on its equipment. The company decided to record the understatement in its accounts. The following entry was made:

Amortization Expense	40,000	
Accumulated Amortization		40,000

4. The president of Durkovitch used his expense account to purchase a pre-owned Mercedes-Benz SL500 solely for personal use. The following entry was made:

Automobiles	68,000	
Cash		68,000

5. Land was purchased on April 30 for $200,000. This amount was recorded in the Land account. On December 31, the land would have cost $240,000, so the following entry was made:

Land	40,000	
Gain on Land		40,000

Instructions

(a) In each of the situations above, discuss the appropriateness of the journal entry in terms of generally accepted accounting principles and assumptions.

(b) Prepare the journal entries needed to correct any inappropriate application of GAAP in each of the situations above.

P11–5A Santa's Christmas Tree Farm grows pine, fir, and spruce trees. The company cuts and sells the trees for cash during the Christmas season. The majority of the trees are exported to the U.S. The remaining trees are sold to local tree lot operators.

Discuss application of
revenue recognition and
matching principles.
(SO 5) C

It normally takes about 12 years for a tree to grow to a suitable size. The average selling price for a mature tree is $24. The owner of Santa's Christmas Tree Farm believes that the company should recognize revenue at the rate of $2 a year ($24 ÷ 12 years) for each tree that it cuts. The biggest cost of this business is the cost of fertilizing, pruning, and maintaining the trees over the 12-year period. These costs average $22 a tree and the owner believes they should also be spread over the 12-year period.

Instructions

(a) Do you agree with the proposed revenue recognition policy for Santa's Christmas Tree Farms? Explain why or why not. Use the revenue recognition guidelines to explain when you believe revenue should be recognized for this tree-farming business.

(b) When should the cost of fertilizing, pruning, and maintaining the trees be recognized? Explain.

P11–6A Cosky Construction Company is involved in a long-term construction contract to build an office building. The estimated cost is $20 million and the contract price is $28 million. Additional information follows:

Calculate revenue,
expense, and gross
profit—percentage-of-
completion and completed-
contract methods.
(SO 5) AP

Year	Cash Collections	Actual Costs Incurred
2003	$ 4,500,000	$3,000,000
2004	10,000,000	9,000,000
2005	7,000,000	5,000,000
2006	6,500,000	3,000,000

The project is completed in 2006.

Instructions

(a) Prepare a schedule to determine the revenue, expense, and gross profit in each year of the contract, using the percentage-of-completion method.

(b) How would your answer in (a) change if Cosky used the completed-contract method rather than the percentage-of-completion method? What are the benefits of using percentage-of-completion?

(c) Assume instead that the actual costs were $7 million in 2005 and that at the end of 2005 Cosky revised its total estimated costs to $24 million. Also assume actual costs in 2006 were $5 million. Calculate the impact this will have on the total gross profit. Calculate the revenue and gross profit to be recognized in 2005 and 2006 given these changes to the total estimated cost and the actual costs.

Calculate gross profit and comment—percentage-of-completion method.
(SO 5) AP

P11–7A Kamloops Construction Company has a contract for the construction of a new health and fitness centre. It is accounting for this project using the percentage-of-completion method. The contract amount is $2.5 million and the cost of construction is initially expected to total $1.4 million. The actual costs incurred are shown below for the three-year life of the project:

Year	Actual Costs Incurred
2004	$550,000
2005	500,000
2006	350,000

Instructions

(a) Calculate the amount of gross profit to be recognized in each year.

(b) Comment on the above results.

(c) What if Kamloops Construction receives less cash in each of the first two years from this contract than the amount it has recognized as revenue? Is it still appropriate to recognize the amount of revenue calculated in the percentage-of-completion schedules? Explain.

Calculate gross profit—instalment method.
(SO 5) AP

P11–8A Aasen Construction sold apartments it had constructed to Mattson Management Company for $2.5 million. Aasen's cost to construct the apartments was $1.55 million. Appropriately, Aasen uses the instalment method because collection is uncertain. Additional information follows:

Year	Cash Collections
2004	$ 900,000
2005	1,150,000
2006	450,000

Instructions

(a) Determine the gross profit for each year using the instalment method.

(b) Repeat (a) assuming the construction cost was $1.75 million.

Calculate gross profit and comment—instalment method.
(SO 5) AP

P11–9A Dave's Deep Discount Furniture Store makes many of its sales on long-term instalment contracts. It accounts for these using the instalment method because collectibility is uncertain. During 2002, Dave's had $850,000 of instalment sales. The related cost of goods sold was $527,000. The instalment contracts called for the customers' payments to be made as follows:

Year	Payment
2002	$170,000
2003	200,000
2004	200,000
2005	200,000
2006	80,000

The company collected the payments for 2002 through 2004 exactly as scheduled above. However, in 2005 and 2006 things were quite different:

1. Collections in 2005 were only $170,000. Nevertheless, the company was hopeful that the amounts in arrears would soon be collected.

2. Collections in 2006 were only $40,000, and the company conceded that none of the amounts in arrears (neither the $30,000 from 2005 nor the $40,000 from 2006) would ever be collected.

Instructions

(a) Calculate the amount of gross profit to be recognized in the years 2002 through 2004.

(b) Calculate the amount of gross profit to be recognized in 2005. (*Hint:* Note that the overall gross profit expected to be earned on these instalment sales has not been changed by the year's events. You can follow the usual instalment method procedures in this situation.)

(c) Calculate the amount of gross profit (if any) to be recognized in 2006. (*Hint:* Note that the overall gross profit earned on these instalment sales has been changed by this year's developments. You should begin by calculating the overall gross profit actually realized on these sales, and then compare it to the cumulative amount already recognized in the years 2002 through 2005.)

(d) Comment on the above results.

P11–10A A friend of yours, Ryan Konotopsky, has come to you looking for some answers about financial statements. Ryan tells you that he is thinking about opening a movie theatre in his home town. Before doing so, he wants to find out how much sales he could expect to make from food concessions as opposed to ticket sales. He wants to know what portion of ticket sales he could expect for children, youth, and seniors, who pay less, versus adults, who pay the highest admission rate. He also wants to know how much profit he would make on ticket sales versus sales at the concession stands, and the average wage per employee.

Comment on accounting constraints. (SO 6) C

Ryan knows that Empire Theatres operates in many cities and towns in Atlantic Canada. He downloaded the financial statements of Empire Company Limited from the Internet. He noticed that the company's income statement reported revenues for the year ended April 30, 2003, of $10.6 billion and cost of sales, selling, and administrative expenses of $10 billion. He read through Empire Company Limited's annual report and learned that Empire Theatres is just one part of the investments division of the company. There are food distribution and real estate divisions as well.

Ryan is disillusioned when he cannot find many details about Empire Theatres in the annual report. He has come to you looking for explanations.

Instructions

What are two constraints in accounting? What impact have these constraints had on the financial reporting by Empire Theatres?

Problems: Set B

P11–1B Many high-tech companies report continued losses, yet their share prices skyrocket. **Research in Motion Limited**, maker of wireless personal digital products, is an interesting example. The company has consistently recorded losses of increasing sizes, and reported an accumulated deficit of $170 million in fiscal 2003. Its share price was as high as $202 per share in February 2000 and as low as $15 in September 2002. By February 2004, Research in Motion's shares had rebounded somewhat and were trading at $133 per share.

Comment on relevance and reliability. (SO 3) C

Instructions

(a) Explain why investors in companies like Research in Motion are willing to pay such high prices for shares of a company that has reported losses regularly. Include in your answer a discussion of the trade-off between relevance and reliability.

(b) What might have happened that caused investors to reduce the amount they were willing to pay for a share of the company from $202 per share to $15 per share?

(c) What might have happened that caused investors to increase the amount they were willing to pay for a share of the company from $15 per share to $133 per share?

P11–2B A friend of yours, Emily Collis, recently completed an undergraduate degree in science and has just started working with a Canadian biotechnology company. Emily tells you that the owners of the business are trying to secure new sources of financing which are needed for the company to proceed with development of a new health-care product. Emily says that her boss told her the company has to put together a report to present to potential investors.

Comment on objective and qualitative characteristics of financial reporting. (SO 3) C

Emily thinks that the company's report should include the detailed scientific findings related to the Phase I clinical trials for this product. "I know that the biotech industry sometimes has only a 10% success rate with new products," she says to you, "but if we report all the scientific findings, everyone will see what a sure success this is going to be!

"The president was talking about the importance of following some set of accounting principles. We shouldn't have to follow those. What they need to realize is that we have scientific results that are quite encouraging, some of the most talented employees around, and the start of some really great customer relationships. We haven't made any sales yet, but we will. We just need the funds to get through all the clinical testing and get government approval for our product. Then these investors will be quite happy that they bought into our company early!"

Instructions

(a) What is the objective of financial reporting? Explain to Emily how her proposal meets or does not meet this objective.

(b) Comment on how Emily's suggestions for what to report to potential investors conform to the qualitative characteristics of accounting information. Do you think that the things Emily wants to include in the information for investors will conform to generally accepted accounting principles?

Identify principle or assumption violated. Prepare correct entries.
(SO 4, 5) AN

P11–3B Jivraj and Juma are accountants at Desktop Computers. They disagree over the following transactions that occurred during the calendar year 2005:

1. Desktop purchased equipment for $35,000 at a going-out-of-business sale. The equipment was worth $45,000. Jivraj believes that the following entry should be made:

Equipment	45,000	
Cash		35,000
Gain on Acquisition of Equipment		10,000

2. Land costing $60,000 was appraised at $90,000. Jivraj suggests the following journal entry.

Land	30,000	
Gain on Appreciation of Land		30,000

3. Amortization for the year was $18,000. Since net income is expected to be lower this year, Jivraj suggests deferring amortization to a year when there is more net income.

4. Desktop bought a custom-made piece of equipment for $36,000. This equipment has a useful life of six years. Desktop amortizes equipment using the double declining-balance method. "Since the equipment is custom-made, it will have no resale value. It shouldn't be amortized but instead should be expensed immediately," argues Jivraj. "Besides, it provides for lower net income." Jivraj suggests the following entry:

Equipment Expense	36,000	
Cash		36,000

5. Jivraj suggests that the company building should be reported on the balance sheet at the lower of cost and market value. Market value is $15,000 less than cost.

6. On December 20, 2005, Desktop hired a marketing consultant to design and implement a marketing plan in 2006. The contract amount is $45,000 payable in three instalments in 2006. Jivraj argues that the contract must be recorded in 2005 because the company is legally obligated for the full amount. Jivraj suggest the following:

Marketing Expense	45,000	
Accounts Payable		45,000

7. In September 2005, Desktop sold 100 computers to college students for $1,000 each. Each student signed an instalment contract in which the student agreed to pay $500 in July 2006 and another $500 in July 2007. Jivraj argues the merchandise has been delivered to the customers and that Desktop should record the following in 2005:

Accounts Receivable	100,000	
Sales		100,000

Juma disagrees with Jivraj on each of the above situations.

Instructions

For each transaction, indicate why Juma disagrees. Identify the accounting principle or assumption that would be violated if Jivraj's suggestions were used. Prepare the correct journal entry for each transaction, if any.

P11–4B Presented below are a number of business transactions that occurred during the current year for SGI Company:

Prepare correct entries.
(SO 4, 5) AN

1. Materials were purchased on March 31 for $65,000. This amount was entered in the Materials Inventory account. On December 31, the materials would have cost $80,000, so the following entry was made:

Materials Inventory	15,000	
Gain on Inventory		15,000

2. An order for $30,000 was received from a customer for products on hand. This order is to be shipped on January 9 next year. The following entry was made:

Accounts Receivable	30,000	
Sales		30,000

3. The president of SGI used her expense account to purchase a pre-owned Saab 9000 solely for personal use. The following entry was made:

Miscellaneous Expense	44,000	
Cash		44,000

4. At a fire sale, equipment worth $250,000 was acquired at a cost of $210,000. It had soot and smoke damage, but was otherwise in good order. The following entry was made:

Equipment	250,000	
Cash		210,000
Gain on Purchase of Equipment		40,000

5. Because the general level of prices decreased during the current year, SGI determined that its equipment and amortization were overstated by $25,000. The following entry was made:

Accumulated Amortization	25,000	
Equipment		25,000

Instructions

(a) In each situation, discuss the appropriateness of the journal entries in terms of generally accepted accounting principles and assumptions.
(b) Prepare the journal entries needed to correct any inappropriate application of GAAP in each of the situations above.

P11–5B Superior Salmon Farm raises salmon for sale to supermarket chains and restaurants. The current average selling price for a mature salmon is $6.

Discuss application of revenue recognition and matching principles.
(SO 5) C

It normally takes three years for the fish to grow to a saleable size. During that period the fish must be fed and closely monitored to ensure they are healthy and free of disease. Their habitat must also be maintained. These costs average $4.50 per fish over the three-year growing period.

The owner of Superior Salmon Farm believes the company should recognize revenue at a rate of $2 a year ($6 ÷ 3 years) for each fish that it harvests. The owner argues that since the demand for salmon is increasing as more people become aware of the health benefits of the omega-3 fatty acids present in salmon, the selling price of this fish can only increase in the future.

Instructions

(a) Do you agree with the proposed revenue recognition policy for Superior Salmon Farm? Explain why or why not. Use the revenue recognition guidelines to explain when you believe the revenue should be recognized for this salmon farming business.
(b) When should the cost of feeding, monitoring, and maintaining healthy fish and a proper habitat be recognized? Explain.

P11–6B MacNeil Construction Company is involved in a long-term construction contract to build a shopping centre. The centre has a total estimated cost of $30 million, and a contract price of $38 million. Additional information follows:

Year	Cash Collections	Actual Costs Incurred
2003	$ 6,000,000	$ 5,500,000
2004	8,500,000	7,000,000
2005	10,500,000	10,000,000
2006	13,000,000	7,500,000

The shopping centre is completed in 2006 as scheduled. All cash collections related to the contract are received.

Instructions

(a) Prepare a schedule to determine the revenue, expense, and gross profit for each year of the long-term construction contract, using the percentage-of-completion method.

(b) How would your answer in (a) change if MacNeil used the completed-contract method rather than the percentage-of-completion method?

(c) Assume instead that the actual costs were $12 million in 2005 and that at the end of 2005 MacNeil revised its total estimated costs to $34 million. Also assume actual costs in 2006 were $9.5 million. Calculate the impact this will have on the total gross profit. Calculate the revenue and gross profit to be recognized in 2005 and 2006 given these changes to the total estimated cost and the actual costs.

P11–7B Hamilton Construction Company has a contract for the construction of a new recreation centre. It accounts for this project using the percentage-of-completion method. The contract amount is $3 million and the cost of construction is expected to total $2.2 million.

The actual costs incurred are shown below for the three-year life of the project:

Year	Actual Costs Incurred
2004	$ 650,000
2005	1,000,000
2006	550,000

Instructions

(a) Calculate the amount of revenue, expense, and gross profit to be recognized in each of 2004, 2005, and 2006.

(b) Comment on the above results.

(c) What if Hamilton Construction receives less cash in each of the first two years from this contract than the amount it has recognized as revenue? Is it still appropriate to recognize the amount of revenue calculated in the percentage-of-completion schedules? Explain.

P11–8B The Scotia Trawler Shipyard builds custom trawlers. During its first year of operations, it signed a two-year contract to build a 42-foot trawler for Jim McLeod. The sale price was $750,000. Scotia's cost to construct the boat was estimated to be $500,000. Additional information follows:

Year	Cash Collections	Actual Costs Incurred
2005	$350,000	$300,000
2006	400,000	200,000

Instructions

(a) Prepare a schedule to determine the gross profit for each year, using the percentage-of-completion method.

(b) Prepare a schedule to determine the gross profit for each year, using the instalment method.

(c) Which method is more appropriate for the Scotia Trawler Shipyard to use? Explain your reasoning.

P11–9B Fran's Furniture Warehouse makes many of its sales on long-term instalment contracts. It accounts for these using the instalment method because collectibility is uncertain. During 2003, Fran's had $950,000 of instalment sales. The related cost of goods sold was $560,500. The required payments per the instalment contracts and the actual payments received are as follows:

Year	Contract Payments	Actual Payments
2003	$125,000	$125,000
2004	200,000	200,000
2005	200,000	200,000
2006	200,000	175,000
2007	225,000	0

1. In 2006, when actual collections were less than the amount specified in the instalment contracts, Fran's Furniture Warehouse was still hopeful that the amount in arrears would soon be collected.
2. At the end of 2007, Fran's Furniture Warehouse determined that the amount in arrears from 2006 and 2007 was uncollectible.

Instructions

(a) Calculate the amount of gross profit to be recognized in the years 2003 though 2005.
(b) Calculate the amount of gross profit to be recognized in 2006. (*Hint:* Note that the overall gross profit expected to be earned on these instalment sales has not been changed by the year's events. You can follow the usual instalment method procedures in this situation.)
(c) Calculate the amount of gross profit (if any) to be recognized in 2007. (*Hint:* Note that the overall gross profit earned on these instalment sales has been changed by this year's developments. You should begin by calculating the overall gross profit actually realized on these sales, and then compare it to the cumulative amount recognized already in the years 2003 through 2005.)
(d) Comment on the above results.

P11–10B Under GAAP, no separate disclosure is required on the income statement for the cost of goods sold (the cost of merchandise sold to customers). Because this disclosure is not specifically required, less than half of reporting companies disclose their cost of goods sold separately on their income statement. Most companies include it with other expenses, as **Sears Canada Inc.** did in its income statement for the year ended December 31, 2002:

Comment on accounting constraints.
(SO 6) C

Cost of merchandise sold, operating, administrative,
    and selling expenses $6.1 billion

Instructions

(a) Why do you think Sears does not report its cost of merchandise sold separately on its income statement? Comment on how this disclosure would meet the objective of financial reporting.
(b) What are the two constraints in accounting? Does either of these constraints likely have an impact on Sears' reporting policy for cost of merchandise sold? Give an example of how each constraint might affect Sears' reporting of its financial information.

Continuing Cookie Chronicle

(Note: This is a continuation of the Cookie Chronicle from Chapters 1 through 10.)

Natalie's biggest competitor is Trial Appliances. Trial Appliances sells a fine European mixer similar to the one that customers are able to buy from Cookie Creations. Natalie estimates that Trial Appliances sells twice as many mixers as she does. Trial Appliances also sells microwaves, dishwashers, washing machines, and refrigerators. Natalie believes that one of the major reasons Trial Appliances sells the number of mixers that it does is because it sells all of its appliances on an extended payment plan.

Natalie knows that Trial Appliances sells its mixers for $1,100. She also knows that under the extended payment plan approximately $275 (25%) is collected in the year the mixer is sold, $550 (50%) is collected the year after the appliance is sold, and the remaining $275 (25%) is collected in the third year. Trial Appliances sells approximately 65 mixers a year and tries to keep a gross profit margin of approximately 50%.

Natalie comes to you to ask about the accounting for revenues when mixers are sold on an extended payment plan. She would really like to generate more sales revenues and cash flow. Based on her discussions with the sales manager at Trial Appliances, she believes that she could sell more mixers if she offered her customers the option of paying over an extended period of time.

Natalie asks you the following questions:

1. I currently sell 32 mixers a year at $1,025 apiece. My cost of goods sold averages $566 per mixer. What is my gross profit margin?
2. I've heard that sometimes revenue cannot be recorded until the cash is collected. What are the guidelines that determine when revenue should be recorded? How will these guidelines affect me if I start selling mixers on an extended payment plan?
3. What are some of the advantages and disadvantages of giving my customers the option of paying through an extended payment plan?

Instructions

(a) Answer Natalie's questions.
(b) Natalie would like more information about her annual gross profit if she decides to implement an extended payment plan similar to the one offered by Trial Appliances. Assume that she sells 32 mixers in year 1 and that all the customers use the extended payment plan. Calculate the amount of gross profit to be recorded in years 1, 2, and 3 if she recognizes revenue (1) at the point of sale, and (2) on the instalment basis. (For this calculation, assume there are no additional sales in years 2 and 3 and that 25% of the amount due is collected in year 1, 50% is collected in year 2, and the remaining 25% is collected in year 3).
(c) Do you think Natalie should offer her customers the option of paying through an extended payment plan?

Cumulative Coverage—Chapters 6 to 11

Johan Company and Nordlund Company are competing businesses. Both began operations six years ago and they are quite similar in most respects. The current balance sheet data for the two companies are as follows:

	Johan Company	Nordlund Company
Cash	$ 50,300	$ 48,400
Accounts receivable	309,700	312,500
Allowance for doubtful accounts	(13,600)	0
Merchandise inventory	463,900	520,200
Property, plant, and equipment	245,300	257,300
Accumulated amortization	(107,650)	(189,850)
Total assets	$947,950	$948,550
Current liabilities	$440,200	$436,500
Long-term liabilities	78,000	80,000
Total liabilities	518,200	516,500
Owner's equity	429,750	432,050
Total liabilities and owner's equity	$947,950	$948,550

You have been engaged as a consultant to conduct a review of the two companies. Your goal is to determine which of them is in a stronger financial position. Your review of their financial statements quickly reveals that the two companies have not followed the same accounting principles. The differences, and your conclusions regarding them, are summarized below:

1. Johan Company has used the allowance method of accounting for bad debts. A review shows that the amount of its write-offs each year has been quite close to the allowances that have been provided. It seems reasonable to have confidence in its current estimate of bad debts.

   Nordlund Company has been somewhat slow to recognize its uncollectible accounts. Based on an aging analysis and review of its accounts receivable, it is estimated that $14,000 of its existing accounts will become uncollectible.
2. Johan Company has determined the cost of its merchandise inventory using the LIFO cost flow assumption. The result is that its inventory appears on the balance sheet at an amount that is below its current replacement cost. Based a detailed physical examination of its merchandise on hand, the current replacement cost of its inventory is estimated at $500,000.

Nordlund Company has used the FIFO cost flow assumption of valuing its merchandise inventory. The result is that its ending inventory appears on the balance sheet at an amount that quite closely approximates its current replacement cost.

3. Johan Company estimated a useful life of 12 years and a residual value of $30,000 for its property, plant, and equipment, and has been amortizing them on a straight-line basis.

Nordlund Company has the same type of property, plant, and equipment. However, it estimated a useful life of 10 years and a residual value of $10,000. It has been amortizing its property, plant, and equipment using the double declining-balance method.

Based on engineering studies of these types of property, plant, and equipment, you conclude that Nordlund's estimates and method for calculating amortization are more appropriate.

Instructions

(a) Where would you find the above information on the two companies' accounting principles? Be specific about what information would be available and where you would find it.

(b) Discuss how the full disclosure principle and the cost-benefit constraint have affected what was included or not included in each company's financial statements.

(c) What is the objective of financial reporting? Why might your client want to determine which company has the stronger financial position?

(d) Using similar accounting principles for both companies, revise the balance sheets presented above. Has the quality of accounting information been increased for one particular company by preparing these revised statements?

(e) Write a report for your client on which company is in a stronger financial position.

BROADENING YOUR PERSPECTIVE

Financial Reporting and Analysis

 Practice Tools

Financial Reporting Problem

BYP11–1 Refer to the Notes to Consolidated Financial Statements for **The Forzani Group Ltd.**, in Appendix A.

Instructions

(a) Subsection (h) of Note 2, Significant Accounting Policies, describes Forzani's store-opening expenses. Explain how the company's treatment of these expenses relates to the matching principle. Can you think of an alternative treatment of these expenses?

(b) Subsection (p) of Note 2, Significant Accounting Policies, describes Forzani's comparative figures. Do you think this additional disclosure was necessary? Explain why or why not, referring to the appropriate generally accepted accounting principles in your answer.

(c) Note 13, Sale of Investment, refers to the company's sale of a wholesale distribution operation. What accounting principles and constraints are reflected in this disclosure?

(d) Note 18 provides information about a transaction with a company officer. Why might it be important for readers of the financial statements to be aware of this transaction?

Interpreting Financial Statements

BYP11–2 Today, companies must compete in a global economy. For example, Canada's oldest candy company, **Ganong Bros., Limited**, which has been making chocolates since 1873, must compete with **Nestlé S.A.**, among others. Nestlé, a Swiss company, although best known for its chocolates and confections, is also the largest food company in the world. Comparing companies such as Ganong and Nestlé can pose some challenges. Consider the following excerpt from the notes to Nestlé's financial statements:

NESTLÉ GROUP
Notes to the Financial Statements (partial)
December 31, 2002

Accounting policies
- Accounting convention and accounting standards

The Consolidated accounts comply with International Financial Reporting Standards (IFRS) issued by the International Accounting Standards Board (IASB) and with the Standing Interpretations issued by the International Financial Reporting Interpretations Committee (IFRIC) of the IASB.

The accounts have been prepared on an accrual basis and under the historical cost convention. . . All significant consolidated companies have a 31ˢᵗ December accounting year-end. All disclosures required by the 4ᵗʰ and 7ᵗʰ European Union company law directives are provided.

Instructions

Discuss the implications of each of these items in terms of the effect it might have (positive or negative) on your ability to compare Nestlé to Ganong. (*Hint:* In your answer, include a discussion of relevant principles and assumptions in financial reporting.)

Accounting on the Web

BYP11–3 Revenue recognition is a critical area for standard-setters. This case reviews the revenue recognition policies of three Canadian companies.

Instructions

Specific requirements of this Internet case are available on the Weygandt website.

Critical Thinking

Collaborative Learning Activity

BYP11–4 Hague Industries has two operating divisions—Devany Construction Division and Security Equipment Division. Both divisions maintain their own accounting systems and methods of revenue recognition.

Devany Construction Division

During the fiscal year ending November 30, 2005, Devany Construction Division has one construction project in progress. A $30-million contract for construction of a civic centre was granted on June 19, 2005. Construction begins on August 1, 2005. Estimated costs of completion at the contract date are $25 million over a two-year period. By November 30, 2005, construction costs of $6.75 million have been incurred.

The construction costs to complete the remainder of the project are reviewed on November 30, 2005. They are estimated to amount to $20.25 million because of an expected decline in raw materials costs.

Revenue recognition is based on the percentage-of-completion method.

Security Equipment Division

Security Equipment Division works through manufacturers' agents in various cities. Orders for alarm systems, and down payments, are forwarded from the agents. The division ships the goods FOB destination directly to customers (usually police departments and security-guard companies). Customers are billed directly for the balance due.

The firm receives orders for $7 million of goods during the fiscal year ending November 30, 2005. Down payments of $500,000 are received, and goods with a selling price of $6.5 million are billed and shipped. Commissions of 8% of the product price are paid to the agents after the goods are shipped to the customers. The goods are covered under warranty for 90 days after shipment. Warranty returns have been about 2% of sales.

Revenue is recognized at the point of sale by this division.

Instructions

With the class divided into groups, do the following:

(a) There are various methods of revenue recognition. Define and describe each of the following methods of revenue recognition. Indicate the circumstances under which each of them follows generally accepted accounting principles.

    1. Point of sale   3. Completed-contract

    2. Percentage-of-completion   4. Instalment

(b) Calculate the amount of revenue to be recognized in the fiscal year 2005 for each operating division of Hague Industries, in accordance with generally accepted accounting principles.

Communication Activity

BYP11–5 The Algonquin College of Applied Arts and Technology has over 11,000 full-time students at campuses in Ottawa, Pembroke, and Perth. About 40% of Algonquin College's revenues come from provincial government grants. The college received $8.5 million from the Province of Ontario in the year ended March 31, 2003, to construct a new building for the School of Transportation and Building Trades. It was scheduled for completion in January 2004. In addition, the college received $4.5 million during the same fiscal year to enhance the quality of the college's programs and services.

One of the difficulties in receiving provincial grants is to match expenses against revenues in the right fiscal year. For example, the funding for the new building was received in fiscal 2003 but will not all be spent until fiscal 2004. Tuition fees from the increased capacity in the School of Transportation and Building Trades will not be received until 2004 and will cover multiple years. The funding for quality assurance was received in fiscal 2003, but it may take up to five years to see the results of this funding in the college's programs and services. Even then, there will be no way to directly relate increased revenues in the future to the expenses incurred now to improve quality.

Instructions

Write a letter covering the following points:

(a) Why is the matching principle important in accounting for Algonquin College's revenues and expenses?

(b) How should the college account for the $8.5 million received to construct the new building for the School of Transportation and Building Trades? In what period(s) should the college match the revenues and expenses related to this project?

(c) How should the college account for the $4.5 million received to improve quality? In what period(s) should the college match the revenues and expenses related to this project?

(d) Give some examples of a situation in which the matching principle might be difficult to apply at your own college or university.

Ethics Case

BYP11–6   When the CICA issues new accounting recommendations, the required implementation date is usually 12 months or more after the date of publication. Early implementation is encouraged.

Carol DesChenes, an accountant at Grocery Online.com, discusses with her financial vice-president the need for early implementation of a recently issued recommendation. She says it will result in a much fairer presentation of the company's financial position. When the financial vice-president determines that early implementation would adversely affect reported net income for the year, he strongly discourages Carol from implementing the recommendation until it is required.

Instructions
(a) Who are the stakeholders in this situation?
(b) What, if any, are the ethical considerations in this situation?
(c) What could Carol gain by supporting early implementation? Who might be affected by the decision against early implementation?

Answers to Self-Study Questions
1. a   2. d   3. c   4. c   5. a   6. a   7. c   8. c   9. c   10. b

Answer to Forzani Review It Question 2
Deloitte & Touche, Forzani's auditors, state that the financial statements are presented fairly, in all material respects, in accordance with Canadian generally accepted accounting principles.

 Remember to go back to the Navigator Box at the beginning of the chapter to check off your completed work.

concepts for review >>

Before studying this chapter, you should understand or, if necessary, review:

a. The cost principle of accounting. (Ch. 1, p. 7)
b. The statement of owner's equity. (Ch. 1, p. 20)
c. How to make closing entries and prepare the post-closing trial balance. (Ch. 4, pp. 158–163)
d. The steps in the accounting cycle. (Ch. 4, p. 164–165)
e. The format of a classified balance sheet. (Ch. 4, pp. 167–172)

Partners Work Together for Success

SASKATOON, Sask.—When chartered accountants Glen Bailey and Clare Heagy founded their partnership back in 1983, they knew that working together would benefit both them and their clients. Mr. Heagy had been a partner in a national firm and had a roster of clients; Mr. Bailey was just starting out but had specialized training in taxation. By combining their talents and resources, they soon built a thriving practice serving a wide range of Saskatchewan businesses.

Today the partnership has expanded to include four partners and a staff of 15. Mr. Bailey says the firm's success is rooted in a clear understanding of what partnership entails and everyone pulling their weight.

"When we got started we drew up an agreement that basically covered how the business would be operated, splitting of income, draws of money, and provisions around death, disability, or withdrawal of partners," he recalls. The agreement also recognized the fact that Mr. Heagy had brought in the initial client base and included a provision for a fee to be paid to him on withdrawal, over and above the value of his assets.

A few years later, in 1988, Richard Altrogge joined the partnership, initially as an associate. "After a while, we admitted him as a junior partner under a system that allowed him to become an equal partner through an injection of cash equal to the net book value of the assets when his billings reached a pro rata share of total revenues," says Mr. Bailey.

The firm was then a three-way partnership for a number of years. When Mr. Heagy retired in 1998, Richard Matchett, who had begun working for the firm as an employee, became a junior partner, followed by Alan Ashdown.

In 2002, the province of Saskatchewan passed legislation allowing professionals to incorporate. At that point the structure of the partnership was modified. "We each set up our own professional corporation and rolled our interests in the partnership into those," explains Mr. Bailey. "We're still a partnership, but technically we're a partnership of corporations." The firm now bears the name Heagy Bailey Altrogge Matchett LLP.

"A partnership is much like a marriage," concludes Mr. Bailey. "You're going to have problems, but if all the partners do their part and work together, you have the best chance of success."

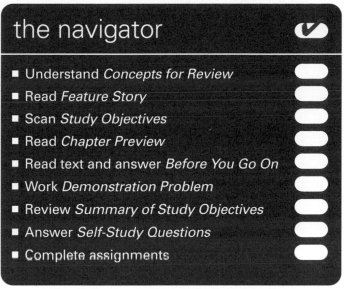

the navigator ✔

- Understand *Concepts for Review*
- Read *Feature Story*
- Scan *Study Objectives*
- Read *Chapter Preview*
- Read text and answer *Before You Go On*
- Work *Demonstration Problem*
- Review *Summary of Study Objectives*
- Answer *Self-Study Questions*
- Complete assignments

c h a p t e r 1 2
Accounting for Partnerships

study objectives >>

the navigator ✔

After studying this chapter, you should be able to:

1. Describe the characteristics of the partnership form of business organization.
2. Describe and generate the accounting entries for the formation of a partnership.
3. Apply various bases to divide net income or net loss.
4. Describe and illustrate the form and content of partnership financial statements.
5. Prepare and explain the effects of the entries when a new partner is admitted.
6. Prepare and explain the effects of the entries when a partner withdraws from the firm.
7. Prepare the entries to record the liquidation of a partnership.

It is not surprising that Glen Bailey and Clare Heagy decided to use the partnership form of organization when they started their accounting practice. They saw an opportunity to combine their expertise and better leverage their resources. In this chapter, we will discuss why the partnership form of organization is often chosen. We will also explain the major issues in accounting for partnerships.

The chapter is organized as follows:

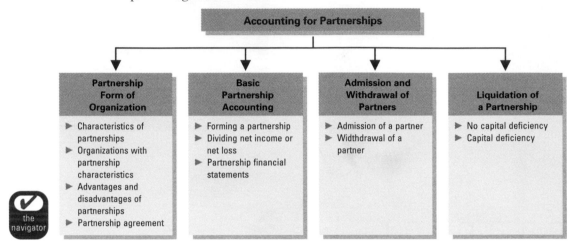

Partnership Form of Organization

All provinces in Canada have a *Partnership Act* which provides the basic rules for the formation and operation of partnerships. These acts define a **partnership** as two or more people who do business with the intention of making a profit. This does not necessarily mean that there must be a profit—just that profit is the objective. Partnerships are common in professions such as accounting, advertising, law, or medicine. Professional partnerships can vary in size from two partners to thousands.

There are different forms of partnership organizations. The most common is the general partnership. Unless otherwise indicated, our discussion in this chapter focuses on the general partnership organization.

Characteristics of Partnerships

study objective 1

Describe the characteristics of the partnership form of business organization.

Partnerships are fairly easy to form. Although they can be formed simply by a verbal agreement, it is far better to have a legal, written agreement outline the rights and obligations of the partners, as in the feature story. Partners who have not put their agreement in writing have found that the absence of a written agreement can sometimes lead to later difficulties.

The principal characteristics of the partnership form of business organization are shown in Illustration 12-1, and are explained in the following sections.

Illustration 12-1 ◄

Partnership characteristics

Association of Individuals

The voluntary association of two or more individuals in a partnership may be based on an act as simple as a handshake. It is highly recommended, however, that the agreement be in writing.

A partnership is a legal entity for certain purposes. For instance, property (land, buildings, equipment) can be owned in the name of the partnership. The firm can sue or be sued. A partnership is also an accounting entity for financial reporting purposes. Thus, the personal assets, liabilities, and transactions of the partners are excluded from the accounting records of the partnership, just as they are in a proprietorship.

Co-Ownership of Property

Partnership assets are owned jointly by the partners. If the partnership is dissolved, the assets do not legally return to the original contributor. Each partner has a claim on total assets equal to the balance in his or her respective capital account. This claim does not give a right to specific assets that an individual partner contributed to the firm. Similarly, if a partner invests a building in the partnership that is valued at $100,000 and the building is later sold at a gain of $20,000, that partner does not receive the entire gain.

Division of Income

Just as property is co-owned, so is partnership net income (or net loss). The partners specify how the partnership net income (loss) will be divided when they form the partnership, just as they did in the feature story. If the division isn't specified, net income (loss) is assumed to be shared equally. We will learn more about dividing partnership income in a later section of this chapter.

The net income of a partnership is not taxed as a separate entity. Instead, each partner's share is personally taxable. This share of income is recorded on the partner's personal income tax return and taxed at his or her personal income tax rate regardless of the amount withdrawn from the partnership during the year.

Limited Life

A partnership does not have an unlimited life. Any change in ownership dissolves the partnership. **Partnership dissolution** occurs whenever a partner withdraws (whether voluntarily or involuntarily through death, incapacitation, or retirement) or a new partner is admitted. Dissolution of a partnership does not necessarily mean that the business ends. If the continuing partners agree, operations can continue without interruption through the formation of a new partnership.

Mutual Agency

Mutual agency means that each partner acts for the partnership when doing partnership business. The action of any partner is binding on all other partners. This is true even when partners exceed their authority, so long as the act appears appropriate for the partnership. For example, a partner of an accounting firm who purchases a building creates a binding contract in the name of the partnership, even if the partnership agreement denies this authority. On the other hand, if a partner in a law firm were to buy a snowmobile for the partnership, the act would not be binding on the partnership, because the purchase is unrelated to the business.

Unlimited Liability

Each partner is **jointly and severally (individually) liable** for all partnership liabilities. If one partner incurs a liability, the other partners are also held responsible. Creditors' claims are first on partnership assets. If these are insufficient, the claims then attach to the personal resources of any partner, regardless of that partner's equity in the partnership. Because each partner is responsible for all the debts of the partnership, each partner is said to have **unlimited liability**.

Unlimited liability and mutual agency can combine for disastrous results. An unethical or incompetent partner can commit the partnership to a deal which could ultimately bankrupt the partnership assets. The creditors may then be able to seek recourse from the partners' personal assets—the assets of *all* the partners and not just those of the partner who committed the partnership to the misguided deal. As Mr. Bailey says in the feature story, "A partnership is much like a marriage." Consequently, an individual must be extremely cautious in selecting a partner.

Partners can avoid unlimited liability by forming a limited liability partnership, as they did in the feature story. We will discuss limited liability partnerships in the next section.

Organizations with Partnership Characteristics

Because of the fear of unlimited liability, special forms of business organizations have been created that include many partnership characteristics but that modify the characteristic of unlimited liability. These special forms include limited partnerships and limited liability partnerships.

Limited Partnerships (LP)

In a **limited partnership** one or more of the partners have unlimited liability. This type of partner is called a **general partner**. A general partner normally contributes work and experience to the partnership and is authorized to manage and represent the partnership. The general partner's liability for the debts of the partnership is unlimited.

In addition to the general partner(s), one or more partners have limited liability for the debts of the partnership. This type of partner is called a **limited partner**. Limited partners normally provide cash or assets to the partnership. A limited partner's liability for the debts of the partnership is limited to the amount of capital he or she contributed. This type of organization is identified in its name with the words "Limited Partnership," "Ltd.," or "LP."

Limited partnerships are normally used by businesses that provide income tax shelters for investors, such as real estate investment trusts (REIT), rental properties, and sports ventures. For example, the Calgary Flames are organized as a limited partnership. In this type of partnership, sports fans (or investors) contribute money that they can use as a deduction on their personal income tax returns. Investors must exercise caution, however, in investing in limited partnerships solely for the tax deduction. The tax deductions are limited, and as with any investment, the investment should be made for sound financial reasons, and not solely as an income tax deduction.

Limited Liability Partnerships (LLP)

Most professionals such as lawyers, doctors, and accountants form a **limited liability partnership** or "LLP." In the feature story, Heagy Bailey Altrogge Matchett operates as a limited liability partnership. The largest LLP in the world is PricewaterhouseCoopers. With more than 8,000 partners, this accounting and professional services firm earns fees of nearly $14 billion in 142 countries.

A limited liability partnership is designed to protect innocent partners from negligence claims resulting from the acts of another partner. That is, partners in an LLP continue to have unlimited liability for their own negligence but have limited liability for other partners' negligence. In addition to remaining personally liable for their own actions, partners also are liable for the actions of those they directly supervise and control.

Advantages and Disadvantages of Partnerships

Why do people choose partnerships? Often, it is to **combine the skills and resources** of two or more individuals. For example, the partners of Heagy Bailey Altrogge Matchett LLP are able to work together and share office space and accounting knowledge. They can also divide among the partners different areas of responsibility and expertise—assurance, taxation, and business valuation, for example.

A partnership is **easily formed and is relatively free from government regulations and restrictions**. Also, decisions can be made quickly on important matters that affect the firm. There is no board of directors that must be consulted.

On the other hand, partnerships also have some disadvantages: **mutual agency, limited life,** and **unlimited liability** in general partnerships. Unlimited liability is particularly troublesome. Many individuals fear they may lose not only their initial investment, but also their personal assets if those assets are needed to pay partnership creditors. As a result, partnerships often find it difficult to obtain large amounts of investment capital. That is one reason why the largest business enterprises in Canada are corporations, not partnerships.

The advantages and disadvantages of the general partnership form of business organization are summarized in Illustration 12-2:

Advantages	Disadvantages
Combines skills and resources of two or more individuals	Mutual agency
Easily formed	Limited life
Relatively free of government regulations and restrictions	Unlimited liability
Ease of decision-making	

Illustration 12-2 ◄

Advantages and disadvantages of a general partnership

on Test.

V.I.P.

Partnership Agreement

Ideally, the agreement of two or more individuals to form a partnership should be in the form of a written contract, known as the **partnership agreement**. The partnership agreement contains such basic information as the name and principal location of the firm, the purpose of the business, and the date of inception. In addition, relationships among the partners must be specified, such as:

1. The names and capital contributions of partners
2. The rights and duties of partners   *on. Test-*
3. The basis for sharing net income or net loss
4. Provisions for withdrawal of assets
5. Procedures for submitting disputes to arbitration
6. Procedures for the withdrawal, or addition, of a partner
7. The rights and duties of surviving partners if a partner dies

We cannot overemphasize the importance of a written contract. If a partnership agreement does not exist, the provisions of the *Partnership Act* will apply, which may not be what the partners want. The partnership agreement should be written with care to anticipate all possible situations, contingencies, and disagreements.

ACCOUNTING IN ACTION ▶ Business Insight

A partnership may be created unintentionally. For example, the *Partnership Act* for British Columbia states that if you receive a share of income from a business, you will be considered a partner in the business unless evidence exists to the contrary. In B.C., then, it would be wise to have a formal agreement that specifies the partners of a firm. Without one, you may be part of a partnership without knowing it!

BEFORE YOU GO ON . . .

▶Review It

1. What are the distinguishing characteristics of a partnership?
2. How can partners limit their liability?
3. What are the principal advantages and disadvantages of a partnership?
4. What are the major items in a partnership agreement?
5. The Forzani Group Ltd. originally started as a partnership when Calgary Stampeder John Forzani and three of his teammates (which included two of his brothers) started Forzani's Locker Room in 1974. Why do you suppose they changed to the corporate form of organization in 1993? The answer to this question is at the end of the chapter.

Related exercise material: BE12–1 and E12–1.

Basic Partnership Accounting

We now turn to the basic accounting for partnerships. The major accounting issues relate to forming the partnership, dividing income or loss, and preparing financial statements.

Forming a Partnership

Each partner's initial investment in a partnership is entered in the partnership records. These investments should be recorded at the **fair market value of the assets at the date of their transfer to the partnership**. The values given must be agreed to by all of the partners.

To illustrate, assume that M. Gan and K. Sin combine their proprietorships on January 2 to start a partnership named Interactive Software. The firm will specialize in developing financial-modelling software packages. Gan and Sin have the following assets before forming the partnership:

| | Book Value | | Market Value | |
	Gan	Sin	Gan	Sin
Cash	$ 8,000	$ 9,000	$ 8,000	$ 9,000
Office equipment	5,000		4,000	
Accumulated amortization	(2,000)			
Accounts receivable		4,000		4,000
Allowance for doubtful accounts		(700)		(1,000)
	$11,000	$12,300	$12,000	$12,000

※ Always use Market value.

The entries to record the investments are:

Capital = investments.

		Investment of M. Gan		
Jan.	2	Cash	8,000	
		Office Equipment	4,000	
		M. Gan, Capital		12,000
		To record investment of Gan.		
		Investment of K. Sin		
	2	Cash	9,000	
		Accounts Receivable	4,000	
		Allowance for Doubtful Accounts		1,000
		K. Sin, Capital		12,000
		To record investment of Sin.		

A	=	L	+	PE
+8,000				+12,000
+4,000				

Cash flows: +8,000

A	=	L	+	PE
+9,000				+12,000
+4,000				
−1,000				

Cash flows: +9,000

Note that neither the original cost of the office equipment ($5,000) nor its book value ($5,000 – $2,000) is recorded by the partnership. Instead, the equipment is recorded at its fair market value of $4,000. Because the equipment has not yet been used by the partnership, there is no accumulated amortization.

In contrast, the gross claims on customers ($4,000) are carried forward to the partnership. The allowance for doubtful accounts is adjusted to $1,000 to arrive at a net realizable value of $3,000. A partnership may start with an allowance for doubtful accounts, because it will continue to collect existing accounts receivable, some of which are expected to be uncollectible.

After the partnership has been formed, the accounting for transactions is similar to the accounting for any other type of business organization. For example, all transactions with outside parties, such as the performance of services and payment for them, should be recorded in the same way for a partnership as for a proprietorship.

The steps in the accounting cycle that are described in Chapter 4 for a proprietorship also apply to a partnership. For example, a partnership journalizes and posts transactions, prepares a trial balance, journalizes and posts adjusting entries, and prepares an adjusted trial balance. However, there are minor differences in journalizing and posting closing entries and in preparing financial statements, as explained in the following sections. The differences occur because there is more than one owner.

Helpful hint The cost principle applies. Cash and the fair market value of noncash assets are recorded at the date of acquisition. The fair market value is what the assets would have cost if they had been purchased at that time.

Accounting Cycle Tutorial

Dividing Net Income or Net Loss

study objective 3

Apply various bases to divide net income or net loss.

Partnership net income or net loss is shared equally unless the partnership agreement indicates a different division. The same basis of division usually applies to both net income and net loss. It is customary to refer to this basis as the **income ratio**. It is also known as the income and loss ratio, or the profit and loss ratio. A partner's share of net income or net loss is recognized in the accounts through closing entries.

Closing Entries

As in the case of a proprietorship, four entries are required in preparing closing entries for a partnership:

1. Debit each individual revenue account for its balance and credit Income Summary for total revenues.
2. Debit Income Summary for total expenses and credit each individual expense account for its balance.
3. Debit Income Summary for its balance (which should equal the net income amount) and credit each partner's capital account for his or her share of net income. Conversely, credit Income Summary and debit each partner's capital account for his or her share of net loss.
4. Debit each partner's capital account for the balance in that partner's drawings account, and credit each partner's drawings account for the same amount.

The first two entries are the same as in a proprietorship. The last two entries are different because (1) there are two or more owners' capital and drawings accounts, and (2) it is necessary to divide net income (or net loss) among the partners.

To illustrate closing entries, we will assume, for simplicity, that Interactive Software has one revenue and one expense account. Sales Revenue totalled $100,000 and Operating Expenses totalled $68,000 for the year ended December 31, 2005. The partners, M. Gan and K. Sin, share net income and net loss equally. Drawings for the year were Gan, $8,000, and Sin, $6,000. The closing entries are as follows:

A	=	L	+	PE
				−100,000
				+100,000

Cash flows: no effect

A	=	L	+	PE
				−68,000
				+68,000

Cash flows: no effect

A	=	L	+	PE
				−32,000
				+16,000
				+16,000

Cash flows: no effect

A	=	L	+	PE
				−8,000
				−6,000
				+8,000
				+6,000

Cash flows: no effect

Date	Account	Debit	Credit
Dec. 31	Sales Revenue	100,000	
	Income Summary		100,000
	To close revenue to income summary.		
31	Income Summary	68,000	
	Operating Expenses		68,000
	To close expenses to income summary.		
31	Income Summary ($100,000 − $68,000)	32,000	
	M. Gan, Capital ($32,000 × 50%)		16,000
	K. Sin, Capital ($32,000 × 50%)		16,000
	To close net income to capital accounts.		
31	M. Gan, Capital	8,000	
	K. Sin, Capital	6,000	
	M. Gan, Drawings		8,000
	K. Sin, Drawings		6,000
	To close drawings accounts to capital accounts.		

As in a proprietorship, the partners' capital accounts are permanent accounts. Revenue, expense, income summary, and the partners' drawings accounts are temporary accounts.

Income Ratios

As noted earlier, the partnership agreement should specify the basis for sharing net income or net loss. The following are typical income ratios:

1. A fixed ratio, expressed as a proportion (2:1), a percentage (67% and 33%), or a fraction ($\frac{2}{3}$ and $\frac{1}{3}$).
2. A ratio based either on capital balances at the beginning or end of the year, or on average capital balances during the year.

3. Salaries to partners and the remainder in a fixed ratio.
4. Interest on partners' capital balances and the remainder in a fixed ratio.
5. Salaries to partners, as well as interest on partners' capital balances, and the remainder in a fixed ratio.

The goal is to agree to a basis that fairly reflects the partners' capital investment and service to the partnership.

A fixed ratio is easy to apply, and it may be an equitable basis in some circumstances. Assume, for example, that Hughes and Lane are partners. Each contributes the same amount of capital, but Hughes expects to work full-time in the partnership, while Lane expects to work only half-time. Accordingly, the partners agree to a fixed ratio of two-thirds to Hughes and one-third to Lane.

A ratio based on capital balances may be appropriate when the funds invested in the partnership are the critical factor. Capital balances may also be fair when a manager is hired to run the business and the partners do not plan to take an active role in daily operations.

The three remaining income ratios (items 3, 4, and 5 in the list above) recognize differences among partners specifically. These ratios provide salary allowances for time worked and interest allowances for capital invested. Any remaining net income or net loss is allocated using a fixed ratio. Caution needs to be used in working with these types of income ratios. **These ratios are used only for the calculations that divide net income or net loss among partners.**

Salaries to partners and interest on partners' capital balances should not be recorded as expenses of the partnership. For a partnership, as with other entities, salaries expense is for the cost of services performed by employees. Likewise, interest expense relates to the cost of borrowing from creditors. As owners, partners are not considered either employees or creditors. Some partnership agreements permit partners to make monthly withdrawals of cash based on their salary allowance. These may or may not be the same as the salary allowance specified in the income ratio. In such cases, the withdrawals are debited to the partner's drawings account. They are not debited to Salaries Expense.

ACCOUNTING IN ACTION ► Business Insight

Partners in large public accounting firms can make substantial incomes. A few senior partners may earn as much as $1 million a year. However, the average earnings of partners are more likely to be in the $300,000 range. The compensation of partners in most large partnerships differs in both form and substance from the compensation of a corporate executive. Partners are not guaranteed an annual salary, nor are they granted stock options. Compensation depends entirely on each year's operating results, which could be positive (net income) or negative (net loss). Also, substantial investment is required of each partner. This capital is at risk for the partner's entire career—often 25 to 30 years—without an established return. Upon leaving, it is repayable to the partner without an adjustment for inflation or appreciation in value.

Salaries, Interest, and Remainder in a Fixed Ratio

Under one income ratio (item 5 in the list above), salaries and interest must be allocated before the remainder is divided according to the specified fixed ratio. This is true even if the salary and interest provisions exceed net income. It is also true even if the partnership has suffered a net loss for the year.

To illustrate this income ratio, assume that Sara King and Ray Lee are partners in the Kingslee Company. The partnership agreement provides for (1) salary allowances of $8,400 to King and $6,000 to Lee, (2) interest allowances of 10% on capital balances at the beginning of the year, and (3) the remainder to be distributed equally. Capital balances on January 1 were King $28,000 and Lee $24,000. For the year ended December 31, 2005, partnership net income is $22,000. The division of net income for the year ended December 31, 2005, is as follows:

Illustration 12-3 ▶

Division of net income

KINGSLEE COMPANY Division of Net Income Year Ended December 31, 2005			
	Sara King	Ray Lee	Total
Net income			$22,000
Salary allowance	$ 8,400	$6,000	14,400
Remaining income			7,600
Interest allowance			
King ($28,000 × 10%)	2,800		
Lee ($24,000 × 10%)		2,400	5,200
Remaining income			2,400
Fixed ratio			
King ($2,400 × 50%)	1,200		
Lee ($2,400 × 50%)		1,200	2,400
Remaining income			0
Division of net income	$12,400	$9,600	$22,000

The entry to record the division of net income is:

A	=	L	+	PE
				−22,000
				+12,400
				+9,600

Cash flows: no effect

Dec. 31	Income Summary	22,000	
	Sara King, Capital		12,400
	Ray Lee, Capital		9,600
	To close net income to partners' capital accounts.		

Now let's look at a situation in which the salary and interest allowances are greater than net income or there is a loss. Assume that Kingslee Company reports a net loss of $18,000. In this case, the salary and interest allowances create a total deficiency of $37,600 ($18,000 + $14,400 + $5,200). This deficiency is divided equally among the partners as shown below:

Illustration 12-4 ▶

Division of net loss

KINGSLEE COMPANY Division of Net Loss Year Ended December 31, 2005			
	Sara King	Ray Lee	Total
Net loss			$(18,000)
Salary allowance	$ 8,400	$ 6,000	14,400
Remaining loss			(32,400)
Interest allowance			
King ($28,000 × 10%)	2,800		
Lee ($24,000 × 10%)		2,400	5,200
Remaining loss			(37,600)
Fixed ratio			
King ($37,600 × 50%)	(18,800)		
Lee ($37,600 × 50%)		(18,800)	(37,600)
Remaining loss			0
Division of net loss	$ (7,600)	$(10,400)	$(18,000)

The salary and interest allowances are calculated first, as in the preceding example, regardless of whether the partnership reports a net income or a net loss. Any remaining excess or deficiency is then allocated to the partners.

The journal entry to record the division of the net loss would be as follows:

Dec. 31	Sara King, Capital	7,600	
	Ray Lee, Capital	10,400	
	Income Summary		18,000
	To close net loss to partners' capital accounts.		

A = L + PE
-7,600
-10,400
+18,000

Cash flows: no effect

Partnership Financial Statements

The financial statements of a partnership are similar to those of a proprietorship. The differences are due to the number of owners involved.

The income statement for a partnership is identical to the income statement for a proprietorship. The allocation (division) of the partnership net income or loss is often disclosed as a separate schedule or note to the statement.

The statement of equity for a partnership is called the **statement of partners' capital**. Its function is to explain the changes in each partner's capital account and in total partnership capital during the year. As in a proprietorship, changes in capital may result from three causes: additional capital investments, drawings, and each partner's share of the net income or net loss.

The statement of partners' capital for Kingslee Company is shown in Illustration 12-5. It is based on the division of $22,000 of net income in Illustration 12-3. The statement includes assumed data for the investments and drawings.

study objective 4

Describe and illustrate the form and content of partnership financial statements.

Illustration 12-5 ◄

Statement of partners' capital

KINGSLEE COMPANY
Statement of Partners' Capital
Year Ended December 31, 2005

	Sara King	Ray Lee	Total
Capital, January 1	$28,000	$24,000	$52,000
Add: Investments	2,000	0	2,000
Net income	12,400	9,600	22,000
	42,400	33,600	76,000
Less: Drawings	7,000	5,000	12,000
Capital, December 31	$35,400	$28,600	$64,000

The statement of partners' capital is prepared from the income statement and the partners' capital and drawings accounts.

The balance sheet for a partnership is the same as for a proprietorship, except for the equity section. In a proprietorship, the equity section of the balance sheet is called **owner's equity**. A one-line capital account is reported for the owner. In a partnership, the capital balances of each partner are shown in the balance sheet, in a section called **partners' equity**. The partners' equity section in Kingslee Company's balance sheet appears in Illustration 12-6.

Illustration 12-6 ►

Partners' equity section of
a partnership balance sheet

KINGSLEE COMPANY Balance Sheet (partial) December 31, 2005		
Liabilities and Partners' Equity		
Total liabilities (assumed amount)		$115,000
Partners' equity		
Sara King, Capital	$35,400	
Ray Lee, Capital	28,600	64,000
Total liabilities and partners' equity		$179,000

It is impractical for large partnerships to report each individual partner's equity separately. For reporting purposes, these amounts are usually aggregated in the balance sheet.

BEFORE YOU GO ON . . .

►Review It

1. How should a partner's initial investment of assets be valued?
2. What are the closing entries for a partnership?
3. What types of income ratios may be used in a partnership?
4. How do partnership financial statements differ from proprietorship financial statements?

►Do It

LeMay Company reports net income of $44,000 for the year ended May 31. The partnership agreement provides for a salary allowance of $30,000 to L. Lee and $24,000 to R. May. The remainder is to be shared on a 60:40 basis (60% to Lee, 40% to May). L. Lee asks for your help to divide the net income between the two partners and prepare the closing entry.

Action Plan

- Calculate net income to be divided, ignoring any salary or interest allowances.
- Allocate the salary allowance first, followed by the interest allowance, if any.
- Apply the partners' income ratios to the remaining income or deficiency.
- Prepare the closing entry distributing net income or loss among the partners' capital accounts.

Solution

The division of net income is as follows:

	L. Lee	R. May	Total
Net income			$44,000
Salary allowance	$30,000	$24,000	54,000
Remaining deficiency			(10,000)
Fixed ratio			
Lee (60% × $10,000)	(6,000)		
May (40% × $10,000)		(4,000)	(10,000)
Remaining deficiency			0
Division of net income	$24,000	$20,000	$44,000

The closing entry for net income is as follows:

May 31	Income Summary	44,000	
	L. Lee, Capital		24,000
	R. May, Capital		20,000
	To close net income to partners' capital accounts.		

Related exercise material: BE12–2, BE12–3, BE12–4, BE12–5, BE12–6, BE12–7, E12–2, E12–3, and E12–4.

Admission and Withdrawal of Partners

We have seen how the basic accounting for a partnership works. We now look at how to account for a common occurrence in partnerships—the addition or withdrawal of a partner.

Admission of a Partner

The admission of a new partner results in the legal dissolution of the existing partnership and the beginning of a new one. From an economic standpoint, the admission of a new partner (or partners) may be of minor significance to the continuity of the business. For example, in large public accounting or law firms, partners are admitted without any change in operating policies. To recognize the economic effects, it is only necessary to open a capital account for each new partner. In most cases, the accounting records of the predecessor partnership will continue to be used by the new partnership.

A new partner may be admitted by either (1) purchasing the interest of an existing partner, or (2) investing assets in the partnership, as shown in Illustration 12-7. The former involves only a transfer of capital among the partners who are part of the transaction: the total capital of the partnership is not affected. The latter (an investment of assets) increases both the partnership's net assets (total assets less total liabilities) and total capital.

> **study objective 5**
>
> Prepare and explain the effects of the entries when a new partner is admitted.

How Partners Can Be Admitted

1. Purchase of a partner's interest

2. Investment of assets in the partnership

Illustration 12-7 ◀

Ways of adding partners

Purchase of a Partner's Interest

The admission by purchase of an interest is a personal transaction between one or more existing partners and the new partner. Each party acts as an individual, separate from the partnership entity. The price paid is negotiated by the individuals involved. It may be equal to or different from the partner's capital in the accounting records of the partnership. The purchase price passes directly from the new partner to the partner who is giving up part or all of his or her ownership claims. Any money or other consideration exchanged is the personal property of the participants and not the property of the partnership.

Accounting for the purchase of an interest is straightforward. In the partnership, only the transfer of a partner's capital is recorded. **The old partner's capital account is debited for the ownership claims that have been given up. The new partner's capital account is credited with the ownership interest purchased.** Total assets, total liabilities, and total capital remain unchanged, as do all individual asset and liability accounts.

Helpful hint In a purchase of an interest, the partnership is not a participant in the transaction. No cash is contributed to the partnership.

To illustrate, assume that on July 1 L. Carson agrees to pay $10,000 each to two partners, D. Arbour and D. Baker, for one-third of their interest in the Arbour-Baker partnership. At the time of Carson's admission, each partner has a $30,000 capital balance. Both partners, therefore, give up $10,000 ($\frac{1}{3}$ × $30,000) of their capital. The entry to record the admission of Carson is as follows:

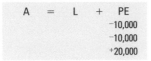

Cash flows: no effect

July	1	D. Arbour, Capital	10,000	
		D. Baker, Capital	10,000	
		L. Carson, Capital		20,000
		To record admission of Carson by purchase.		

The effect of this transaction on the partners' capital accounts is shown below:

D. Arbour, Capital		D. Baker, Capital		L. Carson, Capital	
10,000	Bal. 30,000	10,000	Bal. 30,000		20,000
	Bal. 20,000		Bal. 20,000		Bal. 20,000

Each partner now has a $20,000 ending capital balance. Net assets and total capital remain unchanged at $60,000 (net assets = partners' equity; $60,000 = $20,000 + $20,000 + $20,000). Arbour and Baker continue as partners in the firm, but the capital interest of each has changed from $30,000 to $20,000. The cash paid by Carson goes directly to the individual partners and not to the partnership.

Regardless of the amount paid by Carson for the one-third interest, the entry above would be exactly the same. If Carson pays $12,000 each to Arbour and Baker for one-third of their interest in the partnership, the above entry is still made.

Investment of Assets in a Partnership

The admission of a partner by an investment of assets is a transaction between the new partner and the partnership. It is often referred to simply as **admission by investment**. This transaction **increases both the net assets and the total capital of the partnership**. In the feature story, Richard Altrogge was admitted as a partner by investment, which increased both assets and capital.

To illustrate, assume that instead of purchasing a partner's interest as illustrated in the previous section, Carson invests $30,000 in cash in the Arbour-Baker partnership for a one-third capital interest. In this case, the entry is:

A = L + PE
+30,000   +30,000

↑ Cash flows: +30,000

July	1	Cash	30,000	
		L. Carson, Capital		30,000
		To record admission of Carson by investment.		

Both net assets and total capital increase by $30,000. The effect of this transaction on the partners' capital accounts is shown below:

D. Arbour, Capital		D. Baker, Capital		L. Carson, Capital	
	Bal. 30,000		Bal. 30,000		30,000
	Bal. 30,000		Bal. 30,000		Bal. 30,000

Remember that Carson's one-third capital interest might not result in a one-third income ratio. Carson's income ratio should be specified in the new partnership agreement. It may or may not be equal to the one-third capital interest.

The different effects of an admission by purchase of an interest or by investment are shown in the comparison of the net assets and capital balances below.

Admission by Purchase of an Interest		Admission by Investment	
Net assets	$60,000	Net assets	$90,000
Capital		Capital	
D. Arbour	$20,000	D. Arbour	$30,000
D. Baker	20,000	D. Baker	30,000
L. Carson	20,000	L. Carson	30,000
Total capital	$60,000	Total capital	$90,000

When an interest is purchased, the total net assets and the total capital of the partnership do not change. In contrast, when a partner is admitted by investment, both the total net assets and the total capital change.

In the case of admission by investment, complications occur when the new partner's investment differs from the capital equity acquired. When those amounts are not the same, the difference is considered a bonus either (1) to the existing (old) partners or (2) to the new partner.

Bonus to Old Partners. The existing partners may be unwilling to admit a new partner without receiving a bonus. In an established firm, existing partners may insist on a bonus as compensation for the work they have put into the partnership over the years.

Two accounting factors explain why a bonus may be necessary. First, total partners' capital equals the **net book value** of the recorded net assets of the partnership. When the new partner is admitted, the fair market values of assets such as land and buildings may be higher than their book values. The bonus will help make up the difference between fair market value and net book value. Second, when the partnership has been profitable, goodwill may exist. But the goodwill is not recorded among the assets or reflected in total partners' capital. In such cases, the new partner is usually willing to pay the bonus to become a partner.

A bonus to old partners results when the new partner's investment in the partnership is greater than the capital credit on the date of admittance. The bonus results in an increase in the capital balances of the old partners. It is allocated to them on the basis of their income ratios before the admission of the new partner.

To illustrate, assume that the Bart-Simpson partnership, owned by Sam Bart and Hal Simpson, has total capital of $120,000. Bart has a capital balance of $72,000; Simpson has a capital balance of $48,000. Lisa Trent acquires a 25% ownership (capital) interest in the partnership by making a cash investment of $80,000 on November 1. The procedure for determining Trent's capital credit and the bonus to the old partners is as follows:

1. Determine the total capital of the new partnership. Add the new partner's investment to the total capital of the old partnership. In this case, the total capital of the new firm is $200,000, calculated as follows:

Total capital of existing partnership	$120,000
Investment by new partner, Trent	80,000
Total capital of new partnership	$200,000

2. Determine the new partner's capital credit. Multiply the total capital of the new partnership by the new partner's ownership interest.

    Trent's capital credit ($200,000 × 25%) $50,000

3. Determine the amount of the bonus. Subtract the new partner's capital credit from the new partner's investment.

    Bonus ($80,000 − $50,000) $30,000

4. Allocate the bonus to the old partners on the basis of their income ratios: Assuming the ratios are Bart 60% and Simpson 40%, the allocation of the bonus to the old partners is:

To Bart ($30,000 × 60%)	$18,000	
To Simpson ($30,000 × 40%)	12,000	$30,000

The entry to record the admission of Trent on November 1 follows:

A	=	L	+	PE
+80,000				+18,000
				+12,000
				+50,000

Cash flows: +80,000

Nov. 1	Cash		80,000	
	Sam Bart, Capital			18,000
	Hal Simpson, Capital			12,000
	Lisa Trent, Capital			50,000
	To record admission of Trent and bonuses to old partners.			

The before and after effects of the bonus to the old partners are shown in the comparison of the net assets and capital balances below:

	Bonus to Old Partners	
	Before Bonus	After Bonus
Net assets	$120,000	$200,000
Capital		
Bart	$ 72,000	$ 90,000
Simpson	48,000	60,000
Trent	0	50,000
Total capital	$120,000	$200,000

In summary, $80,000 cash was invested in the partnership by Lisa Trent for a $50,000 capital credit, and the $30,000 bonus was allocated to the partners' capital accounts as follows: $18,000 to Sam Bart and $12,000 to Hal Simpson.

Bonus to New Partner. A bonus to a new partner results when the new partner's investment in the partnership is less than his or her capital credit. This may occur when the new partner possesses resources or special attributes that are desired by the partnership. For example, the new partner may be able to supply cash that is urgently needed for expansion or to meet maturing debts. Or the new partner may be a recognized expert or authority in a relevant field. An engineering firm, for example, may be willing to give a renowned engineer a bonus to join the firm. Or the partners of a restaurant may offer a bonus to a sports celebrity in order to add the athlete's name to the partnership. A bonus to a new partner may also result when recorded net book values on the partnership books are higher than their market value.

A bonus to a new partner results in a decrease in the capital balances of the old partners. The amount of the decrease for each partner is based on the income ratios before the admission of the new partner. To illustrate, assume that Lisa Trent invests $20,000 in cash for a 25% ownership interest in the Bart-Simpson partnership on November 1. Using the four procedures described in the preceding section, the calculations for Trent's capital credit and bonus are:

1. Determine the total capital of the new partnership:

Total capital of existing partnership	$120,000
Investment by new partner, Trent	20,000
Total capital of new partnership	$140,000

2. Determine the new partner's capital credit: Multiply the total capital of the new partnership by the new partner's ownership interest.

Trent's capital credit ($140,000 × 25%) $35,000

3. Determine the amount of the bonus: Subtract the new partner's capital credit from the new partner's investment. The result in this case is ($15,000). In the Bonus to Old Partners section on the previous page, this difference was a positive amount and the bonus was allocated to the old partners. Here, the difference is a negative amount, so the bonus is allocated to the new partner from the existing partners' capital accounts.

Bonus ($20,000 − $35,000) $(15,000)

4. Allocate the bonus from the old partners on the basis of their income ratios. With the same ratios of Bart 60% and Simpson 40%, the allocation of the bonus to the new partner is:

From Bart ($15,000 × 60%) $9,000
From Simpson ($15,000 × 40%)   6,000 $15,000

The entry to record the admission of Trent on November 1 in this case is:

Nov. 1	Cash	20,000	
	Sam Bart, Capital	9,000	
	Hal Simpson, Capital	6,000	
	Lisa Trent, Capital		35,000
	To record Trent's admission and bonus to new partner.		

A	−	L	+	PE
+20,000				−9,000
				−6,000
				+35,000

Cash flows: +20,000

The before and after effects of the bonus to the new partner are shown in the comparison of the net assets and capital balances below:

	Bonus to New Partner	
	Before Bonus	After Bonus
Net assets	$120,000	$140,000
Capital		
Bart	$ 72,000	$ 63,000
Simpson	48,000	42,000
Trent	0	35,000
Total capital	$120,000	$140,000

In summary, $20,000 cash was invested in the partnership by Lisa Trent for a $35,000 capital credit, and the $15,000 bonus was allocated from the partners' capital accounts as follows: $9,000 from Sam Bart and $6,000 from Hal Simpson.

Withdrawal of a Partner

Now let's look at the opposite situation—the withdrawal of a partner. A partner may withdraw from a partnership voluntarily, by selling his or her equity in the firm. He or she may withdraw involuntarily, by reaching mandatory retirement age, by expulsion, or by dying. The withdrawal of a partner, like the admission of a partner, legally dissolves the partnership. However, it is customary to record only the economic effects of the partner's withdrawal, while the partnership reorganizes itself and continues to operate.

As indicated earlier, the partnership agreement should specify the terms of withdrawal. Often, however, the withdrawal of a partner occurs outside of the partnership agreement. For example, when the remaining partners are anxious to remove an uncontrollable partner from the firm, they may agree to pay the departing partner much more than was specified in the original partnership agreement.

The withdrawal of a partner may be accomplished by payment from partners' personal assets or payment from partnership assets, as shown in Illustration 12-8. The former affects only the partners' capital accounts but not total capital. The latter decreases the total net assets and total capital of the partnership.

study objective 6

Prepare and explain the effects of the entries when a partner withdraws from the firm.

Illustration 12-8 ▶
Ways of dropping partners

How Partners Can Withdraw

1. Payment from partners' personal assets

2. Payment from partnership assets

Payment from Partners' Personal Assets

✱ only the capital is affected

Withdrawal by payment from partners' personal assets is a personal transaction between the partners. It is the direct opposite of admitting a new partner who purchases a partner's interest. Payment to the departing partner is made directly from the remaining partners' personal assets. **Partnership assets are not involved in any way, and total capital does not change.** The effect on the partnership is limited to a transfer of the partners' capital balances.

To illustrate, assume that Javad Dargahi, Dong Kim, and Robert Viau have capital balances of $25,000, $15,000, and $10,000, respectively. The partnership equity totals $50,000. Dargahi and Kim agree to buy out Viau's interest. Each agrees to pay Viau $8,000 in exchange for one-half of Viau's total interest of $10,000 on February 1. The entry to record the withdrawal is as follows:

A	=	L	+	PE						
				−10,000	Feb. 1	Robert Viau, Capital			10,000	
				+5,000		Javad Dargahi, Capital				5,000
				+5,000		Dong Kim, Capital				5,000
						To record purchase of Viau's interest.				

Cash flows: no effect

The effect of this transaction on the partners' capital accounts is shown below:

Javad Dargahi, Capital		Dong Kim, Capital		Robert Viau, Capital	
	Bal. 25,000		Bal. 15,000		Bal. 10,000
	5,000		5,000	10,000	
	Bal. 30,000		Bal. 20,000		Bal. 0

Net assets and total capital remain the same at $50,000 (Dargahi, Capital, $30,000 + Kim, Capital, $20,000). All that has happened is a reallocation of capital amounts. Note also that the $16,000 paid to Viau personally is not recorded. Viau's capital is debited for only $10,000, not the $16,000 cash that he received. Similarly, both Dargahi and Kim credit their capital accounts for only $5,000, not the $8,000 they each paid.

After Viau's withdrawal, Dargahi and Kim will share net income or net loss equally unless they specifically indicate another income ratio in the partnership agreement.

Payment from Partnership Assets

Withdrawal by payment from partnership assets is a transaction that involves the partnership. Both partnership net assets and total capital are decreased. Using partnership assets to pay for a withdrawing partner's interest is the **reverse of admitting a partner through the investment of assets in the partnership**.

In accounting for a withdrawal by payment from partnership assets, asset revaluations should not be recorded. Recording a revaluation to the fair market value of the assets at the time of a partner's withdrawal violates the cost principle, which requires assets to be stated at original cost. It is also a departure from the going concern assumption, which assumes that the entity will continue indefinitely. The terms of the partnership contract should not dictate the accounting for this event.

Instead, any difference between the amount paid and the withdrawing partner's capital balance should be considered a bonus to the departing partner or a bonus to the remaining partners.

Bonus to Departing Partner. A bonus may be paid to a departing partner under any of these situations:

1. The fair market value of partnership assets is more than their net book value.
2. There is unrecorded goodwill resulting from the partnership's superior earnings record.
3. The remaining partners are anxious to remove the partner from the firm.

The bonus is deducted from the remaining partners' capital balances on the basis of their income ratios at the time of the withdrawal.

In our feature story, Mr. Heagy received a bonus when he retired from the partnership. In his particular case, this bonus was specified in the partnership agreement to recognize the fact that he had brought in the initial client base for the firm in 1983.

To illustrate a bonus to a departing partner, assume that the following capital balances exist in the RST partnership: Fred Roman, $50,000; Dee Sand, $30,000; and Betty Terk, $20,000. The partners share income in the ratio of 3:2:1, respectively. Terk retires from the partnership on March 1 and receives a cash payment of $25,000 from the firm. The procedure for determining the bonus to the departing partner and the allocation of the bonus to the remaining partners is as follows:

1. Determine the amount of the bonus: Subtract the departing partner's capital balance from the cash paid by the partnership.

    Bonus ($25,000 − $20,000) $5,000

2. Allocate payment of the bonus by the remaining partners on the basis of their income ratios: The ratios of Roman and Sand are 3:2. Thus, the allocation of the $5,000 bonus is:

    From Roman ($5,000 × $\frac{3}{5}$) $3,000
    From Sand ($5,000 × $\frac{2}{5}$)   2,000 $5,000

The entry to record the withdrawal of Terk on March 1 is as follows:

Mar. 1	Betty Terk, Capital	20,000	
	Fred Roman, Capital	3,000	
	Dee Sand, Capital	2,000	
	Cash		25,000
	To record withdrawal of, and bonus to, Terk.		

A	=	L	+	PE
−25,000				−20,000
				−3,000
				−2,000

Cash flows: −25,000

The remaining partners, Roman and Sand, will recover the bonus given to Terk as the undervalued assets are used or sold.

Bonus to Remaining Partners. The departing partner may give a bonus to the remaining partners under the following situations:

1. Recorded assets are overvalued.
2. The partnership has a poor earnings record.
3. The partner is anxious to leave the partnership.

In such cases, the cash paid to the departing partner will be less than the departing partner's capital balance. **The bonus is allocated (credited) to the capital accounts of the remaining partners on the basis of their income ratios.**

To illustrate, assume, instead of the example above, that Terk is paid only $16,000 for her $20,000 equity when she withdraws from the partnership on March 1. In that case, the calculations are as follows:

1. Determine the amount of the bonus: Subtract the departing partner's capital balance from the cash paid by the partnership. In the Bonus to Departing Partner section above, this difference was a positive amount and the bonus was allocated to the departing partner. Here, the difference is a negative amount, so the bonus is allocated to the remaining partners:

    Bonus ($16,000 − $20,000) $(4,000)

2. Allocate the payment of the bonus to the remaining partners on the basis of their income ratios. Roman and Sand share income in a ratio of 3:2. The allocation of the $4,000 bonus is:

    To Roman ($4,000 × $\frac{3}{5}$) $2,400
    To Sand ($4,000 × $\frac{2}{5}$)   1,600 $4,000

The entry to record the withdrawal on March 1 follows:

A	=	L	+	PE
−16,000				−20,000
				+2,400
				+1,600

Cash flows: −16,000

Mar. 1	Betty Terk, Capital	20,000	
	Fred Roman, Capital		2,400
	Dee Sand, Capital		1,600
	Cash		16,000
	To record withdrawal of Terk and bonus to remaining partners.		

Death of a Partner

The death of a partner dissolves the partnership. But provision is generally made in the partnership agreement for the surviving partners to continue operations. When a partner dies, the partner's equity at the date of death normally has to be determined. This is done by (1) calculating the net income or loss for the year to date, (2) closing the books, and (3) preparing the financial statements.

The death of the partner may be recorded by either of the two methods described earlier in the section for the withdrawal of a partner: payment from the partners' personal assets or payment from the partnership assets. That is, one or more of the surviving partners may agree to purchase the deceased partner's equity from their personal assets. Or, partnership assets may be used to settle with the deceased partner's estate. To facilitate payment from partnership assets, many partnerships obtain life insurance policies on each partner. The partnership is named as the beneficiary. The proceeds from the insurance policy on the deceased partner are then used to settle with the estate.

In both instances—payment from partners' personal assets or payment from partnership assets—the entries to record the death (withdrawal) of the partner are similar to those presented earlier.

BEFORE YOU GO ON . . .

►Review It

1. How does the accounting for admission in a partnership by purchase of an interest differ from the accounting for admission by an investment of assets?
2. Contrast the accounting for withdrawal of a partner by payment from (a) personal assets, and (b) partnership assets.

►Do It

Chandler, Phoebe, and Ross have a partnership, in which they share income and loss equally.. There ✳ Do it. is a $40,000 balance in each capital account. Record the journal entries on September 1 for each of the independent events listed below:

1. Chandler, Phoebe, and Ross agree to admit Rachel as a new one-quarter interest partner. Rachel pays $10,000 in cash directly to each partner.
2. Chandler, Phoebe, and Ross agree to admit Rachel as a new one-quarter interest partner. Rachel contributes $40,000 to the partnership.
3. Phoebe withdraws from the partnership and receives $30,000 of partnership cash.
4. Phoebe withdraws from the partnership. Chandler and Ross each pay Phoebe $25,000 out of their personal assets.

Action Plan

- Recognize that the admission by purchase (or withdrawal by sale) of a partnership interest is a personal transaction between one or more existing partners and the new (or withdrawing) partner.
- Recognize that the admission by investment (or withdrawal by payment) of partnership assets is a transaction between the new (or withdrawing) partner and the partnership.

Solution

1. Sept. 1	Chandler, Capital	10,000	
	Phoebe, Capital	10,000	
	Ross, Capital	10,000	
	Rachel, Capital		30,000
	To record admission of Rachel by purchase.		
2. Sept. 1	Cash	40,000	
	Rachel, Capital		40,000
	To record admission of Rachel by investment.		
3. Sept. 1	Phoebe, Capital	40,000	
	Cash		30,000
	Chandler, Capital		5,000
	Ross, Capital		5,000
	To record withdrawal of Phoebe and bonus to remaining partners.		
4. Sept. 1	Phoebe, Capital	40,000	
	Chandler, Capital		20,000
	Ross, Capital		20,000
	To record purchase of Phoebe's interest.		

Related exercise material: BE12–8, BE12–9, BE12–10, BE12–11, E12–5, E12–6, E12–7, and E12–8.

✔ the navigator

NO → # Liquidation of a Partnership

The liquidation of a partnership terminates the business. It involves selling the assets of the firm, paying liabilities, and distributing any remaining assets to the partners. Liquidation may result from the sale of the business by mutual agreement of the partners or from bankruptcy. A **partnership liquidation** ends both the legal and the economic life of the entity.

Before the liquidation process begins, the accounting cycle for the partnership must be completed for the final operating period. This includes the preparation of adjusting entries, a trial balance, financial statements, closing entries, and a post-closing trial balance. Only balance sheet accounts should be open as the liquidation process begins.

In liquidation, the sale of noncash assets for cash is called realization. Any difference between the net book value and the cash proceeds is called the **gain or loss on realization**. To liquidate a partnership, it is necessary to follow these steps:

1. Sell noncash assets for cash and recognize any gain or loss on realization.
2. Allocate any gain or loss on realization to the partners, based on their income ratios.
3. Pay partnership liabilities in cash.
4. Distribute the remaining cash to partners, based on their capital balances.

Each of the steps must be performed in sequence, and **creditors must be paid before partners receive any cash distributions**. Each step must also be recorded by an accounting entry.

When a partnership is liquidated, all partners may happen to have credit balances in their capital accounts. This situation is called **no capital deficiency**. Alternatively, one or more of the partners' capital accounts may have a debit balance. This situation is called a **capital deficiency**. To illustrate each of these conditions, assume that the Ace Company is liquidated on April 15, 2005, when its ledger shows the assets, liabilities, and partners' equity accounts in Illustration 12-9 below.

Illustration 12-9 ▶

Account balances prior to liquidation

ACE COMPANY Balance Sheet April 15, 2005			
Assets		**Liabilities and Partners' Equity**	
Cash	$ 5,000	Notes payable	$15,000
Accounts receivable	15,000	Accounts payable	16,000
Inventory	18,000	R. Aube, Capital	15,000
Equipment	35,000	P. Chordia, Capital	17,800
Accumulated amortization—		W. Elliott, Capital	1,200
equipment	(8,000)		
	$65,000		$65,000

NO → ## No Capital Deficiency

The partners of Ace Company agree to liquidate the partnership on the following terms: (1) the noncash assets of the partnership will be sold to Moriyama Enterprises for $75,000 cash, and (2) the partnership will pay its partnership liabilities. The income ratios of the partners are 3:2:1 for Aube, Chordia, and Elliott. The steps in the liquidation process are as follows:

1. The noncash assets (accounts receivable, inventory, and equipment) are sold on April 18 for $75,000. The net book value of these assets is $60,000 ($15,000 + $18,000 + $35,000 − $8,000). Thus, a gain of $15,000 is realized on the sale, and the following entry is made:

(1)		
Apr. 18	Cash	75,000	
	Accumulated Amortization—Equipment	8,000	
	Accounts Receivable		15,000
	Inventory		18,000
	Equipment		35,000
	Gain on Realization		15,000
	To record realization of noncash assets.		

A = L + PE
+75,000   +15,000
+8,000
−15,000
−18,000
−35,000

Cash flows: +75,000

2. The gain on realization of $15,000 is allocated to the partners based on their income ratios, which are 3:2:1 (or $\frac{3}{6}$, $\frac{2}{6}$, and $\frac{1}{6}$). The entry is:

(2)		
Apr. 18	Gain on Realization	15,000	
	R. Aube, Capital ($15,000 × $\frac{3}{6}$)		7,500
	P. Chordia, Capital ($15,000 × $\frac{2}{6}$)		5,000
	W. Elliott, Capital ($15,000 × $\frac{1}{6}$)		2,500
	To allocate gain to partners' capital accounts.		

A = L + PE
−15,000
+7,500
+5,000
+2,500

Cash flows: no effect

3. Partnership liabilities consist of notes payable, $15,000, and accounts payable, $16,000. Creditors are paid in full on April 23 by a cash payment of $31,000. The entry follows:

(3)		
Apr. 23	Notes Payable	15,000	
	Accounts Payable	16,000	
	Cash		31,000
	To record payment of partnership liabilities.		

A = L + PE
−31,000   −15,000
          −16,000

Cash flows: −31,000

4. The remaining cash is distributed to the partners on April 25 based on their **capital balances**. After the entries in the first three steps are posted, all partnership accounts will have zero balances except for four accounts: Cash, $49,000; R. Aube, Capital, $22,500; P. Chordia, Capital, $22,800; and W. Elliott, Capital, $3,700, as shown below:

Cash		R. Aube, Capital	P. Chordia, Capital	W. Elliot, Capital
Bal. 5,000		Bal. 15,000	Bal. 17,800	Bal. 1,200
(1) 75,000	(3) 31,000	(2) 7,500	(2) 5,000	(2) 2,500
Bal. **49,000**		Bal. **22,500**	Bal. **22,800**	Bal. **3,700**

The entry to record the distribution of cash on April 25 is:

(4)		
Apr. 25	R. Aube, Capital	22,500	
	P. Chordia, Capital	22,800	
	W. Elliott, Capital	3,700	
	Cash		49,000
	To record distribution of cash to partners.		

A = L + PE
−49,000   −22,500
             −22,800
             −3,700

Cash flows: −49,000

After this entry is posted, all partnership general ledger accounts will have zero balances.

A word of caution: **Cash should not be distributed to partners on the basis of their income-sharing ratios.** On this basis, Aube would receive $\frac{3}{6}$, or $24,500. This would produce an incorrect debit balance of $2,000. While the income ratio is the proper basis for allocating net income or loss and any gains or losses on the realization of assets, it is not a proper basis for making the final distribution of cash to the partners.

No   →   # Capital Deficiency

Helpful hint These entries are the same as those in the No Capital Deficiency section except for the loss on realization.

A capital deficiency may be caused by recurring net losses, excessive drawings, or losses from the realization during liquidation. To illustrate, assume that Ace Company is almost bankrupt. The partners decide to liquidate by having a going-out-of-business sale on April 18. Merchandise is sold at substantial discounts, and the equipment is sold at auction. Cash proceeds from these sales and collections from customers total only $42,000. The loss on liquidation is $18,000 ($60,000 in net book value − $42,000 in proceeds). The steps in the liquidation process are as follows:

1. The entry for the realization of noncash assets is recorded on April 18:

A   =   L   +   PE
+42,000   −18,000
+8,000
−15,000
−18,000
−35,000

↑ Cash flows: +42,000

	(1)		
Apr. 18	Cash	42,000	
	Accumulated Amortization—Equipment	8,000	
	Loss on Realization	18,000	
	Accounts Receivable		15,000
	Inventory		18,000
	Equipment		35,000
	To record realization of noncash assets.		

2. The loss on realization is allocated to the partners on the basis of their income ratios of 3:2:1 and recorded as follows:

A   =   L   +   PE
                    −9,000
                    −6,000
                    −3,000
                    +18,000

Cash flows: no effect

	(2)		
Apr. 18	R. Aube, Capital ($18,000 × $\frac{3}{6}$)	9,000	
	P. Chordia, Capital ($18,000 × $\frac{2}{6}$)	6,000	
	W. Elliott, Capital ($18,000 × $\frac{1}{6}$)	3,000	
	Loss on Realization		18,000
	To allocate loss to partners' capital accounts.		

3. Partnership liabilities are paid on April 23 and recorded:

A   =   L   +   PE
−31,000   −15,000
           −16,000

↓ Cash flows: −31,000

	(3)		
Apr. 23	Notes Payable	15,000	
	Accounts Payable	16,000	
	Cash		31,000
	To record payment of partnership liabilities.		

4. After posting of the three entries, two accounts will have debit balances: Cash, $16,000, and W. Elliott, Capital, $1,800. Two accounts will have credit balances: R. Aube, Capital, $6,000, and P. Chordia, Capital, $11,800. All four accounts are shown below:

Cash		R. Aube, Capital		P. Chordia, Capital		W. Elliot, Capital	
Bal. 5,000		(2) 9,000 | Bal. 15,000		(2) 6,000 | Bal. 17,800		(2) 3,000 | Bal. 1,200	
(1) 42,000 | (3) 31,000		Bal. **6,000**		Bal. **11,800**		Bal. **1,800**	
Bal. **16,000**							

Elliott has a capital deficiency of $1,800. He therefore owes the partnership $1,800. Aube and Chordia have a legally enforceable claim for that amount against Elliott's personal assets. The distribution of cash is still made on the basis of capital balances. But the amount will vary depending on how Elliott's deficiency is settled. Two alternatives for settling are presented next.

Payment of Deficiency

If the partner with the capital deficiency pays the amount owed to the partnership, the deficiency is eliminated. To illustrate, assume that Elliott pays $1,800 to the partnership on April 24. The entry and account balances are as follows:

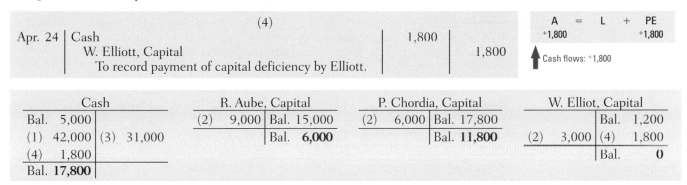

Apr. 24	Cash		1,800	
	W. Elliott, Capital			1,800
	To record payment of capital deficiency by Elliott.			

A = L + PE
+1,800   +1,800
Cash flows: +1,800

Cash		R. Aube, Capital		P. Chordia, Capital		W. Elliot, Capital	
Bal. 5,000		(2) 9,000	Bal. 15,000	(2) 6,000	Bal. 17,800		Bal. 1,200
(1) 42,000	(3) 31,000		Bal. **6,000**		Bal. **11,800**	(2) 3,000	(4) 1,800
(4) 1,800							Bal. 0
Bal. **17,800**							

The cash balance of $17,800 is now equal to the credit balances in the capital accounts (Aube $6,000 + Chordia $11,800). Cash is distributed on the basis of these balances on April 25, and the following entry is made:

Apr. 25	R. Aube, Capital		6,000	
	P. Chordia, Capital		11,800	
	Cash			17,800
	To record distribution of cash to partners.			

A = L + PE
−17,800   −6,000
            −11,800
Cash flows: −17,800

After this entry is posted, all accounts will have zero balances.

Nonpayment of Deficiency

If a partner with a capital deficiency is unable to pay the amount owed to the partnership, the partners with credit balances must absorb the loss. The loss is allocated on the basis of the income ratios that exist between the partners with credit balances. For example, the income ratios of Aube and Chordia are 3:2 (or $\frac{3}{5}$ and $\frac{2}{5}$), respectively. The following entry would be made to remove Elliott's capital deficiency on April 25:

(4)			
Apr. 25	R. Aube, Capital ($1,800 × $\frac{3}{5}$)		1,080	
	P. Chordia, Capital ($1,800 × $\frac{2}{5}$)		720	
	W. Elliott, Capital			1,800
	To record write-off of capital deficiency.			

A = L + PE
            −1,080
            −720
            +1,800
Cash flows: no effect

After posting this entry, the cash balance of $16,000 now equals the sum of the credit balances in the capital accounts (Aube $4,920 + Chordia $11,080) as shown below:

Cash		R. Aube, Capital		P. Chordia, Capital		W. Elliot, Capital	
Bal. 5,000		(2) 9,000	Bal. 15,000	(2) 6,000	Bal. 17,800		Bal. 1,200
(1) 42,000	(3) 31,000	(4) 1,080		(4) 720		(2) 3,000	(4) 1,800
Bal. **16,000**			Bal. **4,920**		Bal. **11,080**		Bal. 0

The entry to record the distribution of cash follows:

Apr. 25	R. Aube, Capital		4,920	
	P. Chordia, Capital		11,080	
	Cash			16,000
	To record distribution of cash to partners.			

A = L + PE
−16,000   −4,920
            −11,080
Cash flows: −16,000

After this entry is posted, all accounts will have zero balances.

BEFORE YOU GO ON . . .

▶Review It

1. What are the steps in liquidating a partnership?
2. What basis is used in making the final distribution of cash to the partners?

▶Do It

Hinton, Kinnear, and Smistad LLP dissolved their partnership as of August 31. Prior to liquidation, the three partners shared income and losses in the ratio of 2:3:4. After the books were closed on August 31, the following summary accounts remained:

Cash	$ 6,000	Hinton, Capital	$20,000
Noncash assets	110,000	Kinnear, Capital	30,000
Liabilities	25,000	Smistad, Capital	41,000

On September 24, the partnership sold the remaining noncash assets for $74,000 and paid the liabilities. None of the partners are able to pay any capital deficiency, if one exists. Prepare the journal entries to record the (1) sale of noncash assets, (2) allocation of any gain or loss on realization, (3) payment of liabilities, and (4) distribution of cash to the partners.

Action Plan

- Calculate the gain or loss by comparing cash proceeds to the book value of assets.
- Allocate any gain or loss to each partner's capital account using the income ratios.
- Record the final distribution of cash to each partner to eliminate the balance in each capital account. Do not distribute cash using the income ratio.

Solution

1. Sept.24	Cash	74,000	
	Loss on Realization	36,000	
	Noncash Assets		110,000
	To record realization of noncash assets.		
2. Sept. 24	Hinton, Capital ($36,000 × $\frac{2}{9}$)	8,000	
	Kinnear, Capital ($36,000 × $\frac{3}{9}$)	12,000	
	Smistad, Capital ($36,000 × $\frac{4}{9}$)	16,000	
	Loss on Realization		36,000
	To allocate loss to partners' capital accounts.		
3. Sept. 24	Liabilities	25,000	
	Cash		25,000
	To record payment of liabilities.		
4. Sept. 24	Hinton, Capital ($20,000 − $8,000)	12,000	
	Kinnear, Capital ($30,000 − $12,000)	18,000	
	Smistad, Capital ($41,000 − $16,000)	25,000	
	Cash ($6,000 + $74,000 − $25,000)		55,000
	To record distribution of cash to partners.		

Related exercise material: BE12–12, BE12–13, BE12–14, E12–9, E12–10, and E12–11.

Demonstration Problem

Additional
Demonstration
Problems

On January 1, 2005, the capital balances in Hollingsworth Company are Lois Holly, $26,000, and Jim Worth, $24,000. For the year ended December 31, 2005, the partnership reports net income of $30,000. The income ratio provides for salary allowances of $12,000 for Holly and $10,000 for Worth, with the remainder distributed equally. Neither partner had any drawings in 2005.

In 2006, assume that the following independent transactions occur on January 1:

1. Donna Reichenbacher purchases one-half of Lois Holly's capital interest from Holly for $25,000.
2. Marsha Mears is admitted with a 25% capital interest by a cash investment of $40,000.
3. Stan Wells is admitted with a 35% capital interest by a cash investment of $35,000.

Instructions

(a) Prepare a schedule showing the distribution of net income in 2005.
(b) Journalize the division of 2005 net income and its distribution to the partners.
(c) Journalize each of the independent transactions that occurred on January 1, 2006.

Solution to Demonstration Problem

(a)

Division of Net Income

	Lois Holly	Jim Worth	Total
Net income			$30,000
Salary allowance	$12,000	$10,000	22,000
Remaining income			8,000
Lois Holly ($8,000 × 50%)	4,000		
Jim Worth ($8,000 × 50%)		4,000	8,000
Remaining income			0
Division of net income	$16,000	$14,000	$30,000

(b)

Dec. 31	Income Summary	30,000	
	Lois Holly, Capital		16,000
	Jim Worth, Capital		14,000
	To close net income to partners' capital accounts.		

Lois Holly, Capital		Jim Worth, Capital	
	26,000		24,000
	16,000		14,000
	42,000		38,000

(c)

1. Jan.	1	Lois Holly, Capital ($42,000 × 50%)	21,000	
		Donna Reichenbacher, Capital		21,000
		To record purchase of one-half of Holly's interest.		

2. Jan.	1	Cash	40,000	
		Lois Holly, Capital ($10,000 × 50%)		5,000
		Jim Worth, Capital ($10,000 × 50%)		5,000
		Marsha Mears, Capital		30,000
		To record admission of Mears by investment and bonus to old partners.		

Total capital after investment: $120,000
   (Holly, $42,000; Worth $38,000; Mears investment, $40,000)
Mears' capital credit (25% × $120,000) $30,000
Bonus to old partners ($40,000 – $30,000) $10,000

Action Plan

- Allocate the partners' salaries (and interest, if any) first. Divide the remaining net income among the partners, based on the income ratio.
- Journalize the division of net income in a closing entry.
- Recognize the admission by purchase of a partnership interest as a personal transaction between an existing partner and the new partner.
- Recognize the admission by investment of partnership assets as a transaction between the new partner and the partnership.

3. Jan.	1	Cash	35,000	
		Lois Holly, Capital ($5,250 × 50%)	2,625	
		Jim Worth, Capital ($5,250 × 50%)	2,625	
		Stan Wells, Capital		40,250
		To record admission of Wells by investment and		
		bonus to new partner.		

Total capital after investment: $115,000
(Holly, $42,000; Worth, $38,000; Wells investment, $35,000)
Wells' capital credit (35% × $115,000) $40,250
Bonus to Wells ($35,000 − $40,250) $(5,250)

Summary of Study Objectives

1. *Describe the characteristics of the partnership form of business organization.* The principal characteristics of a partnership are (a) the association of individuals, (b) mutual agency, (c) co-ownership of property, (d) limited life, and (e) unlimited liability.

2. *Describe and generate the accounting entries for the formation of a partnership.* When a partnership is formed, each partner's initial investment should be recorded at the fair market value of the assets at the date of their transfer to the partnership.

3. *Apply various bases to divide net income or net loss.* Net income or net loss is divided on the basis of the income ratio, which may be any of the following: (a) a fixed ratio, (b) a ratio based on beginning, ending, or average capital balances, (c) salaries allocated to partners and the remainder in a fixed ratio, (d) interest on partners' capital balances and the remainder in a fixed ratio, and (e) salaries allocated to partners, interest on partners' capital balances, and the remainder in a fixed ratio.

4. *Describe and illustrate the form and content of partnership financial statements.* The financial statements of a partnership are similar to those of a proprietorship. The principal differences are that (a) the statement of owners' equity is called the statement of partners' equity, and (b)

each partner's capital is usually reported on the balance sheet or in a supporting schedule.

5. *Prepare and explain the effects of the entries when a new partner is admitted.* The entry to record the admission of a new partner by purchase of a partner's interest affects only partners' capital accounts. The entry to record the admission by investment of assets in the partnership (a) increases both net assets and total capital, and (b) may result in the recognition of a bonus to either the old partners or the new partner.

6. *Prepare and explain the effects of the entries when a partner withdraws from the firm.* The entry to record a withdrawal from the firm when payment is made from partners' personal assets affects only partners' capital accounts. The entry to record a withdrawal when payment is made from partnership assets (a) decreases net assets and total capital, and (b) may result in recognizing a bonus to either the departing partner or the remaining partners.

7. *Prepare the entries to record the liquidation of a partnership.* When a partnership is liquidated, it is necessary to record (a) the sale of noncash assets, (b) the allocation of the gain or loss on realization, (c) the payment of partnership liabilities, and (d) the distribution of cash to the partners on the basis of their capital balances.

Glossary

 Key Term Matching Activity

Admission by investment Admission of a partner by an investment of assets in the partnership. Both partnership net assets and total capital increase. (p. 584)

Admission by purchase of an interest Admission of a partner through a personal transaction between one or more existing partners and the new partner. It does not change total partnership assets or total capital. (p. 583)

Capital deficiency A debit balance in a partner's capital account after the allocation of a gain or loss in a liquidation of a partnership. Capital deficiencies can be repaid,

or allocated among the remaining partners. (p. 592)

Income ratio The basis for dividing both net income and net loss in a partnership. (p. 577)

Limited liability partnership (LLP) A partnership in which partners are given limited liability for other partners' negligence. (p. 575)

Limited partnership (LP) A partnership in which one or more general partners have unlimited liability, and one or more partners have limited liability for the obligations of the partnership. (p. 574)

No capital deficiency A situation where all partners have credit balances after the allocation of a gain or a loss on liquidation of a partnership. (p. 592)

Partnership An association of two or more individuals to carry on as co-owners of a business for profit. (p. 572)

Partnership agreement A written contract that expresses the voluntary agreement of two or more individuals in a partnership. (p. 576)

Partnership dissolution A change in the number of partners that dissolves the partnership. It does not necessarily terminate the business. (p. 574)

Partnership liquidation An event that ends both the legal and economic life of a partnership. (p. 592)

Statement of partners' capital The equity statement for a partnership that shows the changes in each partner's capital balance, and in total partnership capital, during the year. (p. 581)

Withdrawal by payment from partners' personal assets Withdrawal of a partner by a personal transaction between partners. It does not change total partnership assets or total capital. (p. 588)

Withdrawal by payment from partnership assets Withdrawal of a partner by a transaction that decreases both partnership net assets and total capital. (p. 589)

Self-Study Questions

Chapter 12 Self-Test

Answers are at the end of the chapter.

(SO 1) K 1. Which of the following is not a characteristic of a partnership?
 (a) Taxable entity
 (b) Co-ownership of property
 (c) Mutual agency
 (d) Limited life

(SO 1) K 2. The advantages of a general partnership do not include:
 (a) ease of formation.
 (b) unlimited liability.
 (c) little government regulation.
 (d) ease of decision-making.

(SO 2) K 3. Upon formation of a partnership, each partner's initial investment of assets should be recorded at its:
 (a) net book value.   (c) fair market value.
 (b) original cost.   (d) liquidation value.

(SO 3) AP 4. The ABC Company reports net income of $60,000. If partners A, B, and C have an income ratio of 50%, 30%, and 20%, respectively, C's share of the net income is:
 (a) $12,000.   (c) $30,000.
 (b) $18,000.   (d) $60,000.

(SO 3) AP 5. Using the data in question 4, what is B's share of net income if each partner also receives a $10,000 salary allowance?
 (a) $16,000   (c) $20,000
 (b) $19,000   (d) $25,000

(SO 4) K 6. Which of the following statements about partnership financial statements is true?
 (a) Details of the distribution of net income are shown in the cash flow statement.
 (b) The distribution of net income is shown on the balance sheet.
 (c) Partner capital balances are usually shown in the income statement.
 (d) The statement of owners' equity is called the statement of partners' capital.

(SO 5) AP 7. R. Ranken purchases 50% of L. Lars' capital interest in the Kim & Lars partnership for $22,000. The capital balances of Kim and Lars are $40,000 and $30,000, respectively. Ranken's capital balance after the purchase is:
 (a) $15,000.   (c) $22,000.
 (b) $20,000.   (d) $35,000.

(SO 5) AP 8. Capital balances in the DEA partnership are Delano, Capital, $60,000; Egil, Capital, $50,000; and Armand, Capital, $40,000. The income ratio is 5:3:2. The DEAR partnership is formed by admitting Ranger to the firm with a cash investment of $60,000 for a 25% capital interest. The bonus to be credited to Armand, Capital, in admitting Ranger is:
 (a) $1,500.   (c) $7,500.
 (b) $3,750.   (d) $10,000.

(SO 6) AP 9. Capital balances in the TERM partnership are Takako, Capital, $50,000; Endo, Capital, $40,000; Reiko, Capital, $30,000; and Maeda, Capital, $20,000. The income ratio is 4:3:2:1. Maeda withdraws from the firm after receiving $29,000 in cash from the partnership. Endo's capital balance after recording the withdrawal of Maeda is:
 (a) $36,000.   (c) $38,000.
 (b) $37,000.   (d) $40,000.

(SO 7) AP 10. Partners Aikawa, Ito, and Mori shared an income ratio of 2:1:3 in the AIM Company. After AIM was liquidated, $12,000 cash remained and the balances in the partners' capital accounts were as follows: Aikawa, $10,000 Cr.; Ito, $5,000 Cr.; and Mori, $3,000 Dr. How much cash would be distributed to Aikawa, assuming Mori does not repay his capital deficiency?
 (a) $8,000   (c) $9,000
 (b) $8,500   (d) $10,000

Questions

(SO 1) C 1. The characteristics of a partnership include the following: (a) association of individuals, (b) limited life, and (c) co-ownership of property. Explain each of these terms.

(SO 1) C 2. Carla Cardosa is confused about the partnership characteristics of (a) mutual agency, and (b) unlimited liability. Explain these two characteristics to Carla.

(SO 1) C 3. K. Nasser and T. Yoko are considering a business venture. They ask you to explain the advantages and disadvantages of the partnership form of organization.

(SO 1) C 4. (a) Identify two other types of business organizations having partnership characteristics.
(b) How do these types of business organizations differ from partnerships?

(SO 1) C 5. (a) What items should be specified in a partnership agreement?
(b) What is the importance of having this agreement in writing?

(SO 2) K 6. (a) When a partner invests assets in a partnership, how is the value of the contributed assets measured for accounting purposes?
(b) Is this practice consistent with the cost principle? Explain.

(SO 2) C 7. Ingrid and Hartmut are transferring the assets from each of their sole proprietorships into a partnership. These assets include accounts receivable and equipment. Explain what happens to the balance in the allowance for doubtful accounts and accumulated amortization contra accounts in recording these accounts.

(SO 3) C 8. R. Hay, S. Innis, and L. Joyce have a partnership called Express Wings. There is a dispute among the partners. Hay has invested twice as much as the other two partners. She believes net income and net losses should be shared in accordance with the capital contributions. The partnership agreement does not specify the division of profits and losses. How will net income and net loss be divided?

(SO 3) C 9. S. Hark and R. Green are discussing how income and losses should be divided in a partnership they plan to form. What factors should be considered in determining the division of net income or net loss?

(SO 3) C 10. H. Astro and S. Sund share partnership net income and net loss equally. (a) Which accounts are debited and credited to record the division of net income between the partners? (b) If Astro withdraws $30,000 in cash for personal use, which accounts are debited and credited?

(SO 3) C 11. What is the relationship between the salary allowance used in allocating net income among partners, and cash withdrawals by the partners? Explain.

(SO 4) C 12. Are the financial statements of a partnership similar to those of a proprietorship? Explain.

(SO 5) C 13. Holly Canter decides to pay $50,000 for a one-third interest in a partnership. What effect does this transaction have on the partnership net assets?

(SO 5) AP 14. R. Minoa decides to invest $25,000 in a partnership for a one-sixth capital interest. How much do the partnership's net assets increase? Does Minoa also acquire a one-sixth income ratio through this investment?

(SO 5) C 15. Explain why a new partner may be willing to pay a bonus as part of the cost of investing in an existing partnership.

(SO 5) C 16. Your roommate argues that partnership assets should be revalued to their fair values when a new partner is admitted. Why is this generally not done?

(SO 6) C 17. Under what circumstances will a departing partner grant the remaining partners a bonus when withdrawing from a partnership?

(SO 6) C 18. What is the purpose of a partnership obtaining life insurance policies on each of the partners?

(SO 7) C 19. How does the liquidation of a partnership differ from the dissolution of a partnership?

(SO 7) C 20. Joe and Jean are discussing the liquidation of a partnership. Joe maintains that all cash should be distributed to partners on the basis of their income ratios. Is he correct? Explain.

(SO 7) C 21. In continuing their discussion, Jean says that even in the case of a capital deficiency, all cash should still be distributed on the basis of capital balances. Is Jean correct? Explain.

Brief Exercises

Identify partnership terminology.
(SO 1) K

BE12–1 The following terms were introduced in this chapter.
1. Admission by investment
2. Salary allowance
3. Capital deficiency
4. Limited liability partnership
5. General partnership
6. Partnership liquidation
7. Withdrawal by payment from partners' personal assets
8. Income ratio
9. Mutual agency

Match the above terms with the following descriptions:

(a) ____ Partners have limited liability.
(b) ____ Partners have unlimited liability.
(c) ____ It is the basis for dividing net income and loss.
(d) ____ Partnership assets and capital increase with the change in partners.
(e) ____ Partnership assets and capital stay the same with the change in partners.
(f) ____ Actions of partners are binding on all other partners.
(g) ____ It is a compensation for differences in personal effort put into the partnership.
(h) ____ There is a debit balance in a partner's capital account.
(i) ____ Partnership is terminated.

BE12–2 R. Alfredo and B. Panos decide to organize the All-Star partnership. Alfredo invests $15,000 cash. Panos contributes $10,000 cash and equipment having a book value of $3,500. The equipment has an original cost of $8,000 and a current fair market value of $6,000. Prepare the entry to record each partner's investment in the partnership on July 10, 2005.

Record formation of partnership.
(SO 2) AP

BE12–3 C. Held and G. Kamp decide to merge their proprietorships into a partnership called HeldKamp Company. Immediately before the merger, the balance sheet of Kamp Co. shows the following:

Accounts receivable	$16,000	
Less: allowance for doubtful accounts	1,200	$14,800
Equipment	$20,000	
Less: accumulated amortization	8,000	12,000

Prepare partial opening balance sheet.
(SO 2) AP

The partners agree that the net realizable value of the receivables is $12,500. The fair market value of the equipment is $10,000. Indicate how these items should appear in the opening balance sheet of the partnership on December 31, 2005.

BE12–4 Brung & Rohls Co. reports net income of $70,000 for the year ended March 31, 2005. The income ratios are Brung 60% and Rohls 40%. Indicate the division of net income to each partner. Prepare the entry to distribute the net income.

Calculate and record division of net income.
(SO 3) AP

BE12–5 MET Co. reports net income of $60,000. Partner salary allowances are Moses, $10,000; Eaton, $5,000; and Talty, $5,000. Indicate the division of net income to each partner. The income ratio is 5:3:2.

Calculate division of net income.
(SO 3) AP

BE12–6 S&T Co. reports net income of $24,000. Interest allowances for the partners are Siebrasse, $6,000, and Tong, $5,000. Salary allowances are Siebrasse, $15,000, and Tong, $10,000. The remainder is shared equally. Show the distribution of income.

Calculate division of net income.
(SO 3) AP

BE12–7 The medical practice of Drs. Jarratt and Bramstrup had the following general ledger account balances at April 30, 2005, its fiscal year end:

Cash	$10,000	Dr. Jarratt, drawings	$ 5,000
Equipment	55,000	Dr. Bramstrup, capital	15,000
Accumulated amortization		Dr. Bramstrup, drawings	5,000
—equipment	15,000	Fees earned	65,000
Note payable, due 2006	20,000	Operating expenses	50,000
Dr. Jarratt, capital	10,000		

Prepare financial statements.
(SO 4) AP

Prepare the year-end partnership financial statements, assuming the doctors share income or loss equally.

BE12–8 In ABC Co., the capital balances of the partners are Ali, $30,000; Babson, $25,000; and Carter, $20,000. The partners share income equally. Dutton is admitted to the firm by purchasing one-half of Carter's interest for $15,000 on June 9, 2005. Journalize the admission of Dutton to the partnership. How would the entry change if Dutton paid $8,000 instead of $15,000?

Record admission of partner.
(SO 5) AP

BE12–9 In the EZ Co., the capital balances of the partners are Edie, $40,000; and Zane, $30,000. The partners share income equally. Kerns is admitted to the firm on October 1, 2005, with a 45% interest by a cash investment of $42,000. Journalize the admission of Kerns. What would the journal entry be if Kerns had paid $65,000 for a 45% interest?

Record admission of partner.
(SO 5) AP

Record withdrawal of partner.
(SO 6) AP

BE12–10 The capital balances of the partners in DEB Co. are Ditka, $40,000; Embs, $30,000; and Boyd, $25,000. The partners share income equally. Ditka and Embs each agree to pay Boyd $12,000 from their personal assets to receive 50% each of Boyd's equity. Journalize the withdrawal of Boyd on December 31, 2004.

Record withdrawal of partner.
(SO 6) AP

BE12–11 Data for DEB Co. are presented in BE12–10. Instead of a payment from personal assets, assume that Boyd receives $32,000 from partnership assets in withdrawing from the firm. Journalize the withdrawal of Boyd on December 31, 2004. What would the journal entry be if Boyd received $20,000 cash instead of $32,000?

Record partnership liquidation.
(SO 7) AP

BE12–12 On November 15, 2005, the account balances in the Greenscape Partnership were Cash, $5,000; Other Assets, $11,000, Dupuis, Capital, $9,000; Dueck, Capital, $6,000; and Veitch, Capital, $1,000. The three partners share income and losses equally. The other assets are sold for $14,000 cash. Prepare journal entries to (a) record the sale of the other assets, (b) distribute any resulting gain or loss to the capital accounts, and (c) record the final distribution of cash to the partners.

Record partnership liquidation.
(SO 7) AP

BE12–13 Data for the Greenscape Partnership are presented in BE12–12. Assume that the other assets were sold for $8,000 cash instead of $14,000. Prepare journal entries to (a) record the sale of the other assets, (b) distribute any resulting gain or loss to the capital accounts, and (c) record the final distribution of cash to the partners.

Record partnership liquidation.
(SO 7) AP

BE12–14 Prior to the distribution of cash to the partners on September 30, 2005, the accounts in the MEL Company are as follows: Cash, $31,000; McDonald, Capital, $18,000 (Cr.); El Bayouni, Capital, $16,000 (Cr.); and Lodge, Capital, $3,000 (Dr.). The income ratios are 5:3:2, respectively.

Instructions

(a) Prepare the entry on September 30 to record (1) Lodge's payment of $3,000 in cash to the partnership, and (2) the distribution of cash to the partners.
(b) Prepare the entry on September 30 to record (1) the absorption of Lodge's capital deficiency by the other partners, and (2) the distribution of cash to the partners.

Exercises

Determine form of organization.
(SO 1) AN

E12–1 Presented below are three independent situations:

1. Angelique Gloss and David Deutsch, students looking for summer employment, open a home meal replacement business. Each day, they prepare nutritious, ready-to-bake meals, which they sell to people on their way home from work.
2. Joe Daigle and Cathy Goodfellow own a ski repair business and a ski shop. They have decided to combine their businesses. They expect that within the coming year they will need significant funds to expand their operations.
3. Three business professors have formed a business to offer income tax services to the community. They expect to hire students during the busy season.

Instructions

In each of the above situations, explain whether the partnership form of organization is the most appropriate one for the business. Explain your reasoning.

Record formation of partnership.
(SO 2) AP

Interactive Homework

E12–2 Ted Karl has owned and operated a proprietorship for several years. On January 1, he decides to terminate this business and become a partner in the firm of Kurl and Karl. Karl's investment in the partnership consists of $15,000 in cash and the following assets of the proprietorship: accounts receivable of $14,000 less an allowance for doubtful accounts of $2,000, and equipment of $20,000 less accumulated amortization of $4,000. It is agreed that the net realizable value of accounts receivable should be $10,000 for the partnership. The fair market value of the equipment is $17,000. The partnership will also assume responsibility for Karl's accounts payable of $6,000.

Instructions

Journalize Karl's admission to the firm of Kurl and Karl.

E12–3 R. Huma and W. How have capital balances on January 1, 2004, of $50,000 and $40,000, respectively. The partnership income-sharing agreement provides for (1) salary allowances of $20,000 for Huma and $12,000 for How, (2) interest at 10% on beginning capital balances, and (3) remaining income or loss to be shared 75% by Huma and 25% by How.

Calculate and record division of income.
(SO 3) AP

Instructions

(a) Prepare a schedule showing the division of net income for the year ended June 30, 2005, assuming net income is (1) $55,000, and (2) $30,000.

(b) Journalize the allocation of net income in each of the situations in (a).

E12–4 In Schott Co., beginning capital balances of the partners on January 1, 2005, are M. Salz, $20,000, and C. Toni, $18,000. During the year, drawings were Salz, $8,000, and Toni, $5,000. Net income was $33,000. Salz and Toni share income based on a 3:1 ratio.

Prepare statement of partners' capital and partial balance sheet.
(SO 4) AP

Instructions

(a) Prepare the statement of partners' capital for the year.

(b) Prepare the partners' equity section of the balance sheet at December 31, 2005.

E12–5 T. Halo, K. Rose, and J. Lamp share income on a 5:3:2 basis. They have capital balances of $30,000, $26,000, and $15,000, respectively, when R. Zahn is admitted to the partnership on July 1 of the current year.

Record admission of partner.
(SO 5) AP

Instructions

Prepare the journal entry to record the admission of Zahn under each of the following assumptions:

(a) Zahn purchases 50% of Halo's equity for $19,000.

(b) Zahn purchases 50% of Rose's equity for $12,000.

(c) Zahn purchases 33% of Lamp's equity for $9,000.

E12–6 Joe Keho and Mike McLain share income on a 4:2 basis, respectively. They have capital balances of $90,000 and $70,000, respectively, when Ed Kehler is admitted to the partnership on January 1, 2005.

Record admission of partner.
(SO 5) AP

Interactive Homework

Instructions

Prepare the journal entry to record the admission of Ed Kehler on January 1 under each of the following assumptions:

(a) Kehler invests $100,000 cash for a 25% ownership interest.

(b) Kehler invests $35,000 cash for a 25% ownership interest.

E12–7 Julie Lane, Sara Miles, and Amber Noll have capital balances of $50,000, $40,000, and $30,000, respectively. The income ratio is 5:3:2. Assume Noll withdraws from the partnership on December 31 of the current year under each of the following separate conditions:

Record withdrawal of partner.
(SO 6) AP

1. Lane and Miles agree to purchase Noll's equity by paying $17,000 each from their personal assets. Each purchaser receives 50% of Noll's equity.

2. Miles agrees to purchase all of Noll's equity by paying $27,000 cash from her personal assets.

3. Lane agrees to purchase all of Noll's equity by paying $33,000 cash from her personal assets.

Instructions

Journalize the withdrawal of Noll under each of the above assumptions.

E12–8 Dale Nagel, Keith White, and Dan Neal have capital balances of $95,000, $75,000, and $60,000, respectively. They share income or loss on a 5:3:2 basis. Assume White withdraws from the partnership on September 30, 2005, under each of the following separate conditions:

Record withdrawal of partner.
(SO 6) AP

Interactive Homework

1. White is paid $82,000 in cash from partnership assets.

2. White is paid $66,000 in cash from partnership assets.

Instructions

Journalize the withdrawal of White under each of the above assumptions.

E12–9 At December 31, Baylee Company has cash of $15,000, equipment of $140,000, accumulated amortization of $60,000, liabilities of $55,000, and the following partners' capital balances: Bayer, $30,000, and Leech, $10,000. The firm is liquidated on December 31, 2005. Cash of $120,000 is received for the equipment. Bayer and Leech have income ratios of 55% and 45%, respectively.

Calculate amounts paid on liquidation of partnership.
(SO 7) AP

Instructions

Calculate how much will be paid to each of the partners when the firm is liquidated on December 31, 2005.

Record partnership liquidation.
(SO 7) AP

E12–10 Data for the Baylee Company partnership are presented in E12–9.

Instructions

Prepare the entries to record (a) the sale of equipment, (b) the allocation to the partners of the gain or loss on liquidation, (c) the payment of creditors, and (d) the distribution of cash to the partners.

Record partnership liquidation.
(SO 7) AP

Interactive Homework

E12–11 Ole Low, Arnt Olson, and Stig Lokum decided to liquidate the LOL partnership on December 31, 2005 and go their separate ways. The partners share income and losses equally. As at December 31, the partnership had cash of $20,900, noncash assets of $114,500, and liabilities of $15,000. Prior to selling their noncash assets the partners had capital balances of $45,500, $63,200, and $11,700, respectively. After selling the noncash assets for $66,500 and paying all creditors, $72,400 cash remained in the partnership.

Instructions

(a) Calculate the balance in each of the partners' capital accounts after allocating the loss from the sale of the noncash assets and paying the liabilities..
(b) Assume that all of the partners have the personal resources to cover a deficit in their capital accounts. Prepare journal entries to record any cash receipts from the partners to cover any existing deficit and to record the final distribution of cash.
(c) Now assume that the partners do not have the personal resources to cover a deficit in their capital accounts. Prepare journal entries to allocate any deficit to the remaining partners and to record the final distribution of cash.

Problems: Set A

Discuss partnership characteristics.
(SO 1) AN

P12–1A The **Calgary Flames Limited Partnership** is owned by seven partners. In addition to operating the Calgary Flames hockey franchise, the partnership also operates the Pengrowth Saddledome, a 17,159-seat arena that is home to the Flames.

The Flames reported revenue of US$47.0 million in 2002 and a net loss of US$3.7 million. Consequently, the partnership has investigated other ways of bringing in additional cash to the organization. One possibility considered was to build and operate a casino in the Saddledome.

Instructions

Discuss why you think the owners of the Calgary Flames chose to organize as a partnership. Do you think this form of organization will serve the Flames well in the future?

Record formation of partnership and prepare balance sheet.
(SO 2, 4) AP

P12–2A The post-closing trial balances of two proprietorships on January 1, 2005, follow:

	Domic Company		Dasilva Company	
	Dr.	Cr.	Dr.	Cr.
Cash	$ 14,000		$12,000	
Accounts receivable	17,500		26,000	
Allowance for doubtful accounts		$ 3,000		$ 4,400
Merchandise inventory	26,500		18,400	
Equipment	45,000		29,000	
Accumulated amortization—equipment		24,000		11,000
Notes payable		20,000		15,000
Accounts payable		20,000		31,000
I. Domic, capital		36,000		
P. Dasilva, capital				24,000
	$103,000	$103,000	$85,400	$85,400

Domic and Dasilva decide to form a partnership on January 1 with the following agreed-upon valuations for the noncash assets contributed by each:

	Domic Company	Dasilva Company
Accounts receivable	$17,500	$26,000
Allowance for doubtful accounts	4,500	4,000
Merchandise inventory	30,000	20,000
Equipment	23,000	18,000

All cash will be transferred to the partnership. The partnership will also assume all the liabilities of the two proprietorships. It is also agreed that Domic will invest $15,000 cash and Dasilva will invest $9,000 cash.

Instructions

(a) Prepare separate journal entries to record the transfer of each proprietorship's assets and liabilities to the partnership on January 1, 2005.
(b) Journalize the additional cash investment by each partner.
(c) Prepare a balance sheet for the partnership at January 1, 2005.

P12–3A On June 30, 2005, Jainacom and 3D Gaming, two separate proprietorships which develop computer games, agree to combine their operations and form a partnership. The new partnership will be known as Blackend. Jainacom doesn't have any assets worth transferring into the new partnership. The owner, P. Jaina, agrees to invest sufficient cash so the opening balances of the two capital accounts are equal. R. Olsen is the owner of 3D Gaming. 3D Gaming transfers the following assets and liabilities into the partnership at fair market values:

Prepare opening balance sheet.
(SO 2, 4) AP

	Net Book Value	Fair Market Value
Cash	$ 9,000	$ 9,000
Accounts receivable	20,000	18,000
Allowance for doubtful accounts	1,000	1,500
Computer hardware and software	50,000	16,500
Accumulated amortization— computer hardware and software	30,000	
Accounts payable	15,000	15,000
Notes payable	25,000	25,000

Instructions

Prepare a balance sheet for the Blackend partnership at June 30, 2005.

P12–4A At the end of its first year of operations, December 31, 2005, the CNW Company's accounts show the following:

Calculate and record division of net income. Prepare statement of partners' capital.
(SO 3, 4) AP

Partner	Drawings	Capital
Jackie Chapman	$12,000	$33,000
Cathy Nelson	9,000	20,000
Heather Weir	4,000	10,000

The capital balance represents each partner's initial capital investment. Net income or net loss for 2005 has not been closed to the partners' capital accounts.

Instructions

(a) Prepare a schedule showing the division of net income for 2005 under each of the following assumptions:
   1. Net income is $33,000. Income is shared 3:2:1 (Chapman, Nelson, Weir).
   2. Net income is $30,000. Nelson and Weir are given salary allowances of $10,000 and $8,000, respectively. The remainder is shared equally.
   3. Net income is $25,200. Each partner is allowed interest of 10% on beginning capital balances. Nelson and Weir are given a $15,000 salary allowance each. The remainder is shared equally.
(b) Prepare the entry to record the division of net income calculated in (a) for each of the three assumptions.
(c) Prepare a statement of partners' capital for the year under assumption 1 in (a) above.

Allocate income. Prepare income statement, statement of partners' equity, and closing entries.
(SO 2, 3, 4) AP

P12–5A Veda Storey and Gordon Rogers have a partnership agreement which includes the following provisions for sharing net income or net loss:

1. A salary allowance of $30,000 to Storey and $15,000 to Rogers
2. An interest allowance of 10% on capital balances at the beginning of the year
3. The remainder to be divided between Storey and Rogers on a 3:2 basis

The capital balances on January 1, 2005, for Storey and Rogers were $80,000 and $100,000, respectively. During 2005, the Storey Rogers Partnership had sales of $330,000, cost of goods sold of $190,000, operating expenses of $100,000, V. Storey drawings of $40,000, and G. Rogers drawings of $30,000.

Instructions

(a) Prepare an income statement for the Storey Rogers Partnership for the year ended December 31, 2005.
(b) Prepare a schedule to show how net income will be allocated to the two partners.
(c) Prepare a statement of partners' equity for the year ended December 31, 2005.
(d) Prepare closing entries on December 31, 2005.
(e) How would income be divided if there was a dispute between the partners and there was no written partnership agreement?

Record admission of partner.
(SO 5) AP

P12–6A At April 30, partners' capital balances in the SOS Company are as follows: R. Smistad, $36,000; K. Osborne, $24,200; and W. Smistad, $59,800. The income-sharing ratio is 3:2:4. On May 1, the SOSO Company is formed by admitting N. Ortiz to the firm as a partner.

Instructions

(a) Journalize the admission of Ortiz under each of the following independent assumptions:
    1. Ortiz purchases 50% of W. Smistad's ownership interest by paying W. Smistad $32,000 cash.
    2. Ortiz purchases 50% of Osborne's ownership interest by paying Osborne $10,000 cash.
    3. Ortiz invests $47,000 cash in the partnership for a 40% ownership interest.
    4. Ortiz invests $33,330 in the partnership for a 20% ownership interest.
(b) Assume Osborne's capital balance is $22,200 after admitting Ortiz to the partnership by investment. If Osborne's ownership interest is 15% of total partnership capital after the admission of Ortiz, what were (1) Ortiz's cash investment, and (2) the bonus to the new partner?

Record withdrawal of partner.
(SO 6) AP

P12–7A On December 31, the capital balances and income ratios in the FJA Company are as follows:

Partner	Capital Balance	Income Ratio
H. Fercho	$70,000	60%
P. Jiang	30,000	30%
R. Antoni	24,500	10%

Instructions

(a) Journalize the withdrawal of Antoni under each of the following independent assumptions:
    1. Each of the remaining partners agrees to pay $14,000 cash from personal funds to purchase Antoni's ownership equity. Each receives 50% of Antoni's equity.
    2. Jiang agrees to purchase Antoni's ownership interest for $20,000 cash.
    3. From partnership assets, Antoni is paid $29,600.
    4. Antoni is paid $17,300 from partnership assets.
(b) Assuming Jiang's capital balance after Antoni's withdrawal is $32,200, what were (1) the total bonuses to the remaining partners, and (2) the cash paid by the partnership to Antoni?

Prepare and post entries for partnership liquidation.
(SO 7) AP

P12–8A The partners in Cottage Country Company decide to liquidate the firm when the balance sheet shows the following:

COTTAGE COUNTRY COMPANY
Balance Sheet
April 30, 2005

Assets		Liabilities and Partners' Equity	
Cash	$ 28,000	Notes payable	$14,000
Accounts receivable	19,000	Accounts payable	24,000
Allowance for doubtful accounts	(1,000)	Wages payable	2,000
Merchandise inventory	28,000	A. Hoffer, capital	25,000
Equipment	17,000	K. Lonseth, capital	11,200
Accumulated amortization—equipment	(10,000)	D. Posca, capital	4,800
	$ 81,000		$81,000

The partners share income and loss 5:3:2 (Hoffer, Lonseth, Posca). During the process of liquidation, the transactions below were completed in the sequence shown:

1. A total of $48,000 was received from converting noncash assets into cash on May 2, 2005.
2. Liabilities were paid in full on May 6, 2005.
3. Cash was paid to the partners on May 9, 2005.

Instructions

(a) Prepare the entries to record the transactions.
(b) Post the transactions to the cash and capital accounts.

P12–9A On June 1, 2005, the musical partnership of James, Lars, Kirk, and Robert decides to separate and liquidate the partnership. The partners have capital balances of $1 million each except for Robert, whose capital balance is $600,000. Cash, noncash assets, and liabilities total $900,000, $5.8 million, and $3.1 million, respectively. The four partners share income and loss equally.

Record liquidation of partnership.
(SO 7) AP

Instructions

Journalize the liquidation of the partnership under each of the following independent assumptions:

(a) The noncash assets are sold for $3.5 million cash, the liabilities are paid, and the remaining cash is paid to the partners.
(b) The noncash assets are sold for $2.5 million cash and the liabilities are paid. The partner with the debit capital balance pays the amount owed to the partnership and the remaining cash is paid to the partners.
(c) The noncash assets are sold for $2.5 million cash and the liabilities are paid. The partner with the debit capital balance is unable to pay the amount owed to the partnership. The cash is paid to the three other partners.

Problems: Set B

P12–1B The **Clearwater Seafoods Limited Partnership** was created in July 2002 to acquire the seafood business of Clearwater Fine Foods Incorporated. Clearwater Fine Foods Incorporated owns the general partnership units; the limited partnership units are owned by the publicly traded Clearwater Seafoods Income Fund.

Discuss partnership characteristics.
(SO 1) AN

The Clearwater Seafoods Limited Partnership harvests, processes, and distributes fresh and frozen fish and shellfish throughout Asia, Europe, and North America.

On December 31, 2002, the partnership reported total assets of $289.9 million and unit holders' (partners) equity of $110.3 million.

Instructions

Discuss why you think the owners of the Clearwater Seafoods Limited Partnership chose to organize as a partnership. Do you think this form of organization will serve them well in the future?

P12–2B The post-closing trial balances of two proprietorships on January 1, 2005, are presented below:

Record formation of partnership and prepare balance sheet.
(SO 2, 4) AP

	Visanji Company		Vanbakel Company	
	Dr.	Cr.	Dr.	Cr.
Cash	$ 9,500		$ 6,000	
Accounts receivable	15,000		23,000	
Allowance for doubtful accounts		$ 2,500		$ 4,000
Merchandise inventory	28,000		17,000	
Equipment	50,000		30,000	
Accumulated amortization—equipment		24,000		13,000
Notes payable		20,000		
Accounts payable		25,000		37,000
F. Visanji, capital		31,000		
P. Vanbakel, capital				22,000
	$102,500	$102,500	$76,000	$76,000

Visanji and Vanbakel decide to form the Varsity Company partnership with the following agreed-upon valuations for the noncash assets contributed by each :

	Visanji Company	Vanbakel Company
Accounts receivable	$15,000	$23,000
Allowance for doubtful accounts	3,500	5,000
Merchandise inventory	32,000	24,000
Equipment	31,000	18,000

All cash will be transferred to the partnership on January 1. The partnership will also assume all the liabilities of the two proprietorships. Further, it is agreed that Visanji will invest $4,000 cash. Vanbakel will invest $10,000 cash.

Instructions

(a) Prepare separate journal entries to record the transfer of each proprietorship's assets and liabilities to the partnership on January 1, 2005.
(b) Journalize the additional cash investment by each partner.
(c) Prepare a balance sheet for the partnership at January 1, 2005.

Prepare opening balance sheet.
(SO 2, 4) AP

P12–3B The post-closing trial balances of two proprietorships on January 1, 2005, are presented below:

	Elias Company		Geist Company	
	Dr.	Cr.	Dr.	Cr.
Cash	$ 19,000		$ 18,000	
Accounts receivable	25,000		33,000	
Allowance for doubtful accounts		$ 2,500		$ 5,000
Merchandise inventory	38,000		30,000	
Equipment	60,000		35,000	
Accumulated amortization—equipment		34,000		28,000
Notes payable		30,000		
Accounts payable		35,000		47,000
I. Elias, capital		40,500		
K. Geist, capital				36,000
	$142,000	$142,000	$116,000	$116,000

Elias and Geist decide to form the Elias Geist Company with the following agreed-upon valuations for the noncash assets contributed by each:

	Elias Company	Geist Company
Accounts receivable	$25,000	$33,000
Allowance for doubtful accounts	4,000	6,000
Merchandise inventory	35,000	31,000
Equipment	31,000	28,000

All cash will be transferred to the partnership, and the partnership will assume all the liabilities of the two proprietorships. The partners also agree that each partner should contribute an equal amount to the partnership. After transferring their proprietorship assets and liabilities to the partnership, one of them will contribute additional cash from her personal assets to bring her capital account balance up to the balance in the other partner's capital account.

Instructions

Prepare a balance sheet for the partnership at January 1, 2005.

P12–4B At the end of its first year of operations, on December 31, 2005, LBS Company's accounts show the following:

Partner	Drawings	Capital
Sue Little	$23,000	$90,000
Debra Bartlet	14,000	60,000
Dorothy Sawka	10,000	50,000

Calculate and record division of net income. Prepare statement of partners' capital. (SO 3, 4) AP

The capital balance represents each partner's initial capital investment. Net income or net loss for 2005 has not been closed to the partners' capital accounts.

Instructions

(a) Journalize the entry to record the division of net income for the year 2005 under each of the following separate assumptions:
   1. Net income is shared in the ratio of their initial investments. Net income is $47,000.
   2. Net income is $34,000. Bartlet and Sawka are given salary allowances of $15,000 and $10,000, respectively. The remainder is shared equally.
   3. Net income is $23,000. Each partner is allowed interest of 10% on beginning capital balances. Sawka is given a $15,000 salary allowance. The remainder is shared equally.
(b) Prepare a schedule showing the division of net income under assumption 3 in (a) above.
(c) Prepare a statement of partners' capital for the year under assumption 2 in (a) above.

P12–5B Terry Lam and Chris Tan have a partnership agreement which includes the following provisions regarding sharing net income or net loss:

Allocate income. Prepare income statement, statement of partners' equity, and closing entries. (SO 2, 3, 4) AP

   1. A salary allowance of $40,000 to Lam and $25,000 to Tan
   2. An interest allowance of 8% on capital balances at the beginning of the year
   3. The remainder to be divided between Lam and Tan on a 4:2 basis

The capital balances on January 1, 2005, for Lam and Tan were $110,000 and $130,000, respectively. During 2005, the Lam Tan Partnership had sales of $445,000, cost of goods sold of $295,000, operating expenses of $100,000, T. Lam drawings of $40,000, and C. Tan drawings of $30,000.

Instructions

(a) Prepare an income statement for the Lam Tan Partnership for the year ended December 31, 2005.
(b) Prepare a schedule to show how net income will be allocated to the two partners.
(c) Prepare a statement of partners' equity for the year ended December 31, 2005.
(d) Prepare closing entries on December 31, 2005.
(e) What would happen if one of the partners died and there was no written partnership agreement?

P12–6B At September 30, partners' capital balances in NEW Company are A. Nolan, $62,000; D. Elder, $48,000; and T. Wuhan, $14,000. The income-sharing ratio is 5:4:1. On May 1, the NEWS Company is formed by admitting C. Santos to the firm as a partner.

Record admission of partner. (SO 5) AP

Instructions

(a) Journalize the admission of Santos under each of the following independent assumptions:
   1. Santos purchases 50% of Wuhan's ownership interest by paying Wuhan $16,000 in cash.
   2. Santos purchases $33\frac{1}{3}$% of Elder's ownership interest by paying Elder $15,000 in cash.
   3. Santos invests $75,000 for a 30% ownership interest.
   4. Santos invests $40,000 for a 35% ownership interest.
(b) Assume that Nolan's capital balance is $64,400 after Santos is admitted to the partnership by investment. If Nolan's ownership interest is 35% of total partnership capital, what were (1) Santos' cash investment, and (2) the bonus to the old partners?

Record withdrawal of partner.
(SO 6) AP

P12–7B On December 31, the capital balances and income ratios in the VKD Company are as follows:

Partner	Capital Balance	Income Ratio
B. Vuong	$60,000	50%
G. Khan	40,000	30%
R. Dixon	30,000	20%

Instructions

(a) Journalize the withdrawal of Dixon under each of the following independent assumptions:
  1. Each of the continuing partners agrees to pay $18,000 cash from personal funds to purchase Dixon's ownership equity. Each receives 50% of Dixon's equity.
  2. Khan agrees to purchase Dixon's ownership interest for $25,000 cash.
  3. Dixon is paid $36,000 from partnership assets.
  4. Dixon is paid $26,000 from partnership assets.
(b) If Vuong's capital balance after Dixon's withdrawal is $64,375, what were (1) the total bonus to the remaining partners, and (2) the cash paid by the partnership to Dixon?

Prepare and post entries for partnership liquidation.
(SO 7) AP

P12–8B The partners in the Omni Company decide to liquidate the firm when the balance sheet shows the following:

OMNI COMPANY
Balance Sheet
May 31, 2005

Assets		Liabilities and Partners' Equity	
Cash	$ 27,500	Notes payable	$ 13,500
Accounts receivable	25,000	Accounts payable	27,000
Allowance for doubtful accounts	(1,000)	Wages payable	3,800
Merchandise inventory	34,500	L. Sciban, capital	33,000
Equipment	21,000	V. Subra, capital	21,000
Accumulated amortization—equipment	(5,500)	C. Werier, capital	3,200
Total	$101,500	Total	$101,500

The partners share income and loss 4:3:2 (Sciban, Subra, Werier). During the process of liquidation, the following transactions were completed in the sequence shown:

1. A total of $50,000 was received from converting noncash assets into cash.
2. Liabilities were paid in full.
3. Werier paid her capital deficiency.
4. Cash was paid to the partners with credit balances.

Instructions

(a) Prepare the entries to record the transactions.
(b) Post the transactions to the cash and capital accounts.
(c) Assume that Werier is unable to pay the capital deficiency. (1) Prepare the entry to allocate Werier's debit balance to Sciban and Subra. (2) Prepare the entry to record the final distribution of cash.

Record liquidation of partnership.
(SO 7) AP

P12–9B On September 1, 2005, the CGA accounting partnership of M. Broski and B. Hazle separated and liquidated the partnership. The partners Broski and Hazle share income and loss in a 1:3 ratio. Just before the liquidation, the partnership balance sheet showed the following:

BROSKI AND HAZLE
Balance Sheet
September 1, 2005

Assets		Liabilities and Partners' Equity	
Cash	$ 80,000	Accounts payable	$ 50,000
Office equipment	85,000	M. Broski, capital	50,000
Accumulated amortization	(50,000)	B. Hazle, capital	15,000
	$115,000		$115,000

Instructions

Journalize the liquidation of the partnership under each of the following independent assumptions:

(a) The equipment is sold for $43,000 cash, the accounts payable are paid, and the remaining cash is paid to the two partners.

(b) The equipment is scrapped and the accounts payable are paid. Hazle pays his capital deficiency and the remaining cash is distributed to the partners.

(c) The equipment is sold for $2,500 cash and the accounts payable are paid. Hazle does not pay his capital deficiency. The remaining cash is distributed to Broski.

Continuing Cookie Chronicle

(Note: This is a continuation of the Cookie Chronicle from Chapters 1 through 11.)

Natalie's high school friend, Katy Peterson, has been operating a bakery for approximately 18 months. Because Natalie has been so successful operating Cookie Creations, Katy would like to have Natalie become her partner. Katy believes that together they will create a thriving cookie-making business.

Natalie is quite happy with her current business set-up. Up until now, she had not considered joining forces with anyone. From past meetings with Katy, however, Natalie has gathered the following information about Katy's business and compared it to her own results:

- The current fair values of assets and liabilities of both businesses are as follows:

	The Baker's Nook	Cookie Creations
Cash	$ 1,500	$10,000
Accounts receivable	5,000	500
Allowance for doubtful accounts	(750)	0
Merchandise inventory	450	1,130
Equipment	7,500	1,000
Bank loan payable	10,000	0

All assets would be transferred into the partnership. The partnership would assume all of the liabilities of the two proprietorships. The bank loan is due February 17, 2006.

- Katy operates her business from leased premises. She has just signed a lease for 12 months. Monthly rent will be $1,000. Katy's landlord has agreed to draw up a new lease agreement that would be signed by both partners.

- Katy graduated from cooking school. She has no assets and has significant amounts of student loans and credit card debt. Natalie's assets consist of investments in Canada Savings Bonds. Natalie has no personal liabilities.

- Katy would like to make a monthly drawing of $1,000 so she can repay her personal debt.

- Katy has also mentioned to Natalie that she would like to buy a van that she would use for both personal and business purposes. (Katy does not have a vehicle of her own.) The car dealership has agreed to sell the vehicle to the partnership as long as both Natalie and Katy sign the loan agreement on behalf of the partnership.

- Katy is reluctant to have a partnership agreement drawn up. She thinks it's a waste of both time and money. As Katy and Natalie have been friends for a long time, Katy is confident that all problems can be easily resolved over a nice meal.

Natalie believes that it may be a good idea to establish a partnership with Katy. She comes to you with the following questions:

1. Do I really need a formalized partnership agreement drawn up? What would be the point of having one if Katy and I agree on all major decisions? What type of information should the partnership agreement contain?

2. I would like to have Katy contribute the same amount of capital as I am contributing. My grandmother is willing to lend Katy the necessary cash. How much would my grandmother have to lend her? (Hint: How much cash, in addition to the amount in Katy's proprietorship, would Katy have to invest in the partnership so that Natalie and Katy have the same capital balances?)

3. Katy has a lot of personal debt. Should this affect my decision about whether or not to go forward with this business venture? Why or why not?

4. What other issues should I consider before I say yes or no to Katy?

Instructions:

(a) Answer Natalie's questions.

(b) Assume that Natalie and Katy go ahead and form a partnership called Cookie Creations and More on November 1, 2005, and that Katy borrows the cash from Natalie's grandmother. Prepare a balance sheet for the partnership on November 1, 2005.

(c) Assume the partnership earns $9,000 in the first year of operations. Assume also that Katy and Natalie agree to share income by allowing a salary allowance of $6,000 for Katy and $4,000 for Natalie with the remainder distributed equally. Finally, assume Katy withdraws $12,000 during the year and that Natalie does not make any withdrawals. (1) Prepare a schedule showing the distribution of net income for the year ended October 31, 2006. (2) Prepare a statement of partners' capital for the year ended October 31, 2006.

BROADENING YOUR PERSPECTIVE

Financial Reporting and Analysis

Practice
Tools

Financial Reporting Problem

BYP12–1 The **Shelter Restaurant (Moose Jaw) Limited Partnership** was organized in 1987 to hold the title to rental properties. The balance sheet and notes to its financial statements include the following excerpts:

SHELTER RESTAURANT (MOOSE JAW) LIMITED PARTNERSHIP
Balance Sheet (partial)
December 31, 2002

Limited partners' equity	
Original investment	$405,000
Surplus	162,076
	$567,076

SHELTER RESTAURANT (MOOSE JAW) LIMITED PARTNERSHIP
Notes to the Financial Statements
December 31, 2002

6. **Liability of Limited Partners**

   The Limited Partnership Agreement provides that the General Partner has unlimited liability for the debts and obligations of the Limited Partnership. The liability of each Limited Partner is limited to the amount of capital contributed or agreed to be contributed plus the Limited Partner's share of undistributed income.

Instructions

(a) What are the advantages to the company of operating as a limited partnership rather than as a general partnership?

(b) Using the balance sheet information provided above, specify how much the limited partners' liability is restricted to in dollars.

(c) Do you think that new partners would likely be added by purchase of a partner's interest or by investment of assets in the partnership, or both? What entries are likely made when new partners are added to the limited partnership?

Accounting on the Web

BYP12–2 This case discusses the reasons why so many small accounting firms find it beneficial to merge or adopt alliances with larger accounting partnerships.

Instructions
Specific requirements of this Internet case are available on the Weygandt website.

Critical Thinking

Collaborative Learning Activity

BYP12–3 Benoît Goyette and Liu Xiaoyan, two professionals in the finance department, have worked for the Leasing Solutions Company for a number of years. Ben and Liu have decided that, with their financial expertise, they should start their own company to provide consulting services to individuals interested in leasing equipment. One form of organization they are considering is a partnership.

If they start a partnership, each of them plans to contribute $60,000 cash. In addition, Liu has a used computer that originally cost $5,500 which she intends to invest in the partnership. The computer has a current market value of $1,500. Ben has furniture that he intends to invest in the partnership. The furniture originally cost $4,000 and has a current market value of $3,000.

Although both Ben and Liu are financial wizards, they do not know a great deal about how a partnership operates. As a result, they have come to you for advice.

Instructions
With the class divided into groups, answer the following questions:

(a) What are the major advantages and disadvantages of operating a business as a general partnership? As a limited liability partnership?

(b) What type of document is needed for a partnership? What information should this document contain?

(c) Prepare journal entries to record the investment of each partner.

(d) Both Ben and Liu plan to work full-time in the new partnership. They believe that net income or net loss should be shared equally. However, they are wondering how they can provide compensation to Ben for his additional investment of the furniture. What would you tell them?

(e) Ben and Liu have worked together for a number of years. Ben's skills complement Liu's and vice versa. If one of them dies, it will be very difficult for the other to maintain the business, not to mention pay the deceased partner's estate for his or her partnership interest. What concerns would you have if you were either Ben or Liu?

Communication Activity

BYP12–4 You are an expert in the field of forming partnerships. Dr. Konu Chatterjie and Dr. Sheila Unger want to establish a partnership to practice medicine. They are going to meet with you to discuss their plans. Prior to the meeting, you will send them a letter discussing the issues they need to consider before their visit.

Instructions

Write a letter, in good form, to be sent to Konu and Sheila. In it, provide an overview of the various aspects of a partnership agreement and the issues that need to be addressed in order for the agreement to be a well-thought-out document.

Ethics Case

BYP12–5 Susan and Erin operate a spa as partners who share profits and losses equally. The success of their business has exceeded their expectations and it is operating quite profitably. Erin is anxious to maximize profits. She schedules appointments from 8 a.m. to 6 p.m. daily and she even works weekends to accommodate regular customers. Susan schedules her appointments from 9 a.m. to 5 p.m. and does not work weekends. Susan regularly makes significantly larger withdrawals of cash than Erin does, but she says, "Erin, you needn't worry; I never make a withdrawal without you knowing about it, so it is properly recorded in my drawings account and charged against my capital at the end of the year." Susan's withdrawals to date are double Erin's.

Instructions

(a) Who are the stakeholders in this situation?
(b) Identify the problems with Susan's actions, and discuss the ethical considerations related to her actions.
(c) How might the partnership agreement be designed to accommodate the differences in Susan's and Erin's work and withdrawal habits?

Answers to Self-Study Questions

1. a   2. b   3. c   4. a   5. b   6. d   7. a   8. a   9. b   10. a

Answer to Forzani Review It Question 5

Mutual agency, limited life, unlimited liability, and co-ownership of property are major characteristics of a partnership. As a company like The Forzani Group grows in size, it is difficult for it to remain a partnership, because of these factors. The corporate form of organization separates ownership and management and makes it easier to raise capital. The unlimited liability of a partnership hinders raising capital because owners may lose not only their initial investment but also their personal assets if those assets are needed to pay partnership creditors.

 Remember to go back to the Navigator Box at the beginning of the chapter to check off your completed work.

concepts for review >>

the navigator

Before studying this chapter, you should understand or, if necessary, review:
a. The differences between the three forms of business organization. (Ch. 1, pp. 9–10 and pp. 12–13)
b. The content of the equity section of the balance sheet for a proprietorship (Ch. 1, pp. 11–12) and for a partnership. (Ch. 12, pp. 581–582)
c. How to prepare closing entries for a proprietorship (Ch. 4, pp. 157–158) and for a partnership (Ch. 12, p. 578)

Student Savvy Pays Off for Research In Motion

WATERLOO, Ont.—In 1984, University of Waterloo co-op engineering student Mike Lazaridis incorporated Research In Motion Limited (RIM) with partner Douglas Fregin.

The company sold its first wireless e-mail system in 1987—a large, clunky system with a very small market. But Lazaridis knew the potential of the technology was great. "Wireless data was something I believed in," he explains. Through the late 1980s and early 1990s, RIM designed and built products such as interactive pagers, wireless PC cards, and wireless radio modems it marketed to other manufacturers to incorporate into various products.

In 1996, the company was poised for a major expansion. RIM's 1997 initial public offering (IPO) raised more than $100 million from the sale of 13.8 million common shares, issued at $7.25 on the Toronto Stock Exchange (TSX).

The financing was used to build, and then expand, a new production facility in Waterloo. It also helped fund sales and marketing and, especially, expand research and development activities. That R&D focus paid off when, in 1999, RIM launched what has become its signature product, the wildly successful BlackBerry wireless hand-held device.

This sleek "e-mail on steroids" quickly became a must-have item not only for techno-wizards but for stockbrokers and others whose business depends on time-sensitive information.

In 1999, RIM's revenues soared to $70 million and its income to $9.5 million. Its share price went on a roller-coaster ride, trading as high as $260 and as low as $50 on the TSX during the year. The same year also saw RIM get a listing on the Nasdaq market, the big kids' playground for high-tech firms. An additional public share offering

Research In Motion: www.rim.net

followed in October 2000 when its share price was around US$100. Today, RIM's shares trade at around $45 on the TSX and US$34 on the Nasdaq.

In 2003, RIM recorded revenues of US$306.7 million. Its annual report lists US$704.7 million of shareholders' equity (US$874.3 million of share capital and a deficit of US$169.6 million). The company continues to grow—it now has nearly 2,000 employees—fuelled by its significant R&D investments and grants.

But in an industry characterized by hype, RIM and Lazaridis himself retain a certain Canadian modesty. Lazaridis is known to still drop by former professor Mohamed Elmasry's office at the University of Waterloo for advice. This low-key approach is reflected in RIM's culture and its focus on devices that help customers use the computers and e-mail accounts they already have.

the navigator

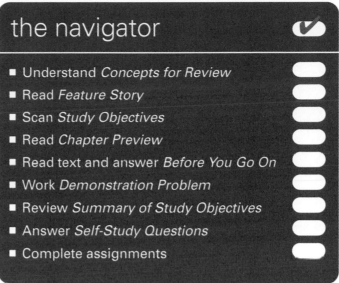

the navigator

- Understand *Concepts for Review*
- Read *Feature Story*
- Scan *Study Objectives*
- Read *Chapter Preview*
- Read text and answer *Before You Go On*
- Work *Demonstration Problem*
- Review *Summary of Study Objectives*
- Answer *Self-Study Questions*
- Complete assignments

chapter | 13

c h a p t e r 1 3

Corporations: Organization and Share Capital Transactions

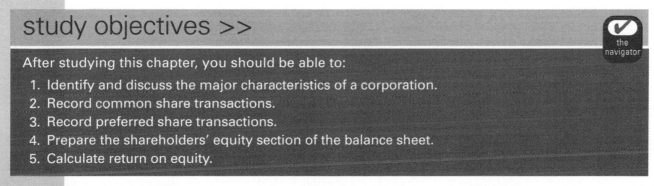

study objectives >>

After studying this chapter, you should be able to:

1. Identify and discuss the major characteristics of a corporation.
2. Record common share transactions.
3. Record preferred share transactions.
4. Prepare the shareholders' equity section of the balance sheet.
5. Calculate return on equity.

Incorporated companies can start out small and grow large, as Research In Motion has. It should not be surprising, then, that the corporation is the dominant form of business organization. In this chapter, we will explain the essential features of a corporation and the accounting for a corporation's share capital transactions. In Chapter 14, we will look at other issues related to accounting for corporations.

The chapter is organized as follows:

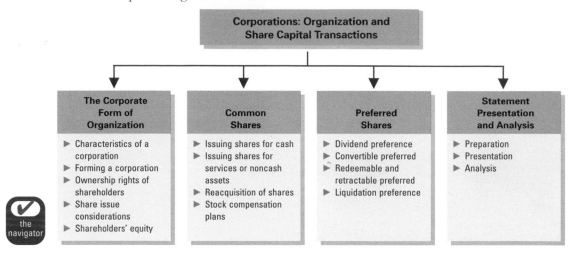

M.C. Question.

The Corporate Form of Organization

Helpful hint In Canada, you can tell whether a company is incorporated by looking at its name. The words "Limited" (Ltd.), "Incorporated" (Inc.), or "Corporation" (Corp.) follow the name of an incorporated company.

A corporation is a legal entity that is separate and distinct from its owners, who are known as shareholders. As a legal entity, a corporation has most of the rights and privileges of a person. It must respect laws and it must pay income tax. The major exceptions are privileges that only a living person can exercise, such as the right to vote or to hold public office.

Corporations may be classified in a variety of ways. Two common classifications are by purpose and by ownership. A corporation may be organized for the purpose of making a **profit** or it may be **not-for-profit** (also known as nonprofit). Corporations for profit include well-known companies such as Cineplex Odeon Corporation, The Forzani Group Ltd., and Maple Leaf Foods Inc. Not-for-profit corporations are organized for cultural, social, charitable, medical, educational, and religious purposes. Examples are Big Brothers/Big Sisters, the Canadian National Institute for the Blind, the Canadian Chamber of Commerce, the Red Cross, and the Society for the Prevention of Cruelty to Animals.

In classification by ownership, a distinction is made between publicly held and privately held corporations. A **publicly held corporation** may have thousands of shareholders. Its shares are usually traded in an organized securities market, such as the Toronto Stock Exchange. Most of the largest Canadian corporations are publicly held. Examples of publicly held corporations are Canadian Pacific Railway Company, The Forzani Group Ltd., and Sears Canada Inc. In contrast, a **privately held corporation**, often called a closely held corporation, usually has only a few shareholders. It does not offer its shares for sale to the general public. Privately held companies are generally much smaller than publicly held companies, although there are notable exceptions such as McCain Foods, The Jim Pattison Group, and the Irving companies. Research In Motion, in our feature story, was a privately held corporation until it offered its shares for sale to the public in 1997 and became publicly held.

Characteristics of a Corporation

Many characteristics distinguish corporations from proprietorships and partnerships. The most important of these characteristics are explained below.

① Separate Legal Existence

As an entity separate and distinct from its owners, the corporation acts under its own name rather than in the name of its shareholders. Research In Motion, for example, may buy, own, and sell property. It may borrow money and enter into legally binding contracts in its own name. It may also sue or be sued, and it pays income tax as a separate legal entity.

2 diff people.

Remember that in a proprietorship or partnership, the acts of the owners (partners) bind the proprietorship or partnership. In contrast, the acts of owners (shareholders) do not bind a corporation unless these individuals are also duly appointed agents of the corporation. For example, if you owned shares of Research In Motion, you would not have the right to purchase a new production facility unless you were appointed an agent of the corporation.

② Limited Liability of Shareholders

Since a corporation is a separate legal entity, creditors only have access to corporate assets to have their claims repaid to them. The liability of shareholders is normally limited to their investment in the corporation. Creditors have no legal claim on the personal assets of the shareholders unless fraud has occurred. Even in bankruptcy, shareholders' losses are generally limited to their capital investment in the corporation.

③ Transferable Ownership Rights

Ownership of a corporation is held in shares of capital. These are transferable units. Shareholders may dispose of part or all of their interest (ownership) in a corporation simply by selling their shares. Remember that the transfer of an ownership interest in a proprietorship or partnership, in contrast, requires the consent of each owner or partner. In a corporation, the transfer of shares is entirely decided by the shareholder. It does not require the approval of either the corporation or other shareholders.

← *can change ownership anytime.*

The transfer of ownership rights between shareholders has no effect on the operating activities of the corporation. Nor does it affect the corporation's assets, liabilities, and total equity. The transfer of these ownership rights is a transaction between individual shareholders. The company does not participate in such transfers after it has initially issued the share capital.

④ Ability to Acquire Capital

It is relatively easy for a large corporation to obtain capital by issuing shares. Buying shares in a corporation is often attractive to an investor because a shareholder has limited liability and shares are easily transferable. Also, many individuals can become shareholders by investing small amounts of money. For these reasons, a successful corporation's ability to obtain capital is virtually unlimited.

⑤ Continuous Life

Most corporations have an unlimited life. Since a corporation is a separate legal entity, its continuance as a going concern is not affected by the withdrawal, death, or incapacity of a shareholder, employee, or officer. As a result, a successful enterprise can have a continuous and indefinite life. For example, the Hudson's Bay Co., Canada's oldest corporation, was founded in 1670 and is still going strong.

Corporation goes on doesn't matter what happens

⑥ Corporation Management

Shareholders legally own the corporation. But they manage the corporation indirectly through a board of directors they elect. The board, in turn, decides on the operating policies of the company and selects officers—such as a president and one or more vice-presidents—to execute policy and to perform daily management functions. Douglas Fregin and Mike Lazaridis, introduced in our feature story, are both officers of Research In Motion's board of directors, along with one other management director and three independent directors.

The organizational structure of a corporation enables a company to hire professional managers to run the business. On the other hand, the separation of ownership and management prevents owners from having an active role in managing the company, which is difficult for some owners to accept.

ACCOUNTING IN ACTION ► Ethics Insight

In the wake of Enron's collapse, many people asked, "Where was the board of directors?" The Enron board claimed that it was kept in the dark by management and the auditors. Some have speculated that the collapse of Enron was not so much because of problems with accounting principles as because of board culture and leadership. This situation highlighted the need for adequate selection and training of independent directors. Corporate governance reforms now encourage directors to ask the hard questions of management and the auditors, and to work with management to set the ethical tone for the corporation.

⑦ Government Regulations

Canadian companies may be incorporated federally, under the terms of the *Canada Business Corporations Act*, or provincially, under the terms of a provincial business corporations act. Federal and provincial laws specify the requirements for issuing shares, distributing income to shareholders, and reacquiring shares. Similarly, provincial securities commissions' regulations govern the sale of share capital to the general public. Respecting federal, provincial, and securities regulations increases costs and complexity for corporations.

⑧ Income Tax

Neither proprietorships nor partnerships pay entity income tax. Each owner's (or partner's) share of income from these organizations is reported on his or her personal income tax return. Income tax is then paid by the individual on this amount. Corporations, on the other hand, must pay federal and provincial income taxes as separate legal entities. These taxes can be substantial. They can amount to as much as 45% of taxable income.

There are income tax deductions available to some corporations. With eligible deductions, or other corporate tax incentives, a corporation's tax rate may be reduced to between 15% and 25%. This tax rate is much lower than the tax rate for the same amount of income earned by an individual.

In some circumstances, an advantage of incorporation is the deferral of personal income tax. The shareholders of a corporation do not pay tax on corporate income until it is distributed to them. Shareholders pay tax on cash dividends, which are pro rata distributions of net income. Many people argue that corporate income is taxed twice (double taxation)—at the corporate level and again at the individual level. This is not exactly true, however, as individuals receive a dividend tax credit to reduce some of the tax burden.

To determine whether incorporating will result in more or less income tax for a proprietorship or partnership, it is wise to seek expert advice. Income tax laws are complex, and care in tax planning is essential for any business venture.

Illustration 13-1 summarizes the advantages and disadvantages of a corporation compared to a proprietorship or partnership.

Advantages	Disadvantage
• Corporation management—professional managers • Separate legal existence • Limited liability of shareholders • Potential for deferred or reduced income tax • Transferable ownership rights • Ability to acquire capital • Continuous life	• Corporation management—ownership separated from management • Increased cost and complexity to follow government regulations • Potential for additional income tax

Illustration 13-1 ◄

Advantages and disadvantages of a corporation

It is worth noting that many of these advantages and disadvantages depend on the size of the corporation. For example, in a small private (closely held) corporation, such as the Diab Corner Grocery Store Ltd., it is just as hard to sell shares of ownership, or to acquire capital, as it is for an unincorporated business. The limited liability feature also makes it harder for a small corporation to obtain loans. Lenders often require officers to personally guarantee the loans, which eliminates the limited liability advantage.

Forming a Corporation

As previously mentioned, a company can incorporate federally or provincially. The federal government and the majority of provinces file **articles of incorporation** to incorporate a company, although other methods also exist.

Articles of incorporation contain information such as (1) the name and purpose of the proposed corporation, (2) the amounts and kinds of share capital to be authorized and the number of shares, (3) the names and addresses of the incorporators, and (4) the location of the corporation's head office. Anyone can apply to incorporate a company, as long as he or she is over the age of 18, of sound mind, and not bankrupt.

After receiving its articles of incorporation—essentially the constitution of the company—the corporation establishes by-laws. The by-laws set the internal rules and procedures for operations. Corporations engaged in interprovincial commerce must also obtain a licence from each province they do business in. The licence forces the corporation's operating activities to respect the laws of the province.

The costs of forming a corporation are called **organization costs**. These costs include legal fees, accounting fees, and registration costs. It may be argued that organization costs should be capitalized as they have an asset life equal to the life of the corporation. However, most companies expense organization costs in the year they occur. Determining the amount and timing of future benefits is so difficult that the conservative approach of expensing these costs immediately is more justifiable.

Ownership Rights of Shareholders

Once it is incorporated, the company may begin selling ownership rights in the form of shares. The shares of the company are divided into different classes, such as Class A, Class B, and so on. The rights and privileges assigned to each class of shares are stated in the articles of incorporation. The different classes are usually identified by the generic terms **common shares** and **preferred shares**. When a corporation has only one class of shares, this class has the rights and privileges of **common shares**. Each common share gives the shareholder the ownership rights shown in Illustration 13-2.

Illustration 13-2 ▶
Ownership rights of
shareholders

Shareholders have the right to:

1. Vote in the election of the board of directors at an annual meeting. Vote on actions that require shareholders' approval.

2. Share the corporate income by receiving dividends.

Dividends

3. Share in the assets upon liquidation, in proportion to their holdings. (This claim is called a **residual claim** because the owners are paid with assets remaining after all claims have been paid.)

A **share certificate** proves that a shareholder owns shares. The face of the certificate shows the name of the corporation, the shareholder's name, the class and special features of the shares, the number of shares owned, and the signatures of duly authorized corporate officials. Certificates should be prenumbered to facilitate accountability. They may be issued for any quantity of shares.

ACCOUNTING IN ACTION ▶ @–Business Insight

Paper share certificates will soon be as scarce as hula hoops. The Canadian Capital Markets Association has recommended that most, if not all, stock certificates be converted into an electronic format. Trading with paper certificates is unwieldy and is blocking the move to settle share trades in one day. Some countries, such as France and Denmark, have already eliminated the use of physical certificates. The U.S. plans to move to electronic stock certificates by the end of 2005.

Share Issue Considerations

Alternative terminology
Issued also means *sold*.

When Research In Motion first issued shares in 1997, it had to make a number of decisions. How many shares should be authorized for sale? How should the shares be issued? At what price should the shares be issued? What value should be assigned to the shares? These questions are answered in the following sections.

Authorized Share Capital

A corporation's **authorized shares**—that is, the total number of shares a company is allowed to sell—is indicated in its articles of incorporation. It may be specified as an unlimited amount or a certain number (e.g., 500,000 shares authorized). More than three-quarters of public companies with share capital in Canada have an unlimited amount of authorized shares. Research In Motion has an unlimited number of shares authorized.

If a number is specified, the amount of authorized shares normally anticipates a company's initial and later capital needs. **Issued shares** are the authorized shares that have been sold.

If a corporation has issued all of its authorized shares, it must obtain legislative approval to amend its articles of incorporation before it can issue additional shares. To determine the number of unissued shares that can be issued without amending the articles of incorporation, the total shares issued are subtracted from the total authorized. For example, if

Advanced Micro Corp. is authorized to sell 100,000 common shares but has issued only 80,000 shares, 20,000 shares remain unissued. If Advanced Micro had an unlimited amount of common shares authorized, an unlimited number of shares would remain unissued.

The authorization of share capital does not result in a formal accounting entry, because the event has no immediate effect on either assets or shareholders' equity. However, disclosure of the authorized and issued shares is required in the shareholders' equity section of the balance sheet.

Issue of Shares

A corporation can issue common shares either directly to investors or indirectly through an investment dealer (brokerage house) that specializes in bringing securities to the attention of potential investors. Direct issue is typical in closely held companies. Indirect issue is customary for a publicly held corporation, such as Research In Motion in our feature story.

The first time a corporation's shares are offered to the public, the offer is called an **initial public offering (IPO)**. The company receives the cash (less any issue fees) from the sale of the IPO shares whether done by a direct or indirect issue. The company's assets (cash) increase, and its shareholders' equity (share capital) also increases.

Once these shares have been initially issued, they continue trading on the **secondary market**. That is, investors buy and sell shares from each other, rather than from the company. When shares are sold among investors, there is no impact on the company's financial position. The company receives no additional assets, and it issues no additional shares. The only change in the company records is the name of the shareholder, not the number of shares issued.

In Canada, shares are offered for sale to the public (whether through an IPO or through the secondary market) using organized securities exchanges, such as the Toronto Stock Exchange (TSX) or the Montréal Exchange (MX).

How does a corporation like Research In Motion in our opening story set the price for its initial issue of shares? Among the factors to be considered are (1) the company's anticipated future earnings, (2) its expected dividend rate per share, (3) its current financial position, (4) the current state of the economy, and (5) the current state of the securities market. The subject can be complex and is usually taught in a finance course.

Market Value of Shares

After the initial issue of new shares, the market price per share changes according to the interaction between buyers and sellers. In general, the price follows the trend of a company's income and dividends. Factors beyond a company's control (such as an embargo on oil, changes in interest rates, the outcome of an election, and war) can also influence market prices.

For each listed security, the financial press reports the highest and lowest prices of the shares for the year; the annual dividend rate; the highest, lowest, and closing prices for the day; and the net change over the previous day. The total volume of shares traded on a particular day, the dividend yield, and price-earnings ratios are also reported. A recent listing for Research In Motion from the Toronto Stock Exchange is shown below:

365-day		stock	sym	div	high /bid	low /ask	close	chg	vol 100s	yld	p/e ratio
high	low										
47.80	13.19	Research In Motion	RIM		45.86	44.41	45.12	-0.49	4175		

Research In Motion's shares have traded as high as $47.80 and as low as $13.19 during the past year. The stock's ticker symbol is "RIM." Research In Motion does not pay an annual dividend, as the blank space in the "div" column shows. The highest, lowest, and closing prices for the date shown were $45.86, $44.41, and $45.12 per share, respectively. The closing share price decreased $0.49 from the previous day. The trading volume was 417,500 shares. Since Research In Motion does not pay any dividend, there is no dividend yield ("yld"). The dividend yield reports the rate of return an investor earned from dividends by dividing the dividend by the share price. There also is no reported price-earnings ("p/e") ratio (share price divided by earnings per share) because Research In Motion currently has a loss per share, rather than earnings per share.

No Par Value Shares *always use it.*

Years ago, par or stated value was used to determine the **legal capital** per share that must remain invested in the business for the protection of corporate creditors. Corporations with par or stated value shares were required to sell their shares at par or stated value or above. Consequently, most companies assigned their par or stated value shares a very low value.

The usefulness of par or stated value as a protective device to creditors was questionable because this assigned value was usually immaterial compared to the value of the company's shares—even at the time of issue. For example, Reebok's par value is 1 cent per share, yet a new share issue by Reebok would sell today at a **market value** of $34 per share. Thus, par or stated value had no relationship with market value and in the vast majority of cases was an immaterial amount. Today, the use of par or stated values for shares is either not required or is prohibited by companies incorporating federally, as well as by companies incorporating in most Canadian provinces. Par value shares are still issued in some other countries, however, including the United States.

No par value shares are shares that have not been assigned a preset value. Instead, the entire proceeds received upon issue of the shares are considered to be legal capital. If shares have no par value, then the questionable practice of using par value as a basis for legal capital never arises. Whenever shares are issued in this chapter, we will assume that they have no par value.

Shareholders' Equity

The shareholders' equity section of a corporation's balance sheet includes (1) share capital (contributed capital) and (2) retained earnings (earned capital). **Share capital** consists of amounts contributed to the corporation by shareholders in exchange for shares of ownership. Other amounts can also be contributed by, or accrue to, shareholders which, along with share capital, form the total **contributed capital** of the corporation. We will learn more about other sources of contributed capital later in this chapter. **Retained earnings** are earned capital (cumulative net income less losses and amounts distributed to shareholders) that has been retained for future use. A negative amount of retained earnings is called a deficit.

The distinction between share capital and retained earnings is important from both a legal and an economic point of view. As mentioned in the previous section, share capital is the legal capital that must be held in the business. Retained earnings, however, can be distributed to shareholders as dividends (similar to owner's drawings) or retained in the company for operating requirements.

We will discuss the accounting for share capital in this chapter. Retained earnings and dividends will be discussed in more detail in the next chapter.

BEFORE YOU GO ON

►Review It

1. What are the advantages and disadvantages of a corporation compared to a proprietorship or partnership?
2. To a corporation, what is the significance of the amount of authorized shares? Issued shares?
3. How does the sale of shares affect a company in an initial public offering? Afterwards, in the secondary market?
4. Distinguish between share capital and retained earnings.

Related exercise material: BE13–1, BE13–2, BE13–3, and E13–1.

Common Shares

Let's now look at how to account for common share transactions. Common shares may be sold for cash or exchanged for noncash assets. Shares may also be reacquired from investors. We will discuss each of these transactions in the following sections.

study objective 2

Record common share transactions.

Issuing Shares for Cash

Shares are most commonly issued in exchange for cash. As discussed earlier, when no par value common shares are issued, the entire proceeds from the issue become legal capital. To illustrate the issue of common shares, assume that Hydroslide is authorized to issue an unlimited number of no par value common shares. It issues 1,000 of these shares for $1 per share on January 12. The entry to record this transaction is as follows:

Jan. 12	Cash	1,000	
	Common Shares		1,000
	To record issue of 1,000 common shares.		

A = L + SE
+1,000 +1,000

↑ Cash flows: +1,000

Issuing Shares for Services or Noncash Assets

Shares may also be issued for services (compensation to lawyers or consultants) or for noncash assets (land, buildings, and equipment). In such cases, what cost should be recognized in the exchange transaction? To comply with the cost principle in a noncash transaction, cost is the cash equivalent price. The cash equivalent price is the fair market value of the consideration given up. If this amount cannot be determined, we look to the fair market value of the consideration received to determine the cash equivalent price, and thus the cost.

To illustrate, assume that lawyers have helped Hydroslide incorporate. They have billed the company $5,000 for their services. On January 18, they agree to accept 4,000 common shares in payment of their bill. At the time of the exchange, the market price for the shares is $1. In this case, the shares should be recorded at the market value of the consideration given up, which is 4,000 shares worth $1 per share, and not the amount of the bill, which is $5,000. Accordingly, the entry is as follows:

Jan. 18	Legal Fees Expense	4,000	
	Common Shares		4,000
	To record issue of 4,000 common shares to lawyers.		

A = L + SE
          −4,000
          +4,000

Cash flows: no effect

Assume now that a newly incorporated company issues 10,000 shares on October 1 to acquire land recently advertised for sale at $80,000. At the time of the acquisition, the company's shares have not established a reliable market value. In this case, the land would be recorded as follows at the market value of the consideration received, $80,000:

A	=	L	+	SE
+80,000				+80,000

Cash flows: no effect

Oct.	1	Land	80,000	
		Common Shares		80,000
		To record issue of 10,000 common shares for land.		

V.I.P.

Reacquisition of Shares

V.I.P.

Companies can purchase their own shares on the open market. A corporation may acquire shares to meet any of the following objectives:

1. To increase trading of the company's shares in the securities market in the hopes of enhancing its market value
2. To reduce the number of shares issued and thereby increase earnings per share
3. To have additional shares available to reissue to officers and employees under bonus and stock compensation plans
4. To have additional shares available for use in the acquisition of other companies
5. To comply with percentage share ownership requirements (i.e., limit foreign ownership)

Another less frequent reason for a company to buy its own shares is when management wants to eliminate hostile shareholders by buying them out. Canadian Occidental Petroleum Ltd. (CanOxy) repurchased nearly half of its shares in 2000 to stop the Los Angeles–based Occidental Petroleum Corp. from taking over its huge Syncrude oil sands project in northern Alberta.

When a federally incorporated company reacquires its own shares, the repurchased shares must be retired and cancelled. This effectively restores the shares to the status of authorized but unissued shares. Some provincially incorporated companies are allowed to hold reacquired shares for future use. Shares held for this purpose are called **treasury shares**. Treasury share transactions are rare in Canada and are only permitted in restricted circumstances.

To illustrate the accounting for reacquired shares, assume that Hydroslide, Inc. now has a total of 25,000 common shares issued and a balance in its common shares account of $50,000. On September 23, Hydroslide purchases and cancels 5,000 of its common shares.

Recall that when a long-lived asset is retired, the cost of the asset must be credited and any difference between the proceeds received and the original cost is recorded as a gain or loss. Similarly, the cost of the common shares reacquired and retired must be determined and that amount deleted (debited) from Common Shares. The difference between the price paid to reacquire the shares and their original cost is essentially a "gain" or "loss" on reacquisition. However, companies cannot realize a gain or suffer a loss from share transactions with their own shareholders, so these amounts are not reported on the income statement. They are seen instead as an excess or deficiency belonging to the original shareholders and are reported as an increase or decrease in the shareholders' equity section of the balance sheet.

In order to determine the cost of the common shares reacquired, it is necessary to calculate an average cost per share. It is impractical, and often impossible, to determine the cost of each individual common share reacquired. An average cost per common share is therefore calculated by dividing the balance in the common shares account by the number of shares issued. In the case of Hydroslide, the average cost of the common shares, immediately before the reacquisition, is $2 per share ($50,000 ÷ 25,000).

The accounting for the reacquisition of shares is different depending on whether the shares are reacquired by paying less than the average cost or more than the average cost.

Reacquisition below Cost

To illustrate the reacquisition of common shares at a price less than their average cost, assume that Hydroslide reacquired its 5,000 common shares at a price of $1.50 per share. Since the average cost of the shares was $2 per share, a $0.50 ($2.00 − $1.50) additional contribution to shareholders' equity results, as shown below:

Sept. 23	Common Shares (5,000 × $2)	10,000	
	Contributed Capital—Reacquisition of Shares		2,500
	Cash (5,000 × $1.50)		7,500
	To record reacquisition and retirement of 5,000 common shares.		

A = L + SE
−7,500   −10,000
            +2,500

Cash flows: −7,500

After this entry, Hydroslide still has an unlimited number of shares authorized, but only 20,000 (25,000 − 5,000) shares issued, and a balance of $40,000 ($50,000 − $10,000) in Common Shares. The difference between the average cost of the shares and the amount paid to repurchase them is credited to a new shareholders' equity account for the contributed capital from the reacquisition of shares. This account is reported as shareholders' equity, along with the share capital, to indicate the total capital contributed by the shareholders. The cash in the entry was paid to the various shareholders the shares were repurchased from.

Reacquisition above Cost

If Hydroslide had paid $2.50 per share to reacquire 5,000 of its common shares, rather than $1.50 per share as assumed above, there would be a debit to the shareholders' equity account for the difference between the price paid to reacquire the shares and their average cost. If there is any balance in the contributed capital account from previous reacquisitions, this amount would first be reduced (debited). However, contributed capital cannot be reduced below zero. In other words, contributed capital can never have a negative, or debit, balance. Instead, any excess debit deficiency amount would be recorded in Retained Earnings.

The journal entry to record the reacquisition and retirement of Hydroslide's common shares at $2.50 per share is as follows:

Sept. 23	Common Shares (5,000 × $2)	10,000	
	Retained Earnings	2,500	
	Cash (5,000 × $2.50)		12,500
	To record reacquisition and retirement of 5,000 common shares.		

A = L + SE
−12,500   −10,000
             −2,500

Cash flows: −12,500

In this entry, Hydroslide is assumed to have no existing balance in a contributed capital account. After this entry, Hydroslide still has 20,000 (25,000 − 5,000) shares issued and a balance of $40,000 ($50,000 − $10,000) in its common shares account.

The only difference in the accounting for a reacquisition at below or above the average cost has to do with recording the difference and the amount of cash paid. If the shares are reacquired at a price below the average cost, the difference is credited to a contributed capital account. If the shares are reacquired at a price above the average cost, the difference is debited first to the contributed capital account for any prior reacquisition below cost of the same class of shares, and secondly to the retained earnings account if there is no credit balance remaining in the contributed capital account.

Stock Compensation Plans

We mentioned above that companies sometimes repurchase shares to issue them to officers and employees under stock compensation plans. Stock compensation plans reward employees with options to buy shares, encouraging employees to act in a way that maximizes share prices. A **stock option** is a right granted by a company to an employee to buy a specified number of the company's shares at a specified price during a specified time period. When the market price of the shares exceeds the option price, the employee gains by exercising the option (buying the shares).

Stock option plans are a common way of increasing compensation—especially for corporate executives. Of the companies surveyed in a recent year, 98% reported using stock-based compensation plans. It has been estimated that stock options account, on average, for up to 80% of executive compensation. In some instances, stock options account for significantly more. For example, Frank Stronach, Chair of Magna International Inc., earned a salary of $314,000 in 2002 and received stock options valued at $51.8 million.

Over the last few years, no subject in financial accounting has received as much press as accounting for stock options. While there is no doubt in anyone's mind that stock options are valuable, it is very difficult to measure the actual value of the compensation. Consequently, until recently, stock options were disclosed only in the notes to the financial statements, and not recorded as an expense. This resulted in a situation where literally billions of dollars of compensation provided to employees was not recorded as a compensation expense, significantly overstating earnings. For example, Toronto-based Imax Corp. reported a net income of US$11.9 million in 2002. Had Imax expensed its stock options, it would have reported a net loss of US$1.2 million.

All of this has now changed. In a move towards more transparent financial reporting, Canadian public companies are now required to record stock-based compensation as an expense in their financial statements. This move, effective January 1, 2004, made Canada the first major country to require expensing of stock-based compensation.

The Forzani Group Ltd., along with some other companies, voluntarily started to expense stock options in 2003. Forzani reported an expense on its statement of operations of $1,608,000 related to stock-based compensation in its interim financial statements for the nine months ended November 2, 2003.

Accounting standard-setters in Europe and the United States are also expected to require companies to begin expensing stock options, one year later, in 2005.

ACCOUNTING IN ACTION ▶ Business Insight

Lavish executive options packages of the late 1990s may have provided too much incentive for senior executives to manage share prices. Some say that steps taken to boost revenues and hide losses in the corporate scandals of the past few years were taken in order to give executives time to cash in their stock options before the signs of decline were seen. At the very least, stock options forced executives to focus on short-term results, instead of long-term implications and the company's survival.

This is a moot point now. Plummeting share values and closer scrutiny of stock options have meant that the portion of executive compensation coming from stock options has declined compared to other forms of compensation. Right now, most stock options are worth far less than their current option price. Repricing options for company employees has been all but ruled out by irate shareholders, who would not benefit from such a move. And buying back options is not realistic for cash-strapped companies.

This has made stock options unattractive to many who hold them and of questionable value as a long-term financial reward that ties together shareholder and management interests.

BEFORE YOU GO ON . . .

►Review It

1. Explain the accounting for an issue of common shares for cash.
2. Explain the accounting for an issue of common shares for services or noncash assets.
3. Did The Forzani Group Ltd. repurchase any of its own shares in fiscal 2003? The answer to this question is at the end of this chapter.
4. Which financial statements, if any, do stock options affect?

►Do It

Victoria Corporation begins operations on March 1 by issuing 100,000 common shares for cash at $12 per share. On March 15, it issues 5,000 common shares to its lawyers in settlement of their bill of $65,000. The shares continue to trade at $12 per share on March 15. On June 1, Victoria repurchases 10,000 of its own shares at $10 per share.

Do it
V.I.P.

Action Plan

- Credit the account Common Shares for the entire share issue proceeds.
- Use the cash equivalent price when shares are issued for services. The cash equivalent price is equal to the fair market value of what is given up. If this amount cannot be determined, use the fair market value of what is received.
- Calculate the average cost per share by dividing the balance in Common Shares by the number of shares issued.
- Debit Common Shares for the average cost of the reacquired shares. If the reacquisition price is below the average cost, credit the difference to a contributed capital account. If the reacquisition price is above the average cost, debit the difference to Retained Earnings unless there is an existing balance in a contributed capital account from prior reacquisitions and retirements.

Solution

Mar. 1	Cash	1,200,000	
	Common Shares (100,000 × $12)		1,200,000
	To record issue of 100,000 shares at $12 per share.		
15	Legal Fees Expense	60,000	
	Common Shares (5,000 × $12)		60,000
	To record issue of 5,000 shares for lawyers' fees.		
June 1	Common Shares (10,000 × $12)	120,000	
	Contributed Capital—Reacquisition of Shares		20,000
	Cash (10,000 × $10)		100,000
	To record reacquisition and retirement of 10,000 common shares at an average cost of $12 ($1,260,000 ÷ 105,000).		

Related exercise material: BE13–4, BE13–5, BE13–6, BE13–7, E13–2, E13–3, and E13–4.

Preferred Shares

A corporation may issue preferred shares in addition to common shares. **Preferred shares** have contractual provisions that give them a preference, or priority, over common shares in certain areas. Typically, preferred shareholders have priority over (1) dividends (distributions of income) and (2) assets in the event of liquidation. They generally do not have voting rights. A recent survey indicated that nearly one-third of Canadian companies have preferred shares.

Like common shares, preferred shares may be issued for cash or for noncash assets. They can also be reacquired. The entries for all these transactions are similar to the entries for common shares. When a company has more than one class of shares, the transactions for each class should be recorded in separate accounts.

Assume that Staudinger Corporation issues 10,000 preferred shares for $12 cash per share on January 28. The entry to record the issue is as follows:

A	=	L	+	SE
+120,000				+120,000

↑ Cash flows: +120,000

Jan. 28	Cash	120,000	
	Preferred Shares		120,000
	To record the issue of 10,000 preferred shares.		

The preferred shares account is used to record the issue of preferred shares. As with common shares, no par value shares are most commonly issued. In the shareholders' equity section, preferred shares are presented first because of their dividend and liquidation preferences over common shares.

Some typical features of preferred shares, including dividend and liquidation preferences, are discussed next.

Dividend Preference

As indicated before, corporate income is distributed to **preferred shareholders before it goes to common shareholders**. For example, if the dividend rate on preferred shares is $5 per share, common shareholders will not receive any dividends in the current year until preferred shareholders have received $5 per share. The first claim to dividends does not, however, guarantee the payment of dividends. Dividends depend on many factors, such as adequate retained earnings and the availability of cash.

Preferred shares often contain a **cumulative dividend** feature. This means that preferred shareholders must be paid both current year dividends and any unpaid prior year dividends before common shareholders receive dividends. When preferred shares are cumulative, preferred dividends that are not declared in a given period are called **dividends in arrears**. When preferred shares are not cumulative (known as noncumulative), a dividend unpaid in any year is lost forever. The majority of preferred shares issued today are noncumulative.

To illustrate the cumulative dividend feature, assume that Staudinger's 10,000 preferred shares have a $3.50 cumulative dividend. The per share dividend amount is usually given as an **annual** amount, similar to interest rates. So, Staudinger's annual total dividend is $35,000 (10,000 × $3.50 per share). If dividends are two years in arrears, preferred shareholders are entitled to receive the following dividends:

Dividends in arrears ($35,000 × 2)	$ 70,000
Current year dividends	35,000
Total preferred dividends	$105,000

No distribution can be made to common shareholders until this entire preferred dividend is paid. In other words, dividends cannot be paid on common shares while any preferred shares are in arrears.

Dividends in arrears are not considered a liability. No payment obligation exists until a dividend is declared by the board of directors. However, the amount of dividends in arrears should be disclosed in the notes to the financial statements. This enables investors to assess the potential impact of this future declaration on the corporation's financial position.

Even though there is no requirement to pay an annual dividend, companies that do not meet their dividend obligations are not looked upon favourably by the investment community. When discussing one company's failure to pay its cumulative preferred dividend, a financial officer noted, "Not meeting your obligations on something like that is a major black mark on your record." The accounting entries for dividends are explained in Chapter 14.

Convertible Preferred

As an investment, preferred shares are even more attractive when there is a conversion privilege. **Convertible preferred shares** give shareholders the option of exchanging preferred shares for common shares at a specified ratio.

Convertible preferred shares are bought by investors who want the greater security of preferred shares but who also want the option of conversion if the market value of the common shares increases significantly.

To illustrate, assume that Ross Industries Inc. issues 1,000 convertible preferred shares at $100 per share. One share of preferred is convertible into 10 shares of common. The current market price of the common shares is $9 per share. At this point, holders of the preferred shares would not want to convert, because they would exchange preferred shares worth $100,000 (1,000 × $100) for common shares worth only $90,000 (10,000 × $9). However, if the price of the common shares were to increase above $10 per share, conversion would be advantageous for the preferred shareholders.

To record the conversion, the cost of the preferred shares is transferred to the common shares account. As with the reacquisition of shares, it is seldom possible to determine the original cost of the preferred shares converted. An average cost per share is therefore calculated by dividing the balance in the preferred shares account by the number of shares issued, as at the transaction date.

To illustrate, assume that the 1,000 preferred shares of Ross Industries with an average cost of $100 per share are converted into 10,000 common shares when the market values of the two classes of shares are $101 and $12 per share, respectively, on June 10. The entry to record the conversion is:

V.I.P.

June 10	Preferred Shares	100,000	
	Common Shares		100,000
	To record conversion of 1,000 preferred shares into 10,000 common shares.		

A	=	L	+	SE
				−100,000
				+100,000

Cash flows: no effect

Note that the average cost (which is the same as the original cost in this example) of the preferred shares is used to record the conversion. **The market values of the shares are not considered in recording the transaction**, because the corporation has not received any assets equal to fair market value. Therefore, the conversion of preferred shares does not result in either a gain or loss to the corporation.

Redeemable and Retractable Preferred

Many preferred shares are issued with a redemption or call feature. **Redeemable (or callable) preferred shares** give the issuing corporation the right to purchase the shares from shareholders at specified future dates and prices. The redemption feature enables a corporation to eliminate the preferred shares when it is advantageous to do so.

Often, shares that are redeemable are also convertible. Sometimes, companies will redeem or call their preferred shares to induce investors to convert those preferred shares into common shares.

Retractable preferred shares are similar to redeemable preferred shares except that the shareholders can redeem shares at their option instead of the corporation's. This usually occurs at an arranged price and date.

When preferred shares are redeemable or retractable, the distinction between equity and debt begins to blur. Redeemable and retractable preferred shares are similar in some

Helpful hint The two features differ in terms of benefit. *Redeemable* is at the option of the corporation. *Retractable* is at the option of the shareholder.

ways to debt. They both offer a rate of return to the investor, and with the redemption of the shares, they both offer a repayment of the principal investment.

Contractual arrangements of this sort are known as **financial instruments**. The CICA requires companies to present financial instruments in accordance with their economic substance rather than their form. That is, redeemable and retractable preferred shares are usually presented in the *liabilities* section of the balance sheet rather than in the equity section. This is because they often have more of the features of debt than of equity.

Companies are issuing an increasing number of shares with innovative preferences. Some have the attributes of both debt and equity; others have the attributes of both common and preferred shares. Accounting for such financial instruments presents unique challenges to accountants. Further discussion of this topic is left to an intermediate accounting course.

Liquidation Preference

Most preferred shares also have a preference on corporate assets if the corporation fails. This means that assets will be used to pay the preferred shareholders first if the corporation goes bankrupt. This feature provides security for the preferred shareholders. The preference to assets may be for the legal capital of the shares or for a specified liquidating value. The liquidation preference establishes the respective claims of creditors and preferred shareholders.

BEFORE YOU GO ON . . .

▶**Review It**

1. Compare the normal rights and privileges of common and preferred shareholders.
2. Distinguish between cumulative and noncumulative dividends.
3. Distinguish between convertible, redeemable, and retractable preferred shares.

Related exercise material: BE13–8, BE13–9, E13–5, and E13–6.

Statement Presentation and Analysis

study objective 4

Prepare the shareholders' equity section of the balance sheet.

In this section, we will review the preparation and presentation of the shareholders' equity section and then learn how to use this information to calculate an important profitability measure—the return on equity ratio.

Preparation

In the shareholders' equity section of the balance sheet, contributed capital and retained earnings are reported.

Contributed Capital

Within contributed capital, two classifications are recognized:

1. **Share capital.** This category consists of preferred and common shares. Because of the additional rights they give, preferred shares are shown before common shares. The legal value (e.g., no par value), number of shares authorized, and number of shares issued are reported for each class of shares.

2. **Additional contributed capital.** This category includes amounts contributed from reacquiring and retiring shares. It can also include amounts paid in excess of stated or par values, if such values exist. As mentioned earlier, this is not the common practice in Canada, where most shares have no par value. Other situations not discussed in this textbook can also result in additional contributed capital. If a company has a variety of sources of additional contributed capital, it is important to distinguish each source.

In most cases, there will be no additional contributed capital. The caption "share capital" is therefore used more often than "contributed capital."

Retained Earnings

Retained earnings are the cumulative net income (or loss) since incorporation that has been retained in the company (i.e., not distributed to shareholders). Each year, net income is added (or a net loss is deducted) and dividends are deducted from the opening retained earnings balance to determine the ending retained earnings amount. Dividends are amounts distributed to shareholders—they are similar to drawings by an owner in a proprietorship. We will learn more about dividends in the next chapter.

As in a proprietorship, revenue and expense accounts (which combine to produce net income or loss) and the dividends account are temporary accounts which accumulate transactions for the period. At the end of each period, these accounts are closed, just as their corresponding accounts in a proprietorship are: (1) individual revenue and expense accounts are closed to Income Summary, (2) the income summary account is closed to retained earnings, and (3) dividends are closed to retained earnings. Note that the income summary account is not closed to the owner's capital account, as it is in a proprietorship. Instead, in a corporation it is closed to the retained earnings account, as is the dividends account.

For example, assume for simplicity that Zaboschuk Inc. has three temporary accounts at its December 31 year end: Service Revenue, $500,000; Operating Expenses, $290,000; and Dividends, $80,000. The closing entries follow:

Dec. 31	Service Revenue	500,000			A = L + SE
	Income Summary		500,000		-500,000
	To close revenue to income summary.				+500,000
31	Income Summary	290,000			Cash flows: no effect
	Operating Expenses		290,000		-290,000
	To close expenses to income summary.				+290,000
31	Income Summary	210,000			Cash flows: no effect
	Retained Earnings		210,000		-210,000
	To close income summary to retained earnings.				+210,000
31	Retained Earnings	80,000			Cash flows: no effect
	Dividends		80,000		-80,000
	To close dividends to retained earnings.				+80,000

After these entries are posted, the retained earnings account (a permanent account) is up to date in the general ledger. It is this ending balance that is reported in the shareholders' equity section of the balance sheet. This ending balance becomes the opening balance for the next period. The statement of retained earnings, similar to the statement of owner's equity in a proprietorship, reconciles the opening and ending balances in each period. We will learn how to prepare the statement of retained earnings in the next chapter.

Cash flows: no effect

Presentation

The assumed shareholders' equity section of Zaboschuk Inc., shown on the next page, includes most of the accounts discussed in this chapter. Zaboschuk's preferred shares section discloses that the dividend rate is $9 per annum, 10,000 preferred shares of no par value have been authorized, and 6,000 shares are issued. This means 4,000 shares are still available for issue at some point in the future. The common shares are no par value with an unlimited amount of shares authorized. To date, 400,000 shares have been issued. Zaboschuk also reports additional contributed capital of $60,000, earned when reacquiring common shares, and retained earnings of $1,058,000.

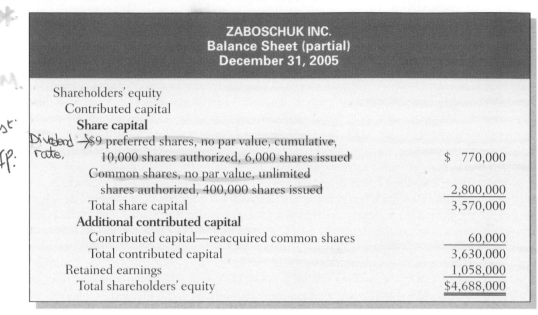

ZABOSCHUK INC.
Balance Sheet (partial)
December 31, 2005

Shareholders' equity
  Contributed capital
    Share capital
      $9 preferred shares, no par value, cumulative,
        10,000 shares authorized, 6,000 shares issued $ 770,000
      Common shares, no par value, unlimited
        shares authorized, 400,000 shares issued   2,800,000
      Total share capital   3,570,000
    Additional contributed capital
      Contributed capital—reacquired common shares   60,000
      Total contributed capital   3,630,000
  Retained earnings   1,058,000
  Total shareholders' equity $4,688,000

Analysis

study objective 5

Calculate return on equity.

There are many valuable ratios that can be determined from the shareholders' equity section of the balance sheet. One of the most important is the return on equity ratio.

Return on Equity

Return on equity, also known as return on investment, is considered by many to be *the* most important measure of a firm's profitability and efficiency. This ratio is used by management and investors to evaluate how many dollars are earned for each dollar invested by the shareholders. It can be used to compare investment opportunities in the marketplace.

Return on equity is a widely published figure. The highest return on equity among Canada's top 1,000 corporations in a recent year was reported by Laniuk Industries, an Alberta oil and gas company, which reported a return on equity of 238%. The lowest was reported by Ontario-based MDR Switchview Global Networks, which reported a negative 617%.

The following illustration calculates the return on equity ratio for The Forzani Group ($ in thousands):

Illustration 13-3 ▶

Return on equity

Net Income	÷	Average Shareholders' Equity	=	Return on Equity
$30,531	÷	$\dfrac{\$203,723 + \$132,045}{2}$	=	18.2%

Forzani's return on equity, at 18.2%, is slightly above the industry average, which is 15.4%. Return on equity can vary significantly by company and by industry.

Calculations can be done to produce a return on equity for common shareholders only. This is done by dividing net income by the shareholders' equity that belongs to the common shareholders (total shareholders' equity less preferred dividends).

BEFORE YOU GO ON . . .

► Review It

1. Distinguish between contributed capital and retained earnings.
2. Explain how to calculate the return on equity.

Related exercise material: BE13–10, BE13–11, BE13–12, E13–7, E13–8, E13–9, and E13–10.

Demonstration Problem

The Rolman Corporation is authorized to issue an unlimited number of no par value common shares and 100,000 no par value, $6 cumulative, convertible preferred shares. Each preferred share is convertible into 7.5 common shares. In its first year, the company had the following share transactions:

Jan. 10 Issued 400,000 common shares at $8 per share.
July 1 Issued 100,000 common shares in exchange for land. The land had an asking price of $900,000. The shares were currently selling on the Toronto Stock Exchange at $8.25 per share.
Sept. 1 Issued 20,000 preferred shares at $50 each.
Dec. 1 Converted 4,000 preferred shares into 30,000 common shares. The common shares were selling on the Toronto Stock Exchange at $9 per share on that date.

Additional
Demonstration
Problems

✗ DO iͨ

Instructions

(a) Journalize the transactions.
(b) Prepare the shareholders' equity section, assuming the company has retained earnings of $900,000 at December 31, 2005.

Solution to Demonstration Problem

(a)

Jan. 10	Cash	3,200,000	
	Common Shares (400,000 × $8)		3,200,000
	To record issue of 400,000 shares at $8 each.		
July 1	Land	825,000	
	Common Shares (100,000 × $8.25)		825,000
	To record issue of 100,000 shares for land.		
Sept. 1	Cash	1,000,000	
	Preferred Shares (20,000 × $50)		1,000,000
	To record issue of 20,000 preferred shares at $50 each.		
Dec. 1	Preferred Shares (4,000 × $50)	200,000	
	Common Shares		200,000
	To record conversion of 4,000 preferred shares into 30,000 common shares.		

Action Plan

• Credit Common Shares for the full amount of the proceeds from the issue of no par value shares.

• Fair market value should be used in a noncash transaction.

• Use separate accounts for each type or class of shares.

• Record the conversion of shares at book value, not market value.

• Keep track of the number of shares issued.

(b)

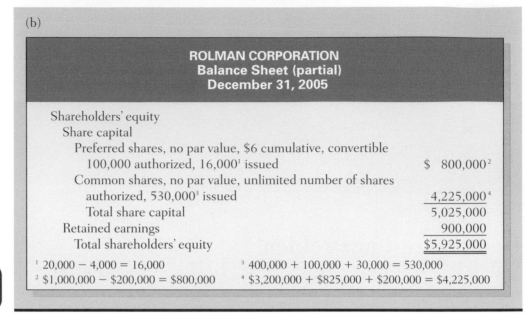

ROLMAN CORPORATION
Balance Sheet (partial)
December 31, 2005

Shareholders' equity	
Share capital	
Preferred shares, no par value, $6 cumulative, convertible	
100,000 authorized, 16,000[1] issued	$ 800,000[2]
Common shares, no par value, unlimited number of shares	
authorized, 530,000[3] issued	4,225,000[4]
Total share capital	5,025,000
Retained earnings	900,000
Total shareholders' equity	$5,925,000

[1] 20,000 − 4,000 = 16,000   [3] 400,000 + 100,000 + 30,000 = 530,000
[2] $1,000,000 − $200,000 = $800,000   [4] $3,200,000 + $825,000 + $200,000 = $4,225,000

the navigator

Summary of Study Objectives

1. *Identify and discuss the major characteristics of a corporation.* The major characteristics of a corporation are as follows: separate legal existence, limited liability of shareholders, transferable ownership rights, ability to acquire capital, continuous life, corporation management, government regulations, and entity income tax.

2. *Record common share transactions.* When no par value shares are issued for cash, the entire proceeds from the issue become legal capital and are credited to the common shares account. When shares are issued for assets or services, the fair market value of the consideration given up is used if it can be easily determined. If not, the fair market value of the consideration received is used.

When shares are reacquired, the average cost is debited to the common shares account. If the shares are reacquired at a price below the average cost, the difference is credited to a contributed capital account. If the shares are reacquired at a price above the average cost, the difference is debited first to the contributed capital account if a balance exists, and secondly to the retained earnings account.

the navigator

3. *Record preferred share transactions.* The accounting for preferred shares is similar to the accounting for common shares. Preferred shares have contractual provisions that give them priority over common shares in certain areas. Typically, preferred shareholders have priority over (1) dividends, and (2) assets in the event of liquidation. They usually do not have voting rights. In addition, preferred shares may be convertible, redeemable, and/or retractable. Convertible preferred shares allow their holder to convert them into common shares at a specified ratio. The redemption feature gives the issuing corporation the right to purchase the shares from shareholders at specified future dates and prices. Retractable preferred shares give shareholders the option of selling their shares to the corporation at specified future dates and prices. Redeemable and retractable preferred shares are often more like debt than equity.

4. *Prepare the shareholders' equity section of the balance sheet.* In the shareholders' equity section, contributed capital and retained earnings are reported. Within contributed capital, two classifications may be shown if applicable: share capital and additional contributed capital.

5. *Calculate return on equity.* Return on equity is calculated by dividing net income by average shareholders' equity. It is an important measure of a firm's profitability and efficiency.

Glossary

Key Term Matching Activity

Authorized shares The amount of share capital that a corporation is authorized to sell, as indicated in its articles of incorporation. This amount may be unlimited or specified. (p. 622)

Contributed capital The total amount of cash paid or other assets contributed by shareholders in exchange for share capital. (p. 624)

Convertible preferred shares Preferred shares that the shareholder can convert into common shares at a specified ratio. (p. 631)

Corporation A business organized as a legal entity, separate and distinct from its owners, under corporation law. (p. 618)

Cumulative dividend A feature of preferred shares that entitles the shareholder to receive current and unpaid prior year dividends before common shareholders receive any dividends. (p. 630)

Initial public offering (IPO) The initial offering of a corporation's shares to the public. (p. 623)

Issued shares The portion of authorized shares that has been sold. (p. 622)

Legal capital The amount per share that must be retained in the business for the protection of corporate creditors. (p. 624)

No par value shares Share capital that has not been assigned a specific value. All the proceeds from the sale of no par value shares are treated as legal capital. (p. 624)

Organization costs Costs incurred in the formation of a corporation. (p. 621)

Preferred shares Share capital that has contractual preferences over common shares. (p. 629)

Privately held corporation A corporation that has only a few shareholders. Its shares are not available for sale to the general public. (p. 618)

Publicly held corporation A corporation that may have thousands of shareholders. Its shares are usually traded on an organized securities market. (p. 618)

Redeemable (callable) preferred shares Preferred shares that give the issuer the right to purchase the shares from shareholders at specified future dates and prices. (p. 631)

Retained earnings Net income after subtracting net losses and dividends distributed to shareholders since incorporation. If negative (i.e., a debit balance), it is called a deficit. (p. 624)

Retractable preferred shares Preferred shares that give the shareholder the right to sell the shares to the issuer at specified future dates and prices. (p. 631)

Return on equity Net income expressed as a percentage of average shareholders' equity. (p. 634)

Share capital The amount paid to the corporation by shareholders in exchange for shares of ownership. (p. 624)

Stock option A right granted to purchase a specified number of shares at a specified price during a specified time period. (p. 628)

Self-Study Questions

Chapter 13 Self-Test

Answers are at the end of the chapter.

(SO 1) K 1. Which of the following is not a major advantage of a corporation?
(a) Separate legal existence
(b) Continuous life
(c) Government regulations
(d) Transferable ownership rights

(SO 1) AP 2. Cossette Corporation has 100,000 common shares authorized and 75,000 common shares issued. How many more shares is Cossette allowed to sell?
(a) 0   (c) 75,000
(b) 25,000   (d) 100,000

(SO 2) AP 3. ABC Corporation issues 1,000 common shares at $12 per share. In recording the transaction, a credit is made to:
(a) Gain on Sale of Shares for $12,000.
(b) Common Shares for $12,000.
(c) Equity Investment—ABC Common Shares for $12,000.
(d) Retained Earnings for $12,000.

(SO 2) C 4. A company will buy back its own shares:
(a) to force the share price up.
(b) to force the share price down.
(c) to increase the number of shares available for dividends.
(d) to save cash.

(SO 2) AP 5. A company has Contributed Capital—Reacquisition of Shares, $50,000, and Retained Earnings, $500,000. If it repurchases common shares for $120,000 which have an average cost of $100,000, the journal entry to record the acquisition would include:
(a) a debit to Contributed Capital—Reacquisition of Shares, $20,000.
(b) a debit to Contributed Capital—Reacquisition of Shares for $50,000 and a credit to Retained Earnings for $30,000.
(c) a debit to Retained Earnings of $20,000.
(d) a debit to Common Shares of $120,000.

(SO 3) K 6. Preferred shares may have priority over common shares *except* in:
(a) dividends.
(b) assets in the event of liquidation.
(c) conversion.
(d) voting.

(SO 3) AP 7. If 10,000 convertible preferred shares are converted to 20,000 common shares at a time when the cost of the preferred is $10 per share, the market value of the preferred is $15 per share, and the market value of the common is $9 per share:
(a) Common Shares would be credited for $180,000.
(b) Common Shares would be credited for $100,000.
(c) Preferred Shares would be debited for $150,000.
(d) No entry would be recorded.

(SO 4) K 8. Which of the following is reported in the shareholders' equity section?
(a) Retained earnings
(b) Common shares
(c) Contributed capital—reacquisition of shares
(d) All of the above

9. The shareholders' equity section of a balance sheet will never report: (SO 4) C
(a) a debit balance in a contributed capital account.
(b) a debit balance in a share capital account.
(c) a debit balance in a retained earnings account.
(d) both (a) and (b).

10. If a company's net income is $35,000, its share capital, $500,000, its retained earnings, $200,000, and its net sales, $1,000,000, its return on equity is: (SO 5) AN
(a) 3.5%.   (c) 7%.
(b) 5%.   (d) 17.5%.

Questions

(SO 1) C 1. Pat Kabza, a student, asks for your help in understanding the following characteristics of a corporation: (a) separate legal existence, (b) limited liability of shareholders, and (c) transferable ownership rights. Explain these characteristics to Pat.

(SO 1) C 2. (a) Your friend R. Cedras cannot understand how income taxation can be both an advantage and a disadvantage for a corporation. Clarify this problem.
(b) Identify and explain two other advantages and disadvantages of a corporation.

(SO 1) C 3. (a) The following terms relate to forming a corporation: (1) articles of incorporation, and (2) organization costs. Explain the terms.
(b) Cary Brant believes a corporation must be incorporated federally if it wishes to operate in more than one province. Is Cary correct? Explain.

(SO 1) K 4. What are the basic ownership rights of common shareholders?

(SO 1) C 5. What factors help determine the market value of shares?

(SO 1) C 6. Explain why the majority of companies in Canada issue no par value shares rather than par or stated value shares.

(SO 1) K 7. Identify the two principal components of shareholders' equity and explain what each component represents.

(SO 1) AP 8. Jean-Guy LeBlanc purchases 100 common shares of Innovate.com for $10 per share from the company's initial public offering. Subsequently, Jean-Guy purchases 200 more Innovate.com common shares for $15 each on the Toronto Stock Exchange, using his own Web Broker account. Explain the impact each of these transactions will have on Innovate.com's assets, liabilities, and shareholders' equity.

9. **Abitibi-Consolidated Inc.'s** share price fell 11% in one year from $10.66 in September 2002 to $9.48 in September 2003. Explain the effect of this decline in share price on Abitibi's financial statements. (SO 1) AP

10. Land appraised at $80,000 is purchased by issuing 1,000 common shares. The market price of the shares at the time of the exchange is $90 per share. Should the land be recorded at $80,000 or $90,000? Explain. (SO 2) AP

11. For what reasons might a company repurchase some of its shares? (SO 2) C

12. Wilmor, Inc. purchases 1,000 of its own previously issued common shares. What effect does this transaction have on (a) total assets, (b) total liabilities, and (c) total shareholders' equity? (SO 2) C

13. XYZ Corp. has reacquired some of its common shares at a price less than their average cost. The company's president argues that this difference is in essence a gain and should be reported on the income statement. Is this appropriate? Explain. (SO 3) C

14. Jeff argues that stock compensation plans are an excellent way to reward employees because it doesn't cost the company anything to give the stock options. Is Jeff right? (SO 3) C

15. Explain the principal differences between common shares and preferred shares. (SO 3) C

16. Preferred shares may be cumulative. Discuss this feature. (SO 3) C

17. (a) What are dividends in arrears? (SO 3) C
(b) How are they reported in the financial statements?
(c) Under what circumstances is a dividend reported as a liability?

(SO 3) C 18. A preferred shareholder converts her convertible preferred shares into common shares. What effect does this have on the corporation's (a) total assets, (b) total liabilities, and (c) total shareholders' equity?

(SO 4) C 19. Indicate how each of the following accounts should be classified in the shareholders' equity section:
(a) Common Shares
(b) Retained Earnings
(c) Contributed Capital—Reacquired Common Shares
(d) Preferred Shares

20. In assessing a corporation's profitability, why is it (SO 5) C necessary to compare net income to shareholders' equity? Why is it not enough to just examine the amount of net income?

Brief Exercises

BE13–1 For each characteristic listed, identify which type of business organization(s) best fits the description. There may be more than one answer in some cases. The first one has been done for you as an example.

Characteristic	Proprietorship	Partnership	Corporation
1. Continuous life			X
2. Unlimited liability			
3. Ease of formation			
4. Entity income taxes			
5. Ability to acquire capital			
6. Shared skills and resources			
7. Fewer government regulations			
8. Separation of ownership and management			
9. Owners' acts are binding			
10. Transferable ownership rights			

Distinguish between the characteristics of a proprietorship, partnership, and corporation.
(SO 1) C

BE13–2 The share prices of dozens of high-tech companies soared in early to mid-2000. Take, for example, **NHC Communications Inc.**, located in Quebec. Its share price went from a low of $0.08 to a high of $22, an increase of 27,500%! Yet NHC reported a loss of $2.18 million and a 33% negative return on equity in this same period. Why do you think shareholders were anxious to pay increasing amounts for NHC's shares?

Evaluate factors affecting share price.
(SO 1) C

BE13–3 The share prices of technology companies started dropping like stones in the early 2000s. **Nortel Networks'** share price, for example, dropped from a 52-week high of $124.50 in July 2000 to a low of $0.70 in September 2002. What is the impact of this drop in share price on Nortel's financial position? What is the impact of this drop in share price on Nortel's shareholders?

Evaluate impact of share price on financial position.
(SO 1) C

BE13–4 On June 1, Eagle Inc. issues 2,000 common shares at a cash price of $6 per share. On June 15, Eagle issues an additional 1,000 shares for $7 cash per share. Journalize the issues of the shares.

Record issue of common shares.
(SO 2) AP

BE13–5 Spiro Inc.'s common shares are actively traded at a market value of $14 per share. On December 20, Spiro issues 5,000 shares to purchase land advertised for sale at $80,000. Journalize the issue of the shares for acquiring the land.

Record issue of shares in noncash transaction.
(SO 2) AP

BE13–6 The Quebec-based international paper company **Cascades Inc.** repurchased 238,400 of its own common shares in 2002 and cancelled them. The share repurchase resulted in a debit of $1 million to the common shares account and a debit of $3 million to the retained earnings account. How much did Cascades pay, on average, to repurchase its shares? What was the initial issue price of the shares, on average? Why do you think Cascades likely repurchased some of its own shares?

Discuss share repurchase.
(SO 2) AP

BE13–7 Enviro Corporation reported the following on its January 31, 2005, balance sheet: Common Shares, no par value, unlimited number of shares authorized, 35,000 shares issued, $122,500. On February 15, 2005, it paid cash to reacquire 5,000 of these shares. Journalize the

Record reacquisition of shares.
(SO 2) AP

reacquisition of the shares assuming the company paid $14,500. Then assume the company instead paid $18,750 to reacquire the shares. This is the first time Enviro Corporation has reacquired any of its shares.

Record issue of preferred shares.
(SO 3) AP

BE13–8 First Nations Inc. issues 5,000 preferred shares for cash at $110 per share on January 28. Journalize the issue of the preferred shares.

Record conversion of preferred shares.
(SO 3) AP

BE13–9 In March, Spiral Corporation issues 40,000 preferred shares for $100 each. These shares are convertible into four common shares for each preferred share. Both the common and the preferred shares are listed on the Toronto Stock Exchange. In October, when the preferred shares are trading at $103 each, and the common shares are at $27.50 each, 10,000 of the preferred shares are converted into common shares. Journalize the conversion of the preferred shares.

Prepare shareholders' equity section.
(SO 4) AP

BE13–10 Kaposi Corporation has the following accounts at December 31, 2005: Common Shares, no par value, unlimited number of shares authorized, 5,000 shares issued, $50,000; Preferred Shares, $8 cumulative, no par value, unlimited number of shares authorized, 800 shares issued, $20,000; and Retained Earnings, $29,000. Prepare the shareholders' equity section of the balance sheet.

Record closing entries.
(SO 4) AP

BE13–11 At December 31, Enviro Corporation reports revenues of $2 million and expenses of $1.5 million. Prepare the entries required to close revenue and expenses.

Calculate return on equity.
(SO 5) AP

BE13–12 **Sleeman Breweries Ltd.** reported the following selected information for the year ended December 31, 2002 (in thousands): net sales, $157,053; net income, $12,321; beginning shareholders' equity, $73,088; and ending shareholders' equity, $90,197. Calculate the return on equity.

Exercises

Interpret stock market listing.
(SO 1) AN

E13–1 Presented below is a stock market listing for **Canadian Pacific Railway** (CP) common shares.

| 365-day | | | | | high | low | | | vol | | p/e |
high	low	stock	sym	div	/bid	/ask	close	chg	100s	yld	ratio
34.73	27.98	CPRailway	CP	0.51	34.73	34.30	34.55	+.06	3862	1.5	17.0

Instructions
Answer the following questions:
(a) What is the highest price CP shares traded for during the last year? The lowest?
(b) How many CP common shares were sold on the trading day of the listing?
(c) If you had purchased 1,000 common shares at CP's high price of the day in the above listing, what would be the total cost of your share purchase?
(d) What would be your likely motivation for purchasing these shares—future dividend income or price increase?
(e) What was the closing price of CP common shares on the previous day?
(f) Why are the 365-day high and the high/bid values the same?

Record issue of common shares.
(SO 2) AP

E13–2 During its first year of operations, the Algonquin Corporation had the following transactions for its common shares:

Jan. 10 Issued 75,000 shares for cash at $5 per share.
July   1 Issued 50,000 shares for cash at $6.50 per share.

Instructions
(a) Journalize the transactions.
(b) Calculate the average issue price per share.

E13–3 As an accountant for the CGA firm of Bell and Whistle, you encounter the following situations when performing the accounting for different clients:

1. The Ruth Corporation is a closely held corporation whose shares are not publicly traded. On December 5, the corporation acquired land by issuing 5,000 common shares. The owner's asking price for the land was $120,000. The fair market value of the land was $115,000.
2. The Hache Corporation is a publicly held corporation whose common shares are traded on the Toronto Stock Exchange. On June 1, it acquired land by issuing 20,000 shares. At the time of the exchange, the land was advertised for sale at $250,000. The shares were selling at $11 per share.

Record issue of shares in noncash transactions.
(SO 2) AP

Interactive Homework

Instructions

Prepare the journal entries for each of the situations above.

E13–4 **Wendy's International, Inc.** repurchased 525,000 common shares in February 2003 for US$13.2 million. Wendy's also has a stock option plan for employees and directors to purchase the company's common shares. It makes no recognition of the options in its financial statements until they are exercised.

Discuss share repurchase and stock options.
(SO 2) C

Instructions

(a) Explain how a repurchase of shares affects the number of shares authorized and issued, and the market value of the remaining shares.
(b) Speculate on why Wendy's may have repurchased its shares.
(c) What is the financial impact of not recognizing stock options in the financial statements when the options are first issued? Identify any accounts that you believe are understated or overstated.
(d) If Wendy's was a Canadian company, would its accounting for stock options be any different in fiscal 2004?

E13–5 Moosonee Co. Ltd. was incorporated on January 5, 2005, and is authorized to issue an unlimited number of common and preferred shares. The company entered into the following share transactions during its first year:

Record issue and reacquisition of shares.
(SO 2, 3) AP

Interactive Homework

Jan. 6 Issued 200,000 common shares for cash at $1.50 per share.
      8 Issued 16,000 common shares to lawyers as payment for a bill of $25,000 for services performed in helping the company to incorporate.
     12 Issued 34,000 common shares for $51,000 cash.
Mar. 17 Issued 1,000 $7 preferred shares for cash at $105 per share.
Jul. 18 Issued 1 million common shares for $2 million cash.
Nov. 17 Reacquired 10,000 common shares for cash at $1.75 per share.

Instructions

(a) Journalize the above transactions.
(b) Assume instead that on November 17 the company paid $2.45 per share to reacquire the shares. Prepare the journal entry to record this transaction.

E13–6 Kerr Corporation has 10,000 preferred shares which had been issued at $100 per share. Each share is convertible into five common shares. On November 15, when the market values of the two classes of shares are $110 and $25, respectively, 2,000 preferred shares are converted into common shares.

Record conversion of preferred shares.
(SO 3) AP

Instructions

(a) Journalize the conversion of the 2,000 shares.
(b) Repeat (a) assuming that the market values at conversion are $95 and $25, respectively.
(c) Repeat (a) assuming that each share is convertible into eight common shares.

Answer questions about
shareholders' equity
section.
(SO 2, 3, 4) S

Interactive Homework

E13–7 The shareholders' equity section of Shumway Corporation at December 31 is as follows:

SHUMWAY CORPORATION
Balance Sheet (partial)
December 31, 2005

Shareholders' equity
  Share capital
    Preferred shares, $5 cumulative, no par value, unlimited
      number of shares authorized, 10,000 shares issued $ 600,000
    Common shares, no par value, 750,000 shares authorized,
      600,000 shares issued   1,800,000
    Total share capital   2,400,000
  Retained earnings   1,158,000
  Total shareholders' equity $3,558,000

Instructions

From a review of the shareholders' equity section, answer these questions:

(a) What was the average per share selling price of the preferred shares? Common shares?
(b) How many additional common shares will Shumway be able to sell if it wishes to raise additional equity financing?
(c) What is the total annual dividend on preferred shares?
(d) If dividends of $100,000 were in arrears on the preferred shares, what would be the balance reported for retained earnings?

Classify financial statement
accounts.
(SO 4) AP

E13–8 The ledger of Val d'Or Corporation contains the following selected accounts:

1. Cash
2. Common shares
3. Contributed capital—reacquired common shares
4. Gain on sale of property, plant, and equipment
5. Patents
6. Preferred shares
7. Retained earnings
8. Legal fees expense

Instructions

Using the following table headings, indicate whether or not each of the above accounts should be reported in the shareholders' equity section of the balance sheet. If yes, indicate whether the account should be reported as share capital, additional contributed capital, or retained earnings. If not, indicate in which financial statement (balance sheet or income statement) and in which section the account should be reported. The first account has been done for you as an example.

| | Shareholders' Equity | | | Other | |
| | Contributed Capital | | | | |
Account	Share Capital	Additional Contributed Capital	Retained Earnings	Financial Statement	Classification
1. Cash				Balance sheet	Current asset

Prepare shareholders'
equity section of balance
sheet. Calculate return on
equity.
(SO 4, 5) AP

E13–9 Reitmans reported the following selected accounts and information, as at February 1, 2003:

REITMANS (CANADA) LIMITED
Selected Financial Data
February 1, 2003
(in thousands)

Class A non-voting shares, unlimited authorized, 13,839,564 issued	$ 12,046
Common shares, unlimited authorized, 3,360,000 issued	482
Dividends	6,876
Net income	24,535
Retained earnings, February 2, 2002	213,334
Total shareholders' equity, February 2, 2002	225,579

Instructions

(a) Prepare the shareholder's equity section of the balance sheet for Reitmans as at February 1, 2003.
(b) Calculate Reitmans' return on equity at February 1, 2003.

E13–10 Presented below are some of the terms discussed in this chapter.

Identify terminology.
(SO 1, 2, 3, 4, 5) C

Interactive Homework

1. Publicly held corporations
2. Cumulative dividends
3. No par value shares
4. Articles of incorporation
5. Initial public offering
6. Organization costs
7. Common shares
8. Market value
9. Secondary market
10. Preferred shares
11. Authorized shares
12. Issued shares
13. Retained earnings
14. Stock option
15. Share capital

Instructions

For each description, write the number of the term it matches. Not every number will necessarily be used.

(a) _____ A right granted by a corporation to an investor (often an employee) to purchase a specified number of shares at a specified price during a specified time period
(b) _____ The type of corporation whose shares are traded in an organized security market, such as the Toronto Stock Exchange
(c) _____ Legal fees, accounting fees, and registration costs incurred in forming a company
(d) _____ Includes information such as the amounts and kinds of share capital to be authorized
(e) _____ The maximum number of shares a corporation is allowed to sell
(f) _____ The first time a corporation's shares are offered to the public
(g) _____ Where investors buy and sell shares from each other, rather than from the company
(h) _____ The element of shareholders' equity that is increased by net income and decreased by net losses
(i) _____ The class of shares that normally does not have voting power
(j) _____ Shares that have not been assigned a preset value
(k) _____ The amount contributed to the corporation by shareholders in exchange for shares of ownership
(l) _____ A feature that ensures that unpaid dividends on preferred shares must be paid prior to common shareholders' receiving a dividend

Problems: Set A

P13–1A Presented below are five independent situations:

Determine forms of business organization.
(SO 1) AN

1. Three physics professors have formed a business to improve the speed of information transfer over the Internet. Each has contributed an equal amount of cash and knowledge to the venture. While their approach looks promising, they are concerned about the legal liabilities that their business might confront.
2. Joseph LeBlanc, a student looking for summer employment, opened a bait shop in a small shed on a local fishing dock.
3. Robert Steven and Tom Cheng each own separate shoe manufacturing businesses. They have decided to combine their businesses. They expect that within the coming year, they will need significant funds to expand their operations.
4. Darcy Becker, Ellen Sweet, and Meg Dwyer recently graduated with marketing degrees. They have been friends since childhood. They have decided to start a consulting business focused on marketing sporting goods over the Internet.
5. Hervé Gaudet wants to rent portable DVD players and DVDs in airports across the country. His idea is that customers will be able to rent equipment and DVDs at one airport, watch the DVDs on their flight, and return the equipment and DVDs at their destination airport. This will require a substantial investment in equipment and DVDs, as well as in employees and locations in each airport. Hervé has no savings or personal assets. He wants to maintain control over the business.

Instructions

In each case, explain what form of organization the business is likely to take—proprietorship, partnership, or corporation. Give reasons for your choice.

Answer questions about shareholders' equity section.
(SO 2, 3, 4) AP

P13–2A The shareholders' equity section of Maple Corporation, after closing the books on December 31, 2005, presented the following information:

MAPLE CORPORATION
Balance Sheet (partial)
December 31, 2005

Shareholders' equity
  Contributed capital
    Share capital
      $7 cumulative preferred shares, unlimited
        number authorized, 12,000 shares issued $1,200,000
      Common shares, no par value, 500,000 shares
        authorized, 100,000 shares issued   1,000,000
    Total share capital   2,200,000
    Additional contributed capital
      Contributed capital——reacquired common shares   40,000
    Total contributed capital   2,240,000
  Retained earnings
    January 1, 2005 $500,000
    Net income   175,000   675,000
  Total shareholders' equity $2,915,000

Instructions

(a) What was the average per share selling price of the preferred shares? Of the common shares?
(b) What is the annual total preferred share dividend requirement, stated in dollars?
(c) What was the total amount of dividends, if any, declared by Maple Corporation in 2005?
(d) Assuming that there were no dividends in arrears at the beginning of 2005, are there any dividends in arrears at the end of 2005? If so, for what amount?
(e) Assume the full amount in the Contributed Capital – Reacquired Common Shares account relates to the reacquisition of 20,000 common shares during 2005 and that no new common shares were issued during the year. How much did Maple Corporation pay to reacquire those shares?

Record and post share transactions. Prepare share capital section.
(SO 2, 3, 4) AP

P13–3A The Wetland Corporation was organized on January 1, 2005. It is authorized to issue an unlimited number of $8 no par value preferred shares and an unlimited number of no par value common shares. The following transactions were completed during the first year:

Jan. 10 Issued 80,000 common shares for cash at $4 per share.
Mar.   1 Issued 5,000 preferred shares for cash at $115 per share.
Apr.   1 Issued 22,000 common shares for land. The asking price of the land was $100,000. The fair market value of the land was $90,000. The market value of the common shares was $4.25 per share on this date.
June 20 Issued 78,000 common shares for cash at $4.50 per share.
Aug.   1 Issued 10,000 common shares to lawyers in payment of their bill of $50,000 for services performed in helping the company organize. The market value of the common shares was $4.75 on this date.
Sept. 1 Issued 10,000 common shares for cash at $5 per share.
Nov.   1 Issued 1,000 preferred shares for cash at $117 per share.

Instructions

(a) Journalize the transactions.
(b) Open general ledger accounts and post to the shareholders' equity accounts.
(c) Prepare the share capital section of shareholders' equity at December 31, 2005.

P13–4A Remmers Corporation is authorized to issue 10,000 shares of no par value, $10 convertible, preferred shares and 200,000 no par value common shares. Each preferred share is convertible into 10 common shares. On January 1, 2005, the ledger contained the following shareholders' equity balances:

Record and post
shareholders' equity
transactions. Prepare
shareholders' equity
section.
(SO 2, 3, 4) AP

Preferred shares (4,000 shares)	$ 440,000
Common shares (70,000 shares)	1,050,000
Retained earnings	300,000

During 2005, the following transactions occurred:

Feb. 1 Issued 1,100 preferred shares for land having a fair market value of $125,000. The market value of the shares on this date was $115 per share.

Mar. 1 Issued 1,400 preferred shares for cash at $120 per share.

July 1 Holders of 1,000 preferred shares converted the shares into 10,000 common shares. The market value of the preferred shares was $125 per share. The market value of the common shares was $13 per share.

Sept. 1 Issued 500 preferred shares for a patent. The asking price of the patent was $70,000. The market value of the preferred shares was $125 per share.

Dec. 1 Holders of 1,000 preferred shares converted the shares into 10,000 common shares. Market values were as follows: preferred shares, $125, and common shares, $16.

Dec. 31 Total revenues and expenses for the year were $400,000 and $250,000, respectively. No dividends were declared.

Instructions

(a) Prior to 2005, what was the average price at which the preferred shares were issued?
(b) Journalize the transactions that occurred during 2005 and the closing entries.
(c) Enter the beginning balances in the accounts and post the journal entries to the shareholders' equity accounts.
(d) Prepare the shareholders equity section of the balance sheet at December 31, 2005.

P13–5A The following shareholders' equity accounts, arranged alphabetically, are in the ledger of Branch Inc. on January 1, 2005:

Show impact of
transactions on accounts.
(SO 2, 3, 4) AP

Common Shares (no par value, unlimited authorized, 150,000 issued)	$2,400,000
Preferred Shares ($6, cumulative, convertible, 100,000 authorized, 5,000 issued)	350,000
Retained Earnings	1,276,000

Branch Inc. had the following transactions during the year:

1. Issued 1,000 common shares for $23 cash per share.
2. Reacquired 10,000 common shares for $25 cash each.
3. Shareholders converted 1,000 preferred shares into 4,000 common shares. The market value per preferred share was $80, per common share, $24.
4. Issued 1,000 common shares for land. The market value of each common share was $25, of the land, $23,500.
5. Issued 100 preferred shares for $72 cash per share.
6. Did not pay the preferred share dividend during the year.

Instructions

For each of the above transactions, indicate whether, and by how much, each item in the table provided will be increased (+), decreased (−), or not affected (NA). The first transaction has been done for you as an example.

			Shareholders' Equity		
		Preferred	Common	Other Contributed	Retained
Assets	Liabilities	Shares	Shares	Capital	Earnings
1. +$23,000	NA	NA	+$23,000	NA	NA

Record and post share transactions, and prepare shareholders' equity. Calculate return on equity. (SO 2, 3, 4, 5) AP

P13–6A The shareholders' equity accounts of Chung Corporation at January 1, 2005, were as follows:

Preferred Shares (no par value, $10 noncumulative, 5,000 shares authorized, 3,000 shares issued)	$ 320,000
Common Shares (no par value, unlimited number of shares authorized, 200,000 shares issued)	1,425,000
Retained Earnings	488,000

During 2005, the corporation had the following transactions and events related to its shareholders' equity:

Feb. 1 Issued 5,000 common shares for $32,500.
July 20 Issued 1,000 preferred shares for $107,000.
Sept. 3 Issued 2,000 common shares for a patent valued at $12,250.
Nov. 17 Reacquired 10,000 common shares for $5.75 cash per share.

Instructions

(a) Journalize the transactions.
(b) Prepare summary closing entries, assuming revenues totalled $480,000 and expenses totalled $220,000.
(c) Enter the beginning balances in the accounts and post the journal entries to the shareholders' equity accounts.
(d) Prepare a shareholders' equity section of the balance sheet at December 31, 2005.
(e) Calculate the return on equity for 2005.

Calculate return on equity. (SO 5) AN

P13–7A **Canadian Tire Corporation** reported the following selected information:

CANADIAN TIRE CORPORATION
December 31
(in millions)

	2002	2001	2000
Net income	$ 202.4	$ 176.7	$ 148.0
Shareholders' equity	1,806.9	1,603.7	1,459.4

Instructions

(a) Calculate Canadian Tire's return on equity for 2002 and 2001. Comment on whether its return on equity has improved or deteriorated.
(b) The return on equity for Canadian Tire's industry is 19% in 2002. Compare Canadian Tire's performance to the industry average for this year.

Prepare balance sheet; calculate return on equity. (SO 4, 5) AP

P13–8A **Santa's Village Limited**, located in Ontario, has the following selected accounts, listed in alphabetical order, as at October 31, 2002:

SANTA'S VILLAGE LIMITED
Selected Accounts
October 31, 2002

Accounts payable and accrued liabilities	$ 124,186
Accounts receivable	13,419
Accumulated amortization—property, plant, and equipment	4,786,497
Bank loan payable (short-term)	90,000
Cash	19,104
Common shares, unlimited authorized, 252,980 issued	711,994
Current income taxes receivable	118,988
Current portion of long-term debt	161,379
Dividends	25,298
Future income tax liability (long-term)	245,000
Inventory	42,942
Long-term debt	1,123,727
Net loss	59,988
Prepaid expenses	48,735
Property, plant, and equipment	8,097,216
Retained earnings, November 1, 2001	1,182,907

Instructions

(a) Prepare a classified balance sheet for Santa's Village.

(b) Calculate the return on equity for Santa's Village. Total shareholder's equity at October 31, 2001, was $1,894,901.

Problems: Set B

P13–1B Presented below are five independent situations:

(a) Dawn Addington, a student looking for summer employment, opened a vegetable stand along a busy local highway. Each morning, she buys produce from local farmers, then sells it in the afternoon as people return home from work.

(b) Joseph LeBlanc and Sabra Surkis each own separate bike shops. They have decided to combine their businesses and try to expand their operations to include skis and snowboards. They expect that, within the coming year, they will need significant funds to expand their operations.

(c) Three chemistry professors have formed a business to employ bacteria to clean up toxic waste sites. Each has contributed an equal amount of cash and knowledge to the venture. The use of bacteria in this situation is experimental, and legal obligations could result.

(d) Abdur Rahim has run a successful, but small, co-operative health and organic food store for over twenty years. The increased sales of his own store have made him believe that the time is right to open a chain of health and organic food stores across the country. Of course, this will require a substantial investment in inventories and property, plant, and equipment, as well as employees and other resources. Abdur has no savings or personal assets.

(e) Mary Emery and Richard Goedde recently graduated with advanced degrees in economics. They have decided to start a consulting business focused on teaching the basics of international economics to small business owners interested in international trade.

Instructions

In each case, explain what form of organization the business is likely to take—proprietorship, partnership, or corporation. Give reasons for your choice.

P13–2B The shareholders' equity section of Moreau Corporation, after closing on December 31, 2005, presented the following information:

Determine forms of business organization. (SO 1) AN

Answer questions about shareholders' equity section. (SO 1, 2, 3, 4) AP

MOREAU CORPORATION
Balance Sheet (partial)
December 31, 2005

Shareholders' equity		
Share capital		
$5 cumulative preferred shares, no par value, unlimited number of shares authorized, ? shares issued		$3,150,000
Common shares, no par value, unlimited number of shares authorized, 250,000 shares issued		1,000,000
Total share capital		4,150,000
Retained earnings		
January 1, 2005	$500,000	
Net income	175,000	
Reacquisition of common shares	(56,250)	
Dividends—preferred	(150,000)	468,750
Total shareholders' equity		$4,618,750

There are no dividends in arrears at the end of 2004 or 2005.

Instructions

(a) How many preferred shares were issued at December 31, 2005?
(b) What was the average selling price of the preferred shares, on a per share basis? Of the common shares?
(c) Assume that in 2005 the only change in the number of common shares issued was the reacquisition of 25,000 shares. How much did Moreau Corporation pay to reacquire those shares?
(d) In terms of the limited liability characteristic of a corporation, what is the dollar amount of the investment that is subject to liability (legal capital) for the preferred shareholders? For the common shareholders?

Record and post share transactions. Prepare share capital section.
(SO 2, 3, 4) AP

P13–3B The Highland Corporation was organized on January 1, 2005. It is authorized to issue an unlimited number of $3 no par value preferred shares, and an unlimited number of no par value common shares. The following transactions were completed during the first year:

Jan. 10 Issued 100,000 common shares for cash at $2 per share.
Mar. 1 Issued 10,000 preferred shares for cash at $42 per share.
Apr. 1 Issued 25,000 common shares for land. The appraised value of the land was $67,000. The market value of the common shares was $2.50 per share on this date.
May 1 Issued 75,000 common shares for cash at $3 per share.
July 24 Issued 10,000 common shares to lawyers in payment of their bill of $39,000 for services rendered in helping the company organize. The market value of the common shares was $3.50 on this date.
Sept. 1 Issued 16,800 common shares for $60,000 cash and used equipment. The equipment originally cost $10,000. It now has a net book value of $4,000 and a fair market value of $5,000. The common shares issued had a market value of $4 per share.
Nov. 1 Issued 2,000 preferred shares for cash at $54 per share.

Instructions

(a) Journalize the transactions.
(b) Open general ledger accounts and post to the shareholders' equity accounts.
(c) Prepare the share capital section of shareholders' equity at December 31, 2005.

Record and post shareholders' equity transactions. Prepare shareholders' equity section. Calculate return on equity.
(SO 2, 3, 4, 5) AP

P13–4B Denison Corporation is authorized to issue 10,000 no par value, $10 convertible, preferred shares and 125,000 no par value common shares. Each preferred share is convertible into eight common shares. On January 1, 2005, the ledger contained the following shareholders' equity balances:

Preferred shares (5,000 shares)	$ 525,000
Common shares (70,000 shares)	1,050,000
Retained earnings	300,000

During 2005, the following transactions occurred:

Feb. 6 Issued 1,250 preferred shares for a building having a fair market value of $132,000. The market value of the shares on this date was $110 per share.
July 15 Holders of 2,000 preferred shares converted the shares into 16,000 common shares. Market values were as follows: preferred shares, $122, and common shares, $16.
Aug. 22 Issued 750 preferred shares for land. The asking price of the land was $99,000. The market value of the preferred shares was $125 per share.
Nov. 1 Holders of 1,000 preferred shares converted the shares into 8,000 common shares. Market values were as follows: preferred shares, $127, and common shares, $18.
Dec. 31 Total revenues and expenses for the year were $600,000 and $340,000, respectively. No dividends were declared.

Instructions

(a) Journalize the transactions and the closing entries.
(b) Enter the beginning balances in the accounts and post the journal entries to the shareholders' equity accounts.
(c) Prepare a shareholders' equity section of the balance sheet at December 31, 2005.
(d) Calculate the company's return on equity for 2005.

P13–5B The following shareholders' equity accounts, arranged alphabetically, are in the ledger of Talty Inc. on January 1, 2005:

Show impact of transactions on accounts. (SO 2, 3, 4) AP

Common shares (no par value, unlimited authorized, 500,000 issued)	$4,000,000
Preferred shares ($8, cumulative, convertible 100,000 authorized, 4,000 issued)	600,000
Retained earnings	1,958,000

Talty Inc. had the following transactions during the year:

1. Issued 10,000 common shares for $11 cash per share.
2. Issued 500 common shares in exchange for a piece of equipment. The market value of the shares was $12 per share, of the equipment, $6,500.
3. Shareholders converted 2,000 preferred shares into 20,000 common shares. The market value per preferred share was $160, per common share, $16.50.
4. Issued 1,000 preferred shares for $160 cash per share.
5. Reacquired 500 preferred shares for $145 cash each.
6. The preferred share dividend was paid at the end of the year.

Instructions

For each of the above transactions, indicate whether, and by how much, each item in the table provided will be increased (+), decreased (−), or not affected (NA). The first transaction has been done for you as an example.

			Shareholders' Equity			
	Assets	Liabilities	Preferred Shares	Common Shares	Other Contributed Capital	Retained Earnings
1.	+$110,000	NA	NA	+$110,000	NA	NA

P13–6B The shareholders' equity accounts of the Daoust Corporation on January 1, 2005, were as follows:

Record and post share transactions, and prepare shareholders' equity section. Calculate return on equity. (SO 2, 3, 4, 5) AP

Preferred shares (no par value, $6 cumulative, 10,000 shares authorized, 8,000 issued)	$ 500,000
Common shares (no par value, unlimited number of shares authorized, 1 million issued)	2,750,000
Retained earnings	1,816,000

During 2005, the corporation had the following transactions and events related to its shareholders' equity:

Feb. 1 Issued 25,000 common shares for $81,250.
Sept. 3 Issued 7,000 common shares for equipment valued at $28,000.
Oct. 25 Reacquired 5,000 common shares for $21,250 cash.

No dividends were declared during the year and the preferred dividends are one year in arrears.

Instructions

(a) Journalize the transactions.
(b) Prepare summary closing entries, assuming revenue totalled $965,000 and expenses totalled $590,000.
(c) Enter the beginning balances in accounts and post the journal entries to the shareholders' equity accounts.
(d) Prepare a shareholders' equity section at December 31, 2005, including the disclosure of the preferred dividends in arrears.
(e) Calculate the return on equity for 2005.

P13–7B Scars Canada Inc. reported the following selected information:

Calculate return on equity. (SO 5) AN

SEARS CANADA INC.
December 31
(in millions)

	2002	2001	2000
Net income	$ 52.2	$ 94.1	$ 225.8
Shareholders' equity	1,646.9	1,619.9	1,549.3

Instructions

(a) Calculate Sears' return on equity for 2002 and 2001. Comment on whether its return on equity has improved or deteriorated.

(b) The return on equity for Sears' industry is 11.6% in 2002. Compare Sears' performance to the industry average for this year.

Prepare balance sheet; calculate return on equity. (SO 4, 5) AP

P13–8B Andrés Wines Ltd., with wineries across Canada, has the following selected accounts, listed in alphabetical order, as at March 31, 2003:

ANDRÉS WINES LTD.
Selected Accounts
March 31, 2003
(in thousands)

Accounts payable and accrued liabilities	$10,855
Accounts receivable	10,466
Accumulated amortization—property, plant, and equipment	36,008
Bank indebtedness	15,444
Class A shares, nonvoting, unlimited authorized, 3,741,082 issued	4,110
Class B shares, voting, convertible into Class A shares, unlimited authorized, 1,002,972 issued	401
Current portion of long-term debt	2,420
Dividends	2,971
Dividends payable	743
Future income tax liability (long-term)	5,675
Goodwill	21,324
Income and other taxes payable	2,218
Inventories	47,239
Long-term debt	22,130
Net earnings	6,929
Other assets (long-term)	400
Prepaid expenses	1,344
Property, plant, and equipment	87,241
Retained earnings, April 1, 2002	64,052

Instructions

(a) Prepare a classified balance sheet for Andrés Wines.

(b) Calculate the return on equity for Andrés Wines. Total shareholder's equity at March 31, 2002 was $68,560,000.

Continuing Cookie Chronicle

(Note: This is a continuation of the Cookie Chronicle from Chapters 1 through 12.)

Natalie's friend, Curtis Lesperance, decides to meet with Natalie after hearing that her discussions about a possible business partnership with her friend Katy Peterson have failed. (Natalie had decided that forming a partnership with Katy, a high school friend, would hurt their friendship. Natalie had also concluded that she and Katy were not compatible to operate a business venture together.)

Because Natalie has been so successful with Cookie Creations and Curtis has been just as successful with his coffee shop, they both conclude that they could benefit from each other's business expertise. Curtis and Natalie next evaluate the different types of business organization, and because of the advantage of limited personal liability, decide to form a corporation.

Curtis has operated his coffee shop for two years. He buys coffee, muffins, and cookies from a local supplier. Natalie's business consists of giving cookie-making classes and selling fine European mixers. The plan is for Natalie to use the premises Curtis currently rents to give her cookie-making classes and demonstrations of the mixers that she sells. Natalie will also hire, train, and supervise staff hired to bake cookies and muffins sold in the coffee shop. By offering her classes on the premises, Natalie will save on travelling time going from one place to another. Another advantage is that the coffee shop will provide one central location for selling the mixers.

The current fair values of the assets of both businesses are as follows:

Description	Curtis' Coffee	Cookie Creations
Cash	$7,500	$10,000
Accounts receivable	100	500
Merchandise inventory	450	1,130
Equipment	2,500	1,000

Combining forces will also allow Natalie and Curtis to pool their resources and buy a few more assets to run their new business venture.

Curtis and Natalie then meet with a lawyer and form a corporation on November 1, 2005 called Cookie & Coffee Creations Ltd. The articles of incorporation state that there will be two classes of shares the corporation is authorized to issue, one class designated as common, the other class designated as preferred. An unlimited number of shares are authorized for the common shares; 10,000 shares are authorized for the preferred shares.

The assets held by each of their sole proprietorships will be transferred into the corporation at current market value. Curtis will receive 10,550 common shares and Natalie will receive 12,630 common shares in the corporation.

Natalie and Curtis are very excited about this new business venture. They come to you with the following questions:

1. Curtis' Dad and Natalie's grandmother are interested in investing $5,000 each in the business venture. We are considering issuing them preferred shares. What would be the advantage of issuing them preferred shares instead of common shares?

2. Our lawyer has spoken to us about a cumulative dividend feature on preferred shares. We're really happy to have our family behind our new business venture. What would be the advantages and disadvantages of issuing each of them cumulative preferred shares?

3. Our lawyer has sent us a bill for $750. When we talked the bill over with her, she said that she would be willing to receive common shares in our new corporation instead of cash. We would be happy to issue her shares, but we're a bit worried about accounting for this transaction. Can we do this? If so, how do we determine how many shares to give to her?

Instructions:

(a) Answer Natalie and Curtis' questions.

(b) Prepare the journal entries required on November 1, 2005, the date when Natalie and Curtis transfer the assets of their respective businesses into Cookie & Coffee Creations Ltd.

(c) Assume that Cookie & Coffee Creations Ltd. issues 1,000 $6 cumulative preferred shares to Curtis' Dad and the same number to Natalie's grandmother, in both cases for $5,000. Also assume that Cookie & Coffee Creations Ltd. issues 750 common shares to its lawyer. Prepare the journal entries required for each of these transactions that also occurred on November 1.

(d) Prepare the opening balance sheet for Cookie & Coffee Creations Ltd. as at November 1, 2005, including the journal entries in (b) and (c) above.

Financial Reporting and Analysis

Practice
Tools

Financial Reporting Problem

BYP13–1 The shareholders' equity section for **The Forzani Group Ltd.** is shown in the Consolidated Balance Sheet in Appendix A. You will also find data related to this case in the notes to the financial statements.

Instructions

(a) How many classes of shares does Forzani have? For each class of shares, specify how many shares are authorized and issued at February 2, 2003.
(b) What was the average cost of the common (Class A) shares at the end of fiscal 2003?
(c) Forzani issued additional common shares when employees exercised stock options in 2003. What amount (consideration) did it record for this share issue? Was this amount equivalent to the compensation value that the employees received or will receive?
(d) Forzani's return on equity was calculated for fiscal 2003 in Illustration 13-3. Calculate the company's return on equity for fiscal 2002. The shareholders' equity at January 28, 2001, was $316,886. Was there an improvement or deterioration in this ratio from 2002 to 2003?

Interpreting Financial Statements

BYP13–2 Talisman Energy Inc., headquartered in Calgary, explores for, develops, and produces crude oil, natural gas, and natural gas liquids. Talisman's authorized share capital includes an unlimited number of common shares with no par value.

During the 2002 fiscal year, Talisman repurchased 3,847,500 common shares for a total of $220 million. The following additional information is also available for the year ended December 31 ($ and number of shares in millions except price per share):

	2002	2001
Net income	$ 524	$ 733
Total assets	11,594	10,819
Total liabilities	7,092	6,693
Common shares	2,785	2,831
Total shareholders' equity	4,502	4,126
Number of common shares	131	134
Return on equity	11.4%	19.3%
Return on assets	5.2%	8.6%
Market price per share	56.85	60.50

Instructions

(a) What are some of the reasons why a company repurchases its own shares?
(b) During the year, Talisman debited retained earnings $136 million for the repurchase of its common shares. Were Talisman's common shares repurchased for more, or less, than their average cost? Prepare the journal entry to record this repurchase.
(c) Discuss the change in Talisman's profitability from 2001 to 2002.
(d) What are some of the factors that may influence Talisman's market price?

Accounting on the Web

BYP13–3 Originally incorporated in 1878, the **Toronto Stock Exchange (TSX)** is the second-largest stock exchange in North America. It is Canada's largest capital market, accounting for 95% of all equity trading in Canada. This case explores the TSX website to learn more about the exchange, stock market terminology, indices, and processes. We also learn how to use this website to obtain a current share quote for a listed company.

Instructions

Specific requirements of this Internet case are available on the Weygandt website.

Critical Thinking

Collaborative Learning Activity

BYP13–4 The annual meeting for Resolute Corporation has been in progress for some time. The chief financial officer is presently reviewing the company's financial statements. She is explaining the items that make up the shareholders' equity section of the balance sheet for the current year. The shareholders' equity section at December 31, 2005, is as follows:

RESOLUTE CORPORATION
Balance Sheet (partial)
December 31, 2005

Shareholders' equity		
Contributed capital		
Share capital		
$8 preferred shares, authorized 1 million shares,		
cumulative, no par value, 6,000 shares issued	$ 600,000	
Common shares, unlimited number of shares authorized,		
no par value, 3 million shares issued	28,000,000	
Total share capital	28,600,000	
Additional contributed capital		
Contibuted capital—reacquisition of common shares	50,000	
Total contributed capital	28,650,000	
Retained earnings	900,000	
Total shareholders' equity	$29,550,000	

The shareholders have raised a number of questions regarding the shareholders' equity section of Resolute Corporation's balance sheet at the meeting.

Instructions

With the class divided into groups, answer the following questions from shareholders as if you were the chief financial officer for Resolute Corporation:

(a) "What does the cumulative provision related to the preferred shares mean?"
(b) "What is the total annual dividend for the preferred shares?"
(c) "I thought the common shares were presently selling at $12 per share. Yet, the shares have an average share price of $9.33 ($28,000,000 ÷ 3,000,000). How can this be?"
(d) "The company repurchased common shares during the year. I don't see this reported in the equity section. Where is it reported?"
(e) "Did the company pay more, or less, than the average cost of the common shares when it repurchased them?"

Communication Activity

BYP13–5 Canada's standard-setters announced that companies must record the cost of stock options as compensation expense in their income statements effective January 1, 2004. Other countries, including European nations and the United States, are still studying this issue, although they are also expected to require companies to expense stock options in the near future.

A number of companies throughout the world have voluntarily started to expense stock options. Still others disagree with the proposed standard, believing that options are too complicated to measure.

Instructions

Write a memo to the standard-setters, explaining whether or not this new standard will benefit you as an investor. Include in your memo comments about whether the early adoption of this standard in Canada will facilitate, or complicate, the comparison of financial statements of companies from different countries over the next year or so.

Ethics Case

BYP13–6 The R&D division of Simplex Chemical Corp. has just developed a chemical to sterilize the voracious mountain pine beetles that are invading Western Canada's forests. The president of Simplex is anxious to get the chemical to market. Simplex's profits need a boost and his job is in jeopardy because of decreasing sales and profits. Simplex has an opportunity to sell this chemical in several Central American countries, where the laws are much more relaxed than in Canada.

The director of Simplex's R&D division strongly recommends further laboratory testing for side effects of this chemical on other insects, birds, animals, plants, and even humans. He cautions the president, "We could be sued from all sides if the chemical has tragic side effects that we didn't even test for in the labs." The president answers, "We can't wait an additional year for your lab tests. We can avoid losses from such lawsuits by establishing a separate, wholly owned corporation to shield Simplex Corp. We can't lose any more than our investment in the new corporation, and we'll invest just the patent covering this chemical. We'll reap the benefits if the chemical works and is safe, and avoid the losses from lawsuits if it's a disaster."

The following week Simplex creates a new wholly owned corporation called Pinebeetle Inc. It sells the chemical patent to it for $10 and watches the spraying begin.

Instructions

(a) Who are the stakeholders in this situation?
(b) Are the president's motives and actions ethical?
(c) Can Simplex shield itself against losses of Pinebeetle Inc.?

Answers to Self-Study Questions
1. c　2. b　3. b　4. a　5. a　6. d　7. b　8. d　9. d　10. b

Answer to Forzani Review It Question 3
Forzani did not acquire any of its own shares in fiscal 2003. As detailed in Note 9, shares were issued, but not reacquired.

Remember to go back to the Navigator Box at the beginning of the chapter to check off your completed work.

concepts for review >>

Before studying this chapter, you should understand or, if necessary, review:

  a. How to prepare an income statement and statement of owner's equity. (Ch. 3, pp. 118–119)

  b. How to account for share transactions. (Ch. 13, pp. 625–627)

  c. The rights of preferred shareholders to dividends. (Ch. 13, p. 630)

  d. The form and content of the shareholders' equity section of the balance sheet. (Ch. 13, pp. 632–634)

  e. How to calculate return on equity. (Ch. 13, pp. 634–635)

Taking Stock of Business

Transcontinental Inc.: www.transcontinental.com

MONTREAL, Que.—There's always something hot off the press at Transcontinental Inc. As one of North America's largest commercial printers, the Montreal-based company prints flyers, direct marketing materials, books, and newspapers, including *The Globe and Mail* and *La Presse*. It also publishes consumer magazines such as *Canadian Living*, *TV Guide*, *Elle Québec* and *Elle Canada* as well as a number of community newspapers across Canada.

In 1976, partners Rémi Marcoux, Claude Dubois, and André Kingsley purchased a small printing company called Imprimerie Trans-Continental that specialized in flyers and inserts. Two years later, the company expanded into distribution and changed its name to Transcontinental Group. The company then entered publishing with the acquisition of the economic weekly *Les Affaires*. From there, it continued to grow through acquisitions. Its shares began trading on the Montreal Stock Exchange in 1984 and the Toronto Stock Exchange the following year.

Today, Transcontinental employs over 12,000 people in Canada, the U.S., and Mexico and is one of the country's leading printers of newspapers, books, magazines, and other commercial products. In 2003, it reported cash of $89 million, revenues of $1.9 billion, retained earnings of $473 million, and shareholders' equity of $869 million.

Transcontinental has done well over the years. By diversifying its customer base and focusing on niche markets, it has been able to maintain a strong balance sheet. In April 2003, the company split its common shares two-for-one, increasing the number of its Class A Subordinate Voting Shares from 35.2 million to 70.4 million, and the number of Class B Shares from 9.1 million to 18.2 million.

"Our stock had doubled in price over the previous 24 months," explains Daniel Denault, vice president and chief financial officer of Transcontinental. "The split makes it more affordable to retail investors and improves liquidity."

In the two years leading up to the move, Transcontinental's share price had gone from $18 to $42. At the time of the split, which took effect on April 8, 2003, the price had dipped to $33, following announcements from industry giant Quebecor about decreasing demand for certain printed products and over capacity in the industry. After the split, the shares began trading around $16. By May, the price had climbed back up to $19, reaching $26 by February 2004.

Only time will tell how Transcontinental's share price will fare in the long run. Since the stock split, the volume of transactions has increased. For now, says Mr. Denault, "The move sends a positive signal from management that earnings momentum will continue and that there's still good growth ahead."

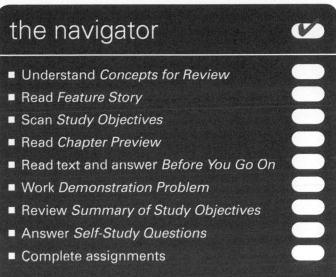

the navigator

■ Understand *Concepts for Review*
■ Read *Feature Story*
■ Scan *Study Objectives*
■ Read *Chapter Preview*
■ Read text and answer *Before You Go On*
■ Work *Demonstration Problem*
■ Review *Summary of Study Objectives*
■ Answer *Self-Study Questions*
■ Complete assignments

chapter 14

Corporations: Dividends, Retained Earnings, and Income Reporting

study objectives >>

After studying this chapter, you should be able to:

1. Prepare the entries for cash dividends, stock dividends, and stock splits, and compare their financial impact.
2. Illustrate the proper form and content of corporation income statements.
3. Prepare a statement of retained earnings.
4. Prepare and analyse the shareholders' equity section of a balance sheet.

As a corporation grows, it is not unusual for its share price to rise rapidly. Many corporations split their stock—as Transcontinental did in the feature story—in order to reduce their share price. A reduced share price makes a company's shares more affordable for current and potential shareholders, which should result in even more demand for the company's shares.

This chapter discusses dividends, stock splits, corporation income statements, retained earnings, and key earnings and dividend ratios. The chapter is organized as follows:

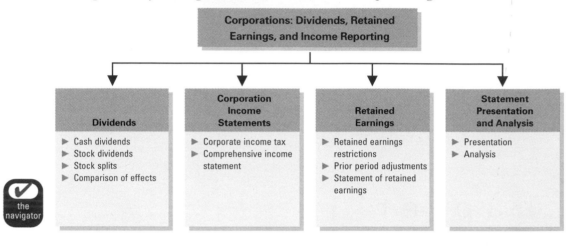

Dividends

study objective 1

Prepare the entries for cash dividends, stock dividends, and stock splits, and compare their financial impact.

A dividend is a pro rata (equal) distribution of a portion of a corporation's retained earnings to its shareholders. "Pro rata" means that if you own, say, 10% of the shares, you will receive 10% of the dividend. The most common types of dividends are, first, cash dividends, and, second, stock dividends. They are the focus of our discussion about dividends.

Investors are very interested in a company's dividend practices. However, fewer and fewer companies are paying dividends consistently. According to the Toronto Stock Exchange, only 57 Canadian companies have paid dividends non-stop for the past 25 years, compared to 100 companies 20 years ago. The Bank of Montreal has the longest unbroken dividend record, as it started in 1829—more than 175 years ago.

In the financial press, dividends are reported as an annual dollar amount per share, even though it is usual to pay dividends quarterly. For example, Transcontinental in our feature story has an annual dividend rate of $0.14 on both its Class A and Class B shares. The dividend is paid quarterly at a rate of $0.035 ($0.14 ÷ 4) per share.

Cash Dividends

A **cash dividend** is a pro rata distribution of cash to shareholders. For a corporation to pay a cash dividend, it must have all of the following:

1. **Enough retained earnings.** Dividends are normally paid out of retained earnings, which represent the undistributed cumulative income and losses of the corporation. Although laws governing cash dividends vary by jurisdiction, in general a deficit cannot be created by the declaration of the dividend.
2. **Enough cash.** Having enough retained earnings does not necessarily indicate a company's ability to pay a dividend. For example, Transcontinental, with a retained

earnings balance of $473 million, could legally pay a dividend of $473 million. But Transcontinental's cash balance is only $89 million. In order to pay the dividend, Transcontinental would need to raise additional cash through the sale of other assets or through additional financing.

Before declaring a cash dividend, a company's board of directors must carefully consider current and future demands on the company's cash resources. In some cases, current (or planned future) liabilities may make a cash dividend inappropriate.

3. **A declaration of dividends.** A company does not pay dividends unless its board of directors decides to do so, at which point the board "declares" the dividend. The board of directors has full authority to determine the amount of income to be distributed in the form of a dividend and the amount to be retained in the business. Dividends do not accrue like interest on a note payable. They are not a liability until they are declared.

The amount and timing of a dividend are important issues. The payment of a large cash dividend could lead to liquidity problems for the company. On the other hand, a small dividend—or a missed dividend—may cause unhappiness among shareholders. Many of them expect to receive a reasonable cash payment from the company on a periodic basis. Most companies declare and pay cash dividends quarterly.

Entries for Cash Dividends

Three dates are important for dividends: (1) the declaration date, (2) the record date, and (3) the payment date. Normally, there are two to four weeks between each date and the next one. For example, at its September 11, 2003 (declaration date) meeting, the board of directors of Transcontinental voted a quarterly dividend of $0.035 per share on Class A and Class B shares. These dividends were then paid on October 27, 2003 (payment date) to shareholders of record at the close of business on October 6, 2003 (record date). Accounting entries were required on two of the dates—the declaration date and the payment date.

On the **declaration date**, a company's board of directors formally declares (authorizes) the cash dividend and announces it to shareholders. Declaring a cash dividend commits the corporation to a legal obligation. The obligation is binding and cannot be rescinded (reversed). An entry is required to recognize the decrease in retained earnings and the increase in the current liability Dividends Payable.

To illustrate, assume that on December 1, 2005, the directors of Media General declare a $0.50 per share cash dividend on 100,000 common shares. The dividend is $50,000 (100,000 × $0.50). The entry to record the declaration is as follows:

	Declaration Date		
Dec. 1	Cash Dividends—Common	50,000	
	Dividends Payable		50,000
	To record declaration of cash dividend.		

A	=	L	+	SE
		+50,000		−50,000

Cash flows: no effect

Note that Dividends Payable is a current liability. It will normally be paid within the next month.

Instead of debiting the account Cash Dividends, some accountants debit Retained Earnings directly in order to avoid a later closing entry. Use of the dividends account, however, provides additional information in the ledger. Also, a company may have separate dividend accounts for each class of shares or for each type of dividend. When a dividend account is used, its balance is transferred to Retained Earnings at the end of the year by a closing entry. Whatever account is used for the dividend declaration, the effect is the same: retained earnings are decreased and the current liability is increased.

On the **record date**, ownership of the shares is determined so that the corporation knows who to pay the dividend to. The records maintained by the corporation supply this information. In the interval between the declaration date and the record date, the cor-

Helpful hint Between the declaration date and the record date, the number of shares remains the same. The purpose of the record date is to identify the persons or entities that will receive the dividend, not to determine the total amount of the dividend liability.

poration updates its share ownership records. Remember that shares trade among investors on organized stock markets after an initial public offering, and not between the company and its investors.

For Media General, assume the record date is December 22. No entry is required on this date because the corporation's liability recognized on the declaration date is unchanged.

On the **payment date**, dividend cheques are mailed to shareholders and the payment of the dividend is recorded. The entry on January 20, the assumed payment date, is shown below:

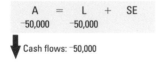

		Payment Date		
Jan. 20	Dividends Payable		50,000	
	Cash			50,000
	To record payment of cash dividend.			

Note that payment of the dividend reduces both current assets and current liabilities. It has no effect on shareholders' equity. The cumulative effect of the **declaration and payment** of a cash dividend is to **decrease both shareholders' equity (through retained earnings) and total assets (through cash)**.

Allocating Cash Dividends between Preferred and Common Shares

As explained in Chapter 13, preferred shares have priority over common shares in regard to dividends. A dividend priority does not guarantee that dividends will be paid. It simply means that if dividends are declared, preferred dividends must be paid before dividends can be paid on common shares.

To illustrate, assume that at December 31, 2005, IBR Inc. has 1,000 $8-cumulative preferred shares. It also has 50,000 common shares. At December 31, 2005, the directors declare a $6,000 cash dividend. The required annual preferred dividend is $8,000 (1,000 × $8). In this case, the entire $6,000 dividend amount goes to preferred shareholders because of their dividend preference. The entry to record the declaration of the dividend is as follows:

Dec. 31	Cash Dividends—Preferred		6,000	
	Dividends Payable			6,000
	To record partial cash dividend to preferred shareholders.			

Because of the cumulative feature, dividends of $2 per share are in arrears on preferred shares for 2005. These dividends must be paid to preferred shareholders before they receive their current year dividend in 2006, or in any subsequent year. Dividends in arrears are not recorded as a liability (until declared). They should be disclosed in the financial statements.

At December 31, 2006, IBR declares a $50,000 cash dividend. The allocation of the dividend to the two share classes is as follows:

Total dividend		$50,000
Allocated to preferred shares		
Dividends in arrears, 2005 (1,000 × $2)	$2,000	
2006 dividend (1,000 × $8)	8,000	10,000
Remainder allocated to common shares		$40,000

The entry to record the declaration of the dividend is:

Dec. 31	Cash Dividends—Preferred	10,000	
	Cash Dividends—Common	40,000	
	Dividends Payable		50,000
	To record declaration of cash dividends.		

A	=	L	+	SE
		+50,000		−10,000
				−40,000

Cash flows: no effect

What if IBR's preferred shares were not cumulative? In that case, preferred shareholders would have received only $8,000 in dividends in 2006. Common shareholders would have received $42,000.

In most cases, a company does not declare a combined dividend amount for both classes of shares, as we have with IBR's declaration of a $50,000 total cash dividend. Rather, it would declare a specified dividend, say $8,000 (or $8 per share), payable to the preferred shareholders, and a specified dividend, say $40,000 (or $0.80 per share), payable to the common shareholders. We used a combined dividend to emphasize the priority that preferred shareholders have when dividend allocations are determined.

Stock Dividends

A **stock dividend** is a pro rata distribution to shareholders of the corporation's own shares. Whereas a cash dividend is paid in cash, a stock dividend is distributed (paid) in shares. A stock dividend results in a decrease in retained earnings and an increase in share capital. There is no change in *total* assets, liabilities, or shareholders' equity.

To illustrate a stock dividend, assume that you have a 2% ownership interest in IBR Inc. You own 1,000 of its 50,000 common shares. If IBR declares a 10% stock dividend, it would issue 5,000 additional shares (50,000 × 10%). You would receive 100 shares (2% × 5,000 or 10% × 1,000). Would your ownership interest change? No, it would remain at 2% (1,100 ÷ 55,000). You now own more shares, but your ownership interest has not changed. Illustration 14-1 shows the effect of a stock dividend for shareholders.

Helpful hint Dividends were declared by 57% of the companies surveyed by *Financial Reporting in Canada*. Of these, less than 3% were stock dividends.

Before stock dividend **After stock dividend**

"I owned 1,000 shares before and I own 1,100 shares now, but I still own only 2% of the company!"

Illustration 14-1 ◄

Effect of stock dividend for shareholders

From the company's point of view, no cash has been paid, and no liabilities have been assumed. What are the purposes and benefits of a stock dividend? A corporation generally issues stock dividends for one or more of the following reasons:

1. To satisfy shareholders' dividend expectations without spending cash.
2. To increase the marketability of the corporation's shares. When the number of shares increases, the market price per share decreases. Decreasing the market price makes it easier for investors to purchase the shares.
3. To emphasize that a portion of shareholders' equity has been permanently retained in the business and is unavailable for cash dividends.

The size of the stock dividend and the value to be assigned to each share are determined by the board of directors when the dividend is declared. The *Canada Business Corporations Act* recommends that directors of federally incorporated companies assign the **market value per share** for stock dividends at the declaration date, which is what most companies do.

v.I.P. ## Entries for Stock Dividends

To illustrate the accounting for stock dividends, assume that IBR Inc. has a balance of $300,000 in retained earnings. On June 30, 2005, it declares a 10% stock dividend on its 50,000 common shares. The current market value of its shares is $15 per share. The number of shares to be issued is 5,000 (10% × 50,000). The total amount to be debited to Stock Dividends is $75,000 (5,000 × $15). The entry to record the declaration of the stock dividend is as follows:

A = L + SE
  +75,000
  −75,000

Cash flows: no effect

June 30	Stock Dividends—Common	75,000	
	Common Stock Dividends Distributable		75,000
	To record declaration of 10% stock dividend.		

Helpful hint Note that the dividend account title uses the word "Distributable," not "Payable."

At the declaration date, Stock Dividends is increased by the market value of the shares issued; Common Stock Dividends Distributable is increased by the same amount. Common Stock Dividends Distributable is a **shareholders' equity account**. It is not a liability, because assets will not be used to pay the dividend. If a balance sheet is prepared before the dividend shares are issued, the distributable account is reported under share capital.

As with cash dividends, no entry is required at the record date. When the dividend shares are issued on August 5, the account Common Stock Dividends Distributable is debited and the account Common Shares is credited:

A = L + SE
      −75,000
      +75,000

Cash flows: no effect

Aug. 5	Common Stock Dividends Distributable	75,000	
	Common Shares		75,000
	To record issue of 5,000 common shares in a		
	stock dividend.		

Effects of Stock Dividends

How do stock dividends affect shareholders' equity? They **change the composition of shareholders' equity**, because a portion of retained earnings is transferred to share capital. However, **total shareholders' equity remains the same**. The number of shares issued has also increased. These effects are shown below for IBR Inc.:

	Before Stock Dividend	After Stock Dividend
Shareholders' equity		
Preferred shares	$100,000	$100,000
Common shares	500,000	575,000
Retained earnings	300,000	225,000
Total shareholders' equity	$900,000	$900,000
Number of common shares	50,000	55,000

In this example, the account Common Shares is increased by $75,000 and Retained Earnings is decreased by the same amount. Total shareholders' equity remains unchanged. Preferred Shares is not affected by the common stock dividend.

Stock Splits

A stock split, like a stock dividend, involves the issue of additional shares to shareholders according to their percentage ownership. However, a stock split is usually much larger than a stock dividend. The purpose of a stock split is to increase the marketability of the shares by lowering the market value per share. A lower market value increases investor interest and makes it easier for the corporation to issue additional shares.

The effect of a split on market value is generally inversely proportional to the size of the split. Sometimes, due to increased investor interest, the share price rises beyond its intended split value. For example, in the feature story, Transcontinental's share price fell from $33 to $16 after a two-for-one stock split. One month later, its share price had climbed to $19.

In a stock split, the number of shares is increased by a specified proportion. For example, in a two-for-one split, one share is exchanged for two shares. **A stock split does not have any effect on share capital, retained earnings, or shareholders' equity.** But the number of shares increases.

> **Helpful hint** Some companies with penny shares do a reverse stock split, i.e., one for-two, to increase the market value per share.

These effects are shown below for IBR Inc. For the illustration, we assume that, instead of a 10% stock dividend, IBR splits its 50,000 common shares on a two-for-one basis.

	Before Stock Split	After Stock Split
Shareholders' equity		
Preferred shares	$100,000	$100,000
Common shares	500,000	500,000
Retained earnings	300,000	300,000
Total shareholders' equity	$900,000	$900,000
Number of common shares	50,000	100,000

A stock split does not affect the balances in any shareholders' equity accounts. Therefore, it is not necessary to journalize a stock split. Only a memo entry noting the details of the split is needed.

ACCOUNTING IN ACTION ▶ Business Insight

A wave of reverse stock splits is under way as many companies—particularly in the struggling technology sector—try to turn around sinking share prices. Some companies have seen their share prices fall to the point where they're in jeopardy of being delisted from stock market exchanges. Reverse stock splits—where the number of shares is reduced by exchanging some multiple of shares for a single share—appear to be an attractive and inexpensive method of boosting a company's share price. Handheld-maker Palm, Inc. was forced to take this route to ensure its shares didn't fall into penny-stock status and trade below the Nasdaq's $1 minimum price in 2002. Palm's reverse stock split exchanged 20 shares for one share.

Comparison of Effects

Significant differences between stock splits, stock dividends, and cash dividends (after payment) are shown in Illustration 14-2. In the illustration, "NE" means "no effect."

Illustration 14-2 ▶

Effects of cash dividends, stock dividends, and stock splits

	Cash Dividend	Stock Dividend	Stock Split
Total assets	Decrease	NE	NE
Total liabilities	NE	NE	NE
Total shareholders' equity	Decrease	NE	NE
Total share capital	NE	Increase	NE
Total retained earnings	Decrease	Decrease	NE
Number of shares	NE	Increase	Increase
% of shareholder ownership	NE	NE	NE

BEFORE YOU GO ON . . .

▶Review It

1. What entries are made for cash dividends on (a) the declaration date, (b) the record date, and (c) the payment date?
2. Contrast the effects of a stock dividend and a two-for-one stock split on shareholders' equity and the number of shares.
3. Did The Forzani Group declare any dividends or stock splits in 2003? The answer to this question is at the end of the chapter.

▶Do It

Sing CD Corporation has had five years of record earnings. Due to this success, the market price of its 500,000 common shares tripled from $15 to $45 per share. During this period, the Common Shares account remained the same at $2 million. Retained Earnings increased from $1.5 million to $10 million. President Bill Zerter is considering either (1) a 10% stock dividend, or (2) a two-for-one stock split. He asks you to show the before-and-after effects of each option on the accounts Common Shares and Retained Earnings and the number of shares.

Action Plan

- Calculate the stock dividend effect on retained earnings by multiplying the stock dividend percentage by the number of existing shares to determine the number of new shares to be issued. Multiply the number of new shares by the market price of the shares.
- A stock dividend increases the number of shares and affects both Common Shares and Retained Earnings.
- A stock split increases the number of shares but does not affect Common Shares and Retained Earnings.

Solution

With a 10% stock dividend (option 1), the stock dividend amount is $2,250,000 [(500,000 × 10%) × $45]. The new balance in common shares is $4,250,000 ($2,000,000 + $2,250,000) and in retained earnings is $7,750,000 ($10,000,000 − $2,250,000).

With a stock split (option 2), the account balances in Common Shares and Retained Earnings after the stock split are the same as they were before: $2,000,000 and $10,000,000, respectively.

The comparative balances are as follows:

	Original Balances	After Stock Dividend	After Stock Split
Common shares	$ 2,000,000	$ 4,250,000	$ 2,000,000
Retained earnings	10,000,000	7,750,000	10,000,000
Total shareholders' equity	$12,000,000	$12,000,000	$12,000,000
Number of shares	500,000	550,000	1,000,000

Related exercise material: BE14–1, BE14–2, BE14–3, BE14–4, BE14–5, E14–1, E14–2, and E14–3.

Corporation Income Statements

The income statement helps users to evaluate the past performance of managers and to estimate future cash flows. **Income statements for corporations are the same as the statements for proprietorships or partnerships except for one thing: the reporting of income tax.**

study objective 2

Illustrate the proper form and content of corporation income statements.

Corporate Income Tax

For income tax purposes, a corporation is a separate legal entity. As a result, **income tax expense** is reported in a separate section of the corporation income statement, which is located before net income. The condensed income statement for Leads Inc. shown below shows a typical presentation. Note that the corporation reports "Income before income tax" before "Income tax expense."

LEADS INC. Income Statement Year Ended December 31, 2005	
Sales	$800,000
Cost of goods sold	600,000
Gross profit	200,000
Operating expenses	50,000
Income from operations	150,000
Other revenues	10,000
Other expenses	4,000
Income before income tax	**156,000**
Income tax expense	46,800
Net income	$109,200

Income tax is calculated annually on the income of the corporation, but must be estimated and remitted monthly. Therefore, the year-end current liability on the balance sheet is usually much less than the income tax expense reported for the period on the income statement. Most small businesses have three months (two months for larger companies) after year end to remit any balance due without penalty (or to request any refund). They have six months after their fiscal year end to file their completed income tax return, called a T2.

The final determination of income tax expense (or recovery) and liability (or receivable) usually results in an adjusting entry. Assume Leads had originally estimated its income tax would total $42,000. It remitted monthly instalments to the Canada Customs and Revenue Agency in the amount of $3,500 per month ($42,000 ÷ 12). At year end, Leads actually reports taxable income of $156,000, with a total income tax liability of $46,800. Assuming it has already recorded and remitted $42,000 of income tax, the required adjusting entry for $4,800 ($46,800 − $42,000) will be as follows:

Dec. 31	Income Tax Expense	4,800	
	Income Tax Payable		4,800
	To adjust estimated income tax expense to actual.		

$$A = L + SE$$
$$+4,800 \quad -4,800$$

Cash flows: no effect

Leads' income statement reports income before income tax of $156,000 and income tax expense of $46,800. The balance sheet reports a current liability of $4,800, due three months after year end.

Interperiod Tax Allocation

Income taxes are, in reality, far more complicated than the preceding presentation implies. As discussed in earlier chapters, the objectives for revenues and expenses for accounting purposes differ from the objectives for revenues and expenses for income tax purposes. Because of this, timing differences often occur. Transactions are sometimes recorded in one period for accounting purposes (in order to determine income tax expense) and in another period for income tax purposes (to determine income tax payable). These timing differences result in **future income taxes**.

Alternative terminology
Future income taxes are also known as *deferred income taxes.*

Future income taxes are discussed at length in intermediate accounting courses. For now it should be said that the income tax expense amount presented in many financial statements is usually divided between the amount currently due or receivable and the amount due or receivable in the future. The act of dividing the amounts is called **interperiod tax allocation**. An illustration of interperiod income tax allocation is presented in the income statement of The Forzani Group in Appendix A.

Intraperiod Tax Allocation

Helpful hint   *Intra* means within the current year's income statement; *inter* means between two or more income statements.

Intraperiod tax allocation refers to associating income taxes in a specified period with their related item of income. This can be contrasted with **interperiod tax allocation**, in which income taxes are allocated between two or more periods. Under intraperiod tax allocation, the relevant income tax expense or saving is associated with each non-typical item, as we will learn in the next section of this chapter for corrections of prior period errors and changes in accounting principles. Intraperiod tax allocation discloses useful information to statement users about the income tax effects of these adjustments. The general concept is "let the tax follow the income or loss."

No
Comprehensive Income Statement

Another type of income statement, called the **comprehensive income statement**, will soon also be required. This comprehensive income statement will include not only net income reported on the traditional income statement but also certain kinds of income transactions that currently bypass the income statement and are reported directly in the shareholders' equity section of the balance sheet.

What should be reported on the income statement and what should be reported as an adjustment to shareholders' equity has been the subject of debate for many years. Currently, all revenues, expenses, gains, and losses recognized during a period are reported on the income statement, with a few exceptions. These exceptions, which include items we will not be studying in this course, are excluded from net income and reported directly in shareholders' equity. For example, translation gains and losses on foreign currency (a topic studied in advanced accounting) are currently reported as a separate component of shareholders' equity. In future, these types of gains and losses will be presented as a separate component of comprehensive income. In addition, a proposed new accounting standard that we will learn about in Chapter 16 will result in unrealized gains and losses on certain types of investments when it is approved. Unrealized gains and losses are currently reported as an adjustment of shareholders' equity and would also be presented in the comprehensive income statement.

Comprehensive income, then, will include all increases and decreases to shareholders' equity during a period except those changes resulting from the sale or repurchase of shares and from the payment of dividends. By combining items traditionally reported in the income statement with other income items that are presented elsewhere, the profitability of a company can be more easily determined on an "all-inclusive" basis.

Comprehensive income statements have been used in the United States for many years. They are currently scheduled to be provided by Canadian companies for fiscal years commencing on or after October 1, 2005, as part of the standards harmonization efforts we learned about in Chapter 11. The comprehensive income statement will be presented along with the other four financial statements we've studied to date: income statement, statement of retained earnings, balance sheet, and cash flow statement.

ACCOUNTING IN ACTION ▶ International Insight

Financial analysts welcome the move to present comprehensive income. The Global Financial Reporting Advocacy Committee of the Association for Investment Management and Research made the following comment in a letter to the International Accounting Standards Board supporting the move to harmonize comprehensive income: "We consider income to include all of an enterprise's wealth changes except those engendered from transactions with its owners. We have profound misgivings about the increasing number of wealth changes that elude disclosure on the income statement. ... Financial statement users need in one place all the data reporting an enterprise's economic activity, which they then may sort out to suit their own purposes."

Source: Letter to the International Accounting Standards Board, September 9, 2003.

BEFORE YOU GO ON . . .

▶Review It

1. What is the unique feature of a corporation income statement?
2. Distinguish between interperiod and intraperiod tax allocation.
3. What is comprehensive income?

Related exercise material: BE14–6.

the navigator

Retained Earnings

As you learned in Chapter 13, **retained earnings** are the cumulative total since incorporation of net income (less losses) less any declared dividends. In other words, they are the earnings that have been retained or kept in the business. The following illustration shows a simple statement of retained earnings for Leads Inc. In it, we've assumed that Leads had an opening retained earnings balance of $500,000 and declared $25,000 of cash dividends during the year.

study objective 3

Prepare a statement of retained earnings.

v · P.

LEADS INC. Statement of Retained Earnings Year Ended December 31, 2005	
Retained earnings, January 1	$500,000
Add: Net income	109,200
	609,200
Less: Cash dividends	25,000
Retained earnings, December 31	$584,200

Each year, net income is added (or a net loss is deducted) and dividends are deducted from the opening retained earnings balance to determine the ending retained earnings amount. Similar to in a proprietorship, revenue and expense accounts (which make up net income) and dividends accounts are temporary accounts and are closed to retained earnings at the end of each period to bring the general ledger account Retained Earnings up to date. The ending Retained Earnings balance at December 31 will become the opening Retained Earnings amount, dated January 1, for the 2006 fiscal year.

The balance in Retained Earnings is part of the shareholders' claim on the total assets of the corporation. It does not, though, represent a claim on any specific asset. Nor can the amount of retained earnings be associated with the balance of any individual asset account. For example, a $100,000 balance in Retained Earnings does not mean that there should be $100,000 in Cash. The reason is that the cash resulting from the excess of revenues over expenses and dividends may have been used to purchase buildings, equipment, and other assets, or to pay liabilities. To illustrate the fact that the retained earnings and cash amounts may be quite different, the table below shows recent amounts of retained earnings and cash (including cash equivalents) for selected companies in a recent year.

	(in millions)	
Company	Retained Earnings	Cash
Air Canada	$(3,280)	$558
Canadian Tire	973	579
Reitmans	231	31
Saputo	547	0

Recall that Retained Earnings is a shareholders' equity account whose normal balance is a credit. A debit (negative) balance in Retained Earnings, such as has been reported by Air Canada, is identified as a **deficit**. It is reported as a deduction in the shareholders' equity section, as follows:

AIR CANADA
Balance Sheet (partial)
December 31, 2002
(in millions)

Shareholders' equity	
Share capital	$ 977
Contributed surplus	15
Deficit	(3,280)
Total shareholders' equity	$(2,288)

A negative total shareholders' equity, such as that reported by Air Canada, is sometimes called a shareholders' *deficiency*, rather than shareholders' *equity*. Air Canada uses the term shareholders' equity in its financial statements. Of course, a company cannot operate very long with a shareholders' deficiency by whatever name, which is why Air Canada is currently restructuring its operations under creditor protection.

Retained Earnings Restrictions

Helpful hint *Financial Reporting in Canada* reported in a recent year that 8% of the companies surveyed have restrictions on their retained earnings.

The balance in Retained Earnings is generally available for dividend declarations. Of course it would not be prudent for a company to declare a dividend equal to its balance in Retained Earnings. A company must retain enough net assets to sustain its operations. In some cases there may be specific **retained earnings restrictions**. These make a portion of the balance unavailable for dividends. Restrictions generally are of one or more of the following types:

1. **Contractual restrictions.** Long-term debt contracts may restrict retained earnings as a condition for the loan. The restriction limits the use of corporate assets for the

payment of dividends. This increases the likelihood that the corporation will be able to meet required loan payments.

2. **Voluntary restrictions.** The board of directors may voluntarily create retained earnings restrictions for specific purposes. For example, the board may authorize a restriction for future plant expansion. By reducing the amount of retained earnings available for dividends, the company makes more cash available for the planned expansion.

Retained earnings restrictions are generally disclosed in the notes to the financial statements.

Prior Period Adjustments

Suppose that a corporation's books have been closed and the financial statements have been issued. The corporation then discovers that a material error has been made in reporting net income of a prior year. Or suppose that the corporation changes an accounting policy that affects the comparison of prior year figures. How should these situations be recorded in the accounts and reported in the financial statements of prior periods?

When a correction of an error or a change in accounting principle results, the accounting treatment is similar:

1. The corrected amount or new principle should be used in reporting the results of operations of the current year.
2. The cumulative effect of the correction or change should be disclosed as an adjustment to opening retained earnings net of (after subtracting) applicable income tax.
3. All prior period financial statements should be corrected or restated to make comparison easier.
4. The effects of the change should be detailed and disclosed in a note to the statements.

An adjustment of financial results for prior periods is only appropriate in two circumstances: (1) when correcting an error related to a prior period, and (2) when changing an accounting principle. Let's now look in more detail at the accounting for each of these.

Correction of Prior Period Errors

M.C.

The correction of a prior period error in previously issued financial statements is made directly to Retained Earnings since the effect of the error is now in this account. The revenues and expenses (net income) for the previous period have been recorded in Retained Earnings through the journalizing and posting of closing entries.

To illustrate the correction of a prior period error, assume that Graber Inc. discovers in 2005 that it overstated its cost of goods sold in 2004 by $10,000 as a result of errors in counting inventory. These errors overstated expenses and understated income before income tax by $10,000. If we assume an income tax rate of 30%, income tax expense would be understated by $3,000 ($10,000 × 30%). The overall effect on net income is to understate it by $7,000 ($10,000 − $3,000). In other words, net income is understated by the difference after tax [$10,000 × (100% − 30%)].

The following table details this effect, using assumed data for revenues and expenses:

Helpful hint Normally, errors made in the year are discovered and corrected before the financial statements for the year are issued. Thus, corrections of prior period errors rarely happen.

	Incorrect	Correct	Difference
Revenues	$900,000	$900,000	$ 0
Expenses	550,000	540,000	10,000
Income before income tax	350,000	360,000	10,000
Income tax expense (30%)	105,000	108,000	3,000
Net income	$245,000	$252,000	$ 7,000

On the balance sheet, current assets (Merchandise Inventory) and retained earnings are also understated. The entry for the correction on December 31, 2005, is as follows:

A	=	L	+	SE
+10,000		+3,000		+7,000

Cash flows: no effect

Dec. 31	Merchandise Inventory	10,000	
	Income Tax Payable		3,000
	Retained Earnings		7,000
	To adjust for overstatement of cost of goods sold in a prior period.		

A credit to an income statement account, in this case Cost of Goods Sold, instead of Retained Earnings, would be incorrect because the error is for a prior year. Recall that income statement accounts are temporary accounts that are closed at the end of each year to the Retained Earnings account.

Prior period corrections are reported in the statement of retained earnings, net of associated income tax. Corrections are added to (or deducted from, depending on the error) the beginning Retained Earnings balance. This results in an adjusted beginning balance. Assuming Graber has a beginning balance of $800,000 in Retained Earnings, the correction is reported as follows:

GRABER INC.
Statement of Retained Earnings (partial)
Year Ended December 31, 2005

Balance, January 1, as previously reported	$800,000
Add: Correction for overstatement of cost of goods sold	
in 2004, net of $3,000 income tax expense	7,000
Balance, January 1, as adjusted	807,000

If the 2004 financial results are presented with the 2005 financial statements for comparative purposes, the 2004 amounts would be restated using the correct cost of goods sold expense and inventory amounts. An appropriately cross-referenced note should show the impact of the correction. It would also note the fact that the prior year's statements have been restated.

Change in Accounting Principle

▶Ethics note

Changes in accounting principles should result in financial statements that are more informative for statement users. They should not be used to artificially improve the company's reported performance and financial position.

To make comparisons easier, financial statements for the current period should be prepared using the same accounting principles that were used for the preceding period. This improves comparability. That is, there is a general presumption that generally accepted accounting principles are consistently applied from period to period.

This does not mean, however, that accounting principles can never change. A **change in accounting principle** (also known as a change in accounting policy) occurs when the principle used in the current year is different from the one used in the previous year. A change in accounting principle is permitted when the new generally accepted accounting principle results in a more appropriate presentation of events or transactions in the financial statements.

Examples of a change in accounting principle include a change in amortization method (e.g., declining-balance to straight-line) and a change in inventory cost flow assumption (e.g., FIFO to average cost). Often the CICA forces a change in accounting principle. One of the most significant changes required by the CICA was the requirement for goodwill and other intangible assets with indefinite lives to no longer be amortized, and instead be tested annually for impairment.

The effect of a change in accounting principle on prior period earnings can be significant. When Transcontinental adopted the new impairment accounting principle in 2001, it recorded a goodwill impairment loss of $20 million. This resulted in the restatement of opening retained earnings as at November 1, 2001, from $253.9 million to $233.9 million.

Like the correction of a prior period error, the cumulative effect of a change in accounting principle on net income is reported, net of applicable income tax, as an adjustment to the opening balance of retained earnings. To illustrate, assume that at the beginning of 2005, Graber changes from the straight-line method of amortization for equipment to the declining-balance method. The equipment was purchased on January 1, 2001. The cumulative effect of this change is to increase amortization expense and decrease the net book value of the equipment (because of the increase in accumulated amortization) for the years 2001 to 2004.

Retained earnings are affected by the change in amortization expense as is income tax expense. Both affect net income of the prior periods. Assume that the total increase in amortization expense during the period 2001–2004 amounts to $24,000. This decreases income before income tax by $24,000. If the company had a 30% tax rate, the after-tax effect of the change would be $16,800 [$24,000 × (100% − 30%)]. The entry to record this change in accounting principle follows:

Dec. 31	Income Tax Payable (or Recoverable)	7,200	
	Retained Earnings	16,800	
	Accumulated Amortization		24,000
	To record retroactive effect of change in amortization method.		

A	=	L	+	SE
−24,000		−7,200		−16,800

Cash flows: no effect

The presentation of this change in the statement of retained earnings is similar to the correction of prior period errors. The presentation is shown in the following illustration:

GRABER INC.
Statement of Retained Earnings (partial)
Year Ended December 31, 2005

Balance, January 1, as previously reported	$800,000
Add: Correction for overstatement of cost of goods sold in 2004, net of $3,000 income tax expense	7,000
Less: Cumulative effect of change in amortization method, net of $7,200 income tax savings	(16,800)
Balance, January 1, as adjusted	790,200

Any financial statements from prior years which are presented for comparative purposes would be restated using the declining-balance method of amortization. Graber's income statement would also show amortization expense for the current year on a declining-balance basis (i.e., using the new method of amortization). Accumulated amortization on the balance sheet would be calculated as though declining-balance had always been used. An appropriately cross-referenced note to the statements should detail the impact of the change and the fact that prior years' statements have been restated.

Statement of Retained Earnings

The **statement of retained earnings** shows the changes in retained earnings during the year. The statement is prepared from the Retained Earnings account. Transactions and events that affect retained earnings are shown in Illustration 14-3.

Illustration 14-3 ▶

Debits and credits to
retained earnings

Retained Earnings	
Debits (Decreases)	Credits (Increases)
1. Correction of a prior period error that overstated income 2. Cumulative effect of a change in accounting principle that decreased income 3. Net loss 4. Cash dividends 5. Stock dividends 6. Reacquisition of shares	1. Correction of a prior period error that understated income 2. Cumulative effect of a change in accounting principle that increased income 3. Net income

As indicated, net income increases retained earnings and a net loss decreases retained earnings. Prior period adjustments—a correction of an error or a change in accounting principle—may either increase or decrease retained earnings. Both cash and stock dividends decrease retained earnings. Stock splits do not affect retained earnings, so they do not appear in this list of transactions.

You will recall as well from Chapter 13 that gains and losses from the reacquisition of shares are reported as shareholders' equity transactions, not income statement transactions. Gains, which occur when shares are reacquired at a price lower than the average issue price, create contributed capital. Losses, which occur when shares are reacquired at a price higher than the average issue price, first reduce contributed capital, and then retained earnings.

The statement of retained earnings for Graber, using assumed data for net income and dividends and incorporating the prior period adjustments just discussed, follows.

GRABER INC.
Statement of Retained Earnings (partial)
Year Ended December 31, 2005

Balance, January 1, as previously reported		$ 800,000
Add: Correction for overstatement of cost of goods sold in 2004, net of $3,000 income tax expense		7,000
Less: Cumulative effect of change in amortization method, net of $7,200 income tax savings		(16,800)
Balance, January 1, as adjusted		790,200
Add: Net income		549,800
		1,340,000
Less: Cash dividends	$100,000	
Stock dividends	200,000	300,000
Balance, December 31		$1,040,000

Some companies combine the statement of retained earnings with their income statement, instead of presenting them separately. For example, The Forzani Group does this in its Consolidated Statements of Operations and Retained Earnings, as shown in Appendix A. However, the majority of companies present a separate statement of retained earnings.

BEFORE YOU GO ON ...

► Review It

1. How are retained earnings restrictions reported?
2. Distinguish between a correction of a prior period error and a change in accounting principle.
3. What are the principal sources of debits and credits to the Retained Earnings account?

► Do It

Vega Corporation has retained earnings of $5,130,000 on January 1, 2005. During the year, the company earns $2,000,000 of net income. It declares and pays a $250,000 cash dividend. In 2005, Vega records an adjustment of $275,000, less $95,000 of applicable income tax, for an overstatement resulting from a mathematical error affecting 2004 ending inventory. Prepare a statement of retained earnings for the year ended December 31, 2005.

Action Plan

• A statement of retained earnings begins with retained earnings as reported at the end of the previous year.
• Add or subtract any prior period adjustments to arrive at the adjusted opening Retained Earnings balance.
• Add net income and subtract dividends declared to arrive at the ending balance in Retained Earnings.

Solution

VEGA CORPORATION
Statement of Retained Earnings
Year Ended December 31, 2005

Balance, January 1, as previously reported	$5,130,000
Less: Correction for overstatement of ending inventory, net of $95,000 applicable income tax	(180,000)
Balance, January 1, as adjusted	4,950,000
Add: Net income	2,000,000
	6,950,000
Less: Cash dividend	250,000
Balance, December 31	$6,700,000

Related exercise material: BE14–7, BE14–8, BE14–9, E14–4, E14–5, and E14–6.

the navigator

Statement Presentation and Analysis

Shares are generally purchased by investors for potential capital gains (market price appreciation) or for potential income (dividends). Consequently, investors are interested in the shareholders' equity section of the balance sheet and profitability measures using this information. In the next sections, we will review the statement presentation and analysis of shareholders' equity.

study objective 4

Prepare and analyse the shareholders' equity section of a balance sheet.

Presentation

The shareholders' equity section of the balance sheet of Graber Inc., based on assumed data, is as follows.

GRABER INC.
Balance Sheet (partial)
December 31, 2005

Shareholders' equity		
Contributed capital		
Share capital		
$9 preferred shares, no par value, cumulative,		
10,000 shares authorized, 6,000 shares issued		$ 630,000
Common shares, no par value, unlimited number		
of shares authorized, 400,000 shares issued	$3,000,000	
Common stock dividends distributable	50,000	3,050,000
Total share capital		3,680,000
Additional contributed capital		
Contributed capital—reacquired common shares		50,000
Total contributed capital		3,730,000
Retained earnings (Note X)		1,040,000
Total shareholders' equity		$4,770,000

Note X: Loan agreements contain, among other covenants, a restriction on the payment of dividends, which limits future dividend payments to 75% of net income.

Instead of presenting a detailed shareholders' equity section in the balance sheet, many companies detail the components of the shareholders' equity accounts in the notes to the statements. Refer to The Forzani Group's note 9 in Appendix A for an illustration of this type of presentation.

Analysis

For the shareholder, profitability can be measured by the return on equity ratio introduced in Chapter 13. Shareholders and potential investors are also interested in a company's earnings performance and dividend record.

Earnings Performance

Two ratios related to income are frequently reported in the financial press. They are widely used by shareholders and potential investors in evaluating the profitability of a company. The first ratio—a convenient measure of earnings—is the **earnings per share** ratio. Earnings per share disclosures are required for publicly held companies and recommended for private companies. Investors and others link earnings per share to the market price per share. This relationship produces the second ratio—the **price-earnings ratio**.

Earnings Per Share. Earnings per share (EPS) indicates the net income earned by each common share. Thus, **earnings per share is reported only for common shares**. When a company has both preferred and common shares, the current year's dividend declared on preferred shares is subtracted from net income to determine the income available to common shareholders. Illustration 14-4 shows the formula for calculating EPS.

V.I.P

Illustration 14-4 ▶

Earnings per share formula

Net Income Minus Preferred Dividends	÷	Weighted Average Number of Common Shares	=	Earnings per Share
($30,531,000 − $0)	÷	$30,082,408	=	$1.01

To illustrate the calculation of earnings per share above, we have used data from Forzani's 2003 financial statements reproduced in Appendix A. Forzani's net income of $30,531,000 is divided by the weighted average number of common shares, 30,082,408, to determine its earnings per share of $1.01.

In determining the numerator of the earnings per share calculation ($30,531,000), note that Forzani had no preferred dividends to subtract from net income. If it did, any preferred dividends declared for the current year would be subtracted from net income to determine the income available for the common shareholders. In addition, note that if preferred shares are cumulative, the dividend is deducted whether or not it is declared.

For the denominator of the earnings per share calculation (30,082,408), the weighted average number of shares is used instead of the ending balance. If there is no change in the number of common shares issued during the year, the weighted average number of shares will be the same as the ending balance. If new shares are issued in the year, these shares are adjusted for the fraction of the year they are outstanding to determine the weighted average number of shares. This is done because the issue of shares during the period changes the amount of net assets on which income can be earned.

To illustrate the calculation of the weighted average number of common shares, assume that a company had 100,000 common shares on January 1, and issued an additional 10,000 shares on October 1. The weighted average number of shares for the year would be calculated as follows:

Date	Actual Number	Fraction of Year	Weighted Average
Jan. 1	100,000	$\times \frac{12}{12} =$	100,000
Oct. 1	10,000	$\times \frac{3}{12} =$	2,500
	110,000		102,500

As illustrated, 110,000 shares were actually issued by the end of the year. Of these, 100,000 were outstanding for the full year and are allocated a full weight, 12 months out of 12. As 10,000 of the shares have only been outstanding for three months (from October 1 to December 31), they are weighted for $\frac{3}{12}$ of the year, resulting in 2,500 weighted shares. In total, the company's weighted average number of shares is 102,500 for the year. In the next calendar year, the 110,000 shares would receive a full weight (unless some of these shares are repurchased) because all 110,000 shares would be outstanding for the entire year.

Complex Capital Structure. When a corporation has securities that may be converted into common shares, it is said to have a **complex capital structure**. Two examples of such securities are convertible preferred shares and stock options, which, when exercised, will reduce or dilute the earnings per share.

Two earnings per share figures are calculated when a corporation has a complex capital structure. The first earnings per share figure is called **basic earnings per share**. The earnings per share amount we calculated in Illustration 14-4 is known as basic earnings per share. All public companies must report basic earnings per share on the face of their income statement. As determined in Illustration 14-4, Forzani reports basic earnings per share of $1.01 on its income statement for 2003.

The second earnings per share figure is called **fully diluted earnings per share**. This figure calculates *hypothetical* earnings per share as though *all* dilutive securities are converted into common shares, even though they have not been. Forzani, which has stock options, is considered to have a complex capital structure. It reports fully diluted earnings per share of $0.96 in 2003. Note that fully diluted earnings per share will always be lower than basic earnings per share.

The calculation of fully diluted earnings per share is complex. In addition, the determination of the weighted average number of shares for both basic and fully diluted earnings per share becomes more complicated when there are stock dividends and stock splits during the year. Further discussion of these and other earnings per share complexities is left to an intermediate accounting course.

Price-Earnings Ratio. Comparisons of earnings per share across companies are not very meaningful because of the wide variations in the numbers of shares among companies and in the share prices. In order to compare earnings across companies, we calculate the **price-earnings (PE) ratio**. The price-earnings ratio is a frequently quoted statistic that measures **the ratio of the market price of each common share to its earnings per share**.

To illustrate, we will calculate the price-earnings ratio for The Forzani Group Ltd. Forzani's earnings per share for the year ended February 2, 2003, was $1.01 as shown in Illustration 14-4. Its market price at year end was $16.85. Illustration 14-5 shows Forzani's price-earnings ratio.

Illustration 14-5 ▶

Calculation of price-earnings ratio

Market Price per Share	÷	Earnings per Share	=	Price-Earnings Ratio
$16.85	÷	$1.01	=	17 times

This ratio indicates that Forzani's shares are trading at 17 times earnings. The PE ratio reflects investors' assessment of a company's future earnings. The ratio of price to earnings will be higher if investors think that current income levels will continue or increase. It will be lower if investors think that income will decline.

Dividend Record

One way that companies reward investors for their investment is to pay dividends. The **payout ratio** tells you what percentage of income the company is distributing to its shareholders. If the number is very high, consider it a danger signal—it could mean the company is failing to reinvest enough of its income in its operations. A high payout ratio can also mean the company's income is falling or that it is trying to attract investors who find little else to get excited about.

The payout ratio is calculated by dividing total cash dividends by net income. This ratio can also be expressed on a per share basis by dividing common dividends per share by earnings per share. The formula to calculate the payout ratio is shown in Illustration 14-6.

Illustration 14-6 ▶

Calculation of payout ratio

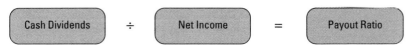

Cash Dividends	÷	Net Income	=	Payout Ratio

Forzani's payout ratio is zero. As mentioned earlier, it paid no dividends in 2003.

Like most ratios, the payout ratio varies with the industry. Real estate investment trusts pay out almost all their income because of a provision in the law that exempts them from income tax if they do so. Utilities also have high payout ratios. By contrast, companies that have high growth rates generally have low payout ratios because they reinvest most of their net income in the company.

ACCOUNTING IN ACTION ▶ Business Insight

Investors like to see a steady payout ratio. This was evident when Sherritt International Corp.'s share price dropped 14% as investors expressed their dismay at news that the natural resources company planned to discontinue its quarterly dividend because its income had been hurt by the declining price of commodities. "If you start the cut [the dividend], you're pulling the rug out from under investors," said one market analyst. "It's a tough time to be taking that stability away from your investors."

Source: Caroline Alphonso, "Dividend Cuts Raise Investor Ire," *Globe and Mail*, November 28, 2001, B1.

BEFORE YOU GO ON . . .

▶Review It

1. Explain how to calculate earnings per share.
2. How is the weighted average number of shares calculated?
3. Explain how the price-earnings ratio relates to the earnings per share ratio.
4. What ratio provides information about a company's dividend record?

▶Do It

Shoten Limited reported net income of $249,750 on its October 31, 2005, year-end income statement. The shareholders' equity section of its balance sheet reported 3,000 $2-cumulative preferred shares and 50,000 common shares. Of the common shares, 40,000 were outstanding at the beginning of the year, 15,000 shares were issued on March 1, and 5,000 shares were repurchased on August 1. Calculate Shoten's earnings per share.

Action Plan

- Adjust the shares for the fraction of the year outstanding to determine the weighted average number of shares.
- Subtract the preferred dividends from net income to determine the income available for common shareholders.
- Divide the income available for common shareholders by the weighted average number of shares to calculate the earnings per share.

Solution

Weighted average number of shares:

Date	Actual Number	Fraction of Year	Weighted Average
Nov. 1	40,000	$\times \frac{12}{12} =$	40,000
Mar. 1	15,000	$\times \frac{8}{12} =$	10,000
Aug. 1	(5,000)	$\times \frac{3}{12} =$	(1,250)
	50,000		48,750

Earnings per share:

$$\frac{\$249,750 - \$6,000 \ [3,000 \times \$2]}{48,750} = \$5$$

Related exercise material: BE14–10, BE14–11, BE14–12, BE14–13, E14–7, E14–8, E14–9, E14–10, E14–11, and E14–12.

the navigator

Demonstration Problem

Additional Demonstration Problems

On January 1, 2005, Fuso Corporation had the following shareholders' equity accounts:

$5 preferred shares, no par value, unlimited number authorized, 10,000 issued	$1,000,000
Common shares, no par value, unlimited number authorized, 260,000 issued	3,120,000
Retained earnings	3,200,000

During the year, the following transactions occurred:

Mar. 10 Declared quarterly cash dividend to preferred shareholders of record on March 31, payable April 15.

Apr. 15 Paid the quarterly cash dividend to preferred shareholders.

June 1 Announced a 2-for-1 stock split of the common shares. Immediately prior to the split, the share price was $10 per share.

June 10 Declared quarterly cash dividend to preferred shareholders of record on June 30, payable July 15.

July 15 Paid the quarterly cash dividend to preferred shareholders.

Aug.   1 Declared a 5% stock dividend to common shareholders of record on August 25, distributable September 8. On August 1, the share price was $12 per share.

Sept. 8 Issued the common shares for the stock dividend.

      10 Declared quarterly cash dividend to preferred shareholders of record on September 30, payable October 15.

Oct. 15 Paid the quarterly cash dividend to preferred shareholders.

Dec. 10 Declared quarterly cash dividend to preferred shareholders of record on December 31, payable January 15.

      31 Determined that net income for the year was $600,000.

Instructions

(a) Record the above transactions and the closing entries for the Income Summary and dividend accounts.

(b) Prepare the shareholders' equity section of the balance sheet at December 31, 2005.

Action Plan

- Keep a running total of the number of shares issued.
- Remember that dividend rates are expressed as annual amounts.
- Make journal entries for dividends on the declaration and payment dates, but not on the record date.
- Adjust the number of shares for the stock split, but make no journal entry.
- Apply the stock dividend percentage to the number of shares issued. Multiply the new shares to be issued by the market value of the shares.

Solution to Demonstration Problem

(a)

Mar. 10	Cash Dividend—Preferred	12,500	
	Dividend Payable		12,500
	To record quarterly preferred dividend ($5 ÷ 4 = $1.25; $1.25 × 10,000).		
Apr. 15	Dividend Payable	12,500	
	Cash		12,500
	To record payment of quarterly preferred dividend.		
June 1	Memo entry only about 2-for-1 stock split. Now 520,000 (260,000 × 2) common shares.		
10	Cash Dividend—Preferred	12,500	
	Dividend Payable		12,500
	To record quarterly preferred dividend ($5 ÷ 4 = $1.25; $1.25 × 10,000).		
July 15	Dividend Payable	12,500	
	Cash		12,500
	To record payment of quarterly preferred dividend.		
Aug. 1	Stock Dividend—Common	312,000	
	Stock Dividend Distributable		312,000
	To record stock dividend to common shareholders (520,000 × 5% = 26,000; 26,000 × $12).		
Sept. 8	Stock Dividend Distributable	312,000	
	Common Shares		312,000
	To record issue of 26,000 additional common shares with stock dividend. Now 546,000 common shares.		
10	Cash Dividend—Preferred	12,500	
	Dividend Payable		12,500
	To record quarterly preferred dividend ($5 ÷ 4 = $1.25; $1.25 × 10,000).		
Oct. 15	Dividend Payable	12,500	
	Cash		12,500
	To record payment of quarterly preferred dividend.		
Dec. 10	Cash Dividend—Preferred	12,500	
	Dividend Payable		12,500
	To record quarterly preferred dividend ($5 ÷ 4 = $1.25; $1.25 × 10,000).		

Dec. 31	Income Summary	600,000	
	Retained Earnings		600,000
	To close Net Income to Retained Earnings.		
31	Retained Earnings	362,000	
	Cash Dividend—Preferred		50,000
	Stock Dividend—Common		312,000
	To close dividend accounts to Retained Earnings.		

(b)

FUSO CORPORATION
Balance Sheet (Partial)
December 31, 2005

Shareholders' equity
  Share capital
    $5 preferred shares, no par value, unlimited number
      authorized, 10,000 issued $1,000,000
    Common shares, no par value, unlimited number authorized,
      546,000 issued ($3,120,000 + $312,000)   3,432,000
                                   4,432,000
  Retained earnings ($3,200,000 + $600,000 − $362,000) 3,438,000
  Total shareholders' equity $7,870,000

Summary of Study Objectives

1. *Prepare the entries for cash dividends, stock dividends, and stock splits, and compare their financial impact.* Entries for both cash and stock dividends are required at the declaration date and the payment or distribution date. There is no entry for a stock split. Cash dividends reduce assets and shareholders' equity (retained earnings). Stock dividends reduce retained earnings and increase common shares, but have no impact on total shareholders' equity. Stock splits reduce the market price of the shares, and increase the number of shares issued, but have no impact on the financial position of the company.

2. *Illustrate the proper form and content of corporation income statements.* The form and content of corporation income statements are similar to the statements of proprietorships and partnerships with one exception. Income tax expense must be reported in a separate section before net income in the corporation's income statement. The proposed new comprehensive income statement will report all increases and decreases to shareholders' equity during a period except changes resulting from the sale or repurchase of shares and from the payment of dividends.

3. *Prepare a statement of retained earnings.* Additions to retained earnings include net income, corrections of understatements of prior years' net income, and increases due to the cumulative effect of a change in accounting principle. Deductions consist of net loss, corrections of overstatements of prior years' net income, decreases due to the cumulative effect of a change in accounting principle, cash and stock dividends, and losses from the reacquisition of shares.

4. *Prepare and analyse the shareholders' equity section of a balance sheet.* A shareholders' equity section consists of two subsections: share capital and retained earnings. It should also include notes to the financial statements that explain adjustments to opening retained earnings, restrictions on retained earnings, and dividends in arrears, if any.

Profitability measures used to analyse shareholders' equity include return on equity (discussed in Chapter 13), earnings per share, the price-earnings ratio, and the payout ratio.

Earnings (loss) per share is calculated by dividing net income (loss) available to the common shareholders by the weighed average number of common shares. The price-earnings ratio is calculated by dividing the market price per share by the earnings per share. The payout ratio is calculated by dividing cash dividends by net income.

Glossary

Key Term Matching Activity

Basic earnings per share The net income (or loss) earned by each common share. It is calculated by subtracting any preferred dividends declared from net income and dividing the result by the weighted average number of common shares. (p. 675)

Cash dividend A pro rata (equal) distribution of cash to shareholders. (p. 658)

Change in accounting principle The use of a generally accepted accounting principle in the current year that is different from the one used in the preceding year. (p. 670)

Comprehensive income statement A statement that reports all increases and decreases to shareholders' equity during a period except changes resulting from the sale or repurchase of shares and from the payment of dividends. (p. 666)

Correction of a prior period error The correction of an error in previously issued financial statements. (p. 669)

Declaration date The date the board of directors formally declares a dividend and announces it to shareholders. (p. 659)

Deficit A debit (negative) balance in retained earnings. (p. 668)

Dividend A distribution of cash or shares by a corporation to its shareholders on a pro rata (equal) basis. (p. 658)

Earnings per share (EPS) The net income (or loss) earned by each common share. (p. 674)

Fully diluted earnings per share Earnings per share adjusted for the maximum possible dilution that would occur if dilutive securities were converted into common shares. (p. 675)

Interperiod tax allocation The allocation of income tax expense between two or more periods to record the amount which is currently due and the amount which is due in the future (deferred). (p. 666)

Intraperiod tax allocation The procedure of associating income tax expense with the specific item that directly affects the income tax for the period. (p. 666)

Payment date The date cash dividend cheques are mailed to shareholders. For a stock dividend, the date the shares are distributed to shareholders. (p. 660)

Payout ratio Measures the percentage of earnings distributed in the form of cash dividends. It is calculated by dividing cash dividends by net income. (p. 676)

Price-earnings (PE) ratio The ratio of the price of a common share to earnings per common share. (p. 676)

Record date The date when ownership of shares is determined for dividend purposes. (p. 659)

Retained earnings restrictions Circumstances that make a portion of retained earnings currently unavailable for dividends. (p. 668)

Statement of retained earnings A financial statement that shows the changes in retained earnings during the year. (p. 671)

Stock dividend A pro rata (equal) distribution of the corporation's own shares to shareholders. (p. 661)

Stock split The issue of additional shares to shareholders according to their percentage ownership. A stock split results in a reduction in the legal value per share. (p. 663)

Weighted average number of shares The number of common shares outstanding during the year, with any shares purchased or issued during the year weighted by the fraction of the year for which they have been outstanding. (p. 675)

Self-Study Questions

Chapter 14 Self-Test

Answers are at the end of the chapter.

(SO 1) K 1. Entries for cash dividends are required on the:
   (a) declaration date and payment date.
   (b) record date and payment date.
   (c) declaration date, record date, and payment date.
   (d) declaration date and record date.

(SO 1) K 2. Which of the following statements about stock dividends is true?
   (a) A stock dividend increases total shareholders' equity.
   (b) A stock dividend decreases total shareholders' equity.
   (c) Market value per share is usually assigned to the dividend shares.
   (d) A stock dividend ordinarily will have no effect on total share capital.

3. Which of the following statements about a 3-for-1 stock split is true?   **(SO 1) K**
   (a) It will triple the market value of the shares.
   (b) It will triple the amount of total shareholders' equity.
   (c) It will have no effect on total shareholders' equity.
   (d) It requires the company to distribute cash.

(SO 2) K 4. Corporation income statements may be the same as the income statements for unincorporated companies, except for:
(a) gross profit.   (c) operating income.
(b) income tax expense.   (d) net sales.

(SO 3) K 5. Which of the following are not reported in a statement of retained earnings?
(a) Cash and stock dividends
(b) Stock splits
(c) Corrections of errors in income of prior periods
(d) Changes in accounting principles

(SO 3) K 6. Which of the following can cause a restriction in retained earnings?
(a) Long-term debt covenant terms
(b) A change in accounting principle
(c) A correction of a prior period error
(d) All of the above

(SO 3) K 7. A prior period adjustment is:
(a) reported in the income statement.
(b) reported directly in the shareholders' equity section.
(c) reported in the statement of retained earnings as an adjustment to the opening balance of Retained Earnings.
(d) reported in the statement of retained earnings as an adjustment to the ending balance of Retained Earnings.

(SO 4) AP 8. Wreck Cove Inc. had 100,000 common shares on January 1. It issued an additional 24,000 shares on June 1 and repurchased 10,000 shares on October 1. What is Wreck Cove's weighted average number of shares?
(a) 57,000   (c) 114,000
(b) 111,500   (d) 116,500

(SO 4) AP 9. The Breau Corporation reported net income, $24,000; weighted average number of common shares, 6,000; and a share market price of $60. It had no preferred shares. What were its earnings per share and price-earnings ratios?
(a) $4 and 15 times   (c) $10 and 6 times
(b) $6 and 10 times   (d) $15 and 4 times

(SO 4) C 10. Bernard Dupuis is nearing retirement and would like to invest in shares that will provide a steady income. Bernard should choose shares with a:
(a) high earnings per share.
(b) high price-earnings ratio.
(c) high payout ratio.
(d) high return on equity.

Questions

(SO 1) C 1. (a) What is a dividend?
(b) "Dividends must be paid in cash." Do you agree? Explain.

(SO 1) C 2. Robin O'Malley maintains that enough cash is the only requirement for the declaration of a cash dividend. Is Robin correct? Explain.

(SO 1) C 3. (a) Three dates are important in connection with cash dividends. Identify these dates and explain their significance to the corporation and its shareholders.
(b) Identify the journal entry (if any) that is made for a cash dividend on each of the above dates.

(SO 1) C 4. What is the impact of cumulative preferred shares compared to noncumulative preferred shares on the payment of dividends to common shareholders?

(SO 1) C 5. Contrast the effects of a cash dividend and a stock dividend on (a) a corporation's balance sheet and (b) an individual shareholder's personal financial position.

(SO 1) C 6. Jill Simmons asks, "Since stock dividends don't change anything, why declare them?" What is your answer to Jill?

(SO 1) C 7. In April 2002, **Call-Net Enterprises Inc.**, parent of Sprint Canada, announced a 20-to-1 reverse stock split. Prior to the split the share price was $0.50 per share. Explain why Call-Net might have undertaken this reverse stock split.

(SO 1) C 8. The board of directors is considering either a stock split or a stock dividend. It understands that total shareholders' equity will remain the same under either action. However, it is not sure of the different effects of the two types of actions on the components of shareholders' equity: common shares and retained earnings. Explain the differences to the directors.

(SO 2) C 9. What is the difference between income statements for corporations and income statements for proprietorships and partnerships? Why does this difference exist?

(SO 2) C 10. Nels Olsen, who owns many investments in common shares, says, "I don't care what a company's net income is. The balance sheet tells me everything I need to know!" How do you respond to Nels?

(SO 2) K 11. How is comprehensive income different from net income?

(SO 3) AP 12. ABC Corporation has a Retained Earnings balance of $240,000 on January 1. During the year, a correction of a prior period error of $90,000 before income tax of 25% is recorded because of the understatement of amortization in the prior period. Show the presentation of this information in the statement of retained earnings.

(SO 3) C 13. Under what circumstances is it appropriate to record an adjustment of the results of prior periods? How are these adjustments reported in the financial statements?

(SO 3) C   14. What is the purpose of a retained earnings restriction? How are retained earnings restrictions generally reported in the financial statements?

(SO 3) C   15. Identify the events that result in increases (credits) and decreases (debits) to Retained Earnings.

(SO 3) C   16. When studying for an accounting test, a fellow student says, "Changes in accounting principles are reported in the statement of retained earnings." Is your friend correct, or should he study harder?

(SO 4) C   17. Omar Radhah believes that both the beginning and ending balances in Retained Earnings are shown in the shareholders' equity section of the balance sheet. Is Omar correct? Explain.

(SO 4) AP   18. Indicate how each of the following accounts should be classified in the shareholders' equity section of the balance sheet. (a) Common Shares, (b) Preferred

Shares, (c) Stock Dividends Distributable, (d) Contributed Capital—Reacquisition of Shares, and (e) Retained Earnings

(SO 4) C   19. Why is the weighted average number of common shares used in earnings per share calculations?

(SO 4) C   20. The Hanwell Corporation has both common and preferred shares. The company's accountant argues that it is only necessary to subtract the preferred share dividends from net income in the earnings per share calculation if preferred share dividends have been declared that year. Is the accountant correct? Discuss.

(SO 4) C   21. Holding all other factors constant, indicate whether each of the following is generally considered favourable or unfavourable by a potential investor: (a) an increase in earnings per share, (b) a decrease in the price-earnings ratio, and (c) an increase in the payout ratio

Brief Exercises

Record cash dividend.
(SO 1) AP

BE14–1 The Boudin Corporation has 50,000 common shares. It declares a $2 per share cash dividend on November 1 to shareholders of record on December 1. The dividend is paid on December 31. Prepare the entries on the appropriate dates to record the cash dividend.

Allocate dividends to preferred and common shareholders.
(SO 1) AP

BE14–2 Mertz Corporation has 100,000 $8-cumulative preferred shares and 550,000 common shares. In the first year of operations, it paid total dividends of $450,000. In the second year, the company paid total dividends of $1,500,000. Calculate the dividend payment to the preferred and common shareholders for both years. How would this differ if the preferred shares were noncumulative?

Record stock dividend.
(SO 1) AP

BE14–3 Patina Corporation has 80,000 common shares. It declares a 10% stock dividend on December 1 when the market value per share is $15. The dividend shares are issued on December 31. Prepare the entries for the declaration and distribution of the stock dividend.

Compare cash dividend, stock dividend, and stock split.
(SO 1) AP

BE14–4 Indicate whether each of the following transactions would increase (+), decrease (−), or have no effect (NE) on total assets, total liabilities, and total shareholders' equity:

Transaction	Assets	Liabilities	Shareholders' Equity
(a) Declared and paid a cash dividend.			
(b) Declared and distributed a stock dividend.			
(c) Split stock 3-for-1.			

Analyse impact of stock split.
(SO 1) AP

BE14–5 Pella Corporation has 10,000 common shares when it announces a 4-for-1 stock split. Before the split, the shares had a market value of $140 per share. After the split, how many shares will be issued? What will be the approximate market price per share?

Record income tax and prepare income statement.
(SO 2) AP

BE14–6 For the year ended May 31, 2005, Osbern Inc. earned $2 million in revenues and incurred $1.6 million of expenses. The company has a 30% income tax rate. Prepare (a) the journal entry to record income taxes, assuming no previous accruals, and (b) the income statement.

BE14–7 For the year ending December 31, 2005, Cadien Inc. reports net income of $150,000 and dividends of $85,000. Prepare the statement of retained earnings for the year, assuming the balance in Retained Earnings on January 1, 2005, was $260,000.

Prepare statement of retained earnings.
(SO 3) AP

BE14–8 On January 1, 2005, Ouellet, Inc. changed from the straight-line method of amortization to the declining-balance method. The cumulative effect of the change was to increase prior years' amortization by $70,000. The income tax rate is 35%. Prepare a journal entry to record this change in accounting principle.

Record change in accounting principle.
(SO 3) AP

BE14–9 Ouellet, Inc. reported retained earnings of $337,500 on December 31, 2004. For the year ended December 31, 2005, the company had net income of $195,000 and declared and paid dividends of $67,000. Using this information and the data for Ouellet in BE14–8, prepare a statement of retained earnings.

Prepare statement of retained earnings with prior period adjustment.
(SO 3) AP

BE14–10 Ménard Corporation has these accounts at December 31, 2005: Common Shares, no par value, unlimited number authorized, 5,000 issued, $50,000; Stock Dividend Distributable, $15,000; and Retained Earnings, $29,000. Of the retained earnings, $20,000 has been restricted because of loan agreements. Prepare the shareholders' equity section of the balance sheet.

Prepare shareholders' equity section.
(SO 4) AP

BE14–11 Darlin Corporation reports net income of $370,000 and 200,000 common shares.
(a) Calculate the earnings per share.
(b) Assume that Darlin also has cumulative preferred dividends for the current year of $20,000 that were declared and paid. Recalculate the earnings per share.
(c) Assume that the preferred dividends referred to in part (b) were not declared and paid. What difference would this make in calculating the earnings per share?

Calculate earnings per share, with and without preferred shares.
(SO 4) AP

BE14–12 Lake Limited had 40,000 common shares on January 1, 2005. On April 1, 8,000 shares were repurchased. On August 31, 12,000 shares were issued. Calculate the number of shares at December 31, 2005, and the weighted average number of shares for 2005.

Calculate weighted average number of shares.
(SO 4) AP

BE14–13 Wang, Inc. reported earnings per share of $5. Its common shares were selling at $52.50 per share. During the same year, the company paid a $1.50 per share cash dividend. Calculate the price-earnings ratio and the payout ratio.

Calculate price-earnings and payout ratios.
(SO 4) AP

Exercises

E14–1 The Oshawa Corporation was organized on January 1, 2004. During its first year, the corporation issued 2,000 preferred shares and 100,000 common shares. At December 31 of each year, the company declared the following cash dividends: for 2004, $6,000; for 2005, $11,000; for 2006, $28,000; and for 2007, $9,000.

Allocate dividends to preferred and common shareholders.
(SO 1) AP

Interactive Homework

Instructions
(a) Show the allocation of dividends to preferred and common shareholders for each year, assuming the preferred share dividend is $4 and noncumulative.
(b) Show the allocation of dividends to preferred and common shareholders for each year, assuming the preferred share dividend is $5 and cumulative.
(c) Journalize the declaration of the cash dividend for the year 2006 under each of part (a) and (b).

E14–2 Laine Inc. is considering following one of three courses of action: (1) paying a $1 cash dividend, (2) distributing a 5% stock dividend, or (3) effecting a 2-for-1 stock split. The current market price is $14 per share.

Compare cash dividend, stock dividend, and stock split.
(SO 1) AP

Interactive Homework

Instructions
Assist Laine in making its decision about which course of action to take by completing the following chart (treat each possibility independently):

	Before Action	After Cash Dividend	After Stock Dividend	After Stock Split
Total assets	$1,250,000			
Total liabilities	$ 50,000			
Common shares	800,000			
Retained earnings	400,000			
Total shareholders' equity	1,200,000			
Total liabilities and shareholders' equity	$1,250,000			
Number of common shares	80,000			

Prepare correcting entries for dividends and stock split.
(SO 1) AP

E14–3 Before preparing financial statements for the current year, the chief accountant for Kaufel Ltd. discovered the following errors in the accounts:

1. The declaration and payment of a $25,000 cash dividend was recorded as a debit to Dividends Expense of $25,000 and a credit to Cash of $25,000.
2. A 10% stock dividend (1,000 shares) was declared on the common shares when the market value per share was $10. The only entry made was as follows: (Dr.) Retained Earnings $10,000 and (Cr.) Dividend Payable $10,000. The shares have not been issued.
3. The company declared a 4-for-1 stock split involving the issue of 400,000 $2 preferred shares for 100,000 $8 preferred shares. The market value of the preferred shares prior to the split was $60. The split was recorded as a debit to Retained Earnings of $6 million and a credit to Preferred Shares of $6 million.

Instructions
Prepare the correcting entries.

Record dividends and indicate statement presentation.
(SO 1, 3) AP

E14–4 On January 1, Wei Corporation had 75,000 common shares. During the year, the following occurred:

Apr.   1 Issued 5,000 additional common shares for $16 per share.
June 15 Declared a cash dividend of $1 per share to shareholders of record on June 30.
July 10 Paid the $1 cash dividend.
Aug. 21 Declared a 5% stock dividend to the shareholders of record on September 5, distributable on September 20. The market value of the common shares was $18 per share.
Sept.20 Issued the shares for the stock dividend. The market value of the common shares was $18.50 per share.
Dec.   1 Issued 3,000 additional common shares for $19 per share.
        15 Declared a cash dividend of $1.25 per share to shareholders of record on December 31.

Instructions
(a) Prepare the entries required to record the above transactions.
(b) How are dividends and dividends payable reported in the financial statements prepared at December 31, Wei's year end?

Prepare combined income statement and statement of retained earnings.
(SO 2, 3) AP

E14–5 Coaldale Ltd. has an August 31 fiscal year end. On August 31, 2004, Coaldale had retained earnings of $283,000. The company has a 20% income tax rate. Included in the company's trial balance at August 31, 2005, are the following:

Cost of goods sold	$512,050	Interest expense	$ 9,200
Cash dividends	42,480	Operating expenses	232,750
Dividends payable	10,620	Sales	931,000

Instructions
Prepare a combined multiple-step income statement and statement of retained earnings for the year ended August 31, 2005.

E14–6 On January 1, 2005, Windsor Corporation had retained earnings of $580,000. During the year, Windsor had the following selected transactions:

1. Declared cash dividends, $120,000.
2. Corrected overstatement of 2004 net income because of amortization error, $35,000.
3. Earned income before income taxes of $390,000.
4. Declared stock dividends, $60,000.
5. Reacquired 20,000 common shares for $45,000 more than the original issue price. This was the first time the company had ever reacquired its own shares.

Prepare statement of retained earnings.
(SO 3) AP

Interactive Homework

Instructions

Prepare a statement of retained earnings for the year ended December 31, 2005. The company has a 40% income tax rate.

E14–7 During 2005, Kettle Creek Corporation had the following transactions and events:

1. Declared a cash dividend.
2. Issued common shares for cash.
3. Completed a 3-for-1 stock split.
4. Declared a stock dividend.
5. Made a prior period correction for an overstatement of net income.
6. Issued the common shares required by the stock dividend declaration in (4) above.
7. Paid the cash dividend declared in (1) above.
8. Repurchased common shares for less than their initial issue price.

Indicate effects of transactions on shareholders' equity.
(SO 1, 3, 4) AP

Instructions

Indicate the effect(s) of each of the above items on the subdivisions of shareholders' equity. Present your answer in tabular form with the following columns. Use "I" for increase, "D" for decrease, and "NE" for no effect. Item 1 is given as an example.

	Contributed Capital			
Item	Share Capital	Additional	Retained Earnings	Total Shareholders' Equity
1.	NE	NE	D	D

E14–8 On January 1, 2005, Knowledge Corporation had an unlimited number of no par value common shares authorized, of which 150,000 had been issued for $1,500,000, and retained earnings of $750,000. The company issued 50,000 common shares at $14 on July 1, and declared a 3-for-2 stock split on September 30 when the market value was $18 per share. The company earned net income of $410,000 for the year.

Record stock dividend; prepare shareholders' equity section.
(SO 1, 4) AP

Instructions

(a) Journalize the declaration of a 15% stock dividend on December 10, 2005, when the market value is $15 per share.
(b) Prepare the shareholders' equity section at December 31, 2005, assuming that the stock dividend has not yet been distributed.

E14–9 The following account information appears in the ledger of Byung-Kee Inc. after the books are closed at December 31, 2005:

Prepare shareholders' equity section.
(SO 4) AP

Common Shares (no par value, unlimited number of shares authorized, 300,000 shares issued)	$300,000
Common Stock Dividends Distributable	75,000
$8 Preferred Shares (no par value, cumulative, unlimited number of shares authorized, 2,000 shares issued)	150,000
Retained Earnings	900,000

Instructions

Prepare the shareholders' equity section of the balance sheet at December 31, 2005, assuming $100,000 of retained earnings is restricted for a plant expansion.

Calculate earnings per share.
(SO 4) AP

E14–10 At December 31, 2005, Morse Corporation has 2,000 $8-cumulative preferred shares and 100,000 common shares. Morse's net income for the year is $547,000.

Instructions

Calculate the earnings per share under each of the following independent assumptions. (Round to two decimals.)
(a) The dividend to preferred shareholders was declared.
(b) The dividend to preferred shareholders was not declared.
(c) $10,000 of preferred dividends in arrears from 2004 were declared and paid in 2005 in addition to the 2005 preferred dividend.
(d) Assume instead that the preferred shares are noncumulative and that $10,000 of preferred dividends were declared and paid during the year.

Calculate earnings per share.
(SO 4) AP

Interactive Homework

E14–11 Chinook Corporation reported net income of $339,950 for its November 30, 2005, year end. Cash dividends of $75,000 on the common shares and of $45,000 on the preferred shares were declared during the year. The following changes in common shares also occurred:

Dec. 1, 2004	The opening number of common shares was 60,000.
Feb. 28, 2005	Sold 10,000 common shares for $200,000 cash.
May 31, 2005	Reacquired 5,000 shares for $90,000 cash.
Nov. 1, 2005	Issued 15,000 common shares in exchange for land with a market value of $310,000.

Instructions

(a) Calculate the income available for the common shareholders.
(b) Calculate the weighted average number of common shares for the year.
(c) Calculate the earnings per share for the year.
(d) Why is it necessary to calculate a weighted average number of shares? Why not use the number of shares at the end of the year?

Calculate ratios.
(SO 4) AP

E14–12 The following financial information is available for the **Bank of Montreal** as at October 31 (in millions, except for per share amounts):

	2002	2001	2000
Net income	$1,417	$1,471	$1,857
Preferred share dividend (total)	$79	$80	$101
Weighted average number of common shares	491	511	531
Dividends per common share	$1.20	$1.12	$1.00
Market price per common share	$24.59	$21.37	$23.19

Instructions

Calculate the earnings per share, price-earnings ratio, and payout ratio for each of the three years. Comment on the Bank of Montreal's earnings and dividend performance.

Problems: Set A

Indicate impact of equity transactions.
(SO 1, 3, 4) AN

P14–1A Savary Island Development Inc. has 200,000 common shares issued on November 1, 2004, the beginning of the fiscal year. Juanita Tolentino is the president and largest shareholder, owning 20% of the common shares. On November 1, the shares were trading on the Toronto Stock Exchange for $8 per share. The November 1 balances in Common Shares and Retained Earnings were $1,000,000 and $250,000, respectively.

You are provided with the following information about selected events and transactions that occurred during the fiscal year ended October 31, 2005:

Jan.	1	Savary Island issued another 50,000 common shares in order to finance a new development project. The shares were sold for $9 cash per share. Juanita purchased 10,000 of these shares in order to maintain her 20% interest in the company.
May	1	The company effected a 3-for-2 stock split when the company's shares were trading at $12.75 per share. After the split, each share was trading at $8.50.

Aug. 31 Savary Island declared and issued a 3% stock dividend. The shares were trading at $9 just prior to the announcement.

Oct. 31 The share price at the close of business was $10.

Instructions

Starting with the November 1, 2004 opening balances, indicate the impact of each transaction on the following:

(a) The balance of retained earnings
(b) The number of shares issued
(c) The number of shares held by Juanita Tolentino
(d) The share price
(e) The market value of Juanita Tolentino's portfolio of common shares

P14–2A The condensed balance sheet of Laporte Corporation reports the following amounts:

Compare impact of cash and stock dividends on company and shareholder. (SO 1) AN

LAPORTE CORPORATION
Balance Sheet (partial)
June 30, 2005

Total assets	$15,500,000
Liabilities and shareholders' equity	
Total liabilities	$ 5,500,000
Shareholders' equity	
Common shares, unlimited number authorized,	
400,000 shares issued, no par value	2,000,000
Retained earnings	8,000,000
Total shareholders' equity	10,000,000
Total liabilities and shareholders' equity	$15,500,000

Laporte wishes to assess the impact of two possible dividend alternatives on the corporation and its shareholders:

1. Payment of a $1.50 per share cash dividend
2. Distribution of a 5% stock dividend. The market price of the common shares is currently $30 per share.

Instructions

(a) Determine the impact on assets, liabilities, shareholders' equity (common shares and retained earnings), and the number of shares of each of the two alternatives.
(b) 1. Assess the impact of each alternative on a shareholder who currently owns 1,000 common shares at a cost of $28,000. Which alternative is more beneficial for the shareholder?
    2. How would shareholders record their receipt of the cash dividend or stock dividend on their own records?

P14–3A The shareholders' equity accounts of Tmao, Inc. at January 1, 2005, are as follows:

Prepare statement of retained earnings. (SO 1, 3) AP

TMAO INC.
Balance Sheet (partial)
January 1, 2005

Shareholders' equity	
$9 preferred shares, no par value, unlimited number authorized,	
4,000 shares issued	$ 400,000
Common shares, no par value, unlimited number authorized,	
160,000 shares issued	800,000
Retained earnings	450,000
Total shareholders' equity	$1,650,000

The company has a 30% income tax rate. During 2005, the company had the following transactions and events:

July 1 Declared a $0.25 cash dividend to common shareholders.
Aug. 1 Discovered a $70,000 overstatement of 2004 amortization.
Sept. 1 Paid the cash dividend declared on July 1.
Dec. 1 Declared a 10% common stock dividend when the market value of the shares was $12

per share.

Dec. 15 Declared the annual cash dividend to preferred shareholders, payable January 31, 2006.
    31 Determined that net income before income taxes for the year was $350,000.

Instructions

Prepare a statement of retained earnings for the year ended December 31, 2005. There are no preferred dividends in arrears.

Prepare income statement and statement of retained earnings.
(SO 2, 3) AP

P14–4A The ledger of Hyperchip Corporation at November 30, 2005, contains the following summary data:

Amortization expense	$ 355,000
Cash dividends	162,500
Common shares (32,500 issued)	325,000
Cost of goods sold	7,280,000
Net sales	9,124,000
Operating expenses	1,120,000
Other expenses	83,000
Other revenues	48,000
Retained earnings, December 1, 2004	755,000

Your analysis reveals the following additional information:

1. The company has a 40% income tax rate.
2. During the year, Hyperchip decided to change its amortization method from straight-line to declining-balance. The cumulative effect of the change on prior years' income was a decrease of $57,000 before income tax. (Assume that amortization under the new method is correctly included for the current year in the above data.)
3. Included in the operating expenses above is $69,500 of expenses that should have been recorded in the previous year when they were incurred. The error was made because last year the company had an inexperienced accountant who thought it was correct to wait and record expenses when they were paid.
4. No shares were issued during the year.

Instructions

(a) Prepare a multiple-step income statement for the year ended November 30, 2005.
(b) Calculate earnings per share for the year ended November 30, 2005.
(c) Prepare a statement of retained earnings for the year ended November 30, 2005.

Record and post transactions; prepare shareholders' equity section.
(SO 1, 3, 4) AP

P14–5A On January 1, 2005, Cedeno Inc. had the following shareholders' equity balances:

CEDENO INC.
Balance Sheet (partial)
January 1, 2005

Shareholders' equity

Common shares, no par value (unlimited number of shares authorized, 1,000,000 shares issued)	$3,000,000
Stock dividends distributable	400,000
Retained earnings	1,200,000
Total shareholders' equity	$4,600,000

During 2005, the following transactions and events occurred:

Jan. 20 Issued 100,000 common shares as a result of a 10% stock dividend declared on December 15, 2004.
Feb. 12 Issued 60,000 common shares for cash at $5 per share.
Mar. 31 Corrected an error that had understated the cost of goods sold for 2004 by $60,000.
Nov. 2 Reacquired 10,000 shares for $5.50 cash each.
Dec. 31 Declared and paid a cash dividend of $0.25 per share.
    31 Earned net income of $400,000.

The company has a 40% income tax rate.

Instructions

(a) Journalize the transactions and summary closing entries for net income and dividends.
(b) Enter the beginning balances, and post the entries in (a) to the shareholders' equity accounts. (*Note:* Open additional shareholders' equity accounts as needed.)
(c) Prepare the shareholders' equity section of the balance sheet at December 31, 2005.

P14–6A On January 1, 2005, LeBlanc Corporation had the following shareholders' equity accounts:

Record and post transactions; prepare shareholders' equity section.
(SO 1, 4) AP

LEBLANC CORPORATION
Balance Sheet (partial)
January 1, 2005

Shareholders' equity

Common shares (no par value, unlimited number of shares authorized, 90,000 shares issued)	$1,100,000
Retained earnings	540,000
Total shareholders' equity	$1,640,000

During the year, the following transactions occurred:

Jan. 15 Declared a $1 cash dividend per share to shareholders of record on January 31, payable February 15.

Feb. 15 Paid the dividend declared in January.

Apr. 15 Declared a 10% stock dividend to shareholders of record on April 30, distributable May 15. On April 15, the market price of each share was $23.

May 15 Issued the shares for the stock dividend.

July 1 Announced a 2-for-1 stock split. The market price per share prior to the announcement was $30.

Dec. 1 Declared a $0.60 per share cash dividend to shareholders of record on December 15, payable January 10, 2006.

31 Determined that net income before income taxes for the year was $250,000. The company has a 25% income tax rate.

Instructions

(a) Journalize the transactions and the summary closing entries for net income and dividends.
(b) Enter the beginning balances and post the entries in part (a) to the shareholders' equity accounts. (*Note:* Open additional shareholders' equity accounts as needed.)
(c) Prepare the shareholders' equity section of the balance sheet at December 31, 2005.

P14–7A After the books have been closed, the ledger of Jajoo Corporation at December 31, 2005, contains the following shareholders' equity accounts:

Allocate dividend. Prepare statement of retained earnings and shareholders' equity section.
(SO 1, 3) AP

Preferred shares (10,000 shares issued)	$1,100,000
Common shares (400,000 shares issued)	2,000,000
Contributed capital—reacquisition of common shares	450,000
Common stock dividend distributable	170,000
Retained earnings	2,390,000

A review of the accounting records reveals the following:

1. Both the common and preferred shares have no par value and an unlimited number of shares authorized.
2. The preferred shares are noncumulative with an $11 dividend. The 10,000 shares were issued on January 15, 2003. No dividend was paid to the preferred shareholders in 2003 or 2004.
3. The January 1 balance in Retained Earnings was $2,450,000.
4. On January 15, reacquired 20,000 common shares for $7.50 cash per share.
5. On October 1, 100,000 common shares were sold for cash at $8 per share.
6. A cash dividend of $650,000 was declared and properly allocated to Preferred Shares and Common Shares on November 1.
7. On December 31, a 5% common stock dividend was declared when the market price per share was $8.50.
8. Net income for the year was $760,000.
9. On December 31, 2005, the directors authorized a $100,000 restriction of retained earn-

ings for a plant expansion.

Instructions

(a) Calculate the allocation of the cash dividend to preferred and common shareholders.

(b) Prepare a statement of retained earnings for the year ended December 31, 2005.

(c) Prepare the shareholders' equity section of the balance sheet at December 31, 2005.

Calculate earnings per share.
(SO 4) AP

P14–8A The shareholders' equity accounts of Blue Bay Logistics Ltd. on April 1, 2004, the beginning of the fiscal year, appear below:

$8 preferred shares (20,000 shares issued)	$1,800,000
Common shares (500,000 shares issued)	3,750,000
Retained earnings	1,550,000
Total shareholders' equity	$7,100,000

During the year, the following transactions occurred:

1. On June 1, 2004, the company reacquired 12,000 common shares for $9 cash per share.
2. On July 1, 2004, the company issued 50,000 common shares for $9.50 cash per share.
3. On September 30, 2004, Blue Bay paid $78,000 to reacquire 8,000 common shares.
4. An additional 60,000 common shares were issued on January 31, 2005, in exchange for land. The market value of the common shares issued was $10 per share.
5. Net income for the year ended March 31, 2005, was $975,000.

Instructions

(a) Calculate the weighted average number of common shares for the year.

(b) Assume the preferred shares are cumulative and one year in arrears:

    1. Calculate the earnings per share if no preferred dividends are declared during the year.

    2. Calculate the earnings per share if the preferred share dividends for the current and prior year are declared during the year.

(c) Assume the preferred shares are not cumulative:

    1. Calculate the earnings per share if no preferred share dividends are declared during the year.

    2. Calculate the earnings per share if the company declares a preferred share dividend for $80,000.

    3. Calculate the earnings per share if the company declares a total of $535,000 of dividends. (*Hint:* First allocate the dividend between the preferred and common shareholders.)

Calculate ratios and comment.
(SO 4) AP

P14–9A The following selected information is available for the **Canadian National Railway Company (CN)** (in millions, except for market price per common share):

	December 31, 2002	December 31, 2001
Weighted average number of common shares	196.7	192.1
Net income	$571	$727
Common cash dividends	$170	$150
Preferred cash dividends	$6	$12
Market price per common share	$64.83	$76.18

Instructions

(a) Calculate the following ratios for CN for 2002 and 2001:

    1. Earnings per share

    2. Price-earnings ratio

    3. Payout ratio (for common shares only)

(b) Comment on the above ratios for 2002 compared to those for 2001.

Problems: Set B

P14–1B   Gull Lake Enterprises Inc. had 100,000 common shares at July 1, 2004, the beginning of its fiscal year. Mark Bradbury is the president and largest shareholder and owns 25% of the common shares. On July 1, the common shares were trading on the Toronto Stock Exchange for $25 per share. Gull Lake Enterprises' Common Shares and Retained Earnings accounts had opening balances of $2,000,000 and $350,000, respectively.

Indicate impact of equity transactions.
(SO 1, 3, 4) AN

You are provided with the following information about selected events and transactions that occurred during the year ended June 30, 2005:

Aug. 31, 2004 The company declared and issued a 4% stock dividend. The shares were trading at $28 per share on that day.

Dec.   1, 2004 The company issued another 20,000 common shares. This issue was needed in order to finance new product development. Mark Bradbury acquired 5,000 of these shares to keep his 25% interest in the shares of the company. The market value of the shares was $30 per share.

Mar. 31, 2005 The company's shares were trading at $26 per share and the company effected a 2-for-1 stock split. After the stock split, each share was trading at $13.

June 30, 2005 The share price at the close of business on June 30, 2005, was $10.50.

Instructions

Starting with the July 1, 2004 opening balances, indicate the impact of each transaction on the following:

(a) The balance of retained earnings
(b) The number of shares issued
(c) The number of shares held by Mark Bradbury
(d) The share price
(e) The market value of Mark Bradbury's portfolio of common shares

P14–2B   The condensed balance sheet of Erickson Corporation reports the following amounts:

Compare impact of cash dividend, stock dividend, and stock split on company and shareholder.
(SO 1) AN

ERICKSON CORPORATION
Balance Sheet (partial)
January 31, 2005

Total assets		$8,000,000
Liabilities and shareholders' equity		
Liabilities		$1,500,000
Shareholders' equity		
Common shares, unlimited number authorized,		
500,000 issued, no par value	$3,000,000	
Retained earnings	3,500,000	6,500,000
Total liabilities and shareholders' equity		$8,000,000

Erickson Corporation wishes to assess the impact of three possible alternatives on the corporation and its shareholders. The market price of the common shares is currently $20 per share. The alternatives are (1) a payment of a $1.20 per share cash dividend, (2) distribution of a 6% stock dividend, or (3) a 2-for-1 stock split. The market price is anticipated to fall to $10 per share after the stock split.

Instructions

(a) Determine the impact on assets, liabilities, shareholders' equity (common shares and retained earnings), and the number of shares involved under each of the three alternatives.
(b) Assume an Erickson shareholder currently owns 2,000 common shares at a cost of $35,000. Which alternative is more beneficial for the shareholder? Assess the impact of each alternative.

Prepare statement of
retained earnings.
(SO 1, 3) AP

P14–3B The condensed balance sheet of Kanada Inc. reports the following amounts:

KANADA INC.
Balance Sheet (partial)
September 30, 2004

Shareholders' equity

$7 preferred shares, cumulative, no par value, unlimited number
authorized, 6,000 shares issued $ 465,000

Common shares, no par value, unlimited number
authorized, 225,000 issued   900,000

Retained earnings   540,000

Total shareholders' equity $1,905,000

Kanada has a 35% income tax rate. During the following fiscal year, Kanada had these transactions and events:

Dec. 31, 2004 Declared a $0.20 cash dividend to common shareholders.
Jan.   31, 2005 Paid the cash dividend declared on Dec. 31.
Mar. 14, 2005 Declared a 4% common stock dividend when the market value of the shares was $10 per share.
Apr.   5, 2005 Distributed the common stock dividend declared on Mar. 14.
July   7, 2005 Decided to change from declining-balance amortization to straight-line amortization. The cumulative effect of the change on prior years' net income was an increase of $33,000 before income tax.
Aug.   1, 2005 Discovered a $54,000 understatement of cost of goods sold in the prior year's income statement.
Sept. 20, 2005 Declared the annual cash dividend payable to the preferred shareholders, payable on October 25. There were no dividends in arrears.
        25, 2005 Declared a 2-for-1 reverse stock split.
        30, 2005 Determined that net income before income taxes was $284,000.

Instructions

Prepare a statement of retained earnings for the year ended September 30, 2005.

Prepare income statement
and statement of retained
earnings.
(SO 2, 3) AP

P14–4B The ledger of Coquitlam Corporation at December 31, 2005, contains the following summary data:

Cash dividends	$ 125,000
Cost of goods sold	962,500
Operating expenses	180,625
Other expenses	28,000
Other revenues	47,000
Retained earnings, January 1, 2005	642,000
Sales	1,750,000

Your analysis reveals the following additional information:

1. The company has a 35% income tax rate.
2. In 2004 the company incorrectly recorded operating expenses of $62,700 that should have been recorded as operating expenses in 2005. This error has not been corrected in the above amounts.
3. During the year, Coquitlam decided to change its inventory cost flow assumption from weighted average to FIFO. The cumulative effect of the change on prior years' income was an increase of $38,200 before income tax. (Assume that cost of goods sold under FIFO is correctly calculated for the current year in the above data.)
4. There were 100,000 common shares on January 1, 2005. On April 1, 2005, Coquitlam issued an additional 25,000 shares for $25 cash per share.

Instructions

(a) Prepare a multiple-step income statement for the year ended December 31, 2005.
(b) Calculate earnings per share for the year ended December 31, 2005.
(c) Prepare a statement of retained earnings for the year ended December 31, 2005.

P14–5B The shareholders' equity accounts of Fryman Ltd. at January 1, 2005, are as follows:

Record and post transactions; prepare shareholders' equity section.
(SO 1, 3, 4) AP

FRYMAN LTD.
Balance Sheet (partial)
January 1, 2005

Shareholders' equity

Preferred shares, no par value, unlimited number authorized,		
12,000 shares issued		$ 800,000
Common shares, no par value, unlimited number authorized,		
250,000 shares issued		500,000
Contributed capital—reacquired common shares		100,000
Retained earnings		900,000
Total shareholders' equity		$2,300,000

During 2005, the company had the following transactions and events:

July   7 Declared a $0.50 cash dividend on common shares.
Aug.   1 Discovered a $45,000 overstatement of 2004 amortization. The company has a 30% income tax rate.
Sept. 1 Paid the cash dividend declared on July 7.
Dec.   1 Declared a 10% stock dividend on common shares when the market value of the shares was $18 per share.
      15 Declared a $4.50 cash dividend on preferred shares, payable January 15, 2006. The preferred shares are noncumulative.
      31 Determined that net income for the year was $395,000.
      31 Recognized a $200,000 restriction of retained earnings for a plant expansion.

Instructions

(a) Journalize the transactions and summary closing entries.
(b) Enter the beginning balances in the accounts and post to the shareholders' equity accounts. (*Note*: Open additional shareholders' equity accounts as needed.)
(c) Prepare the shareholders' equity section of the balance sheet at December 31, 2005.

P14–6B On January 1, 2005, Asaad Corporation had the following shareholders' equity accounts:

Record and post transactions; prepare shareholders' equity section.
(SO 1, 4) AP

ASAAD CORPORATION
Balance Sheet (partial)
January 1, 2005

Shareholders' equity

Common shares (no par value, unlimited number of shares	
authorized, 75,000 shares issued)	$1,700,000
Retained earnings	600,000
Total shareholders' equity	$2,300,000

During the year, the following transactions occurred:

Feb.   1 Declared a $1 cash dividend per share to shareholders of record on February 15, payable March 1.
Mar.   1 Paid the dividend declared in February.
Apr.   1 Announced a 3-for-1 stock split. Prior to the split, the market price per share was $36.
July   1 Declared a 6% stock dividend to shareholders of record on July 15, distributable July 31. On July 1, the market price of the shares was $16 per share.
      31 Issued the shares for the stock dividend.
Dec.   1 Declared a $0.40 per share dividend to shareholders of record on December 15, payable January 5, 2006.
      31 Determined that net income before income taxes for the year was $350,000. The company has a 25% income tax rate.

Instructions

(a) Journalize the transactions and summary closing entries for net income and dividends.
(b) Enter the beginning balances, and post the entries in (a) to the shareholders' equity accounts. (*Note*: Open additional shareholders' equity accounts as needed.)
(c) Prepare the shareholders' equity section of the balance sheet at December 31, 2005.

Allocate dividend. Prepare statement of retained earnings and shareholders' equity section. Calculate ratios.
(SO 1, 3, 4) AP

P14–7B The post-closing trial balance of Michaud Corporation at December 31, 2005, contains the following shareholders' equity accounts:

Preferred shares (15,000 shares issued)	$ 750,000
Common shares (250,000 shares issued)	3,000,000
Retained earnings	1,133,000

A review of the accounting records reveals the following:

1. Preferred shares are cumulative with dividends of $4 per share.
2. An unlimited number of no par value preferred and common shares is authorized.
3. The January 1 balance in Retained Earnings was $1,150,000.
4. On April 1, 25,000 common shares were reacquired for $16 per share.
5. On September 1, the company discovered an error of $60,000 that understated amortization expense in 2004. The net-of-tax effect was properly debited to Retained Earnings. The company has a 30% income tax rate.
6. A cash dividend of $370,000 was declared and properly allocated to preferred and common shareholders on October 1. No dividends were paid to preferred shareholders in 2004.
7. The market value per share on December 31, 2005, was $18.
8. Net income for the year was $495,000.
9. On December 31, 2005, the directors authorized the disclosure of a $200,000 restriction of retained earnings for a plant expansion.

Instructions

(a) Calculate the allocation of the cash dividend to preferred and common shareholders.
(b) Prepare a statement of retained earnings for the year.
(c) Prepare the shareholders' equity section of the balance sheet as at December 31, 2005.
(d) Calculate the earnings per share.
(e) Calculate the price-earnings ratio as at December 31, 2005.

Calculate earnings per share.
(SO 4) AP

P14–8B The shareholders' equity accounts of Gualtieri Inc. on August 1, 2004, the beginning of the fiscal year, appear below:

$4 preferred shares (25,000 shares issued)	$1,250,000
Common shares (350,000 shares issued)	3,750,000
Retained earnings	2,250,000
Total shareholders' equity	$7,250,000

During the year, the following transactions occurred:

1. On November 30, 2004, the company issued 40,000 common shares for $18 cash per share.
2. On February 1, 2005, the company reacquired 6,000 common shares for $19 cash per share.
3. On March 1, 2005, Gualtieri issued 30,000 common shares in exchange for equipment. The market value of the common shares issued was $600,000.
4. An additional 6,600 common shares were reacquired July 31, 2005, for $19 per share.
5. Net income for the year ended July 31, 2005, was $1,025,000.

Instructions

(a) Calculate the weighted average number of common shares for the year.
(b) Assume the preferred shares are cumulative and one year in arrears:
   1. Calculate the earnings per share if no preferred dividends are declared during the year.
   2. Calculate the earnings per share if the preferred share dividends for the current and prior year are declared during the year.
(c) Assume the preferred shares are not cumulative:
   1. Calculate the earnings per share if no preferred share dividends are declared during the year.
   2. Calculate the earnings per share if the company declares a preferred share dividend of $60,000.
   3. Calculate the earnings per share if the company declares a total of $375,000 of dividends. (*Hint*: First allocate the dividend between the preferred and common shareholders.)
(d) Why is it important to use a weighted average number of shares in the earnings per share calculations? Why not just use the number of shares issued at year end?

P14–9B The following selected information is available for the **National Bank of Canada** for the year ended October 31:

Calculate ratios and comment.
(SO 4) AN

(in millions, except for market price)	2002	2001
Weighted average number of common shares	186.6	189.9
Net income	$429	$563
Common cash dividends	$174	$156
Preferred cash dividends	$21	$35
Average common shareholders' equity	$3,612	$3,480
Market price per common share	$29.39	$24.25

Instructions

(a) Calculate the following ratios for 2002 and 2001:
   1. Payout ratio   3. Price-earnings ratio
   2. Earnings per share   4. Return on common shareholders' equity
(b) Comment on the above ratios for 2002, in comparison to the prior year.

Continuing Cookie Chronicle

(Note: This is a continuation of the Cookie Chronicle from Chapters 1 through 13.)

After establishing their company's fiscal year end to be October 31, Natalie and Curtis began operating Cookie & Coffee Creations Ltd. on November 1, 2005. As at that date, after the issues of shares, the share capital section of the company's balance sheet was as follows:

Share capital
   $6 cumulative preferred shares, no par value,
      10,000 shares authorized, 2,000 shares issued $10,000
   Common shares, no par value, unlimited number
      of shares authorized, 23,930 shares issued   23,930

The company had the following selected transactions during its first year of operations:

2006
Jan.   1 Issued an additional 500 preferred shares to Natalie's brother for $2,500 cash.
June 30 Repurchased 750 shares issued to the lawyer, for $500 cash. The lawyer had decided to retire and wanted to liquidate all of her assets.
Oct. 15 The company had a very successful first year of operations and as a result declared dividends of $25,000, payable November 15, 2006. (Indicate the amounts payable to the preferred shareholders and to the common shareholders.)
Oct. 31 The company earned revenues of $462,500 and incurred expenses of $406,500 (excluding income tax). Record income tax expense, assuming the company has a 20% income tax rate.

Instructions

(a) Prepare the journal entries to record each of the above transactions.
(b) Prepare all of the closing entries required on October 31, 2006.
(c) Prepare the statement of retained earnings for the year ended October 31, 2006.
(d) Prepare the shareholders' equity section of the balance sheet as at October 31, 2006.
(e) Calculate the earnings per share.

Cumulative Coverage—Chapters 13 and 14

Cyber Force Corp.'s post-closing trial balance at December 31, 2004, is presented below:

CYBER FORCE CORP.
Post-Closing Trial Balance
December 31, 2004

	Debit	Credit
Cash	$ 45,820	
Inventory	138,485	
Equipment	144,950	
Accumulated amortization—equipment		$ 43,485
Income taxes payable		25,500
Notes payable (due on July 1, 2007)		75,000
$7 preferred shares, no par value, cumulative, unlimited number authorized, 350 issued		35,000
Common shares, no par value, unlimited number authorized, 100,000 issued		100,000
Retained earnings		50,270
	$329,255	$329,255

Other information:

1. The preferred share dividends were one year in arrears on December 31, 2004.
2. Cyber Force uses straight-line amortization. The equipment on hand from December 31, 2004, had a total estimated 10-year useful life and no residual value.
3. The company has a 25% income tax rate.

The following transactions (in summary form) occurred during 2005:

1. Cash sales were $845,750, and cost of goods sold was $490,535. (Cyber Force uses a perpetual inventory system.)
2. Cash purchases of inventory were $510,650.
3. Cash payments for operating expenses were $192,060.
4. A cash payment of interest on a note payable on December 31, 2005, was for $6,000.
5. The income taxes payable from December 31, 2004, were paid.
6. On March 1, 2005, 6,000 common shares were issued in exchange for equipment with a fair market value of $15,750. The market value of the shares issued on that date was $16,600. The equipment had an expected useful life of 8 years and no residual value.
7. On October 1, 2005, 10,000 common shares were reacquired for $2.65 per share.
8. On December 1, 2005, the preferred share dividends were declared and paid.
9. On December 31, 2005, a $0.25 per share dividend was declared on the common shares, payable on January 10, 2006.

Instructions

(a) Prepare and post journal entries for the above events. Remember to include an adjusting entry for amortization and for income tax expense.
(b) Prepare an adjusted trial balance at December 31, 2005.
(c) Prepare a multiple-step income statement, a statement of retained earnings, and a classified balance sheet.
(d) Prepare closing entries.
(e) Calculate the basic earnings per share.

Financial Reporting and Analysis

Practice
Tools

Financial Reporting Problem

BYP14–1 Refer to the consolidated financial statements and accompanying notes for **The Forzani Group Ltd.** reproduced in Appendix A.

Instructions

(a) During the year ended February 2, 2003, how many new common shares were issued to the general public? To employees exercising stock options?
(b) At February 2, 2003, what percentage of the company's assets was financed by shareholders' equity? At January 27, 2002?
(c) Did Forzani report any prior period adjustments in fiscal 2003 or 2002?
(d) Basic earnings per share for 2003 was reported in the chapter in Illustration 14-6. How much was basic earnings per share for 2002? Did earnings per share improve or deteriorate in 2003?
(e) How much (if anything) was paid or distributed in dividends during fiscal 2003 and 2002? Why might a company choose *not* to pay dividends?

Interpreting Financial Statements

BYP14–2 The Jean Coutu Group (PJC) Inc. operates a network of retail drug stores in Canada and the United States. In September 2002, Jean Coutu declared, for the third time in its history, a 2-for-1 stock split of its Class A subordinate voting shares and Class B shares. At May 31, 2003, the company's year end, the total number of Class A shares issued was 102,569,550 and Class B shares totalled 124,000,000. Both share classes are considered common shares.

The following information is also available (in thousands, except for share price data):

	2003	2002
Net income	$163,622	$139,879
Average shareholders' equity	982,964	888,993
Cash dividends	27,134	21,404
Share price	15.71	19.12
Weighted average number of shares	226,053	225,176

Instructions

(a) Explain the different effects that a cash dividend and stock split would have on Jean Coutu's financial position and number of shares.
(b) Why do you think Jean Coutu has split its Class A and Class B shares in the past?
(c) If the market price for a share before the stock split in September 2002 was $32.95, what do you think the market price for a share would be immediately after the stock split?
(d) Calculate the return on equity, earnings per share, price-earnings ratio, and payout ratio for 2003 and 2002. Comment on the company's profitability.

Accounting on the Web

BYP14–3 SEDAR (System for Electronic Document Analysis and Retrieval) contains securities filings by Canadian public companies. This includes financial statements, annual reports, prospectuses, press releases, and other public company filings. This case reviews a selection of documents on this website and on the stock exchange website to obtain information about a company's equity and shares.

Instructions
Specific requirements of this Internet case are available on the Weygandt website.

Critical Thinking

Collaborative Learning Activity

BYP14–4 The Track Corporation is a diversified manufacturer of tires and vinyl products. Selected financial data, in millions of dollars, for a recent two-year period were as follows.

	Current Year	Prior Year
Net income	$209.9	$ 83.6
Cumulative effect on prior years' income of change in amortization method from straight-line to declining-balance	(2.7)	
Cash dividends	8.8	9.8
Stock dividends	43.3	37.0
Retained earnings, end of year	560.4	405.3

The notes to the company's financial statements indicate that the weighted average number of common shares was 25,179,000 for the current year and 23,651,000 for the prior year.

Instructions
With the class divided into groups, do the following:
(a) Explain whether the cumulative effect of the change in amortization method should be treated as an adjustment of the current year's income or as an adjustment to opening retained earnings.
(b) Calculate the earnings per share data for the company for each year.
(c) Discuss the reasons why a company might decide to issue a stock dividend rather than a cash dividend.
(d) Prepare a statement of retained earnings for the current year.

Communication Activity

BYP14–5 Earnings per share is the most commonly cited financial ratio and share prices rise and fall in reaction to a company's earnings per share. The price-earnings ratio is also published in many newspapers' stock market listings.

Instructions
Write a memo explaining why earnings per share and the price-earnings ratio are so important to investors. Explain how both ratios are calculated and how they relate to each other. Include in your memo an explanation of how to interpret a high or low price-earnings ratio.

Ethics Case

BYP14–6 Flambeau Corporation has paid 60 consecutive quarterly cash dividends (15 years' worth). The last six months, however, have been a real cash drain on the company as profit margins have been greatly narrowed by increasing competition. With a cash balance sufficient to meet only day-to-day operating needs, the president, Vince Ramsey, has decided that a stock dividend instead of a cash dividend should be declared. He tells Flambeau's financial vice-president, Janice Rahn, to issue a press release stating that the company is extending its consecutive dividend record with the issue of a 10% stock dividend. "Write the press release to convince the shareholders that the stock dividend is just as good as a cash dividend," he orders. "Just watch our share price rise when we announce the stock dividend. It must be a good thing if that happens."

Instructions
(a) Who are the stakeholders in this situation?
(b) Is there anything unethical about Ramsey's intentions or actions?
(c) As a shareholder, which would you rather receive—a cash dividend or a stock dividend? Why?

Answers to Self-Study Questions
1. a   2. c   3. c   4. b   5. b   6. a   7. c   8. b   9. a   10. c

Answer to Forzani Review It Question 3
Forzani did not declare any dividends or stock splits in 2003.

Remember to go back to the Navigator Box at the beginning of the chapter to check off your completed work.

concepts for review >>

Before studying this chapter, you should understand or, if necessary, review:

a. What a current liability is. What a long-term liability is. (Ch. 4, pp. 170–171 and Ch. 10, p. 484)

b. How to record adjusting entries for interest expense. (Ch. 3, p. 110)

c. How to record entries for the issue of notes payable and related interest expense. (Ch. 10, pp. 485–486).

Investing in Higher Education

MONTREAL, Que.—When Concordia University needed cash for a major expansion project in 2002, the institution did something it had never done before—it raised part of the funds by selling bonds. At $225 million, Concordia's issue remains the largest Canadian university bond offering to date, though it was not the first of its kind.

The initiative is part of a trend that began in 2001 with the University of Toronto, which raised $160 million, followed by UBC's offering worth $125 million. Faced with rising enrolments and dwindling resources from provincial governments, post-secondary institutions are turning to the private sector to help finance upgrades and repairs.

Today, at least half a dozen institutions across the country have raised a combined total of nearly $1 billion through bonds, including U of T, UBC, York, McMaster, Concordia, and McGill. Still others are talking of doing the same.

By issuing bonds, universities pay less interest than they would have to pay with a bank loan. And unlike bank loans, which usually have to be renegotiated every few years, the interest rate for a bond offering is locked in for the duration of the term.

Concordia offered a series of 40-year unsecured bonds with an interest rate of 6.55% paid semi-annually and a minimum purchase of $150,000—effectively gearing the debenture towards large institutional investors such as pension and mutual funds.

Dominion Bond Rating Service gave the school a credit rating of A, while Moody's Investors Service assigned it an A1. Just like credit ratings for individuals, these ratings reflect a school's ability to meet its financial obligations. They are affected by many factors, including the school's age, size, and location, as well as

Concordia University: www.concordia.ca

factors affecting its regular funding from tuition fees, government grants, and donations.

The money raised by Concordia will be used to help finance a $351-million project involving the construction of three new buildings and various improvements to existing facilities. Work is slated for completion by 2006.

Some universities have considered the bond option and rejected it, and critics point out that not-for-profit organizations in general should not be going into debt. But so far investors have decided otherwise. The handful of Canadian university bond offerings to date have sold out fast—in some cases within hours—paving the way for others to follow suit.

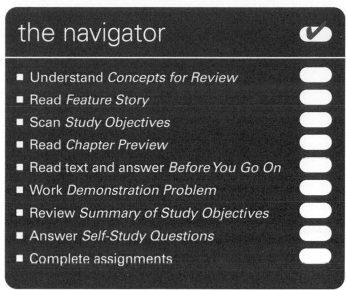

the navigator ✔

- Understand *Concepts for Review*
- Read *Feature Story*
- Scan *Study Objectives*
- Read *Chapter Preview*
- Read text and answer *Before You Go On*
- Work *Demonstration Problem*
- Review *Summary of Study Objectives*
- Answer *Self-Study Questions*
- Complete assignments

chapter 15
Long-Term Liabilities

study objectives >>

After studying this chapter, you should be able to:

1. Describe the advantages and illustrate the impact of issuing bonds instead of common shares.
2. Prepare the entries for the issue of bonds and the recording of interest expense.
3. Prepare the entries when bonds are retired.
4. Account for long-term notes payable.
5. Contrast the accounting for operating leases and capital leases.
6. Explain and illustrate the methods for the financial statement presentation and analysis of long-term liabilities.
7. Apply the straight-line method of amortizing bond discounts and premiums (Appendix 15A).
8. Apply the effective-interest method of amortizing bond discounts and premiums (Appendix 15B).

As you can see from the feature story, Concordia University chose to issue bonds to fund its building projects. The bonds are classified as **long-term liabilities** because they are obligations that are not due within the next year. In this chapter, we will explain the accounting for the major types of long-term liabilities reported on the balance sheet. These liabilities include bonds, long-term notes, and lease obligations.

The chapter is organized as follows:

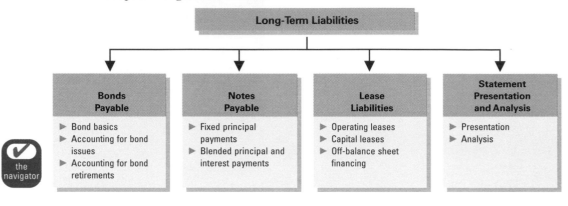

Bonds Payable

Bonds are a form of interest-bearing note payable. They are issued by corporations, universities, and governments. Unlike Concordia University's bonds, which had a minimum purchase of $150,000 and were aimed at large investors, bonds are usually sold in small denominations ($1,000 or multiples of $1,000). As a result, bonds attract many investors.

Bond Basics

In the next few sections, we will look at some basic questions about bonds, including why and how they are issued and traded. We will also introduce you to some bond terminology and explain how to account for bond issues and retirements.

Why Issue Bonds?

study objective 1

Describe the advantages and illustrate the impact of issuing bonds instead of common shares.

A corporation may use long-term financing other than bonds, such as notes payable and leasing. These other forms of financing involve finding an individual, company, or financial institution that is willing to supply the needed funds. Notes payable and leasing rarely provide enough money for a plant expansion or major projects like new buildings. In addition, as noted in the feature story, Concordia University will pay less interest with bonds than it would have to pay with a note payable.

To obtain large amounts of long-term capital, corporate management usually must decide whether to issue common shares (equity financing) or bonds (debt financing). For a corporation seeking long-term financing, bonds offer some advantages over common shares, as shown in Illustration 15-1.

Illustration 15-1 ◄

Advantages of bond financing over common shares

Bond Financing	
	1. Shareholder control is not affected. Bondholders do not have voting rights, so shareholders keep full control of the company.
	2. Income tax savings result. Bond interest is deductible for income tax purposes. Dividends are not.
	3. Earnings per share may be higher. Although bond interest expense reduces net income, earnings per share is often higher under bond financing because no additional common shares are issued

V.I.P.

To illustrate the potential effect on earnings per share, assume that Microsystems Inc. is considering two plans for financing the construction of a new $5-million plant. Plan A is to issue 200,000 common shares at $25 per share. Plan B is to issue $5 million of 6% bonds at face value. Income before interest and income tax resulting from the new plant will be $1.5 million. Income tax is expected to be 45%. Microsystems currently has 100,000 common shares. The effects on earnings per share for each plan are shown below:

	Plan A Issue Shares	Plan B Issue Bonds
Income before interest and income tax	$1,500,000	$1,500,000
Interest expense (6% × $5,000,000)	0	300,000
Income before income tax	1,500,000	1,200,000
Income tax expense (45%)	675,000	540,000
Net income	$ 825,000	$ 660,000
Issued shares	300,000	100,000
Earnings per share	**$2.75**	**$6.60**

Note that net income is $165,000 lower with long-term debt financing (bonds). However, earnings per share is higher, because there are 200,000 fewer shares.

After seeing this illustration, one might ask why companies don't rely exclusively on debt financing rather than equity. Debt has one major disadvantage. **Interest must be paid on a periodic basis and the principal (face value) of the bonds must be paid at maturity.** In contrast, if common shares are issued, a company is not required to pay dividends or repay the shareholders' investment.

Types of Bonds

Bonds may have many different features. The common types of bonds are described below.

Secured and Unsecured Bonds. **Secured bonds** have specific assets of the issuer pledged as collateral for the bonds. **Unsecured bonds** are issued against the general credit of the borrower. There are no assets used as collateral. These bonds, also called **debenture bonds**, are used by large corporations with good credit ratings. For example, Concordia University's bonds are unsecured debenture bonds.

M.C.

Term and Serial Bonds. Bonds that mature (are due for payment) at a single specified future date are called **term bonds**. In contrast, bonds that mature in instalments are called **serial bonds**. The Concordia University bonds referred to in the feature story are term bonds, due in 40 years.

Registered and Bearer Bonds. Bonds issued with the name of the owner are called **registered bonds**. Interest payments on registered bonds are made by cheque or direct deposit to registered bondholders. Canada Savings Bonds, issued by the federal government each fall, are an example of registered bonds. Bonds that are not registered are called **bearer (or coupon) bonds**. Holders of bearer bonds must send in coupons to receive interest payments. Bearer bonds may be transferred directly to another party. In contrast, the transfer of registered bonds requires the cancellation of the bonds by the institution and the issue of new bonds. Most bonds issued today are registered bonds.

Convertible Bonds. Bonds that can be converted into shares by the bondholder are called **convertible bonds**. Convertible bonds have features that are attractive to both the bondholder and the issuer. The conversion gives bondholders an opportunity to benefit if the market price of the common shares increases. As well, the bondholder receives interest on the bond until a decision is made to convert it. For the issuer, the bonds sell at a higher price and pay a lower rate of interest than comparable debt securities that do not have a conversion option.

Redeemable/Retractable Bonds. Bonds that can be retired by the issuer at a stated dollar amount before they mature are known as **redeemable bonds** or **callable bonds**. **Retractable bonds** are bonds which can be redeemed before maturity by the bondholder. Both redeemable and retractable bonds can be retired at a specified amount before they mature. The key distinction is that redeemable bonds can be retired at the option of the issuer (the borrower) and retractable bonds can be retired at the option of the bondholder (the investor).

ACCOUNTING IN ACTION ▶ Business Insight

Bond-rating agencies, such as Moody's Investors Service and the Dominion Bond Rating Service, help investors assess the risk level or creditworthiness of bonds. The highest quality bonds are graded as Aaa bonds; superior quality, Aa; and good quality, A. The credit scale descends to C, and finally to the D or default category. Generally, bonds rated below Bbb (or its equivalent) are referred to as junk bonds. Junk bonds are considered speculative and have a higher risk of default.

Moody's Investors Service also adds numbers (1, 2, and 3) to each grade category from A to C to further distinguish credit risk. So in the feature story, the Concordia University bonds were rated A1 by Moody's, which indicates that the bonds are of good quality and have a low credit risk.

Issuing Procedures

In a corporation, approval by the board of directors (and sometimes the shareholders) is required before bonds can be issued. In authorizing the bond issue, the board of directors must state the number of bonds to be authorized, the total face value, the contractual interest rate, and the maturity date. Similar to issues of share capital, the total bond authorization often exceeds the number of bonds actually issued. This is done intentionally to help ensure that the company will have the flexibility it needs to meet future cash requirements by selling more bonds.

The **face value** is the amount of principal the company (the issuer) must pay at the maturity date. The **contractual interest rate** is the rate used to determine the amount of cash interest the borrower pays and the investor receives. Usually, the contractual rate is stated as an annual rate and interest is paid semi-annually. For example, the contractual interest rate on Concordia University's bonds is 6.55% a year, but interest is paid semi-annually (6.55% × $\frac{6}{12}$). The **maturity date** is the date that the final payment is due to the investor from the company. All of these details are included in a **bond certificate**, which is issued to investors to provide evidence of an investor's credit claim against the company.

Alternative terminology
Face value is also called *par value*, or *maturity value*. The contractual interest rate is commonly known as the *coupon*, or *stated, interest rate*.

Bond Trading

Corporate bonds, like share capital, are traded on organized securities exchanges. Thus, bondholders have the opportunity to convert their bonds into cash at any time by selling the bonds at the current market price. The following illustration shows bond prices and yields, which are published daily in the financial press:

Issuer	Coupon	Maturity Date	Bid Price	Ask Price	Bid Yld	Ask Yld	Yield Chg
Bell CDA	6.150	2009-Jun-15	106.89	106.95	4.75	4.74	+0.047

This bond listing for a recent issue of Bell Canada bonds indicates that these bonds have a contractual (coupon) interest rate of 6.15% per year. It also states that the bonds mature on June 15, 2009. **Bond prices are quoted as a percentage of the face value of the bonds, which are usually sold in denominations of $1,000.** In this particular case, the bid price of 106.89 means $1,068.90 ($1,000 × 106.89%) was bid for one of the bonds by an investor interested in buying them. The asking price of 106.95 means $1,069.50 ($1,000 × 106.95%) was the price an investor interested in selling these bonds was asking for.

The yield, or market interest rate, on the bonds is 4.75% or 4.74%, depending on the bid or ask price. Note that because the market interest rate is lower than the contractual interest rate, these bonds are selling at a premium. We will learn more about market interest rates and bond premiums later in the chapter. The yield change, 0.47%, is the change in the ask yield from the previous closing date. In this case, Bell Canada's bond asking price is 0.047 points higher than yesterday's, which was 4.69%.

Transactions between a bondholder and other investors **are not journalized by the issuing corporation.** If Vinod Thakkar sells his Bell Canada bonds to Julie Tarrel, the issuing corporation, Bell Canada, does not journalize the transaction. While the issuer (or its trustee) does keep records of the names of bondholders in the case of registered bonds, a corporation makes journal entries only when it issues or buys back bonds.

> **Helpful hint** Most bonds sell in denominations of $1,000, but they can be of any value, such as $100 or $5,000 or $10,000.

Determining the Market Value of Bonds

If you were an investor wanting to purchase a bond, how would you determine how much to pay? To be more specific, assume that Candlestick Inc. issues a zero-interest bond (pays no interest) with a face value of $1 million due in 20 years. For this bond, the only cash you receive is a million dollars at the end of 20 years. Would you pay a million dollars for this bond? We hope not! A million dollars received 20 years from now is not the same as a million dollars received today.

The reason you should not pay a million dollars relates to the time value of money. If you had a million dollars today, you could invest it. From that investment, you would earn interest. At the end of 20 years, your investment would be worth much more than a million dollars. If someone were going to pay you a million dollars 20 years from now, you would want to find out its equivalent today. In other words, you would want to determine how much must be invested today at current interest rates to have a million dollars in 20 years. That amount—what must be invested today at a given rate of interest over a specified time—is called the **present value**.

The present value of a bond is the value at which it should sell in the marketplace. Market value, therefore, is a function of the three factors that determine present value: (1) the dollar amounts to be received, (2) the length of time until the amounts are received, and (3) the market interest rate. The **market interest rate** is the rate investors demand for lending their money. This rate is also commonly known as the **effective interest rate** or **yield**. The process of finding the present value is called discounting the future amounts.

To illustrate, assume that on January 1, 2005, Candlestick issues $1 million of 5% bonds due in five years, with interest payable semi-annually. The purchaser of the bonds would receive two cash inflows: (1) the **principal** of $1 million to be paid at maturity, and

(2) ten $25,000 **interest payments** ($1,000,000 × 5% × $\frac{6}{12}$ months) over the term of the bonds. Illustration 15-2 shows the time diagram for both cash flows:

Illustration 15-2 ▶

Time diagram showing cash flows

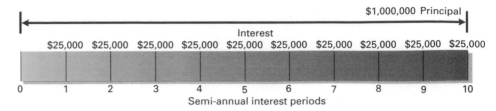

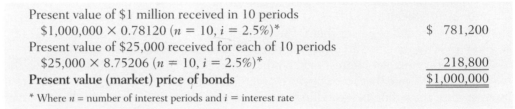

The current market value of a bond is equal to the present value of all the future cash inflows promised by the bond. The present values of these amounts are as shown below:

Present value of $1 million received in 10 periods	
$1,000,000 × 0.78120 ($n = 10$, $i = 2.5\%$)*	$ 781,200
Present value of $25,000 received for each of 10 periods	
$25,000 × 8.75206 ($n = 10$, $i = 2.5\%$)*	218,800
Present value (market) price of bonds	$1,000,000

* Where n = number of interest periods and i = interest rate

Study Aids

The present value of the bonds always equals the principal when the market interest rate is the same as the contractual interest rate, as it is in this case.

Tables are available to determine the present value factors used (e.g., 0.78120 and 8.75206), or these values can be determined mathematically using a calculator. There is further discussion of present value concepts in the Study Aids section of the Student Navigator CD that accompanies this textbook.

BEFORE YOU GO ON . . .

▶Review It

1. What are the advantages of bond financing over common share financing?
2. Explain the differences between each of these types of bonds: secured versus unsecured, term versus serial, registered versus bearer, and redeemable versus retractable.
3. Explain the terms "face value," "contractual interest rate," "market interest rate," and "maturity date."

Related exercise material: BE15–1, BE15-12, E15-1, and E15–2.

Accounting for Bond Issues

study objective 2

Prepare the entries for the issue of bonds and the recording of interest expense.

Bonds may be issued at face value, below face value (at a discount), or above face value (at a premium).

Issuing Bonds at Face Value

To illustrate the accounting for bonds, let's continue the example discussed in the last section, where Candlestick Inc. issues one thousand $1,000 ($1 million), five-year, 5% bonds on January 1, 2005, at 100 (100% of face value). The entry to record the sale is as follows:

A = L + SE
+1,000,000 +1,000,000

↑ Cash flows: +1,000,000

Jan.	1	Cash	1,000,000	
		Bonds Payable		1,000,000
		To record sale of bonds at face value.		

Bonds payable are reported in the long-term liabilities section of the balance sheet because the maturity date (January 1, 2010) is more than one year away.

Over the term (life) of the bonds, entries are required for bond interest. Interest on bonds payable is calculated in the same manner as interest on notes payable, as explained in Chapter 10. Interest is payable semi-annually on January 1 and July 1 on the bonds described above. Interest of $25,000 ($1,000,000 × 5% × $\frac{6}{12}$) must be paid on July 1, 2005. The following is the entry for the interest payment, assuming no previous accrual of interest:

July 1	Bond Interest Expense	25,000	
	Cash		25,000
	To record payment of bond interest.		

A = L + SE
−25,000   −25,000

Cash flows: −25,000

At December 31, Candlestick's year end, an adjusting entry is required to recognize the $25,000 of interest expense incurred since July 1. The entry is as follows:

Dec. 31	Bond Interest Expense	25,000	
	Bond Interest Payable		25,000
	To accrue bond interest.		

A = L + SE
+25,000   −25,000

Cash flows: no effect

Bond interest payable is classified as a current liability because it is scheduled for payment within the next year (in fact, it is due the next day in this case). When the interest is paid on January 1, 2006, Bond Interest Payable is debited and Cash is credited for $25,000.

Discount or Premium on Bonds

The previous illustration assumed that the contractual interest rate paid on the bonds and the market interest rate of the bonds were the same. Recall that the contractual interest rate is the rate applied to the face value of the bonds to arrive at the interest paid in a year. The market interest rate is the rate investors demand for loaning funds to the corporation. When the contractual interest rate and the market interest rate are the same, bonds sell at face value, as shown in the preceding section.

However, market interest rates change daily. They are influenced by the type of bond issued, the state of the economy, current industry conditions, and the company's performance. The contractual and market interest rates often differ. As a result, bonds sell below or above face value.

To illustrate, suppose that investors have one of two options: (1) purchase bonds that have just been issued with a contractual interest rate of 6%, or (2) purchase bonds issued at an earlier date with a lower contractual interest rate of 5%. If the bonds are of equal risk, investors will choose the 6% investment. To make the investments equal, investors will demand a rate of interest higher than the 5% contractual interest rate provided in option 2. But investors cannot change the contractual interest rate. What they can do is pay less than the face value for the bonds. By paying less for the bonds, investors can effectively obtain the market interest rate of 6%. In these cases, **bonds sell at a discount**.

On the other hand, the market interest rate may be lower than the contractual interest rate. In that case, investors will have to pay more than face value for the bonds. That is, if the market interest rate is 4% and the contractual interest rate is 5%, the issuer will require more funds from the investors. In these cases, **bonds sell at a premium**.

These relationships are shown in Illustration 15-3.

Illustration 15-3 ▶

Interest rates and bond prices

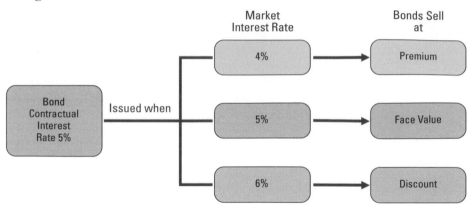

Issuing bonds at an amount different from face value is quite common. By the time a company prints the bond certificates and markets the bonds, it will be a coincidence if the market rate and the contractual rate are the same. Thus, the sale of bonds at a discount does not mean that the issuer's financial strength is suspect. Nor does the sale of bonds at a premium indicate exceptional financial strength.

Issuing Bonds at a Discount

To illustrate the issue of bonds at a discount, assume that on January 1, 2005, Candlestick sells $1 million of five-year, 5% bonds at 95.7345 (95.7345% of face value). Interest is payable on July 1 and January 1. The entry to record the issue is as follows:

A = L + SE
+957,345   −42,655
+1,000,000

Cash flows: +957,345

Jan.	1	Cash ($1,000,000 × 95.7345%)	957,345	
		Discount on Bonds Payable ($1,000,000 − $957,345)	42,655	
		Bonds Payable		1,000,000
		To record sale of bonds at a discount.		

Although Discount on Bonds Payable has a debit balance, it is not an asset. Rather, it is a **contra liability account**. This account is **deducted from bonds payable** on the balance sheet, as shown below:

CANDLESTICK INC.
Balance Sheet (partial)
January 1, 2005

Long-term liabilities		
Bonds payable	$1,000,000	NBV
Less: Discount on bonds payable	42,655	$957,345

The $957,345 represents the **carrying (or book) value** of the bonds. On the date of issue, this amount equals the market price of the bonds.

The issue of bonds at a discount (below face value) makes the total cost of borrowing higher than the bond interest paid. That is, the issuing corporation must pay not only the contractual interest rate over the term of the bonds, but also the face value (rather than the issue price) at maturity. Therefore, the difference between the issue price ($957,345) and the face value ($1,000,000) of the bonds—the discount ($42,655)—is an **additional cost of borrowing**. This additional cost should be recorded as bond interest expense over the life of the bonds.

The total cost of borrowing $957,345 for Candlestick Inc. is $292,655, calculated as follows:

Bonds Issued at a Discount

Semi-annual interest payments
$$(\$1,000,000 \times 5\% \times \tfrac{6}{12} = \$25,000 \times 10 \text{ periods}) \qquad \$250,000$$
Add: Bond discount ($1,000,000 − $957,345) 42,655
Total cost of borrowing $292,655

To follow the matching principle, the total cost should be allocated to expense over the life of the bonds. The $25,000 is recorded as interest expense every semi-annual period for five years (10 semi-annual periods). The bond discount is also allocated to interest expense over the 10 periods—this allocation is called **amortizing the discount**.

Two methods are commonly used to allocate this discount to interest expense: (1) the straight-line method, and (2) the effective-interest method. Procedures to apply these methods are shown in Appendix 15A and Appendix 15B to this chapter.

Whatever method is chosen to amortize the discount, amortization of the discount will increase the amount of interest expense reported each period. That is, after amortizing the discount, the amount of interest expense reported in a period will exceed the contractual interest amount.

As the discount is amortized, its balance will decline until it reaches zero at maturity. Therefore, the carrying value of the bonds will increase until at maturity the carrying value of the bonds equals their face value. This is shown in Illustration 15-4.

Illustration 15-4 ▼
Amortization of bond discount

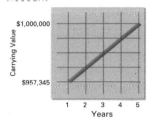

Issuing Bonds at a Premium

The issue of bonds at a premium can be illustrated by assuming the Candlestick bonds are sold at 104.4915 (104.4915% of face value) rather than at 95.7345.

The entry to record the sale would be as follows:

Jan. 1	Cash ($1,000,000 × 104.4915%)	1,044,915	
	Bonds Payable ($1,044,915 − $1,000,000)		1,000,000
	Premium on Bonds Payable		44,915
	To record sale of bonds at a premium.		

A = L + SE
+1,044,915   +1,000,000
+44,915

↑ Cash flows: +1,044,915

A premium on bonds payable is **added to bonds payable** on the balance sheet, as shown below:

CANDLESTICK INC.
Balance Sheet (partial)
January 1, 2005

Long-term liabilities		
Bonds payable	$1,000,000	
Add: Premium on bonds payable	44,915	$1,044,915

Helpful hint Both discount and premium accounts are valuation accounts. A discount account is a contra-type valuation account (its balance is deducted from Bonds Payable). A premium account is an adjunct-type valuation account (its balance is added to the balance of Bonds Payable).

The sale of bonds above face value causes the total cost of borrowing to be **less than the bond interest paid**. The bond premium is considered **a reduction in the cost of borrowing**. The total cost of borrowing $1,044,915 for Candlestick Inc. is $205,085 calculated as follows:

Bonds Issued at a Premium		
Semi-annual interest payments		
($1,000,000 × 5% × $\frac{6}{12}$ = $25,000 × 10 periods)	$250,000	
Less: Bond premium ($1,044,915 − $1,000,000)	44,915	
Total cost of borrowing	$205,085	

To follow the matching principle, the total cost should be allocated to expense over the life of the bonds. The $25,000 is recorded as interest expense every semi-annual period for five years (10 semi-annual periods). The bond premium is also allocated to interest expense over the 10 periods—this allocation is called **amortizing the premium**.

The same two methods used to allocate bond discounts are used to allocate bond premiums to interest expense: (1) the straight-line method, and (2) the effective-interest method. Procedures to apply these methods are shown in Appendix 15A and Appendix 15B to this chapter.

Whatever method is chosen to amortize the premium, amortization of the premium will decrease the amount of interest expense reported each period. That is, after amortizing the premium, the amount of interest expense reported in a period will be less than the contractual interest amount.

As the premium is amortized, its balance will decline until it reaches zero at maturity. Therefore, the carrying value of the bonds will decrease until at maturity the carrying value of the bonds equals their face value. This is shown in Illustration 15-5.

Illustration 15-5 ▼

Amortization of bond premium

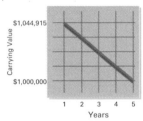

BEFORE YOU GO ON . . .

▶Review It

1. What journal entry is made to record the issue of bonds payable of $1 million at 100? At 96? At 102?
2. Why do bonds sell at a discount? At a premium? At face value?
3. Explain why bond discounts and premiums are amortized.
4. When bonds are issued at a discount, does the carrying value increase or decrease over the life of the bond? When issued at a premium?

▶Do It

Over the total life of recently issued bonds, contractual interest is determined to be $50,000 and interest expense, $52,000. Answer the following questions: (1) Were the bonds sold at a premium or at a discount? (2) After recording the interest expense, will the bond carrying value increase or decrease?

Action Plan

- Understand the effects that the amortization of a bond discount or bond premium has on bond interest expense and on the carrying value of the bond.
- Remember that bond discount amortization increases both bond interest expense and the carrying value of the bond.
- Remember that bond premium amortization decreases both bond interest expense and the carrying value of the bond.

Solution

Interest expense is $2,000 greater than the interest paid. This difference is equal to the discount amount that must be amortized. (1) The bonds were sold at a discount. (2) Recording interest expense and amortizing the bond discount will decrease Discount on Bonds Payable and increase the carrying value of the bonds.

Related exercise material: BE15–3, BE15–4, BE15–5, and E15–3.

Accounting for Bond Retirements

Bonds may be retired either when they mature or when they are redeemed (purchased on the open market) by the issuing corporation before they mature. These transactions are explained in the following sections.

Redeeming Bonds at Maturity

Regardless of the issue price of bonds, the carrying value of the bonds at maturity will equal their face value. Assuming that the interest for the last interest period has been paid and recorded, the entry to record the redemption of the Candlestick bonds at maturity, January 1, 2010, is as follows:

Jan.	1	Bonds Payable	1,000,000	
		Cash		1,000,000
		To record redemption of bonds at maturity.		

A = L + SE
−1,000,000 −1,000,000

Cash flows: −1,000,000

Redeeming Bonds before Maturity

A company may decide to retire bonds before maturity to reduce interest cost or to remove debt from its balance sheet. If the company purchases the bonds on the open market, it pays the going market price. If the bonds are redeemable, the company will pay investors an amount specified at the time of issue, known as the call price or redemption price.

When bonds are retired before maturity, it is necessary to (1) update any unrecorded interest, (2) eliminate the carrying value of the bonds at the redemption date, (3) record the cash paid, and (4) recognize the gain or loss on redemption. The carrying value of the bonds is the face value of the bonds less the unamortized bond discount, or plus the unamortized bond premium, at the redemption date.

To illustrate, assume that Candlestick sells its bonds at a premium as described in the last section. It retires its bonds at 103 at the end of the fourth year (eighth period) after paying the semi-annual interest. Assume that the carrying value of the bonds at the redemption date is $1,008,983. That is, the face value of the bonds is $1,000,000 and the unamortized premium is $8,983. The following is the entry to record the redemption at the end of the eighth interest period (January 1, 2009):

Jan.	1	Bonds Payable	1,000,000	
		Premium on Bonds Payable	8,983	
		Loss on Bond Redemption	21,017	
		Cash ($1,000,000 × 103%)		1,030,000
		To record redemption of bonds at 103.		

A = L + SE
−1,030,000 −1,000,000 −21,017
−8,983

Cash flows: −1,030,000

The loss of $21,017 is the difference between the cash paid of $1,030,000 and the carrying value of the bonds of $1,008,983. This is very similar to the calculation of a loss or gain on the sale of property, plant, and equipment. In both cases, cash is compared to carrying value. However, the determination of whether a loss or a gain results naturally differs, depending on whether you are selling property, plant, and equipment (assets) or purchasing bonds (liabilities). For example, when you sell an asset, you gain when the cash received is greater than the carrying value. When you retire a liability, you gain when the cash paid is less than the carrying value.

Illustration 15-6 ▶

Comparison of asset and liability gain and loss

Property, Plant, and Equipment	Bonds Payable
Sale price	Purchase price
– Carrying value	– Carrying value
Gain (loss)	Loss (gain)

Losses and gains on bond redemption are reported separately in the income statement.

Converting Bonds into Common Shares

Convertible bonds have features that are attractive to both bondholders and the issuer (company). The conversion often gives bondholders an opportunity to benefit if the market price of the common shares increases. Until conversion, though, the bondholders receive interest on the bond. For the issuer, the bonds sell at a higher price and pay a lower rate of interest than comparable debt securities without the conversion option.

A convertible bond has two basic aspects. First, it is a liability because of the agreement to repay the principal upon maturity of the bond. Second, it is equity, since the bondholder has the right to convert the bonds to shares. These two aspects—liability and equity—must be recorded and presented separately on the balance sheet.

With bonds like these, the distinction between debt financing and equity financing blurs. For example, convertible bonds, especially convertible redeemable bonds, can be converted into equity at a specified time. In such cases, the company may never have to repay the principal amount of the bonds. These and other innovative debt financing options are known as financial instruments. Accounting for financial instruments is complex and is left to future accounting courses.

BEFORE YOU GO ON . . .

▶Review It

1. Explain the accounting for the redemption of bonds at maturity and before maturity.
2. Distinguish between gains or losses from the sale of property, plant, and equipment and the redemption of bonds.
3. Why are convertible bonds considered both a liability and an equity item?

▶Do It

R & B Inc. issues $500,000 of 10-year bonds at a premium. Prior to maturity, on June 30 when the carrying value of the bonds is $508,000, the company redeems the bonds at 101. Prepare the entry to record the redemption of the bonds.

Action Plan

- Update any unrecorded interest.
- Eliminate the carrying value of the bonds. Remove the balances from the accounts Bonds Payable and Premium on Bonds Payable.
- Record the cash paid.
- Calculate and record the gain or loss (the difference between the cash paid and the carrying value).

Solution

There is a $3,000 gain on redemption. The cash paid, $505,000, is lower than the carrying value of $508,000 ($500,000 + $8,000). The entry is as follows:

June 30	Bonds Payable	500,000	
	Premium on Bonds Payable	8,000	
	Gain on Bond Redemption		3,000
	Cash ($500,000 × 101%)		505,000
	To record redemption of bonds at 101.		

Related exercise material: BE15–6 and E15–4.

Notes Payable

study objective 4

Account for long-term notes payable.

The use of long-term notes payable in debt financing is common. Long-term notes payable are similar to short-term notes payable except that the terms of the notes exceed one year. In periods of unstable interest rates, the interest rate on long-term notes may be tied to changes in the market rate. An example of this is The Forzani Group's long-term borrowing rate, which is based on prime plus 1.5% to 2%. Prime is the interest rate that banks charge their most creditworthy customers. It is usually set slightly above the Bank of Canada rate, the lending rate at which financial institutions borrow.

A long-term note may be unsecured or secured. A secured note pledges title to specific assets as security for the loan. Secured notes are commonly known as mortgages. A **mortgage note payable** is widely used by individuals to purchase homes. It is also used by many companies to acquire property, plant, and equipment.

Just Read it

While short-term notes are normally repayable in full at maturity, most long-term notes are repayable in a series of periodic payments. These payments are known as **instalments** and are paid monthly, quarterly, semi-annually, or at another defined period. Each payment consists of (1) interest on the unpaid balance of the loan, and (2) a reduction of loan principal. Payments generally take one of two forms: (1) fixed principal payments plus interest, or (2) blended principal and interest payments. Let's look at each of these payment patterns in more detail.

Fixed Principal Payments

Instalment notes with fixed principal payments are repayable in **equal periodic amounts**, **plus interest**. Interest may be either **fixed** or **floating**. A fixed interest rate will be constant over the term of the note. A floating (or variable) interest rate will change with fluctuating market rates.

To illustrate, assume that on January 1, 2005, Belanger Ltée issues a $120,000, 7%, five-year note payable to obtain financing for a new research laboratory. The terms provide for equal monthly instalment payments of $2,000 ($120,000 ÷ 60 periods) on the first of each month, plus interest of 7% on the outstanding principal balance. Monthly interest expense is calculated by multiplying the outstanding principal balance by the interest rate. For the first payment date—February 1—interest expense is $700 ($120,000 × 7% × $\frac{1}{12}$ mos.). Note that the 7% is an annual interest rate and must be adjusted for the monthly time period. The cash payment of $2,700 for the month of February is the total of the instalment payment, $2,000, which is applied against the principal, plus the interest, $700.

The entries to record the note payable and the first instalment payment one month later are as follows:

A = L + SE
+120,000 +120,000

Cash flows: +120,000

A = L + SE
−2,700 −2,000 −700

Cash flows: −2,700

Jan.	1	Cash		120,000	
		Notes Payable			120,000
		To record five-year, 7% note payable.			
Feb.	1	Interest Expense		700	
		Notes Payable		2,000	
		Cash			2,700
		To record monthly payment on note.			

An instalment payment schedule is a useful tool to help organize this information and assist in the preparation of journal entries. The instalment payment schedule for the first few months for Belanger Ltée, rounded to the nearest dollar, is shown in Illustration 15-7.

Illustration 15-7 ▶

Instalment payment schedule—fixed principal payment

BELANGER LTÉE
Instalment Payment Schedule—Fixed Principal Payment

Interest Period	(A) Cash Payment (B + C)	(B) Interest Expense (D × 7% × $\frac{1}{12}$)	(C) Reduction of Principal ($120,000 ÷ 60)	(D) Principal Balance (D − C)
Jan. 1				$120,000
Feb. 1	$2,700	$700	$2,000	118,000
Mar. 1	2,688	688	2,000	116,000
Apr. 1	2,677	677	2,000	114,000

Column A, the cash payment, is the total of the instalment payment, $2,000, plus the interest. The cash payment changes each period because the interest changes. Column B determines the interest expense, which decreases each period because the principal balance, on which interest is calculated, decreases. Column C is the instalment payment of $2,000, which is applied against the principal. The instalment payment is constant each period in a "fixed principal payment plus interest" pattern. Column D is the principal balance, which decreases each period by the amount of the instalment payment.

In summary, with fixed principal payments, the interest decreases each period (as the principal decreases). The portion applied to the reduction of loan principal stays constant, but because of the decreasing interest, the total payment decreases.

Blended Principal and Interest Payments

Instalment notes with blended principal and interest payments are repayable in **equal periodic amounts, including interest.** Blended principal and interest payments result in changing amounts of interest and principal applied to the loan. As with fixed principal payments, the interest decreases each period (as the principal decreases). In contrast to fixed principal payments, the portion applied to the loan principal increases each period.

To illustrate, assume that instead of fixed principal payments, Belanger Ltée repays its $120,000, 7% note payable in equal monthly instalments of $2,376. As with the fixed principal payments illustrated above, monthly interest expense is calculated by multiplying the outstanding principal balance by the interest rate. For the first payment date—February 1—interest expense is $700 ($120,000 × 7% × $\frac{1}{12}$ mos.). The instalment payment of $2,376 is fixed for each month, and includes interest and principal amounts which will vary. In February, the principal balance will be reduced by $1,676, which is the difference between the instalment payment of $2,376 and the interest amount of $700.

The entries to record the note payable and the first instalment payment one month later are as follows:

Jan.	1	Cash	120,000	
		Notes Payable		120,000
		To record five-year, 7% note payable.		
Feb.	1	Interest Expense	700	
		Notes Payable	1,676	
		Cash		2,376
		To record monthly payment on note.		

A	=	L	+	SE
+120,000		+120,000		

Cash flows: +120,000

A	=	L	+	SE
-2,376		-1,676		-700

Cash flows: -2,376

An instalment payment schedule can also be prepared for blended principal and interest payments. Illustration 15-8 shows the instalment payment schedule for the first few months for Belanger Ltée, rounded to the nearest dollar.

BELANGER LTÉE
Instalment Payment Schedule—Blended Principal and Interest

Interest Period	(A) Cash Payment	(B) Interest Expense (D × 7%)($\frac{1}{12}$)	(C) Reduction of Principal (A − B)	(D) Principal Balance (D − C)
Jan. 1				$120,000
Feb. 1	$2,376	$700	$1,676	118,324
Mar. 1	2,376	690	1,686	116,638
Apr. 1	2,376	680	1,696	114,942

Illustration 15-8 ◄

Instalment payment schedule—blended principal and interest

They use present value.

Study Aids

Column A, the cash payment, is specified and is the same for each period. The amount of this cash payment can actually be calculated using present value techniques discussed further in the Study Aids section of the Student Navigator CD that accompanies this textbook. Column B determines the interest expense, which decreases each period because the principal balance on which interest is calculated decreases. Column C is the amount by which the principal is reduced. This is the difference between the cash payment of $2,376 and the interest for the period. Consequently, this amount will increase each period. Column D is the principal balance, which decreases each period by a varying amount, that is, by the reduction of the principal amount from Column C.

With both types of instalment notes payable, as with any other long-term note payable, **the reduction in principal for the next year must be reported as a current liability.** The remaining unpaid principal is classified as a long-term liability.

BEFORE YOU GO ON . . .

►**Review It**

1. Distinguish between short-term and long-term notes payable.
2. Explain the accounting for long-term notes payable.

►**Do It**

On December 31, 2005, Tian Inc. issued a $500,000, 8%, 15-year mortgage note payable. The terms provide for semi-annual blended instalment payments of $28,915, principal and interest, on June 30 and December 31. Prepare the journal entries required to record the issue of the note on December 31, 2005, and the first two payments on June 30, 2006, and December 31, 2006.

✳ Do it.

Action Plan

- Multiply the interest rate by the principal balance at the beginning of the period to determine interest expense. Don't forget to adjust for the partial period ($\frac{6}{12}$ months).
- Record the mortgage payments, recognizing that each payment consists of (1) interest on the unpaid loan balance, and (2) a reduction of the loan principal.

Solution

Dec. 31, 2005	Cash	500,000	
	Mortgage Notes Payable		500,000
	To record issue of 8%, 15-year mortgage		
	note payable.		
June 30, 2006	Interest Expense ($500,000 × 8% × $\frac{6}{12}$)	20,000	
	Mortgage Notes Payable ($28,915 − $20,000)	8,915	
	Cash		28,915
	To record monthly payment on note.		
Dec. 31, 2006	Interest Expense		
	[($500,000 − $8,915) × 8% × $\frac{6}{12}$)]	19,643	
	Mortgage Notes Payable ($28,915 − $19,643)	9,272	
	Cash		28,915
	To record monthly payment on note.		

the navigator

Related exercise material: BE15–7, BE15–8, E15–5, and E15–6.

Lease Liabilities

A lease is a contractual arrangement between a **lessor** (owner of a property) and a **lessee** (renter of a property). It grants the right to use specific property for a period of time in return for cash payments. The two main types of leases are operating leases and capital leases.

ACCOUNTING IN ACTION ▶ Business Insight

Leasing is big business in Canada. How big? Lease financing is estimated to be more than $100 billion. In a recent year, 25% of the machinery and equipment purchased was financed by lease. Nearly half of new vehicles sold in Canada are leased. The reasons often stated for leasing include favourable income tax treatment, increased flexibility, and increased cash flow.

NO⇒ Operating Leases

Helpful hint *Financial Reporting in Canada notes that 74% of the companies surveyed reported operating leases and 40% reported capital leases.*

Rental of an apartment and rental of a car are examples of operating leases. An operating lease implies temporary use of the property by the lessee. The lessor continues to own the property. The lease (or rental) payments are recorded as an expense by the lessee and as revenue by the lessor. For example, assume that a sales representative for Western Inc. leases a car from Hertz Car Rental at the airport on July 17. Hertz charges a total of $275. The entry by the lessee, Western Inc., would be as follows:

A	=	L	+	SE
−275				−275

↓ Cash flows: −275

July 17	Car Rental Expense	275	
	Cash		275
	To record payment of lease rental charge.		

The lessee may have other costs during the lease period. For example, in the case above, the lessee may pay for gas and insurance. These costs are also reported as an expense.

^{wo}→Capital Leases

In some cases, the lease contract transfers all the benefits and risks of ownership to the lessee. Such a lease effectively results in a purchase of the property. This type of lease is called a **capital lease**. The name comes from the fact that the present value of the cash payments for the lease are capitalized and recorded as an asset. Illustration 15-9 shows the major difference between an operating and a capital lease.

Operating lease

Lessor has substantially all of the benefits and risks of ownership.

Capital lease

Lessee has substantially all of the benefits and risks of ownership.

Illustration 15-9 ◀

Types of leases

The lessee must classify the lease as a capital lease and record the purchase as an asset if **any one** of the following conditions exists:

1. **The lease transfers ownership of the property to the lessee.** *Rationale*: If, during or at the end of the lease term, the lessee receives ownership of the asset or can purchase the asset at a price substantially below its fair market value (called a bargain purchase option), the leased asset should be reported as an asset on the lessee's books.
2. **The lease term is equal to 75% or more of the economic life of the leased property.** *Rationale*: If the lease term is for much of the asset's useful life, the asset has effectively been purchased and should be recorded by the lessee.
3. **The present value of the lease payments equals or exceeds 90% of the fair market value of the leased property.** *Rationale*: If the present value of the lease payments is equal to, or almost equal to, the fair market value of the asset, the lessee has essentially purchased the asset. As a result, the leased asset should be recorded on the books of the lessee.

To illustrate, assume that Fortune Ltd. decides to lease new equipment on November 27. The lease period is four years and the economic life of the leased equipment is estimated to be five years. The present value of the lease payments is $190,000 and the fair market value of the equipment is $200,000. There is no transfer of ownership during the lease term.

In this example, Fortune has essentially purchased the equipment. Conditions (2) and (3) have been met. First, the lease term is 80% (4/5), which is ≥ 75% of the economic life of the asset. Second, the present value of cash payments is 95% ($190,000 ÷ $200,000), which is ≥ 90% of the equipment's fair market value. The entry to record the transaction is as follows:

A	=	L	+	SE
+190,000		+190,000		

Cash flows: no effect

Nov. 27	Leased Asset—Equipment	190,000	
	Lease Liability		190,000
	To record leased asset and lease liability.		

The leased asset is reported on the balance sheet under property, plant, and equipment. **The portion of the lease liability expected to be paid in the next year is reported as a current liability. The remainder is classified as a long-term liability.**

Off-Balance Sheet Financing

Most lessees do not like to report leases on their balance sheets. Why? Because the lease liability increases the company's total liabilities. This, in turn, may make it more difficult for the company to obtain needed funds from lenders. As a result, some companies attempt to keep leased assets and lease liabilities off the balance sheet by not meeting any of the three conditions listed on the previous page. This practice of keeping liabilities off the balance sheet is called **off-balance sheet financing**.

Off-balance sheet financing is of significant concern to users of financial statements. The bankruptcy of Enron Corporation—the largest bankruptcy in corporate history—demonstrated how much damage can result when a company does not properly record or disclose all of its debts.

To reduce these concerns, companies are required to report their operating lease obligations in a note to the financial statements. This allows analysts and other financial statement users to adjust ratios such as debt to total assets (which we will learn about later in the next section of this chapter) by adding leased assets and lease liabilities if this treatment is considered more appropriate.

ACCOUNTING IN ACTION ▶ Business Insight

New and innovative off-balance sheet financing arrangements are surfacing every day, designed to help companies deal with deregulation, foreign exchange and interest rate volatility, income tax changes, and other factors. These types of arrangements include loan commitments, financial guarantees, options, synthetic leases, and asset securitizations. Accounting standard-setters are struggling to keep up with disclosure requirements for these evolving financial instruments as investors and regulators increasingly question the merits of these transactions. One senior analyst noted, "I look at off-balance sheet financing from an investor's point of view. All material liabilities must be front and centre."

Source: "CFO Roundtable Webcast Debates the Future of Off-Balance Sheet Financing," *Business Wire,* January 21, 2003.

BEFORE YOU GO ON . . .

▶Review It

1. What is the difference in accounting for an operating lease and a capital lease?
2. What is off-balance sheet financing? Give some examples of off-balance sheet financing.
3. Does The Forzani Group have any capital and/or operating leases? The answer to this question is at the end of the chapter.

Related exercise material: BE15–9 and E15–7.

Statement Presentation and Analysis

Presentation

Long-term liabilities are reported in a separate section of the balance sheet, immediately after current liabilities, as shown below with assumed data:

study objective 6

Explain and illustrate the methods for the financial statement presentation and analysis of long-term liabilities.

ANY COMPANY LTD.
Balance Sheet (partial)
December 31, 2005

Long-term liabilities		
Bonds payable, 10%, due in 2012	$1,000,000	
Less: Discount on bonds payable	80,000	$ 920,000
Mortgage notes payable, 11%, due in 2018		500,000
Lease liability		540,000
Total long-term liabilities		$1,960,000

Full disclosure of debt is very important. Summary data are usually presented in the balance sheet and detailed data (interest rates, maturity dates, conversion privileges, and assets pledged as collateral) are shown in a supporting schedule or in the notes to the financial statements. The current maturities of long-term debt should be reported under current liabilities if they will be paid from current assets.

Analysis

Long-term creditors and shareholders are interested in a company's long-term solvency. Of particular concern is the company's ability to pay interest when it is due and to repay its debt at maturity. The debt to total assets and interest coverage ratios explained below provide information about a company's ability to meet its debt obligations.

Debt to Total Assets

Debt to total assets measures the percentage of the total assets provided by creditors. It is calculated—using data from Forzani's financial statements (in thousands)—as shown in Illustration 15-10, by dividing total liabilities (both current and long-term) by total assets. The higher the percentage of debt to total assets, the greater the risk that the company may be unable to meet its maturing obligations.

on Test.

Illustration 15-10 ◀

Debt to total assets

Total Liabilities	÷	Total Assets	=	Debt to Total Assets
$303,089	÷	$506,812	=	59.8%

What this means is that nearly 60% of Forzani's assets are financed by creditors. The remainder, 40%, have been financed by shareholders. One should be very careful in comparing debt to total asset ratios among companies in different industries. The debt to total asset ratios can vary significantly because different capital structures are appropriate for different industries.

Interest Coverage

Alternative terminology The interest coverage ratio is also commonly known as the *times interest earned ratio*.

The debt to total assets ratio must be interpreted in light of the company's ability to handle its debt. That is, a company might have a high debt to total assets ratio but still be able to easily pay its interest payments. Alternatively, a company may have a low debt to total assets ratio and struggle to cover its interest payments. A useful ratio to supplement the debt to total assets ratio is the interest coverage ratio.

The **interest coverage** ratio indicates the company's ability to meet interest payments as they come due. It is calculated by dividing income before interest expense and income tax expense by interest expense. The numerator is often abbreviated and called **EBIT**, which stands for "earnings before interest and tax." EBIT can be calculated by adding back interest expense and income tax expense to net income. Because these amounts were originally deducted to determine net income, adding them back has the effect of cancelling them.

Illustration 15-11 calculates interest coverage for Forzani ($ in thousands).

Illustration 15-11 ▶

Interest coverage

on Test.

Net Income + Interest Expense + Income Tax Expense (EBIT)	÷	Interest Expense	=	Interest Coverage
$30,531 + $4,354 + $19,932	÷	$4,354	=	12.6 times

Even though Forzani's debt to total assets ratio is nearly 60%, the company appears well equipped to handle its interest payments in 2003. Its EBIT can cover interest charges 12.6 times.

BEFORE YOU GO ON . . .

▶Review It

1. How are liabilities presented on the balance sheet?
2. What information about long-term liabilities should be disclosed in the notes to the financial statements?
3. How are the debt to total assets and interest coverage ratios calculated? Explain how they should be interpreted together.

Related exercise material: BE15–10, BE15–11, E15–8, and E15–9.

APPENDIX 15A ▶ STRAIGHT-LINE AMORTIZATION

study objective 7

Apply the straight-line method of amortizing bond discounts and premiums.

To follow the matching principle, bond discounts or premiums must be allocated to expense in each period in which the bonds are outstanding. There are two commonly used amortization methods to do so: the straight-line method and the effective-interest method (discussed in Appendix 15B). The **straight-line method of amortization** is the simpler of the two. It allocates the same amount to interest expense in each interest period. The amount is determined as shown in Illustration 15A-1.

Illustration 15A-1 ▶

Calculation of amortization using straight-line method

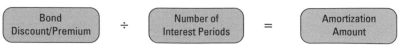

Bond Discount/Premium	÷	Number of Interest Periods	=	Amortization Amount

Amortizing a Bond Discount

To illustrate the straight-line method of amortizing a bond discount, we will continue to use Candlestick Inc. from earlier in the chapter as an example. As you recall from the "Issuing Bonds at a Discount" section, Candlestick issued $1 million of five-year, 5% bonds at $957,345. Interest is payable semi-annually on July 1 and January 1.

In this example, the bond discount is $42,655. Semi-annual amortization of this discount is $4,265.50 ($42,655 ÷ 10 six-month periods), using the straight-line method. The entry to record the payment of bond interest and the amortization of bond discount on the first interest date (July 1, 2005) is as follows:

July 1	Bond Interest Expense	29,265.50	
	Discount on Bonds Payable		4,265.50
	Cash ($1,000,000 × 5% × $\frac{6}{12}$)		25,000.00
	To record payment of bond interest and		
	amortization of bond discount.		

A = L + SE
−25,000.00 +4,265.50 −29,265.50

Cash flows: −25,000

Note that it is the *interest payment*, and not the *interest expense*, that is calculated by applying the contractual interest rate for the period (5% × $\frac{6}{12}$) to the face value of the bonds. The interest expense includes both the interest payment ($25,000) and the bond discount amortization ($4,265.50). Recall from our chapter discussion that the bond discount is part of the cost of borrowing.

At December 31, Candlestick's year end, the adjusting entry is recorded as follows:

Dec. 31	Bond Interest Expense	29,265.50	
	Discount on Bonds Payable		4,265.50
	Bond Interest Payable		25,000.00
	To record accrued bond interest and		
	amortization of bond discount.		

A = L + SE
+4,265.50 −29,265.50
+25,000.00

Cash flows: no effect

Over the term of the bonds, the balance in Discount on Bonds Payable will decrease semi-annually by the same amortization amount until it reaches zero at the maturity date of the bonds. The carrying value of the bonds at maturity will be equal to the face value.

A bond discount amortization schedule, as shown in Illustration 15A-2 on the following page, is a useful tool to organize and summarize this information. The schedule shows the interest payment, interest expense, discount amortization, and carrying value of the bonds for each interest period. Note that the carrying value of the bonds increases by $4,265.50 each period until it reaches the face value of $1 million at the end of period 10 (January 1, 2010).

We have highlighted columns (A), (B), and (C) in the amortization schedule shown in Illustration 15A-2 to emphasize their importance. These three columns provide the numbers for each year's journal entries. They are the primary reason for preparing the schedule. Column (A) provides the amount of the credit to Cash (or Interest Payable). Column (B) shows the debit to Bond Interest Expense. And column (C) is the credit to Discount on Bonds Payable.

CANDLESTICK INC.
Bond Discount Amortization Schedule
Straight-Line Method

Semi-Annual Interest Period	(A) Interest Payment ($1,000,000 × 5% × $\frac{6}{12}$)	(B) Interest Expense (A + C)	(C) Discount Amortization ($42,655 ÷ 10)	(D) Unamortized Discount (D − C)	(E) Bond Carrying Value ($1,000,000 − D)
Issue date (Jan. 1, 2005)				$42,655.00	$ 957,345.00
1 (July 1)	$ 25,000	$ 29,265.50	$ 4,265.50	38,389.50	961,610.50
2 (Jan. 1, 2006)	25,000	29,265.50	4,265.50	34,124.00	965,876.00
3 (July 1)	25,000	29,265.50	4,265.50	29,858.50	970,141.50
4 (Jan. 1, 2007)	25,000	29,265.50	4,265.50	25,593.00	974,407.00
5 (July 1)	25,000	29,265.50	4,265.50	21,327.50	978,672.50
6 (Jan. 1, 2008)	25,000	29,265.50	4,265.50	17,062.00	982,938.00
7 (July 1)	25,000	29,265.50	4,265.50	12,796.50	987,203.50
8 (Jan. 1, 2009)	25,000	29,265.50	4,265.50	8,531.00	991,469.00
9 (July 1)	25,000	29,265.50	4,265.50	4,265.50	995,734.50
10 (Jan. 1, 2010)	25,000	29,265.50	4,265.50	0.00	1,000,000.00
	$250,000	$292,655.00	$42,655.00		

Column (A) remains constant because the face value of the bonds ($1,000,000) is multiplied by the semi-annual contractual interest rate each period.
Column (B) is calculated as the interest paid (Column A) plus the discount amortization (Column C).
Column (C) indicates the discount amortization each period, which stays constant.
Column (D) decreases each period by the same amount of discount amortization until it reaches zero at maturity.
Column (E) increases each period by the same amount of discount amortization until it equals the face value at maturity.

Illustration 15A-2 ▲

Bond discount amortization schedule—straight-line method

No →

Amortizing a Bond Premium

The amortization of a bond premium parallels that of a bond discount. In the chapter example, Candlestick issued $1 million of 5% bonds at a premium of $44,915. The premium amortization for each interest period is $4,491.50 ($44,915 ÷ 10). The entry to record the first payment of interest on July 1 follows:

```
A   =   L    +   SE
−25,000.00  −4,491.50  −20,508.50

  Cash flows: −25,000
```

July 1	Bond Interest Expense		20,508.50	
	Premium on Bonds Payable		4,491.50	
	Cash ($1,000,000 × 5% × $\frac{6}{12}$)			25,000.00
	To record payment of bond interest			
	and amortization of bond premium.			

As we learned earlier in the chapter, a bond premium reduces the cost of borrowing. Consequently, the interest expense account is effectively increased (debited) for the interest payment ($25,000) and decreased (credited) for the premium amortization in the same entry. Note that interest expense is credited, rather than a revenue or other account.

At December 31, the adjusting entry is:

```
A   =   L    +   SE
        −4,491.50  −20,508.50
        +25,000.00

Cash flows: no effect
```

Dec. 31	Bond Interest Expense		20,508.50	
	Premium on Bonds Payable		4,491.50	
	Bond Interest Payable			25,000.00
	To record accrued bond interest			
	and amortization of bond premium.			

Over the term of the bonds, the balance in Premium on Bonds Payable will decrease semi-annually by the same amount until it reaches zero at maturity. Carrying values *increase* to maturity value with a bond discount and *decrease* to maturity value with a bond premium.

A bond premium amortization schedule, as shown in Illustration 15A-3, shows interest expense, premium amortization, and the carrying value of the bonds for each interest period. The interest expense recorded each period for the Candlestick bonds is $20,508.50 under the straight-line method. This is the amount of the interest payment ($25,000) reduced by the premium amortization ($4,491.50). Note also that the carrying value of the bonds decreases by $4,491.50 each period until it reaches the face value of $1 million at the end of period 10.

Illustration 15A-3 ▼

Bond premium amortization schedule—straight-line method

CANDLESTICK INC.
Bond Premium Amortization Schedule
Straight-Line Method

Semi-Annual Interest Period	(A) Interest Payment ($1,000,000 × 5% × $\frac{6}{12}$)	(B) Interest Expense (A − C)	(C) Premium Amortization ($44,915 ÷ 10)	(D) Unamortized Premium (D − C)	(E) Bond Carrying Value ($1,000,000 + D)
Issue date (Jan. 1, 2005)				$44,915.00	$1,044,915.00
1 (July 1)	$ 25,000	$ 20,508.50	$ 4,491.50	40,423.50	1,040,423.50
2 (Jan. 1, 2006)	25,000	20,508.50	4,491.50	35,932.00	1,035,932.00
3 (July 1)	25,000	20,508.50	4,491.50	31,440.50	1,031,440.50
4 (Jan. 1, 2007)	25,000	20,508.50	4,491.50	26,949.00	1,026,949.00
5 (July 1)	25,000	20,508.50	4,491.50	22,457.50	1,022,457.50
6 (Jan. 1, 2008)	25,000	20,508.50	4,491.50	17,966.00	1,017,966.00
7 (July 1)	25,000	20,508.50	4,491.50	13,474.50	1,013,474.50
8 (Jan. 1, 2009)	25,000	20,508.50	4,491.50	8,983.00	1,008,983.00
9 (July 1)	25,000	20,508.50	4,491.50	4,491.50	1,004,491.50
10 (Jan. 1, 2010)	25,000	20,508.50	4,491.50	0	1,000,000.00
	$250,000	$205,085.00	$44,915.00		

Column (A) remains constant because the face value of the bonds ($1,000,000) is multiplied by the semi-annual contractual interest rate each period.
Column (B) is calculated as the interest paid (Column A) less the premium amortization (Column C).
Column (C) indicates the premium amortization each period, which stays constant.
Column (D) decreases each period by the same amount of premium amortization until it reaches zero at maturity.
Column (E) decreases each period by the same amount of premium amortization until it equals the face value at maturity.

APPENDIX 15B ► EFFECTIVE-INTEREST AMORTIZATION

To follow the matching principle, bond discounts or premiums must be allocated to expense in each period in which the bonds are outstanding. There are two commonly used amortization methods to do so: the straight-line method (discussed in Appendix 15A) and the effective-interest method. The **effective-interest method of amortization** calculates interest expense by multiplying the carrying value of the bonds by the market interest rate in effect at the time the bonds were issued. Expressed as a percentage, this market interest rate is also known as the **effective interest rate**.

Under the effective-interest method, the amortization of a bond discount or bond premium results in periodic interest expense equal to a constant percentage of the carrying

study objective 8

Apply the effective-interest method of amortizing bond discounts and premiums.

value of the bonds. The effective-interest method results in varying amounts of amortization and interest expense each period but a constant percentage rate. The straight-line method results in constant amounts of amortization and interest expense each period but a varying percentage rate. The following illustration shows this by using data from selected interest periods of the bond premium amortization schedule shown in Appendix 15A, in Illustration 15A-3.

Illustration 15B-1 ▶

Interest percentage rates under straight-line method

CANDLESTICK INC. **Interest Expense Percentage** **Straight-Line Method**			
Semi-Annual Interest Period	Interest Expense (B)	Bond Carrying Value at Beg. of Period (E)	Interest Expense as a Percentage of Carrying Value (B ÷ E)
1	$20,508.50	$1,044,915.00	1.96%
2	20,508.50	1,040,432.50	1.97%
3	20,508.50	1,035,932.00	1.98%
10	20,508.50	1,004,491.50	2.04%

The effective-interest method is considered conceptually superior to the straight-line method because the interest expense as a percentage of carrying value remains the same in each interest period.

Both the straight-line and effective-interest methods of amortization result in the same total amount of interest expense over the term of the bonds. Both methods are acceptable to use unless **the amounts are materially different each interest period. If this occurs, the effective-interest method is required under generally accepted accounting principles**.

The following steps are required under the effective-interest method:

1. Calculate the **bond interest expense**: Multiply the carrying value of the bonds at the beginning of the interest period by the market (effective) interest rate.
2. Calculate the **bond interest paid** (or accrued): Multiply the face value of the bonds by the contractual interest rate.
3. Calculate the **amortization amount**: Determine the difference between the amounts calculated in steps (1) and (2).

These steps are shown in Illustration 15B-2.

Illustration 15B-2 ▶

Calculation of amortization using effective-interest method

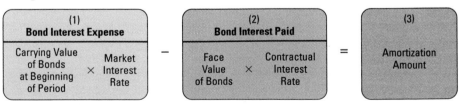

No →Amortizing a Bond Discount

To illustrate the effective-interest method of bond discount amortization, we will continue to use Candlestick Inc. from earlier in the chapter as an example. As you recall, Candlestick issued $1 million of five-year, 5% bonds. Interest is payable semi-annually on July 1 and January 1.

The bonds are issued to yield a market interest rate of 6%. Using time value of money techniques, we determine that the bonds will sell for $957,345 (95.7345% of face value).

Present value of $1 million received in 10 periods
  $1,000,000 × 0.74409 (n = 10, i = 3%)* $744,090
Present value of $25,000 received for each of 10 periods
  $25,000 × 8.53020 (n = 10, i = 3%)   213,255
Present value (market) price of bonds $957,345

  *Where n = number of interest periods and i = interest rate

This market price results in a bond discount of $42,655 ($1,000,000 − $957,345).

For the first interest period, the bond interest expense is $28,720, calculated by multiplying the carrying value of the bonds at the beginning of the period by the market interest rate ($957,345 × 6% × $\frac{6}{12}$). The interest payment, $25,000, is the same regardless of which method is used. It is calculated by multiplying the face value of the bonds by the contractual interest rate ($1,000,000 × 5% × $\frac{6}{12}$). The amortization is not a specific calculation as it is in the straight-line amortization method. It is simply the difference between the interest expense and the interest paid ($28,720 − $25,000 = $3,720). The interest payment will remain constant each period while the interest expense and amortization will change with the carrying value.

A bond discount amortization schedule, as shown in Illustration 15B-3, makes it easier to record the interest expense and the discount amortization. For simplicity, amounts have been rounded to the nearest dollar in this schedule.

Illustration 15B-3 ▼

Bond discount amortization schedule—effective-interest method

CANDLESTICK INC.
Bond Discount Amortization Schedule
Effective-Interest Method

Semi-Annual Interest Period	(A) Interest Payment ($1,000,000 × 5% × $\frac{6}{12}$)	(B) Interest Expense (E × 6% × $\frac{6}{12}$)	(C) Discount Amortization (B − A)	(D) Unamortized Discount (D − C)	(E) Bond Carrying Value ($1,000,000 − D)
Issue date (Jan. 1, 2005)				$42,655	$ 957,345
1 (July 1)	$ 25,000	$ 28,720	$ 3,720	38,935	961,065
2 (Jan. 1, 2006)	25,000	28,832	3,832	35,103	964,897
3 (July 1)	25,000	28,947	3,947	31,156	968,844
4 (Jan. 1, 2007)	25,000	29,065	4,065	27,091	972,909
5 (July 1)	25,000	29,187	4,187	22,904	977,096
6 (Jan. 1, 2008)	25,000	29,313	4,313	18,591	981,409
7 (July 1)	25,000	29,442	4,442	14,149	985,851
8 (Jan. 1, 2009)	25,000	29,576	4,576	9,573	990,427
9 (July 1)	25,000	29,713	4,713	4,860	995,140
10 (Jan. 1, 2010)	25,000	29,860*	4,860	0	1,000,000
	$250,000	$292,655	$42,655		

Column (A) remains constant because the face value of the bonds ($1,000,000) is multiplied by the semi-annual contractual interest rate each period.
Column (B) is the bond carrying value at the beginning of the period multiplied by the semi-annual market interest rate.
Column (C) indicates the discount amortization each period.
Column (D) decreases each period by the amortization amount until it reaches zero at maturity.
Column (E) increases each period by the amortization amount until it equals the face value at maturity.
* $6 difference due to rounding.

Note that interest expense as a percentage of carrying value remains constant at 3% (6% × $\frac{6}{12}$ mos.).

Columns A, B, and C provide information for the required journal entries. For the first interest period, the entry to record the payment of interest and amortization of bond discount by Candlestick is as follows:

$$A = L + SE$$
$$-25,000 \quad +3,720 \quad -28,720$$

Cash flows: −25,000

July 1	Bond Interest Expense ($957,345 × 6% × $\frac{6}{12}$)	28,720	
	Discount on Bonds Payable		3,720
	Cash ($1,000,000 × 5% × $\frac{6}{12}$)		25,000
	To record payment of bond interest and amortization of bond discount.		

Recall from our chapter discussion that a bond discount increases the cost of borrowing. Consequently, the interest expense includes both the interest payment ($25,000) and the bond discount amortization ($3,720).

For the second interest period, at Candlestick's year end, the following adjusting entry is made:

$$A = L + SE$$
$$+3,832 \quad -28,832$$
$$+25,000$$

Cash flows: no effect

Dec. 31	Bond Interest Expense ($961,065 × 6% × $\frac{6}{12}$)	28,832	
	Discount on Bonds Payable		3,832
	Bond Interest Payable ($1,000,000 × 5% × $\frac{6}{12}$)		25,000
	To record accrued bond interest and amortization of bond discount.		

Amortizing a Bond Premium

The amortization of a bond premium by the effective-interest method is similar to the procedures described for a bond discount.

Using our previous example, assume that Candlestick Inc. issues its $1 million of five-year, 5% bonds on January 1, 2005, with interest payable on July 1 and January 1. In this case, the bonds are issued to yield a market interest rate of 4%. Using time value of money techniques, we determine that the bonds will sell for $1,044,915 (104.4915% of face value).

Present value of $1 million received in 10 periods	
$1,000,000 × 0.82035 ($n = 10, i = 2$)*	$ 820,350
Present value of $25,000 received for each of 10 periods	
$25,000 × 8.98259 ($n = 10, i = 2$)	224,565
Present value (market) price of bonds	$1,044,915

*Where n = number of interest periods and i = interest rate

This market price results in a premium of $44,915 ($1,044,915 − $1,000,000).

The bond premium amortization schedule is shown in Illustration 15B-4. Figures have been rounded to the nearest dollar for simplicity.

CANDLESTICK INC.
Bond Premium Amortization Schedule
Effective-Interest Method

Semi-Annual Interest Period	(A) Interest Payment ($1,000,000 × 5% × 6/12)	(B) Interest Expense (E × 4% × 6/12)	(C) Premium Amortization (A − B)	(D) Unamortized Premium (D − C)	(E) Bond Carrying Value ($1,000,000 + D)
Issue date (Jan. 1, 2005)				$44,915	$1,044,915
1 (July 1)	$ 25,000	$ 20,898	$ 4,102	40,813	1,040,813
2 (Jan. 1, 2006)	25,000	20,816	4,184	36,629	1,036,629
3 (July 1)	25,000	20,733	4,267	32,362	1,032,362
4 (Jan. 1, 2007)	25,000	20,647	4,353	28,009	1,028,009
5 (July 1)	25,000	20,560	4,440	23,569	1,023,569
6 (Jan. 1, 2008)	25,000	20,471	4,529	19,040	1,019,040
7 (July 1)	25,000	20,381	4,619	14,421	1,014,421
8 (Jan. 1, 2009)	25,000	20,288	4,712	9,709	1,009,709
9 (July 1)	25,000	20,194	4,806	4,903	1,004,903
10 (Jan. 1, 2010)	25,000	20,097*	4,903	0	1,000,000
	$250,000	$205,085	$44,915		

Column (A) remains constant because the face value of the bonds ($1,000,000) is multiplied by the semi-annual contractual interest rate each period.
Column (B) is the bond carrying value at the beginning of the period multiplied by the semi-annual market interest rate.
Column (C) indicates the premium amortization each period.
Column (D) decreases each period by the amortization amount until it reaches zero at maturity.
Column (E) decreases each period by the amortization amount until it equals the face value at maturity.
* $1 difference due to rounding.

Note that interest expense as a percentage of carrying value remains constant at 2% (4% × $\frac{6}{12}$ mos.).

The entry on the first interest date is as follows:

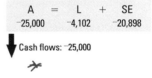

Illustration 15B-4 ▲
Bond premium amortization schedule—effective-interest method

	July 1	Bond Interest Expense ($1,044,915 × 4% × $\frac{6}{12}$)	20,898	
		Premium on Bonds Payable	4,102	
		Cash ($1,000,000 × 5% × $\frac{6}{12}$)		25,000
		To record payment of bond interest and amortization of bond premium.		

A = L + SE
−25,000   −4,102   −20,898

Cash flows: −25,000

As we learned earlier in the chapter, a bond premium reduces the cost of borrowing. Consequently, the interest expense account is effectively increased (debited) for the interest payment ($25,000) and decreased (credited) for the bond premium amortization ($4,102) in the same entry. Note that interest expense is credited, rather than a revenue or other account.

For the second period, the following adjusting entry is made. While the interest expense and amortization amounts vary, the cash payment is a constant $25,000 every interest period.

Dec. 31	Bond Interest Expense ($1,040,813 × 4% × $\frac{6}{12}$)	20,816	
	Premium on Bonds Payable	4,184	
	Bond Interest Payable ($1,000,000 × 5% × $\frac{6}{12}$)		25,000
	To record accrued bond interest and amortization of bond premium.		

A = L + SE
−4,184   −20,816
+25,000

Cash flows: no effect

Note that the amount of periodic interest expense decreases over the life of the bond when the effective-interest method is applied to bonds issued at a premium. This is because a constant percentage is applied to a decreasing bond carrying value to calculate interest expense. The carrying value is decreasing because of the amortization of the premium.

Demonstration Problem 1

Additional Demonstration Problems

On January 1, 2005, Feng Inc. issued $500,000 of 7%, 10-year bonds at 93. Interest is payable semi-annually on January 1 and July 1. Feng's year end is June 30. Five years later, on January 1, 2010, Feng redeemed all of these bonds at 90. The carrying value of the bonds at that time was $482,500.

Instructions

(a) Prepare the journal entry to record the issue of the bonds on January 1, 2005.
(b) Prepare the journal entry to accrue the first interest payment on June 30. Assume that the amortization amount for the first interest period is $1,750.
(c) Show the presentation of the liability on Feng's balance sheet on June 30, 2005.
(d) Prepare the journal entry to record the redemption of the bonds on January 1, 2010.

Action Plan

- To calculate the proceeds, multiply the face value by the issue price, expressed as a percentage (e.g., 93%).
- Compare the face value of the bonds to the proceeds to determine if the bonds are issued at a discount or premium. A discount occurs when the proceeds are less than the face value.
- Record and report the discount on bonds as a contra liability account.
- Record the amortization of the bond discount as an increase in interest expense.
- Compare the redemption price of the bonds to their carrying value to determine if a gain or a loss resulted.

Solution to Demonstration Problem

(a)

2005			
Jan. 1	Cash ($500,000 × 93%)	465,000	
	Discount on Bonds Payable	35,000	
	Bonds Payable		500,000
	To record issue of 7%, 10-year bonds.		

(b)

June 30	Bond Interest Expense ($1,750 + $17,500)	19,250	
	Discount on Bonds Payable		1,750
	Bond Interest Payable ($500,000 × 7% × $\frac{6}{12}$)		17,500
	To record accrual of semi-annual interest.		

(c)

FENG INC.
Balance Sheet (partial)
June 30, 2005

Long-term liabilities	
Bonds payable	$500,000
Less: Discount on bonds payable ($35,000 − $1,750)	33,250
	$466,750

(d)

2010			
Jan. 1	Bonds Payable	500,000	
	Discount on Bonds Payable ($500,000 − $482,500)		17,500
	Cash ($500,000 × 90%)		450,000
	Gain on Bond Redemption ($482,500 − $450,000)		32,500
	To record redemption of bonds.		

Demonstration Problem 2

Snyder Software Inc. successfully developed a new spreadsheet program. To produce and market the program, the company needed $500,000 of additional financing. On December 31, 2005, Snyder issued a $500,000, 12%, 15-year mortgage note payable. The terms provide for semi-annual blended instalment payments of $36,324, principal and interest, on June 30 and December 31.

Instructions

Round your answers to the nearest dollar.

(a) Prepare a payment schedule for the first four instalment payments.
(b) Prepare the entry for the issue of the note on December 31, 2005.
(c) Prepare the entry to record the first instalment payment on June 30, 2006.
(d) Indicate the current and noncurrent amounts for the mortgage note payable at December 31, 2006.

Solution to Demonstration Problem 2

(a)

Semi-Annual Interest Period	Cash Payment	Interest Expense	Reduction of Principal	Principal Balance
Issue Date (Dec. 31, 2005)				$500,000
1 (June 30, 2006)	$36,324	$30,000[1]	$6,324[2]	493,676[3]
2 (Dec. 31)	36,324	29,621	6,703	486,973
3 (June 30, 2007)	36,324	29,218	7,106	479,867
4 (Dec. 31)	36,324	28,792	7,532	472,335

[1] $500,000 \times 12\% \times \frac{6}{12} = \$30,000$
[2] $\$36,324 - \$30,000 = \$6,324$
[3] $\$500,000 - \$6,324 = \$493,676$

(b)

2005			
Dec. 31	Cash	500,000	
	Mortgage Note Payable		500,000
	To record issue of mortgage note payable.		

(c)

2006			
June 30	Interest Expense	30,000	
	Mortgage Note Payable	6,324	
	Cash		36,324
	To record interest and instalment payment on mortgage note payable.		

(d) The current liability is $14,638 ($7,106 + $7,532).
The long-term liability is $472,335.
The total liability is $486,973, the balance at the end of the second period, December 31, 2006.

Action Plan

- Determine the interest expense for the mortgage by multiplying the semi-annual interest rate by the principal balance at the beginning of the period. The reduction of principal is the difference between the cash payment and the interest expense amounts.
- Recognize that as the principal amount decreases, so does the interest expense.
- Record mortgage payments, recognizing that each payment consists of (1) interest on the unpaid loan balance, and (2) a reduction of the loan principal.

Summary of Study Objectives

1. *Describe the advantages and illustrate the impact of issuing bonds instead of common shares.* Bonds may be sold to many investors. They offer the following advantages over common shares: (a) shareholder control is not affected, (b) income tax savings result, (c) the borrower may benefit from leverage, and (d) earnings per share may be higher.

2. *Prepare the entries for the issue of bonds and the recording of interest expense.* When bonds are issued, Cash is debited for the cash proceeds and Bonds Payable is credited for the face value of the bonds. The accounts Premium on Bonds Payable and Discount on Bonds Payable are used to show the bond premium or bond discount. Bond discounts and premiums are amortized to interest expense over the life of the bond. The amortization of a bond discount increases interest expense. The amortization of a bond premium decreases interest expense.

3. *Prepare the entries when bonds are retired.* When bonds are redeemed at maturity, Cash is credited and Bonds Payable is debited for the face value of the bonds. When bonds are redeemed before maturity, it is necessary to (a) update any unrecorded interest, (b) eliminate the carrying value of the bonds at the redemption date, (c) record the cash paid, and (d) recognize the gain or loss on redemption.

4. *Account for long-term notes payable.* Long-term notes are repayable in a series of payments. Each payment consists of (1) interest on the unpaid balance of the loan, and (2) a reduction of the loan principal. These payments can be either (1) fixed principal payments or (2) blended principal and interest payments.

5. *Contrast the accounting for operating leases and capital leases.* For an operating lease, lease (or rental) payments are recorded as an expense by the lessee (renter).

For a capital lease, the lessee records the asset and related obligation at the present value of the future lease payments.

6. *Explain and illustrate the methods for the financial statement presentation and analysis of long-term liabilities.* The nature and amount of each long-term debt should be reported in the balance sheet or in the notes accompanying the statements. The long-term solvency of a company may be analysed by calculating two ratios. Debt to total assets indicates the proportion of company assets financed by debt. Interest coverage measures a company's ability to meet its interest payments as they come due.

7. *Apply the straight-line method of amortizing bond discounts and premiums (Appendix 15A).* Amortization is calculated under the straight-line method by dividing the bond discount or premium by the number of interest periods. Interest expense is calculated by multi-

plying the face value of the bonds by the contractual interest rate. The straight-line method of amortization results in a constant amount of amortization and interest expense each period, but a varying percentage rate.

8. *Apply the effective-interest method of amortizing bond discounts and premiums (Appendix 15B).* Amortization is calculated under the effective-interest method as the difference between the interest paid and the interest expense. Interest paid is calculated by multiplying the face value of the bonds by the contractual interest rate. Interest expense is calculated by multiplying the carrying value of the bonds at the beginning of the interest period by the market interest rate. The effective-interest method of amortization results in varying amounts of amortization and interest expense each period, but a constant percentage rate of interest.

Glossary

Key Term Matching Activity

Bearer (coupon) bonds Bonds that are not registered. (p. 704)

Bonds A form of interest-bearing note payable issued by corporations, universities, and governments. (p. 702)

Bond certificate A legal document indicating the name of the issuer, the face value of the bond, and other data such as the contractual interest rate and maturity date of the bond. (p. 704)

Capital lease A contractual arrangement that transfers all the benefits and risks of ownership to the lessee, so that the lease effectively results in a purchase of the property. (p. 717)

Contractual interest rate Rate used to determine the amount of interest the borrower pays and the investor receives. (p. 704)

Convertible bonds Bonds that permit bondholders to convert them into common shares. (p. 704)

Debenture bonds Bonds issued against the general credit of the borrower. Also called unsecured bonds. (p. 703)

Debt to total assets The ratio of total liabilities to total assets. Indicates the proportion of assets financed by debt. (p. 719)

Discount (on bonds payable) The difference that results when the selling price of the bonds is less than the face value of the bonds. This occurs when the market interest rate is greater than the contractual interest rate. (p. 707)

EBIT Earnings before interest and tax, calculated as net income + interest expense + income tax expense. (p. 720)

Effective-interest method of amortization A method of amortizing bond discount or bond premium that results in periodic interest expense equal to a constant

percentage of the carrying value of the bonds. (p. 723)

Face value The amount of principal the issuer must pay at the maturity date of the bond. (p. 704)

Interest coverage A measure of a firm's ability to meet its interest obligations. It is calculated by dividing income before interest expense and income tax expense (EBIT) by interest expense. (p. 720)

Market (effective) interest rate The rate investors require for lending money to a corporation. (p. 705)

Maturity date The date on which the final payment on a bond is due from the bond issuer to the investor. (p. 704)

Mortgage note payable A long-term note that pledges title to specific assets as security for a loan. (p. 713)

Off-balance sheet financing The intentional effort by a company to structure its financing arrangements so as to avoid showing liabilities on its books. (p. 718)

Operating lease A contractual arrangement that gives the lessee temporary use of the property, with continued ownership of the property by the lessor. (p. 716)

Premium (on bonds payable) The difference that results when the selling price of the bonds is greater than the face value of the bonds. This occurs when the market interest rate is less than the contractual interest rate. (p. 707)

Redeemable bonds Bonds that the issuer can redeem at a stated dollar amount prior to maturity. Also known as callable bonds. (p. 704)

Registered bonds Bonds issued in the name of the owner. (p. 704)

Retractable bonds Bonds that the bondholder can redeem at a stated dollar amount prior to maturity. (p. 704)

Secured bonds Bonds that have specific assets of the issuer pledged as collateral. (p. 703)

Serial bonds Bonds that mature in instalments. (p. 703)

Straight-line method of amortization A method of amortizing bond discount or bond premium that allocates the same amount to interest expense in each interest period. (p. 720)

Term bonds Bonds that mature at a single specified future date. (p. 703)

Unsecured bonds Bonds issued against the general credit of the borrower. Also called debenture bonds. (p. 703)

Note: All Questions, Exercises and Problems below with an asterisk (*) relate to material in Appendices 15A and 15B.

Self-Study Questions

Chapter 15 Self-Test

Answers are at the end of the chapter.

(SO 1) K 1. The term used for bonds that are unsecured is:
(a) redeemable bonds.
(b) retractable bonds.
(c) debenture bonds.
(d) convertible bonds.

(SO 2) K 2. If bonds are issued at a premium, it indicates that:
(a) the contractual interest rate exceeds the market interest rate.
(b) the market interest rate exceeds the contractual interest rate.
(c) the contractual interest rate and the market interest rate are the same.
(d) no predictable relationship exists between the two rates.

(SO 2) AP 3. On January 1, 2005, Scissors Corp. issues $200,000 of five-year, 7% bonds at 97. The entry to record the issue of the bonds would include a:
(a) debit to Cash for $200,000.
(b) debit to Bonds Payable for $200,000.
(c) debit to Discount on Bonds Payable for $6,000.
(d) credit to Premium on Bonds Payable for $6,000.

(SO 3) AP 4. Gester Corporation redeems its $100,000 face value bonds at 105 on January 1, after the payment of semi-annual interest. The carrying value of the bonds at the redemption date is $103,745. The entry to record the redemption will include a:
(a) credit of $3,745 to Premium on Bonds Payable.
(b) debit of $1,255 to Loss on Bond Redemption.
(c) credit of $1,255 to Gain on Bond Redemption.
(d) debit of $105,000 to Cash.

(SO 4) AP 5. Zhang Inc. issues a $497,000, 10%, three-year instalment note payable on January 1. The note will be paid in three annual blended instalments of $200,000, each payable at the end of the year. What is the amount of interest expense that should be recognized by Zhang in the second year?
(a) $16,567   (c) $49,700
(b) $34,670   (d) $347,600

(SO 5) C 6. The lease term for Lease A is equal to 90% of the estimated economic life of the leased property. The lease term for Lease B is equal to 60% of the estimated economic life of the leased property. Assuming no other conditions are met, how should the lessee classify these leases?

Lease A	Lease B
(a) Operating lease	Capital lease
(b) Operating lease	Operating lease
(c) Capital lease	Operating lease
(d) Capital lease	Capital lease

(SO 6) AP 7. In a recent year, Yung Kee Corporation had net income of $150,000, interest expense of $30,000, and income tax expense of $20,000. What was Yung Kee's interest coverage ratio?
(a) 5.0 times   (c) 6.0 times
(b) 5.7 times   (d) 6.7 times

(SO 7) AP *8. On January 1, Hurley Corporation issues $500,000 of five-year, 6% bonds at 96 with interest payable on July 1 and January 1. The entry on July 1 to record the payment of bond interest and the amortization of bond discount using the straight-line method will include a:
(a) debit to Interest Expense, $15,000.
(b) debit to Interest Expense, $30,000.
(c) credit to Discount on Bonds Payable, $4,000.
(d) credit to Discount on Bonds Payable, $2,000.

(SO 7) AP *9. For the bonds issued in question 8, above, what is the carrying value of the bonds at the end of the third interest period?
(a) $474,000   (c) $486,000
(b) $484,000   (d) $492,000

(SO 8) AP *10. On January 1, Dias Corporation issued $2 million of five-year, 7% bonds with interest payable on July 1 and January 1. The bonds sold for $1,918,880. The market rate of interest for these bonds was 8%. Assuming the effective-interest method is used, on the first interest date the debit entry to Bond Interest Expense (rounded to the nearest dollar) is for:
(a) $67,161.   (c) $76,755.
(b) $70,000.   (d) $80,000.

Questions

(SO 1) C   1. What are long-term liabilities? Give three examples.

(SO 1) C   2. (a) As a source of long-term financing, what are the major advantages of bonds over common shares?
(b) What are the major disadvantages of using bonds for long-term financing?

(SO 1) C   3. The following terms are important in issuing bonds: (a) face value, (b) contractual interest rate, and (c) market interest rate. Explain each of these terms.

(SO 1) C   4. Describe the two major obligations a company has to pay after it issues bonds.

(SO 1) C   5. What is a convertible bond? Discuss the advantages of a convertible bond from the standpoint of (a) the bondholders, and (b) the issuing corporation.

(SO 2) AP   6. Assume that Stoney Inc. sold bonds with a face value of $100,000 for $98,000. Was the market interest rate equal to, less than, or greater than the bonds' contractual interest rate? Explain.

(SO 2) C   7. La Mi and Jack Dalton are discussing how the market price of a bond is determined. La believes that the market price of a bond is solely the function of the amount of the principal payment at the end of the term of the bond. Is she right? Discuss.

(SO 2) C   8. How is the carrying value of a bond calculated if the bond is sold at a discount? How does this amount change over the life of the bond?

(SO 2) C   9. How is the carrying value of a bond calculated if the bond is sold at a premium? How does this amount change over the life of the bond?

(SO 2) C   10. How will the total cost of borrowing be affected if a bond is sold (a) at a discount and (b) at a premium? Explain when this cost of borrowing should be recorded and identify the related generally accepted accounting principle.

(SO 3) AP   11. Which accounts are debited and which are credited if a bond issue originally sold at a premium is redeemed before maturity at 97?

(SO 4) C   12. What are the typical differences between short-term and long-term notes payable?

(SO 4) C   13. Distinguish between instalment notes payable with fixed principal payments and those with blended principal and interest payments.

(SO 4) AP   14. Doug Bareak, a friend of yours, has recently purchased a home for $200,000. He paid $20,000 down and financed the remainder with a 20-year, 5% mortgage, payable in blended payments of principal and interest at $1,290 per month. At the end of the first month, Doug received a statement from the bank indicating that only $390 of the principal was paid during the month. At this rate, he calculated that it will take over 38 years to pay off the mortgage. Explain why this is not the case.

(SO 5) C   15. (a) What is a lease agreement?
(b) What are the two major types of lease?
(c) Distinguish between the two types of leases.

(SO 5) AP   16. Rasch Corporation entered into an agreement to lease computers from Elgin Electronics Inc. The annual lease payments of $47,900 have a present value of $186,300. What is the impact on Rasch's balance sheet if it accounts for the lease as an operating lease as opposed to a capital lease?

(SO 6) C   17. What is off-balance sheet financing? Provide two examples of off-balance sheet financing.

(SO 6) K   18. In general, what are the requirements for the financial statement presentation of long-term liabilities?

(SO 6) C   19. Huan Yue is wondering why the debt to total assets and interest coverage ratios are calculated. Answer her question and explain why the debt to total assets ratio should never be interpreted without referring to the interest coverage ratio.

(SO 7, 8) C *20. Distinguish between the straight-line and effective-interest methods of amortizing a discount and a premium on bonds payable.

(SO 8) C   *21. Julia Amant is explaining the advantages of the effective-interest method of bond amortization to her accounting staff. What should Julia be saying?

(SO 8) AP *22. Summit Corporation issues $400,000 of 9%, five-year bonds on January 1, 2003, at 104. If Summit uses the effective-interest method to amortize the premium, will the annual interest expense increase or decrease over the life of the bonds? Explain.

Brief Exercises

BE15–1 Olga Inc. is considering two alternatives to finance its construction of a new $2-million plant at the beginning of the year:

(a) Issue 200,000 common shares at a market price of $10 per share.
(b) Issue $2 million of 8% bonds at face value.

Complete the following table for the year, and indicate which alternative is better:

Compare financing alternatives—common shares versus bonds. (SO 1) AP

	Issue Shares	Issue Bonds
Income before interest and income tax	$1,000,000	$1,000,000
Interest expense	_____	_____
Income before income tax		
Income tax expense (30%)	_____	_____
Net income	$ _____	$ _____
Weighted average number of shares	_____	500,000
Earnings per share	_____	_____

BE15–2 Carvel Corp. issued $500,000 of five-year, 8% bonds with interest payable semi-annually. How much did Carvel receive from the sale of these bonds if the market interest rate was:

(a) 7%? [Present value factors if $n = 10$ and $i = 3.5\%$ are 0.70892 (present value of 1) and 8.31661 (present value of an annuity of 1)

(b) 8%? [Present value factors if $n = 10$ and $i = 4\%$ are 0.67556 (present value of 1) and 8.11090 (present value of an annuity of 1)

(c) 10%? [Present value factors if $n = 10$ and $i = 5\%$ are 0.61391 (present value of 1) and 7.72173 (present value of an annuity of 1)

Calculate present value of bond. (SO 1) AP

BE15–3 Presented below are some of the terms discussed in this chapter:

Identify bond terminology. (SO 1, 2) C

1. Contractual interest rate
2. Carrying value of bonds
3. Market value
4. Bond premium
5. Bond discount
6. Market interest rate
7. Maturity date
8. Bond certificate

Instructions

The following statements describe one or more of these terms. Identify by number the term described by the statement.

(a) _____ A function of the dollar amounts to be received, the length of time until the amounts are received, and the market interest rate.

(b) _____ The difference between the face value and the selling price of the bonds that occurs when the market interest rate is less than the contractual interest rate.

(c) _____ The rate used to calculate the semi-annual interest payments.

(d) _____ Includes information such as the maturity date, face value, and contractual interest rate.

(e) _____ The date the principal and final interest payment is due to the investor from the company.

(f) _____ The rate investors demand for lending their money.

(g) _____ The difference that results when the face value is greater than the selling price of the bonds.

(h) _____ The amortization of the bond discount or premium causes this number to change over the life of the bond.

BE15–4 Keystone Corporation issued one thousand 9%, five-year, $1,000 bonds dated March 1, 2005, at 100. (a) Prepare the journal entry to record the sale of these bonds on March 1. (b) Prepare the journal entry to record the first interest payment on September 1, 2005, if interest is payable semi-annually. Assume no previous accrual of interest. (c) Prepare the adjusting journal entry on December 31, 2005, Keystone's year end, to record the interest expense.

Record bond transactions. (SO 2) AP

Record issue of bonds. Show balance sheet presentation. (SO 2) AP

BE15–5 Refer to data presented in BE15–4 for Keystone Corporation's bond issue.

(a) Prepare the journal entry to record the sale of these bonds assuming that the bonds were issued at 98, rather than 100.

(b) Prepare the journal entry to record the sale of these bonds assuming that the bonds were issued at 102, rather than 100.

(c) Show the balance sheet presentation of the bonds on March 1, 2005, if the bonds were issued at (1) 100, (2) 98, and (3) 102.

(d) What will the carrying value be at maturity, March 1, 2010, under each of the three issue prices?

Record redemption of bonds. (SO 3) AP

BE15–6 The balance sheet for Hathaway Corporation reports the following information on July 1, 2005:

HATHAWAY CORPORATION
Balance Sheet (partial)
July 1, 2005

Long-term liabilities		
Bonds payable	$1,000,000	
Less: Discount on bonds payable	60,000	$940,000

Hathaway redeems these bonds at 99 on July 1, 2005. Prepare the journal entry to record the redemption.

Record note transactions. (SO 4) AP

BE15–7 Eyre Inc. issues a $300,000, 8%, 10-year mortgage note payable on November 30, 2005, to obtain financing for a new building. The terms provide for monthly payments. Prepare the entries to record the mortgage loan on November 30, 2005, and the first two payments on December 31, 2005, and January 31, 2006, assuming:

(a) the payment is a fixed principal payment of $2,500.

(b) the payment is a blended principal and interest payment of $3,639.83.

Prepare instalment schedule for notes payable. (SO 4) AP

BE15–8 You qualify for a $10,000 loan from the Canada Student Loans Program to help finance your education. Once you graduate, you start repaying this note payable at an interest rate of 10%. The monthly cash payment is $132.15, principal and interest, for 120 payments (10 years). Prepare an instalment payment schedule for the first three payments.

Record operating and capital leases. (SO 5) AP

BE15–9 Prepare the journal entries that the lessee should make to record the following transactions:

1. The lessee makes a lease payment of $7,000 to the lessor in an operating lease transaction.

2. Chang Corp. leases a new building from Bracer Construction, Inc. The present value of the lease payments is $600,000. The lease is a capital lease.

Prepare long-term liabilities section of balance sheet. (SO 6) AP

BE15–10 Long-term liability items are presented below for Waugh Corporation at December 31, 2005. Prepare the long-term liabilities section of the balance sheet for Waugh Corporation.

Bonds payable, due 2007	$900,000
Discount on bonds payable	45,000
Lease liability	50,000
Notes payable, due 2009	80,000

Calculate debt ratios. (SO 6) AP

BE15–11 Molson Inc.'s financial statements contained the following selected data at March 31, 2002 (in millions):

Total assets	$2,178.9
Total liabilities	1,261.3
Interest expense	52.1
Income tax expense	0.5
Net income	246.7

Calculate Molson's (a) debt to total assets, and (b) interest coverage ratios.

Record bond transactions, using straight-line method of amortization. (SO 2, 7) AP

*BE15–12** On January 1, 2005, Dominic Ltd. issues $2 million of 10-year, 8% bonds at 96, with interest payable on July 1 and January 1. The straight-line method is used to amortize the bond discount.

(a) Prepare the journal entry to record the sale of these bonds on January 1, 2005.
(b) Prepare the journal entry to record interest expense and bond discount amortization on July 1, 2005.

*BE15–13 Abela Inc. issues $5 million of five-year, 9% bonds at 103 on January 1, 2005, with interest payable on July 1 and January 1. The straight-line method is used to amortize the bond premium.

    (a) Prepare the journal entry to record the sale of these bonds on January 1, 2005.
    (b) Prepare the journal entry to record interest expense and bond premium amortization on July 1, 2005.

Prepare bond transactions, using straight-line method of amortization. (SO 2, 7) AP

*BE15–14 Niagara Corporation issued $100,000 of five-year, 8.5% bonds on April 1, 2004, with interest payable on October 1 and April 1. The bonds were issued at $106,237 to yield a market interest rate of 7%. Answer the following questions:

    (a) How much interest expense would Niagara record on each of the first two interest payment dates (October 1, 2004, and April 1, 2005) if it used the straight-line method of bond amortization?
    (b) How much interest expense would Niagara record on each of the first two interest payment dates if it used the effective-interest method of bond amortization?

Compare amortization for bonds, using straight-line and effective-interest methods. (SO 7, 8) AP

*BE15–15 A partial bond discount amortization schedule for Chiasson Corp. is presented below. Chiasson uses the effective-interest method of amortization.

Record bond transactions and answer questions, using effective-interest method of amortization. (SO 2, 8) AP

Semi-Annual Interest Period	Interest Payment	Interest Expense	Discount Amortization	Unamortized Discount	Bond Carrying Value
Issue Date				$62,311	$937,689
1	$45,000	$46,884	$1,884	60,427	939,573
2	45,000	46,979	1,979	58,448	941,552

    (a) Prepare the journal entry to record the payment of interest and the discount amortization at the end of period 1.
    (b) What is the contractual interest rate on the bonds? The market interest rate?
    (c) Explain why interest expense is greater than interest paid.
    (d) Explain why interest expense will increase each period.
    (e) Outline the advantages of using the effective-interest method rather than the straight-line method of amortization.

Exercises

E15–1 Charter Airlines is considering two alternatives to finance the purchase of a fleet of airplanes. These alternatives are (1) to issue 60,000 common shares at $45 per share, and (2) to issue 10-year, 9% bonds at face value for $2.7 million.

    It is estimated that the company will earn $600,000 before interest and income tax as a result of this purchase. The company has an income tax rate of 30%. It has 90,000 common shares issued prior to the new financing.

Compare financing alternatives—common shares versus bonds. (SO 1) AN

Instructions
Compare the effect on net income and earnings per share for these two methods of financing.

E15–2 Central College is about to issue $1 million of 10-year bonds that pay a 7% annual interest rate, with interest payable semi-annually. The market interest rate is 6%. How much will Central receive for the sale of these bonds? How much would it receive if the market rate was 7%? If it was 8%?

    Present value factors that may help you answer this question follow:

Calculate present value of bonds. (SO 1) AP

Interest	PV of $1		PV of an Annuity	
Rate	n = 10	n = 20	n = 10	n = 20
3%	0.74409	0.55368	8.53020	14.87747
3.5%	0.70892	0.50257	8.31661	14.21240
4%	0.67556	0.45639	8.11090	13.59033
6%	0.55839	0.31180	7.36009	11.46992
7%	0.50835	0.25842	7.02358	10.59401
8%	0.46319	0.21455	6.71008	9.81815

Record bond transactions, using straight-line method of amortization.
(SO 2) AP

E15–3 On January 1, 2004, Laramie Corporation issued $200,000 of 10-year, 8.5% bonds at face value. Interest is payable semi-annually on July 1 and January 1. Laramie uses the straight-line method of amortization.

Instructions

Prepare journal entries to record the following:
  (a) The issue of the bonds on January 1, 2004
  (b) The payment of interest on July 1, 2004, assuming interest is not accrued on June 30
  (c) The accrual of interest on December 31, 2004
  (d) The payment of interest on January 1, 2005

Record redemption of bonds.
(SO 3) AP

E15–4 Two separate situations are presented below:

  1. Ernst Corporation retired $120,000 of 7% bonds on June 30, 2005. The carrying value of the bonds at the date of redemption was $117,500.
  2. Young, Inc. retired $150,000 face value 10.5% bonds on June 30, 2005. The carrying value of the bonds at the date of redemption was $152,000.

Instructions

  (a) Assume that in each case the company paid 103 to retire the bonds. Prepare the appropriate journal entry to record the redemption for each company.
  (b) Assume that in each case the company paid 96 to retire the bonds. Prepare the appropriate journal entry to record the redemption for each company.

Record mortgage note payable.
(SO 4) AP

E15–5 Ste. Anne Corp. receives $150,000 on December 31, 2004, when it issues a $150,000, 8%, 20-year mortgage note payable to finance the construction of a building. The terms provide for semi-annual instalment payments on June 30 and December 31.

Instructions

Prepare the journal entries to record the mortgage loan and the first two instalment payments assuming:

  (a) the payment is a fixed principal payment of $3,750.
  (b) the payment is a blended principal and interest payment of $7,578.52.

Prepare instalment payment schedule and record note payable.
(SO 4) AP

E15–6 On January 1, 2004, Wolstenholme Corp. borrows $9,000 by signing a three-year, 8.25% note payable. The note is repayable in three equal instalments of $3,508.07 on December 31 of each year.

Instructions

  (a) Prepare an instalment payment schedule for the note.
  (b) Prepare journal entries to record the loan and the three instalment payments.

Record operating lease and capital lease.
(SO 5) AP

E15–7 Two separate situations are presented below:

  1. Ready Car Rental leased a car to Dumfries Company for one year. Terms of the operating lease agreement call for monthly payments of $525, beginning on May 21.
  2. On January 1, 2005, InSynch.com entered into an agreement to lease 60 computers from Hi-Tech Electronics. The terms of the lease agreement require three annual rental payments of $39,648 (including 9.5% interest) beginning on December 31, 2005. The present value of the three rental payments is $99,474. InSynch.com considers this a capital lease.

Instructions

(a) Prepare the appropriate journal entry to be made by Dumfries Company for the first lease payment.

(b) Prepare the journal entry to record the lease agreement on the books of InSynch.com on January 1, 2005.

(c) Explain the rationale behind the different accounting treatment of operating and capital leases.

E15–8 **Maple Leaf Foods Inc.'s** financial statements for 2002 contain the following selected data (in thousands):

Analyse liquidity and solvency.
(SO 6) AN

Current assets	$ 681,682	Net income	$84,686
Total assets	2,189,247	Income tax expense	54,947
Current liabilities	597,003	Interest expense	56,289
Total liabilities	1,457,346		

Instuctions

(a) Calculate the following valucs:

    1. Working capital   3. Debt to total assets

    2. Current ratio   4. Interest coverage

(b) The notes to Maple Leaf Foods' financial statements show that the company has future operating lease commitments totalling $250,229,000. Discuss the implications these unrecorded obligations have for the analysis of Maple Leaf Foods' liquidity and solvency.

E15–9 The adjusted trial balance for Priya Corporation at the end of the current year, July 31, 2004, contained the following:

Prepare long-term liabilities section of balance sheet.
(SO 6) AP

Bond interest payable	$ 9,000	Premium on bonds payable	$31,500
Lease liability	79,500	Note payable	75,000
Bonds payable, due 2013	180,000		

Of the lease liability amount, $11,000 is due within the next year. Of the note payable amount, $15,000 is due on November 17, 2004, and the balance is due in 2009.

Instructions

(a) Prepare the long-term liabilities section of the balance sheet as at July 31, 2004.

(b) Indicate the proper balance sheet classification for the accounts listed above that do not belong in the long-term liabilities section.

*E15–10** **Bhog Limited** issued $300,000 of 20-year, 9% bonds on January 1, 2004, at 103. Interest is payable semi-annually on July 1 and January 1. Bhog uses straight-line amortization.

Record bond transactions, using straight-line method of amortization.
(SO 2, 3, 7) AP

Interactive Homework

Instructions

Prepare the journal entries to record the following:

(a) The issue of the bonds

(b) The payment of interest and the amortization on July 1, 2004, assuming that interest was not previously accrued

(c) The accrual of interest and the amortization on December 31, 2023

(d) The redemption of the bonds at maturity, January 1, 2024

*E15–11** **Jyoti Inc.** issued $200,000 of 10-year, 6% bonds on December 31, 2004, for $187,000. Interest is payable semi-annually on June 30 and December 31. Jyoti uses the straight-line method to amortize any bond premium or discount.

Record bond transactions, using straight-line method of amortization.
(SO 2, 3, 7) AP

Instructions

Prepare the journal entries to record the following:

(a) The issue of the bonds on December 31, 2004

(b) The payment of intcrest and the amortization on June 30, 2005

(c) The payment of interest and the amortization on December 31, 2005

(d) The redemption of the bonds at maturity, assuming interest for the last interest period has been paid and recorded

Record bond transactions, using effective-interest method of amortization. (SO 2, 8) AP

*E15–12 Québec Corporation issued $650,000 of 10-year, 8.5% bonds on January 1, 2004, for $719,285. This price resulted in a market interest rate of 7% on the bonds. Interest is payable semi-annually, on July 1 and January 1. Québec uses the effective-interest method to amortize bond premium or discount and has a December 31 year end.

Instructions

Prepare the journal entries (rounded to the nearest dollar) to record the following:

(a) The issue of the bonds on January 1, 2004
(b) The payment of interest and the amortization on July 1, 2004
(c) The accrual of interest and the amortization on December 31, 2004

Record bond transactions, using effective-interest method of amortization. (SO 2, 8) AP

Interactive Homework

*E15–13 Tagawa Corporation issued $600,000 of 10-year, 7% bonds on January 1, 2004, for $559,231. This price resulted in an effective interest rate of 8% on the bonds. Interest is payable semi-annually on July 1 and January 1. Tagawa uses the effective-interest method to amortize bond premium or discount and has a December 31 year end.

Instructions

Prepare the journal entries (rounded to the nearest dollar) to record the following:

(a) The issue of the bonds on January 1, 2004
(b) The payment of interest and the amortization on July 1, 2004
(c) The accrual of interest and the amortization on December 31, 2004

Problems: Set A

Record bond transactions. (SO 2, 3) AP

P15–1A The following section is taken from Disch Corp.'s balance sheet at December 31, 2004:

Current liabilities	
Bond interest payable	$ 72,000
Long-term liabilities	
Bonds payable, 9%, due January 1, 2009	1,600,000

Interest is payable semi-annually on January 1 and July 1.

Instructions

(a) Journalize the payment of the bond interest on January 1, 2005.
(b) Assume that on January 1, 2005, after paying interest, Disch redeems bonds having a face value of $400,000. The redemption price is 104. Record the redemption of the bonds.
(c) Journalize the payment of the bond interest on July 1, 2005, on the remaining bonds.
(d) Prepare the adjusting entry on December 31, 2005, to accrue the interest on the remaining bonds.

Record bond transactions. Show balance sheet presentation. (SO 2, 3, 6) AP

P15–2A On May 1, 2004, MEM Corp. issued $800,000 of 9%, five-year bonds at face value. The bonds were dated May 1, 2004, and pay interest annually on May 1. Financial statements are prepared annually on December 31.

Instructions

(a) Prepare the journal entry to record the issue of the bonds.
(b) Prepare the adjusting entry to record the accrual of interest on December 31, 2004.
(c) Show the balance sheet presentation on December 31, 2004.
(d) Prepare the journal entry to record the payment of interest on May 1, 2005.
(e) Prepare the adjusting entry to record the accrual of interest on December 31, 2005.
(f) Assume that on January 1, 2006, MEM pays the accrued bond interest and redeems all of the bonds. The redemption price is 101. Record the payment of interest and redemption of the bonds.

Record bond and note transactions. Show balance sheet presentation. (SO 2, 4, 6) AP

P15–3A Myron Corporation is building a new state-of-the-art production and assembly facility for $12 million. To finance the facility, it issued $12 million of 6%, 10-year bonds at 98.5 on December 31, 2005. They pay interest December 31 and June 30. Myron has a December 31 year end.

Myron also purchased a new piece of equipment to be used in its new facility. The $750,000 piece of equipment was purchased with a $50,000 down payment and with cash received through a $700,000, 6%, four-year mortgage note payable issued on October 1, 2005. The terms provide for quarterly blended instalment payments of $49,536 on December 31, March 31, June 30, and September 30.

Instructions

Round all calculations to the nearest dollar.

(a) Prepare the journal entry to record the issue of the bonds on December 31, 2005.
(b) Prepare all necessary journal entries related to the notes payable for 2005.
(c) Show the balance sheet presentation for these obligations for December 31, 2005. (*Hint*: Be sure to distinguish between the current and long-term portions of the note.)

P15–4A Kinyae Electronics issues a $500,000, 9%, 10-year mortgage note on December 31, 2004, to help finance a plant expansion. The terms provide for semi-annual blended instalment payments of $38,438. Payments are due on June 30 and December 31.

Prepare instalment payment schedule and record mortgage note payable. Show balance sheet presentation.
(SO 4, 6) AP

Instructions

Round all calculations to the nearest dollar.

(a) Prepare an instalment payment schedule for the first two years.
(b) Prepare the entries for (1) the mortgage loan, and (2) the first two instalment payments.
(c) Show how the total mortgage liability should be reported on the balance sheet at December 31, 2005. (*Hint*: Remember to divide the liability between long-term and current portions.)

P15–5A Isabelle Moreau has just approached a venture capitalist for financing for her new business venture, the development of a local ski hill. On April 1, 2004, the lenders loaned the company $100,000 at an annual interest rate of 10%. The loan is repayable over five years in annual instalments of $26,380, principal and interest, due each March 31. The first payment is due March 31, 2005. The ski hill company's year end will be March 31.

Record note transactions. Show balance sheet presentation.
(SO 4, 6) AP

Instructions

(a) Prepare all journal entries for the ski hill company for the first two fiscal years ended March 31, 2005, and March 31, 2006.
(b) Show the balance sheet presentation of the note payable as at March 31, 2005. (*Hint*: Remember to distinguish between the current and long-term portions of the note).

P15–6A Three different lease transactions are presented below for Manitoba Enterprises. Assume that all lease transactions start on January 1, 2005. Manitoba does not receive title to the properties leased during the lease term or at the end of it.

Analyse and record various lease situations. Discuss financial statement presentation.
(SO 5) AP

Type of property	Bulldozer	Truck	Furniture
Lease term	4 years	6 years	3 years
Estimated economic life	8 years	7 years	5 years
Yearly rental	$13,000	$15,000	$4,000
Fair market value of leased asset	$80,000	$85,000	$27,500
Present value of the lease rental payments	$48,000	$74,000	$10,500

Instructions

(a) Are the leases above operating or capital leases? Explain your reasoning for each lease.
(b) How should each of the lease transactions be recorded in 2005?
(c) What would appear on the balance sheet for Manitoba Enterprises for each of the lease contracts?

P15–7A Loblaw Companies Limited reported the following selected comparative information in its 2002 financial statements (in millions):

Calculate and analyse debt ratios.
(SO 6) AN

	2002	2001
Total assets	$11,110	$10,025
Total liabilities	6,986	6,456
Interest expense	161	158
Income tax expense	414	372
Net income	728	563

Instructions

(a) Calculate Loblaw's debt to total assets and interest coverage ratios for each year.
(b) What conclusions concerning Loblaw's long-term solvency can be drawn from the ratios calculated in (a)?

Record bond transactions, using straight-line method of amortization. Show balance sheet presentation. (SO 2, 6, 7) AP

*P15–8A Ecomdrive Corporation sold $1.5 million of 10-year, 7% bonds on January 1, 2004. The bonds were dated January 1, 2004, and pay interest on July 1 and January 1. Ecomdrive uses the straight-line method to amortize any bond premium or discount. Ecomdrive's year end is December 31.

Instructions

(a) Prepare all the necessary journal entries to record the issue of the bonds and bond interest expense for 2004, assuming that the bonds sold at (1) 102 and (2) 94.
(b) Show the balance sheet presentation for each bond issue assumption at December 31, 2004.

Record bond transactions, using straight-line method of amortization. Show balance sheet presentation. (SO 2, 6, 7) AP

*P15–9A Easter Electric sold $4.5 million of 8-year, 9% bonds on January 1, 2004. The bonds were sold at 103.5. The bonds were dated January 1 and pay interest on July 1 and January 1. Easter Electric uses the straight-line method to amortize any bond premium or discount. Easter Electric's year end is December 31.

Instructions

(a) Prepare the journal entry to record the issue of the bonds on January 1, 2004.
(b) Prepare a bond amortization schedule for the first four interest periods.
(c) Prepare the journal entries for interest and amortization in 2004 and 2005.
(d) Show the balance sheet presentation of the bond liability at December 31, 2005.

Record bond transactions, using straight-line method of amortization. (SO 2, 3, 7) AP

*P15–10A The following is taken from the Walenda Oil Ltd. balance sheet at December 31, 2004:

WALENDA OIL LTD.
Balance Sheet (partial)
December 31, 2004

Current liabilities		
Bond interest payable		$ 96,000
Long-term liabilities		
Bonds payable, 8%, due January 1, 2014	$2,400,000	
Less: Discount on bonds payable	81,000	2,319,000

The bonds were initially issued January 1, 2004 at a discount of $90,000. Interest is payable semi-annually on January 1 and July 1. Walenda uses straight-line amortization for any bond premium or discount and has a December 31 year end.

Instructions

Round all calculations to the nearest dollar.

(a) Journalize the payment of bond interest on January 1, 2005.
(b) Prepare the entry to amortize the bond discount and to pay the interest due on July 1, 2005. Assume no interest is accrued on June 30.
(c) Assume that after paying interest on July 1, 2005, Walenda redeems bonds that have a face value of $600,000. Record the redemption of the bonds at a price of 102.
(d) Prepare the adjusting entry at December 31, 2005, to amortize the bond discount and accrue interest on the remaining bonds.

Record bond transactions, using effective-interest method of amortization. (SO 2, 8) AP

*P15–11A On July 1, 2004, Global Satellites issued $1.2 million face value, 7%, 10-year bonds at $1,118,462. This price resulted in a market interest rate of 8% on the bonds. Global uses the effective-interest method to amortize any bond premium or discount. The bonds pay semi-annual interest on July 1 and January 1. Global has a December 31 year end.

Instructions

Round all calculations to the nearest dollar.

(a) Prepare the journal entry to record the issue of the bonds on July 1, 2004.
(b) Prepare an amortization table for this bond issue through December 31, 2005 (three interest periods).
(c) Prepare the journal entry to record the accrual of interest and the amortization on December 31, 2004.

(d) Prepare the journal entry to record the payment of interest and the amortization on July 1, 2005.
(e) Prepare the journal entry to record the accrual of interest and the amortization on December 31, 2005.

*P15–12A On July 1, 2004, Webhancer Corp. issued $2 million face value, 6%, 10-year bonds at $2,155,890. This price resulted in a 5% market interest rate on the bonds. Webhancer uses the effective-interest method to amortize any bond premium or discount. The bonds pay semi-annual interest on each July 1 and January 1. Webhancer has a December 31 year end.

Record bond transactions, using effective-interest method of amortization. Show balance sheet presentation. Answer analytical questions. (SO 2, 6, 8) AN

Instructions

(a) Prepare the journal entries to record the following transactions:
 1. The issue of the bonds on July 1, 2004
 2. The accrual of interest and the amortization on December 31, 2004
 3. The payment of interest and the amortization on July 1, 2005
 4. The accrual of interest and the amortization on December 31, 2005
(b) Show the proper balance sheet presentation for the liability for bonds payable on the December 31, 2005, balance sheet.
(c) Write answers to the following questions in letter form:
 1. What amount of interest expense is reported for 2005?
 2. Would the bond interest expense reported in 2005 be the same, greater, or less if the straight-line method of amortization were used?
 3. What is the total cost of borrowing over the life of the bonds?
 4. Would the total bond interest expense be greater, the same, or less if the straight-line method of amortization were used?

Problems: Set B

P15–1B The following section is taken from Peppermint Patty Ltd.'s balance sheet at December 31, 2004:

Record bond transactions. (SO 2, 3) AP

Current liabilities
  Bond interest payable $ 8,000
Long-term liabilities
  Bonds payable, 8%, due January 1, 2010   200,000

Interest is payable semi-annually on January 1 and July 1.

Instructions

(a) Journalize the payment of the bond interest on January 1, 2005.
(b) Assume that on January 1, 2005, after paying interest, Peppermint Patty redeems bonds having a face value of $50,000. The redemption price is 102. Record the redemption of the bonds.
(c) Journalize the payment of the bond interest on July 1, 2005, on the remaining bonds.
(d) Prepare the adjusting entry on December 31, 2005, to accrue the interest on the remaining bonds.

P15–2B On October 1, 2004, PFQ Corp. issued $600,000 of 6%, 10-year bonds at face value. The bonds were dated October 1, 2004, and pay interest annually on October 1. Financial statements are prepared annually on December 31.

Record bond transactions. Show balance sheet presentation. (SO 2, 3, 6) AP

Instructions

(a) Prepare the journal entry to record the issue of the bonds on October 1, 2004.
(b) Prepare the adjusting entry to record the accrual of interest on December 31, 2004.
(c) Show the balance sheet presentation on December 31, 2004.
(d) Prepare the journal entry to record the payment of interest on October 1, 2005.
(e) Prepare the adjusting entry to record the accrual of interest on December 31, 2005.
(f) Assume that on January 1, 2006, PFQ pays the accrued bond interest and redeems all of the bonds. The redemption price is 103. Record the payment of interest and redemption of the bonds.

Record bond and note transactions. Show balance sheet presentation. (SO 2, 4, 6) AP

P15–3B Atwater Corporation is building a new state-of-the-art production and assembly facility for $10 million. To finance the facility, it issued $10 million of 8%, five-year bonds at 102.5 on December 31, 2005. They pay interest on December 31 and June 30. Atwater has a December 31 year end.

Atwater also purchased a new piece of equipment to be used in its new facility. The $550,000 piece of equipment was purchased with a $50,000 down payment and with cash received through the issue of a $500,000, 8%, three-year mortgage note payable issued on October 1, 2005. The terms provide for quarterly blended instalment payments of $47,280 on December 31, March 31, June 30, and September 30.

Instructions

Round all calculations to the nearest dollar.

(a) Prepare the journal entry to record the issue of the bonds on December 31, 2005.
(b) Prepare all necessary journal entries related to the notes payable for 2005.
(c) Show the balance sheet presentation for these obligations for December 31, 2005. (*Hint:* Be sure to distinguish between the current and long-term portions of the note.)

Prepare instalment payment schedule and record mortgage note payable. Show balance sheet presentation. (SO 4, 6) AP

P15–4B Elite Electronics issues a $350,000, 7.5%, 10-year mortgage note on December 31, 2005. The proceeds from the note will be used to finance a new research laboratory. The terms of the note provide for semi-annual instalment principal payments of $17,500, plus interest. Payments are due on June 30 and December 31.

Instructions

Round all calculations to the nearest dollar.

(a) Prepare an instalment payment schedule for the first two years.
(b) Prepare the entries for (1) the mortage loan, and (2) the first two instalment payments.
(c) Show how the mortgage liability should be reported on the balance sheet at December 31, 2005. (*Hint:* Remember to report any current portion separately from the long-term liability.)

Record note transactions. Show balance sheet presentation. (SO 4, 6) AP

P15–5B Peter Furlong has just approached a venture capitalist for financing for his sailing school. The lenders are willing to loan Peter $50,000 at a high-risk annual interest rate of 18%. The loan is payable over three years in instalments of $3,635, blended as to principal and interest. Payments are due at the end of every other month (that is, six times per year). Peter receives the loan on May 1, 2006, the first day of his fiscal year. Peter makes the first payment on June 30, 2006. The sailing school's year end is April 30.

Instructions

(a) Prepare all journal entries for the sailing school for the first six months of the fiscal year, that is, from May 1, 2006, through October 31, 2006.
(b) Show the balance sheet presentation of the note payable at October 31, 2006. (*Hint:* Remember to distinguish between the current and long-term portions of the note.)

Analyse and record various lease situations. Discuss financial statement presentation. (SO 5) AP

P15–6B Presented below are three different lease transactions that occurred for Klippert Inc. in 2005. Assume that all lease contracts start on January 1, 2005. Klippert does not receive title to any of the properties leased during the lease term or at the end of it.

Type of property	Computer	Delivery equipment	Automobile
Yearly rental	$8,000	$4,200	$3,700
Lease term	6 years	4 years	2 years
Estimated economic life	7 years	7 years	5 years
Fair market value of lease asset	$44,000	$19,000	$11,000
Present value of the lease rental payments	$41,000	$13,000	$6,400

Instructions

(a) Which of the leases above are operating leases and which are capital leases? Explain.
(b) How should the lease transaction for each of the above companies be recorded in 2005?
(c) Describe how the transaction would be reported on the income statement and balance sheet of each company at the end of 2005.

Calculate and analyse debt ratios. (SO 6) AN

P15–7B **Shoppers Drug Mart Corporation** reported the following selected information in its financial statements (in thousands):

	2002	2001
Total assets	$3,131,059	$3,043,316
Total liabilities	1,533,560	1,652,755
Interest expense	79,011	209,119
Income tax expense	135,688	74,538
Net income	208,584	7,179

Instructions

(a) Calculate Shoppers Drug Mart's debt to total assets and interest coverage ratios for each year.

(b) What conclusions concerning Shoppers Drug Mart's long-term solvency can be drawn from the ratios calculated in (a)?

(c) Shoppers Drug Mart has total operating lease commitments of $1.1 billion. Explain the impact an operating lease has on a company's solvency ratios. Does this information change any of your conclusions in (b)?

*P15–8B** Eatsleepmusic Inc. sold $1.5 million of 10-year, 8% bonds on April 1, 2004. The bonds were dated April 1 and pay interest on April 1 and October 1. Eatsleepmusic uses the straight-line method to amortize any bond premium or discount and has a December year end.

Instructions

(a) Prepare all the necessary journal entries to record the issue of the bonds and bond interest expense for 2004, assuming that the bonds sold at (1) 102 and (2) 97.

(b) Show the balance sheet presentation for each bond issue assumption at December 31, 2004.

Record bond transactions, using straight-line method of amortization. Show balance sheet presentation. (SO 2, 6, 7) AP

*P15–9B** Kyberpass Corp. sold $3.5 million of 20-year, 8.5% bonds on April 1, 2004. They were sold at 98.5. The bonds were dated April 1, 2004, and pay interest on October 1 and April 1. Kyberpass uses the straight-line method to amortize any bond premium or discount. Kyberpass's year end is December 31.

Instructions

(a) Prepare the journal entry to record the issue of the bonds on April 1, 2004.

(b) Prepare a bond amortization schedule for the first two interest periods.

(c) Prepare the journal entries:

1. for payment of interest and amortization of bond premium or discount on October 1, 2004.
2. for accrual of interest and amortization of bond premium or discount on December 31, 2004.
3. for payment of interest and amortization of bond premium or discount on April 1, 2005.

(d) Show the balance sheet presentation of the bond liability at December 31, 2004.

Record bond transactions, using straight-line method of amortization. Show balance sheet presentation. (SO 2, 6, 7) AP

*P15–10B** The following is taken from the Balzac Coal Limited balance sheet at December 31, 2004:

Calculate interest rate on bonds. Record bond transactions, using straight-line method of amortization. (SO 2, 3, 7) AP

BALZAC COAL LIMITED
Balance Sheet (partial)
December 31, 2004

Current liabilities		
Bond interest payable (for six months, from July 1 to December 31)		$ 108,000
Long-term liabilities		
Bonds payable, due January 1, 2009	$3,600,000	
Add: Premium on bonds payable	48,000	3,648,000

The bonds were initially issued on January 1, 2004 at a $60,000 premium. Interest is payable semi-annually on January 1 and July 1. Balzac Coal uses straight-line amortization for any bond premium or discount and has a December 31 year end.

Instructions

Round all calculations to the nearest dollar.

(a) Calculate the contractual rate of interest on these bonds.

(b) Prepare the entry to amortize the bond premium and pay the interest due on July 1, 2005, assuming no accrual of interest on June 30.

(c) Assume that after paying interest on July 1, 2005, Balzac Coal redeems bonds having a face value of $1.44 million. The redemption price paid is 101. Record the redemption of the bonds.

(d) Prepare the adjusting entry at December 31, 2005, to amortize the bond premium and to accrue interest on the remaining bonds.

Record bond transactions, using effective-interest method of amortization. (SO 2, 8) AP

*P15–11B On July 1, 2004, Ponasis Corporation issued $1.5 million face value, 6%, 10-year bonds at $1,616,917. This price resulted in a market interest rate of 5%. Ponasis uses the effective-interest method to amortize any bond premium or discount. The bonds pay semi-annual interest on July 1 and January 1. Ponasis has a December 31 year end.

Instructions

Round all calculations to the nearest dollar.

(a) Prepare the journal entry to record the issue of the bonds on July 1, 2004.

(b) Prepare an amortization table for this bond issue through December 31, 2005 (three interest periods).

(c) Prepare the journal entry to record the accrual of interest and the amortization on December 31, 2004.

(d) Prepare the journal entry to record the payment of interest and the amortization on July 1, 2005.

(e) Prepare the journal entry to record the accrual of interest and the amortization on December 31, 2005.

Record bond transactions, using effective-interest method of amortization. Show balance sheet presentation. Answer analytical questions. (SO 2, 6, 8) AN

*P15–12B On July 1, 2004, Waubonsee Ltd. issued $2.2 million face value, 5%, 10-year bonds at $2,036,357. This price resulted in a market interest rate of 6% on the bonds. Waubonsee uses the effective-interest method to amortize any bond premium or discount. The bonds pay semi-annual interest on July 1 and January 1. Waubonsee has a December 31 year end.

Instructions

(a) Prepare the journal entries to record the following transactions:

1. The issue of the bonds on July 1, 2004
2. The accrual of interest and amortization on December 31, 2004
3. The payment of interest and the amortization on July 1, 2005
4. The accrual of interest and amortization on December 31, 2005

(b) Show the proper balance sheet presentation for the liability for the bonds payable on the December 31, 2005, balance sheet.

(c) Write answers to the following questions in letter form:

1. What amount of interest expense is reported for 2005?
2. Would the bond interest expense reported in 2005 be the same as, greater than, or less than the amount that would be reported if the straight-line method of amortization were used? Explain the reason for your answer.
3. Determine the total cost of borrowing over the life of the bond.
4. Would the total bond interest expense be greater than, the same as, or less than the total interest expense that would be reported if the straight-line method of amortization were used?
5. Compare the advantages and disadvantages of the straight-line method to those of the effective-interest method.

Continuing Cookie Chronicle

(Note: This is a continuation of the Cookie Chronicle from Chapters 1 through 14.)

Natalie and Curtis have been experiencing great demand for their cookies and muffins. As a result, they are now thinking about buying a commercial oven. The cost of this oven is estimated at $14,000, and the company already has $5,000 set aside for the purchase. Natalie and Curtis have met with the bank manager. She is willing to lend Cookie & Coffee Creations Ltd. $9,000 on November 1, 2006, for a period of three years at a 5% interest rate. The bank manager has set out the following two payment alternatives:

Alternative 1: The terms provide for equal semi-annual instalment payments of $1,500 on May 1 and November 1 of each year, plus interest on the outstanding principal balance.

Alternative 2: The terms provide for equal blended semi-annual instalment payments of $1,634, including interest and principal, on May 1 and November 1 of each year.

Natalie and Curtis ask you to determine the better payment alternative.

Instructions

(a) Prepare instalment payment schedules for each of the alternatives for the full term of the loan. (Use the schedules in Illustrations 15-7 and 15-8 as your model.)

(b) Prepare the journal entry required for the purchase of the oven and the issue of the note payable on November 1, 2006.

(c) Prepare the journal entries required for the first three payments under each alternative.

(d) Determine the current portion of the note payable and the long-term portion of the note payable as of November 1, 2007, under each alternative.

(e) Recommend a payment plan and state your reasons.

BROADENING YOUR PERSPECTIVE

Financial Reporting and Analysis

 Practice Tools

Financial Reporting Problem

BYP15–1 Refer to the consolidated financial statements and notes of **The Forzani Group Ltd.** in Appendix A.

Instructions

(a) What was Forzani's long-term debt at February 2, 2003? What was the increase (decrease) in total long-term debt from January 27, 2002?

(b) Does Forzani separate the current portion due from its long-term debt? If so, how much of its long-term debt is currently due?

(c) What kind of long-term debt does Forzani have?

(d) Does Forzani have any off-balance sheet financing that you can determine?

(e) Forzani's debt to total assets and interest coverage ratios for fiscal 2003 were calculated in Illustrations 15-10 and 15-11 in the chapter. Calculate these ratios for fiscal 2002. Comment on whether Forzani's solvency improved or deteriorated in 2003.

Interpreting Financial Statements

BYP15–2 **Reitmans (Canada) Limited** and **La Senza Corporation** are two specialty women's clothing merchandisers. Here are financial data for both companies at February 1, 2003 (in thousands):

	Reitmans	La Senza
Total current assets	$134,185	$109,562
Beginning total assets	279,336	245,258
Ending total assets	419,570	234,609
Total current liabilities	79,915	61,171
Total liabilities	174,049	90,253
Net sales	752,494	289,100
Interest expense	2,656	2,094
Income tax expense	12,548	5,945
Net income (loss)	24,535	(3,775)

Instructions

(a) Calculate the working capital and current ratio for each company. Discuss their relative liquidity.
(b) Calculate the debt to total assets and interest coverage for each company. Discuss their relative solvency.
(c) The notes to the financial statements indicate that many of the retail stores' furniture and fixtures and the like are leased using operating leases. Discuss the implications of these operating leases for each company's solvency.
(d) Calculate the asset turnover, return on assets, and profit margin for each company. Comment on each company's relative profitability.

Accounting on the Web

BYP15–3 Bonds have complex terminology associated with them. In this question, we review the Bonds Online website and explore a glossary of bond terms.

Instructions

Specific requirements of this Internet case are available on the Weygandt website.

Critical Thinking

Collaborative Learning Activity

BYP15–4 On January 1, 2003, Landry Corporation issued $6,000,000 of five-year, 8% bonds at 96. The bonds pay interest semi-annually on July 1 and January 1. By January 1, 2005, the market rate of interest for bonds of similar risk to those of Landry Corporation had risen. As a result, the market value of the Landry bonds was $5,000,000 on January 1, 2005—which is below their carrying value of $5,856,000. Barbara Landry, president of the company, suggests repurchasing all of these bonds in the open market at the $5,000,000 price. To do so, the company will have to issue $5,000,000 (face value) of new 10-year 6% bonds. The president asks you, as the company controller, "What is the feasibility of my proposed repurchase plan?"

Instructions

With the class divided into groups, do the following:
(a) Prepare the journal entry to retire the five-year bonds on January 1, 2005. Prepare the journal entry to issue the new 10-year bonds.
(b) Write a short memo to the president in response to her request for advice. List the economic factors that you believe should be considered in her repurchase proposal.

Communication Activity

BYP15–5 Finn Berge, president of the Blue Marlin, is thinking of issuing convertible bonds to finance an expansion of his business. He has asked you to discuss the advantages and disadvantages of convertible bonds over common share financing.

Instructions

Write a memo to the president, answering his request.

Ethics Case

BYP15–6 Enron Corporation—once the world's largest electronic trader in natural gas and electricity—was one of the largest corporate bankruptcies in American history. Just weeks before it filed for bankruptcy, the company admitted that it had shifted billions of dollars in debt off its balance sheets and into a variety of complex partnerships.

One journalist wrote that "The Enron practice of shifting liabilities off the books to more than 3,500 subsidiaries raised so many red flags that you'd think you were in a military parade somewhere in China." Yet, Enron and its auditors argued vehemently that the "special purpose entity" partnerships they used were in accordance with U.S. GAAP and fully disclosed, even if not recorded in the books.

Instructions

(a) Who are the stakeholders in this situation?
(b) Explain how shifting debt off the balance sheet might mislead investors.
(c) Do you think that management has an obligation to ensure that a company's accounting and disclosure is relevant to its users, even if it follows GAAP?

Answers to Self-Study Questions

1. c   2. a   3. c   4. b   5. b   6. c   7. d   *8. d   *9. c   *10. c

Answer to Forzani Review It Question 3

Forzani does not have any capital leases. It does, however, have an operating lease for land (see Building on Leased Land reported in note 3). Note 11 reports the company's commitments for this lease over the next five years.

 Remember to go back to the Navigator Box at the beginning of the chapter to check off your completed work.

concepts for review >>

Before studying this chapter, you should understand or, if necessary, review:

a. How to record an issue of bonds. (Ch. 15, pp. 706–710)

b. How to calculate and record interest. (Ch. 3, p. 110, Ch. 8, p. 399, and Ch. 15, pp. 706–710 and 713–715)

c. Where temporary and long-term investments are classified on a balance sheet. (Ch. 4, pp. 167–169)

Students Learn and Earn

Portfolio Management Foundation: www.sauder.ubc.ca/pmf

VANCOUVER, B.C.—Jessica Lu and the other six fund managers of the Portfolio Management Foundation (PMF) in Vancouver face the pressures typical of the investment industry. They research and write detailed reports on potential investments. They balance risk and return on the $2.5 million in assets they oversee. And they regularly defend their decisions in high-pressure meetings with a demanding board of trustees.

But they also have to worry about how the 30 hours a week they spend at the office are affecting their grades.

Ms. Lu and her colleagues are undergraduate students at the University of British Columbia's Sauder School of Business. They are part of a program begun in 1986 in which students manage a substantial endowment of real money in the real marketplace.

As a teaching tool, the program is a great success. Former PMF participants can be found working in the investment industry from New York to Hong Kong, often with such top names as Merrill Lynch, CIBC World Markets, and Scotia Capital.

But perhaps more surprisingly, the PMF is a success as an investment fund as well. The core of its asset pool was originally about $1 million in donations from alumni and corporations. It has grown to over $2.5 million since then, while covering the program's expenses, which include summer work terms in Vancouver and Toronto for the student managers.

It's no surprise that several other Canadian universities have instituted similar programs. At McGill University, 12 teams of undergraduate commerce and graduate MBA students manage funds of about $250,000 each as part of the one-year Applied Investment Program—the largest student fund management program in Canada in terms of the number of students involved.

At the University of New Brunswick, 13 undergraduate and MBA business students manage a $1.3-million civil-service pension fund for the New Brunswick Investment Management Corp. as part of a two-semester course. And at Concordia University's John Molson School of Business, 16 undergraduate students enrolled in the two-year Kenneth Wood Portfolio Management Program manage approximately $1 million. In addition to supporting costs, proceeds are used to fund scholarships—a pretty good investment itself when you consider the results of these programs!

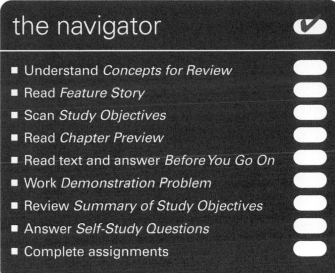

the navigator

- Understand *Concepts for Review*
- Read *Feature Story*
- Scan *Study Objectives*
- Read *Chapter Preview*
- Read text and answer *Before You Go On*
- Work *Demonstration Problem*
- Review *Summary of Study Objectives*
- Answer *Self-Study Questions*
- Complete assignments

chapter 16
Investments

study objectives >>

the navigator

After studying this chapter, you should be able to:

1. Identify the reasons why corporations invest in debt and equity securities.
2. Distinguish between temporary and long-term investments.
3. Explain and illustrate the accounting for debt investments.
4. Explain and illustrate the accounting for equity investments.
5. Describe the purpose and usefulness of consolidated financial statements.
6. Indicate how debt and equity investments are valuated and reported on the financial statements.

Investments can include debt and equity, and can be made by individuals or corporations. Investments can be bought for a short or long period of time. They can be made as either a passive investment, as in our feature story, or to control a company. As you will see in this chapter, the way in which a company accounts for its investments is determined by a number of factors.

The chapter is organized as follows:

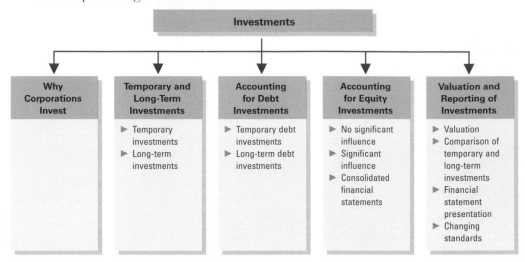

Why Corporations Invest

Helpful hint Money market instruments include certificates of deposit issued by banks, money market certificates issued by banks and credit institutions, treasury bills issued by governments, and high-quality commercial paper issued by corporations.

Corporations generally buy investments in **debt securities** (money-market instruments and bonds) and **equity securities** (preferred and common shares) for one of three reasons. First, a corporation may have **excess cash** that it does not immediately need. For example, many companies experience seasonal fluctuations in sales which can lead to idle cash until purchases are made for the next busy season. Until the cash is needed, these companies may invest the excess funds to earn a greater return than they would get by just holding the funds in the bank.

When investing excess cash for short periods of time, corporations invest in debt securities—usually money-market instruments which are low-risk and highly liquid. It is generally unwise to invest short-term excess cash in equity securities, because share prices can drop suddenly and dramatically. If a company does invest excess cash in shares and the price of the shares falls just before the company needs the cash again, it will be forced to sell its equity investment at a loss.

A second reason some companies buy investments is to **generate investment income**. The Portfolio Management Foundation in our feature story invests its funds in debt and equity securities for this purpose. Debt securities generate interest income. Equity securities generate dividend income. Although some common shares pay dividends, most companies buy preferred shares to get dividends.

Companies also invest in debt and equity securities hoping that they can sell them at a higher price than they originally paid for them. They speculate that the investment will increase in value and result in a gain when sold.

A third reason companies invest is for **strategic reasons**. A company may buy an interest in another company in a related or new industry to become part of that industry. Or a company might buy another company in the same industry as itself. The purchase of a company that is in the industry, but involved in a different activity, is called a **vertical** acquisition. In a **horizontal acquisition**, the purchased company is in the same activity as the company buying it.

In 2001, The Forzani Group bought Sport Mart Inc. This was a horizontal acquisition because Sport Mart is in the same industry as Forzani and sells similar products.

In summary, businesses invest in other companies for the reasons shown in Illustration 16-1.

Reason	Typical Investment
To house excess cash until needed	Low-risk, high-liquidity, short-term debt securities
To generate investment income	Debt securities (money-market instruments and bonds) and equity securities (preferred and common shares)
To meet strategic goals	Common shares of companies in a related industry or an unrelated industry that the company wishes to enter

In the "To generate investment income" row: I need 1,000 treasury bills by tonight.

Illustration 16-1 ◄
Why businesses invest

Temporary and Long-Term Investments

In addition to being classified as debt or equity investments, investments are also categorized as temporary or long-term investments.

study objective 2

Distinguish between temporary and long-term investments.

Temporary Investments

Temporary investments ordinarily consist of money-market instruments, debt securities (corporate, government, and university bonds), and equity securities (preferred and common shares). In order to be classified as temporary, these investments must be (1) **readily marketable**, and (2) **intended to be converted into cash** in the near future. When debt and/or equity securities of several different corporations or institutions are held, the group of securities is called an **investment portfolio**.

Alternative terminology
Temporary investments are also called *marketable securities* or *short-term investments.*

Readily Marketable

An investment is readily marketable when it can be sold easily whenever the need for cash arises. Money-market instruments meet this criterion because they can easily be sold to other investors. Shares and bonds that are traded on organized securities exchanges, such as the Toronto Stock Exchange, are readily marketable. They can be bought and sold daily. In contrast, there may be only a limited market for the securities issued by small corporations and no market at all for the securities of a privately held company.

Intent to Convert

"Intent to convert" means that management intends to sell the investment when the need for cash arises. It is the intention to sell that determines whether or not the investment is classified as temporary, not the length of time it is held. For example, a Christmas tree farmer may invest idle cash in a money-market fund after the Christmas season and intend to sell this temporary investment to finance supplies and labour needed to get ready for the next Christmas season. This investment is considered temporary even if the Christmas tree farm does not need to convert the investment into cash as intended.

Long-Term Investments

Long-term investments can also consist of debt securities (corporate, government, and university bonds) and equity securities (preferred and common shares). To determine whether a debt or equity security is a temporary or long-term investment, we test the investment against the temporary investment criteria. Investments that do not meet both investment criteria—readily marketable and intent to convert—are long-term investments.

The majority of the Portfolio Management Foundation's investments are long-term. PMF holds less than 5% in money-market instruments. The remainder of the fund is invested in debt securities of Canadian and foreign issuers and equity securities in Canada and the United States.

Accounting for Debt Investments

study objective 3

Explain and illustrate the accounting for debt investments.

Debt investments are investments in money-market instruments, as well as investments in corporate, government, and university bonds. As we just learned, these investments may be classified as temporary or long-term. The accounting for debt investments can differ depending on whether the investments are temporary or long-term.

Temporary Debt Investments

In accounting for debt investments, entries are required to record (1) the acquisition, (2) the interest revenue, and (3) the sale.

Money-Market Instruments

Money-market instruments can include term deposits and treasury bills, as well as other forms of instruments. All are relatively safe, temporary investments which allow a company to earn a higher interest rate than can normally be earned on a regular bank account balance.

Recording Acquisitions. Assume that Cheung Corporation has an excess of cash on hand. On November 30, 2005, it purchases a $5,000 three-month term deposit, which pays an annual interest rate of 2%. The entry to record Cheung's temporary investment is as follows:

A   =   L   +   SE
+5,000
–5,000

Cash flows: –5,000

Nov. 30	Temporary Debt Investment—Term Deposit	5,000	
	Cash		5,000
	To record purchase of three-month, 2% term deposit.		

Recording Interest. Cheung Corporation's year end is December 31. Most term deposits pay a fixed interest rate on maturity, although variable interest rates are also possible.

Assuming that Cheung's term deposit pays a fixed interest rate at maturity, it is necessary to accrue $8 of interest for the month of December ($5,000 × 2% × $\frac{1}{12}$, rounded to the nearest dollar).

Dec. 31	Interest Receivable	8	
	Interest Revenue		8
	To accrue interest on term deposit.		

| A | = | L | + | SE |
| +8 | | | | +8 |

Cash flows: no effect

Recording Maturity. On February 28, 2006, when the term deposit matures, it is necessary to (1) update the interest for the latest period, and (2) record the receipt of cash and the elimination of the term deposit. Most banks credit the company's bank account directly for the interest and principal amounts when a term deposit matures unless asked to do otherwise.

Feb. 28	Cash	5,025	
	Interest Receivable		8
	Interest Revenue ($5,000 × 2% × $\frac{2}{12}$)		17
	Temporary Debt Investment—Term Deposit		5,000
	To record maturation of term deposit.		

A	=	L	+	SE
+5,025				+17
−8				
−5,000				

Cash flows: +5,025

If the company does not require the cash when the term deposit matures, it may reinvest it by buying another term deposit. In such cases, two separate entries should be recorded. One entry, as above, records the maturation of the first term deposit and interest earned. The second entry records the acquisition of the new term deposit, which will have a different maturity date and may also have a different interest rate.

Bonds

The recording of temporary investments in bonds differs from the recording of money-market instruments in three respects: the determination of cost, the timing of the receipt of interest, and the sale of the bond. First, the cost of the bond often includes additional costs such as brokerage fees, whereas money-market instruments rarely do since they are usually bought directly from a bank. Second, bond investments receive interest semi-annually, while money-market investments receive interest only at maturity. Finally, bonds are usually for a much longer term than money-market instruments, which means they are often sold before they mature when the need for cash arises, which can result in gain or loss.

We will review the entries for the acquisition of bonds, the receipt and accrual of interest revenue, and the sale of bonds in the next sections.

Recording Acquisitions. At acquisition, the cost principle applies. Cost includes all expenses to acquire these investments, such as the price paid plus brokerage fees (commissions), if any.

Assume that Kuhl Corporation acquires 50 Doan Inc. 8%, 10-year, $1,000 bonds on January 1, 2005, for $51,000, including brokerage fees of $1,000. Kuhl Corporation, as the bondholder, is known as the **investor**. Doan Inc., as the issuer of the bonds, is known as the **investee**. The bonds pay interest semi-annually, on July 1 and January 1. The entry to record the investment follows:

Jan. 1	Temporary Debt Investment—Doan Bonds	51,000	
	Cash		51,000
	To record purchase of 50 Doan bonds.		

A	=	L	+	SE
+51,000				
−51,000				

Cash flows: −51,000

Recording Interest. The bonds pay interest of $2,000 (50 × $1,000 = $50,000; $50,000 × 8% × $\frac{6}{12}$) semi-annually on July 1 and January 1. The following entry records the receipt of interest on July 1:

A	=	L	+	SE
+2,000				+2,000

↑ Cash flows: +2,000

July	1	Cash	2,000	
		Interest Revenue		2,000
		To record receipt of interest on Doan bonds.		

If Kuhl's fiscal year ends on December 31, it is necessary to accrue the interest of $2,000 earned since July 1. The adjusting entry is as follows:

A	=	L	+	SE
+2,000				+2,000

Cash flows: no effect

Dec. 31	Interest Receivable	2,000	
	Interest Revenue		2,000
	To accrue interest on Doan bonds.		

Note that the interest receivable is reported as a current asset in the balance sheet. The interest revenue is reported as other revenue in the income statement.

When the interest is received on January 1, 2006, the entry is as follows:

A	=	L	+	SE
+2,000				
−2,000				

↑ Cash flows: +2,000

Jan.	1	Cash	2,000	
		Interest Receivable		2,000
		To record receipt of accrued interest.		

A credit to interest revenue at this time would be incorrect. Why? Because the interest revenue was earned and accrued in the previous accounting period.

Recording Sales. When the bonds are sold, it is necessary to (1) update any unrecorded interest up to the date of sale, (2) debit cash for the net proceeds received, (3) credit the investment account for the cost of the bonds, and (4) record any gain or loss on sale. Any difference between the net proceeds from the sale of the bonds (the sales price less brokerage fees) and their original cost is recorded as a gain or loss.

Assume, for example, that Kuhl receives net proceeds of $55,000 on the sale of the Doan bonds on January 1, 2006, after receiving (and recording) the interest due. Since the debt securities cost $51,000, a gain of $4,000 has been realized. The entry to record the sale follows:

A	=	L	+	SE
+55,000				+4,000
−51,000				

↑ Cash flows: +55,000

Jan.	1	Cash	55,000	
		Temporary Debt Investment—Doan Bonds		51,000
		Gain on Sale of Investment in Doan Bonds		4,000
		To record sale of Doan Inc. bonds.		

A gain on the sale of debt investments is reported as other revenue in the income statement.

Long-Term Debt Investments

The accounting for temporary debt investments and for long-term debt investments is similar. The major exception is when there is a debt investment in bonds and the bonds are purchased at a premium or discount. As we saw in Chapter 15, this results when a bond is purchased above its face value (at a premium) or below its face value (at a discount).

For temporary investments, any bond premium or discount is combined and recorded along with the face value of the investment in the temporary debt investment account. That is, a bond premium or discount is not separately recorded when the investment is a temporary one. In addition, no premium or discount is amortized to Interest Revenue.

This is because the bonds are held for a short period of time and any misstatement of interest revenue is not significant.

In contrast, for long-term investments, if there is any bond premium or discount, it is separately recorded, similar to what we learned in Chapter 15 for long-term bond liabilities. Any premium or discount is amortized to Interest Revenue over the remaining term of the bonds. If there is a bond premium, interest revenue is reduced by the amortization amount. If there is a bond discount, interest revenue is increased by the amortization amount. Like the issuer of the bonds, the investor uses either the straight-line or the effective-interest method of amortization. The straight-line method was explained in Chapter 15 in Appendix 15A, the effective-interest method in Appendix 15B.

Illustration 16-2 compares the entries for a temporary debt investment and a long-term debt investment in bonds. In this illustration, Khadr Inc. has bought ABC Corporation bonds with a face value of $100,000 at a price of 101. In the first set of entries, it is assumed that the bonds were bought as a temporary investment. In the second set of entries, it is assumed that the bonds were instead bought as a long-term investment.

As explained above, the distinction between the two sets of entries relates to the separate recording of the premium. Premiums are not separately recorded in temporary investments, but are in long-term investments.

Illustration 16-2 ▼
Comparison of temporary and long-term investment

	Temporary Investment					Long-Term Investment		
Jan. 1	Temporary Debt Investment—ABC Bonds	101,000			Jan. 1	Long-Term Debt Investment—ABC Bonds	100,000	
	Cash		101,000			Premium on Bonds	1,000	
	To record purchase of ABC bonds as a temporary investment.					Cash		101,000
						To record purchase of ABC bonds as a long-term investment.		

Recording for the Investor and Investee

Recording a long-term investment in bonds (an asset) is basically the opposite of recording long-term bonds payable (a liability) discussed in Chapter 15. Using the Khadr bond example introduced above, Illustration 16-3 compares the initial recording of the bonds as an investment for Khadr Inc. (the investor) and the recording of the bonds as a liability for ABC Corporation (the investee).

Illustration 16-3 ▼
Comparison of long-term bond investment and liability

	Khadr Inc. (Investor)					ABC Corporation (Investee)		
Jan. 1	Long-Term Debt Investment —ABC Bonds	100,000			Jan. 1	Cash	101,000	
	Premium on Bonds	1,000				Premium on Bonds		1,000
	Cash		101,000			Bonds Payable		100,000
	To record purchase of ABC bonds as a long-term investment.					To record issue of bonds.		

Note that the premium on the bonds is recorded as a debit for the investor, Khadr bond, and as a credit for the investee, ABC Corporation. Recall from Chapter 15 that premium accounts are credits and added to the bond payable liability to determine the bond carrying value. Discount accounts are debits and deducted from the bond payable liability. Even though the premium account is debited in the investment entry, it is still called a premium, and not a discount. The following table summarizes the initial recording of bond discounts and premiums, depending on whether bonds are treated as an investment or as a liability:

	Investment (Investor)	Liability (Investee)
Bond	Debit	Credit
Discount	Credit	Debit
Premium	Debit	Credit

BEFORE YOU GO ON . . .

▶Review It

1. Why might a company make investments in debt or equity securities?
2. What criteria must be met for an investment to be classified as temporary?
3. What entries are required for a temporary investment in money-market instruments? In bonds?
4. How does the accounting for a temporary debt investment differ from that for a long-term debt investment?
5. How does the initial recording of a long-term bond investment by an investor differ from that for a long-term bond issue by an investee?

▶Do It

The Wang Corporation had the following transactions for temporary debt investments:

Jan. 1 Purchased 30 5%, $1,000 Hillary Corp. bonds for $29,500, plus brokerage fees of $900. Interest is payable semi-annually on July 1 and January 1.
July 1 Received semi-annual interest on Hillary Corp. bonds.
July 1 Sold 15 Hillary Corp. bonds for $14,650, less $400 of brokerage fees.

(a) Journalize the transactions for Wang Corporation.
(b) Prepare the adjusting entry for the accrual of interest on December 31, Wang's year end.

Action Plan

• Record bond investment at cost, including brokerage fees.
• When bonds are sold, (1) update any unrecorded interest and (2) credit the investment account for the cost of the bonds.
• Record any difference between the cost and the net proceeds as a gain or loss: Gain = proceeds > cost; loss = proceeds < cost.

Solution

(a)

Jan.	1	Temporary Debt Investment—Hillary Bonds ($29,500 + $900)	30,400	
		Cash		30,400
		To record purchase of 30 Hillary Corp. bonds.		
	1	Cash (30 × $1,000 = $30,000; $30,000 × 5% × $\frac{6}{12}$)	750	
		Interest Revenue		750
		To record receipt of interest on Hillary Corp. bonds.		
	1	Cash ($14,650 − $400)	14,250	
		Loss on Sale of Investment in Hillary Bonds	950	
		Temporary Debt Investment—Hillary Bonds ($30,400 × $\frac{15}{30}$)		15,200
		To record sale of 15 Hillary Corp. bonds.		

(b)

Dec. 31		Interest Receivable	375	
		Interest Revenue (15 × $1,000 = $15,000; $15,000 × 5% × $\frac{6}{12}$)		375
		To accrue interest on Hillary Corp. bonds.		

the navigator

Related exercise material: BE16–1, BE16–2, E16–1, and E16–2.

Accounting for Equity Investments

Equity investments are investments in the share capital—common and/or preferred—of other corporations. As we learned earlier in this chapter, preferred shares are usually held to earn dividend income. Either common or preferred shares can also be held for share price appreciation. Common shares can also be held to influence relationships between companies.

The accounting for equity investments is based on how much influence the investor has over the operating and financial affairs of the issuing corporation (the investee). Illustration 16-4 shows the guidelines for the levels of influence.

Investor's Ownership Interest in Investee's Common Shares	Presumed Influence on Investee	Accounting Guidelines
Less than 20%	Insignificant	Cost method
20% or more	Significant	Equity method

Illustration 16-4 ◄

Accounting guidelines for equity investments

All temporary equity investments are accounted for using the cost method. If the intent is to sell the equity investment if the need for cash arises, then little or no influence exists. Long-term equity investments are accounted for by either the cost method or the equity method, depending on the amount of influence.

When an investor owns 20% or more of the common shares of another company, the investor is generally presumed to exercise a significant influence over the decisions of the investee company.

The presumed influence may be reduced by other circumstances. For example, a company that acquires a 25% interest in a "hostile" takeover may not have significant influence over the investee.

Among the questions that should be answered to determine an investor's influence are these: (1) Does the investor have representation on the investee's board of directors? (2) Does the investor participate in the investee's policy-making process? (3) Are there material transactions between the investor and investee? (4) Are the common shares held by other shareholders concentrated or dispersed? In other words, companies are required to use judgement instead of blindly following the guidelines. On the following pages, we will explain and illustrate the application of each guideline.

No Significant Influence

In accounting for equity investments where there is no significant influence (normally holdings of less than 20%), the cost method is used. Under the **cost method**, the investment is recorded at cost and revenue is recognized only when cash dividends are received. UBC's Portfolio Management Foundation in our feature story has nearly two-thirds of its assets invested in equities. It would use the cost method to account for these investments. The entries for equity investments under the cost method are explained next. They are identical regardless of whether the investment is temporary or long-term.

Recording Acquisitions of Shares

Helpful hint The entries for investments in common shares also apply to investments in preferred shares.

At acquisition, the cost principle applies. Cost includes all expenses to acquire these investments, such as the price paid plus any brokerage fees (commissions). Assume, for example, that on July 1, 2005, St. Amand Corporation (the investor) acquires 1,000 common shares (10% ownership) of Beal Corporation (the investee) at $40 per share plus brokerage fees of $500 as a long-term investment. The entry for the purchase is as follows:

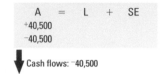

A = L + SE
+40,500
−40,500

Cash flows: −40,500

July 1	Long-Term Equity Investment—Beal Common Shares	40,500	
	Cash [(1,000 × $40) + $500]		40,500
	To record purchase of 1,000 common shares of Beal Corporation.		

While the investor, St. Amand Corporation, must record this acquisition, no entry is required at this time by Beal Corporation. Recall that shares, once issued, are traded among investors. St. Amand Corporation did not purchase these shares directly from Beal Corporation. It purchased them from investors on organized stock exchanges, such as the Toronto Stock Exchange.

Recording Dividends

During the time the shares are held, entries are required for any cash dividends received. If a $2 per share dividend is received by St. Amand Corporation on December 1, the entry is as follows:

A = L + SE
+2,000   +2,000

Cash flows: +2,000

Dec. 1	Cash (1,000 × $2)	2,000	
	Dividend Revenue		2,000
	To record receipt of cash dividend.		

Dividend revenue is reported under other revenues in the income statement. Unlike interest, dividends do not accrue before they are declared. There are therefore no adjusting entries to accrue dividends.

Recording Sales of Shares

When shares are sold, the difference between the net proceeds from the sale (the sale price less brokerage fees) and the cost of the shares is recognized as a gain or loss. Assume that St. Amand receives net proceeds of $39,500 on the sale of its Beal common shares on October 10, 2006. Because the shares cost $40,500, a loss of $1,000 has been incurred. The entry to record the sale follows:

A = L + SE
+39,500   −1,000
−40,500

Cash flows: +39,500

Oct. 10	Cash	39,500	
	Loss on Sale of Equity Investment	1,000	
	Long-Term Equity Investment—Beal Common Shares		40,500
	To record sale of Beal common shares.		

The loss is reported under other expenses in the income statement. A gain on sale would be reported as other revenue.

ACCOUNTING IN ACTION ▶ @–Business Insight

Amazon.com's website receives many "hits" each day. Because of this, Amazon earns significant revenue by allowing other companies to advertise there. Many of them pay with shares since dot.coms often have very little cash. When Amazon receives the shares, it debits Equity Investment and credits Unearned Revenue for the market value of the shares on the day they are received. It then recognizes revenue over the life of the advertising agreement.

Significant Influence

When an investor company owns only a small portion of the shares of another company, the investor cannot exercise control over the investee. But when an investor owns at least 20% of the common shares of a corporation, it is presumed that the investor has significant influence over the financial and operating activities of the investee and plans to hold the investment for the long term. The investor probably also has a representative on the investee's board of directors. Through that representative, the investor begins to exercise some control over the investee. The investee company, to some extent, becomes part of the investor company.

Of course, when an investor owns more than 50% of the common shares of a corporation, it has more than significant influence—it has control. Either way, when an investor owns more than 20% of the common shares of another company, unless there is other evidence to the contrary, it will be able to exercise significant influence or total influence over the investee.

When Forzani bought Sport Mart, it bought 100% of its common shares. Because it had control over the decisions made by Sport Mart, it used an approach called the equity method to account for its investment. Under the equity method, **the investor records its share of the net income of the investee in the same year the income is earned**. An alternative might be to delay recognizing the investor's share of net income until a cash dividend is declared. But that approach would ignore the fact that the investor and investee are, in some sense, one company, which means the investor benefits from the investee's net income.

Under the **equity method**, the investment in common shares is initially recorded at cost. After that, the investment account is adjusted annually to show the investor's equity in the investee. Each year, the investor does the following: (1) It increases (debits) the investment account and increases (credits) revenue for its share of the investee's net income.[1] (2) The investor also decreases (credits) the investment account when dividends are received. The investment account is reduced for dividends received because the net assets of the investee are decreased when a dividend is paid.

> **Helpful hint** Under the equity method, revenue is recognized on the accrual basis—i.e., when it is earned by the investee.

Recording Acquisitions of Shares

Assume that Milar Corporation acquires 30% of the common shares of Beck Corporation for $120,000 on January 1, 2005. Milar is assumed to have significant influence over Beck. The following entry records this transaction:

Jan.	1	Long-Term Equity Investment—Beck Common Shares	120,000	
		Cash		120,000
		To record purchase of Beck common shares.		

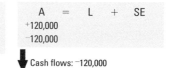

A = L + SE
+120,000
−120,000

Cash flows: −120,000

Recording Investment Revenue and Dividends

For 2005, Beck reports net income of $100,000. It declares and pays a $40,000 cash dividend. Milar is required to record (1) its share of Beck's income, $30,000 (30% × $100,000), and (2) the reduction in the investment account for the dividends received, $12,000 ($40,000 × 30%). The entries are as follows:

---

[1] Or the investor increases (debits) a loss account and decreases (credits) the investment account for its share of the investee's net loss.

A   =   L   +   SE
+30,000   +30,000

Cash flows: no effect

A   =   L   +   SE
+12,000
−12,000

▲ Cash flows: +12,000

	(1)		
Dec. 31	Long-Term Equity Investment—Beck Common Shares	30,000	
	Revenue from Investment in Beck		30,000
	To record 30% equity in Beck's net income.		
	(2)		
31	Cash	12,000	
	Long-Term Equity Investment—Beck Common Shares		12,000
	To record dividends received.		

After the transactions for the year have been posted, the investment and revenue accounts will show the following:

Long-Term Equity Investment—Beck Common Shares				Revenue from Investment in Beck	
Jan. 1	120,000				Dec. 31 30,000
Dec. 31	30,000	Dec. 31	12,000		
Dec. 31 Bal. 138,000					

During the year, the investment account has increased by $18,000 ($138,000 − $120,000). This $18,000 is Milar's 30% equity in the $60,000 increase in Beck's retained earnings ($100,000 − $40,000). In addition, Milar will report $30,000 of revenue from its investment, which is 30% of Beck's net income of $100,000.

The difference between income reported under the cost method and under the equity method can be significant. For example, if Milar were assumed not to have significant influence, it would report only $12,000 of dividend revenue (30% × $40,000) using the cost method. Illustration 16-5 compares the journal entries used to record these investment transactions. First, it is assumed that the cost method (no significant influence) is used by Milar. Then we assume that the equity method (as discussed in this section) is used.

Illustration 16-5 ▼

Comparison of cost and equity method journal entries

Cost Method				Equity Method			
Acquisition				*Acquisition*			
Long-Term Equity Investment—Beck	120,000			Long-Term Equity Investment—Beck	120,000		
Cash			120,000	Cash			120,000
Investee reports net income				*Investee reports net income*			
No entry				Long-Term Equity Investment—Beck		30,000	
				Revenue from Investment in Beck			30,000
Investee pays dividends				*Investee pays dividends*			
Cash		12,000		Cash		12,000	
Dividend Revenue			12,000	Long-Term Equity Investment—Beck			12,000

BEFORE YOU GO ON . . .

▶Review It

1. Compare the accounting for temporary equity investments and long-term equity investments under the cost method.
2. Compare the accounting entries for equity investments for which ownership has (a) no significant influence, and (b) significant influence.

▶Do It

Two separate situations are presented below:

1. CJW Inc. acquired 5% of the 400,000 common shares of Stillwater Corp. as a long-term investment at a total cost of $6 per share on May 18, 2005. On August 30, Stillwater declared

and paid a $0.10 per share dividend. On December 31, Stillwater reported net income of $244,000 for the year.

2. Dumas, Inc. obtained significant influence over North Sails by buying 40% of North Sails' 60,000 common shares at a cost of $12 per share on January 1, 2005. On April 15, North Sails declared and paid a cash dividend of $0.75 per share. On December 31, North Sails reported net income of $120,000 for the year.

Prepare all necessary journal entries for 2005 for (1) CJW Inc., and (2) Dumas, Inc.

Action Plan

- Use the cost method for ownership where no significant influence exists (normally less than 20% of the common shares of another corporation).
- Under the cost method, recognize investment income when dividends are declared.
- Use the equity method for ownership where significant influence is presumed (normally 20% or more of the common shares of another corporation).
- Under the equity method, recognize investment income when the investee declares net income. The distribution of dividends is not income, but rather reduces the equity investment.

Solution

(1) CJW Inc.: Cost Method

May 18	Long-Term Equity Investment—Stillwater Common Shares (400,000 × 5% = 20,000; 20,000 × $6)	120,000	
	Cash		120,000
	To record purchase of 20,000 shares of Stillwater Corp.		
Aug. 30	Cash	2,000	
	Dividend Revenue ($0.10 × 20,000)		2,000
	To record receipt of cash dividend.		
Dec. 31	No entry to record investee's net income.		

(2) Dumas, Inc.: Equity Method

Jan. 1	Long-Term Equity Investment—North Sails Common Shares (60,000 × 40% = 24,000; 24,000 × $12)	288,000	
	Cash		288,000
	To record purchase of 24,000 shares of North Sails.		
Apr. 15	Cash	18,000	
	Long-Term Equity Investment—North Sails Common Shares ($0.75 × 24,000)		18,000
	To record receipt of cash dividend.		
Dec. 31	Long-Term Equity Investment—North Sails Common Shares ($120,000 × 40%)	48,000	
	Revenue from Investment in North Sails		48,000
	To record 40% equity in North Sails' net income.		

Related exercise material: BE16–3, BE16–4, BE16–5, BE16–6, E16–3, E16–4, and E16–5.

Consolidated Financial Statements

study objective 5

Describe the purpose and usefulness of consolidated financial statements.

A company that owns more than 50% of, or controls, the common shares of another company is known as the **parent company**. The company whose shares are owned by the parent company is called the **subsidiary company**. Because of its share ownership, the parent company has a **controlling interest** in the subsidiary company. Voting control can also occur with share ownership of less than 50%, depending on how widely dispersed share ownership is and other factors mentioned previously.

As mentioned in the previous section, when a company controls the common shares of another company, the equity method is used by the parent company to account for its investment in the accounting records. In addition, **for financial reporting purposes only**, **consolidated financial statements** are prepared.

Consolidated financial statements present the total assets and liabilities controlled by the parent company. Consolidated statements are prepared in addition to the financial statements for the individual parent and subsidiary companies. For example, Forzani uses the equity method to account for its investment in Sport Mart in its own individual statements. But, for external reporting, Forzani consolidates Sport Mart's results with its own financial statements. Under this approach, the individual assets and liabilities of Sport Mart are included with those of The Forzani Group.

Consolidated statements are useful because they indicate the size and range of operations of the companies under common control. Consolidation is a complex topic dealt with in advanced accounting courses.

ACCOUNTING IN ACTION ► Business Insight

The top five subsidiary companies in Canada, ranked by revenue, are listed below. In all cases, the major shareholder controls the subsidiary's shares. The percentage ownership is indicated in parentheses.

Rank	Subsidiary	Parent
1	Loblaw, Toronto	George Weston (61%)
2	Power Financial, Montreal	Power Corp. of Canada (67%)
3	Great-West Lifeco, Winnipeg	Power Financial (82%)
4	Celestica, Toronto	Onex (84%)
5	Bell Canada, Montreal	BCE (100%)

BEFORE YOU GO ON . . .

►Review It

1. When a company has a controlling interest in another company, what method of accounting should it use for the investment?
2. What is the purpose of consolidated financial statements?
3. Are The Forzani Group's financial statements consolidated? If so, what percentage does it own of its subsidiary companies? The answers to these questions are provided at the end of this chapter.

Related exercise material: E16–6.

Valuation and Reporting of Investments

study objective 6

Indicate how debt and equity investments are valuated and reported on the financial statements.

We have learned how to account for debt and equity investments. However, another step is required before these investments can be reported in the financial statements. In the next section, we will apply the lower of cost and market valuation rule to temporary and long-term investments. Then, before we learn how to present them in the financial statements, we will summarize the key differences in accounting and valuating temporary and long-term investments. Finally, we will look at some evolving standards that will impact the accounting for, and presentation of, investments in the future.

Valuation

The value of debt and equity investments may change greatly during the time they are held. For example, in a recent one-year period, Forzani's share price hit a low of $14.40

and a high of $23.25—a percentage change of more than 60%. If prices fluctuate so much, what value should equity investments be given at the balance sheet date?

Valuation could be at cost, at market value, or at the lower of cost and market value. Some argue that market value is the best valuation because it is the expected realizable value. **Market value** is the amount for which a security can be sold in a normal market. Others say, however, that unless the investment is going to be sold soon, the market value is not relevant because the price will likely change again. **Conservatism** resolves this issue by requiring the application of the **lower of cost and market (LCM)** rule.

You were introduced to the LCM rule in Chapter 6, for inventories. Just as inventories are reported at the lower of their cost and market values, so too are investments. If the market value of the investments falls below their cost, this potential loss should be recognized when it becomes known, so that decision-makers have access to timely information. Use of the LCM rule varies, depending on whether the investment is temporary or long-term.

Temporary Investments

To illustrate the valuation of temporary debt and equity investments, assume that on December 31, 2005, Plano Corporation's investment portfolio has the following costs and market values:

Investments	Cost	Market Value	Gain (Loss)
Bell Canada bonds	$ 50,000	$ 48,000	$(2,000)
Nexfor shares	90,000	91,000	1,000
Total	$140,000	$139,000	$(1,000)

The LCM rule is normally applied to the total portfolio and not to individual investments. Applying LCM individually would result in an overly conservative valuation for what is already a conservative rule.

The adjusting entry for Plano Corporation is as follows:

Dec. 31	Loss on Decline in Value of Investments	1,000	
	Allowance to Reduce Cost to Market Value		1,000
	To record loss in value of temporary investments.		

A	=	L	+	SE
−1,000				−1,000

Cash flows: no effect

The decline in value from cost to market is reported as a loss on the income statement (in the other expenses section).

A valuation allowance account, Allowance to Reduce Cost to Market Value, is used to record the difference between the cost and market value of the securities. By using this **contra asset account**, the company can keep a record of its original investment cost. The actual cost is needed to determine the gain or loss when individual securities are sold. The allowance account balance is deducted from the cost of the temporary investments to arrive at the lower of cost and market valuation reported on the balance sheet.

The allowance account is carried forward into future accounting periods, in a manner similar to the Allowance for Doubtful Accounts, which offsets Accounts Receivable. No entries are made to the Allowance to Reduce Cost to Market Value account during the period. At the end of each reporting period, the balance in the account is adjusted to the difference between cost and market value (assuming market is lower than cost). If the market value rises above the cost, the allowance account is adjusted to a zero balance. The valuation allowance account should never have a debit balance. This would result in the recognition of a gain. Remember that while conservatism allows losses to be recognized before realization, gains are not recognized until they are realized.

Long-Term Investments

Helpful hint Note that while an allowance is used to record declines in market value below cost in the total portfolio of temporary investments, individual long-term investments are directly written down if the decline is permanent.

Because long-term investments have longer maturities than temporary investments, **their carrying values are not adjusted to reflect temporary fluctuations in market values.** If market value falls substantially below cost and the decline is considered permanent, the investment must be reduced to its market value. This value becomes the investment's new cost base. Any write-down to market value is directly credited to the investment account, as no later recovery in value is expected.

To illustrate, assume that Hébert Corporation purchased 10,000 shares of Bre-X Minerals Ltd. at a cost of $20 per share, as a long-term investment. These shares are now worthless as Bre-X went out of business. The adjusting entry for Hébert to record the $200,000 loss is as follows:

A   =   L   +   SE
−200,000   −200,000

Cash flows: no effect

Dec. 31	Loss on Decline in Value of Investment	200,000	
	Long-Term Equity Investment—Bre-X Minerals Shares		200,000
	To record loss on long-term investment in Bre-X shares.		

ACCOUNTING IN ACTION ▶ Business Insight

JDS Uniphase Corporation's eye-popping US$56-billion loss in 2001 represented a hangover from a high-priced acquisition binge to build up the optical equipment market—a spending spree that came back to haunt the company. This loss amounts to the equivalent of a stack of US$10,000 bills 2.3 times the height of the CN Tower.

Massive write-offs of investments contributed to the fibre-optics supplier's loss. In hindsight, the company grossly overpaid for its acquisitions. A senior technology analyst said at the time, "The market has devalued the companies significantly, so they're revaluating those assets at current market valuations."

Source: Showwei Chu, "Buying Binge Blamed for Startling JDS Loss," *Globe and Mail,* July 27, 2001, B1.

Comparison of Temporary and Long-Term Investments

In this chapter, we have learned how to record the acquisition and sale of debt and equity investments. We have also learned how to record the investment revenue on these investments and how to valuate them for reporting purposes. The following illustration provides a summary overview of some of the key distinctions found in accounting for temporary and long-term debt investments.

Illustration 16-6 ▼

Comparison of temporary and long-term debt investments

	Debt Investments				
	Temporary			Long-Term	
Acquisition	Record at cost, including brokerage fees:			Record at cost, including brokerage fees:	
	Temporary Debt Investment	XX		Long-Term Debt Investment	XX
	Cash		XX	Premium (dr.) [or Discount (cr.)]	XX
				Cash	XX
Investment revenue	Interest earned recorded as revenue:			Interest earned recorded as revenue. Premium or discount, if any, amortized (not illustrated):	
	Cash or Interest Receivable	XX		Cash or Interest Receivable	XX
	Interest Revenue		XX	Interest Revenue	XX
Valuation	Value at lower of cost or market:			Record permanent declines in market value only:	
	Loss on Decline in Value of Investment	XX		Loss on Decline in Value of Investment	XX
	Allowance to Reduce Cost to Market Value		XX	Long-Term Debt Investment	XX

Recording temporary and long-term debt investments differs in two main respects. First, any premium or discount on bonds is recorded separately for long-term debt investments but not for temporary debt investments. Consequently, there is no premium or discount amortization recorded for temporary investments. For long-term investments, any premium or discount is amortized to interest revenue. Secondly, any declines in market value below cost are recorded using a contra account for temporary investments. This contra account can be reversed for increases in market value until it reaches a zero (equal to cost) balance. Only permanent declines in market values are recorded for long-term investments and the investment account is written down directly, rather than using a contra account. No subsequent increases in market value are recorded.

Illustration 16-6 compares some of the key distinctions in accounting for temporary and long-term equity investments.

Illustration 16-7 ▼

Comparison of temporary and long-term equity investments

	Equity Investments		
	Temporary	**Long-Term**	
	Cost Method	Cost Method	Equity Method
Acquisition	Record at cost, including brokerage fees:	Record at cost, including brokerage fees:	Record at cost, including brokerage fees:

	Temporary Equity Investment XX
	  Cash XX
		Long-Term Equity Investment XX
		  Cash XX
			Long-Term Equity Investment XX
			  Cash XX

Investment revenue	Dividends received recorded as revenue:	Dividends received recorded as revenue:	Dividends received recorded as reduction of equity investment; proportionate share of net income recorded as revenue:

	Cash XX
	  Dividend Revenue XX
		Cash XX
		  Dividend Revenue XX
			Cash XX
			  Long-Term Equity Investment XX
			Long-Term Equity Investment XX
			  Revenue from Equity Investment XX

Valuation	Value at lower of cost or market:
	Loss on Decline in Value of Investment XX
	  Allowance to Reduce Cost to Market Value XX
		Record permanent declines in market value only:
		Loss on Decline in Value of Investment XX
		  Long-Term Equity Investment XX
			Record permanent declines in market value only:
			Loss on Decline in Value of Investment XX
			  Long-Term Equity Investment XX

Temporary and long-term equity investments held without significant influence are recorded similarly, using the cost method. The only difference relates to the recording of any declines in market value below cost. As with debt investments, declines for temporary equity investments are recorded using a contra account. This contra account can be reversed for increases in market value until it reaches a zero (equal to cost) balance. Only permanent declines in market values are recorded for long-term investments and the investment account is written down directly, rather than using a contra account. No subsequent increases in market value are recorded.

The accounting for long-term equity investments differs depending on the amount of influence an investor can exert. If an investor does not have significant influence (ownership usually less than 20%), the cost method is used and the recording is similar to that explained for temporary investments except for the LCM valuation. If an investor has significant influence (ownership usually 20% or more), the equity method is used. The equity method records investment revenue when an investee declares its net income, rather than waiting until the net income is distributed as dividends. When an investee declares dividends, an investor reduces the value of its equity investment. The LCM valuation of long-term equity investments is the same regardless of whether the cost or equity method is used.

Financial Statement Presentation

In the balance sheet, investments must be classified as temporary or long-term. No distinction is made between debt and equity securities for financial reporting purposes. The securities are combined and reported as one portfolio amount for each of the temporary or long-term classifications in the financial statements.

Temporary Investments

Cash, the most liquid asset, is listed first in the current assets section of the balance sheet. Highly liquid temporary investments of a very short-term duration (typically less than three months) are viewed as "near" cash. These temporary investments are commonly combined with cash and reported as a single line item called "**Cash and Cash Equivalents.**"

Other temporary investments rank next in order of liquidity. These are presented in the current assets section immediately following cash and cash equivalents.

Temporary investments are reported at the lower of cost and market value. When they are reported at cost, the market value should also be disclosed, usually in parentheses or in the notes to the financial statements. Often there is a statement that says market approximates cost. When temporary investments are reported at market, as was the case in our example earlier in this chapter, one possible presentation is as follows:

PLANO CORPORATION Balance Sheet (partial) December 31, 2005		
Current assets		
Cash and cash equivalents		$ 42,000
Temporary investments, at cost	$140,000	
Less: Allowance to reduce cost to market value	1,000	
Temporary investments, at market		139,000

More often, however, the allowance is not reported separately. Temporary investments are simply stated to be at the lower of cost and market and presented in one line, similar to the presentation style indicated in Illustration 16-8 on the following page.

Long-Term Investments

Debt and equity securities held for other than temporary investment purposes are classified as long-term investments. Long-term investments are generally reported in a separate section of the balance sheet, immediately below current assets, as shown in Illustration 16-8.

Comprehensive Balance Sheet

Many examples of sections of classified balance sheets have been presented in this and earlier chapters. The balance sheet shown in Illustration 16-8 includes key topics from previous chapters in one place: the issue of long-term bonds, the issue of common shares, and restrictions on retained earnings. From this chapter, the statement includes (highlighted in red) temporary and long-term investments (reported at cost and at equity), and informative descriptions within the statement.

Income Statement

In the income statement, the following investment-related accounts are reported in the non-operating section:

Other Revenue	Other Expenses
Interest Revenue	Los on Sale of Investment
Dividend Revenue	Loss on Decline in Value
Gain on Sale of Investment	of Investment

Illustration 16-8 ◄

Comprehensive balance sheet

ZABOSCHUK CORPORATION
Balance Sheet
December 31, 2005

Assets

Current assets
Cash and cash equivalents		$ 21,000
Temporary investments, at lower of cost and market (market $75,000)		60,000
Accounts receivable	$84,000	
Less: Allowance for doubtful accounts	4,000	80,000
Merchandise inventory		130,000
Prepaid insurance		23,000
Total current assets		314,000

Investments
Debt investments	$100,000	
Equity investments, at cost	50,000	
Equity investments, at equity	150,000	
Total long-term investments		300,000

Property, plant, and equipment
Land		$200,000	
Buildings	$800,000		
Less: Accumulated amortization	200,000	600,000	
Equipment	$180,000		
Less: Accumulated amortization	54,000	126,000	
Total property, plant, and equipment			926,000

Intangible assets
Goodwill	170,000
Total assets	$1,710,000

Liabilities and Shareholders' Equity

Current liabilities
Accounts payable		$ 185,000
Bond interest payable		10,000
Income tax payable		60,000
Total current liabilities		255,000

Long-term liabilities
Bonds payable, 7%, due 2016	$300,000	
Less: Discount on bonds	10,000	
Total long-term liabilities		290,000
Total liabilities		545,000

Shareholders' equity
Common shares, no par value, 200,000 authorized, 80,000 issued	$900,000	
Retained earnings (of which $100,000 is restricted for plant expansion)	265,000	
Total shareholders' equity		1,165,000
Total liabilities and shareholders' equity		$1,710,000

Changing Standards

Accounting for investments is about to change. Canadian standard-setters are expected to require the use of market values to account for some investments in 2005, which would harmonize the valuation and reporting of investments with practices in the United States and internationally.

In addition to accounting for some investments at market value rather than at the lower of cost and market, investments are expected to be reclassified into three broad categories:

1. **Trading securities** are debt or equity investments bought and sold and held mainly for sale in the near term. Trading securities are classified as current assets.
2. **Available-for-sale securities** are debt or equity investments that are held with the intent of selling them sometime in the future. Available-for-sale securities can be classified as either current or long-term assets, depending on management's intent.
3. **Held-to-maturity securities** are debt investments that the investor has the intent and ability to hold to maturity. Held-to-maturity securities are classified as long-term assets.

The revaluation of investments—in particular trading securities and available-for-sale securities—to market value will result in unrealized gains or losses. These are called unrealized because the investments have not been sold. The unrealized gain or loss is the difference between the total cost of the investments and their total market value. These unrealized gains and losses will be reported directly on the income statement, or as an adjustment to shareholders' equity, depending on their classification.

You will recall that in Chapter 14 we learned about another standards change expected soon—the introduction of a comprehensive income statement. The comprehensive income statement will not only include net income reported on the traditional income statement. It will also show some income-type transactions that are not now in the income statement but are reported in the shareholders' equity section of the balance sheet. These include such items as translation gains and losses on foreign currency and unrealized gains and losses on available-for-sale securities.

At the time of writing, these new standards affecting investments and the comprehensive income statement are expected to be introduced as a package later in 2004, and to take effect in October 2005. Many believe that a move to recording some types of investments at market value will be a step forward. They think that reporting investments at market value better represents the underlying economic value of some of the company's assets. Others are dissatisfied: some think the proposed new standards go too far; still others think they do not go far enough.

For now, we just wish to make you aware that these changes are very likely to be introduced soon as part of the standards harmonization efforts we learned about in Chapter 11. However, until these standards are made official, this text will focus on the existing standards that valuate investments at the lower of cost and market and classify investments as temporary and long-term debt and equity investments.

BEFORE YOU GO ON . . .

▶Review It

1. Describe the proper valuation and reporting of temporary and long-term investments on a balance sheet.
2. Where are temporary and long-term investments and related accounts reported on a balance sheet? On an income statement?
3. How might new standards affect the valuation of investments?

Related exercise material: BE16–7, BE16–8, BE16–9, BE16–10, BE16–11, E16–7, E16–8, E16–9, E16–10, E16–11, E16–12, and E16–13.

Demonstration Problem

In its first year of operations, DeMarco Ltd. had the following selected transactions in temporary equity investments:

June 1 Purchased for cash 600 Sanburg common shares at $24 per share plus $300 of brokerage fees.

July 1 Purchased for cash 800 Cey common shares at $33 per share plus $600 of brokerage fees.

Sept. 1 Received a $1 per share cash dividend from Cey Corporation.

Nov. 1 Sold 200 Sanburg common shares for cash at $27 per share less $150 of brokerage fees.

Dec. 15 Received a $0.50 per share cash dividend on Sanburg common shares.

At December 31, the market values per share were $25 for Sanburg and $30 for Cey.

Instructions

(a) Journalize the transactions.

(b) Prepare the adjusting entry at December 31 to report the total investment portfolio at the lower of cost and market value.

Additional
Demonstration
Problems

Solution to Demonstration Problem

(a)

June 1	Temporary Equity Investment—Sanburg Common	14,700	
	Cash [(600 × $24) + $300]		14,700
	To record purchase of 600 Sanburg common shares.		
July 1	Temporary Equity Investment—Cey Common	27,000	
	Cash [(800 × $33) + $600]		27,000
	To record purchase of 800 Cey common shares.		
Sept. 1	Cash (800 × $1)	800	
	Dividend Revenue		800
	To record receipt of $1 per share cash dividend from Cey Corporation.		
Nov. 1	Cash [(200 × $27) − $150]	5,250	
	Temporary Equity Investment—Sanburg Common [(200 ÷ 600) × $14,700)]		4,900
	Gain on Sale of Equity Investments		350
	To record sale of 200 Sanburg common shares.		
Dec. 15	Cash [(600 − 200) × $0.50]	200	
	Dividend Revenue		200
	To record receipt of $0.50 per share dividend from Sanburg.		

(b) The following table shows the relevant values at the end of the fiscal year:

Investment	Cost	Market Value	Gain (Loss)
Sanburg common shares (400)	$ 9,800	$10,000	$ 200
Cey common shares (800)	27,000	24,000	(3,000)
Totals	$36,800	$34,000	$ (2,800)

The lower of cost and market valuation is usually applied to the portfolio as a whole. This results in the following adjusting journal entry:

Dec. 31	Loss on Decline in Value of Temporary Investments	2,800	
	Allowance to Reduce Cost to Market Value		2,800
	To record loss on temporary investments.		

Action Plan

- Recall that cost includes the price paid plus brokerage fees and that net proceeds includes the price received less brokerage fees.
- Record dividend revenue when received (or declared).
- Keep an up-to-date balance of the number of shares purchased and sold.
- Determine the gain or loss by the difference between the net proceeds and the cost of the securities.
- Determine the adjustment to LCM based on the difference between the total cost and total market value of the securities.

the
navigator

Summary of Study Objectives

1. *Identify the reasons why corporations invest in debt and equity securities.* Corporations invest for three main reasons: (a) They have excess cash. (b) They view investments as a revenue source. (c) They have strategic goals such as gaining control of a competitor, promoting strategic alliances, or moving into a new line of business.

2. *Distinguish between temporary and long-term investments.* Temporary investments are securities held by a company that are (a) readily marketable and (b) intended to be exchanged for cash in the near future as the need for cash arises. Investments that do not meet both criteria are classified as long-term investments.

3. *Explain and illustrate the accounting for debt investments.* Entries for investments in debt securities are required when the bonds are purchased, when interest is received or accrued, and when the bonds are sold. The accounting for long-term investments in bonds is the same as that for temporary investments in bonds, except that bond premiums and bond discounts must be recorded separately and amortized.

4. *Explain and illustrate the accounting for equity investments.* Entries for investments in shares are required when the shares are purchased, when dividends are received, and when the shares are sold. When the investor company is not able to exert significant

influence (ownership is usually less than 20%) over the operating and financial policies of the investee company, the cost method is used for both temporary and long-term investments. When significant influence exists (ownership is usually 20% or more) and the investment is long-term, the equity method should be used. When control is exercised (ownership is usually greater than 50%), consolidated financial statements should be prepared for financial reporting purposes.

5. *Describe the purpose and usefulness of consolidated financial statements.* When a company controls the common shares of another company, consolidated financial statements detailing the financial position of the combined entity must be prepared. These statements are useful because they indicate the size and scope of operations of the companies under common control.

6. *Indicate how debt and equity investments are valuated and reported on the financial statements.* Temporary investments are reported as current assets on the balance sheet. These investments are valuated at the lower of cost and market, with market values separately disclosed. Long-term investments are valuated at cost. If the market value is expected to be permanently less than cost, the investment should be written down to market, which now becomes its new cost base.

Glossary

Key Term Matching Activity

Consolidated financial statements Financial statements that present the assets and liabilities controlled by the parent company, and the total profitability of the combined companies. (p. 762)

Controlling interest Ownership of more than 50%, or voting control, of the common shares of another company. (p. 761)

Cost method An accounting method in which the equity investment in shares is recorded at cost. Investment revenue is recognized only when cash dividends are received. (p. 757)

Debt investments Investments in money-market instruments and corporate, government, and university bonds. (p. 752)

Equity investments Investments in the share capital of other corporations. (p. 757)

Equity method An accounting method in which the investment in common shares is initially recorded at cost. The investment account is then adjusted annually to show the investor's equity in the investee. (p. 759)

Investee The corporation that issues (sells) the debt or equity securities. (p. 753)

Investor The corporation that buys the debt or equity securities. (p. 753)

Long-term investments Investments that are not readily marketable or that management does not intend to convert into cash in the near future. (p. 752)

Lower of cost and market (LCM) A conservative rule that states that investments must be carried at the lower of their cost and market value. (p. 763)

Market value Amount for which a security could be sold in a normal market. (p. 763)

Parent company A company that controls, or owns more than 50% of the common shares of, another company. (p. 761)

Subsidiary company A company whose common shares are controlled by another company (usually more than 50% of its common shares are owned by the other company). (p. 761)

Temporary investments Investments that are readily marketable and intended to be exchanged for cash in the near future when the need for cash arises. (p. 751)

Self-Study Questions

Answers are at the end of the chapter.

(SO 1) K 1. Which of the following is not a reason that corporations invest in debt and equity securities?
(a) They have excess cash.
(b) They want to generate losses to reduce income.
(c) They want to generate investment income.
(d) They want to meet strategic goals.

(SO 2) K 2. Temporary investments must be readily marketable and expected to be sold:
(a) within the operating cycle.
(b) within the next year.
(c) within three months.
(d) whenever the need for cash arises.

(SO 2) K 3. Long-term investments:
(a) are expected to be held for more than one year.
(b) are expected to be sold within the next year.
(c) are not intended to be sold in the near future.
(d) consist of debt securities only.

(SO 2) K 4. Debt investments are initially recorded at:
(a) cost.
(b) book value.
(c) market value.
(d) lower of cost and market value.

(SO 3) AP 5. Pryor Corp. receives net proceeds of $42,000 on the sale of debt investments that cost $39,500. This transaction should be reported in the income statement as a:
(a) loss of $2,500 under other expenses.
(b) loss of $2,500 under operating expenses.
(c) gain of $2,500 under other revenues.
(d) gain of $2,500 under operating revenues.

(SO 4) AP 6. The Big K Ranch owns 20% of the Little L Ranch's common shares. The Little L Ranch reported net income of $150,000 and paid dividends of $40,000 this year. How much investment revenue would the Big K Ranch report if it used the cost method to account for this equity investment? The equity method?

(a) $8,000 cost method; $22,000 equity method
(b) $8,000 cost method; $30,000 equity method
(c) $40,000 cost method; $110,000 equity method
(d) $150,000 under both methods

(SO 4) K 7. The equity method of accounting for long-term investments in common shares is normally used when the investor owns:
(a) more than 0% of the investee's common shares.
(b) 20% or more of the investee's common shares.
(c) more than 50% of the investee's common shares.
(d) less than 20% of the investee's common shares.

(SO 5) K 8. Which of the following statements is false? Consolidated financial statements are useful to determine the:
(a) profitability of specific subsidiaries.
(b) total profitability of companies under common control.
(c) range of a parent company's operations.
(d) full extent of the total obligations of companies under common control.

(SO 6) K 9. The account Allowance to Reduce Cost to Market Value is reported as a:
(a) contra asset account on the balance sheet.
(b) contra shareholders' equity account on the balance sheet.
(c) loss on the income statement.
(d) loss on the statement of retained earnings.

(SO 6) AP 10. At the end of the first year of operations, the total cost of the temporary investments portfolio is $120,000. Total market value is $115,000. The financial statements should show:
(a) a $5,000 reduction of a long-term asset in the balance sheet and a loss of $5,000 in the income statement.
(b) a $5,000 reduction of a current asset and a loss of $5,000 in the shareholders' equity section.
(c) a $5,000 reduction of a current asset and a loss of $5,000 in the income statement.
(d) no reduction and no loss.

Questions

(SO 1) K 1. What are the reasons why corporations invest in debt and equity securities?

(SO 2) C 2. Kirk Wholesale Supply owns common shares in **Rogers Wireless Communications Inc.**, which it intends to hold indefinitely because of some negative tax consequences if the investment is sold. Should the investment in Rogers be classified as a temporary investment? Why or why not?

(SO 3) C 3. Osborne Corp. is considering making an investment in Bank of Canada bonds. If Osborne considers this to be a long-term investment instead of a temporary investment, will this have an impact on Osborne's recognition of interest revenue from the investment? Explain why or why not.

(SO 3) C   4. Ann Adler is confused about gains and losses on the sale of debt investments. Explain to Ann (a) how the gain or loss is calculated, and (b) the statement presentation of the gains and losses.

(SO 3) C   5. Clio Ltd. sells an investment in bonds for $45,000. The bonds originally cost $40,000. How should Clio account for the difference in these amounts?

(SO 3, 4) C   6. How is the cost of an equity investment in shares or a debt investment in bonds determined? What is the relevant accounting principle?

(SO 4) AP   7. To acquire Mega Corporation common shares, Duran Ltd. pays $65,000 cash plus $1,500 of broker's fees. Assuming the shares are readily marketable and the company intends to sell them when the need for cash arises, how should this investment be reported on Duran's balance sheet?

(SO 4) K   8. When should a long-term investment in common shares be accounted for by the cost and equity methods?

(SO 4) C   9. How are dividends received from a long-term equity investment accounted for when using (1) the cost method, and (2) the equity method? Explain why this accounting differs.

(SO 4) AP   10. Malon Corporation uses the equity method to account for its ownership of 25% of the common shares of Flynn Packing. During 2005, Flynn Packing reports a net income of $80,000 and declares and pays cash dividends of $10,000. What recognition should Malon give to these events?

(SO 4) K   11. What constitutes "significant influence"? Is it safe to conclude that significant influence exists when a company owns 20% or more of the common shares of another company?

(SO 5) K   12. What are consolidated financial statements? When must they be prepared?

(SO 6) C   13. What is the rationale for using the lower of cost and market rule for reporting investments on the balance sheet?

(SO 6) AP   14. At December 31, G-Products, Inc.'s temporary investments, which cost $74,000, have a market value of $68,000. Indicate how G-Products would report these data in the financial statements prepared on December 31.

(SO 6) C   15. Using the data in question 14, how would G-Products report the data if the investments were long-term and the decline were thought to be temporary? Permanent?

(SO 6) C   16. What is the proper statement presentation of the account Loss on Decline in Value of Temporary Investments?

(SO 6) C   17. What is the purpose of reporting the account Allowance to Reduce Cost to Market Value as a contra asset in the balance sheet?

(SO 6) AP   18. **Hollinger Inc.** reported the following selected data (in thousands) in fiscal 2002: cash and cash equivalents, $188,852; investment in associated companies, at equity, $48,975; marketable investments, at cost, $91,476; other investments, $69,694; investment and other income, $29,729; and net loss in equity accounted companies, $1,233. Identify which financial statement each of these amounts should be reported on and give the relevant classification.

Brief Exercises

Record debt investment transactions.
(SO 3) AP

BE16–1   Toyworks Ltd. has $100,000 of excess cash the company does not need immediately. It decides to invest the cash in the ADR Canadian Money-Market Fund until the money is needed later in the year. Journalize the following transactions:

(a) Buys the money-market fund on March 1, 2005.
(b) Receives notification on March 31, 2005, that $200 interest was earned in March and added to the fund.
(c) Sells the fund on April 30, 2005, and receives $100,401 cash, which includes $201 interest earned in April.

Record debt investment and issue transactions.
(SO 3) AP

BE16–2   Assume that 10-year, 7% bonds are issued at their face value of $50,000 on June 30. Interest is payable semi-annually each June 30 and December 31.

(a) Prepare the journal entries to record the purchase of the debt investment on June 30 and the receipt of the first interest payment on December 31 on the books of the investor, assuming this is a temporary investment.
(b) Prepare the journal entries to record the issue of the debt on June 30 and the first interest payment on December 31 on the books of the issuer.
(c) If the investor had considered this to be a long-term investment instead of a temporary investment, would there be any differences in the journal entries compared to those recorded in (a)?

BE16–3 On August 1, McLain Inc. buys 1,000 Datawave common shares as a temporary investment for $36,000 cash plus brokerage fees of $600. On December 1, McLain sells the shares for $38,000 cash. Journalize the purchase and sale of the investment in common shares.

Record equity investment transactions.
(SO 4) AP

BE16–4 Loop Limited owns 25% of Hook Corporation. For the current year, Hook reports net income of $180,000 and declares and pays a $50,000 cash dividend. Record Loop's equity in Hook's net income and the receipt of dividends from Hook. How much revenue will Loop report?

Record equity investment transactions, using equity method.
(SO 4) AP

BE16–5 Using the data presented in BE16–4, assume that Loop Limited owns only 10% of Hook Corporation. Prepare the journal entries to record the transactions in BE16–4. How much revenue would Loop report now? Explain why this differs from the answer obtained in BE16–4.

Record equity investment transactions, using cost method.
(SO 4) AP

BE16–6 Chan Inc. owns 20% of Dong Ltd.'s common shares. During the year, Dong reported net income of $100,000 and paid a dividend of $20,000. Indicate whether using the equity method instead of the cost method would result in an increase (+), a decrease (−), or no effect (NE) in each of the following categories (assuming Dong's reported net earnings are greater than dividend paid):

Compare financial impact of cost and equity methods.
(SO 4) AP

Balance Sheet			Income Statement		
		Shareholders'			Net
Assets	Liabilities	Equity	Revenues	Expenses	Income

BE16–7 Cost and market value data for the temporary investments of Deal.ca Inc. at December 31, 2005, are $64,000 and $61,000, respectively. Prepare any required adjusting entry to record the securities at the lower of cost and market value. Say if no entry is required.

Record LCM for temporary investments.
(SO 6) AP

BE16–8 For the data presented in BE16–7, show the financial statement presentation of the temporary investments and related accounts.

Show statement presentation.
(SO 6) AP

BE16–9 Duggen Corporation holds equity securities costing $72,000 as a long-term investment. At December 31, 2005, the market value of the securities is $60,000. Assuming the decline in value is not due to temporary market fluctuations, prepare the adjusting entry to record the securities at market value.

Record LCM for long-term investments.
(SO 6) AP

BE16–10 For the data presented in BE16–9, show the financial statement presentation of the long-term investments and related accounts.

Show statement presentation.
(SO 6) AP

BE16–11 Sabre Corporation has the following long-term investments at November 30, 2005: (1) common shares of Sword Co. (10% ownership), original cost $108,000, current market value $120,000; (2) common shares of Epee Inc. (30% ownership), original cost $210,000, equity method valuation $250,000, current market value $253,000; and (3) bonds of Ghoti Corp., original cost $150,000, current market value $175,000. Prepare the long-term investments section of the balance sheet.

Prepare long-term investments section of balance sheet.
(SO 6) AP

Exercises

E16–1 Piper Corporation had the following transactions with temporary debt investments:

Jan. 1 Bought 60 $1,000 Harris Co. 6% bonds for $60,000 cash plus brokerage fees of $900. Interest is payable semi-annually on July 1 and January 1.
July 1 Received semi-annual interest on Harris bonds.
July 1 Sold 30 Harris bonds for $32,000, less $500 of brokerage fees.
Dec. 31 Accrued interest at Piper's year end.

Record debt investment transactions.
(SO 3) AP

Interactive Homework

Instructions

Journalize the transactions.

E16–2 Jackson Ltd. has excess cash at various points in the fiscal year and has a policy of investing these funds in temporary debt investments. During 2005, it enters into the following transactions:

Jan. 2 For $9,938, bought a 90-day T-bill maturing on April 1.
Apr. 1 The T-bill matured and Jackson received $10,000 cash, which included the interest earned on the amount invested.

Record debt investment transactions.
(SO 3) AP

June   1 Invested $40,000 cash in a money-market fund.
       30 Received notification that $75 interest had been earned and added to the fund.
July 31 Received notification that $75 interest had been earned and added to the fund.
Aug. 15 Cashed the money-market fund and received $40,188.
Oct. 31 Bought a three-month, 2.25% term deposit for $24,000.

Instructions

(a) Record journal entries for the above transactions.
(b) Record any accruals necessary on November 30, 2005, Jackson's fiscal year end.

Record equity investment transactions.
(SO 4) AP

E16–3 McCormick Inc. had the following transactions with temporary investments in common shares:

Jan.   1 Bought 1,000 Starr Corporation common shares (5% of the total number of shares) for $105,000 cash plus a $2,000 broker's commission.
July   1 Received a cash dividend of $9 per share.
Dec.   1 Sold 500 Starr common shares for $57,000 cash, less a $1,000 broker's commission.
      31 Received a cash dividend of $9 per share.

Instructions

Journalize the transactions.

Record equity investment transactions; explain income statement presentation.
(SO 4) AP

E16–4 Malea Corporation had the following transactions with temporary equity investments:

Feb.   1 Bought 600 BMO common shares for $23,400 cash plus brokerage fees of $240.
July   1 Received cash dividends of $1 per share on BMO common.
Sept. 1 Sold 300 BMO common shares for $10,800, less brokerage fees of $120.
Dec.   1 Received cash dividends of $1 per share on BMO common.

Instructions

(a) Journalize the transactions.
(b) Explain how dividend revenue and the gain (loss) on sale should be reported in the income statement.

Record equity investment transactions, using cost and equity methods.
(SO 4) AP

Interactive Homework

E16–5 Presented below are two independent situations:

1. Visage Cosmetics Inc. acquires 10% of the 200,000 common shares of Image Fashion Inc. at a total cost of $12 per share on March 18, 2005. On June 30, Image Fashion declares and pays a $75,000 dividend. On December 31, Image Fashion reports net income of $122,000 for the year. At December 31, the market price of Image Fashion is $14 per share. The shares are classified as a long-term investment.
2. Ismail, Inc., acquires 45% of Diner Limited's 30,000 common shares at a total cost of $9 per share on January 1, 2005. On June 15, Diner declares and pays a cash dividend of $35,000. On December 31, Diner reports net income of $75,000 for the year.

Instructions

Prepare all the necessary journal entries for 2005 for (a) Visage Cosmetics Inc., and (b) Ismail, Inc.

Record acquisition and explain accounting for consolidation.
(SO 4, 5) AN

E16–6 In October 2003, **The Bon-Ton Stores Inc.** acquired all the common shares of **Elder-Beerman Corp.** for US$8 per share, which amounted to US$92.8 million cash. The combined company operates 142 stores in 16 different states, making it one of the largest independent retail department stores in the United States.

Instructions

(a) Prepare the journal entry to record Bon-Ton's acquisition of Elder-Beerman on Bon-Ton's books. What entry would Elder-Beerman have made on its books?
(b) Which method—equity or cost—should Bon-Ton use to account for its investment in Elder-Beerman?
(c) Which company is the parent company and which is the subsidiary company?
(d) After the acquisition, the Elder-Beerman stores continued to exist as separate stores. But the Elder-Beerman Corp. shares are no longer traded on the stock exchange and Elder-Beerman's financial results are consolidated with the Bon-Ton Stores' for reporting purposes. Explain why.

E16–7 On November 1, 2004, Lalonde Lteé buys 2,000 shares of Lyman Corporation for $35 per share and 4,000 shares of Kaur Inc. for $25 per share as temporary equity investments. On December 15, Lalonde sells 800 Lyman shares for $50 per share. At December 31, the company's year end, the market value of the Lyman shares is $45 per share and the market value of the Kaur shares is $14 per share. On March 31, 2005, Lalonde sells the remaining Lyman shares for $40 per share. On December 31, 2005, the market value of the Kaur shares is $18 per share.

Record equity investment transactions, including LCM.
(SO 4, 6) AP

Interactive Homework

Instructions

Prepare journal entries to record all transactions, including any required adjusting entries, related to temporary equity investments for Lalonde Lteé for 2004 and 2005.

E16–8 On January 1, Diversity Corporation buys 30% of the voting shares of Bellingham Corporation for $180,000. At December 31, Bellingham declares and pays a $60,000 cash dividend and reports net income of $200,000. Assume Diversity has significant influence over Bellingham.

Record equity investment transactions; determine balance sheet presentation.
(SO 4, 6) AP

Instructions

(a) Journalize the transactions.
(b) Determine the amount to be reported on Diversity's balance sheet and income statement for the investment in Bellingham shares at December 31.
(c) Repeat (b) assuming Diversity does not have significant influence over Bellingham.

E16–9 At December 31, 2005, the temporary investments for Yanik, Inc., are as follows:

Record LCM for temporary investments. Show statement presentation.
(SO 6) AP

Security	Cost	Market Value
A	$18,500	$16,000
B	12,500	14,000
C	23,000	19,000
Totals	$54,000	$49,000

Instructions

(a) Prepare the adjusting entry at December 31, 2005, to report the investment portfolio at the lower of cost and market value.
(b) Show the balance sheet and income statement presentation at December 31, 2005.

E16–10 Data for temporary investments are presented in E16–9. Assume instead that the investments are classified as long-term investments. The declines in value are not due to temporary market fluctuations.

Record LCM for long-term investments. Show statement presentation and prepare memo.
(SO 6) S

Instructions

(a) Prepare the adjusting entry at December 31, 2005, to report the securities in the appropriate manner.
(b) Show the statement presentation at December 31, 2005.
(c) J. Arnet, a member of the board of directors, does not understand why a loss is reported when nothing has been sold. Write a memo to Ms. Arnet which explains the reporting and its purposes.

E16–11 Firstview Corporation has the following data at December 31, 2005:

Record LCM and show statement presentation.
(SO 6) AP

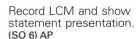

Interactive Homework

	Cost	Market Value
Temporary investments	$125,000	$110,000
Long-term investments	115,000	95,000

Additional information:

1. In previous periods, the market value of temporary investments was always higher than their cost. Consequently, the company does not yet have the account Allowance to Reduce Cost to Market Value.
2. The decline in the market value of the long-term investments is not believed to result from temporary market fluctuations.

Instructions

(a) Prepare the adjusting entries to report each class of securities appropriately.
(b) Indicate the balance sheet and income statement presentation of each class of securities.

Classify balance sheet accounts.
(SO 6) AP

E16–12 You are provided with the following balance sheet accounts of New Bay Inc. as at December 31, 2005:

Accounts payable	$ 35,000
Accounts receivable	65,000
Accumulated amortization—computers	8,000
Accumulated amortization—equipment	11,000
Allowance for doubtful accounts	10,000
Allowance to reduce cost to market value	9,000
Bond interest payable	8,000
Bonds payable, 8%, due 2012	250,000
Cash and cash equivalents	22,000
Common shares, 10,000, no par value	100,000
Computers	12,000
Equipment	22,000
Equity investment (Hemosol Inc. common shares), at equity	50,000
Income tax payable	12,000
Interest receivable	5,000
Long-term debt investment (Aliant Inc. bonds)	180,000
Merchandise inventory	64,000
Premium on bonds payable	18,000
Retained earnings	53,000
Temporary investments, at cost	65,000
Unearned sales revenue	7,000

Instructions

Indicate where each of the above accounts would be classified on New Bay's balance sheet at December 31, 2005.

Identify statement impact of investment transactions.
(SO 6) AN

E16–13 Lai Inc. had the following investment transactions:

1. Bought Chang Corporation preferred shares for cash as a temporary equity investment.
2. Received a stock dividend on Chang preferred shares.
3. Bought Government of Canada bonds for cash as a temporary debt investment.
4. Accrued interest on Government of Canada bonds.
5. Sold Government of Canada bonds for cash at a price less than originally paid.
6. Bought 10% of Xing Ltd. common shares for cash as a long-term equity investment.
7. Received Xing's financial statements, which reported a net loss for the year.
8. Xing declared and paid a cash dividend.
9. Prepared an adjusting entry to record a decline in the market value of the investment portfolio below cost.

Instructions

Using the following table format, indicate whether each of the above transactions would result in an increase (+), decrease (−), or no effect (NE). The first one has been done for you as an example.

	Balance Sheet			Income Statement		
	Assets	Liabilities	Shareholders' Equity	Revenues	Expenses	Net Income
1.	(+/−)	NE	NE	NE	NE	NE

Problems: Set A

P16–1A CASB Incorporated is establishing a new business venture in western Canada. In order to secure necessary start-up capital, it issued 10-year, 7% bonds which pay interest semi-annually on June 30 and December 31. On January 1, 2004, Densmore Consulting Ltd. paid $100,000 for these bonds with a face value of $100,000. At this point in time, Densmore intends to hold the bonds as a long-term investment. On January 1, 2005, Densmore Consulting sold its CASB bonds for $99,000. CASB has a December 31 year end. Densmore has an October 31 year end.

Record debt investment transactions for investor and investee, and comment.
(SO 3) AP

Instructions

(a) Prepare all required entries for the investor, Densmore Consulting.
(b) Prepare all required entries for the investee (issuer), CASB.
(c) Comment on the differences in recording between the investor and the investee.

P16–2A The following Liu Corporation transactions are for long-term investments in bonds:

Record debt investment transactions, including LCM. Show statement presentation.
(SO 3, 6) AP

2004

Jan. 1 Purchased $50,000 of RAM Corp. 6% bonds, at 100.
July 1 Received semi-annual interest on the RAM bonds.
Dec. 31 Accrued interest at year end on the RAM bonds.

2005

Jan. 1 Received semi-annual interest on the RAM bonds.
        1 Sold $25,000 of RAM bonds for $27,500.
July 1 Received the semi-annual interest on the RAM bonds.
Dec. 31 Accrued interest at year end on the RAM bonds.

Instructions

(a) Journalize the transactions.
(b) Assume that the market value of the bonds at December 31, 2005, was $23,000. Prepare any required adjusting entry to properly value the debt investment.
(c) Show the balance sheet presentation of the bonds and interest at December 31, 2005, and indicate where any gain or loss is reported.

P16–3A In January 2005, the management of Rakai Corporation concludes that it has enough cash to purchase temporary investments in debt and equity securities. During the year, the following transactions occur:

Record debt and equity investment transactions, including LCM. Show statement presentation.
(SO 3, 4, 6) AP

Feb. 1 Purchased 850 IBF common shares for $40,000 plus brokerage fees of $800.
Mar. 1 Purchased 500 RST common shares for $18,000 plus brokerage fees of $500.
Apr. 1 Purchased 70 $1,000, 6% CRT bonds for $70,000 plus brokerage fees of $1,200. Interest is payable semi-annually on April 1 and October 1.
July 1 Received a cash dividend of $0.60 per share on the IBF common shares.
Aug. 1 Sold 350 IBF common shares at $42 per share, less brokerage fees of $350.
Sept. 1 Received a $2 per share cash dividend on the RST common shares.
Oct. 1 Received the semi-annual interest on the CRT bonds.
        1 Sold the CRT bonds for $68,000, less $1,500 of brokerage fees.

At December 31, the market values of the IBF and RST common shares were $39 and $30 per share, respectively.

Instructions

(a) Journalize the transactions and post them to each investment account.
(b) Prepare the adjusting entry at December 31, 2005, to report the investments at the lower of cost and market value.
(c) Show the balance sheet presentation of the temporary investments at December 31, 2005.
(d) Identify the income statement accounts involved, and give the statement classification of each account.

Record equity investment transactions, using cost and equity methods. Write memo explaining difference.
(SO 4) S

P16–4A Cardinal Concrete Limited acquired 20% of the common shares of Edra, Inc., on January 1, 2005, by paying $1.2 million for 40,000 shares. Edra declared and paid an $0.80 per share cash dividend on June 30 and again on December 31. Edra reported net income of $800,000 for the year.

Instructions

(a) Prepare the journal entries for Cardinal Concrete for 2005, assuming Cardinal cannot exercise significant influence over Edra.

(b) Prepare the journal entries for Cardinal Concrete for 2005, assuming Cardinal can exercise significant influence over Edra.

(c) The board of directors of Cardinal Concrete is confused about the differences between the cost and equity methods. Write a memo to the board that (1) explains each method, and (2) shows the account balances for both the investment and the related revenue under each method at December 31, 2005.

Record equity investment transactions, using cost and equity methods. Compare statement presentation.
(SO 4, 5, 6) AP

P16–5A Sub Corporation has 500,000 common shares. On January 10, 2005, Par Corporation purchased a block of these shares on the open market at $10 cash per share to hold as a long-term investment. At the end of 2005, Sub Corporation reported net income of $260,000 and declared and paid a $0.25 per share dividend.

This problem involves three independent situations related to the accounting for these investments by Par Corporation:

Situation A: Par purchased 75,000 common shares of Sub.
Situation B: Par purchased 150,000 common shares of Sub.
Situation C: Par purchased all 500,000 common shares of Sub.

Instructions

(a) For each situation, identify the accounting method that should be used by Par to account for this investment in Sub.

(b) For each situation, prepare the journal entries for Par for the year ended December 31, 2005, to record all transactions related to the investment.

(c) For each situation, compare Par's nonconsolidated balance sheet and income statement accounts related to these investments at year end.

(d) In Situation C, what kind of financial statements should be prepared to report the operations of Par and Sub? Whose name will be on the financial statements?

Record equity investment transactions, including LCM. Show statement presentation.
(SO 4, 6) AP

P16–6A On December 31, 2004, Harmon Associates owned the following securities that were being held as long-term investments:

Common Shares	Quantity	Cost
Allain Corp.	2,000	$50,000
Basabe Corp.	6,000	36,000
Crouse Corp.	1,300	24,000

The securities are not held for influence or control over the investees. In 2005, the following transactions occur:

July   1 Received a $1 per share semi-annual cash dividend on Basabe common shares.
Aug.   1 Received a $0.50 per share cash dividend on Allain common shares.
Sept. 1 Sold 2,000 Basabe common shares for cash at $7 per share, less brokerage fees of $300.
Oct.   1 Sold 600 Allain common shares for cash at $27 per share less brokerage fees of $400.
Nov.   1 Received a $1 per share cash dividend on Crouse common shares.
Dec. 15 Received a $0.50 per share cash dividend on Allain common shares.
      31 Received a $1 per share semi-annual cash dividend on Basabe common shares.

At December 31, the market values per share of the common shares were Allain $24, Basabe $6, and Crouse $19.

Instructions

(a) Journalize the 2005 transactions and post them to each long-term investment account.

(b) Prepare the adjusting entry at December 31, 2005, to show the securities at the lower of cost and market value. Assume that any declines are not due to temporary market fluctuations.

(c) Show the balance sheet presentation of the investments at December 31, 2005.

P16–7A The following are in Hi-Tech Inc.'s portfolio of long-term securities at December 31, 2004:

Record equity investment transactions and show statement presentation. (SO 4, 6) AP

	Quantity	Cost
Aglar Corporation common shares	500	$26,000
BAL Corporation common shares	700	42,000
Hicks Corporation preferred shares	600	16,800

Hi-Tech has the following transactions related to the securities during 2005:

Jan.   7 Sold 500 Aglar common shares at $58 per share, less brokerage fees of $700.

     10 Purchased 200 common shares of Miley Corporation at $78 per share plus brokerage fees of $420.

     26 Received a cash dividend of $1.20 per share on BAL common shares.

Feb.   2 Received cash dividends of $2 per share on Hicks preferred shares.

     10 Sold all 600 Hicks preferred shares at $33 per share, less brokerage fees of $180.

Apr. 30 Received 700 BAL common shares as a result of a two-for-one stock split.

July   1 Received a cash dividend of $0.65 per share on BAL common shares.

Aug.   3 Received 20 Miley common shares as the result of a 10% stock dividend.

Sept. 1 Purchased an additional 800 common shares of Miley at $75 per share plus brokerage fees of $700.

Dec. 15 Received a cash dividend of $1.50 per share on Miley common shares.

At December 31, 2005, the market values of the securities are:

BAL common shares	$31 per share
Miley common shares	$72 per share

Instructions

(a) Prepare journal entries to record the transactions.

(b) Post to the investment accounts.

(c) Prepare the adjusting entry at December 31, 2005, to report the individual securities at the lower of cost and market value. Assume that any declines are permanent.

(d) Show the balance sheet presentation of the investments at December 31, 2005.

P16–8A On January 1, 2005, Haidey Inc. purchases common shares of Jordan Cycles Corp. when the shares were trading at $10 per share. Haidey paid no brokerage fees on this purchase and intends to hold these shares as a long-term investment. Jordan Cycles had net income of $400,000 and paid cash dividends of $100,000 during 2005. Jordan Cycles' shares were trading for $12 per share on December 31, 2005.

Analyse information for cost and equity methods. (SO 4, 6) AN

Haidey's accountant prepared a trial balance as at December 31, 2005, under the assumption that Haidey could exercise significant influence over Jordan Cycles. Accordingly, the accountant presented the following information:

HAIDEY INC.
Trial Balance (partial)
December 31, 2005

Long-term equity investment—Jordan Cycles common shares	$575,000
Revenue from investment in Jordan Cycles	100,000

Instructions

(a) What percentage of the Jordan Cycles shares does Haidey own?

(b) What was the amount of the cash dividend that Haidey received from Jordan Cycles during 2005?

(c) How many shares of Jordan Cycles did Haidey purchase on January 1, 2005?

(d) Upon closer examination of the situation, Haidey has determined that it does not have significant influence over Jordan Cycles. What amount will be reported on Haidey's balance sheet at December 31, 2005, with regard to its investment in Jordan Cycles? What will be reported on Haidey's income statement for 2005?

Determine valuation of
equity investments.
(SO 6) AN

P16–9A On January 1, 2005, Sturge Enterprises Inc. held the following investments:

Company	Common Shares	Cost per Share
X Corporation	1,500	$11
Y Corporation	2,000	8

During the year, Sturge makes the following purchases:

Company	Common Shares	Cost per Share
X Corporation	1,000	$10
X Corporation	1,000	8
X Corporation	500	7
Y Corporation	750	9
Z Corporation	2,500	12

The market values of the various securities at year end were as follows:

Company	Market Value per Share
X Corporation	$ 5
Y Corporation	10
Z Corporation	12

Instructions

(a) Calculate the cost of Sturge Enterprises' equity investment portfolio at December 31, 2005.
(b) Calculate the market value of Sturge Enterprises' equity investment portfolio at December 31, 2005.
(c) If Sturge Enterprises considers its entire portfolio to be a temporary investment, what is its LCM valuation?
(d) If Sturge Enterprises decides to classify the X Corporation shares as a long-term investment and classify the Y Corporation and Z Corporation shares as temporary investments, what would be the impact on the income statement? Assume the decline in value for X Corporation is not considered to be permanent.

Prepare balance sheet.
(SO 6) AP

P16–10A The following data, presented in alphabetical order, are taken from the records of Stinson Corporation:

Accounts payable	$ 200,000
Accounts receivable	90,000
Accumulated amortization—building	180,000
Accumulated amortization—equipment	72,000
Allowance for doubtful accounts	6,000
Bonds payable (6%, due 2012)	400,000
Buildings	900,000
Cash and cash equivalents	112,000
Common shares (no par value; unlimited authorized; 300,000 issued)	1,700,000
Discount on bonds payable	20,000
Dividends payable	70,000
Equipment	275,000
Goodwill	200,000
Income tax payable	120,000
Land	500,000
Long-term equity investment—Indira common shares, at equity	270,000
Long-term equity investment—Manitoulin common shares, at cost	360,000
Merchandise inventory, at average cost	170,000
Notes payable (due 2006)	70,000
Preferred shares (no par value; $5 cumulative; 5,000 shares authorized and issued)	200,000
Retained earnings	170,000
Supplies	6,000
Temporary equity investment, at cost (market value $193,000)	185,000
Trademark	100,000

Instructions

Prepare a classified balance sheet at December 31, 2005.

Problems: Set B

P16–1B The following bond transactions occurred for the College of Higher Learning (CHL) and Otutye Ltd.:

Record debt investment transactions for investor and investee. Show statement presentation. (SO 3, 6) AP

2004

Feb.   1 CHL sold $3 million of 7.5%, five-year bonds at 100 to Otutye Ltd. The bonds were dated February 1, 2004, with interest payable semi-annually each August 1 and February 1. The College's and Otutye's year ends are June 30.

June 30 Prepared appropriate year-end adjusting entries.

Aug.   1 Paid the semi-annual interest on the bonds.

2005

Feb.   1 Semi-annual interest payment date.

June 30 Prepared appropriate year-end adjusting entries.

Aug.   1 Semi-annual interest payment date.

Aug.   1 After paying the semi-annual interest on the bonds on this date, CHL decided to repurchase the bonds and retire them. CHL repurchased all $3 million of the bonds from Otutye for $3.1 million cash.

Instructions

(a) Prepare the journal entries for CHL (investee) to record the above bond transactions.
(b) Show how the bond liability would be presented on CHL's June 30, 2005, balance sheet.
(c) Prepare the journal entries for Otutye to record the above bond transactions. Otutye purchased the bonds as a temporary investment.
(d) Show how the debt investment would be presented on Otutye's June 30, 2005, balance sheet.

P16–2B The following Givar Corp. transactions are for long-term investments in bonds.

Record debt investment transactions, including LCM. Show statement presentation. (SO 3, 6) AP

2004

Jan.   1 Purchased $100,000 of Lesley Corporation 5% bonds at 100.

July   1 Received semi-annual interest on Lesley bonds.

Oct. 31 Accrued interest at year end on Lesley bonds.

2005

Jan.   1 Received semi-annual interest on the Lesley bonds.

        1 Sold $25,000 of Lesley bonds for $23,000.

July   1 Received the semi-annual interest on the Lesley bonds.

Oct. 31 Accrued interest at year end on the Lesley bonds.

Instructions

(a) Journalize the transactions.
(b) Assume that the market value of the bonds at October 31, 2005, was $68,000. Prepare any required adjusting entry to properly valuate the debt investment. Assume any decline in market value was permanent.
(c) Show the balance sheet presentation of the bonds and interest at October 31, 2005, and indicate where any gain or loss is reported on the income statement.

P16–3B In January 2005, the management of Mead Ltd. concludes that it has enough cash to purchase temporary investments in debt and equity securities. During the year, these transactions occurred:

Record debt and equity investment transactions, including LCM. Show statement presentation. (SO 3, 4, 6) AP

Feb.   1 Purchased 600 CBF common shares for $32,000 plus brokerage fees of $600.

Mar.   1 Purchased 800 RSD common shares for $20,000 plus brokerage fees of $400.

Apr.   1 Purchased a 90-day treasury bill for $49,600.

June 30 The treasury bill matures and Mead receives $50,000 cash.

July   1 Received a cash dividend of $1 per share on the CBF common shares.

Aug.   1 Sold 200 CBF common shares at $60 per share, less brokerage fees of $200.

Sept. 1 Received a $1 per share cash dividend on the RSD common shares.

Oct.   1 Invested $25,000 in a money-market fund.

At December 31, the fair market values of the CBF and RSD common shares were $50 and $21 per share, respectively. The current value of the money-market fund is $25,115, which includes $115 of interest earned since it was purchased.

Instructions

(a) Journalize the transactions and post them to each investment account.
(b) Prepare the adjusting entry at December 31, 2005, to (1) accrue interest on the money market fund, and (2) report the investment securities at the lower of cost and market.
(c) Show the balance sheet presentation of investment securities at December 31, 2005.
(d) Identify the income statement accounts and give the statement classification of each account.

Record equity investment transactions, using cost and equity methods. Explain difference.
(SO 4) AP

P16–4B DFM Services Ltd. acquired 25% of the common shares of BNA Corporation on January 1, 2005, by paying $800,000 for 50,000 shares. BNA declared and paid $0.20 per share cash dividends on March 15 and September 15. BNA reported net income of $350,000 for the year.

Instructions

(a) Prepare the journal entries for DFM Services for 2005, assuming DFM cannot exercise significant influence over BNA.
(b) Prepare the journal entries for DFM Services for 2005, assuming DFM can exercise significant influence over BNA.
(c) Indicate the investment and income statement account balances at December 31, 2005, under each method of accounting.
(d) Explain why different methods of accounting should be used in parts (a) and (b).

Record equity investment transactions, using cost and equity methods. Compare statement presentation.
(SO 4, 5, 6) AP

P16–5B McReynolds Mariners Limited has 200,000 common shares and a fiscal year which begins on October 1. On October 1, 2004, LeTourneau Enterprises purchases 30% of the common shares of McReynolds Mariners from another shareholder for $40 per share. LeTourneau intends to hold these shares as a long-term investment. On December 31, 2004, McReynolds Mariners issues a 4% common stock dividend when the shares are trading for $42 per share. On May 31, 2005, McReynolds Mariners pays a cash dividend of $2.00 per share to common shareholders. McReynolds Mariners' net income for the year ended September 30, 2005, is $375,000. The market value of each share of McReynolds Mariners at September 30, 2005, is $46.

Instructions

(a) Prepare all entries for LeTourneau Enterprises for the year ended September 30, 2005, assuming that it exercises significant influence over McReynolds Mariners.
(b) Prepare all entries for LeTourneau Enterprises for the year ended September 30, 2005, assuming that it does not exercise significant influence over McReynolds Mariners.
(c) Compare the balance sheet and income statement accounts of LeTourneau Enterprises at September 30, 2005, under the two assumptions.
(d) If LeTourneau had purchased 100% of McReynolds' common shares, what method of accounting for this investment would LeTourneau use? What kind of financial statements should it issue? Whose name would be on the financial statements—LeTourneau's, McReynolds', or both names?

Record equity investment transactions, including LCM. Show statement presentation.
(SO 4, 6) AP

P16–6B On December 31, 2004, Karen Associates owns the following securities that are held as long-term investments. The securities are not held for influence or control of the investees.

Common Shares	Quantity	Cost
Xenos Corp.	3,000	$90,000
Yan Corp.	5,000	45,000
Zhao Corp.	1,500	30,000

In 2005, the following transactions occur:

July   1 Receives a $1 per share semi-annual cash dividend on Yan common shares.
       8 Receives 3,000 Xenos common shares in a two-for-one stock split.
Aug. 1 Receives a $0.50 per share cash dividend on Xenos common shares.
Sept. 1 Sells 1,500 Yan common shares for cash at $8 per share, less brokerage fees of $300.
Oct.   1 Sells 800 Xenos common shares for cash at $19 per share, less brokerage fees of $500.
Dec. 15 Receives a $0.50 per share cash dividend on Xenos common shares.
     31 Receives a $1 per share semi-annual cash dividend on Yan common shares.

At December 31, the market values per share are as follows: Xenos $16, Yan $8, and Zhao $15.

Instructions

(a) Journalize the 2005 transactions and post them to each long-term investment account.
(b) Prepare the adjusting entry at December 31, 2005, to show the securities at the lower of cost and market value. Assume that any declines are permanent.
(c) How would your answer to part (b) differ if the declines were considered to be due to temporary market fluctuations?
(d) Show the balance sheet presentation of the investments at December 31, 2005.

P16–7B The following data are in Big Head Todd Corporation's portfolio of temporary investments at December 31, 2004:

Record equity investment transactions and show statement presentation.
(SO 4, 6) AP

	Quantity	Cost
Alta Corporation common shares	500	$18,500
Brunswick Corporation common shares	700	35,000
Flon Corporation preferred shares	300	26,800

Big Head Todd has the following transactions related to the securities during 2005:

Jan. 7 Sells 500 Alta common shares at $40 per share, less brokerage fees of $700.
　　10 Purchases 200 common shares of Econo Corporation at $53 per share plus brokerage fees of $360.
　　26 Receives a cash dividend of $1.05 per share on Brunswick common shares.
Feb. 2 Receives a cash dividend of $7 per share on Flon preferred shares.
　　10 Sells all 300 Flon preferred shares at $85 per share, less brokerage fees of $360.
Mar. 15 Receives a 10% stock dividend on the Brunswick shares when they are trading at $45 per share.
Sept. 1 Purchases an additional 100 common shares of Econo at $56 per share plus brokerage fees of $400.
Dec. 15 Receives a cash dividend of $1.25 per share on Econo common shares.

At December 31, 2005, the market values of the securities are $42 per share for the Brunswick common shares and $57 per share for the Econo common shares.

Instructions

(a) Prepare journal entries to record the transactions.
(b) Post to the investment accounts.
(c) Prepare the adjusting entry at December 31, 2005, to report the portfolio at the lower of cost and market value.
(d) Show the balance sheet presentation at December 31, 2005.

P16–8B You are presented with the following selected information for Khalil Travel Agency Ltd.:

Analyse information for cost and equity methods.
(SO 4, 6) AN

KHALIL TRAVEL AGENCY LTD.
Balance Sheet (partial)
December 31, 2005

Shareholders' equity	
Common shares, 500,000 shares	
authorized, 180,000 shares issued	$ 900,000
Retained earnings	300,000
Total shareholders' equity	$1,200,000

On January 1, 2005, Stewart Inc. purchased shares of Khalil Travel Agency when the shares were trading at $15 per share. The market value of each share of Khalil Travel Agency at December 31, 2005, was $18.

Stewart intends to hold these shares as a long-term investment. Stewart's bookkeeper prepared an unadjusted trial balance as at December 31, 2005, under the assumption that it could not exercise significant influence over Khalil. Accordingly, the bookkeeper presented the following information:

STEWART INC.
Trial Balance (partial)
December 31, 2005

Long-term equity investment—Khalil Travel Agency common shares	
(market value $648,000)	$540,000
Dividend revenue from investment in Khalil Travel Agency	72,000

Instructions

(a) How many shares of Khalil Travel Agency did Stewart purchase? What percentage of the Khalil Travel Agency shares does Stewart own?

(b) What was the cash dividend paid per share of Khalil Travel Agency?

(c) Stewart determines that it is now able to exercise significant influence over Khalil Travel Agency. The investment will now be carried on Stewart's balance sheet at $600,000 at December 31, 2005. What was the net income of Khalil Travel Agency for the year ended December 31, 2005?

(d) Assuming that Stewart is able to exercise significant influence over Khalil Travel Agency, what amount will Stewart report on its income statement for 2005?

Determine valuation of debt and equity investments.
(SO 6) AN

P16–9B　The following table summarizes information about the temporary and long-term investment portfolios of Daoust Corporation at year end:

	Quantity Purchased	Cost/Security	Market Value/Security
Temporary Investments			
Money-market funds	10,000	$ 10	$ 10
Nortel Networks	5,000	75	3
Microsoft	5,000	120	105
Laidlaw	1,000	5	1
Long-Term Investments			
Government of Canada bonds	1,000	100	120
CIBC bonds	2,000	98	100

Instructions

(a) Calculate the total cost and total market value of each investment portfolio.

(b) At what value should the temporary investment portfolio be reported at year end?

(c) Prepare any required adjusting entry to apply the lower of cost and market rule at year end.

(d) The president of Daoust is speculating about holding Nortel Networks, Microsoft, and Laidlaw for the long term, rather than the short term. She doesn't believe there is any point in selling these shares in the near term until their values recover. What impact would it have on Daoust's income statement if the Microsoft and Laidlaw shares were classified as long-term investments?

　1. Assume first that the decline in market value of these shares is expected to be temporary.

　2. Then assume that the decline in market value is permanent.

Prepare balance sheet.
(SO 6) AP

P16–10B　The following data, presented in alphabetical order, are taken from the records of Vladimir Corporation:

Accounts payable	$ 231,000
Accounts receivable	140,000
Accumulated amortization—building	180,000
Accumulated amortization—equipment	52,000
Allowance for doubtful accounts	14,000
Allowance to reduce temporary investments from cost to market value	20,000
Bond interest payable	13,000
Bonds payable (6.5%, due 2010)	600,000
Building	950,000
Cash	72,000
Common shares (no par value; 500,000 authorized; 220,000 issued)	1,500,000
Dividends payable	80,000
Equipment	275,000
Income tax payable	100,000
Interest receivable	8,000
Land	500,000
Long-term debt investment	200,000
Long-term equity investment—Dion common shares (10% ownership), at cost	278,000

Long-term equity investment—Huston common shares (30% ownership), at equity	$330,000
Merchandise inventory, at FIFO cost	170,000
Notes payable (due 2008)	70,000
Patent (net of amortization)	200,000
Premium on bonds payable	40,000
Prepaid insurance	10,000
Retained earnings ($100,000 restricted for expansion)	413,000
Temporary debt investments, at cost	195,000
Unearned service revenue	15,000

Instructions

Prepare a classified balance sheet at December 31, 2005.

Continuing Cookie Chronicle

(Note: This is a continuation of the Cookie Chronicle from Chapters 1 through 15.)

Natalie has been approached by Ken Thornton, a shareholder of The Beanery Coffee Ltd. Ken wants to retire and would like to sell his 1,000 shares in The Beanery Coffee, which represents 20% of all shares issued. The Beanery is currently operated by Ken's twin daughters, who each own 40% of the common shares. The Beanery not only operates a coffee shop but also roasts and sells beans to retailers, under the name "Rocky Mountain Beanery."

The business has been operating for approximately five years, and in the last two years Ken has lost interest and left the day-to-day operations to his daughters. Both daughters at times find the work at the coffee shop overwhelming. They would like to have a third shareholder involved to take over some of the responsibilities of running a small business. Both feel that Natalie and Curtis are entrepreneurial in spirit and that their expertise would be a welcome addition to the business operation. The twins have also said that they plan to operate this business for another ten years and then retire.

Ken has met with Curtis and Natalie to discuss the business operation. All have concluded that there would be many advantages for Cookie & Coffee Creations Ltd. to acquire an interest in The Beanery Coffee. One of the major advantages would be volume discounts for purchases of coffee bean inventory.

Despite the apparent advantages, Natalie and Curtis are still not convinced that they should participate in this business venture. They come to you with the following questions:

1. We are a little concerned about how much influence we would have in the decision-making process for The Beanery Coffee. Would the amount of influence we have affect how we would account for this investment?
2. Can you think of other advantages of going ahead with this investment?
3. Can you think of any disadvantages of going ahead with this investment?

Instructions

(a) Answer Natalie and Curtis' questions.
(b) Assume that Ken wants to sell his 1,000 shares of The Beanery Coffee for $12,500. Prepare the journal entry required if Cookie & Coffee Creations Ltd. buys Ken's shares.
(c) Assume that Cookie & Coffee Creations Ltd. buys the shares and in the following year The Beanery Coffee earns $50,000 net income and pays $40,000 in dividends. Prepare the journal entries required under both the cost method and the equity method of accounting for this investment.
(d) Identify where this investment would be classified on the balance sheet of Cookie & Coffee Creations Ltd. and explain why. What amount would appear on the balance sheet under each of the methods of accounting for the investment?

Cumulative Coverage—Chapters 13 to 16

Plankton Corporation's trial balance at December 31, 2005, is presented below. All 2005 transactions and adjustments have been recorded except for the items described below the trial balance.

PLANKTON CORPORATION
Trial Balance
December 31, 2005

	Debit	Credit
Cash	$ 18,000	
Accounts receivable	51,000	
Allowance for doubtful accounts		$ 2,550
Merchandise inventory	22,700	
Long-term debt investment—CJS bonds	10,000	
Long-term equity investment—RES common shares at equity	85,000	
Long-term equity investment—SKB common shares at cost	30,000	
Land	120,000	
Building	200,000	
Accumulated amortization—building		40,000
Equipment	40,000	
Accumulated amortization—equipment		15,000
Accounts payable		18,775
Bonds payable (6%, due 2016)		125,000
Common shares, no par value, 100,000 issued		100,000
Retained earnings		75,000
Sales		750,000
Cost of goods sold	365,000	
Operating expenses	180,000	
Interest revenue		375
Interest expense	5,000	
Total	$1,126,700	$1,126,700

Unrecorded transactions and adjustments:

1. On January 7, 2005, Plankton issued 1,000 shares of $2-cumulative, convertible, preferred shares for $25,000 cash.
2. Five hundred of the preferred shares were converted into common shares on October 25, 2005. The conversion ratio is five common shares for one preferred.
3. Declared and paid the appropriate dividend on the preferred shares on December 10, 2005.
4. On December 15, 2005, declared a $0.50 per share cash dividend to the common shareholders of record on December 20, payable on January 3, 2006.
5. The interest payment dates on the bonds payable are March 1 and September 1. An entry to record the interest accrued to December 31, 2005, is required.
6. On November 30, 2005, Plankton obtained a bank loan of $50,000 by issuing a three-year, 6% note payable. Plankton is required to make equal instalment payments (including principal and interest) of $1,520 at the end of each month. The first payment was made on December 31, 2005.
7. On September 2, 2005, purchased 800 common shares of Osborne Inc. as a temporary investment for $23.75 per share plus a $200 brokerage fee.
8. On November 9, 2005, sold 300 of the Osborne shares for $5,700, less a $175 brokerage fee.
9. On December 31, 2005, the market value of the Osborne shares was $17 per share.
10. Plankton owns 40% of RES. RES earned $20,000 and declared and paid dividends of $12,500 in 2005.
11. Plankton owns 5% of SKB. SKB earned $67,000 and declared and paid dividends of $36,000 in 2005.
12. The market values of the RES and SKB shares at December 31, 2005, were higher than their costs.
13. Plankton purchased the CJS 5% bonds at face value. They pay semi-annual interest on April 1 and October 1. An adjustment to accrue interest to December 31, 2005, is required.

Instructions

(a) Prepare journal entries for the items listed above. Add new accounts as necessary.
(b) Prepare an updated trial balance reflecting these transactions at December 31, 2005.
(c) Using the income statement accounts in the trial balance, calculate income before income tax.
(d) Assuming Plankton pays 25% income tax, prepare a journal entry to record income taxes for the year and update the trial balance.
(e) Prepare the income statement for the year ended December 31, 2005.
(f) Prepare a statement of retained earnings for the year ended December 31, 2005.
(g) Prepare a balance sheet at December 31, 2005.
(h) Prepare closing entries on December 31, 2005.

BROADENING YOUR PERSPECTIVE

Financial Reporting and Analysis

 Practice Tools

Financial Reporting Problem

BYP16–1 Refer to the financial statements and accompanying notes for **The Forzani Group Ltd.** presented in Appendix A.

Instructions

(a) Does Forzani report any investments in its consolidated balance sheet in fiscal 2003 and 2002 (see Note 5)? If so, identify what type of investment(s) the company has (temporary or long-term).
(b) Does Forzani report any investment-related income on its statement of operations in fiscal 2003 or 2002?
(c) Does Forzani have any subsidiary companies? If so, what percentage ownership does Forzani hold of these companies (see Note 2)?

Interpreting Financial Statements

BYP16–2 In February 2002, **CTC Acquisition Limited**, a wholly owned subsidiary of **Canadian Tire Corporation, Limited**, acquired 100% of the common shares of **Mark's Work Wearhouse Ltd.** for $110.8 million.

Instructions

(a) Prepare the journal entry that CTC Acquisition made to record the acquisition of the Mark's Work Wearhouse common shares. Assume the purchase was made in cash. What entry would Mark's Work Wearhouse make on its books?
(b) Which method—cost or equity—should CTC Acquisition use to account for its investment in Mark's Work Wearhouse?
(c) Which company is the parent company and which company is the subsidiary company?
(d) Mark's Work Wearhouse financial results have been included in CTC Acquisition's results in the latter's consolidated financial statements. CTC Acquisition's results have been included in Canadian Tire's consolidated financial statements. Explain why these results are consolidated in each company's statements for reporting purposes.

Accounting on the Web

BYP16–3 The Investor Learning Centre of Canada is an independent, not-for-profit organization created by the Canadian Securities Institute. We will now explore the glossary of this site to learn commonly used investment terms.

Instructions

Specific requirements of this Internet case are available on the Weygandt website.

Critical Thinking

Collaborative Learning Activity

BYP16–4 At the beginning of the question-and-answer portion of the annual shareholders' meeting of Réno-Déco Corporation, shareholder Carol Finstrom asks, "Why did management sell its equity investment in AHM Limited at a loss when this company was very profitable during the period its shares were held by Réno-Déco?"

Since president Nathalie Clément has just concluded her speech on the recent success and bright future of Réno-Déco, she is taken aback by this question and responds, "I remember we paid $1.1 million for the shares some years ago, and I am sure we sold those shares at a much higher price. You must be mistaken."

Finstrom retorts, "Well, right here in note number 7 to the financial statements, it shows that 240,000 shares—a 30% interest in AHM—were sold on the last day of the year. Also, it states that AHM earned $550,000 this year and paid out $150,000 in cash dividends. Further, a summary statement indicates that in past years, while Réno-Déco held AHM shares, AHM earned $1.2 million and paid out $500,000 in dividends. Finally, the income statement for this year shows a loss on the sale of AHM shares of $180,000. So, I doubt that I am mistaken."

Red-faced, president Clément turns to you, the vice-president of finance, for answers.

Instructions

With the class divided into groups, answer the following:

(a) What dollar amount did Réno-Déco receive when it sold the AHM shares?
(b) Explain why both shareholder Finstrom and president Clément are correct.

Communication Activity

BYP16–5 Chapperal Corporation has purchased two securities for its portfolio. The first is an equity investment in Ray Corporation, one of its suppliers. Chapperal purchased 10% of Ray with the intention of holding it for a number of years.

The second investment is a purchase of debt securities. Chapperal purchased bonds because its analysts believe that changes in market interest rates will cause these securities to increase in value in a short period of time. Chapperal intends to sell the securities as soon as they have increased in value.

Instructions

Write a memo to Jean Talon, the chief financial officer, explaining how to account for each of these investments. Discuss the implications of this accounting treatment on reported income.

Ethics Case

BYP16–6 Kreiter Financial Services Limited holds a large portfolio of debt and equity securities as an investment. The total market value of the portfolio at December 31, 2005, is greater than its total cost. Some securities have increased in value and others have decreased. Vicki Lemke, the financial vice-president, and Ula Greenwood, the controller, are in the process of classifying the securities in the portfolio for the first time.

Lemke suggests classifying the securities that have increased in value as temporary investments in order to increase net income for the year. She wants to classify the securities that have decreased in value as long-term investments, and attribute the declines to temporary fluctuations in market values. This way, the decreases in value will not affect 2005 net income.

Greenwood disagrees. She recommends classifying the securities that have decreased in value as temporary investments and those that have increased in value as long-term investments. Greenwood argues that the company is having a good year and that recognizing the losses now will help to smooth income for this year. Moreover, for future years, when the company may not be as profitable, it will have built-in gains "held in reserve."

Instructions
 (a) Will classifying the securities as Lemke and Greenwood suggest actually affect income as each says it will?
 (b) Is there anything unethical in what Lemke and Greenwood propose?
 (c) Who are the stakeholders affected by their proposals?

Answers to Self-Study Questions

1. b   2. d   3. c   4. a   5. c   6. a   7. b   8. a   9. a   10. c

Answer to Forzani Review It Question 3

The Forzani Group's financial statements are consolidated. It owns 100% of its subsidiary companies (see Note 2 (a)).

Remember to go back to the Navigator Box at the beginning of the chapter to check off your completed work.

concepts for review >>

Before studying this chapter, you should understand or, if necessary, review:

  a. The difference between the accrual basis and the cash basis of accounting. (Ch. 3, pp. 102–103)
  b. The major items included in a corporation's income statement. (Ch. 14, pp. 665–667)
  c. The major items included in a corporation's balance sheet. (Ch. 16, pp. 766–767)

Looking for the Big Picture in Small Business Loans

TD Canada Trust: www.tdcanadatrust.com

HALIFAX, N.S.—If you're a small business owner or manager, what determines whether or not your loan application is approved? What, exactly, is the person on the other side of that desk looking for?

If that person is Shelley LeBrun, Manager of Small Business Banking at TD Canada Trust in Halifax, the answer is—all kinds of things.

The first thing a loan officer usually asks to see, she says, is the balance sheet, "to see how much equity the company has. Then the income statement, to see if it's actually making any money." But the process, she insists, shouldn't stop there.

The rest of the company's financial statements also help clarify the picture, especially the cash flow statement. Sometimes, for example, a company may not look profitable from its income statement, but its cash flow statement will show that it actually has significant resources available.

"For example, when certain expenses, such as amortization expense, are recorded on the income statement, they can reduce the profit as it appears on the income statement," explains Ms. LeBrun. "However, this has no impact on the amount of cash generated by the business since the asset being amortized was purchased and paid for in prior periods."

There could also be timing differences between the recording on the income statement of revenue earned on a project, for instance, and the actual receipt of cash from the customer.

The bottom line, Ms. LeBrun says, is that "we need to know that the company is able to service the debt. The cash flow statement can show us that. It also gives the bank a good idea of what type of operating line a company may require going forward."

If the cash flow statement, together with previous years' statements and a good business plan, shows the bank that the company is financially sound and can meet its loan payments, then the application is likely to be approved.

"At TD Canada Trust, we try to see the big picture," she explains. Factors like a sound business plan, signed contracts for major orders in the near future, and the owner's personal financial situation—including credit history, net worth, and previous business experience—can all make the difference in getting the small business loan needed for the next step.

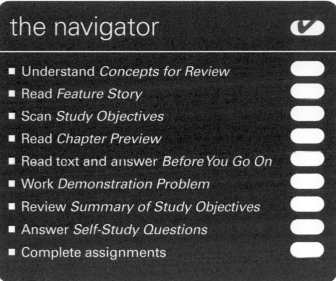

chapter 17
The Cash Flow Statement

study objectives >>

the
navigator

After studying this chapter, you should be able to:

1. Describe the usefulness of the cash flow statement.
2. Distinguish among operating, investing, and financing activities.
3. Prepare a cash flow statement using one of two approaches: (a) the indirect method or (b) the direct method.
4. Analyse the cash flow statement.

As Shelley LeBrun in our feature story indicates, the cash flow statement provides information for decision-making that is not always available from the balance sheet, income statement, and statement of retained earnings. In fact, looking at these three financial statements for some well-known companies, a thoughtful reader might have questions like the following: How did Andrés Wines pay cash dividends in a year in which it had no cash, only bank indebtedness? How did the Student Centre of McGill University buy more than $97,000 of property, plant, and equipment in a year in which it reported a loss of $114,000? How did Capital Sports & Entertainment finance its purchase of the Ottawa Senators? Answers to these and similar questions can be found in this chapter, which presents the cash flow statement.

The chapter is organized as follows:

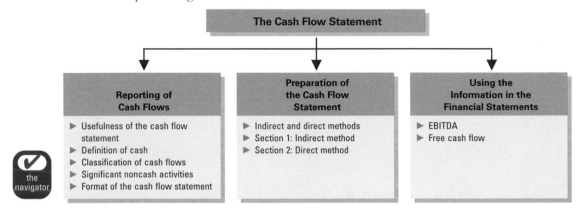

Reporting of Cash Flows

The three financial statements we've studied so far present only partial information about a company's cash flows (cash receipts and cash payments). For example, comparative balance sheets show the increase in property, plant, and equipment during the year, but they do not show how the additions were financed or paid for. The income statement shows net income, but it does not indicate the amount of cash generated by operating activities. Similarly, the statement of retained earnings shows cash dividends declared, but not the cash dividends paid during the year. None of these statements presents a detailed summary of the change in cash as a result of operating, investing, and financing activities during the period.

Usefulness of the Cash Flow Statement

The cash flow statement provides information about the cash receipts, cash payments, and net change in cash that result from operating, investing, and financing activities during a period. Reporting the causes of changes in cash helps investors, creditors, and other interested parties understand what is happening to a company's most liquid resource—its cash.

The information in a cash flow statement should help users assess the following aspects of the company's financial position:

1. **The company's ability to generate future cash flows.** Investors and others examine the relationships between items in the cash flow statement. From these, users can predict the amounts, timing, and uncertainty of future cash flows better than they can from accrual-based data.

2. **The company's ability to pay dividends and meet obligations.** If a company does not have enough cash, employees cannot be paid, debts settled, or dividends paid. Employees, creditors, and shareholders are particularly interested in this statement because it is the only one that shows the flow of cash in a business.

3. **The reasons for the difference between net income and cash provided (used) by operating activities.** Net income provides information on the success or failure of a business. However, some people are critical of accrual-based net income because it requires many estimates, allocations, and assumptions. As a result, the reliability of the number is often challenged. Such is not the case with cash. Many readers of the cash flow statement want to know the reasons for the difference between net income and net cash provided by operating activities. They can then assess for themselves the reliability of the income number.

4. **The investing and financing transactions during the period.** By examining a company's investing and financing transactions, a financial statement reader can better understand why assets and liabilities changed during the period.

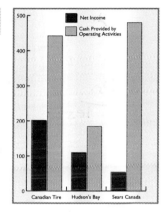

ACCOUNTING IN ACTION ► Business Insight

Variations between net income and cash provided by operating activities are illustrated by the following results for three companies. All are in similar types of retail merchandising and the figures are for the same fiscal year (in millions).

Company	Net Income	Cash Provided by Operating Activities
Canadian Tire	$202.4	$444.3
Hudson's Bay	111.5	182.8
Sears Canada	52.2	486.0

Definition of Cash

The cash flow statement is generally prepared using **cash and cash equivalents** as its basis. You will recall from Chapter 7 that cash equivalents are temporary, highly liquid investments that are both:

1. readily convertible to known amounts of cash, and
2. so near to their maturity that their market value is relatively unaffected by changes in interest rates.

Generally, only investments with original maturities of three months or less qualify under this definition. Examples of cash equivalents are treasury bills, commercial paper (high-quality, short-term corporate debt), and money-market funds. Sometimes short-term or demand loans are deducted from this amount. Cash with restrictions, such as compensating balances, is excluded from cash equivalents. Because a variety of items can be included in cash equivalents, companies should define cash equivalents when they are combined with cash.

Since cash and cash equivalents are viewed as the same, transfers between cash and cash equivalents are not treated as cash receipts and cash payments. That is, such transfers are not reported in the cash flow statement.

Classification of Cash Flows

The cash flow statement classifies cash receipts and cash payments as operating, investing, and financing activities. Transactions and other events that characterize each kind of activity are as follows:

1. **Operating activities** include the cash effects of transactions that create revenues and expenses. They affect net income.

study objective 2

Distinguish among operating, investing, and financing activities.

2. **Investing activities** include (a) acquiring and disposing of investments and long-lived assets, and (b) lending money and collecting the loans. They affect temporary investments that are not cash equivalents, and also affect long-term asset accounts.

3. **Financing activities** include (a) obtaining cash from issuing debt and repaying the amounts borrowed, and (b) obtaining cash from shareholders and providing them with a return on their investment. Financing activities affect short-term notes payable, and long-term liability and equity accounts.

Illustration 17-1 lists typical cash receipts and cash payments in each of the three classifications.

Illustration 17-1 ▶

Typical receipts and payments classified by business activity

*On V.I.P.
On Test.*

Types of Cash Inflows and Outflows
Operating activities—income statement items
Cash inflows:
From the sale of goods or services
From returns on debt investments (interest) and on equity investments (dividends)
Cash outflows:
To suppliers for inventory
To employees for services
To governments for taxes
To lenders for interest
To others for expenses
Investing activities—changes in temporary investments and long-term assets
Cash inflows:
From the sale of property, plant, and equipment
From the sale of debt or equity investments
From the collection of principal on loans to other companies
Cash outflows:
To purchase property, plant, and equipment
To purchase debt or equity investments
To make loans to other companies
Financing activities—changes in short-term notes payable, long-term liabilities, and equity
Cash inflows:
From the sale of shares (preferred and common)
From the issue of debt (bonds and notes)
Cash outflows:
To shareholders as dividends
To redeem long-term debt or reacquire share capital

As you can see, some cash flows related to investing or financing activities are classified as operating activities. For example, receipts of investment revenue (interest and dividends) are classified as operating activities. So are payments of interest to lenders. Why are these considered operating activities? **Because these items are reported in the income statement where results of operations are shown.**

Note the following general guidelines: (1) Operating activities involve income statement items. These items are also affected by noncash working capital accounts (current assets and current liabilities) on the balance sheet. (2) Investing activities involve cash flows resulting from changes in temporary investments and long-term asset items (noncurrent items on the left-hand side of the balance sheet when presented in account form). (3) Financing activities involve cash flows resulting from changes in short-term notes payable and long-term liability and shareholders' equity items (noncurrent items on the right-hand side of the balance sheet when presented in account form).

Illustration 17-2 shows these general guidelines. There are exceptions, as noted above, but these relationships between operating, investing, and financing activities and the income statement and balance sheet are the most common.

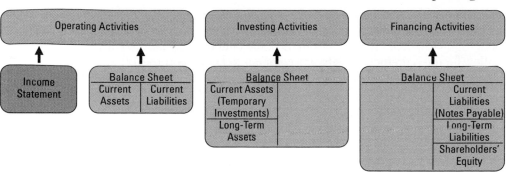

Illustration 17-2 ◀
Operating, investing, and financing activities

Significant Noncash Activities

Not all of a company's significant activities involve cash. The following are examples of significant noncash activities:

1. An issue of common shares to purchase assets
2. A conversion of debt or preferred shares to common shares
3. An issue of debt to purchase assets
4. Exchanges of property, plant, and equipment

    Significant financing and investing activities that do not affect cash are not reported in the body of the cash flow statement. These noncash activities are reported in a separate note, which satisfies the full disclosure principle.

Format of the Cash Flow Statement

The general format of the cash flow statement focuses on the three activities discussed above (operating, investing, and financing). A condensed version of a widely used form of cash flow statement is shown in Illustration 17-3.

Illustration 17-3 ◀
Cash flow statement

COMPANY NAME Cash Flow Statement Period Covered		
Operating activities		
(List of individual inflows and outflows)	$ XX	
Net cash provided (used) by operating activities		$ XXX
Investing activities		
(List of individual inflows and outflows)	$ XX	
Net cash provided (used) by investing activities		XXX
Financing activities		
(List of individual inflows and outflows)	$ XX	
Net cash provided (used) by financing activities		XXX
Net increase (decrease) in cash		XXX
Cash, beginning of period		XXX
Cash, end of period		$ XXX
Note x:		
Noncash investing and financing activities		
(List of significant noncash investing and financing transactions)		$ XXX

    The cash flow statement covers the same period of time as the income statement (e.g., for the year ended). The operating activities section is always first. It is followed by the investing activities and financing activities sections. Individual inflows and outflows from investing and financing activities are reported separately. Thus, the cash outflow for the purchase of equipment is reported separately from the cash inflow from the sale of equipment. Similarly, the cash inflow from the issue of debt is reported separately from the cash outflow for the retirement of debt. If a company did not report the inflows and outflows separately, the investing and financing activities of the company would be unclear. This would make it harder to assess future cash flows.

The reported operating, investing, and financing activities result in net cash being either provided or used by each activity. The amounts of net cash provided or used by each activity are totalled. The result is the net increase (decrease) in cash for the period. This amount is then added to, or subtracted from, the beginning-of-period cash balance. This gives the end-of-period cash balance. Finally, any significant noncash investing and financing activities are reported in a note to the statement.

BEFORE YOU GO ON . . .

▶Review It

1. Why is the cash flow statement useful? What key information does it give?
2. What are cash equivalents?
3. What are the major classifications of cash flows in the cash flow statement? Give an example of each.
4. In its cash flow statement for the year ended February 2, 2003, what amounts are reported by The Forzani Group for (a) cash provided by operating activities, (b) cash used by investing activities, and (c) cash provided by financing activities? The answer to this question is at the end of this chapter.

▶Do It

During its first week of existence, Carrier Molding Ltd. had the following transactions:

1. Issued 100,000 common shares for $800,000 cash.
2. Borrowed $200,000 from the National Bank, signing a five-year note at prime plus 1% interest.
3. Purchased two semi-trailer trucks for $170,000 cash.
4. Paid $12,000 in employee salaries.
5. Collected $20,000 cash for services provided.

Classify each of these transactions by type of cash flow activity. Indicate whether the transaction would be reported as a cash inflow or cash outflow.

Action Plan

- Identify the three types of activities used to report all cash inflows and outflows.
- Report as operating activities the cash effects of transactions that create revenues and expenses, and which are included when net income is determined.
- Report as investing activities transactions to (a) acquire and dispose of investments and productive long-lived assets, and (b) lend money and collect loans.
- Report as financing activities transactions to (a) obtain cash by issuing debt and repay the amounts borrowed, and (b) obtain cash from shareholders and pay them dividends.

Solution

1. Financing activity; cash inflow
2. Financing activity; cash inflow
3. Investing activity; cash outflow
4. Operating activity; cash outflow
5. Operating activity; cash inflow

Related exercise material: BE17–1, BE17–2, BE17–3, E17–1, and E17–2.

Preparation of the Cash Flow Statement

The cash flow statement is prepared differently from the three other basic financial statements. First, it is not prepared from an adjusted trial balance. The statement requires detailed information about the changes in account balances that occurred between two periods of time. An adjusted trial balance will not provide the necessary data. Second, the cash flow statement deals with cash receipts and payments. As a result, **the accrual concept is not used in the preparation of a cash flow statement.**

study objective 3

Prepare a cash flow statement using one of two approaches: (a) the indirect method or (b) the direct method.

The information to prepare this statement usually comes from three sources:

1. **Comparative balance sheet.** Information in the comparative balance sheet indicates the amount of the changes in assets, liabilities, and shareholders' equity from the beginning to the end of the period.
2. **Current income statement.** Information in this statement helps determine the amount of cash provided or used by operating activities during the period.
3. **Additional information.** This includes transaction data that are needed to determine how cash was provided or used during the period.

There are four major steps to prepare the cash flow statement from these data sources as show in Illustration 17-4.

Illustration 17-4 ◄

Steps in preparing the cash flow statement

Step 1: Determine the net cash provided (used) by operating activities by converting net income from an accrual basis to a cash basis.

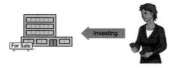

The current year's income statement is analysed, as well as the comparative balance sheet and selected additional information.

Step 2: Determine the net cash provided (used) by investing activities by analysing changes in temporary investment and long-term asset accounts.

Comparative balance sheet data and selected additional information are analysed for their effects on cash.

Step 3: Determine the net cash provided (used) by financing activities by analysing changes in short-term notes payable and long-term liability and equity accounts.

Comparative balance sheet data and selected additional information are analysed for their effects on cash.

Step 4: Determine the net increase (decrease) in cash. Compare the net change in cash with the change in cash reported on the balance sheet to make sure the amounts agree.

The difference between the beginning and ending cash balances can easily be calculated from the comparative balance sheet.

Indirect and Direct Methods

To do step 1, the operating activities section must be converted from an accrual basis to a cash basis. This conversion may be done by one of two methods: (1) the indirect method, or (2) the direct method. The indirect method converts total net income from an accrual basis to a cash basis. The direct method converts each individual revenue and expense account from an accrual basis to a cash basis, thereby identifying specific cash receipts and payments. **Both methods arrive at the same total amount** for "Net cash provided (used) by operating activities." The only difference is which items they disclose. Note that the two different methods affect only the operating activities section. The investing activities and financing activities sections are not affected by the choice of the indirect or direct method.

Most companies use the indirect method. They prefer this method for two reasons: (1) it is easier to prepare, and (2) it focuses on the differences between net income and net cash flow from operating activities. Only a few companies favour the direct method. This method shows operating cash receipts and payments.

The CICA encourages companies to use the direct method of reporting operating activities, but allows either method. Despite the CICA's preference for the direct method, its use is rare in Canada. Less than 1% of Canadian companies use the direct method. The authors of *Financial Reporting in Canada* state: "We continue to be surprised by the failure to use the direct method for presenting this important figure. It is difficult to believe that investors would not find information on the various functional cash flows (e.g., payments to employees) more useful than the information on adjustments required to convert net income into cash flows from operating activities (e.g., amortization expense)."

ACCOUNTING IN ACTION ▶ Business Insight

The cash flow statement ought to be one of the most important tools for any user. But, all too often, the cash flow statement adds little insight to a company's operations. Take, for example, Hudson's Bay Company. The Bay's business is pretty simple. It buys clothes, housewares, and other products, puts them in its stores, and sells them.

When you look at the operating activities section of The Bay's cash flow statement, however, you find references to amortization and "net change in operating working capital." Nowhere does it tell you how much cash The Bay received from shoppers or how much it paid its suppliers.

So why don't companies report this information in their cash flow statement? "It gives material information, so managements don't want to use it," says Richard Rooney, president of Burgundy Asset Management. Mr. Rooney would like to see the direct method of preparing the operating activities section of the cash flow statement be made mandatory. "Something like this is comprehensible, easy to understand and I think it would be harder to fudge—though where there's a will, there's a way."

Source: Derek DeCloet, "Show Investors the Cash Flow," *Financial Post*, March 28, 2002, IN3.

On the following pages, in two separate sections, we describe the use of the two methods. Section 1 explains the indirect method. Section 2 explains the direct method. These sections are independent of each other. When you have finished the section(s) assigned by your instructor, turn to the next topic, "Using the Information in the Financial Statements."

SECTION 1 ► INDIRECT METHOD

To explain and illustrate the indirect method, we will use financial information from Computer Services Corporation to prepare a cash flow statement.

Illustration 17-5 presents Computer Services' current- and previous-year balance sheet, its current-year income statement, and related financial information.

study objective 3a

Prepare a cash flow statement using the indirect method.

Illustration 17-5 ◄

Comparative balance sheet, income statement, and additional information

COMPUTER SERVICES CORPORATION
Balance Sheet
December 31

Assets	2005	2004	Change Increase/Decrease
Current assets			
Cash	$ 55,000	$ 33,000	$ 22,000 Increase
Accounts receivable	20,000	30,000	10,000 Decrease
Inventory	15,000	10,000	5,000 Increase
Prepaid expenses	5,000	1,000	4,000 Increase
Property, plant, and equipment			
Land	130,000	20,000	110,000 Increase
Building	160,000	40,000	120,000 Increase
Accumulated amortization—building	(11,000)	(5,000)	6,000 Increase
Equipment	27,000	10,000	17,000 Increase
Accumulated amortization—equipment	(3,000)	(1,000)	2,000 Increase
Total	$398,000	$138,000	
Liabilities and Shareholders' Equity			
Current liabilities			
Accounts payable	$ 28,000	$ 12,000	$ 16,000 Increase
Income tax payable	6,000	8,000	2,000 Decrease
Long-term liabilities			
Bonds payable	130,000	20,000	110,000 Increase
Shareholders' equity			
Common shares	70,000	50,000	20,000 Increase
Retained earnings	164,000	48,000	116,000 Increase
Total	$398,000	$138,000	

COMPUTER SERVICES CORPORATION
Income Statement
Year Ended December 31, 2005

Sales revenue		$507,000
Cost of goods sold		150,000
Gross profit		357,000
Operating expenses (excluding amortization)	$111,000	
Amortization expense	9,000	
Loss on sale of equipment	3,000	123,000
Income from operations		234,000
Interest expense		42,000
Income before income tax		192,000
Income tax expense		47,000
Net income		$145,000

Additional information for 2005:
1. The company declared and paid a $29,000 cash dividend.
2. The company obtained land by issuing $110,000 of long-term bonds.
3. Equipment costing $25,000 was purchased for cash.
4. The company sold equipment with a book value of $7,000 (cost of $8,000, less accumulated amortization of $1,000) for $4,000 cash.
5. Amortization expense consisted of $6,000 for building and $3,000 for equipment.

We will now apply the four steps to the information provided for Computer Services Corporation.

Step 1: Operating Activities

Determine the Net Cash Provided (Used) by Operating Activities by Converting Net Income from an Accrual Basis to a Cash Basis

To determine net cash provided (or used) by operating activities under the indirect method, **net income is adjusted for items that did not affect cash.**

A useful starting point is to understand **why** net income must be converted to net cash provided by operating activities. Under generally accepted accounting principles, companies use the accrual basis of accounting. As you have learned, this basis requires that revenue be recorded when earned and that expenses be matched against the revenue they were incurred to generate. Earned revenues may include credit sales that have not been collected in cash. Expenses incurred, such as amortization or cost of goods sold, may not have been paid in cash. Thus, under the accrual basis of accounting, net income is not the same as net cash provided by operating activities. Consequently, under the indirect method, accrual-based net income must be adjusted to convert certain items to the cash basis.

The **indirect method** starts with net income and converts it to net cash provided or used by operating activities. Illustration 17-6 shows three types of adjustments that are made to adjust net income for items that affect accrual-based net income but do not affect cash. The first two types of adjustments are found on the income statement. The last type of adjustment—changes to current asset and current liability accounts—is found on the balance sheet.

Illustration 17-6 ▶

Adjustments to convert net income to net cash provided by operating activities

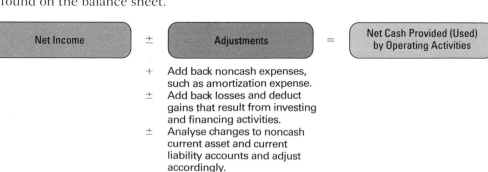

The next three sections explain each type of adjustment.

Amortization Expense

Computer Services' income statement shows an amortization expense of $9,000. Although amortization expense reduces net income, it does not reduce cash. Recall that the entry to record amortization is:

| Amortization Expense | 9,000 | | A = L + SE |
| Accumulated Amortization | | 9,000 | −9,000 −9,000 |

Cash flows: no effect

This entry has no effect on cash, so amortization expense is added back to net income in order to arrive at net cash provided by operating activities:

Operating activities	
Net income	$145,000
Adjustments to reconcile net income to net cash provided by operating activities:	
Amortization expense	**9,000**
Net cash provided by operating activities	154,000

Amortization is often listed in the cash flow statement as the first adjustment to net income. It is important to understand that amortization expense is not added to operating activities as if it were a source of cash. As shown in the journal entry above, amortization does not involve cash. It is added to cancel the deduction created by the amortization expense in the determination of net income.

Gains and Losses on the Sale of Assets

Computer Services' income statement reports a $3,000 loss on the sale of equipment. With the additional information provided, we can reconstruct the journal entry to record the sale of equipment:

Cash	4,000		A = L + SE
Accumulated Amortization	1,000		+4,000 −3,000
Loss on Sale of Equipment	3,000		+1,000
Equipment		8,000	−8,000

Cash flows: +4,000

Illustration 17-1 states that cash received from the sale of long-lived assets should be reported in the investing activities section of the cash flow statement. Consequently, **all gains and losses from investing activities must be eliminated from net income to arrive at cash from operating activities**.

In our example, Computer Services' $3,000 loss should not be included in the operating activities section of the cash flow statement. This amount is eliminated by adding the $3,000 back to net income to arrive at net cash provided by operating activities:

Operating activities		
Net income		$145,000
Adjustments to reconcile net income to net cash provided by operating activities:		
Amortization expense	$9,000	
Loss on sale of equipment	**3,000**	12,000
Net cash provided by operating activities		157,000

If a gain on sale occurs, the gain is deducted from net income in order to determine net cash provided by operating activities. For both a gain and a loss, the actual amount of cash received from the sale is reported as a source of cash in the investing activities section of the cash flow statement.

If we did not eliminate gains and losses and remove them from net income, they would be counted twice—once in the operating activities section (as part of net income), and again in the investing activities section (as part of the cash proceeds from the sale). We explain investing activities later in this chapter.

Gains and losses are also possible in other circumstances, such as when debt is retired. The same adjustment guidelines apply as described for gains and losses on the sale of assets, except that the other side of the transaction is reported in financing activities, rather than investing activities.

Changes in Noncash Current Asset and Current Liability Accounts

A final adjustment in converting net income to net cash provided by operating activities involves examining all changes in current asset and current liability accounts. Most current asset and current liability accounts result from operating activities. For example, accounts receivable indicate credit sales recorded as revenue for which cash collections have not yet been received. Prepaid expenses, such as insurance, reflect insurance that has been paid for, but which has not yet expired and therefore has not been recorded as an expense. Similarly, income tax payable reflects income tax expense incurred by the company but not yet paid.

As a result, we need to adjust net income for these accruals and prepayments to determine net cash provided by operating activities. We do this by analysing the change in each current asset and current liability account to determine each change's impact on net income and cash.

There are situations when current asset and current liability accounts do not result from operating activities. Temporary investments are an example of a current asset that does not relate to operating activities. Temporary investments are shown in the investing activities section of the cash flow statement if they are not part of cash equivalents. Short-term notes payable are an example of a current liability that does not relate to operating activities. These are shown instead in the financing section of the cash flow statement.

Changes in Noncash Current Assets

The adjustments required for changes in noncash current asset accounts are as follows: **increases in current asset accounts are deducted from net income and decreases in current asset accounts are added to net income**, to arrive at net cash provided by operating activities. We will observe these relationships by analysing Computer Services' current asset accounts.

Decrease in Accounts Receivable. When accounts receivable decrease during the year, revenues on an accrual basis are lower than revenues on a cash basis. In other words, more cash was collected during the period than recorded as revenue. Computer Services' accounts receivable decreased by $10,000 (from $30,000 to $20,000) during the year. For Computer Services, this means that cash receipts were $10,000 higher than revenues.

Illustration 17-5 shows that Computer Services had $507,000 in sales revenue reported on its income statement. To determine how much cash was collected in connection with this revenue, it is useful to analyse the accounts receivable account:

	Accounts Receivable		
Jan. 1 Balance	30,000		
Sales revenue	507,000	**Receipts from customers**	**517,000**
Dec. 31 Balance	20,000		

$10,000 net decrease {

If sales revenue (assumed to be sales on account) journalized during the period was $507,000 (Dr. Accounts Receivable; Cr. Sales Revenue), and the change in accounts receivable during the period was a decrease of $10,000, then cash receipts from customers must have been $517,000 (Dr. Cash; Cr. Accounts Receivable).

Consequently, revenues reported on the accrual-based income statement were lower than cash collections. To convert net income to net cash provided by operating activities, the $10,000 decrease in accounts receivable must be added to net income because $10,000 more cash was collected than was reported as accrual-based revenue in the income statement.

When the accounts receivable balance increases during the year, revenues on an accrual basis are higher than cash receipts. Therefore, the amount of the increase in accounts receivable is deducted from net income to arrive at net cash provided by operating activities.

Increase in Inventory. Assuming a perpetual inventory system is being used, the merchandise inventory account is increased by the cost of goods purchased. It is decreased by the cost of goods sold. When inventory increases during the year, the cost of goods purchased is greater than the cost of goods sold expense recorded in the income statement. Any increase in the inventory account must be deducted from net income, in a manner similar to the increase in the accounts receivable account explained above.

Inventory increased by $5,000 for Computer Services Corporation. Because the inventory account is increased by the purchase of goods (Dr. Inventory; Cr. Accounts Payable) and is decreased by the cost of goods sold (Dr. Cost of Goods Sold; Cr. Inventory), Computer Services must have purchased $5,000 more inventory than it sold. Therefore, because cost of goods sold reported on the income statement is $150,000, purchases of merchandise during the year must have been $155,000:

Inventory				
Jan. 1 Balance	10,000			
Purchases	**155,000**	Cost of goods sold	150,000	$5,000 net increase
Dec. 31 Balance	15,000			

To convert net income to net cash provided by operating activities, the $5,000 increase in inventory must be deducted from net income. The increase in inventory means that the cash-based expense must be increased, which has the effect of reducing net income.

This deduction does not completely convert an accrual-based figure to a cash-based figure. It does not tell us how much cash was paid for the goods purchased. It just converts the cost of goods sold to the cost of goods purchased during the year. The analysis of accounts payable—shown later—completes this analysis by converting the cost of goods purchased from an accrual basis to a cash basis.

Increase in Prepaid Expenses. Prepaid expenses increased during the period by $4,000. This means that the cash paid for expenses is higher than the expenses reported on the accrual basis. In other words, cash payments were made in the current period, but expenses have been deferred to future periods. To determine how much cash was paid relative to the operating expenses, it is useful to analyse the prepaid expenses account. Operating expenses, as reported on the income statement, are $111,000. Accordingly, payments for expenses must have been $115,000:

Prepaid Expenses				
Jan. 1 Balance	1,000			
Payments for expenses	**115,000**	Operating expenses	111,000	$4,000 net increase
Dec. 31 Balance	5,000			

To adjust net income to net cash provided by operating activities, the $4,000 increase in prepaid expenses must be deducted from net income to determine the cash paid for expenses. If prepaid expenses decrease, reported expenses are higher than the expenses paid. Therefore, the decrease in prepaid expenses is added to net income to arrive at net cash provided by operating activities.

These adjustments may not completely convert accrual-based expenses to cash-based expenses. For example, if Computer Services Corporation had any accrued expenses payable, these would also have to be considered before we could completely determine the amount of cash paid for operating expenses.

Computer Services does not have any accrued expenses payable related to operating expenses. However, if it did, they would be treated in the same manner as income tax payable, which will we look at in the next section when we adjust for the changes in the current liability accounts. Income tax payable is actually an example of an accrued expense payable; however, it is dealt with separately because income tax expense is reported by itself on the income statement.

The following partial cash flow statement shows the impact on operating activities of changes in noncash current asset accounts, in addition to those adjustments described earlier:

Operating activities		
Net income		$145,000
Adjustments to reconcile net income to net cash		
provided by operating activities:		
Amortization expense	$ 9,000	
Loss on sale of equipment	3,000	
Decrease in accounts receivable	**10,000**	
Increase in inventory	**(5,000)**	
Increase in prepaid expenses	**(4,000)**	13,000
Net cash provided by operating activities		158,000

Changes in Current Liabilities

The adjustments required for changes in current liability accounts are as follows: **increases in current liability accounts are added to net income, and decreases in current liability accounts are deducted from net income**, to arrive at net cash provided by operating activities. We will observe these relationships by analysing Computer Services' current liability accounts, Accounts Payable and Income Tax Payable.

Increase in Accounts Payable. The accounts payable account is increased by purchases of merchandise (Dr. Inventory; Cr. Accounts Payable) and decreased by payments to suppliers (Dr. Accounts Payable; Cr. Cash). We determined the amount of purchases made by Computer Services in the analysis of the inventory account earlier: $155,000. Using this figure, we can now determine that payments to suppliers must have been $139,000:

	Accounts Payable				
			Jan. 1	Balance	12,000
$16,000 net increase	**Payments to suppliers**	**139,000**		Purchases	155,000
			Dec. 31	Balance	28,000

To convert net income to net cash provided by operating activities, the $16,000 increase in accounts payable must be added to net income. The increase in accounts payable means that less cash was paid for the purchases than was deducted in the accrual-based expenses section of the income statement. The addition of $16,000 completes the adjustment required to convert the cost of goods purchased to the cash paid for these goods.

In summary, the conversion of the cost of goods sold on the accrual-based income statement to the cash paid for goods purchased involves two steps: First, the change in the inventory account adjusts the cost of goods sold to the accrual-based figure cost of goods purchased. Second, the change in the accounts payable account adjusts the accrual-based cost of goods purchased to the cash-based payments to suppliers:

Cost of goods sold	$150,000
Add: Increase in inventory	5,000
Cost of goods purchased	155,000
Less: Increase in accounts payable	16,000
Cash payments to suppliers	$139,000

Remember that adjustments to accrual-based expense accounts result in an adjustment in the opposite direction to net income. That is, when an expense account such as Cost of Goods Sold is increased because of an increase in inventory, this amount must be *deducted* from net income. This is because expenses reduce net income. Likewise, when Cost of Goods Sold is decreased because of an increase in accounts payable, this amount must be *added* to net income.

If a periodic inventory system was in use, the accounts for purchases and related expenses, rather than Cost of Goods Sold, would be adjusted in a similar manner for any change in accounts payable. There would be no change in the inventory account throughout the period in a periodic inventory system.

Decrease in Income Tax Payable.

When a company incurs income tax expense but has not yet paid its taxes, it records income tax payable. A change in the income tax payable account reflects the difference between the income tax expense incurred and the income tax actually paid during the year.

Computer Services' income tax payable account decreased by $2,000. This means that the $47,000 of income tax expense reported on the income statement was $2,000 less than the amount of taxes paid during the period of $49,000, as shown in the following T account:

		Income Tax Payable		
		Jan. 1 Balance	8,000	
Payments for income tax	49,000	Income tax expense	47,000	} $2,000 net decrease
		Dec. 31 Balance	6,000	

To adjust net income to net cash provided by operating activities, the $2,000 decrease in income tax payable must be deducted from net income. If the amount of income tax payable had increased during the year, the increase would be added to net income to reflect the fact that income tax expense deducted on the accrual-based income statement was higher than the cash paid during the period.

The partial cash flow statement in Illustration 17-7 shows the impact on operating activities of the changes in current liability accounts, and also shows the adjustments described earlier for amortization expense, gains and losses, and changes in noncash current asset accounts. The operating activities section of the cash flow statement is now complete.

COMPUTER SERVICES CORPORATION
Cash Flow Statement—Indirect Method (partial)
Year Ended December 31, 2005

Operating activities		
Net income		$145,000
Adjustments to reconcile net income to net		
cash provided by operating activities:		
Amortization expense	$ 9,000	
Loss on sale of equipment	3,000	
Decrease in accounts receivable	10,000	
Increase in inventory	(5,000)	
Increase in prepaid expenses	(4,000)	
Increase in accounts payable	**16,000**	
Decrease in income tax payable	**(2,000)**	27,000
Net cash provided by operating activities		172,000

Helpful hint Whether the indirect or direct method (Section 2) is used, net cash provided by operating activities will be the same.

In summary, Illustration 17-7 shows that the accrual-based net income of $145,000 resulted in net cash provided by operating activities of $172,000, after adjustments for noncash items.

Summary of Conversion to Net Cash Provided by Operating Activities—Indirect Method

As shown in the previous pages, the cash flow statement prepared by the indirect method starts with net income. It then adds or deducts items to arrive at net cash provided (or used) by operating activities. The adjustments generally take one of three forms: (1) noncash expenses such as amortization, (2) gains and losses on the sale of assets, and (3) changes in noncash current asset and current liability accounts.

A summary of these changes is provided in Illustration 17-8.

		Adjustment Required to Convert Net Income to Net Cash Provided (Used) by Operating Activities
Noncash charges	Amortization expense	Add
Gains and losses	Gain on sale of asset	Deduct
	Loss on sale of asset	Add
Changes in noncash current asset and current liability accounts	Increase in current asset account	Deduct
	Decrease in current asset account	Add
	Increase in current liability account	Add
	Decrease in current liability account	Deduct

Step 2: Investing Activities

Determine the Net Cash Provided (Used) by Investing Activities by Analysing Changes in Temporary Investment and Long-Term Asset Accounts

Helpful hint Investing and financing activities are measured and reported in the same way under the direct and indirect methods.

Investing activities affect long-term asset accounts, such as property, plant, and equipment, and intangible assets. Temporary investments (other than those classified as cash equivalents) are also reported as investing activities. To determine the investing activities, the balance sheet and additional information provided in Illustration 17-5 must be examined. The change in each noncurrent account (and temporary investments) is analysed to determine what effect, if any, the change had on cash.

Computer Services has three long-term asset accounts that must be analysed: Land, Building, and Equipment.

Increase in Land. Land increased by $110,000 during the year, as reported in Computer Services' balance sheet. The additional information states that this land was purchased through issuing long-term bonds. Issuing bonds for land has no effect on cash, but it is a significant noncash investing and financing activity that must be disclosed in a note to the statement.

Increase in Building. The building account increased by $120,000 during the year. What caused this increase? No additional information has been provided regarding this change. **Whenever unexplained differences in noncurrent accounts occur, we assume the transaction was for cash.** That is, we would assume in this case that a building was acquired, or expanded, for $120,000 cash.

Increase in Accumulated Amortization—Building. Accumulated Amortization increased by $6,000 during the year. As explained in the additional information, this increase resulted from the amortization expense reported on the income statement for the building:

Accumulated Amortization—Building			
	Jan. 1	Balance	5,000
		Amortization expense	6,000
	Dec. 31	Balance	11,000

$6,000 net increase

Amortization expense is a noncash charge and was added back to net income in the operating activities section of the cash flow statement to cancel this charge. No further adjustment or reporting is necessary for amortization related to the building.

Increase in Equipment. Computer Services' equipment account increased by $17,000. The additional information explains that this was a net increase resulting from two different transactions: (1) a purchase of equipment for $25,000 cash, and (2) a sale of equipment that cost $8,000 for $4,000 cash. The T account below shows the reasons for the change in this account during the year:

Equipment					
Jan. 1	Balance	10,000			
	Purchase of equipment	25,000	Cost of equipment sold	8,000	
Dec. 31	Balance	27,000			

$17,000 net increase

The following entries show the details of the equipment transactions:

Equipment	25,000	
Cash		25,000

A = L + SE
+25,000
−25,000

Cash flows: −25,000

Cash	4,000	
Accumulated Amortization	1,000	
Loss on Sale of Equipment	3,000	
Equipment		8,000

A = L + SE
+4,000   −3,000
+1,000
−8,000

Cash flows: +4,000

Each transaction should be reported separately on the cash flow statement. When a net change in a noncurrent balance sheet account has occurred during the year, the individual items that cause the net change should be reported separately. Note that this is different than our practice with current balance sheet accounts, where we report only the net change.

In this particular case, the purchase of equipment should be reported as a $25,000 outflow of cash. The sale of equipment should be reported as a $4,000 inflow of cash. Note that it is the cash proceeds that are reported on the cash flow statement, not the cost of the equipment sold.

Increase in Accumulated Amortization—Equipment.

The accumulated amortization for equipment increased by $2,000. This change does not represent the overall amortization expense for the year. The additional information in Illustration 17-5 helps us determine the details of this change.

	Accumulated Amortization—Equipment			
		Jan. 1	Balance	1,000
Sale of equipment	1,000		Amortization expense	3,000
		Dec. 31	Balance	3,000

$2,000 net increase (bracket grouping the above table)

This account was decreased (debited $1,000) as a result of the sale of equipment, as described earlier. The account was also increased by $3,000 of amortization expense for the current period.

As we have seen, there are two accounts affected by the sale of the equipment on Computer Services' income statement (amortization expense and loss on sale) and two accounts on the balance sheet (equipment and accumulated amortization). In the cash flow statement, it is important to combine the effects of this sale in one place—in the investing activities section.

The amortization expense and loss on sale reported in the income statement are shown as additions to net income in the operating activities section of the cash flow statement. They are added back to net income not because they are sources of cash but because they are noncash charges that must be added to net income to cancel the deduction from operating cash flows.

So, no cash impact of the sale of the equipment ends up being included in the operating activities section. Rather, the cash proceeds received from the sale of the equipment are shown in their entirety in the investing activities section.

The investing activities section of Computer Services' cash flow statement is shown below and reports the changes in the accounts Land, Building, and Equipment:

Investing activities		
Purchase of building	$(120,000)	
Purchase of equipment	(25,000)	
Sale of equipment	4,000	
Net cash used by investing activities		$(141,000)
Note x: Significant noncash investing and financing activities		
Issue of bonds to purchase land		$110,000

Step 3: Financing Activities

Determine the Net Cash Provided (Used) by Financing Activities by Analysing Changes in Short-Term Notes Payable and Long-Term Liability and Equity Accounts

The third step is to analyse the changes in long-term liability and equity accounts, including changes involving short-term notes payable. Computer Services has one long-term liability account, Bonds Payable, and two shareholders' equity accounts: Common Shares and Retained Earnings.

Increase in Bonds Payable. Bonds Payable increased by $110,000. As indicated earlier, land was acquired from the issue of these bonds. This noncash transaction is reported as a note to the cash flow statement because it is a significant financing activity.

Increase in Common Shares. Computer Services' common shares account increased by $20,000. Since no additional information is provided about any reacquisition of shares, we assume that this change relates solely to the issue of additional common shares for cash. This cash inflow is reported in the financing activities section of the cash flow statement.

Increase in Retained Earnings. What caused the net increase of $116,000 in Retained Earnings? This increase can be explained by two factors. First, net income increased retained earnings by $145,000. Second, the additional information provided in Illustration 17-5 indicates that a cash dividend of $29,000 was declared and paid. This information could have also been deduced by analysing the T account:

Retained Earnings				
		Jan. 1 Balance	48,000	
Cash dividend	29,000	Net income	145,000	} $116,000 net increase
		Dec. 31 Balance	164,000	

As noted earlier, these two changes must be reported separately. The net income is therefore reported in the operating activities section of the cash flow statement (and adjusted to a cash basis). The cash dividend paid is reported as a cash outflow in the financing activities section of the statement.

The financing activities section of Computer Services' cash flow statement is shown below and reports the issue of common shares and payment of a dividend:

Financing activities		
Issue of common shares	$ 20,000	
Payment of cash dividend	(29,000)	
Net cash used by financing activities		$(9,000)
Note x: Significant noncash investing and financing activities		
Issue of bonds to purchase land		$110,000

Cash Flow Statement

Using the previous information, we can now combine the sections and present a complete cash flow statement in Illustration 17-9 for Computer Services Corporation. The statement starts with operating activities, follows with investing activities, and continues with financing activities. It concludes with the net change in cash, reconciled to the beginning- and end-of-period cash balances. Finally, a significant noncash investing and financing activity is reported in the note to the statement.

Illustration 17-9 ▶

Cash flow statement—
indirect method

COMPUTER SERVICES CORPORATION
Cash Flow Statement—Indirect Method
Year Ended December 31, 2005

Operating activities		
Net income		$145,000
Adjustments to reconcile net income to net		
cash provided by operating activities:		
Amortization expense	$ 9,000	
Loss on sale of equipment	3,000	
Decrease in accounts receivable	10,000	
Increase in inventory	(5,000)	
Increase in prepaid expenses	(4,000)	
Increase in accounts payable	16,000	
Decrease in income tax payable	(2,000)	27,000
Net cash provided by operating activities		172,000
Investing activities		
Purchase of building	$(120,000)	
Purchase of equipment	(25,000)	
Sale of equipment	4,000	
Net cash used by investing activities		(141,000)
Financing activities		
Issue of common shares	$ 20,000	
Payment of cash dividend	(29,000)	
Net cash used by financing activities		(9,000)
Net increase in cash		22,000
Cash, January 1		33,000
Cash, December 31		$ 55,000
Note x: Significant noncash investing and financing activities		
Issue of bonds to purchase land		$110,000

Computer Services' cash flow statement shows the following: Operating activities **provided** $172,000 of cash. Investing activities **used** $141,000 of cash. Financing activities **used** $9,000 of cash. There was a significant noncash investing and financing activity for $110,000.

Step 4: Net Change in Cash

Determine the Net Increase (Decrease) in Cash. Compare the Net Change in Cash with the Change in Cash Reported on the Balance Sheet to Make Sure the Amounts Agree

The comparative balance sheets in Illustration 17-5 indicate that the net change in cash during the period was an increase of $22,000. The $22,000 net increase in cash reported in the cash flow statement above agrees with this change.

Notice how the cash flow statement links the income statement with the beginning and ending balance sheets. Net income from the income statement is the starting point in determining operating activities. The changes in the balance sheet accounts are explained in terms of their impact on cash. These changes lead to the end-of-period cash balances on the balance sheet and on the cash flow statement.

BEFORE YOU GO ON . . .

▶Review It

1. What is the format of the operating activities section of the cash flow statement for the indirect method?
2. Where is amortization expense shown on a cash flow statement using the indirect method?
3. Where are significant noncash investing and financing activities shown in a cash flow statement? Give some examples.

▶Do It

Presented below is information related to Reynolds Ltd. Use the indirect method to prepare a cash flow statement.

REYNOLDS LTD.
Balance Sheet
December 31

Assets	2005	2004	Change Increase/Decrease	
Cash	$ 54,000	$ 37,000	$ 17,000	Increase
Accounts receivable	68,000	26,000	42,000	Increase
Inventories	54,000	10,000	44,000	Increase
Prepaid expenses	4,000	6,000	2,000	Decrease
Land	45,000	70,000	25,000	Decrease
Buildings	200,000	200,000	0	
Accumulated amortization—buildings	(21,000)	(11,000)	10,000	Increase
Equipment	193,000	68,000	125,000	Increase
Accumulated amortization—equipment	(28,000)	(10,000)	18,000	Increase
Totals	$569,000	$396,000		

Liabilities and Shareholders' Equity				
Accounts payable	$ 23,000	$ 50,000	$ 27,000	Decrease
Accrued expenses payable	10,000	0	10,000	Increase
Bonds payable	110,000	150,000	40,000	Decrease
Common shares	220,000	60,000	160,000	Increase
Retained earnings	206,000	136,000	70,000	Increase
Totals	$569,000	$396,000		

REYNOLDS LTD.
Income Statement
Year Ended December 31, 2005

Sales revenue			$890,000
Cost of goods sold		$465,000	
Operating expenses		221,000	
Loss on sale of equipment		2,000	688,000
Income from operations			202,000
Interest expense			12,000
Income before income tax			190,000
Income tax expense			65,000
Net income			$125,000

Additional information:
1. Operating expenses include an amortization expense of $33,000.
2. Equipment with a cost of $166,000 was bought for cash. Equipment with a cost of $41,000 and a net book value of $36,000 was sold for $34,000 cash.
3. Bonds of $40,000 were redeemed at their face value for cash.

Action Plan

- Determine the net cash provided (used) by operating activities. Operating activities generally relate to revenues and expenses, which are affected by changes in noncash current assets and current liabilities in the balance sheet, and noncash items in the income statement.
- Determine the net cash provided (used) by investing activities. Investing activities generally relate to changes in noncurrent assets.
- Determine the net cash provided (used) by financing activities. Financing activities generally relate to changes in noncurrent liabilities and shareholders' equity accounts.
- Determine the net increase (decrease) in cash. Reconcile to the end-of-period cash balance reported on the balance sheet.

Solution

REYNOLDS LTD.
Cash Flow Statement—Indirect Method
Year Ended December 31, 2005

Operating activities		
Net income		$125,000
Adjustments to reconcile net income to net cash provided by operating activities:		
Amortization expense	$ 33,000	
Loss on sale of equipment	2,000	
Increase in accounts receivable	(42,000)	
Increase in inventories	(44,000)	
Decrease in prepaid expenses	2,000	
Decrease in accounts payable	(27,000)	
Increase in accrued expenses payable	10,000	(66,000)
Net cash provided by operating activities		59,000
Investing activities		
Sale of land	$ 25,000	
Sale of equipment	34,000	
Purchase of equipment	(166,000)	
Net cash used by investing activities		(107,000)
Financing activities		
Redemption of bonds	$ (40,000)	
Issue of common shares	160,000	
Payment of dividends	(55,000) *	
Net cash provided by financing activities		65,000
Net increase in cash		17,000
Cash, January 1		37,000
Cash, December 31		$ 54,000

* $136,000 + $125,000 − $206,000 = $55,000

Related exercise material: BE17–4, BE17–5, BE17–6, BE17–7, BE17–8, BE17–9, E17–3, E17–4, E17–5, E17–6, and E17–7.

Note: This concludes Section 1 on the preparation of the cash flow statement using the indirect method. Unless your instructor assigns Section 2, you should turn to the concluding section of the chapter, "Using the Information in the Financial Statements."

SECTION 2 ▸ DIRECT METHOD

To illustrate the direct method, we will use financial information from Computer Services Corporation to prepare a cash flow statement.

Illustration 17-10 presents Computer Services' current- and previous-year balance sheet, its current-year income statement, and related financial information.

study objective 3b

Prepare a cash flow statement using the direct method.

Illustration 17-10 ◄
Comparative balance sheet, income statement, and additional information

COMPUTER SERVICES CORPORATION
Balance Sheet
December 31

Assets	2005	2004	Change Increase/Decrease
Current assets			
Cash	$ 55,000	$ 33,000	$ 22,000 Increase
Accounts receivable	20,000	30,000	10,000 Decrease
Inventory	15,000	10,000	5,000 Increase
Prepaid expenses	5,000	1,000	4,000 Increase
Property, plant, and equipment			
Land	130,000	20,000	110,000 Increase
Building	160,000	40,000	120,000 Increase
Accumulated amortization—building	(11,000)	(5,000)	6,000 Increase
Equipment	27,000	10,000	17,000 Increase
Accumulated amortization—equipment	(3,000)	(1,000)	2,000 Increase
Total	$398,000	$138,000	
Liabilities and Shareholders' Equity			
Current liabilities			
Accounts payable	$ 28,000	$ 12,000	$ 16,000 Increase
Income tax payable	6,000	8,000	2,000 Decrease
Long-term liabilities			
Bonds payable	130,000	20,000	110,000 Increase
Shareholders' equity			
Common shares	70,000	50,000	20,000 Increase
Retained earnings	164,000	48,000	116,000 Increase
Total	$398,000	$138,000	

COMPUTER SERVICES CORPORATION
Income Statement
Year Ended December 31, 2005

Sales revenue		$507,000
Cost of goods sold		150,000
Gross profit		357,000
Operating expenses (excluding amortization)	$111,000	
Amortization expense	9,000	
Loss on sale of equipment	3,000	123,000
Income from operations		234,000
Interest expense		42,000
Income before income tax		192,000
Income tax expense		47,000
Net income		$145,000

Additional information for 2005:
1. The company declared and paid a $29,000 cash dividend.
2. The company obtained land through the issue of $110,000 of long-term bonds.
3. Equipment costing $25,000 was purchased for cash.
4. The company sold equipment with a book value of $7,000 (cost of $8,000, less accumulated amortization of $1,000) for $4,000 cash.
5. Amortization expense consisted of $6,000 for the building and $3,000 for equipment.

We will now apply the four steps to the information provided for Computer Services Corporation.

Step 1: Operating Activities

Determine the Net Cash Provided (Used) by Operating Activities by Converting Net Income from an Accrual Basis to a Cash Basis

Under the **direct method, net cash provided (or used) by operating activities is calculated by adjusting each item in the income statement from the accrual basis to the cash basis.** To simplify and condense the operating activities section, **only major classes of operating cash receipts and cash payments are reported.** The difference between these cash receipts and cash payments for these major classes is the net cash provided by operating activities. These relationships are shown in Illustration 17-11.

Illustration 17-11 ▶

Major classes of cash receipts and payments

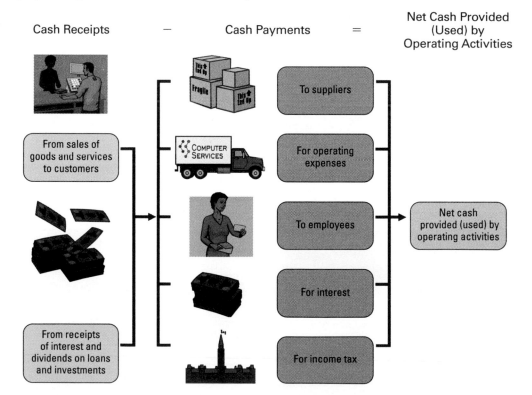

An efficient way to apply the direct method is to analyse the items reported in the income statement in the order in which they are listed. Cash receipts and cash payments related to these revenues and expenses are then determined by adjusting for changes in the related current balance sheet accounts. Most current asset and current liability accounts result from operating activities. For example, accounts receivable indicate credit sales recorded as revenue for which cash collections have not yet been received. Prepaid expenses, such as insurance, reflect insurance that has been paid for, but which has not yet expired and therefore has not been recorded as an expense. Similarly, income tax payable reflects income tax expense incurred by the company but not yet paid.

As a result, we need to adjust revenues and expenses reported on the income statement for these accruals and prepayments to determine the net cash provided by operating activities. To do this, increases in current asset accounts are deducted from revenues and added to expenses to convert accrual-based income statement amounts to cash-based amounts. Conversely, decreases in current asset accounts are added to revenues and deducted from expenses. Increases in current liability accounts are added to revenues and deducted from expenses to convert accrual-based income statement amounts to cash-based amounts. Conversely, decreases in current liability accounts are deducted from revenues and added to expenses.

We explain the reasoning behind these adjustments for Computer Services Corporation, first for cash receipts and then for cash payments, in the following sections.

Cash Receipts

Computer Services has only one source of cash receipts—customers.

Cash Receipts from Customers. The income statement for Computer Services reported sales revenue from customers of $507,000. How much of that was cash receipts? To answer that, it is necessary to consider the change in accounts receivable during the year.

Alternatively, when accounts receivable decrease during the year, revenues on an accrual basis are lower than revenues on a cash basis. In other words, more cash was collected during the period than was recorded as revenue. Computer Services' accounts receivable decreased by $10,000 (from $30,000 to $20,000) during the year. This means that cash receipts were $10,000 higher than revenues. To determine the amount of cash receipts, the decrease in accounts receivable is added to sales revenue.

Thus, cash receipts from customers were $517,000, calculated as in Illustration 17-12:

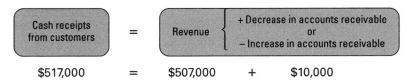

$517,000 = $507,000 + $10,000

Illustration 17-12 ◀

Formula to calculate cash receipts from customers—direct method

Alternatively, when the accounts receivable balance increases during the year, revenues on an accrual basis are higher than cash receipts. In other words, revenues have increased, but not all of these revenues resulted in cash receipts. Therefore, the amount of the increase in accounts receivable is deducted from sales revenues to arrive at cash receipts from customers.

Cash receipts from customers can also be determined from an analysis of the accounts receivable account, as shown below:

Accounts Receivable				
Jan. 1 Balance	30,000			
Sales revenue	507,000	**Receipts from customers**	**517,000**	$10,000 net decrease
Dec. 31 Balance	20,000			

Cash Receipts from Interest and Dividends. Computer Services does not have cash receipts from any source other than customers. If an income statement details other revenue, such as interest and/or dividend revenue, these amounts must be adjusted for any accrued amounts receivable to determine the actual cash receipts. As in Illustration 17-12, increases in accrued receivables would be deducted from accrual-based revenues. Decreases in accrued receivable accounts would be added to accrual-based revenues.

Cash Payments

Computer Services has many sources of cash payments—for suppliers, operating expenses, interest, and income taxes. We will analyse each of these in the next sections.

Cash Payments to Suppliers. Computer Services reported a cost of goods sold, using the perpetual inventory system, of $150,000 on its income statement. How much of that was cash payments to suppliers? To answer that, it is necessary to find the cost of goods purchased for the year. To find purchases, the cost of goods sold is adjusted for the change in inventory. When inventory increases during the year, the cost of goods purchased exceeds the cost of goods sold. To determine the cost of goods purchased, the increase in inventory is added to the cost of goods sold. Any decrease in inventory would be deducted from the cost of goods sold. Computer Services' cost of goods purchased is $155,000 ($150,000 + $5,000).

After the cost of goods purchased is calculated, cash payments to suppliers can be determined. This is done by adjusting the cost of goods purchased for the change in accounts payable. When accounts payable increase during the year, purchases on an accrual basis are higher than they are on a cash basis. To determine cash payments to suppliers, an increase in accounts payable is deducted from the cost of goods purchased. On the other hand, there may be a decrease in accounts payable. That would occur if cash payments to suppliers exceeded purchases. In that case, the decrease in accounts payable is added to the cost of goods purchased.

For Computer Services, cash payments to suppliers were $139,000 ($150,000 + $5,000 = $155,000 − $16,000), as calculated in Illustration 17-13.

Illustration 17-13 ▶

Formula to calculate cash payments to suppliers—direct method

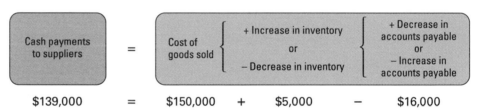

$$\$139,000 \quad = \quad \$150,000 \quad + \quad \$5,000 \quad - \quad \$16,000$$

Cash payments to suppliers (also known as creditors) can also be determined from an analysis of the inventory and accounts payable accounts below:

	Inventory			
Jan. 1 Balance	10,000			
Purchases	155,000	Cost of goods sold	150,000	
Dec. 31 Balance	15,000			

$5,000 net increase

	Accounts Payable			
		Jan. 1 Balance	12,000	
Payments to suppliers	139,000	Purchases	155,000	
		Dec. 31 Balance	28,000	

$16,000 net increase

Cash Payments for Operating Expenses. Operating expenses of $111,000 were reported on Computer Services' income statement. To determine the cash paid for operating expenses, we need to adjust this amount for any changes in prepaid expenses and accrued liabilities.

If prepaid expenses increase during the year, the cash paid for operating expenses will be higher than the operating expenses reported on the income statement. To adjust operating expenses to cash payments for services, any increase in prepaid expenses must be added to operating expenses. On the other hand, if prepaid expenses decrease during the year, the decrease must be deducted from operating expenses.

Operating expenses must also be adjusted for changes in accrued liability accounts (e.g., accrued expenses payable). While some companies record accrued liabilities separately, others combine them with accounts payable. In a merchandising company, such as Computer Services, the accounts payable account is often used only for purchases of merchandise inventory on account. Accrued liability accounts are used for all other payables.

At this point in time, Computer Services does not have any accrued expenses payable related to its operating expenses. If it did, any changes in the accrued expenses payable account would affect operating expenses as follows. When accrued expenses payable increase during the year, operating expenses on an accrual basis are higher than they are on a cash basis. To determine cash payments for operating expenses, an increase in accrued expenses payable is deducted from operating expenses. On the other hand, a decrease in accrued expenses payable is added to operating expenses because the cash payments exceed the operating expenses.

Computer Services' cash payments for operating expenses were $115,000, calculated as in Illustration 17 14.

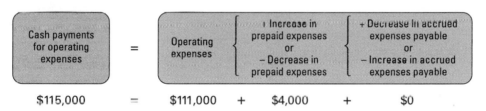

$115,000 = $111,000 + $4,000 + $0

Illustration 17 14 ◄

Formula to calculate cash payments for operating expenses—direct method

Cash payments for operating expenses can also be determined from an analysis of the prepaid expenses account, as shown below:

Prepaid Expenses			
Jan. 1 Balance	1,000		
Payments for expenses 115,000		Operating expenses	111,000
Dec. 31 Balance	5,000		

} $4,000 net increase

Noncash Charges.

Noncash charges on the income statement are not reported on the cash flow statement. Computer Services reports two noncash expenses: amortization expense and a loss on the sale of equipment.

Computer Services' amortization expense in 2005 was $9,000. Recall that the entry to record the amortization would be as follows:

Amortization Expense	9,000	
Accumulated Amortization		9,000

A	=	L	+	SE
−9,000				− 9,000

Cash flows: no effect

This entry has no impact on cash.

Amortization expense was shown separately on Computer Services' income statement. Sometimes amortization expense is included in operating expenses. If the amount for operating expenses includes amortization expense, operating expenses must be reduced by the amount of amortization to determine the cash payments for operating expenses. Other charges to expense that do not require the use of cash, such as bad debt expense, are treated in the same manner as amortization.

The $3,000 loss on the sale of equipment is also a noncash charge. The loss on the sale of equipment reduces net income, but it does not reduce cash. Thus, the loss on the sale of equipment is not reported on the cash flow statement. If there were a gain, it would not be reported either.

Cash Payments to Employees.

Some companies report payments to employees separately, removing these payments from their operating expenses. To determine payments to employees, you would have to know the salary expense amount on the income statement and any salaries payable on the balance sheet. Cash payments to employees would equal the salary expense, plus any decrease (or less any increase) during the period in salaries payable.

Other companies condense their income statements in such a manner that cash payments to suppliers and employees cannot be separated from cash payments for operating expenses (i.e., they do not disclose their cost of goods sold or salary expense separately). Although the disclosure will not be as informative, for reporting purposes it is acceptable to combine these sources of cash payments.

Cash Payments for Interest.

Computer Services reports $42,000 of interest expense on its income statement in Illustration 17-10. This amount equals the cash paid, since the comparative balance sheet indicated no interest payable at the beginning or end of the year.

The relationship among cash payments for interest, interest expense, and changes in interest payable (if any), is shown in Illustration 17-15.

Illustration 17-15 ▶

Formula to calculate cash payments for interest—direct method

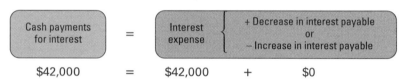

$$\text{Cash payments for interest} = \text{Interest expense} \begin{cases} + \text{Decrease in interest payable} \\ \text{or} \\ - \text{Increase in interest payable} \end{cases}$$

$$\$42,000 = \$42,000 + \$0$$

Cash Payments for Income Tax.

The income statement for Computer Services shows an income tax expense of $47,000 and a decrease in income tax payable of $2,000. When a company incurs income tax expense but has not yet paid its taxes, it records income tax payable. A change in the income tax payable account reflects the difference between income tax expense incurred and income tax actually paid during the year.

The relationship among cash payments for income tax, income tax expense, and changes in income tax payable is shown in Illustration 17-16:

Illustration 17-16 ▶

Formula to calculate cash receipts from customers—direct method

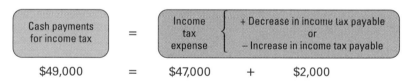

$$\text{Cash payments for income tax} = \text{Income tax expense} \begin{cases} + \text{Decrease in income tax payable} \\ \text{or} \\ - \text{Increase in income tax payable} \end{cases}$$

$$\$49,000 = \$47,000 + \$2,000$$

Computer Services' income tax payable account decreased by $2,000. This means that the $47,000 of income tax expense reported on the income statement was $2,000 less than the $49,000 of taxes paid during the period, as detailed in the following T account:

Income Tax Payable			
		Jan. 1 Balance	8,000
Payments for income tax	**49,000**	Income tax expense	47,000
		Dec. 31 Balance	6,000

$2,000 net decrease {

All of the revenues and expenses in the income statement have now been adjusted to a cash basis. The operating activities section of the cash flow statement is shown in Illustration 17-17.

COMPUTER SERVICES CORPORATION
Cash Flow Statement—Direct Method (partial)
Year Ended December 31, 2005

Operating activities		
Cash receipts from customers		$517,000
Cash payments		
To suppliers	$139,000	
For operating expenses	115,000	
For interest	42,000	
For income tax	49,000	345,000
Net cash provided by operating activities		172,000

Illustration 17-17 ◄
Net cash provided by operating activities—direct method

Helpful hint Whether the direct or indirect method (Section 1) is used, net cash provided by operating activities will be the same.

Step 2: Investing Activities

Determine the Net Cash Provided (Used) by Investing Activities by Analysing Changes in Temporary Investment and Long-Term Asset Accounts

Investing activities affect long-term asset accounts, such as property, plant, and equipment, and intangible assets. Temporary investments (other than those classified as cash equivalents) are also reported as investing activities. To determine the investing activities, the balance sheet and additional information provided in Illustration 17-10 must be examined. The change in each noncurrent account (and temporary investments) is analysed to determine what effect, if any, the change had on cash.

Computer Services has three long-term asset accounts that must be analysed: Land, Buildings, and Equipment.

Helpful hint Investing and financing activities are measured and reported in the same way under the direct and indirect methods.

Increase in Land. Land increased by $110,000 during the year, as reported in Computer Services' balance sheet. The additional information states that this land was purchased through issuing long-term bonds. Issuing bonds for land has no effect on cash, but it is a significant noncash investing and financing activity that must be disclosed in a note to the statement.

Increase in Building. The building account increased by $120,000 during the year. What caused this increase? No additional information has been provided regarding this change. **Whenever unexplained differences in noncurrent accounts occur, we assume the transaction was for cash.** That is, we would assume in this case that a building was acquired, or expanded, for $120,000 cash.

Increase in Accumulated Amortization—Building. Accumulated Amortization increased by $6,000 during the year. As explained in the additional information, this increase resulted from the amortization expense reported on the income statement for the building.

Accumulated Amortization—Building		
	Jan. 1 Balance	5,000
	Amortization expense	6,000
	Dec. 31 Balance	11,000

} $6,000 net increase

As explained earlier, amortization expense is a noncash charge and does not affect the cash flow statement.

Increase in Equipment. Computer Services' equipment account increased by $17,000. The additional information explains that this was a net increase resulting from two different transactions: (1) a purchase of equipment for $25,000 cash, and (2) a sale of equipment that cost $8,000 for $4,000 cash. The T account below shows the reasons for the change in this account during the year:

		Equipment			
Jan. 1	Balance	10,000			
	Purchase of equipment	25,000	Cost of equipment sold		8,000
Dec. 31	Balance	27,000			

$17,000 net increase {

The following entries show the details of the equipment transactions:

A	=	L	+	SE
+25,000				
−25,000				

Equipment	25,000	
Cash		25,000

Cash flows: −25,000

A	=	L	+	SE
+4,000				−3,000
+1,000				
−8,000				

Cash	4,000	
Accumulated Amortization	1,000	
Loss on Sale of Equipment	3,000	
Equipment		8,000

Cash flows: +4,000

Each transaction should be reported separately on the cash flow statement. When a net change in a noncurrent balance sheet account has occurred during the year, the individual items that cause the net change should be reported separately.

In this particular case, the sale of equipment should be reported as a $4,000 inflow of cash. The purchase of equipment should be reported as a $25,000 outflow of cash. Note that it is the cash proceeds that are reported on the cash flow statement, not the cost of the equipment sold.

Increase in Accumulated Amortization—Equipment. The accumulated amortization for equipment increased by $2,000.

	Accumulated Amortization—Equipment			
		Jan. 1	Balance	1,000
Sale of equipment	1,000		Amortization expense	3,000
		Dec. 31	Balance	3,000

$2,000 net increase {

As previously noted, amortization has no impact on cash and does not affect the cash flow statement. The impact of the sale of the equipment was reported as indicated above.

The investing activities section of Computer Services' cash flow statement is shown below and reports the changes in the accounts Land, Building, and Equipment:

Investing activities	
Purchase of building	$(120,000)
Purchase of equipment	(25,000)
Sale of equipment	4,000
Net cash used by investing activities	$(141,000)
Note x: Significant noncash investing and financing activities	
Issue of bonds to purchase land	$110,000

Step 3: Financing Activities

Determine the Net Cash Provided (Used) by Financing Activities by Analysing Changes in Short-Term Notes Payable and Long-Term Liability and Equity Accounts

The third step is to analyse the changes in long-term liability and equity accounts, including changes involving short-term notes payable. Computer Services has one long-term liability account, Bonds Payable, and two shareholders' equity accounts: Common Shares and Retained Earnings.

Increase in Bonds Payable. Bonds Payable increased by $110,000. As indicated earlier, land was acquired from the issue of these bonds. This noncash transaction is reported as a note to the cash flow statement because it is a significant financing activity.

Increase in Common Shares. Computer Services' common shares account increased by $20,000. Since no additional information is provided about any reacquisition of shares, we assume that this change relates solely to the issue of additional common shares for cash. This cash inflow is reported in the financing activities section of the cash flow statement.

Increase in Retained Earnings. What caused the net increase of $116,000 in Retained Earnings? This increase can be explained by two factors. First, net income increased retained earnings by $145,000. Second, the additional information provided in Illustration 17-10 indicates that a cash dividend of $29,000 was declared and paid. This information could have also been deduced by analysing the T account:

		Retained Earnings		
		Jan. 1 Balance	48,000	
Cash dividend	29,000	Net income	145,000	$116,000 net increase
		Dec. 31 Balance	164,000	

Net income is not separately reported in the cash flow statement under the direct method. Rather, the cash components of the items (revenues and expenses) comprising net income are reported in the operating activities section, as we learned earlier. The cash dividend paid is reported as a cash outflow in the financing activities section of the statement.

The financing activities section of Computer Services' cash flow statement is shown below and reports the issue of common shares and payment of a dividend:

Financing activities		
Issue of common shares	$ 20,000	
Payment of cash dividend	(29,000)	
Net cash used by financing activities		($9,000)
Note x: Significant noncash investing and financing activities		
Issue of bonds to purchase land		$110,000

Cash Flow Statement

Using the previous information, we can now combine the sections and present a complete cash flow statement in Illustration 17-18 for Computer Services Corporation. The statement starts with operating activities, follows with investing activities, and continues with financing activities. It concludes with the net change in cash, reconciled to the beginning- and end-of-period cash balances. Finally, a significant noncash investing and financing activity is reported in the note to the statement.

Illustration 17-18 ▶

Cash flow statement—
direct method

COMPUTER SERVICES CORPORATION
Cash Flow Statement—Direct Method
Year Ended December 31, 2005

Operating activities		
Cash receipts from customers		$517,000
Cash payments		
To suppliers	$ 139,000	
For operating expenses	115,000	
For interest	42,000	
For income tax	49,000	(345,000)
Net cash provided by operating activities		172,000
Investing activities		
Purchase of building	$(120,000)	
Purchase of equipment	(25,000)	
Sale of equipment	4,000	
Net cash used by investing activities		(141,000)
Financing activities		
Issue of common shares	$ 20,000	
Payment of cash dividend	(29,000)	
Net cash used by financing activities		(9,000)
Net increase in cash		22,000
Cash, January 1		33,000
Cash, December 31		$ 55,000
Note x: Significant noncash investing and financing activities		
Issue of bonds to purchase land		$110,000

Helpful hint   Note that in the investing and financing activities sections, positive numbers indicate cash inflows (receipts) and negative numbers indicate cash outflows (payments).

Computer Services' cash flow statement shows the following: Operating activities **provided** $172,000 of cash. Investing activities **used** $141,000 of cash. Financing activities **used** $9,000 of cash. There was a significant noncash investing and financing activity for $110,000.

Step 4: Net Change in Cash

Determine the Net Increase (Decrease) in Cash. Compare the Net Change in Cash with the Change in Cash Reported on the Balance Sheet to Make Sure the Amounts Agree

The comparative balance sheets in Illustration 17-10 indicate that the net change in cash during the period was an increase of $22,000. The $22,000 net increase in cash reported in the cash flow statement agrees with this change.

BEFORE YOU GO ON . . .

▶ Review It

1. What is the format of the operating activities section of the cash flow statement using the direct method?
2. Where is amortization expense shown on a cash flow statement using the direct method?
3. Where are significant noncash investing and financing activities shown on a cash flow statement? Give some examples.

▶Do It

Presented below is information related to Reynolds Ltd. Use the direct method to prepare a cash flow statement.

REYNOLDS LTD.
Balance Sheet
December 31

Assets	2005	2004	Change Increase/Decrease
Cash	$ 54,000	$ 37,000	$ 17,000 Increase
Accounts receivable	68,000	26,000	42,000 Increase
Inventories	54,000	10,000	44,000 Increase
Prepaid expenses	4,000	6,000	2,000 Decrease
Land	45,000	70,000	25,000 Decrease
Buildings	200,000	200,000	0
Accumulated amortization—buildings	(21,000)	(11,000)	10,000 Increase
Equipment	193,000	68,000	125,000 Increase
Accumulated amortization—equipment	(28,000)	(10,000)	18,000 Increase
Totals	$569,000	$396,000	

Liabilities and Shareholders' Equity			
Accounts payable	$ 23,000	$ 50,000	$ 27,000 Decrease
Accrued expenses payable	10,000	0	10,000 Increase
Bonds payable	110,000	150,000	40,000 Decrease
Common shares	220,000	60,000	160,000 Increase
Retained earnings	206,000	136,000	70,000 Increase
Totals	$569,000	$396,000	

REYNOLDS LTD.
Income Statement
Year Ended December 31, 2005

Sales revenue		$890,000
Cost of goods sold	$465,000	
Operating expenses	221,000	
Loss on sale of equipment	2,000	688,000
Income from operations		202,000
Interest expense		12,000
Income before income tax		190,000
Income tax expense		65,000
Net income		$125,000

Additional information:

1. Operating expenses include an amortization expense of $33,000.
2. Equipment with a cost of $166,000 was bought for cash. Equipment with a cost of $41,000 and a net book value of $36,000 was sold for $34,000 cash.
3. Bonds of $40,000 were redeemed at their face value for cash.
4. Accounts payable pertain to merchandise suppliers.

Action Plan

- Determine the net cash provided (used) by operating activities. Operating activities generally relate to revenues and expenses shown on the income statement, which are affected by changes in noncash current assets and current liabilities shown on the balance sheet.
- Determine the net cash provided (used) by investing activities. Investing activities generally relate to changes in noncurrent assets.
- Determine the net cash provided (used) by financing activities. Financing activities generally relate to changes in noncurrent liabilities and shareholders' equity accounts.
- Determine the net increase (decrease) in cash. Reconcile to the end-of-period cash balance reported on the balance sheet.

Solution

REYNOLDS LTD.
Cash Flow Statement—Direct Method
Year Ended December 31, 2005

Operating activities
  Cash receipts from customers $848,000[a]
  Cash payments
    To suppliers $(536,000)[b]
    For operating expenses   (176,000)[c]
    For interest   (12,000)
    For income tax   (65,000)   (789,000)
      Net cash provided by operating activities   59,000
Investing activities
    Sale of land $ 25,000
    Sale of equipment   34,000
    Purchase of equipment   (166,000)
      Net cash used by investing activities   (107,000)
Financing activities
    Redemption of bonds $ (40,000)
    Sale of common shares   160,000
    Payment of dividends   (55,000)[d]
      Net cash provided by financing activities   65,000
  Net increase in cash   17,000
  Cash, January 1   37,000
  Cash, December 31 $ 54,000

Calculations:

[a] Cash receipts from customers: $890,000 − $42,000 = $848,000
[b] Payments to suppliers: $465,000 + $44,000 + $27,000 = $536,000
[c] Payments for operating expenses: $221,000 − $33,000 − $2,000 − $10,000 = $176,000
[d] Payment for dividends: $136,000 + $125,000 − $206,000 = $55,000

Related exercise material: BE17–7, BE17–8, BE17–9, BE17–10, BE17–11, BE17–12, BE17–13, BE17–14, E17–8, E17–9, E17–10, E17–11, and E17–12.

Note: This concludes Section 2 on the preparation of the cash flow statement using the direct method. You should now continue with the next—and concluding—section of the chapter, "Using the Information in the Financial Statements."

Using the Information in the Financial Statements

study objective 4

Analyse the cash flow statement.

The cash flow statement provides information about a company's financial health that is not evident from an analysis of the balance sheet or the income statement. Creditors and other users of the cash flow statement are often more concerned with cash flow from operating activities than they are with net income, because they are interested in a company's ability to pay its bills. Two cash flow measures of analysis that contribute to this evaluation are EBITDA and free cash flow.

EBITDA

EBITDA is an important cash-based measure. It is an abbreviation for "**e**arnings **b**efore **i**nterest, **t**ax, **d**epreciation, and **a**mortization." EBITDA is a basic measure of a company's ability to generate cash from operating activities. It is frequently cited in annual reports and in the financial press. It can be calculated, although most companies present this amount directly in their annual reports.

We can calculate EBITDA for The Forzani Group from information provided on its income statement (in thousands):

Net Income	+	Interest Expense	+	Income Tax Expense	+	Amortization Expense	=	EBITDA
$30,531	+	$4,354	+	$19,932	+	$29,624	=	$84,441

Note that although the term EBITDA includes the word "depreciation," no depreciation has been added in the above formula. Few companies in Canada use the term "depreciation," although this term is commonly used in some other countries. In these countries, separate terms are used to distinguish between the allocation of the cost of property, plant, and equipment over their useful lives (known as depreciation) and the allocation of the cost of intangible assets over their useful lives (known as amortization). In Canada, we generally use one term—amortization—for the allocation of the cost of all amortizable assets over their useful lives. So when you see the term EBITDA, you need to understand that depreciation and amortization are usually the same in this country.

Illustration 17-19 ▲
EBITDA

We can clearly see the difference in accrual-based net income and cash-based EBITDA for Forzani. Forzani's net income is $30,531 thousand, but its EBITDA, after significant noncash expenditures have been removed, is nearly three times as high at $84,441 thousand.

Bankers prefer EBITDA because it eliminates the effects of many accounting and financing decisions. Many accrual-based ratios are reproduced using EBITDA instead of net income. Forzani, for example, reports an EBITDA margin in its annual report. An EBITDA margin is similar to the profit margin (which is calculated by dividing net income by net sales), except that EBITDA is used instead of net income in the numerator.

One has to be careful when using EBITDA as a substitute for cash flow from operating activities, however. It ignores several factors, including capital expenditures, which are dealt with in the next cash-based ratio we will discuss—free cash flow.

Free Cash Flow

In the cash flow statement, the amount of cash provided by operating activities is supposed to indicate the company's ability to generate cash. However, this amount fails to take into account the fact that a company must invest in productive assets, such as buildings and equipment, just to maintain its current level of operations. Companies must also keep paying dividends to satisfy investors. One solvency-based measure that helps investors and management understand how much discretionary cash flow a company has is free cash flow. **Free cash flow** is the term used to describe the cash remaining from operating activities after adjustments for capital expenditures and dividends.

Consider the following example. Suppose that Li Ltd. produces and sells 10,000 personal computers this year. It reports $100,000 cash provided by operating activities. In order to maintain production at 10,000 computers, Li then invests $15,000 in equipment. It also chooses to pay $5,000 in dividends. Its free cash flow is therefore $80,000 ($100,000 − $15,000 − $5,000). The company could use this $80,000 to purchase new assets to expand the business or to pay an $80,000 dividend, among other alternatives, while continuing to produce 10,000 computers a year.

We will now use data from Forzani's cash flow statement (in thousands), to further illustrate the calculation of free cash flow.

Cash Provided (Used) by Operating Activities	−	Net Capital Expenditures	−	Dividends Paid	=	Free Cash Flow
$21,013	−	($50,085 − $276)	−	$0	=	$(28,796)

Illustration 17-20 ◄
Free cash flow

The cash provided (used) by operating activities is taken from the operating activities section of the cash flow statement. Net capital expenditures—representing amounts paid for the acquisition of long-lived assets less any recoveries from the sale of these assets—

can be found in the investing activities section of the cash flow statement. Dividends paid, if any, are reported in the financing activities section of the cash flow statement.

Forzani's free cash flow is not "free" at all. It is a negative $28,796 thousand. The cash Forzani produces from operating activities is insufficient to support its current year's capital expenditures. It must therefore finance any deficiency with debt and equity.

Many investors believe that "cash is cash and everything else is accounting." It is important to understand that even if cash flow is less susceptible to management manipulations of estimates and assumptions than is net income, it is not foolproof. For example, management can influence cash flow near year end by timing purchase and sale decisions to occur either after or before the year end, depending on the desired effect.

ACCOUNTING IN ACTION ▶ Business Insight

During the 1990s, analysts increasingly used cash-based measures, such as cash provided by operating activities, instead of, or in addition to, net income. The reason for the change was that they had lost faith in accrual-based measures. Sadly, these days even cash flow isn't always what it seems to be.

Take, for example, Alliance Atlantis Communications Inc. The company reported cash flow *provided* by operating activities of $686.5 million in 2001. Looks impressive, right? However, in 2002, the company's cash flow statement for 2001 was restated to report cash *used* by operating activities of $59.9 million. What happened? Accounting standard-setters decided that money spent to acquire, develop, and produce films and television programs was an operating expense, not an investment. Cash flow didn't actually change, but its reporting did. The moral of this story is that accounting assumptions can alter not only reported earnings, but also cash flow.

Source: Fabrice Taylor, "Show Me the Real Money," *Report on Business Magazine*, November 2002, 109.

BEFORE YOU GO ON . . .

▶Review it

1. Why might an analyst want to supplement accrual-based ratios with cash-based measures?
2. What is the difference between net income and EBITDA?
3. What is the difference between cash from operating activities and free cash flow?
4. What does it mean if a company has a negative free cash flow?

Related exercise material: BE17–15, E17–13, and E17–14.

Demonstration Problem

Additional
Demonstration
Problems

The income statement for the year ended December 31, 2005, for Kosinski Manufacturing Ltd. contains the following condensed information:

KOSINSKI MANUFACTURING LTD. Income Statement Year Ended December 31, 2005		
Sales		$6,583,000
Cost of goods sold	$3,427,000	
Operating expenses	1,469,000	
Amortization expense	880,000	
Loss on sale of machinery	24,000	5,800,000
Income before income tax		783,000
Income tax expense		353,000
Net income		$ 430,000

The following balances are reported on Kosinski's comparative balance sheet at December 31:

KOSINSKI MANUFACTURING LTD.
Balance Sheet (partial)
December 31

	2004	2005	Increase (Decrease)
Cash	$672,000	$130,000	$542,000
Accounts receivable	775,000	610,000	165,000
Inventories	834,000	867,000	(33,000)
Accounts payable	521,000	501,000	20,000

Additional information:

1. Machinery was sold for $270,000 cash at a loss of $24,000.
2. New machinery was purchased during the year for $750,000.
3. Dividends declared and paid in 2005 totalled $200,000.

Instructions

(a) Prepare the cash flow statement using the indirect method.
(b) Prepare the cash flow statement using the direct method.

Solution to Demonstration Problem

(a)

KOSINSKI MANUFACTURING LTD.
Cash Flow Statement—Indirect Method
Year Ended December 31, 2005

Operating activities		
Net income		$ 430,000
Adjustments to reconcile net income to net cash provided by operating activities:		
Amortization expense	$880,000	
Loss on sale of machinery	24,000	
Increase in accounts receivable	(165,000)	
Decrease in inventories	33,000	
Increase in accounts payable	20,000	792,000
Net cash provided by operating activities		1,222,000
Investing activities		
Sale of machinery	$270,000	
Purchase of machinery	(750,000)	(480,000)
Financing activities		
Payment of cash dividends		(200,000)
Net increase in cash		542,000
Cash, January 1		130,000
Cash, December 31		$ 672,000

Action Plan

- Apply the same data to the cash flow statement under both the indirect and direct methods.
- Note the similarities of the two methods: Both methods report the same total amount of cash provided by operating activities. The information in the investing and financing sections is the same in both methods.
- Note the difference between the two methods: The cash flows from operating activities sections report different information.

(b)

KOSINSKI MANUFACTURING LTD.
Cash Flow Statement—Direct Method
Year Ended December 31, 2005

Operating activities		
Cash receipts from customers		$6,418,000 [a]
Cash payments to suppliers		(3,374,000)[b]
Cash payments for operating expenses		(1,469,000)
Cash payment for income tax		(353,000)
Net cash provided by operating activities		1,222,000
Investing activities		
Sale of machinery	$270,000	
Purchase of machinery	(750,000)	(480,000)
Financing activities		
Payment of cash dividends		(200,000)
Net increase in cash		542,000
Cash, January 1		130,000
Cash, December 31		$ 672,000

Direct Method Calculations:

[a] Cash receipts from customers:	
Sales per the income statement	$6,583,000
Deduct: Increase in accounts receivable	165,000
Cash receipts from customers	$6,418,000

[b] Cash payments to suppliers:	
Cost of goods sold per the income statement	$3,427,000
Deduct: Decrease in inventories	33,000
Increase in accounts payable	20,000
Cash payments to suppliers	$3,374,000

the
navigator

Summary of Study Objectives

1. *Describe the usefulness of the cash flow statement.* The cash flow statement provides information about the cash receipts and cash payments resulting from the operating, investing, and financing activities of a company during the period.

2. *Distinguish among operating, investing, and financing activities.* Operating activities include the cash effects of transactions that affect net income. Investing activities include cash flows resulting from changes in temporary investments and long-term asset items. Financing activities include cash flows resulting from changes in short-term notes payable, long-term liability, and shareholders' equity items.

3a. *Prepare a cash flow statement using the indirect method.* The preparation of a cash flow statement involves four major steps: (1) Determine the net cash provided (used) by operating activities by converting net income from an accrual basis to a cash basis. (2) Analyse the changes in temporary investment and noncurrent asset accounts and record them as investing activities, or as significant noncash transactions. (3) Analyse the changes in short-term notes payable and noncurrent liability and equity accounts and record them as financing activities, or as significant noncash transactions. (4) Determine the net increase (decrease) in cash. Compare the net change in cash with the change in cash reported on the balance sheet to make sure the amounts agree.

3b. *Prepare a cash flow statement using the direct method.* The preparation of the cash flow statement involves four major steps: (1) Determine the net cash provided (used) by operating activities by converting each individual revenue and expense from an accrual basis to a cash basis. (2) Analyse the changes in temporary investment and noncurrent asset accounts and record them as investing activities, or as significant noncash transactions. (3) Analyse the changes in short-term notes payable and noncurrent liability and equity accounts and record them as financing activities, or as significant noncash transactions. (4) Determine the net increase (decrease) in cash. Compare the net change in cash with the change in cash reported on the balance sheet to make sure the amounts agree.

4. *Analyse the cash flow statement.* EBITDA, or "earnings before interest, tax, depreciation and amortization," is a proxy measure of a company's ability to generate cash from operating activities. It is calculated by adding interest, income tax, and amortization expenses to net income to remove them from this accrual-based number. Free cash flow is a measure of solvency that indicates the amount of cash a company generated during the current year that is available for the payment of dividends or for expansion. It is calculated by subtracting capital expenditures and dividends from the cash provided by operating activities.

Glossary

Key Term Matching Activity

Cash flow statement A financial statement that provides information about the cash receipts and cash payments of a company during a period, classified as operating, investing, and financing activities. (p. 792)

Direct method A method of determining the net cash provided by operating activities by adjusting each item in the income statement from the accrual basis to the cash basis. (p. 814)

EBITDA Earnings before interest, tax, depreciation, and amortization expenses. (p. 824)

Financing activities Cash flow activities from short-term notes payable and noncurrent liability and equity items. These include (a) obtaining cash from issuing debt and repaying the amounts borrowed, and (b) obtaining cash from shareholders and providing them with a return on their investment. (p. 794)

Free cash flow Cash provided by operating activities less capital expenditures and dividends. (p. 825)

Indirect method A method of preparing a cash flow statement in which net income is adjusted for items that did not affect cash, to determine net cash provided by operating activities. (p. 800)

Investing activities Cash flow activities from temporary investments and noncurrent assets. These include (a) acquiring and disposing of investments and productive long-lived assets, and (b) lending money and collecting on those loans. (p. 794)

Operating activities Cash flow activities that include the cash effects of transactions that create revenues and expenses, and thus affect net income. (p. 793)

Self-Study Questions

Chapter 17 Self-Test

Answers are at the end of the chapter.

(SO 1) K 1. Which of the following remarks about the cash flow statement is incorrect?
   (a) It is a fourth basic financial statement.
   (b) It provides information about the cash receipts and cash payments during a period.
   (c) It reconciles the ending cash account balance to the bank statement balance.
   (d) It provides information about the operating, investing, and financing activities of the business.

(SO 2) K 2. The cash flow statement classifies cash receipts and cash payments by the following activities:
   (a) operating and non-operating.
   (b) operating, investing, and financing.
   (c) financing, operating, and non-operating.
   (d) investing, financing, and non-operating.

3. An example of a cash flow from an operating activity is: (SO 2) C
   (a) a payment of cash to lenders for interest.
   (b) a receipt of cash from the sale of common shares.
   (c) a payment of cash dividends to shareholders.
   (d) a receipt of cash from the issue of a short-term note payable.

4. An example of a cash flow from an investing activity is: (SO 2) C
   (a) a receipt of cash from the issue of bonds.
   (b) a payment of cash to repurchase common shares.
   (c) a receipt of cash from the sale of equipment.
   (d) a payment of cash to suppliers for inventory.

5. An example of a cash flow from a financing activity is: (SO 2) C
   (a) a receipt of cash from the sale of land.
   (b) an issue of debt for cash.
   (c) a purchase of equipment for cash.
   (d) a purchase of inventory on credit.

(SO 2) C 6. Cash dividends paid to shareholders are classified on the cash flow statement as:
(a) operating activities.
(b) investing activities.
(c) financing activities.
(d) a note to the financial statements.

(SO 3a) AP 7. Net income is $132,000. During the year, accounts payable increased by $10,000, inventory decreased by $6,000, and accounts receivable increased by $12,000. Under the indirect method, net cash provided by operating activities is:
(a) $102,000.   (c) $124,000.
(b) $112,000.   (d) $136,000.

(SO 3a) K 8. In determining cash provided by operating activities under the indirect method, noncash charges that are added to net income do not include:
(a) amortization expense.
(b) a gain on the sale of equipment.
(c) a decrease in inventory.
(d) a loss on the sale of equipment.

(SO 3b) AP 9. The beginning balance in accounts receivable is $44,000. The ending balance is $42,000. Sales during the period are $129,000. Cash receipts from customers are:

(a) $127,000.   (c) $131,000.
(b) $129,000.   (d) $141,000.

(SO 3b) C 10. Which of the following items is reported on a cash flow statement prepared using the direct method?
(a) A loss on the sale of a building
(b) An increase in accounts receivable
(c) Amortization expense
(d) Cash payments to suppliers

(SO 4) K 11. EBITDA is an abbreviation for:
(a) earnings before insurance, taxes, debt, and accruals.
(b) employee benefits increased by taxes, debt, and accounts payable.
(c) earnings before interest, tax, depreciation, and amortization expenses.
(d) everything but income tax, debt, and assets.

(SO 4) K 12. Free cash flow provides an indication of a company's ability to:
(a) generate sales.
(b) generate net income.
(c) generate cash for discretionary uses.
(d) generate cash for investments.

Questions

(SO 1) C 1. (a) What is the cash flow statement and why is it useful?
(b) Elisa Botelho maintains that the cash flow statement is an optional financial statement. Do you agree? Explain.

(SO 1) C 2. What questions about cash are answered by the cash flow statement that are not answered by the other statements?

(SO 1) C 3. What are "cash equivalents"? How do cash equivalents affect the cash flow statement?

(SO 1) C 4. Distinguish among the three types of activities reported in the cash flow statement.

(SO 2) C 5. Why is it important to disclose significant noncash transactions? How should they be disclosed?

(SO 2) C 6. Darren and Adriana were discussing the presentation format of the cash flow statement of Rock Candy Corp. Cross-referenced to Rock Candy's cash flow statement was a note entitled "Noncash investing and financing activities." Give two examples of significant noncash transactions that might be reported in this note.

(SO 2) C 7. One of Osman Corporation's shareholders asks at a shareholders' meeting why the company's cash flow statement ends with cash at the end of the period on the balance sheet date and yet the date on the cash flow statement is not the same as the one on the bal-

ance sheet—it seems to cover the entire year.. Explain why the dates of the two statements are not the same.

(SO 2) C 8. Why is it necessary to use a comparative balance sheet, a current income statement, and certain transaction data in preparing a cash flow statement?

(SO 2) C 9. Why is it necessary to convert accrual-based net income to cash-based income when preparing a cash flow statement?

(SO 2) C 10. How can a company's cash balance decrease when the company has earned net income? Conversely, how can cash increase when a company has incurred a net loss?

(SO 2) C 11. If a company reports $500,000 of cash collected from customers on its cash flow statement, would it also report $500,000 of sales on its income statement? Explain why or why not.

(SO 3) C 12. Contrast the advantages and disadvantages of the direct and indirect methods of preparing the cash flow statement. Are both methods acceptable? Which method is preferred by the CICA? Which method is more popular? Why?

(SO 3) C 13. In 2004, Goh Corporation changed its method of reporting operating activities from the indirect method to the direct method in order to make its cash flow statement more informative to its readers. Will this change increase, decrease, or not affect the net cash provided by operating activities?

(SO 3a) C 14. Describe the indirect method for determining net cash provided by operating activities.

(SO 3a) K 15. Identify four items under the indirect method that could be adjustments to reconcile net income to net cash provided by operating activities.

(SO 3a) C 16. Why and how is amortization expense reported in a statement prepared using the indirect method?

(SO 3a) C 17. Explain how the sale of equipment at a gain is reported on a cash flow statement using the indirect method.

18. Describe the direct method for determining net cash provided by operating activities. (SO 3b) C

19. Under the direct method, why is amortization expense not reported in the cash flow from operating activities section? (SO 3b) C

20. What is EBITDA used to measure? Why is it preferred to net income when calculating ratios? (SO 4) C

21. What does free cash flow indicate, and how is it calculated? (SO 4) C

Brief Exercises

BE17–1 For each of the following transactions, indicate whether it will increase (+), decrease (–), or have no effect (NE) on a company's cash flows:

(a) _____ A payment of notes payable
(b) _____ A sale of land for cash
(c) _____ A reacquisition of common shares
(d) _____ A purchase of a long term equity investment
(e) _____ An acquisition of a building by an issue of common shares
(f) _____ An issue of preferred shares for cash
(g) _____ A distribution of a previously declared stock dividend
(h) _____ A collection of accounts receivable

Indicate impact of transaction on cash. (SO 2) AP

BE17–2 Classify the following items as an operating, investing, or financing activity. Assume all items involve cash.

(a) A purchase of equipment
(b) A sale of a building
(c) A retirement of bonds
(d) A payment of dividends
(e) A purchase of inventory
(f) An issue of common shares
(g) An issue of bonds
(h) A sale of a long-term debt investment

Classify transactions by activity. (SO 2) AP

BE17–3 Each of the following items must be considered in preparing a cash flow statement for Survivor Corp. for the year ended December 31, 2005. For each item, state how it should be shown in the cash flow statement.

(a) Issued bonds for $200,000 cash.
(b) Purchased equipment for $150,000 cash.
(c) Sold land costing $20,000 for $30,000 cash.
(d) Declared and paid a $50,000 cash dividend.
(e) Retired $250,000 of bonds by issuing shares.

Indicate statement presentation. (SO 2) AP

BE17–4 Indicate whether each of the following transactions would be added to (+) or subtracted from (−) net income in determining the cash provided (used) by operating activities using the indirect method:

(a) _____ An amortization expense
(b) _____ An increase in accounts receivable
(c) _____ A decrease in inventory
(d) _____ An increase in accounts payable
(e) _____ A decrease in income tax payable
(f) _____ A gain on sale of equipment
(g) _____ A loss on sale of long-term debt investment

Indicate impact on cash from operating activities— indirect method. (SO 3a) AP

BE17–5 Crystal Inc. reported net income of $2.5 million for the year ended December 31, 2005. Amortization expense for the year was $260,000, accounts receivable decreased by $350,000, prepaid expenses increased by $95,000, accounts payable decreased by $280,000, and the company incurred a gain on sale of equipment of $10,000. Calculate the net cash provided (used) by operating activities using the indirect method.

Calculate cash from operating activities— indirect method. (SO 3a) AP

Calculate cash from operating activities—indirect method. (SO 3a) AP

BE17–6 The net income for Dupigne Corporation for the year ended March 31, 2005 was $250,000. For fiscal 2005 amortization expense was $60,000, accounts receivable increased by $19,000, inventory decreased by $17,000, accounts payable increased by $27,000, and the company incurred a loss on sale of equipment of $8,000. Calculate the net cash provided (used) by operating activities using the indirect method.

Calculate dividends paid. (SO 3a, 3b) AP

BE17–7 **Canadian Tire Corporation, Limited** reported net income of $202.4 million for fiscal 2002. Its retained earnings were $973.1 million on January 1 and $1,138.0 million on December 31. It also repurchased shares, which resulted in a $5.9-million reduction to retained earnings in 2002. What amount of dividends was paid by Canadian Tire in 2002?

Calculate cash received from sale of equipment. (SO 3a, 3b) AN

BE17–8 The T accounts for equipment and the related accumulated amortization for Trevis Corporation are as follows:

Equipment					Accumulated Amortization			
Beg. bal.	80,000	Disposals	22,000		Disposals	5,500	Beg. bal.	44,500
Acquisitions	41,600						Amort.	12,000
End. bal.	99,600						End. bal.	51,000

In addition, Trevis' income statement reported a loss on the sale of equipment of $4,900. What amount was reported on the cash flow statement as "cash flow provided by sale of equipment"?

Calculate gain or loss on sale of equipment. (SO 3a, 3b) AN

BE17–9 Illuvatar Limited sold equipment for $11,000 on December 31, 2005. The equipment had been purchased on June 30, 2001, for $50,000, and was being amortized on a straight-line basis over a five-year useful life with no residual value. Calculate the gain or loss on the sale of equipment. Indicate where the gain or loss will be recorded on the cash flow statement using (1) the indirect method, and (2) the direct method.

Calculate cash receipts from customers—direct method. (SO 3b) AP

BE17–10 Westcoast Corporation has accounts receivable of $14,000 at January 1, 2005, and of $24,000 at December 31, 2005. Sales revenues were $470,000 for the year. What is the amount of cash receipts from customers in 2005?

Calculate cash payments for income tax—direct method. (SO 3b) AP

BE17–11 Home Grocery Corporation reported income tax expense of $90,000 in its 2005 income statement, and income tax payable of $14,000 at December 31, 2004, and of $9,000 at December 31, 2005. What was the amount of cash paid for income tax during 2005?

Calculate cash payments for operating expenses—direct method. (SO 3b) AP

BE17–12 For 2005, Linux Corporation reports operating expenses of $100,000, including an amortization expense of $15,000. During the year, prepaid expenses decreased by $6,600 and accrued expenses payable increased by $2,400. Calculate the cash payments for operating expenses in 2005.

Calculate cash payments to suppliers—direct method. (SO 3b) AP

BE17–13 Winter Sportswear Inc. reported a cost of goods sold of $89,000 on its 2005 income statement. It also reported a decrease in inventory of $3,600 and a decrease in accounts payable of $2,700. What amount of cash payments was made to suppliers in 2005?

Prepare cash flow statement—direct method. (SO 3b) AP

BE17–14 The following T account is a summary of the cash account of Baker Corporation:

Cash (Summary Form)

Balance, Jan. 1, 2005	8,000	Payment to reacquire common shares	19,000
Receipts from customers	364,000	Payments to suppliers	200,000
Dividends on equity investments	6,000	Payments for operating expenses	140,000
Proceeds from sale of equipment	36,000	Interest paid	10,000
Proceeds from issue of bonds		Income tax paid	8,000
payable	200,000	Dividends paid	45,000
Balance, Dec. 31, 2005	192,000		

Prepare a cash flow statement for Baker Corporation using the direct method.

Calculate ratios. (SO 4) AP

BE17–15 Jaina Corporation reported cash provided by operating activities of $300,000, cash used by investing activities of $250,000, and cash provided by financing activities of $70,000. Cash spent for property, plant, and equipment during the period was $200,000. In addition, the company reported net income of $131,000, amortization expense of $146,000, interest expense of $10,500, and income tax expense of $44,000. No dividends were paid. Calculate EBITDA and free cash flow.

Exercises

E17–1 Eng Corporation had the following transactions:

Classify transactions by activity.
(SO 2) AP

Transaction	Classification	Cash Inflow or Outflow
1. Purchased a machine for $30,000, giving a long-term note in exchange.		
2. Issued common shares for cash, $50,000.		
3. Collected $16,000 of accounts receivable.		
4. Declared and paid a cash dividend of $25,000.		
5. Sold a long-term investment with a cost of $15,000 for $10,000 cash.		
6. Retired bonds having a carrying value of $200,000 for $175,000.		
7. Paid $18,000 on accounts payable.		
8. Distributed a $45,000 stock dividend, previously declared.		
9. Purchased a temporary investment.		

Instructions

Complete the above table indicating whether each transaction (1) should be classified as an operating activity (O), investing activity (I), financing activity (F), or noncash transaction (NC); and (2) represents a cash inflow, or cash outflow, or has no effect on cash.

E17–2 An analysis of the comparative balance sheet, the current year's income statement, and the general ledger accounts of Fisher Corp. uncovered the following items. Assume all items involve cash unless there is information to the contrary.

Classify transactions by activity.
(SO 2) AP

(a) A purchase of land
(b) A payment of dividends
(c) A sale of a building
(d) An exchange of land for a patent
(e) A redemption of bonds at carrying value
(f) A receipt of interest on notes receivable
(g) An issue of share capital

(h) An issue of bonds for land
(i) A payment of interest on notes payable
(j) A sale of a long-term debt investment
(k) A receipt of dividends on an equity investment
(l) A collection of accounts receivable
(m) A conversion of bonds into common shares

Instructions

Indicate how the above items should be classified in the cash flow statement using these major classifications: operating activity, investing activity, financing activity, and noncash investing and financing activity.

E17–3 Identify whether each of the following transactions will increase (+), decrease (−) or have no effect (NE) on net income and net cash flow provided (used) by operating activities prepared using the indirect method. The first one has been done for you as an example.

Indicate impact on net income and cash from operating activities.
(SO 3a) AP

Interactive Homework

Transaction	Net Income	Net Cash Flow Provided (Used) by Operating Activities
1. Sold merchandise for cash at a price in excess of cost.	+	+
2. Sold merchandise on account at a price in excess of cost.		
3. Purchased merchandise for resale on account.		
4. Paid a cash dividend.		
5. Paid wages not previously accrued.		
6. Accrued wages payable.		
7. Accrued interest receivable.		
8. Recorded amortization expense.		
9. Paid an amount owing on account.		
10. Collected an amount owing from a customer.		
11. Paid for a one-year insurance policy.		

Prepare operating activities section—indirect method. (SO 3a) AP

E17–4 Pesci Limited reported net income of $195,000 for the year ended July 31, 2005. Pesci also reported an amortization expense of $45,000 and a gain of $5,000 on the sale of equipment. The comparative balance sheet shows a decrease in accounts receivable of $15,000 for the year, an increase in accounts payable of $10,000, a decrease in prepaid expenses of $4,000, and a decrease in accrued liabilities of $3,500.

Instructions

Prepare the operating activities section of the cash flow statement for the year ended July 31, 2005. Use the indirect method.

Prepare operating activities section—indirect method. (SO 3a) AP

Interactive Homework

E17–5 The current assets and liabilities sections of Barth Inc.'s balance sheets at December 31, 2004 and 2005, are presented below:

	2005	2004
Current assets		
Cash	$105,000	$ 99,000
Accounts receivable	120,000	89,000
Inventory	161,000	186,000
Prepaid expenses	27,000	32,000
Total current assets	$413,000	$406,000
Current liabilities		
Accrued expenses payable	$ 15,000	$ 5,000
Accounts payable	85,000	92,000
Total current liabilities	$100,000	$ 97,000

Barth's net income for 2005 was $153,000. Amortization expense was $19,000.

Instructions

Prepare the operating activities section of Barth's cash flow statement for the year ended December 31, 2005, using the indirect method.

Prepare operating activities section—indirect method. (SO 3a) AP

E17–6 Savary Limited's comparative balance sheet at December 31, 2005 and 2004, is as follows:

SAVARY LIMITED
Balance Sheet
December 31

Assets	2005	2004
Cash	$ 164,000	$ 85,000
Accounts receivable	750,000	600,000
Inventory	500,000	330,000
Prepaid advertising	18,000	25,000
Equipment and vehicles	1,000,000	1,000,000
Accumulated amortization	(350,000)	(280,000)
Total assets	$2,082,000	$1,760,000
Liabilities and Shareholders' Equity		
Accounts payable	$ 226,000	$ 200,000
Salaries payable	30,000	40,000
Interest payable	26,000	20,000
Notes payable	500,000	350,000
Common shares	400,000	400,000
Retained earnings	900,000	750,000
Total liabilities and shareholders' equity	$2,082,000	$1,760,000

Additional information:

1. Net income for 2005 was $200,000.
2. Cash dividends were declared and paid in 2005.

Instructions

Prepare the operating activities section of the cash flow statement for the year ended December 31, 2005, using the indirect method.

E17–7 Presented below are three accounts that appear in the general ledger of Dupré Corp. during 2005:

Prepare partial cash flow statement—indirect method.
(SO 3a) AP

Equipment

Date		Debit	Credit	Balance
Jan. 1	Balance			160,000
July 31	Purchase of equipment	70,000		230,000
Sept. 2	Cost of equipment constructed	53,000		283,000
Nov. 10	Cost of equipment sold		39,000	244,000

Accumulated Amortization—Equipment

Date		Debit	Credit	Balance
Jan. 1	Balance			71,000
Nov. 10	Accumulated amortization on equipment sold	30,000		41,000
Dec. 31	Amortization expense		28,000	69,000

Retained Earnings

Date		Debit	Credit	Balance
Jan. 1	Balance			105,000
Aug. 23	Dividends (cash)	14,000		91,000
Dec. 31	Net income		67,000	158,000

Instructions

From the postings in the accounts above, indicate how the information is reported by preparing a partial cash flow statement using the indirect method. The loss on the sale of equipment was $6,000.

E17–8 Under the direct method, net cash provided (or used) by operating activities is calculated by adjusting each item in the income statement from the accrual basis to the cash basis.

Indicate impact of transactions on cash from operating activities—direct method.
(SO 3b) AP

Instructions

For each transaction listed below, (a) identify the related income statement account, (b) indicate if the transaction should be added to or deducted from the related income statement account to convert net income to cash from operating activities, and (c) state the title of the resulting cash receipt or payment on the cash flow statement. The first transaction is completed for you as an example.

Transaction	(a) Related Income Statement Account(s)	(b) Add to (+) or Deduct from (−) Income Statement Account	(c) Related Cash Receipt or Payment
(a) Increase in accounts receivable	Net sales	−	Cash receipts from customers
(b) Increase in accounts payable (related to merchandise purchases)			
(c) Decrease in interest payable			
(d) Increase in prepaid insurance			
(e) Increase in inventory			
(f) Increase in income taxes payable			
(g) Decrease in accounts receivable			
(h) Decrease in inventory			

E17–9 McGillis Ltd. has just completed its first year of operations on December 31, 2005. Its income statement showed that McGillis had revenues of $182,000, operating expenses of $88,000, and income tax expense of $31,000. Accounts receivable at year end were $42,000. Accounts payable at year end were $33,000. Assume that the accounts payable were related to operating expenses. There was no income tax paid.

Calculate cash from operating activities—direct method.
(SO 3b) AP

Instructions

Calculate the net cash provided (used) by operating activities using the direct method.

E17–10 The income statement for the Nickerson Corp. shows cost of goods sold of $370,000 and operating expenses (exclusive of amortization) of $250,000. The comparative balance sheet for the year shows that inventory increased by $14,000, prepaid expenses decreased by $4,000,

Calculate cash payments—direct method.
(SO 3b) AP

accounts payable (merchandise suppliers) decreased by $8,000, and accrued expenses payable increased by $4,000.

Instructions

Using the direct method, calculate (a) the cash payments to suppliers and (b) the cash payments for operating expenses.

Calculate operating cash flows—direct method. (SO 3b) AP

E17–11 The following information is taken from the general ledger of Robinson Limited:

Rent:	Rent expense	$ 31,000
	Prepaid rent, January 1	5,900
	Prepaid rent, December 31	9,000
Salaries:	Salaries expense	$ 54,000
	Salaries payable, January 1	10,000
	Salaries payable, December 31	8,000
Sales:	Sales revenue	$190,000
	Accounts receivable, January 1	12,000
	Accounts receivable, December 31	7,000

Instructions

In each of the above cases, calculate the amount that should be reported in the operating activities section of the cash flow statement, using the direct method.

Prepare operating activities section—direct method. (SO 3b) AP

Interactive Homework

E17–12 The accounting records of Flypaper Airlines Inc. reveal the following transactions and events for the year ended March 31, 2005:

Payment of interest	$10,000	Collection of accounts receivable	$192,000
Cash sales	48,000	Payment of salaries and wages	53,000
Receipt of dividend revenue	14,000	Amortization expense	16,000
Payment of income tax	12,000	Proceeds from sale of aircraft	812,000
Net income	38,000	Purchase of equipment for cash	22,000
Payment of accounts payable		Loss on sale of aircraft	3,000
for merchandise	90,000	Payment of dividends	14,000
Payment for land	74,000	Payment of other expenses	28,000

Instructions

Prepare the operating activities section of the cash flow statement, using the direct method. (*Note:* Not all of the above items will be used.)

Prepare cash flow statement—indirect and direct methods. Calculate ratios. (SO 3a, 3b, 4) AP

Interactive Homework

E17–13 The comparative balance sheet for Puffy Ltd. is presented below:

PUFFY LTD.
Balance Sheet
December 31, 2005

	December 31	
Assets	2005	2004
Cash	$ 63,000	$ 22,000
Accounts receivable	85,000	76,000
Inventories	180,000	189,000
Land	75,000	100,000
Equipment	260,000	200,000
Accumulated amortization	(66,000)	(32,000)
Total	$597,000	$555,000
Liabilities and Shareholders' Equity		
Accounts payable	$ 39,000	$ 47,000
Bonds payable	150,000	200,000
Common shares	209,000	174,000
Retained earnings	199,000	134,000
Total	$597,000	$555,000

Additional information:

1. Net income for 2005 was $105,000.
2. Cash dividends of $40,000 were declared and paid.

3. Bonds payable amounting to $50,000 were redeemed for $50,000 cash.
4. Common shares were issued for $35,000 cash.
5. Land was sold at a gain of $5,000.
6. Net sales for the year were $978,000.
7. Cost of goods sold for the year were $751,000.
8. Operating expenses and income tax expense were $43,000 and $50,000, respectively.

Instructions

(a) Prepare a cash flow statement for 2005 using the indirect method.
(b) Prepare a cash flow statement for 2005 using the direct method.
(c) Calculate free cash flow.

E17–14 Toronto-based **Nexfor Inc.** produces specialty papers and pulp, wooden panels, and building products in Canada, the UK, and the U.S. The company reported US$13 million in net income in 2002, an increase of 8% over the US$12 million in net income reported in 2001. It generated cash flow from operating activities of US$146 million, an increase of 38% over the US$106 million generated in 2001. Free cash flow totalled US$102 million in 2002, an increase of 1,600% over free cash flow of US$6 million in 2001.

Discuss cash position.
(SO 4) AN

Instructions

(a) How is it possible that Nexfor can only have US$13 million of net income, but reports cash flow from operating activities of US$146 million?
(b) Explain how Nexfor can increase its cash flow provided by operating activities by 38% when net income only increased 8%.
(c) Explain how Nexfor might have been able to increase its free cash flow by such a large percentage, 1,600%, in one year.

Problems: Set A

P17–1A You are provided with the following transactions that took place during a recent fiscal year:

Classify transactions by activity. Indicate impact on cash and net income.
(SO 2) AP

Transaction	Classification	Cash Inflow or Outflow?	Net Income
1. Recorded amortization expense.			
2. Sold equipment for cash, at a gain.			
3. Sold a long-term investment for cash, at a loss.			
4. Acquired a building by paying 10% in cash and signing a mortgage payable for the balance.			
5. Made principal repayments on the mortgage.			
6. Issued common shares for cash.			
7. Purchased shares of another company for cash, to be held as a long-term equity investment.			
8. Paid cash dividends to common shareholders.			
9. Declared and distributed stock dividends to common shareholders.			
10. Sold inventory on credit, at a price in excess of cost.			
11. Purchased inventory on credit.			
12. Paid wages owing to employees.			

Instructions

Complete the above table by indicating the following for each transaction:

(a) Classify it as an operating activity (O), an investing activity (I), a financing activity (F), or a non-cash transaction (NC).
(b) Specify if the transaction will result in a cash inflow or cash outflow, or have no effect on cash.
(c) Indicate if the transaction will increase (+), decrease (−), or have no effect (NE) on net income.

Calculate cash flows.
(SO 3a, 3b) AP

P17–2A The following selected account balances relate to the property, plant, and equipment accounts of Trudeau Inc. at year end:

	2005	2004
Accumulated amortization—buildings	$337,500	$300,000
Accumulated amortization—equipment	144,000	96,000
Amortization expense	101,500	85,500
Buildings	750,000	750,000
Equipment	300,000	240,000
Land	100,000	60,000
Gain on sale of equipment	1,000	0

Additional information:

Trudeau purchased $80,000 of equipment and $40,000 of land for cash in 2005. Trudeau also sold equipment in 2005.

Instructions

(a) Determine the amounts of any cash inflows or outflows related to the property, plant, and equipment accounts in 2005.

(b) Indicate where each of the cash inflows or outflows identified in (a) would be classified on the cash flow statement.

Calculate cash flows.
(SO 3a, 3b) AP

P17–3A The following selected account balances relate to the shareholder's equity and dividends payable accounts of Valerio Corp. at year end:

	2005	2004
Preferred shares, 2,250 and 2,750 shares for 2005 and 2004, respectively	$225,000	$275,000
Common shares, 55,000 and 40,000 shares for 2005 and 2004, respectively	550,000	400,000
Retained earnings	300,000	100,000
Cash dividends	65,000	50,000
Dividends payable	0	25,000

Additional information for 2005:

1. On March 2, 500 preferred shares were converted to 5,000 common shares.
2. On August 21, 10,000 common shares were issued for cash.

Instructions

(a) What was the amount of net income reported by Valerio Corp. in 2005?

(b) Determine the amounts of any cash inflows or outflows related to the share capital and dividend accounts in 2005.

(c) Indicate where each of the cash inflows or outflows identified in (b) would be classified on the cash flow statement.

P17–4A Presented below is the comparative balance sheet for Cousin Tommy's Toy Company as at December 31:

Prepare cash flow statement—indirect method.
(SO 3a) AP

COUSIN TOMMY'S TOY COMPANY
Balance Sheet
December 31

Assets	2005	2004
Cash	$ 39,000	$ 45,000
Accounts receivable	59,500	62,000
Inventory	151,450	142,000
Prepaid expenses	16,780	21,000
Land	120,000	130,000
Equipment	228,000	155,000
Accumulated amortization—equipment	(45,000)	(35,000)
Building	200,000	200,000
Accumulated amortization—building	(60,000)	(40,000)
	$709,730	$680,000
Liabilities and Shareholders' Equity		
Accounts payable	$ 53,730	$ 40,000
Bonds payable	260,000	300,000
Common shares	200,000	160,000
Retained earnings	196,000	180,000
	$709,730	$680,000

Additional information:

1. Operating expenses include an amortization expense of $42,000.
2. Land was sold for cash, at cost.
3. Cash dividends of $22,000 were paid.
4. Equipment was purchased for $95,000 cash. In addition, equipment costing $22,000 with a net book value of $10,000 was sold for $8,100 cash.
5. Bonds were redeemed at face value by issuing 50,000 common shares.

Instructions

Prepare a cash flow statement for the year ended December 31, 2005, using the indirect method.

P17–5A The income statement of Breckenridge Ltd. is shown below:

Prepare operating activities section—indirect and direct methods.
(SO 3a, 3b) AP

BRECKENRIDGE LTD.
Income Statement
Year Ended November 30, 2005

Sales		$7,200,000
Cost of goods sold		
Beginning inventory	$1,900,000	
Purchases	4,400,000	
Goods available for sale	6,300,000	
Ending inventory	1,400,000	4,900,000
Gross profit		2,300,000
Operating expenses		1,050,000
Income before income tax		1,250,000
Income tax expense		375,000
Net income		$ 875,000

Additional information:

1. Accounts receivable decreased by $200,000 during the year.
2. Prepaid expenses increased by $150,000 during the year.
3. Accounts payable to suppliers of merchandise decreased by $300,000 during the year.
4. Accrued expenses payable decreased by $100,000 during the year.
5. Operating expenses include an amortization expense of $90,000.
6. Income taxes payable increased by $20,000 during the year.

Instructions

(a) Prepare the operating activities section of the cash flow statement for the year ended November 30, 2005, using the indirect method.

(b) Prepare the operating activities section of the cash flow statement for the year ended November 30, 2005, using the direct method.

Prepare operating activities section—indirect and direct methods.
(SO 3a, 3b) AP

P17–6A The income statement of Hanalei International Inc. for the year ended December 31, 2005, reported the following condensed information:

HANALEI INTERNATIONAL INC.
Income Statement
Year Ended December 31, 2005

Revenue		$545,000
Operating expenses		370,000
Income from operations		175,000
Other revenues and expenses		
Gain on sale of equipment	$ 25,000	
Interest expense	(10,000)	15,000
Income before income taxes		190,000
Income tax expense		42,000
Net income		$148,000

Hanalei's balance sheet contained the following comparative data at December 31:

	2005	2004
Accounts receivable	$50,000	$60,000
Prepaid insurance	8,000	5,000
Accounts payable	30,000	41,000
Interest payable	2,000	750
Income taxes payable	8,000	4,500
Unearned revenue	10,000	14,000

Additional information:

1. Operating expenses include $70,000 of amortization expense.
2. Accounts payable relate to operating expenses.

Instructions

(a) Prepare the operating activities section of the cash flow statement for the year ended December 31, 2005, using the indirect method.

(b) Prepare the operating activities section of the cash flow statement for the year ended December 31, 2005, using the direct method.

Prepare cash flow statement—indirect and direct methods.
(SO 3a, 3b) AP

P17–7A Condensed financial data of E-Perform Ltd. appear below:

E-PERFORM LTD.
Balance Sheet
December 31

Assets	2005	2004
Cash	$ 97,800	$ 48,400
Accounts receivable	95,800	33,000
Inventories	112,500	102,850
Prepaid expenses	18,400	6,000
Investments	113,000	94,000
Property, plant, and equipment	270,000	242,500
Accumulated amortization	(50,000)	(52,000)
	$657,500	$474,750

Liabilities and Shareholders' Equity	2005	2004
Accounts payable	$102,000	$ 77,300
Accrued expenses payable	16,500	17,000
Notes payable	85,000	100,000
Common shares	220,000	175,000
Retained earnings	234,000	105,450
	$657,500	$474,750

E-PERFORM LTD.
Income Statement
Year Ended December 31, 2005

Sales		$392,780
Cost of goods sold		135,460
Gross profit		257,320
Operating expenses	$12,410	
Amortization expense	46,500	
Interest expense	4,730	
Loss on sale of equipment	7,500	71,140
Income before income tax		186,180
Income tax expense		45,000
Net income		$141,180

Additional information:

1. New equipment costing $85,000 was purchased for cash during the year.
2. Notes payable matured and were paid off at face value in cash.
3. Old equipment costing $57,500 were sold for $1,500 cash.
4. Accounts payable relate only to merchandise creditors.

Instructions

(a) Prepare a cash flow statement for the year ended December 31, 2005, using the indirect method.
(b) Prepare a cash flow statement for the year ended December 31, 2005, using the direct method.

P17–8A DesRoches Inc. incorporated a repair business on January 1, 2005.

1. On January 1, it issued common shares for $5,000 cash.
2. On the same day, it borrowed $15,000 from a local bank at a 7% interest rate. Principal and interest are repayable in full in two years.
3. DesRoches rented space on January 5, paying rent in advance for three months —January, February, and March—at the rate of $1,000 a month.
4. The company also purchased insurance, effective January 1, for a 12-month period, paying $1,200 in cash.
5. The company rented repair and office equipment on January 1 for $750 a month. It paid January's rent and hopes to be able to purchase this equipment at a later date when its cash flow improves.
6. In January, the company purchased $1,000 of supplies on account. The cost of the supplies remaining at the end of the month was $300.
7. Cash paid on accounts payable during the month totalled $800.
8. During the month, the company provided repair services of $2,500 for cash and $15,000 on account.
9. Accounts receivable collected in cash from customers during January were $12,200.
10. Other operating expenses paid during the month totalled $2,000.
11. Unpaid salaries at the end of the month were $500.

Instructions

(a) Prepare an income statement for the month ended January 31, 2005. (Ignore income taxes.) (*Hint*: You may find it helpful to organize the above information by preparing journal entries or by using T accounts.)
(b) Prepare a cash flow statement, using the direct method, for the month ended January 31, 2005.
(c) Compare the results of the accrual-based statement and the cash-based statement. Which do you think is more useful to decision-makers?

Prepare income statement and cash flow statement—direct method.
(SO 3b) AN

P17–9A The financial statements of Wetaskiwin Ltd. appear below:

WETASKIWIN LTD.
Balance Sheet
December 31, 2005

Assets	2005	2004
Cash	$ 12,000	$ 10,000
Temporary investments	14,000	23,000
Accounts receivable	28,000	14,000
Merchandise inventory	38,000	25,000
Property, plant, and equipment	70,000	78,000
Less: Accumulated amortization	(30,000)	(24,000)
	$132,000	$126,000
Liabilities and Shareholders' Equity		
Accounts payable	$ 29,000	$ 43,000
Income tax payable	15,000	20,000
Notes payable	20,000	10,000
Common shares	25,000	25,000
Retained earnings	43,000	28,000
	$132,000	$126,000

WETASKIWIN LTD.
Income Statement
Year Ended December 31, 2005

Sales	$286,000
Cost of goods sold	194,000
Gross profit	92,000
Operating expenses	34,000
Income from operations	58,000
Loss on sale of equipment	2,000
Interest expense	5,000
Income before income tax	51,000
Income tax expense	15,000
Net income	$ 36,000

Additional information:

1. Equipment was sold during the year for $8,000 cash. This equipment cost $15,000 originally and had a net book value of $10,000 at the time of sale.
2. Additional equipment was purchased for cash.
3. The entire amortization expense is included in operating expenses.
4. Accounts payable relate only to merchandise creditors.
5. Additional notes payable were issued for $15,000 cash.
6. A note payable matured and was paid in cash.
7. The temporary investments of Wetaskiwin are highly liquid and should be considered cash
   equivalents for the purpose of this statement.

Instructions

(a) Prepare a cash flow statement for the year ended December 31, 2005, using the indirect
    method.
(b) Prepare a cash flow statement for the year ended December 31, 2005, using the direct method.
(c) Calculate the following measures:
    1. EBITDA
    2. Free cash flow
(d) Explain why Wetaskiwin should combine its temporary investments with cash when prepar-
    ing the cash flow statement.

Problems: Set B

P17–1B You are provided with the following transactions that took place during a recent fiscal year:

Transaction	Classification	Cash Inflow or Outflow?	Net Income
1. Recorded amortization expense.			
2. Recorded cash proceeds for sale of a patent at a loss.			
3. Recorded cash proceeds for a sale of land at a gain.			
4. Acquired land by issuing common shares.			
5. Paid a cash dividend to preferred shareholders.			
6. Split common shares two for one.			
7. Recorded cash revenues.			
8. Recorded revenues on account.			
9. Purchased inventory for cash.			
10. Purchased inventory on account.			
11. Paid income tax.			
12. Paid an instalment payment on a note payable.			

Classify transactions by activity. Indicate impact on cash and net income. (SO 2) AP

Instructions

Complete the above table by indicating the following for each transaction:

(a) Classify it as an operating activity (O), an investing activity (I), a financing activity (F), or a noncash transaction (NC).
(b) Specify if the transaction will result in a cash inflow or cash outflow, or have no effect on cash.
(c) Indicate if the transaction will increase (+), decrease (−), or have no effect (NE) on net income.

P17–2B The following selected account balances relate to the property, plant, and equipment accounts of Cretien Corp. at year end.

Calculate cash flows. (SO 3a) AP

	2005	2004
Accumulated amortization—buildings	$ 675,000	$ 600,000
Accumulated amortization—equipment	288,000	192,000
Amortization expense	203,000	171,000
Equipment	500,000	480,000
Buildings	1,250,000	1,250,000
Land	250,000	200,000
Loss on sale of equipment	5,000	0

Additional information for 2005:

1. Cretien purchased land for cash.
2. Equipment was sold for cash.
3. Equipment was purchased for $80,000 cash.

Instructions

(a) Determine the amounts of any cash inflows or outflows related to the property, plant, and equipment accounts in 2005.
(b) Indicated where each of the cash inflows or outflows identified in (a) would be classified on the cash flow statement.
(c) Cretien prepares its cash flow statement using the indirect method. What other information related to property, plant, and equipment, in addition to the amounts specified in (b), should be included in the cash flow statement?

P17–3B The following selected account balances relate to the shareholders' equity accounts of Wood Corp. at year end:

Calculate cash flows. (SO 3a, 3b) AP

	2005	2004
Common shares, 10,500 and 10,000 shares, respectively	$168,400	$140,000
Cash dividends	10,000	10,000
Preferred shares, 5,000 shares	125,000	125,000
Stock dividends	8,400	0
Retained earnings	300,000	240,000
Dividends payable	8,000	0

Instructions

(a) What was the amount of net income reported by Wood Corp. in 2005?
(b) Determine the amounts of any cash inflows or outflows related to the shareholders' equity accounts in 2005.
(c) Indicate where each of the cash inflows or outflows identified in (b) would be classified on the cash flow statement.

Prepare cash flow statement—indirect method.
(SO 3a) AP

P17–4B Presented below is the comparative balance sheet for Cortina Limited at December 31:

CORTINA LIMITED
Balance Sheet
December 31

Assets	2005	2004
Cash and cash equivalents	$ 30,000	$ 57,000
Accounts receivable	77,000	64,000
Inventory	192,000	140,000
Prepaid expenses	12,140	16,540
Land	105,000	150,000
Equipment	200,000	175,000
Accumulated amortization—equipment	(60,000)	(42,000)
Building	250,000	250,000
Accumulated amortization—building	(75,000)	(50,000)
	$731,140	$760,540

Liabilities and Shareholders' Equity		
Accounts payable	$ 33,000	$ 45,000
Bonds payable	235,000	265,000
Common shares	280,000	250,000
Retained earnings	183,140	200,540
	$731,140	$760,540

Additional information:

1. Net income for 2005 was $26,890.
2. Operating expenses include an amortization expense of $70,000.
3. Equipment was purchased for $65,000 cash. In addition, equipment costing $40,000 with a net book value of $13,000 was sold for $12,000 cash.
4. Land was sold for cash, at a gain of $5,000.
5. Bonds were converted at face value by issuing 30,000 common shares.
6. Cash dividends were paid during the year.

Instructions

Prepare a cash flow statement for 2005 using the indirect method.

Prepare operating activities section—indirect and direct methods.
(SO 3a, 3b) AP

P17–5B The income statement of Gum San Ltd. is shown below:

GUM SAN LTD.
Income Statement
Year Ended April 30, 2005

Sales		$5,400,000
Cost of goods sold		3,290,000
Gross profit		2,110,000
Operating expenses	$925,000	
Amortization expense	145,000	1,070,000
Income before income taxes		1,040,000
Income tax expense		312,000
Net income		$ 728,000

Additional information:

1. Accounts receivable increased by $510,000 during the year.
2. Inventory decreased by $220,000 during the year.

3. Prepaid expenses increased by $170,000 during the year.
4. Accounts payable to merchandise suppliers increased by $50,000 during the year.
5. Accrued expenses payable decreased by $165,000 during the year.
6. Income taxes payable decreased by $26,000 during the year.

Instructions

(a) Prepare the operating activities section of the cash flow statement for the year ended April 30, 2005, using the indirect method.
(b) Prepare the operating activities section of the cash flow statement for the year ended April 30, 2005, using the direct method.

P17–6B Sable Island Ltd.'s income statement for the year ended December 31, 2005, contained the following condensed information:

Prepare operating activities section—indirect and direct methods.
(SO 3a, 3b) AP

SABLE ISLAND LTD.
Income Statement
Year Ended December 31, 2005

Revenue from fees		$900,000
Operating expenses	$624,000	
Amortization expense	60,000	
Interest expense	5,000	
Loss on sale of equipment	26,000	715,000
Income before income tax		185,000
Income tax expense		46,250
Net income		$138,750

Sable Island's balance sheet contained the following comparative data at December 31:

	2005	2004
Accounts receivable	$47,000	$57,000
Accounts payable	41,000	36,000
Income tax payable	4,000	9,250
Interest payable	1,000	550
Unearned revenue	12,000	9,000

Accounts payable relate to operating expenses.

Instructions

(a) Prepare the operating activities section of the cash flow statement for the year ended December 31, 2005, using the indirect method.
(b) Prepare the operating activities section of the cash flow statement for the year ended December 31, 2005, using the direct method.

Prepare cash flow
statement—indirect and
direct methods.
(SO 3a, 3b) AP

P17–7B Condensed financial data of Galenti, Inc., appear below:

GALENTI, INC.
Balance Sheet
December 31

Assets	2005	2004
Cash	$ 92,700	$ 47,250
Accounts receivable	80,800	21,000
Inventories	121,900	102,650
Prepaid expenses	10,000	16,000
Investments	84,500	107,000
Property, plant, and equipment	290,000	205,000
Accumulated amortization	(49,500)	(40,000)
	$630,400	$458,900

Liabilities and Shareholders' Equity		
Accounts payable	$ 52,700	$ 48,280
Accrued expenses payable	12,100	18,830
Notes payable	140,000	70,000
Common shares	250,000	200,000
Retained earnings	175,600	121,790
	$630,400	$458,900

GALENTI, INC.
Income Statement
Year Ended December 31, 2005

Revenues		
Sales		$305,000
Gain on sale of equipment		8,750
		313,750
Expenses		
Cost of goods sold	$99,460	
Operating expenses	14,670	
Amortization expense	58,700	
Interest expense	2,940	
Loss on sale of investments	7,500	183,270
Income before income tax		130,480
Income tax expense		32,670
Net income		$ 97,810

Additional information:

1. New equipment costing $141,000 was purchased for cash during the year.
2. Equipment with an original cost of $56,000 was sold for $15,550.
3. Notes were issued for cash.
4. Investments were sold at a loss for cash.
5. Accounts payable relate only to merchandise creditors.

Instructions

(a) Prepare a cash flow statement for the year ended December 31, 2005, using the indirect method.
(b) Prepare a cash flow statement for the year ended December 31, 2005, using the direct method.

Prepare income statement
and cash flow statement—
direct method.
(SO 3b) AN

P17–8B You are provided with the following transactions for Great Big Sea Inc. during the year ended July 31, 2005:

1. Sold 1,000 common shares for $75 each.
2. Purchased recording equipment by signing a $200,000, 6% note payable.
3. Recorded amortization for the year on the recording equipment assuming a four-year life, zero residual value, and use of the straight-line method of amortization.
4. Recorded an amount owing for interest on the note payable. Interest is owing for the full year.
5. Paid the amount of interest owing plus $15,000 on the principal of the note.
6. Purchased an inventory of CDs on credit. The invoice was for $75,000.

7. Sold CDs to customers for $200,000. Immediately collected $150,000 from the customers, with the balance on credit.
8. The cost of the CDs that were sold was $42,000.
9. Collected another $8,000 from the customers.
10. Sold a piece of equipment with a cost of $10,000 and accumulated amortization of $2,500 for $6,000. Collected the full $6,000 immediately.
11. Operating expenses of $45,000 were paid in cash.

Instructions

(a) Prepare an income statement for the year ended July 31, 2005. (Ignore income taxes.) (*Hint*: You may find it helpful to organize the above information by preparing journal entries or by using T accounts.)

(b) Prepare a cash flow statement, using the direct method, for the year ended July 31, 2005.

(c) Compare the results of the accrual-based statement and the cash-based statement. Which do you think is more useful to decision-makers?

P17–9B The financial statements of Milk River Ltd. appear below:

Prepare a cash flow statement—indirect and direct methods. Calculate ratios.
(SO 3a, 3b, 4) AP

MILK RIVER LTD.
Balance Sheet
December 31

Assets	2005	2004
Cash	$ 13,000	$ 15,000
Temporary investments	16,000	5,000
Accounts receivable	38,000	4,000
Merchandise inventory	27,000	30,000
Property, plant, and equipment	80,000	78,000
Accumulated amortization	(30,000)	(24,000)
Total	$144,000	$108,000

Liabilities and Shareholders' Equity		
Accounts payable	$ 17,000	$ 15,000
Income taxes payable	1,000	8,000
Notes payable	47,000	33,000
Common shares	18,000	14,000
Retained earnings	61,000	38,000
Total	$144,000	$108,000

MILK RIVER LTD.
Income Statement
Year Ended December 31, 2005

Sales		$242,000
Cost of goods sold		180,000
Gross profit		62,000
Operating expenses		24,000
Income from operations		38,000
Gain on sale of equipment	$1,000	
Interest expense	2,000	1,000
Income before income tax		37,000
Income tax expense		9,250
Net income		$ 27,750

Additional information:

1. Equipment costing $20,000 was purchased in exchange for a note payable.
2. During the year, equipment was sold for $9,500 cash. This equipment had cost $18,000 originally and had a net book value of $8,500 at the time of sale.
3. All amortization expenses are in the operating expenses category.
4. All accounts payable relate to merchandise suppliers.
5. A note payable matured and was paid in cash
6. Milk River's temporary investments are highly liquid and should be considered a cash

equivalent for the purpose of this statement.

Instructions

(a) Prepare a cash flow statement for the year ended December 31, 2005, using the indirect method.
(b) Prepare a cash flow statement for the year ended December 31, 2005, using the direct method.
(c) Calculate the following measures:
    1. EBITDA
    2. Free cash flow
(d) Explain why Milk River should combine its temporary investments with cash when preparing the cash flow statement.

Continuing Cookie Chronicle

(Note: This is a continuation of the Cookie Chronicle from Chapters 1 through 16.)

Natalie is preparing the balance sheet and income statement of Cookie & Coffee Creations Ltd., and she would like you to prepare the cash flow statement. The comparative balance sheet of Cookie & Coffee Creations Ltd. at October 31, 2007, for the years 2007 and 2006, and the income statement for the year ended October 31, 2007, are presented below:

COOKIE & COFFEE CREATIONS LTD.
Balance Sheet
October 31, 2007

Assets	2007	2006
Cash	$ 34,324	$13,050
Accounts receivable	3,250	2,710
Inventory	7,897	7,450
Prepaids	6,300	6,050
Furniture and fixtures	12,500	5,000
Accumulated amortization—furniture and fixtures	(2,000)	(1,000)
Computer equipment	4,000	4,500
Accumulated amortization—computer equipment	(600)	(1,500)
Kitchen equipment	80,000	66,000
Accumulated amortization—kitchen equipment	(22,600)	(6,600)
Total assets	$123,071	$95,660

Liabilities and Shareholders' Equity		
Accounts payable	$ 3,650	$ 2,450
Income taxes payable	10,251	11,200
Dividends payable	28,000	25,000
Salaries payable	2,250	1,280
Interest payable	188	0
Note payable	7,500	0
Preferred shares, $6 cumulative, 3,000 and 2,500 shares issued, respectively	15,000	12,500
Common shares, 23,180 shares issued	23,180	23,180
Contributed capital—reacquisition of shares	250	250
Retained earnings	32,802	19,800
Total liabilities and shareholders' equity	$123,071	$95,660

COOKIE & COFFEE CREATIONS LTD.
Income Statement
Year Ended October 31, 2007

Sales		$485,625
Cost of goods sold		222,694
Gross profit		262,931
Operating expenses		
Amortization expense	$ 17,600	
Salaries and wages expense	147,979	
Other operating expenses	43,186	208,765
Income from operations		54,166
Other expenses		
Interest expense	$ 413	
Loss on sale of computer equipment	2,500	2,913
Income before income tax		51,253
Income tax expense		10,251
Net income		$ 41,002

Additional information:

1. All of the computer equipment was disposed of at the beginning of the year for $500 cash. New computer equipment was then bought for $4,000 cash.
2. Additional kitchen equipment was bought for $14,000 on November 1, 2006. A $9,000 note payable was signed. The terms provide for equal semi-annual instalment payments of $1,500 on May 1 and November 1 of each year, plus interest of 5% on the outstanding principal balance.
3. Additional furniture was bought for $7,500 cash.
4. Dividends were declared to the preferred and common shareholders on October 15, 2007, to be paid on November 15, 2007.
5. Accounts payable relate only to merchandise creditors.
6. Prepaids relate only to other operating expenses.

Instructions:

(a) Prepare a cash flow statement for Cookie & Coffee Creations Ltd. for the year ended October 31, 2007, using the indirect method.
(b) Prepare a cash flow statement for Cookie & Coffee Creations Ltd. for the year ended October 31, 2007, using the direct method.
(c) Calculate the EBITDA and free cash flow amounts.

BROADENING YOUR PERSPECTIVE

Financial Reporting and Analysis

Practice Tools

Financial Reporting Problem

BYP17–1 Refer to the consolidated financial statements for **The Forzani Group Ltd.**, which are reproduced in Appendix A at the end of the textbook.

Instructions

(a) How does Forzani define "cash" for the purpose of its cash flow statement?
(b) What was the amount of increase or decrease in cash for the year ended February 2, 2003?
(c) What were the significant investing activities reported in Forzani's 2003 cash flow statement?

(d) What were the significant financing activities reported in Forzani's 2003 cash flow statement?

(e) Did Forzani report any significant noncash investing and financing activities in 2003?

Interpreting Financial Statements

BYP17–2 Sleeman Breweries Ltd. is Canada's third largest brewery, specializing in craft beers. Sleeman's 2002 balance sheet reported current assets of $52.7 million and current liabilities of $47.6 million, including bank indebtedness (negative cash balance) of $10.5 million.

On a more positive note, Sleeman increased its net income in 2002, from $34.1 million in 2001 to $46.4 million in 2002. It reported EBITDA of $29.9 million. Sleeman reported on its cash flow statement that it generated $13.4 million of cash from operating activities in 2002. The cash flow statement also indicated that Sleeman spent $6.1 million on capital expenditures and paid no dividends.

Instructions

(a) Do you believe that Sleeman's creditors should be worried about its lack of cash? Explain why or why not.

(b) Why do you think Sleeman generated $13.4 million of cash from operating activities but has no cash?

(c) Calculate Sleeman's free cash flow for 2002. Compare this result to its EBITDA and explain what each means.

Accounting on the Web

BYP17–3 This case reviews the cash flows of a company in the telecommunications industry. Its changing share price is evaluated against its cash and income (loss).

Instructions

Specific requirements of this Internet case are available on the Weygandt website.

Critical Thinking

Collaborative Learning Activity

BYP17–4 Greg Rhoda and Debra Sondgeroth are examining Tuktoyaktuk Trading Company's cash flow statement for the year ended January 31, 2006:

TUKTOYAKTUK TRADING COMPANY
Cash Flow Statement
Year Ended January 31, 2006

Cash inflows

From sale of merchandise	$390,000	
From sale of common shares	420,000	
From sale of investment (purchased below)	80,000	
From amortization	55,000	
From issue of note for truck	25,000	
From interest on investment	6,000	
Total sources of cash		$976,000

Cash outflows

For purchase of fixtures and equipment	$320,000	
For merchandise purchased for resale	268,000	
For operating expenses	160,000	
For purchase of investment	75,000	
For purchase of truck by issue of note	25,000	
For interest on note payable	3,000	
Total uses of cash		851,000
Net increase in cash		$125,000

Greg claims that Tuktoyaktuk's cash flow statement is an excellent example of a superb first year because cash increased by $125,000. Debra replies that it was not a superb first year. The year was an operating failure. She says that the statement is incorrectly presented, and that $125,000 is not the actual increase in cash. The cash balance at the beginning of the year was $40,000.

Instructions

With the class divided into groups, answer the following:
(a) With whom do you agree, Greg or Debra? Explain your position.
(b) Prepare a cash flow statement in proper form using the indirect method. There were no changes in any current accounts other than cash.
(c) Prepare a cash flow statement using the direct method.
(d) Would you recommend the payment of a cash dividend this year?

Communication Activity

BYP17–5 Many investors today prefer the cash flow statement to the income statement. They believe that cash-based data are a better measure of performance than accrual-based data because cash-based data are less susceptible to possible income management.

Instructions

Write a brief memo explaining whether or not cash-based data are less susceptible to income management than accrual-based data. In your answer, include an assessment of which financial statement you believe to be the best measure of a company's performance.

Ethics Case

BYP17–6 Paradis Corporation is a wholesaler of automotive parts. It has 10 shareholders who have been paid a total of $1 million in cash dividends for eight consecutive years. The board of directors' policy requires that in order for this dividend to be declared, net cash provided by operating activities, as reported in Paradis' cash flow statement, must be in excess of $1 million. President and CEO Phil Monat's job is secure so long as he produces annual operating cash flows to support the usual dividend.

At the end of the current year, controller Rick Rodgers presents president Monat with some disappointing news. The net cash provided by operating activities is only $970,000. The president says to Rick, "We must get that amount above $1 million. Isn't there some way to increase operating cash flow by another $30,000?" Rick answers, "These figures were prepared by my assistant. I'll go back to my office and see what I can do." The president replies, "I know you won't let me down, Rick."

Upon close scrutiny of the cash flow statement, Rick concludes that he can get the operating cash flows above $1 million by reclassifying a two-year, $60,000 note payable that is listed in the financing activities section as "Proceeds from bank loan—$60,000." He will report the note instead in the operating activities section as an increase in payables. He returns to the president, saying, "You can tell the board to declare its usual dividend. Our net cash flow provided by operating activities is $1.03 million." "Good man, Rick! I knew I could count on you," exults the president.

Instructions

(a) Who are the stakeholders in this situation?
(b) Was there anything unethical about the president's actions? Was there anything unethical about the controller's actions?
(c) Are the board members or anyone else likely to discover the misclassification?

Answers to Self-Study Questions

1. c   2. b   3. a   4. c   5. b   6. c   7. d   8. b   9. c   10. d   11. c   12. c

Answer to Forzani Review It Question 4

Forzani reports the following (in thousands): (a) $21,013 cash provided by operating activities, (b) $49,119 cash used by investing activities, and (c) $28,135 cash provided by financing activities.

Remember to go back to the Navigator Box at the beginning of the chapter to check off your completed work.

concepts for review >>

Before studying this chapter, you should understand or, if necessary, review:

a. The various types of users of financial statement information. (Ch. 1, pp. 3–5)

b. The content and classification of a corporate income statement. (Ch. 14, pp. 665–667)

c. The content and classification of a corporate balance sheet. (Ch. 16, pp. 765–767)

d. The ratios introduced in previous chapters: working capital, current ratio (Ch. 4, p. 174–175); gross profit margin, profit margin (Ch. 5, pp. 234–235); inventory turnover, days sales in inventory (Ch. 6, p. 296); receivables turnover, collection period (Ch. 8, p. 402); asset turnover, return on assets (Ch. 9, p. 456); return on equity (Ch. 13, pp. 634–635); earnings per share, price-earnings, payout (Ch. 14, pp. 674–676); debt to total assets, interest coverage (Ch. 15, pp. 719–720); EBITDA and free cash flow (Ch. 17, pp. 824–826).

Presenting the Whole Picture

TORONTO, Ont.—In the high-stakes world of investments, it's not "who you know" that counts, but rather "what you know." Effective communication enables investors, creditors, and others to tell whether a company is doing well, what its past performance has been, and what its future prospects are. The annual report plays a significant role in keeping a company's stakeholders informed.

While most annual reports follow the same basic format, they vary widely in their presentation, content and, most importantly, the quality of the information they provide. That's where the annual Corporate Reporting Awards play an important role. Jointly sponsored by the Canadian Institute of Chartered Accountants (CICA) and the *National Post*, the Awards aim to recognize the best reporting models in Canada and thereby strengthen corporate reporting in this country. Awards are given to companies which have shown leadership in annual reporting, electronic disclosure, corporate governance disclosure, and sustainable development reporting.

"When the awards program started over 50 years ago, the focus was on the critiquing of a company's annual report," says CICA's president and CEO, David Smith. "While the annual report remains an important communications vehicle for an organization, it is no longer the sole aspect of the awards. Excellence in corporate reporting today also means excellence in corporate governance, electronic disclosure, and sustainable development."

"Truly outstanding," "genuine," and "honest" were just some of the terms the judges used to describe the winner of the Overall Award of Excellence for 2002—Canadian Tire. The judges went even further to describe the report as the "perfect model" of what an annual report should be.

Canadian Institute of Chartered Accountants: www.cica.ca

Just what does that include? For starters, most annual reports generally feature a message from the chairman and CEO, the year's financial statements, a management discussion and analysis, and information about the company directors.

But the judges also consider things such as a statement of objectives, a discussion of the company's performance relative to those objectives, some comparative industry information, information on corporate governance, and layout and design. The judges noted that Canadian Tire's report "communicates well on all levels and features something insightful for everyone, from the avid investor to the general reader."

Communication is, after all, what it's all about. In light of the high-profile corporate scandals of recent years, full disclosure is more important than ever. That means communicating everything—both good news and bad—so investors can make well-informed decisions.

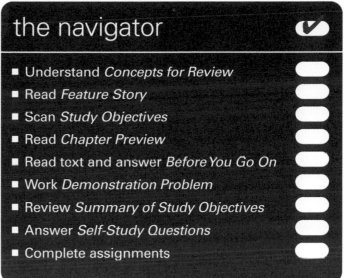

the navigator

- Understand *Concepts for Review*
- Read *Feature Story*
- Scan *Study Objectives*
- Read *Chapter Preview*
- Read text and answer *Before You Go On*
- Work *Demonstration Problem*
- Review *Summary of Study Objectives*
- Answer *Self-Study Questions*
- Complete assignments

chapter 18
Financial Statement Analysis

study objectives >>

the navigator

After studying this chapter, you should be able to:

1. Discuss the need for comparative analysis.
2. Explain and apply horizontal analysis.
3. Explain and apply vertical analysis.
4. Identify and calculate ratios and describe their purpose and use in analysing a company's liquidity, profitability, and solvency.
5. Recognize and illustrate the limitations of financial statement analysis.
6. Understand the concept of earning power, and illustrate how irregular items are presented.

An important lesson can be learned from Canadian Tire's annual report described in our feature story. Effective communication is the key to understanding. This has become even more important in the aftermath of corporate scandals which have created a climate of scepticism about the usefulness of financial reporting.

The purpose of this chapter is to provide you with a comprehensive review of financial statements—a company's primary means of communication. We review all of the decision tools presented in this text and use them to analyse Canadian Tire's financial statements. In addition, we show how difficult it can be to develop high-quality financial numbers, because of the complexities of financial reporting. In particular, we will examine in detail the impact of certain irregular items on financial results and analysis.

The chapter is organized as follows:

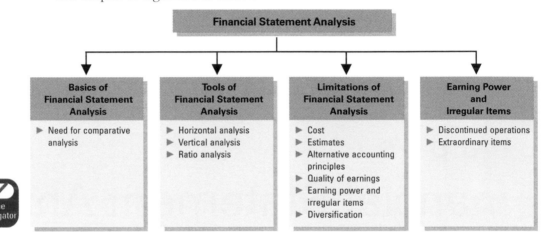

Financial Statement Analysis

Basics of Financial Statement Analysis	Tools of Financial Statement Analysis	Limitations of Financial Statement Analysis	Earning Power and Irregular Items
▶ Need for comparative analysis	▶ Horizontal analysis ▶ Vertical analysis ▶ Ratio analysis	▶ Cost ▶ Estimates ▶ Alternative accounting principles ▶ Quality of earnings ▶ Earning power and irregular items ▶ Diversification	▶ Discontinued operations ▶ Extraordinary items

the navigator

Basics of Financial Statement Analysis

study objective 1

Discuss the need for comparative analysis.

Analysing financial statements involves evaluating three characteristics of a company: its liquidity, its profitability, and its solvency. A short-term creditor, such as a bank, is mostly interested in the ability of the borrower to pay obligations when they come due. The liquidity of the borrower is important because it helps the bank evaluate the safety of a loan. A long-term creditor, such as a bondholder, looks to measures of profitability and solvency that indicate the company's ability to survive over a long period of time. Long-term creditors consider such measures as the amount of debt in the company's capital structure and its ability to meet interest payments. Similarly, shareholders are interested in the profitability and solvency of the company. They want to assess the likelihood of dividends and the growth potential of the shares.

But before we can evaluate a company's liquidity, profitability, and solvency, we must first understand the analysis tools that are available and how we can use them to make effective comparisons. In the next section, we learn how to gather and compare information that will help us do our analysis.

Need for Comparative Analysis

Every item reported in a financial statement has significance. When Canadian Tire reports cash and cash equivalents of $628.2 million on its balance sheet, we know that the company had that amount of cash and cash equivalents on the balance sheet date. However, we do not know if the amount is an increase over prior years, or if it's enough for the company's cash needs. To get this information, the amount of cash must be compared to other financial statement data.

Comparisons can be made on several different bases. The following three are illustrated in this chapter:

1. **Intracompany basis.** This basis compares an item or financial relationship **within a company** in the current year with one or more prior years. Intracompany comparisons are useful for detecting changes in financial relationships and significant trends. For example, Canadian Tire can compare its cash and cash equivalents balance at the end of the current year with last year's balance to find the amount of the increase or decrease. Likewise, Canadian Tire can compare the percentage of cash and cash equivalents to current assets at the end of the current year with the percentage in one or more prior years.

2. **Intercompany basis.** This basis compares an item or financial relationship of one company with the same item or relationship in **one or more competing companies**. Intercompany comparisons are useful for understanding a company's competitive position. For example, Canadian Tire's total sales for the year can be compared with the total sales of one of its major competitors.

   Who are its competitors? Don't be fooled by the name: Canadian Tire sells much more than tires. It sells home, car, sports, and leisure products, in addition to work clothes and casual attire through its subsidiary, Mark's Work Wearhouse. Consequently, it competes with other stores in the retail industry, such as Sears and Wal-Mart.

3. **Industry averages.** This basis compares an item or financial relationship of a company with **industry averages**. These averages are found in annual publications published by financial ratings organizations, such as Dun & Bradstreet, *The Financial Post*, and Statistics Canada. Comparisons with industry averages provide information about a company's relative performance within the industry. For example, Canadian Tire's net income can be compared with the average net income of all companies in the retail industry.

For a comparative analysis to be complete, it must always consider the economic circumstances a company is operating in. Economic measures such as the rates of interest, inflation, and unemployment—to list just a few—can have a big impact on a company's performance. For example, it would be difficult to adequately interpret a company's declining performance if one didn't know that the industry was being affected by an economic recession.

Financial analysis must also include non-financial measures, in addition to financial measures. Some argue that non-financial, or qualitative, measures are even more important than financial, or quantitative, measures in assessing success. Financial measures can only evaluate past performance. Non-financial measures may be better predictors of future performance. Non-financial measures include factors such as customer satisfaction, employee satisfaction, product reputation, innovation, and knowledge resources.

The annual report includes a wealth of both financial and non-financial information. In addition to the financial statement package, other financial information usually includes a management discussion and analysis (MD&A) of the company's financial position and a historical summary of key financial figures and ratios. Non-financial information includes a discussion of the company's mission, goals, and objectives, and its market position, people, and products. The components of an annual report are reviewed in detail on the Student Navigator CD that accompanies this text. As mentioned in our feature story, Canadian Tire's award-winning annual report is the perfect model of what an annual report should be.

Despite its importance, the annual report has recently been receiving less attention as the company's primary communication to its shareholders. Increasingly, companies are using other methods, such as websites and conference calls, to communicate with their shareholders on a timely basis. Because of the need for "continuous" disclosure, the annual report is now just one part of a series of information disclosures that a company makes to its current and future shareholders.

Annual Report Walkthrough

Tools of Financial Statement Analysis

Various tools are used to evaluate the significance of financial statement data. Three commonly used tools follow:

1. **Horizontal analysis** evaluates a series of financial statement data over a period of time.
2. **Vertical analysis** evaluates financial statement data by expressing each item in a financial statement as a percentage of a base amount for the same period of time.
3. **Ratio analysis** expresses the relationship among selected items of financial statement data.

Horizontal analysis is used primarily in intracompany comparisons. Two features in published financial statements make this type of comparison easier. First, each of the financial statements is presented on a comparative basis for a minimum of two years. Second, a summary of selected financial data is presented for a series of five to ten years or more.

Vertical analysis is used in both intracompany and intercompany comparisons. Ratio analysis is used in all three types of comparison. In the following sections, we will explain and illustrate each of the three types of analysis.

Horizontal Analysis

study objective 2

Explain and apply horizontal analysis.

Horizontal analysis, also called **trend analysis**, is a technique for evaluating a series of financial statement data over a period of time. Its purpose is to determine the increase or decrease that has taken place. This change may be expressed as either an amount or a percentage. For example, revenue figures for Canadian Tire are shown below:

CANADIAN TIRE CORPORATION, LIMITED
Revenues (in millions)
Year Ended December 31

2002	2001	2000	1999	1998
$5,944.5	$5,374.7	$5,207.6	$4,728.3	$4,347.3

If we assume that 1998 is the base year, we can measure all percentage increases or decreases from this base period amount by dividing the dollar amount of the change between the year under analysis and the base year by the base year amount, as shown in Illustration 18-1:

Illustration 18-1 ▶

Formula for horizontal analysis of percentage change since base period

$$\text{Percentage change since base period} = \frac{\text{Dollar amount of change}}{\text{Base year amount}}$$

For example, we can determine that revenues for Canadian Tire increased by approximately 9% [($4,728.3 − $4,347.3) ÷ $4,347.3] from 1998 to 1999. Similarly, we can determine that revenues increased by 37% [($5,944.5 − $4,347.3) ÷ $4,347.3] from 1998 to 2002.

Alternatively, we can express revenues as a percentage of the base period amount. This is done by dividing the amount for the specific year we are analysing by the base year amount, as shown in Illustration 18-2:

$$\boxed{\text{Trend percentage in relation to base period}} = \boxed{\frac{\text{Any year amount}}{\text{Base year amount}}}$$

Illustration 18-2 ◄

Formula for horizontal analysis of trend percentage in relation to base year

This analysis for Canadian Tire is presented below for a five-year period with 1998 as the base year:

CANADIAN TIRE CORPORATION, LIMITED Revenues (in millions) Year Ended December 31				
2002	2001	2000	1999	1998
137%	124%	120%	109%	100%

Balance Sheet

To further illustrate horizontal analysis, we will use the financial statements of Hometown Tires and More Inc. Hometown Tires and More is a small, local retail store that directly competes with Canadian Tire. Its two-year condensed balance sheet, showing dollar and percentage changes, is presented in Illustration 18-3.

Illustration 18-3 ◄

Horizontal analysis of balance sheet

HOMETOWN TIRES AND MORE INC. Balance Sheet December 31				
	2002	2001	Increase (Decrease) Amount	Percentage
Assets				
Current assets				
Cash	$ 50,000	$ 55,000	$ (5,000)	(9.1%)
Temporary investments	20,000	35,000	(15,000)	(42.9%)
Accounts receivable	72,500	50,000	22,500	45.0%
Inventory	372,500	325,000	47,500	14.6%
Prepaid expenses	30,000	20,000	10,000	50.0%
	545,000	485,000	60,000	12.4%
Property, plant, and equipment	400,000	450,000	(50,000)	(11.1%)
Intangible assets	55,000	65,000	(10,000)	(15.4%)
	$1,000,000	$1,000,000	$ 0	0.0%
Liabilities				
Current liabilities	$ 337,700	$ 313,500	$24,200	7.7%
Long-term liabilities	400,000	475,000	(75,000)	(15.8%)
	737,700	788,500	(50,800)	(6.4%)
Shareholders' Equity				
Common shares	90,000	90,000	0	0.0%
Retained earnings	172,300	121,500	50,800	41.8%
	262,300	211,500	50,800	24.0%
	$1,000,000	$1,000,000	$ 0	0.0%

The comparative balance sheet above shows that a number of changes have occurred in Hometown Tires and More's financial structure from 2001 to 2002. In the current assets section, accounts receivable increased by $22,500, or 45%, while temporary investments decreased by $15,000, or 42.9%. It looks like Hometown Tires and More may be financing its increase in receivables through its temporary investments. We will look at the income statement in the next section to determine if sales increased proportionately to the receivables increase. If not, this may be an indicator of slow-moving receivables.

Inventory increased by the largest dollar amount, $47,500, or 14.6%. It may have changed because of increased sales—we will investigate this further when we analyse the income statement. Prepaid expenses also increased by 50% in 2002. It is interesting to note that, despite these and other changes, total assets are unchanged from 2001 to 2002.

Current liabilities increased by 7.7%. The increase in current liabilities may be due to the increase in inventory. Changes in current assets and current liabilities usually both move in the same direction—that is, both will increase or both will decrease. In this case, both have risen although current assets have increased more than current liabilities.

Long-term liabilities decreased by $75,000, or 15.8%, in 2002. Hometown Tires and More appears to be using some of its profits to repay its debt. Retained earnings increased by 41.8% in the shareholders' equity section of the balance sheet. This suggests that Hometown Tires and More is financing its business by retaining income, rather than by assuming additional long-term debt.

Income Statement

Illustration 18-4 presents a horizontal analysis of Hometown Tires and More's condensed income statement for the years 2002 and 2001.

Illustration 18-4 ▶

Horizontal analysis of income statement

HOMETOWN TIRES AND MORE INC. Income Statement Year Ended December 31				
			Increase (Decrease)	
	2002	2001	Amount	Percentage
Sales	$2,095,000	$1,960,000	$135,000	6.9%
Sales returns and allowances	98,000	123,000	(25,000)	(20.3%)
Net sales	1,997,000	1,837,000	160,000	8.7%
Cost of goods sold	1,381,000	1,240,000	141,000	11.4%
Gross profit	616,000	597,000	19,000	3.2%
Operating expenses	457,000	440,000	17,000	3.9%
Income from operations	159,000	157,000	2,000	1.3%
Other revenues				
Interest and dividends	9,000	11,000	(2,000)	(18.2%)
Other expenses				
Interest	36,000	40,500	(4,500)	(11.1%)
Income before income tax	132,000	127,500	4,500	3.5%
Income tax expense	50,000	52,500	(2,500)	(4.8%)
Net income	$ 82,000	$ 75,000	$ 7,000	9.3%

Horizontal analysis of the income statement shows the following changes: Sales increased by only 6.9%, while the cost of goods sold increased by 11.4%. Sales returns and allowances were down by 20.3%.

Sales do not appear to have increased at the same rate as receivables. Recall from Illustration 18-3 that receivables increased by 45%. In Illustration 18-4, we see that net sales increased by only 8.7%. Later in the chapter, we will look at the receivables turnover to determine whether receivables are being collected more slowly or not. However, we must be cautious in over-interpreting this increase. This type of business relies substantially on cash sales, not credit sales. Therefore, a relatively small change in receivables can produce a large percentage change.

Recall also that in Illustration 18-3 we observed that inventory increased by 14.6%. The cost of goods sold reported on the income statement appears to have increased also, by 11.4%, even though net sales only increased by 8.7%. We will look at the inventory turnover later in the chapter to determine if these increases are reasonable.

To continue with our horizontal analysis of the income statement, we note that gross profit increased by 3.2%. Operating expenses outpaced this percentage increase at 3.9%. Other revenues and expenses declined. Overall, gross profit and net income both increased, so Hometown Tires and More's profit trend appears favourable.

Statement of Retained Earnings

A horizontal analysis of Hometown Tires and More's comparative statement of retained earnings is presented in Illustration 18-5.

Illustration 18-5 ◄

Horizontal analysis of statement of retained earnings

HOMETOWN TIRES AND MORE INC. Statement of Retained Earnings Year Ended December 31			Increase (Decrease)	
	2002	2001	Amount	Percentage
Retained earnings, Jan. 1	$121,500	$ 76,500	$45,000	58.8%
Add: Net income	82,000	75,000	7,000	9.3%
	203,500	151,500	52,000	34.3%
Less: Dividends	31,200	30,000	1,200	4.0%
Retained earnings, Dec. 31	$172,300	$121,500	$50,800	41.8%

Analysed horizontally, net income increased by $7,000, or 9.3%. This is consistent with the increase shown in the horizontal analysis of the income statement in Illustration 18-4.

Dividends increased by $1,200, or 4%. It is notable that dividends amount to $31,200, which is a fairly large proportion of net income. Management is likely using dividends as part of the company's compensation package, which is not uncommon in small businesses like this.

Ending retained earnings, also shown on the horizontal analysis of the balance sheet in Illustration 18-3, increased by 41.8%. As indicated earlier, the company retained a significant portion of net income to finance its business.

A horizontal analysis of changes from period to period is relatively straightforward and is quite useful. But complications can occur in making the calculations. If an item has no value in a base year and a value in the next year, no percentage change can be calculated. Similarly, if a negative amount appears in the base year and a positive amount exists the following year, or vice versa, no percentage change can be calculated.

We have not included a horizontal analysis of Hometown Tires and More's cash flow statement. Such an analysis is not as useful as the horizontal analyses performed on the balance sheet and income statement. The amounts presented in the cash flow statement (except in the operating activities section) detail the changes between two periods (opening and ending balance sheets). The value of this statement comes from the analysis of where cash came from and what it was used for rather than from comparing these changes to a base amount.

Vertical Analysis

study objective 3

Explain and apply vertical analysis.

Vertical analysis, also called **common size analysis**, is a technique for evaluating financial statement data that expresses each item within a financial statement as a percentage of a base amount. On a balance sheet, we might say that current assets are 54.5% of total assets (total assets being the base amount). Or, on an income statement, we might say that operating expenses are 22.9% of net sales (net sales being the base amount).

Balance Sheet

Alternative terminology
Horizontal analysis is also known as *dynamic analysis*, since it spans years. Vertical analysis is also known as *static analysis*, since it incorporates only one year.

Presented in Illustration 18-6 is the vertical analysis of Hometown Tires and More's comparative balance sheet. The base amount for the asset items is **total assets**. The base amount for the liability and shareholders' equity items is **total liabilities and shareholders' equity, which equals total assets.**

Illustration 18-6 ▶

Vertical analysis of balance sheet

Helpful hint The formula for calculating these balance sheet percentages follows:

$$\frac{\text{Each item on B/S}}{\text{Total assets}} = \%$$

HOMETOWN TIRES AND MORE INC.
Balance Sheet
December 31

	2002 Amount	2002 Percentage	2001 Amount	2001 Percentage
Assets				
Current assets	$ 545,000	54.5%	$ 485,000	48.5%
Property, plant, and equipment	400,000	40.0%	450,000	45.0%
Intangible assets	55,000	5.5%	65,000	6.5%
Total assets	$1,000,000	100.0%	$1,000,000	100.0%
Liabilities				
Current liabilities	$ 337,700	33.8%	$ 313,500	31.4%
Long-term liabilities	400,000	40.0%	475,000	47.5%
Total liabilities	737,700	73.8%	788,500	78.9%
Shareholders' Equity				
Common shares	90,000	9.0%	90,000	9.0%
Retained earnings	172,300	17.2%	121,500	12.1%
Total shareholders' equity	262,300	26.2%	211,500	21.1%
Total liabilities and shareholders' equity	$1,000,000	100.0%	$1,000,000	100.0%

Vertical analysis shows the relative size of each category in the balance sheet. It can also show the percentage change in the individual asset, liability, and shareholders' equity items. For example, we can see that current assets increased from 48.5% of total assets in 2001 to 54.5% of total assets in 2002. Property, plant, and equipment and intangible assets both decreased as relative percentages of total assets—45% in 2001 to 40% in 2002 for property, plant, and equipment and 6.5% in 2001 to 5.5% in 2002 for intangible assets. This decrease is likely due mainly to amortization.

Long-term liabilities decreased from 47.5% to 40%, while retained earnings increased from 12.1% to 17.2% of total liabilities and shareholders' equity between 2001 and 2002. These results reinforce the earlier observation that Hometown Tires and More is financing its growth by retaining earnings, rather than by issuing additional debt.

Income Statement

A vertical analysis of Hometown Tires and More's income statement is shown in Illustration 18-7. The base amount is usually **net sales** on the income statement.

HOMETOWN TIRES AND MORE INC. Income Statement Year Ended December 31				
	2002		2001	
	Amount	Percentage	Amount	Percentage
Sales	$2,095,000	104.9%	$1,960,000	106.7%
Sales returns and allowances	98,000	4.9%	123,000	6.7%
Net sales	1,997,000	100.0%	1,837,000	100.0%
Cost of goods sold	1,381,000	69.2%	1,240,000	67.5%
Gross profit	616,000	30.8%	597,000	32.5%
Operating expenses	457,000	22.9%	440,000	24.0%
Income from operations	159,000	7.9%	157,000	8.5%
Other revenues				
Interest and dividends	9,000	0.5%	11,000	0.6%
Other expenses				
Interest	36,000	1.8%	40,500	2.2%
Income before income tax	132,000	6.6%	127,500	6.9%
Income tax expense	50,000	2.5%	52,500	2.9%
Net income	$ 82,000	4.1%	$ 75,000	4.0%

Illustration 18-7 ◄

Vertical analysis of income statement

Helpful hint The formula for calculating these income statement percentages follows:

$$\frac{\text{Each item on I/S}}{\text{Net Sales}} = \%$$

We can see that the cost of goods sold as a percentage of net sales increased by 1.7% (from 67.5% to 69.2%). Operating expenses declined as a percentage of net sales by 1.1% (from 24% to 22.9%). As a result, income from operations did not change substantially between 2001 and 2002: it declined by 0.6% (from 8.5% to 7.9%). Net income remained relatively unchanged as a percentage of net sales from 2001 to 2002: it increased by 0.1%. Although we saw Hometown Tires and More's net income increase by 9.3% in Illustration 18-4, its profitability is unchanged in comparison to net sales.

A vertical analysis can also be performed on the statement of retained earnings and cash flow statement. However, this is seldom done, because each statement already provides comparative detail of the change between two periods (opening and ending balance sheets).

Intercompany Comparisons

Another benefit of vertical analysis is that it enables you to compare companies of different sizes. For example, Hometown Tires and More's main competitor is Canadian Tire. Using vertical analysis, the condensed balance sheet (or the income statement) of the small local retail company Hometown Tires and More can be more meaningfully compared with the balance sheet (or respective financial statement) of the giant retailer Canadian Tire, as shown in Illustration 18-8.

Illustration 18-8 ▶

Intercompany balance sheet comparison—vertical analysis

Balance Sheets
December 31, 2002
(in thousands)

	Hometown Tires and More		Canadian Tire	
	Amount	Percentage	Amount	Percentage
Assets				
Current assets	$ 545.0	54.5%	$2,314,200	47.5%
Investments and other assets		0.0%	126,700	2.6%
Property, plant and equipment	400.0	40.0%	2,349,700	48.2%
Intangible assets	55.0	5.5%	84,800	1.7%
Total assets	$1,000.0	100.0%	$4,875,400	100.0%
Liabilities				
Current liabilities	$ 337.7	33.8%	$1,583,600	32.5%
Long-term liabilities	400.0	40.0%	1,484,900	30.5%
Total liabilities	737.7	73.8%	3,068,500	63.0%
Shareholders' Equity				
Common shares	90.0	9.0%	668,900	13.7%
Retained earnings	172.3	17.2%	1,138,000	23.3%
Total shareholders' equity	262.3	26.2%	1,806,900	37.0%
Total liabilities and shareholders' equity	$1,000.0	100.0%	$4,875,400	100.0%

Canadian Tire's total assets are 4,875 times greater than the total assets of the much smaller Hometown Tires and More. Vertical analysis eliminates this difference in size. Hometown Tires and More has more current assets and less property, plant, and equipment than Canadian Tire, but not disproportionately so.

Hometown Tires and More has more debt than Canadian Tire, but this is not surprising given that Hometown Tires and More does not have the same access to equity financing as does Canadian Tire. Hometown Tires and More is a privately owned business, with limited share distribution. Accordingly, Hometown Tires and More has a lower equity base than Canadian Tire (26.2% compared to 37%).

Even when comparing companies of vastly different sizes operating in the same industry, there are many things that can be learned by looking at vertically analysed financial statements. The balance sheet is presented above for illustration. The income statement could be similarly analysed. You may wish to attempt this on your own for practice.

BEFORE YOU GO ON . . .

▶ **Review It**

1. Explain the difference between intracompany, intercompany, and industry comparisons.
2. What is horizontal analysis?
3. What is vertical analysis?

▶ **Do It**

Summary financial information for Bonora Corporation is as follows:

	December 31, 2005	December 31, 2004
Current assets	$234,000	$180,000
Property, plant, and equipment (net)	756,000	420,000
Total assets	$990,000	$600,000

Calculate the amount and percentage changes in 2005, using (a) horizontal analysis, assuming 2004 is the base year, and (b) vertical analysis, assuming total assets is the base.

Action Plan

- Horizontal analysis: Find the percentage change by dividing the amount of the increase by the 2004 amount (base year).
- Vertical analysis: Find the percentage change by dividing the specific asset amount by total assets, for each of 2005 and 2004.

Solution

(a) Horizontal analysis:

	Increase in 2005	
	Amount	Percentage
Current assets	$ 54,000	30% [($234,000 − $180,000) ÷ $180,000]
Property, plant, and equipment (net)	336,000	80% [($756,000 − $420,000) ÷ $420,000]
Total assets	$390,000	65% [($990,000 − $600,000) ÷ $600,000]

(b) Vertical analysis:

	2005	2004
Current assets	23.6% ($234,000 ÷ $990,000)	30% ($180,000 ÷ $600,000)
Property, plant, and equipment (net)	76.4% ($756,000 ÷ $990,000)	70% ($420,000 ÷ $600,000)
Total assets	100.0%	100%

Related exercise material: BE18–1, BE18–2, BE18–3, BE18–4, E18–1, E18–2, E18–3, and E18–4.

Ratio Analysis

study objective 4

Identify and calculate ratios and describe their purpose and use in analysing a company's liquidity, profitability, and solvency.

Ratio analysis expresses the relationships between selected items of financial statement data. A **ratio** expresses the mathematical relationship between one quantity and another. The relationship is expressed as either a percentage, a rate, or a simple proportion. To illustrate, Canadian Tire had current assets of $2,314.2 million and current liabilities of $1,583.6 million in 2002. The relationship is determined by dividing current assets by current liabilities. The different ways of expressing the relationship follow:

Percentage: Current assets are 146% of current liabilities.
Rate: Current assets are 1.46 times greater than current liabilities.
Proportion: The relationship of current assets to liabilities is 1.46:1.

For analysis of the primary financial statements, ratios can be classified into three types:

1. **Liquidity ratios.** These measure the short-term ability of the company to pay its maturing obligations and to meet unexpected needs for cash.
2. **Solvency ratios.** These measure the ability of the company to survive over a long period of time.
3. **Profitability ratios.** These measure the operating success of a company for a given period of time.

These three ratio classifications are described and shown in Illustration 18-9.

Illustration 18-9 ▶

Financial ratio classifications

Liquidity Ratios

Measure the short-term ability of the company to pay its maturing obligations and to meet unexpected needs for cash.

Solvency Ratios

Measure the ability of the company to survive over a long period of time.

Profitability Ratios

Measure the income or operating success of a company for a given time.

In previous chapters, we presented liquidity, solvency, and profitability ratios for evaluating the financial condition of a company. In this section, we provide a summary list of these ratios. Chapter and page references to prior discussions are included so you can review any individual ratio. In addition, an example of a comprehensive financial analysis, comparing Hometown Tires and More to Canadian Tire using intracompany, intercompany, and industry comparisons, is provided in the appendix to this chapter.

Liquidity Ratios

Liquidity ratios measure the short-term ability of a company to pay its maturing obligations and to meet unexpected needs for cash. Short-term creditors such as bankers and suppliers are particularly interested in assessing liquidity. Illustration 18-10 lists the liquidity ratios we have covered in this textbook. It is important to remember that these are only examples of commonly used liquidity ratios. You will find more examples as you expand your knowledge of financial analysis.

Illustration 18-10 ▶

Summary of liquidity ratios

Ratio	Formula	Purpose	Discussion
Working capital	Current assets − current liabilities	Measures short-term debt-paying ability.	Ch. 4, p. 172
Current ratio	$\dfrac{\text{Current assets}}{\text{Current liabilities}}$	Measures short-term debt-paying ability.	Ch. 4, p. 172
Inventory turnover	$\dfrac{\text{Cost of goods sold}}{\text{Average inventory}}$	Measures liquidity of inventory.	Ch. 6, p. 296
Days sales in inventory	$\dfrac{\text{365 days}}{\text{Inventory turnover}}$	Measures number of days inventory is on hand.	Ch. 6, p. 296
Receivables turnover	$\dfrac{\text{Net credit sales}}{\text{Average gross receivables}}$	Measures liquidity of receivables.	Ch. 8, p. 402
Collection period	$\dfrac{\text{365 days}}{\text{Receivables turnover}}$	Measures number of days receivables are outstanding.	Ch. 8, p. 402

Solvency Ratios

Solvency ratios measure the ability of a company to survive over a long period of time. Long-term creditors and shareholders are interested in a company's long-term solvency, particularly its ability to pay interest as it comes due and to repay the face value of debt at maturity. Illustration 18-11 lists the solvency ratios we have covered in this textbook.

Ratio	Formula	Purpose	Discussion
Debt to total assets	$\dfrac{\text{Total liabilities}}{\text{Total assets}}$	Measures percentage of total assets provided by creditors.	Ch. 15, p. 719
Interest coverage	$\dfrac{\text{Net income + interest expense}}{\text{+ income tax expense (EBIT)}}$ $\dfrac{}{\text{Interest expense}}$	Measures ability to meet interest payments as they come due.	Ch. 15, p. 720
Free cash flow	Cash provided (used) by operating activities − net capital expenditures − dividends paid	Measures cash available for paying more dividends or for expanding operations.	Ch. 17, p. 825

Illustration 18-11 ◄
Summary of solvency ratios

Profitability Ratios

Profitability ratios measure the operating success of a company for a given period of time. A company's income, or lack of it, affects its ability to obtain debt and equity financing, its liquidity position, and its growth. Creditors and investors alike are therefore interested in evaluating profitability. Profitability is frequently used as the ultimate test of management's operating effectiveness. Illustration 18-12 lists the profitability ratios we have covered in the textbook.

Ratio	Formula	Purpose	Discussion
Gross profit margin	$\dfrac{\text{Gross profit}}{\text{Net sales}}$	Measures margin between selling price and cost of goods sold.	Ch. 5, p. 234
Profit margin	$\dfrac{\text{Net income}}{\text{Net sales}}$	Measures net income generated by each dollar of sales.	Ch. 5, p. 235
Asset turnover	$\dfrac{\text{Net sales}}{\text{Average total assets}}$	Measures how efficiently assets are used to generate sales.	Ch. 9, p. 456
Return on assets	$\dfrac{\text{Net income}}{\text{Average total assets}}$	Measures overall profitability of assets.	Ch. 9, p. 456
Return on equity	$\dfrac{\text{Net income}}{\text{Average shareholders' equity}}$	Measures profitability of shareholders' investment.	Ch. 13, p. 634
Earnings per share	$\dfrac{\text{Net income − preferred dividends}}{\text{Weighted average number of common shares}}$	Measures net income earned on each common share.	Ch. 14, p. 674
Price-earnings ratio	$\dfrac{\text{Market price per share}}{\text{Earnings per share}}$	Measures relationship between market price per share and earnings per share.	Ch. 14, p. 676
Payout ratio	$\dfrac{\text{Cash dividends}}{\text{Net income}}$	Measures percentage of income distributed as cash dividends.	Ch. 14, p. 676
EBITDA	Net income + interest expense + income tax expense + amortization expense	Measures operating profitability on a cash basis.	Ch. 17, p. 825

Illustration 18-12 ◄
Summary of profitability ratios

As analysis tools, ratios can provide clues to underlying conditions that may not be apparent from the individual financial statement components of a particular ratio. However, a single ratio by itself is not very meaningful. Accordingly, ratios must be interpreted alongside the information gained from a detailed review of the financial information, including horizontal and vertical analyses, and non-financial information, as described earlier in the chapter.

BEFORE YOU GO ON . . .

▶Review It

1. What are liquidity ratios? Explain working capital, current ratio, inventory turnover, days sales in inventory, receivables turnover, and collection period.
2. What are solvency ratios? Explain debt to total assets, interest coverage, and free cash flow.
3. What are profitability ratios? Explain gross profit margin, profit margin, asset turnover, return on assets, return on equity, earnings per share, price-earnings ratio, payout ratio, and EBITDA.

the
navigator

Related exercise material: BE18–5, BE18–6, BE18–7, BE18–8, BE18–9, BE18–10, E18–5, E18–6, E18–7, E18–8, E18–9, and E18–10.

Limitations of Financial Analysis

study objective 5

Recognize and illustrate the limitations of financial statement analysis.

Significant business decisions are frequently made by using one or more of the analytical tools illustrated in this chapter. But you should be aware of the limitations of these tools and of the financial statements they are based on.

Cost

Traditional financial statements are based on cost. They are not adjusted for price-level changes. Comparisons of unadjusted financial data from different periods may be invalid due to inflation or deflation. For example, a five-year comparison of Canadian Tire's revenues might show growth of 137%. But this growth trend would be misleading if the general price-level had increased or decreased significantly during the same period.

Estimates

Financial statements contain many estimates. For example, estimates are used to determine the allowance for uncollectible receivables, periodic amortization, and the costs of warranties. To the extent that these estimates are inaccurate or biased, the financial ratios and percentages are inaccurate or biased.

Alternative Accounting Principles

Companies vary in the generally accepted accounting principles they use. Such variations may reduce comparability. For example, Canadian Tire uses the average cost flow assumption. Wal-Mart, one of its competitors, uses LIFO. If inventory is a significant asset to both companies, it is unlikely that their current ratios are comparable. Recall, however, that although the current assets may be different in one or more periods because of the choice of inventory cost flow assumption, in total, over the life of the inventory, there is no difference. We call differences created from alternative accounting principles "artificial" or timing differences.

Also, in an increasing number of industries, competition is global. To evaluate a company's standing, an investor or analyst must make comparisons to companies from other countries. However, due to the many differences in accounting practices, these comparisons can be both difficult and misleading. Although differences in accounting principles might be detectable from reading the notes to the financial statements, adjusting the financial data to compensate for the different principles is difficult, if not impossible, in some cases.

Quality of Earnings

There is intense pressure for publicly traded companies to meet forecasts, especially in a bear market in which stock prices are falling. Managers may try to manipulate income by choosing estimates and accounting principles to manage income. In such cases, the quality of the information content will decrease.

Fortunately, the chief executive officer and chief financial officer of a publicly traded company must ensure, and personally declare, that the reported financial information is accurate, relevant, and understandable. In addition, audit committees are held responsible for quizzing management on the degree of aggressiveness/conservatism applied and the quality of the underlying estimates, accounting principles, and judgements.

Earning Power and Irregular Items

Users of financial statements are interested in the concept of "earning power." Earning power means the normal level of income to be obtained in the future. Earning power differs from actual net income by the amount of non-typical or irregular items. We learned about one type of non-typical item in Chapter 14—a change in accounting principles. In the next section, we will learn about two more types of irregular items—discontinued operations and extraordinary items.

If we compare the performance of one company without irregular items to another company with irregular items, comparability will be affected. Consequently, it is usual to adjust any financial statement items for the impact of irregular items before performing any analysis, be it a horizontal, vertical, or ratio analysis.

Diversification

Diversification in Canadian industry also limits the usefulness of financial analysis. Many firms today are so diversified that they cannot be classified by industry. Canadian Tire, for example, sells home, car, sports, and leisure products. In addition, it is the country's largest independent gasoline retailer. Canadian Tire also sells work clothes and casual attire through its subsidiary, Mark's Work Wearhouse. Consequently, deciding what industry a company is in is actually one of the main challenges to an effective evaluation of its results.

Other companies may appear to be comparable but are not. McCain Foods and Irving-owned Cavendish Farms compete in the frozen potato product field. Yet McCain produces other food products besides french fries, and Irving has many other interests, including oil, newspapers, tissue products, transportation, and shipbuilding.

When companies have significant operations in different lines of business, they are required to report additional disclosures in a **segment information** note to their financial statements. Segment information includes services or product lines and segments located in different countries. Operating income, revenues, and identifiable assets are also reported. Many analysts say that segment information is the most important data in the financial statements. Without it, a comparison of diversified companies is very difficult.

ACCOUNTING IN ACTION ► Ethics Insight

In the wake of a proliferation of corporate scandals, many companies have been scared straight—or at the very least hiring ethics officers to help keep them straight. Regulation has tightened the requirement for ethical financial reporting, including requiring some officers to vouch personally for the accuracy of their financial reports. Ethics officers conduct training courses for employees and watch over potential conflicts of interest. And they work with auditors and the board of directors to help make sure financial statements are accurate.

Of course, ethics programs aren't foolproof. "There isn't much even the most astute ethics officer can do when the board is asleep and senior management is corrupt," says Edward Petry, executive director of the ethics-officer group. However, it is a step in the right direction.

Source: Richard Schmitt, "Firms Scared Straight on Ethics," *Globe and Mail,* November 4, 2002, B9.

BEFORE YOU GO ON . . .

▶Review It

1. What are some limitations of financial analysis?
2. Describe factors that may reduce the quality of earnings.
3. In what way do irregular items limit the comparability of financial information?

Related exercise material: E18–11.

Earning Power and Irregular Items

study objective 6

Understand the concept of earning power, and illustrate how irregular items are presented.

Earning power is net income adjusted for irregular, or non-typical, items. When analysts use income figures in their analysis, they must make sure that net income does not include the "noise" of any irregular revenues and expenses.

For example, suppose that Li Corporation reports that this year's net income is $500,000, but included in that amount is a once-in-a-lifetime gain of $400,000. Using the $500,000 to perform horizontal, vertical, and ratio analyses would be misleading, because the company's earning power is really only $100,000, not $500,000 as reported.

To help determine earning power, irregular items are identified by type on the income statement. Two types of irregular items are reported: (1) discontinued operations and (2) extraordinary items.

Irregular items are reported net of income tax, as we learned for another type of irregular item—a change in accounting principle, reported on the statement of retained earnings. For irregular items affecting the income statement, the applicable income tax expense or income tax saving is shown for income before income tax and for each of the irregular items. The general concept is "Let the tax follow the income or loss."

Discontinued Operations

Discontinued operations refer to the disposal of an identifiable reporting or operating segment of the business. An **identifiable business segment** is a part of a company that can be clearly distinguished, for financial reporting and operating purposes, from the rest of the company. A segment can be a separate subsidiary company, an operating division within the company, or even a group of assets, as long as it is a separate business that can be clearly distinguished from the company as a whole.

Most large corporations have multiple business segments or divisions. For example, Canadian Tire has four business segments that it reports financial and operating information about: Canadian Tire Retail, Canadian Tire Petroleum, Mark's Work Wearhouse, and Canadian Tire Financial Services.

If a company sells a segment of its business, it is reported separately on the income statement as a nonrecurring item called discontinued operations. Note that discontinued operations relate only to the disposal of an identifiable business segment, such as the elimination of an entire line of business or product group. The phasing out of a model or part of a line of business is *not* considered a disposal of a business segment.

For example, Shaw Communications Inc.'s sale of its specialty television and radio media businesses to Corus Entertainment Inc. was reported as discontinued operations. On the other hand, Shaw's sale of its cable operations in Southern Ontario and New Brunswick to Rogers Communications was not reported as discontinued operations, as Shaw continues to operate in the cable industry in other areas of Canada. Gains and losses from Shaw's sale of its cable operations, or from the sale of any other asset, are reported as other revenues or other expenses on the income statement at their gross amount (not net of tax). Such gains and losses form part of the income from continuing operations.

When the disposal of a significant identifiable business segment occurs, the income statement should report both the income (or loss) from continuing operations and the income (or loss) from discontinued operations. The income (loss) from discontinued operations consists of two parts: the income (loss) from these operations and the gain (loss) on disposal of the segment. Both items are presented net of applicable income tax.

To illustrate, assume that Hwa Energy Inc. has revenues of $2.5 million and expenses of $1.7 million from continuing operations in 2005. The company therefore has income before income tax of $800,000. During 2005, Hwa discontinues and sells its unprofitable chemical division. The loss in 2005 from chemical operations is $140,000 ($200,000 less $60,000 income tax, assuming a 30% tax rate). The loss on disposal of the chemical division is $70,000 ($100,000 less $30,000 income tax). The income statement is presented below:

HWA ENERGY INC. Income Statement (partial) Year Ended December 31, 2005		
Revenues		$2,500,000
Expenses		1,700,000
Income before income tax		800,000
Income tax expense		240,000
Income from continuing operations		560,000
Discontinued operations		
Loss from operations of chemical division, net of $60,000 income tax saving	$140,000	
Loss on disposal of chemical division, net of $30,000 income tax saving	70,000	210,000
Net income		$ 350,000

Helpful hint Observe the dual disclosures: (1) the results of operations of the discontinued division (which must be eliminated from the results of continuing operations), and (2) the disposal of the operation.

Note that the caption "Income from continuing operations" is used, and that a section called "Discontinued operations" is added. **In the new section, both the operating loss and the loss on disposal are reported net of applicable income tax.** This presentation clearly indicates the separate effects of continuing operations and discontinued operations on net income. Discontinued operations are relatively common. In a recent year, 17% of the companies surveyed by *Financial Reporting in Canada* reported discontinued operations.

Extraordinary Items

Extraordinary items are events and transactions that meet three conditions. They are:

1. not expected to occur frequently,
2. not typical of normal business activities, and
3. not subject to management's discretion.

To be infrequent, the item should not be expected again in the foreseeable future. To be atypical, the item should be only incidentally related to normal activities. To be outside of management's discretion, the item should not depend on decisions by management or owners.

In reality, extraordinary items are rare. *Financial Reporting in Canada* notes that no public company reported an extraordinary item in recent years. Illustration 18-13 shows the appropriate classification of extraordinary and ordinary items.

Illustration 18-13 ▶

Examples of extraordinary and ordinary items

Extraordinary Items	Ordinary Items
1. Effects of major casualties (acts of God) if rare in the area 	1. Effects of major casualties (acts of God) if frequent in the area 
2. An expropriation (takeover) of property by a government 	2. A write-down of inventories or write-off of receivables 
3. Effects of a newly enacted law or regulation, such as a condemnation action	3. Losses attributable to labour disputes 
4. The destruction of property	4. Gains or losses from the sale of property, plant, and equipment 

All three criteria must be evaluated in terms of the company's environment. The environment includes factors such as industry characteristics and geographic location. For example, the destruction of a Saskatchewan prairie farmer's crops by a tornado would be classified as an extraordinary item because tornados are rare in Saskatchewan. Although they are not unheard of, they occur very infrequently. However, the destruction of a neighbouring Montana farmer's crops by a tornado would not be classified as extraordinary because tornados are experienced more often in Montana. Montana experiences about 11 tornados a year, on average.

Extraordinary items are reported net of income tax in a separate section of the income statement, immediately below discontinued operations. To illustrate, assume that for the construction of a highway in 2005 the government expropriates property held by Hwa Energy Inc. If the loss is $70,000 before applicable income tax of $21,000, the income statement will report a deduction of $49,000, as follows:

HWA ENERGY INC. Income Statement (partial) Year Ended December 31, 2005		
Revenues		$2,500,000
Expenses		1,700,000
Income before income tax		800,000
Income tax expense		240,000
Income from continuing operations		560,000
Discontinued operations		
Loss from operations of chemical division,		
net of $60,000 income tax saving	$140,000	
Loss on disposal of chemical division,		
net of $30,000 income tax saving	70,000	210,000
Income before extraordinary item		350,000
Extraordinary item		
Expropriation of property, net of $21,000		
income tax saving		49,000
Net income		$ 301,000

When there is an extraordinary item to report, the caption "Income before extraordinary item" is added immediately before the section for the extraordinary item. This presentation clearly indicates the effect of the extraordinary item on net income.

What if a transaction or event meets only one or two (but not all) of the criteria for an extraordinary item? In that case, it is reported under either "Other revenues" or "Other expenses" at its gross amount (not net of tax). This is true, for example, of gains (losses) resulting from the sale of property, plant, and equipment, as explained in Chapter 9.

ACCOUNTING IN ACTION ► International Insight

The criteria used to determine if an item is extraordinary or not differ across countries. For example, in the United States extraordinary items do not rule out management involvement. Consequently, in the U.S., extraordinary items are far more frequent than in Canada and can include items such as losses from the retirement of debt that involve decisions made by management.

Canada, Australia, the U.S., and the UK report extraordinary items (they are called "exceptional" in the UK) separately from ordinary items. Many other countries, however, don't distinguish between extraordinary and ordinary items.

BEFORE YOU GO ON . . .

►Review It

1. What is earning power?
2. What irregular items can affect the income statement?
3. What impact do irregular items have on the analysis of financial information?
4. Did The Forzani Group report any irregular items in fiscal 2003? The answer to this question is provided at the end of this chapter.

►Do It

In its 2006 income statement, Qu Ltd. reported a $75,000 loss incurred from closing six of 30 stores, an extraordinary loss of $100,000 from fire, income tax of $135,000 (45% rate), and net income of $165,000. Prepare an income statement, beginning with income before income tax.

Action Plan

- Apply the criteria for discontinued operations to the closure of stores. This closure does not meet the criteria, because Qu continues to operate other stores in the same line of business. The loss should be reported as part of continuing income.
- Apply the criteria for an extraordinary item to the fire loss. This loss meets the criteria since it is infrequent, unusual, and not determined by management.
- Allocate income tax between income from continuing operations and income from atypical (extraordinary) items.
- Report the extraordinary item separately, net of income tax.

Solution

QU LTD.
Income Statement (partial)
Year Ended December 31, 2006

Income before income tax	$400,000
Income tax expense (45%)	180,000
Income before extraordinary item	220,000
Extraordinary loss from fire, net of $45,000 income tax saving	55,000
Net income	$165,000

Related exercise material: BE18–11, BE18–12, BE18–13, and E18–12.

APPENDIX 18A ▶ COMPREHENSIVE ILLUSTRATION OF RATIO ANALYSIS

In previous chapters, we calculated many ratios used to evaluate the liquidity, solvency, and profitability of a company. In this appendix, we provide a comprehensive review of those ratios and discuss some important relationships among them. In this review, we use the following comparisons:

1. **Intracompany comparisons** covering two years (2001 and 2002) for Hometown Tires and More.
2. **Intercompany comparisons** for the year ended December 31, 2002, for Canadian Tire, Hometown Tires and More's principal competitor.
3. **Industry average comparisons** for 2002 for the retail department store industry. For some of the ratios that we use, industry comparisons are not available. These are denoted "n/a."

The financial information shown earlier in the chapter in Illustrations 18-3 through 18-5 has been used to calculate Hometown Tires and More's ratios. You can use these data to review the calculations for each ratio to make sure you understand where the numbers came from. Detailed calculations are not shown for either Canadian Tire or the industry.

Liquidity Ratios

Liquidity ratios measure the ability of a company to pay its current liabilities. Consequently, liquidity ratios focus mainly on the relationships between current assets and current liabilities reported in balance sheet and related accounts on the income statement. Cash provided by operating activities, reported on the cash flow statement, is also useful in assessing liquidity. Liquidity ratios include working capital, the current ratio, receivables turnover, collection period, inventory turnover, and days sales in inventory.

Working Capital

Working capital is the difference between current assets and current liabilities. The 2001 and 2002 working capital figures for Hometown Tires and More, and comparative data, are shown in Illustration 18A-1.

Illustration 18A-1 ◄

Working capital

Working capital = Current assets − Current liabilities

Hometown Tires and More

2002	2001
$545,000 − $337,700 = $207,300	$485,000 − $313,500 = $171,500
Industry Average	Canadian Tire
n/a	$730.6 million

Hometown Tires and More has a positive and increasing working capital: $207,300 in 2002 and $171,500 in 2001. It is not very meaningful to compare this amount to that of the much larger Canadian Tire. In addition, no industry average is available for working capital, nor would any working capital amounts be comparable within the industry.

As we learned in Chapter 4, the current ratio—which expresses current assets and current liabilities as a ratio rather than as an amount—is a more useful indicator of liquidity. It is difficult to compare absolute dollar amounts. In addition, two companies with the same amount of working capital may have very different current ratios.

Current Ratio

The current ratio is a widely used measure of a company's liquidity and short-term debt-paying ability. The ratio is calculated by dividing current assets by current liabilities. The 2002 and 2001 current ratios for Hometown Tires and More, and comparative data, are shown in Illustration 18A-2.

Illustration 18A-2 ◄

Current ratio

$$\text{Current ratio} = \frac{\text{Current assets}}{\text{Current liabilities}}$$

Hometown Tires and More

2002	2001
$\dfrac{\$545,000}{\$337,700} = 1.6{:}1$	$\dfrac{\$485,000}{\$313,500} = 1.5{:}1$
Industry Average	Canadian Tire
1.2:1	1.5:1

What does the ratio actually mean? The 2002 ratio of 1.6:1 means that for every dollar of current liabilities, Hometown Tires and More has $1.60 of current assets. Hometown Tires and More's current ratio has increased slightly in 2002. Its 2002 ratio is slightly higher than Canadian Tire's current ratio of 1.5:1 and quite a bit higher than the industry average of 1.2:1.

The current ratio is only one measure of liquidity. It does not take into account the composition of the current assets. For example, a satisfactory current ratio does not disclose the fact that a portion of the current assets may be tied up in uncollectible accounts receivable or in slow-moving inventory. A dollar of cash is more available to pay bills than a dollar of slow-moving inventory that has yet to be sold and paid for.

Receivables Turnover

Liquidity may be measured by how quickly certain assets can be converted to cash. How liquid, for example, are the receivables? The ratio used to assess the liquidity of the receivables is the receivables turnover. It measures the number of times, on average, receivables are collected during the period. The receivables turnover is calculated by dividing net credit sales (net sales less cash sales) by the average gross receivables.

Assuming that all sales are credit sales, that there is no allowance for doubtful accounts, and that the balance of accounts receivable at the beginning of 2001 is $45,000, the receivables turnover figures for Hometown Tires and More, and comparative data, are shown in Illustration 18A-3.

Illustration 18A-3 ▶

Receivables turnover

Helpful hint Whenever an end-of-period (e.g., balance sheet) figure is compared to a period figure (e.g., income statement or cash flow statement), the end-of-period figure must be averaged so that it approximates the same period of time. Comparisons of end-of-period figures to end-of-period figures, or period figures to period figures, do not require averaging.

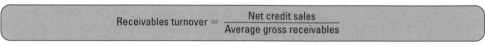

$$\text{Receivables turnover} = \frac{\text{Net credit sales}}{\text{Average gross receivables}}$$

Hometown Tires and More

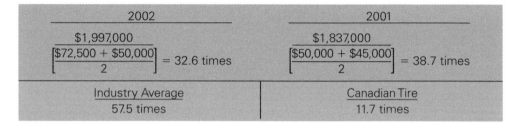

2002	2001
$\dfrac{\$1,997,000}{\left[\dfrac{\$72,500 + \$50,000}{2}\right]} = 32.6$ times	$\dfrac{\$1,837,000}{\left[\dfrac{\$50,000 + \$45,000}{2}\right]} = 38.7$ times
Industry Average	Canadian Tire
57.5 times	11.7 times

Hometown Tires and More's receivables turn over (i.e., are collected) 32.6 times a year. In general, the faster the turnover, the greater the reliability of the current ratio for assessing liquidity.

Hometown Tires and More's receivables turnover declined from 38.7 times in 2001 to 32.6 times in 2002. It is still much higher than Canadian Tire's receivables turnover of 11.7 times a year, but slower than the industry average of 57.5 times a year in 2002.

Why is Hometown Tires and More's receivables turnover so much higher than that of Canadian Tire? Hometown Tires and More likely has few credit sales and therefore few receivables. Most of its sales are for cash. Canadian Tire, on the other hand, has receivables from its franchise stores.

Care must be taken in interpreting this ratio. We assumed that all sales were credit sales, when in fact, this is not a reasonable assumption. Companies do not separately disclose their credit and cash sales. However, intracompany, intercompany, and industry comparisons can still be made, since the same assumption—all sales were credit sales—was applied to Canadian Tire and the industry average.

Collection Period

A popular variant of the receivables turnover is calculated by converting it into a collection period stated in days. This is done by dividing 365 days by the receivables turnover, as shown in Illustration 18A-4.

$$\text{Collection period} = \frac{365 \text{ days}}{\text{Receivables turnover}}$$

Hometown Tires and More

2002	2001
$\dfrac{365 \text{ days}}{32.6} = 11 \text{ days}$	$\dfrac{365 \text{ days}}{38.7} = 9 \text{ days}$
Industry Average 6 days	**Canadian Tire** 31 days

The effectiveness of a company's credit and collection policies is much easier to interpret using the collection period, rather than the receivables turnover ratio. Hometown Tires and More's receivables were collected every 11 days in 2002. Although a decrease from 2001, and not as good as the industry average, this collection period is still excellent and well under the normal 30-day payment period. The general rule is that the collection period should not exceed the credit-term period (the time allowed for payment). Even Canadian Tire's collection period of 31 days is still a reasonable one.

So, despite earlier concerns, receivables management appears to be in good shape for both companies, and the industry. Given the large proportion of cash sales, this is to be expected.

Inventory Turnover

Inventory turnover measures the average number of times the inventory is sold during the period. Its purpose is to measure the liquidity of the inventory. The inventory turnover is calculated by dividing the cost of goods sold by the average inventory.

Assuming that the inventory balance for Hometown Tires and More at the beginning of 2001 was $300,000, its inventory turnover figures, and comparative data, are shown in Illustration 18A-5.

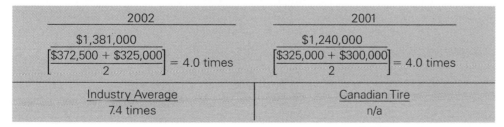

$$\text{Inventory turnover} = \frac{\text{Cost of goods sold}}{\text{Average inventory}}$$

Hometown Tires and More

2002	2001
$\dfrac{\$1,381,000}{\left[\dfrac{\$372,500 + \$325,000}{2}\right]} = 4.0 \text{ times}$	$\dfrac{\$1,240,000}{\left[\dfrac{\$325,000 + \$300,000}{2}\right]} = 4.0 \text{ times}$
Industry Average 7.4 times	**Canadian Tire** n/a

Hometown Tires and More turns (sells) its entire inventory over 4.0 times a year. Its inventory turnover was unchanged between 2001 and 2002. Hometown Tires and More's turnover ratio of 4.0 times is low compared to the industry average of 7.4 times. Generally, the faster inventory is sold, the less cash there is tied up in inventory and the less chance there is of inventory becoming obsolete.

Like many other Canadian companies, Canadian Tire does not separately disclose its cost of goods sold. Consequently, we are unable to calculate its inventory turnover.

Days Sales in Inventory

A variant of inventory turnover is the days sales in inventory. This is calculated by dividing the inventory turnover into 365 days. Hometown Tires and More's days sales in inventory ratios for 2002 and 2001, and comparative data, are shown in Illustration 18A-6.

Illustration 18A-6 ▶

Days sales in inventory

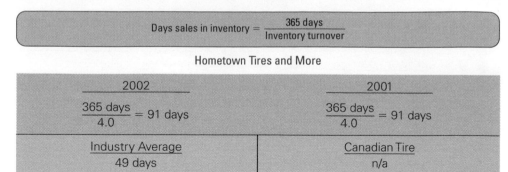

$$\text{Days sales in inventory} = \frac{365 \text{ days}}{\text{Inventory turnover}}$$

Hometown Tires and More

2002	2001
$\frac{365 \text{ days}}{4.0} = 91 \text{ days}$	$\frac{365 \text{ days}}{4.0} = 91 \text{ days}$
Industry Average	Canadian Tire
49 days	n/a

Hometown Tires and More's inventory turnover of 4.0 times divided into 365 days is approximately 91 days. In other words, Hometown Tires and More has 91 days' worth of inventory on hand. This is relatively slow compared to the industry average of 49 days.

It is important to use judgement in interpreting both the inventory turnover and days sales in inventory ratios. Remember that Hometown Tires and More is only one store, while Canadian Tire has 450 stores and the industry is composed of large box stores. Canadian Tire, and other stores in the industry, are large enough to take advantage of just-in-time and other computerized inventory management techniques, whereas Hometown Tires and More likely does not have access to many sophisticated inventory options.

Nonetheless, Hometown Tires and More must keep a close eye on its inventory. It runs the risk of being left with unsaleable inventory, not to mention the additional costs of financing and carrying this inventory over an extended period of time.

Liquidity Conclusion

On an intracompany comparison, Hometown Tires and More's current ratio improved slightly from 2001 to 2002. Although its receivables turnover ratio declined, it is still a strong ratio, and well within the normal collection period. The proportionate increase in the dollar amount of receivables (and prepaid expenses) is likely the reason Hometown Tires and More's current ratio increased. Its inventory turnover remained unchanged.

On an intercompany comparison, Hometown Tires and More's liquidity is better than Canadian Tire's on all counts. Although its current ratio is better than the industry's, this is a bit misleading since both its receivables turnover and inventory turnover are below the industry average. Nonetheless, its receivables management is still strong, and well within normal collection periods. Hometown Tires and More's inventory turnover is significantly below that of the industry, although this may be primarily attributable to the type of goods on hand and the size of the store.

To conclude, Hometown Tires and More's liquidity is good, but it should keep a close eye on its inventory.

Solvency Ratios

While liquidity ratios measure the ability of a company to pay its current liabilities, solvency ratios measure the ability of a company to pay its total liabilities. The debt to total assets and interest coverage ratios provide information about debt-paying ability. In addition, free cash flow provides information about the company's ability to pay additional dividends or invest in new projects.

Debt to Total Assets

Debt to total assets measures the percentage of the total assets provided by creditors. It is calculated by dividing total liabilities (both current and long-term) by total assets. This ratio indicates the company's degree of leverage. It also provides some indication of the company's ability to absorb losses without hurting the interests of its creditors. The higher the percentage of total debt to total assets, the greater the risk that the company may be unable to meet its maturing obligations. The lower the debt to total assets ratio, the more equity "buffer" there is available to creditors if the company becomes insolvent. So, from a creditor's point of view, a low ratio of debt to total assets is desirable.

Helpful hint A popular variant of this ratio is the debt to equity ratio. It is calculated by dividing total debt by shareholders' equity. It compares the percentage of assets provided by creditors to that provided by shareholders.

Hometown Tires and More's 2002 and 2001 ratios, and comparative data, are shown in Illustration 18A-7.

Illustration 18A-7 ◄

Debt to total assets

$$\text{Debt to total assets} = \frac{\text{Total liabilities}}{\text{Total assets}}$$

Hometown Tires and More

2002	2001
$\dfrac{\$737,700}{\$1,000,000} = 73.8\%$	$\dfrac{\$788,500}{\$1,000,000} = 78.9\%$

Industry Average	Canadian Tire
38%	56.8%

A ratio of 73.8% means that creditors have provided 73.8% of Hometown Tires and More's total assets. Conversely, shareholders have financed 26.2% (100% − 73.8%) of the total assets. Although its ratio improved in 2002, Hometown Tires and More's debt to total assets ratio is significantly higher than Canadian Tire's 56.8%, and that of the industry, 38%.

However, as mentioned in the chapter, Hometown Tires and More does not have access to the equity markets since it is privately owned. Consequently, it is not surprising that it relies on debt financing. The more relevant calculation is whether or not it can afford this level of debt. The debt to total assets ratio should never be interpreted without reference to the interest coverage ratio. A company may have a low debt to total assets ratio but be unable to cover its interest payments. Alternatively, a company may have a high debt to total assets ratio but easily be able to cover its interest payments.

Interest Coverage

The interest coverage ratio provides an indication of the company's ability to meet interest payments as they come due. It is calculated by dividing income before interest expense and income tax expense by interest expense. Note that the interest coverage ratio uses income before interest expense and income tax expense. This is often abbreviated as EBIT, which stands for earnings before interest and tax. EBIT represents the amount available to cover interest.

Alternative terminology
The interest coverage ratio is also called the *times interest earned ratio*.

The 2001 and 2000 ratios for Hometown Tires and More, and comparative data, are shown in Illustration 18A-8.

$$\text{Interest coverage} = \frac{\text{Net income} + \text{interest expense} + \text{income tax expense}}{\text{Interest expense}}$$

Hometown Tires and More

2002	2001
$\dfrac{\$82,000 + \$36,000 + \$50,000}{\$36,000} = 4.7$ times	$\dfrac{\$75,000 + \$40,500 + \$52,500}{\$40,500} = 4.2$ times
Industry Average 11.7 times	Canadian Tire 4.8 times

Despite Hometown Tires and More's high debt to total assets ratio, it is able to cover its interest payments. Its income before interest and taxes was 4.7 times the amount needed for interest expense in 2002. Hometown Tires and More's interest coverage improved slightly in 2002, although it is still below that of Canadian Tire at 4.8 times and that of the industry at 11.7 times.

Free Cash Flow

One indication of a company's solvency, as well as of its ability to pay additional dividends or to expand operations, is the amount of excess cash it generates after investing to maintain its current productive capacity and paying current dividends. This amount is referred to as free cash flow.

The cash flow statement was not presented in the chapter for Hometown Tires and More. The additional information necessary to calculate free cash flow is as follows:

	2002	2001
Net cash provided by operating activities	$86,200	$80,000
Net capital expenditures	0	0
Dividends	31,200	30,000

Hometown Tires and More's free cash flow figures for 2002 and 2001, and comparative data, are shown in Illustration 18A-9.

Free cash flow = Cash provided (used) by operating activities − Net capital expenditures − Dividends paid

Hometown Tires and More

2002	2001
$86,200 − $0 − $31,200 = $55,000	$80,000 − $0 − $30,000 = $50,000
Industry Average n/a	Canadian Tire $194.6 million

Hometown Tires and More has "free" cash to invest in additional property, plant, and equipment and to pay its dividends. Still, Canadian Tire's sheer size and national coverage allow it to generate cash at a much faster rate than Hometown Tires and More can. There is no comparable industry average available for free cash flow. And, as noted previously, it is difficult to meaningfully compare absolute dollar amounts for two companies of such different sizes.

Solvency Conclusion

In an intracompany comparison, all of Hometown Tires and More's ratios improved in 2002. Although improvement was apparent within the company, in intercompany and industry comparisons, Hometown Tires and More's solvency was significantly lower than that of Canadian Tire and the industry.

It is important to distinguish between Hometown Tires and More and Canadian Tire in this analysis, as they are very different types of companies. Hometown Tires and More, as a small, privately held company, relies primarily on debt for its financing and has to generate sufficient income to cover its interest payments. In contrast, Canadian Tire, a large public company, relies more on equity for its financing needs. In addition to having to cover interest payments on its debt, Canadian Tire also has to cover dividend payments to meet its shareholders' expectations. Hometown Tires and More has more choice about when to make dividend payments.

Profitability Ratios

Profitability ratios measure the income or operating success of a company for a specific period of time. Income, or the lack of it, affects the company's ability to obtain debt and equity financing. It also affects the company's liquidity position and its ability to grow. Consequently, both creditors and investors are interested in evaluating earning power (profitability). Profitability is frequently used as the ultimate test of management's operating effectiveness. Profitability ratios include the gross profit margin, profit margin, asset turnover, return on assets, return on equity, earnings per share, price-earnings, payout, and EBITDA ratios.

Gross Profit Margin

The gross profit margin is determined by dividing gross profit (net sales less cost of goods sold) by net sales. This ratio indicates a company's ability to maintain an adequate selling price above its cost of goods sold. Gross profit margins should be closely monitored over time.

Hometown Tires and More's gross profit margin figures for 2002 and 2001, and comparative data, are shown in Illustration 18A-10.

Illustration 18A-10 ◀

Gross profit margin

$$\text{Gross profit margin} = \frac{\text{Gross profit}}{\text{Net sales}}$$

Hometown Tires and More

2002	2001
$\frac{\$616,000}{\$1,997,000} = 30.8\%$	$\frac{\$597,000}{\$1,837,000} = 32.5\%$

Industry Average	Canadian Tire
23.5%	n/a

Hometown Tires and More's gross profit margin for 2002 means that 30.8 cents of each dollar of its sales that year went to cover operating expenses and generate a profit. Hometown Tires and More's gross profit margin declined slightly, from 32.5% in 2001 to 30.8% in 2002.

As we mentioned earlier in the inventory section, Canadian Tire does not separately disclose its cost of goods sold or gross profit. Consequently, the gross profit margin cannot be calculated for Canadian Tire.

Hometown Tires and More's gross profit margin is higher than the industry average of 23.5%. This could be the result of several factors. It may be that Hometown Tires and More sells a higher quality of merchandise than do Canadian Tire and other competitors. In addition, prices may be higher in general not only because of increased costs, but also because the company offers a higher level of personal service.

Profit Margin

Alternative terminology
Profit margin is also called the *return on sales*.

Profit margin is a measure of the percentage of each dollar of sales that results in net income. It is calculated by dividing net income by net sales. Hometown Tires and More's profit margin figures, and comparative data, are shown in Illustration 18A-11.

Illustration 18A-11 ▶

Profit margin

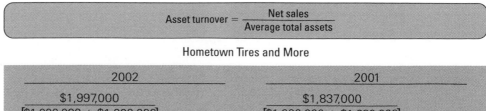

$$\text{Profit margin} = \frac{\text{Net income}}{\text{Net sales}}$$

Hometown Tires and More

2002	2001
$\dfrac{\$82,000}{\$1,997,000} = 4.1\%$	$\dfrac{\$75,000}{\$1,837,000} = 4.1\%$
Industry Average	Canadian Tire
3.3%	3.4%

Hometown Tires and More's profit margin is unchanged from 2001 to 2002, at 4.1% of net sales. It is higher than that of Canadian Tire and the industry. This is consistent with the gross profit margin analysed above. There we speculated that Hometown Tires and More may sell higher quality merchandise, with higher prices and higher margins, than large box stores such as Canadian Tire and others in the industry.

Asset Turnover

Asset turnover measures how efficiently a company uses its assets to generate sales. It is determined by dividing net sales by average total assets. The resulting number shows the dollars of sales produced by each dollar of assets. Assuming that total assets at the beginning of 2001 were $1.09 million, the 2002 and 2001 asset turnover ratios for Hometown Tires and More, and comparative data, are shown in Illustration 18A-12.

Illustration 18A-12 ▶

Asset turnover

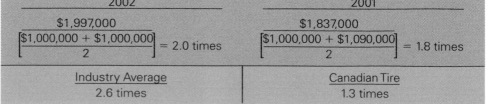

$$\text{Asset turnover} = \frac{\text{Net sales}}{\text{Average total assets}}$$

Hometown Tires and More

2002	2001
$\dfrac{\$1,997,000}{\left[\dfrac{\$1,000,000 + \$1,000,000}{2}\right]} = 2.0 \text{ times}$	$\dfrac{\$1,837,000}{\left[\dfrac{\$1,000,000 + \$1,090,000}{2}\right]} = 1.8 \text{ times}$
Industry Average	Canadian Tire
2.6 times	1.3 times

In 2002, Hometown Tires and More generated $2 of sales for each dollar it had invested in assets. This ratio improved from 2001, when its asset turnover was 1.8 times, or $1.80 of sales for each dollar of assets. Although its 2002 asset turnover is below that of the industry, it is higher than Canadian Tire's asset turnover of 1.3 times.

Return on Assets

An overall measure of profitability is return on assets. This ratio is calculated by dividing net income by average total assets. Hometown Tires and More's return on assets figures for 2002 and 2001, and comparative data, are shown in Illustration 18A-13.

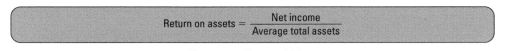

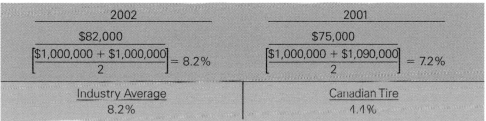

Illustration 18A-13 ◄
Return on assets

Hometown Tires and More's return on assets improved from 2001 to 2002. Its 2002 return of 8.2% is comparable to the industry average. However, it is high in comparison to Canadian Tire's return of 4.4%. Although the percentage is high, it must be analysed in perspective. Hometown Tire and More's earnings improved, and they were strong to begin with. However, they are being compared to a relatively small asset base, so small dollar increases result in large percentage increases.

The return on assets can be further analysed by looking at the profit margin and asset turnover ratios in combination, as shown in Illustration 18A-14.

	Return on Assets		Profit Margin		Asset Turnover
	$\dfrac{\text{Net income}}{\text{Average total assets}}$	=	$\dfrac{\text{Net income}}{\text{Net sales}}$	×	$\dfrac{\text{Net sales}}{\text{Average total assets}}$
2002	8.2%	=	4.1%	×	2.0 times
2001	7.2%	=	4.1%	×	1.76 times

Illustration 18A-14 ◄
Composition of return on assets

With a rounded figure, the calculation for the year 2001 does not work out precisely. If we use Hometown Tires and More's unrounded asset turnover amount of 1.76, instead of the rounded amount of 1.8, we can prove the calculation.

From this breakdown of the return on assets, we learn that Hometown Tires and More's increase in its return on assets has been driven by the improved asset turnover. That is, the sales generating efficiency of Hometown Tires and More's assets improved, which resulted in an improved return on assets. The profitability of each dollar of sales remained unchanged.

Return on Equity

A widely used measure of profitability from the shareholders' viewpoint is the return on equity ratio. This ratio shows how many dollars of net income were earned for each dollar invested by the shareholders. It is calculated by dividing net income by average total

Alternative terminology
Return on equity is also known as *return on investment*.

shareholders' equity. Although we calculate this ratio using total shareholders' equity, it can also be calculated using only the common shareholders' equity if more than one class of shares exists. In such cases, net income is reduced by any preferred dividends to determine the income available for common shareholders. The denominator is the average common shareholders' equity.

Assuming that total shareholders' equity at the beginning of 2001 was $166,500, the return on equity figures for Hometown Tires and More for 2002 and 2001, and comparative data, are shown in Illustration 18A-15.

Illustration 18A-15 ▶

Return on equity

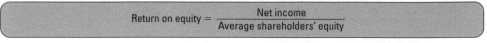

$$\text{Return on equity} = \frac{\text{Net income}}{\text{Average shareholders' equity}}$$

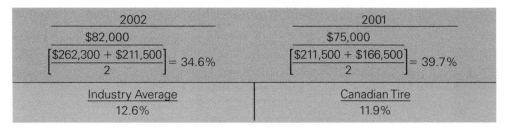

Hometown Tires and More

2002	2001
$82,000	$75,000
$\left[\dfrac{\$262,300 + \$211,500}{2}\right] = 34.6\%$	$\left[\dfrac{\$211,500 + \$166,500}{2}\right] = 39.7\%$
Industry Average	Canadian Tire
12.6%	11.9%

Although declining in 2002, Hometown Tires and More's return on equity is unusually high at 34.6%. The return on equity figures for Canadian Tire and the industry are much lower at 11.9% and 12.6%, respectively.

Note that Hometown Tires and More's 2002 return on equity (34.6%) is much higher than its return on assets (8.2%). The reason is that Hometown Tires and More has made effective use of leveraging, or trading on the equity. Trading on the equity means that the company can earn a higher rate of interest by using borrowed money in its operations than it has to pay on the borrowed money. This enables Hometown Tires and More to use money supplied by creditors to increase the return to the shareholders.

A comparison of the rate of return on total assets to the rate of interest paid for borrowed money indicates the profitability of trading on the equity. Note, however, that trading on the equity is a two-way street. For example, if you borrow money at 7% and earn only 4% on it, you're trading on the equity at a loss rather than a gain. Hometown Tires and More earns more on its borrowed funds than it has to pay in the form of interest. Thus, the return to shareholders exceeds the return on assets, which indicates that shareholders are benefiting from positive leveraging or trading on the equity.

Earnings Per Share (EPS)

Earnings per share is a measure of the net income earned on each common share. It is calculated by dividing the net income available to common shareholders (net income − preferred dividends) by the weighted average number of common shares.

Shareholders usually think in terms of the number of shares they own or plan to buy or sell. Reducing net income to a per share basis provides a useful measure of profitability. This measure is widely used and reported. Because of the importance of the earnings per share ratio, most companies are required to present it directly on the income statement.

Hometown Tires and More has 30,000 common shares issued. There has been no change in this number over the past three years, so the weighted average number of shares is the same. As mentioned previously, Hometown Tires and More's shares are not traded publicly and have a very limited ownership market. The earnings per share figures for Hometown Tires and More for 2002 and 2001, and comparative data, are shown in Illustration 18A-16.

$$\text{Earnings per share} = \frac{\text{Net income} - \text{Preferred dividends}}{\text{Weighted average number of common shares}}$$

Hometown Tires and More

2002	2001
$\dfrac{\$82,000 - \$0}{30,000} = \$2.73$	$\dfrac{\$75,000 - \$0}{30,000} = \$2.50$
Industry Average	Canadian Tire
$1.70	$2.56

Hometown Tires and More's earnings per share increased by $0.23 per share in 2002. This represents a 9% increase over the 2001 earnings per share figure of $2.50. Comparisons to the industry average or Canadian Tire are not meaningful, because of the wide variations in the number of shares among companies. The only meaningful EPS comparison is an intracompany one.

Price-Earnings (PE) Ratio

The price-earnings (PE) ratio is an often-quoted measure of the ratio of the market price of each common share to the earnings per share. The price-earnings ratio reflects investors' assessments of a company's future earnings. It is calculated by dividing the market price per share by earnings per share. Assuming that the market price of Hometown Tires and More's common shares was $5 in both 2002 and 2001, the price-earnings ratios, and comparative data, are shown in Illustration 18A-17.

$$\text{Price-earnings ratio} = \frac{\text{Market price per share}}{\text{Earnings per share}}$$

Hometown Tires and More

2002	2001
$\dfrac{\$5}{\$2.73} = 1.8$ times	$\dfrac{\$5}{\$2.50} = 2.0$ times
Industry Average	Canadian Tire
27.2 times	12.7 times

In 2002, Hometown Tires and More's shares traded at 1.8 times their earnings. This ratio is really not meaningful for Hometown Tires and More, given the restricted trading market for the shares. Hometown Tires and More is a family-owned, privately held company. Its shares are not available to the general public for sale.

Canadian Tire's price-earnings ratio is 12.7 times, which is lower than the industry average of 27.2 times.

In general, a higher price-earnings ratio means that investors favour the company. They are willing to pay more for the shares because they anticipate the company has good prospects for growth and income in the future.

Some investors carefully study price-earnings ratios over time to help them determine when to buy or sell shares. If the highs and lows of a particular share's PE ratio remain constant over several stock market cycles, then these highs and lows can indicate selling and buying points for the shares. They could also mean other things, however, so investors should be very cautious in interpreting PE ratios.

Payout Ratio

The payout ratio measures the percentage of earnings distributed as cash dividends. It is calculated by dividing cash dividends by net income. The 2002 and 2001 payout ratios for Hometown Tires and More, and comparative data, are shown in Illustration 18A-18.

Illustration 18A-18 ▶

Payout ratio

$$\text{Payout ratio} = \frac{\text{Cash dividends}}{\text{Net income}}$$

Hometown Tires and More

2002	2001
$\dfrac{\$31,200}{\$82,000} = 38.0\%$	$\dfrac{\$30,000}{\$75,000} = 40.0\%$
Industry Average	Canadian Tire
15.3%	15.6%

Helpful hint Companies must be cautious about changing their payout ratio too dramatically. Why? Because shareholders buy and hold shares based on the company's historical and expected dividend-paying practices.

Hometown Tires and More's 2002 payout ratio of 38% is more than double the payout ratio of Canadian Tire and the industry. Once again, recall that Hometown Tires and More is a private company, and has discretion as to how much it pays in dividends. It is likely that dividends are high because they are part of management's compensation.

Many companies with stable earnings have high payout ratios. For example, BCE Inc. currently has a 52% payout ratio. Companies that are expanding rapidly normally have low, or no, payout ratios. Research in Motion, for example, has a zero payout ratio.

Earnings Before Interest, Taxes, Depreciation, and Amortization (EBITDA)

An important cash-based measure of profitability is EBITDA, which is an abbreviation for earnings before interest, tax, and depreciation and amortization expenses. Depreciation is the same as amortization for our purposes, although distinctions are made between depreciation and amortization in other countries.

Hometown Tires and More's amortization expense of $60,000 in 2002 and 2001 is combined with its operating expenses in Illustration 18-4 in the chapter. The company's EBITDA figures for 2002 and 2001, and comparative data, are shown in Illustration 18A-19.

Illustration 18A-19 ▶

EBITDA

EBITDA = Net income + Interest expense + Income tax expense + Amortization expense

Hometown Tires and More

2002	2001
$ 82,000	$ 75,000
36,000	40,500
50,000	52,500
60,000	60,000
$228,000	$228,000
Industry Average	Canadian Tire
n/a	$547.7 million

Although Hometown Tires and More's net income improved in 2002, its cash-based earnings, EBITDA, is unchanged. EBITDA is a measure preferred by many creditors because it eliminates the accrual-based effects of many accounting and financing decisions.

Canadian Tire's EBITDA of $547.7 million is much higher than that of Hometown Tires and More. As noted previously, it is difficult to compare absolute numbers for two companies of such different sizes. There is no industry average available for this number.

Profitability Conclusion

In an intracompany comparison, except for the gross profit margin and return on equity, Hometown Tires and More's profitability measures generally improved or remained relatively constant from 2001 to 2002. Some of its market-based ratios declined, such as the price-earnings and payout ratios. However, these ratios have little interpretive value because of the restricted trading of Hometown Tires and More's shares. We therefore ignore these market-based ratios in our intercompany and industry comparisons.

In an intercompany comparison, Hometown Tires and More's profitability measures exceeded those of Canadian Tire. In an industry comparison, Hometown Tires and More's profitability generally exceeded that of the industry except for its asset turnover ratio, which was lower. However, its return on assets ratio was comparable because of its higher profit margin.

Demonstration Problem

The condensed financial statements of Molson Inc. for the years 1999 to 2002, vertically analysed, are presented below:

Additional
Demonstration
Problems

MOLSON INC. Percentage Balance Sheet March 31	2002	2001	2000	1999
Assets				
Current assets	11.1%	11.1%	13.9%	11.4%
Current assets of discontinued operations	0.2%	2.1%	0.6%	4.2%
Noncurrent assets	88.0%	77.0%	84.8%	81.2%
Noncurrent assets of discontinued operations	0.7%	9.8%	0.7%	3.2%
Total assets	100.0%	100.0%	100.0%	100.0%
Liabilities and Shareholders' Equity				
Current liabilities	19.3%	17.5%	19.0%	15.0%
Current liabilities of discontinued operations	0.0%	1.4%	0.2%	4.1%
Noncurrent liabilities	52.4%	52.1%	46.0%	45.3%
Noncurrent liabilities of discontinued operations	2.3%	4.8%	1.8%	3.4%
Total liabilities	74.0%	75.8%	67.0%	67.8%
Shareholders' equity	26.0%	24.2%	33.0%	32.2%
Total liabilities and shareholders' equity	100.0%	100.0%	100.0%	100.0%

MOLSON INC. Percentage Income Statement Year Ended March 31				
	2002	2001	2000	1999
Sales and other revenues	100.0%	100.0%	100.0%	100.0%
Costs and expenses	87.8%	89.5%	104.0%	96.0%
Income (loss) before income taxes	12.2%	10.5%	(4.0%)	4.0%
Income tax expense (recovery)	3.8%	3.1%	(0.3%)	2.3%
Income (loss) from continuing operations	8.4%	7.4%	(3.7%)	1.7%
Income (loss) from discontinued operations	0.0%	(0.2%)	1.4%	9.0%
Net income (loss)	8.4%	7.2%	(2.3%)	10.7%

Instructions

Analyse the significant changes between 1999 and 2002 for Molson.

Action Plan

- Exclude the impact of irregular items in your analysis.
- Look at the percentage comparisons both vertically (within the year) and horizontally (across the years).

Solution to Demonstration Problem

Current assets increased in 2000, and then declined substantially in 2001 before stabilizing in 2002. Molson's current liabilities are a higher percentage of total assets than are its current assets. Current liabilities have generally been increasing, except for in 2001. Except for during that same year, 2001, Molson's noncurrent assets have also been increasing as a percentage of total assets. Noncurrent liabilities have been increasing steadily.

Molson's liquidity and solvency appear to be declining over the four years, with increasing percentages of liabilities. We would have to perform further analyses (e.g., ratio analysis) to determine the reasons for this decline.

In terms of profitability, Molson appears to be controlling its expenses, which have declined, except in 2000. Except for this same year, its profitability (income from continuing operations) also appears to be on the increase.

It is interesting to note the impact that discontinued operations have on Molson's financial position. While these should be excluded from our comparative analysis, one might question whether they are a nonrecurring item or not since discontinued operations appear to be the norm over the last four years rather than the exception. However, except for in 1999, the discontinued operations have not significantly impacted Molson's profitability.

Summary of Study Objectives

1. **Discuss the need for comparative analysis.** Comparative analysis is performed to evaluate a company's liquidity, solvency, and profitability. Comparisons can detect changes in financial relationships and significant trends, and provide insight into a company's competitiveness and relative position in its industry. There are three bases of comparison: (1) intracompany, which compares an item or financial relationship to other data within a company; (2) intercompany, which compares an item or financial relationship of a company to data of one or more competing companies; (3) industry, which compares company data to industry averages.

2. **Explain and apply horizontal analysis.** Horizontal analysis is a technique for evaluating a series of data over

a period of time. The increase or decrease that has taken place is determined, and expressed as either an amount or a percentage.

3. **Explain and apply vertical analysis.** Vertical analysis is a technique for expressing each item within a financial statement as a percentage of a relevant total (base amount).

4. **Identify and calculate ratios and describe their purpose and use in analysing a company's liquidity, profitability, and solvency.** The formula and purpose of each ratio are presented in Illustrations 18-10 (liquidity), 18-11 (solvency), and 18-12 (profitability).

5. *Recognize and illustrate the limitations of financial statement analysis.* The usefulness of analytical tools is limited by the cost basis of accounting, the use of estimates, the application of alternative accounting principles, the quality of earnings, irregular revenues and expenses, and the diversification of companies.

6. *Understand the concept of earning power, and illustrate how irregular items are presented.* Earning power is net income adjusted for irregular, or atypical,

items. Two examples of irregular items are discontinued operations and extraordinary items. Discontinued operations relate to the disposal of an identifiable business segment. Extraordinary items are events and transactions that are infrequent, atypical, and not at the discretion of management. Irregular items such as these are presented on the income statement, net of tax, below "Income from continuing operations" to highlight their infrequent nature.

Glossary

Key Term Matching Activity

Discontinued operations The disposal of an identifiable segment of a business. (p. 870)

Earning power Net income adjusted for irregular, or atypical, items. (p. 870)

Extraordinary items Events and transactions that meet three conditions: (1) infrequent in occurrence, (2) unusual in nature, and (3) not the result of a management decision. (p. 871)

Horizontal analysis A technique for evaluating a series of financial statement data over a period of time to determine the increase (decrease) that has taken place. This increase (decrease) is expressed as either an amount or a percentage. (p. 858)

Identifiable business segment A division or part of a company that can be clearly distinguished, for finan-

cial reporting and operating purposes, from the rest of the company. (p. 870)

Liquidity ratios Measures of the short-term ability of a company to pay its maturing obligations and to meet unexpected needs for cash. (p. 866)

Profitability ratios Measures of the operating success of a company for a specific period of time. (p. 867)

Ratio analysis A technique for evaluating financial statements that expresses the relationship between selected financial statement data. (p. 865)

Solvency ratios Measures of a company's ability to survive over a long period of time. (p. 866)

Vertical analysis A technique for evaluating financial statement data that expresses each item within a financial statement as a percentage of the base amount. (p. 862)

Self-Study Questions

Chapter 18 Self-Test

Answers are at the end of the chapter.

(SO 1) K 1. Comparisons of data within a company are an example of the following comparative basis:
(a) Industry averages   (c) Intercompany
(b) Intracompany   (d) Both (b) and (c)

(SO 2) K 2. In horizontal analysis, each item is expressed as a percentage of the:
(a) net sales amount.
(b) shareholders' equity amount.
(c) total assets amount.
(d) base year amount.

(SO 2) AP 3. Rankin Inlet Corporation reported net sales of $300,000, $330,000, and $360,000 in the years 2004, 2005, and 2006, respectively. If 2004 is the base year, what is the trend percentage for 2006?
(a) 77%   (c) 120%
(b) 108%   (d) 130%

(SO 3) K 4. The following schedule is a display of what type of analysis?

	Amount	Percentage
Current assets	$200,000	25%
Long-lived assets	600,000	75%
Total assets	$800,000	100%

(a) Horizontal analysis   (c) Vertical analysis
(b) Differential analysis   (d) Ratio analysis

5. Which of the following is not a liquidity ratio? **(SO 4) K**
(a) Current ratio   (c) Inventory turnover
(b) Asset turnover   (d) Receivables turnover

6. Which of the following situations would be the most likely indicator that Wang Corporation might have a solvency problem? **(SO 4) AN**
(a) Increasing debt to total assets and interest coverage ratios
(b) Increasing debt to total assets and decreasing interest coverage ratios
(c) Decreasing debt to total assets and interest coverage ratios
(d) Decreasing debt to total assets and increasing interest coverage ratios

(SO 4) AN 7. Which of the following situations is a likely indicator of profitability?
- (a) An increasing price-earnings ratio
- (b) Increasing return on assets, asset turnover, and profit margin ratios
- (c) Decreasing return on equity and payout ratios
- (d) A decreasing gross profit margin and increasing profit margin

(SO 5) K 8. Which of the following is generally not considered to be a limitation of financial analysis?
- (a) Use of estimates
- (b) Use of non-financial performance measures
- (c) Use of cost
- (d) Use of alternative accounting principles

(SO 6) K 9. In reporting discontinued operations, a special section in the income statement should show:

- (a) gains and losses on disposal of the discontinued segment.
- (b) gains and losses from operations of the discontinued segment.
- (c) neither (a) nor (b).
- (d) both (a) and (b).

(SO 6) AP 10. The Dhillon Corporation has net income of $400,000, including a pre-tax extraordinary loss of $125,000. If the income tax rate is 20%, the income statement should show income before and after extraordinary items, respectively, of:
- (a) $300,000 and $400,000.
- (b) $375,000 and $300,000.
- (c) $415,000 and $400,000.
- (d) $500,000 and $400,000.

Questions

(SO 1) C 1. (a) Distinguish among the following bases of comparison: (1) intracompany, (2) intercompany, and (3) industry averages.
(b) Give the principal value of using each of the three bases of comparison individually and together.

(SO 2, 3) C 2. Two methods of financial statement analysis are horizontal analysis and vertical analysis. Explain the difference between these two methods.

(SO 4) K 3. What do the following classes of ratios measure: (a) liquidity ratios, (b) profitability ratios, and (c) solvency ratios?

(SO 4) AN 4. Is a high current ratio always indicative of a company's liquidity? Describe two situations in which a high current ratio might be hiding liquidity problems.

(SO 4) AN 5. Aubut Corporation, a retail store, has a receivables turnover of 4.5 times. The industry average is 6.5 times. Does Aubut have a collection problem with its receivables?

(SO 4) C 6. Loren Foelske is puzzled. His company had a gross profit margin of 40% and a profit margin of 10% in 2005. He feels that this is an indication that the company is doing well. Joan Graham, his accountant, says that more information is needed to determine the firm's financial well-being. Who is correct? Why?

(SO 4) AN 7. Recently, the price-earnings ratio of the **Bank of Nova Scotia** was 11.8 times. The price-earnings ratio of the **Bank of Montreal** was 14.6 times. Which company did investors favour? Explain.

(SO 4) C 8. Which ratio should be used to help answer each of the following questions?
- (a) How efficient is a company at using its assets to produce sales?
- (b) How near to sale is the inventory on hand?
- (c) How many dollars of net income were earned for each dollar invested by the owners?

- (d) How able is a company to meet interest charges as they come due?

(SO 4) AN 9. If you were an investor interested in buying the shares of a company with growth potential, would you look for a company that had high or low price-earnings and payout ratios? If you were interested in buying the shares of a company with income potential, would your answer change? Explain why.

(SO 4) AN 10. Laser Corp.'s cash provided by operating activities in 2005 was double the amount in 2004, but its free cash flow in 2005 was one-half the amount in 2004. Discuss whether or not the decline in free cash flow indicates a decline in the company's solvency.

(SO 4) AN 11. In an effort to increase its profitability, Medicine Hat Inc. revised its sales strategy by reducing the selling price of its merchandise. The result was that sales and net income both increased but the gross profit margin and profit margin both decreased. Discuss whether the president of Medicine Hat Inc. should be concerned about the deterioration in these ratios.

(SO 4) C 12. The return on total assets for Windsor Corporation is 7.6%. During the same year, Windsor's return on equity is 12.8%. What is the explanation for the difference in the two ratios?

(SO 4) C 13. Which two ratios do you think should be of greatest interest in each of the following cases?
- (a) A pension fund considering the purchase of 20-year bonds
- (b) A bank contemplating a short-term loan
- (c) A common shareholder evaluating her investment

(SO 4) C 14. (a) What is meant by trading on the equity?
(b) How would you determine the profitability of trading on the equity?

(SO 5) C 15. Identify and briefly explain the limitations of financial analysis.

(SO 5) AN 16. Give an example of how management might deliberately try to increase income by changing an accounting estimate. How would this affect the quality of the earnings reported?

(SO 5) AP 17. Explain how the choice of one of the following accounting principles over the other raises or lowers a company's net income:
 (a) Use of FIFO instead of average for the inventory cost flow assumption during a period of continuing inflation (rising prices)
 (b) Use of a three-year life for machinery instead of a five-year life
 (c) Use of straight-line amortization instead of declining-balance amortization

(SO 5, 6) C 18. In 2004, Lai Inc. reported a profit margin of 5% before discontinued operations and a profit margin of 8% after discontinued operations. In 2005, the company had no discontinued operations and reported a profit margin of 8%. Has Lai's profit margin improved, deteriorated, or remained constant? Explain.

19. Explain the concept of earning power. What relationship does this concept have to the treatment of irregular items on the income statement? (SO 6) C

20. Why is it important to report discontinued operations and extraordinary items separately from income from continuing operations? (SO 6) C

21. ANR Coal Corp. suffered a significant loss as a result of an unusually difficult and lengthy labour strike during the last fiscal year. The president wants to report this loss as an extraordinary item. Explain whether or not this is appropriate. (SO 6) C

Brief Exercises

BE18–1 Using the following data from the comparative balance sheet of Rioux Ltd. as at December 31, prepare a horizontal analysis:

Prepare horizontal analysis.
(SO 2) AP

	2005	2004
Cash	$ 150,000	$ 175,000
Accounts receivable	600,000	400,000
Inventory	780,000	600,000
Noncurrent assets	3,220,000	2,800,000

BE18–2 Horizontal analysis percentages for Tilden Ltd.'s sales, cost of goods sold, and operating expenses are shown below:

Use horizontal analysis to determine change in net income.
(SO 2) AP

	2005	2004	2003
Sales	96.2%	106.8%	100.0%
Cost of goods sold	102.0	97.0	100.0
Operating expenses	110.6	95.4	100.0

Did Tilden's net income increase, decrease, or remain unchanged over the three-year period? Explain.

BE18–3 Using the same data presented earlier in BE18–1 for Rioux Ltd., prepare a vertical analysis for both years.

Prepare vertical analysis.
(SO 3) AP

BE18–4 Vertical analysis percentages for Waubons Corp.'s sales, cost of goods sold, and operating expenses are shown below:

Use vertical analysis to determine change in net income.
(SO 3) AP

	2005	2004	2003
Sales	100.0%	100.0%	100.0%
Cost of goods sold	59.2	62.4	64.5
Operating expenses	25.0	26.6	27.5

Did Waubons' net income as a percentage of sales increase, decrease, or remain unchanged over the three-year period? Explain

Calculate liquidity ratios.
(SO 4) AP

BE18–5 Topps Company, Inc. is a trading-card and bubble gum company, whose products are sold in more than 50 countries. Selected data taken from the financial statements are as follows (in U.S. thousands):

	March 1, 2003	March 2, 2002
Current assets	$183,743	$183,572
Total assets	261,628	257,950
Current liabilities	42,259	47,183
Total liabilities	64,860	63,896

Calculate (a) the working capital and (b) the current ratio for both years. Did these ratios improve or deteriorate over fiscal 2003?

Evaluate management of accounts receivable.
(SO 4) AN

BE18–6 The following data are taken from **Maple Leaf Foods Inc.'s** financial statements

MAPLE LEAF FOODS INC.
December 31
(in thousands)

	2002	2001	2000
Accounts receivable	$ 243,121	$ 248,064	$ 246,966
Sales (assume on account)	5,075,879	4,775,358	3,943,289

Calculate for each of 2002 and 2001 (a) the receivables turnover and (b) the collection period. Assume terms for all sales are n/45. What conclusion about the management of accounts receivable can be drawn from these data?

Evaluate management of inventory.
(SO 4) AN

BE18–7 The following data are taken from the income statements of Shumway Ltd.:

	2005	2004
Sales	$6,420,000	$6,240,000
Cost of goods sold	4,540,000	4,538,000
Beginning inventory	960,000	837,000
Ending inventory	1,020,000	960,000

Calculate for each year (a) the inventory turnover, and (b) the days sales in inventory. What conclusion concerning the management of the inventory can be drawn from these data?

Calculate profitability ratios.
(SO 4) AP

BE18–8 Staples, Inc. is a large supplier of office products in Canada, the U.S., the UK, Germany, the Netherlands, and Portugal. The company had net income of US$446.1 million and net revenue of US$11,596.1 million for the year ended January 31, 2003. Its total assets were US$5,721.4 million at the beginning of the year and US$4,093.0 million at the end of the year. What are Staples' (a) asset turnover ratio and (b) profit margin ratio?

Calculate solvency ratios.
(SO 4) AP

BE18–9 The Jean Coutu Group Inc. is one of the top three drugstore chains in Canada. Selected financial data (in thousands) are available for the year ended May 31, 2003:

Net income	$ 163,622
Interest expense	25,488
Income tax expense	71,373
Amortization expense	56,293
Total liabilities	703,698
Total assets	1,723,567
Net cash provided by operating activities	213,595
Dividends	27,134
Net capital expenditures	149,603

Calculate the following: (a) debt to total assets, (b) interest coverage, (c) free cash flow, and (d) EBITDA.

Evaluate impact of ratio change.
(SO 4) AN

BE18–10 Assuming all other factors are constant, indicate whether each of the following changes generally signals positive or negative news about a company:

(a) An increase in the profit margin
(b) A decrease in the inventory turnover
(c) An increase in the current ratio
(d) A decrease in the earnings per share
(e) An increase in the price-earnings ratio
(f) An increase in debt to total assets
(g) A decrease in interest coverage

BE18–11 Indicate which of the following items would be reported as an extraordinary item on Thought for Food Corporation's income statement. If the item cannot be reported as an extraordinary item, state which condition or conditions have not been met.

Classify income statement items.
(SO 6) AP

(a) A loss from the sale of short-term investments
(b) A loss due to a labour strike
(c) A loss caused when the Canadian Food Inspection Agency prohibited the manufacture and sale of a product
(d) A loss of inventory from flood damage to a warehouse located on a flood plain that floods every few years
(e) A loss on the write-down of outdated inventory
(f) A loss from a foreign government's expropriation of a production facility
(g) A loss from damage to a warehouse from a minor earthquake

BE18–12 Osborn Corporation discontinued a business segment of its operations in Mexico in 2005. The operating loss from these operations was $300,000 before income tax. The loss on the disposal of these operations was $160,000 before income tax. Osborn's income before income tax was $950,000. The applicable tax rate is 35%. Prepare a partial income statement for Osborn, starting with income before income tax, for the year ended December 31, 2005.

Prepare discontinued operations section.
(SO 6) AP

BE18–13 An inexperienced accountant for Lima Corporation showed the following in Lima's 2005 income statement: income before income taxes and extraordinary item, $300,000, and extraordinary loss from flood (before taxes), $60,000. The extraordinary loss and taxable income are both subject to a 25% tax rate. Prepare an income statement in good format for the year ended November 30, 2005.

Prepare extraordinary item section.
(SO 6) AP

Exercises

E18–1 Financial information for Dressaire Inc. as at December 31 is presented below:

Prepare horizontal analysis.
(SO 2) AP

	2005	2004
Current assets	$120,000	$ 80,000
Noncurrent assets	400,000	350,000
Current liabilities	91,000	70,000
Noncurrent liabilities	144,000	95,000
Common shares	150,000	115,000
Retained earnings	135,000	150,000

Instructions
Prepare a schedule showing a horizontal analysis for 2005, using 2004 as the base year.

E18–2 Operating data for Fleetwood Corporation are presented below:

Prepare vertical analysis.
(SO 3) AP

	2005	2004
Sales	$800,000	$600,000
Cost of goods sold	500,000	390,000
Operating expenses	200,000	156,000
Income tax expense	25,000	13,500
Net income	$ 75,000	$ 40,500

Instructions
Prepare a schedule showing a vertical analysis for the years ended December 31, 2005 and 2004.

Prepare horizontal and vertical analyses of income statement.
(SO 2, 3) AP

Interactive Homework

E18–3 Here are the comparative income statements of Olympic Corporation:

OLYMPIC CORPORATION
Income Statement
Year Ended December 31

	2005	2004
Net sales	$550,000	$550,000
Cost of goods sold	440,000	450,000
Gross profit	110,000	100,000
Operating expenses	58,000	55,000
Income before income tax	52,000	45,000
Income tax	20,800	18,000
Net income	$ 31,200	$ 27,000

Instructions

(a) Prepare a horizontal analysis of the income statement data for Olympic Corporation using 2004 as the base year.

(b) Prepare a vertical analysis of the income statement data for Olympic Corporation for both years.

Prepare horizontal and vertical analyses of balance sheet.
(SO 2, 3) AN

E18–4 The condensed comparative balance sheet of **Mountain Equipment Co-operative**, an outdoor equipment supplier, is presented here:

MOUNTAIN EQUIPMENT CO-OPERATIVE
Balance Sheet
December 31
(in thousands)

	2002	2001
Assets		
Current assets	$40,927	$38,729
Property, plant, and equipment	38,197	39,015
Other assets	417	0
Total assets	$79,541	$77,744
Liabilities and Members' Equity		
Current liabilities	$23,560	$25,110
Long-term liabilities	348	399
Total liabilities	23,908	25,509
Members' equity	55,633	52,235
Total liabilities and members' equity	$79,541	$77,744

Instructions

(a) Prepare a horizontal analysis of the balance sheet for Mountain Equipment Co-op using 2001 as the base year.

(b) Prepare a vertical analysis of the balance sheet data for Mountain Equipment Co-op for 2002 and 2001, using total assets as your base figure.

(c) Comment on any significant changes from 2001 to 2002.

E18–5 Nordstar, Inc. operates hardware stores in several provinces. Selected financial statement data for a recent year are as follows:

Calculate liquidity ratios and compare results.
(SO 4) AN

NORDSTAR, INC.
Balance Sheet (partial)
December 31
(in millions)

	2002	2001
Cash and cash equivalents	$ 30	$ 91
Accounts receivable	676	586
Merchandise inventory	628	586
Prepaid expenses	61	52
Total current assets	$1,395	$1,315
Total current liabilities	$ 710	$ 627

For the year, net credit sales were $3,894 million and the cost of goods sold was $2,600 million.

Instructions

(a) Calculate the liquidity ratios for 2002.
(b) Using the data in Appendix 18A, compare Nordstar's liquidity to the liquidity of (1) Canadian Tire Corporation, Limited, and (2) the industry averages for the retail-department store industry.

E18–6 The following selected ratios are available for Pampered Pets Inc. for the most recent three years:

Evaluate liquidity.
(SO 4) AN

Interactive Homework

	2004	2003	2002
Current ratio	2.6:1	1.4:1	2.1:1
Receivables turnover	6.7 times	7.4 times	8.2 times
Inventory turnover	7.5 times	8.7 times	9.9 times

Instructions

(a) Has the company's collection of its receivables improved or deteriorated over the last three years?
(b) Is the company selling its inventory faster or slower than in past years?
(c) Overall, has the company's liquidity improved or deteriorated over the last three years? Explain.

E18–7 Mwanaki Corp. has the following comparative balance sheet data at December 31:

Calculate ratios.
(SO 4) AP

Interactive Homework

MWANAKI CORP.
Balance Sheet
December 31

	2005	2004
Assets		
Cash	$ 20,000	$ 30,000
Receivables	65,000	60,000
Inventories	60,000	50,000
Property, plant, and equipment	200,000	180,000
	$345,000	$320,000
Liabilities and Shareholders' Equity		
Accounts payable	$ 50,000	$ 60,000
Mortgage payable	100,000	100,000
Common shares	140,000	120,000
Retained earnings	55,000	40,000
	$345,000	$320,000

Additional information for 2005:

1. Net income was $21,000.
2. Sales on account were $420,000. Sales returns and allowances were $20,000.
3. Cost of goods sold was $198,000.

Instructions

Calculate the following ratios at December 31, 2005:

(a) Current ratio	(f) Gross profit margin
(b) Receivables turnover	(g) Return on assets
(c) Collection period	(h) Return on equity
(d) Inventory turnover	(i) Asset turnover
(e) Days sales in inventory	(j) Debt to total assets

Calculate ratios.
(SO 4) AP

Interactive Homework

E18–8 Selected comparative financial data of Canada's #1 bookseller, **Indigo Books & Music Inc.**, are presented here (in thousands):

	March 31	
	2003	2002
Revenue	$779,244	$735,684
Amortization expense	23,894	31,378
Interest expense	14,797	14,358
Income tax expense	1,900	600
Net income	1,425	(47,912)
Total assets	394,777	439,832
Total shareholders' equity	90,364	63,830
Cash provided (used) by operating activities	50,394	(2,574)
Net capital expenditures	14,107	15,364
Dividends paid	0	0
Weighted average number of common shares	22,513	18,552

Instructions

Calculate the following ratios for 2003:

(a) Profit margin	(f) Debt to total assets
(b) Asset turnover	(g) Free cash flow
(c) Return on assets	(h) Earnings per share
(d) Return on equity	(i) EBITDA
(e) Interest coverage	(j) Payout

Calculate ratios.
(SO 4) AP

E18–9 The income statement for the year ended December 31, 2005, of LeFay, Inc., appears below:

LEFAY, INC.
Income Statement
Year Ended December 31, 2005

Sales	$425,000
Cost of goods sold	230,000
Gross profit	195,000
Expenses (including $35,000 amortization, $15,000 interest, and $36,000 income tax)	150,000
Net income	$ 45,000

Additional information:

1. Number of common shares, 30,000.
2. The market price of LeFay, Inc. shares was $15 at the end of 2005.
3. Cash dividends of $21,000 were paid.
4. Net cash provided by operating activities was $98,000.
5. Net capital expenditures were $60,000.

Instructions

Calculate the following ratios for 2005:

(a) Earnings per share	(e) Gross profit margin
(b) Price-earnings	(f) Interest coverage
(c) Payout	(g) EBITDA
(d) Profit margin	(h) Free cash flow

E18–10 Cougar Corporation experienced a fire on December 31, 2005, in which its financial records were partially destroyed. It salvaged some of the records and has figured out the following balances as at December 31:

Calculate amounts from ratios.
(SO 4) AP

	2005	2004
Cash	$ 30,000	$ 10,000
Receivables (net)	72,500	126,000
Inventory	200,000	180,000
Accounts payable	50,000	10,000
Notes payable	30,000	20,000
Common shares	400,000	400,000
Retained earnings	113,500	101,000

Additional information:
1. The inventory turnover is 3.6 times.
2. The return on equity is 19%.
3. The receivables turnover is 9.4 times.
4. The return on assets is 14%.
5. Total assets at December 31, 2004, were $605,000.

Instructions

Calculate the following for Cougar Corporation:
(a) Cost of goods sold for 2005
(b) Net credit sales for 2005
(c) Net income for 2005
(d) Total assets at December 31, 2005

E18–11 The following selected ratios are available for a recent year for **Four Seasons Hotels Inc.** and **Fairmont Hotels & Resorts Inc.**, two large hotel chains headquartered in Toronto:

Analyse ratios.
(SO 4, 5) AN

	Four Seasons	Fairmont	Industry Average
Liquidity			
Current ratio	4.99:1	0.29:1	0.78:1
Receivables turnover	3.4 times	11.6 times	9.4 times
Solvency			
Debt to total assets	17.45%	37.05%	n/a
Interest coverage	n/a	3.30 times	2.10 times
Profitability			
Profit margin	0.58%	7.33%	3.99%
Return on assets	0.2%	2.0%	2.1%

Instructions

(a) Which company is more liquid? Explain.
(b) Which company is more solvent? Explain.
(c) Which company is more profitable? Explain.
(d) Four Seasons operates in 26 countries, while Fairmont operates in five. The Four Seasons manages only luxury hotels, while Fairmont also includes the Delta and Legacy mid-market hotels. Would this information limit the usefulness of your financial analysis in (a) to (c) in any way? Explain why or why not.

E18–12 Davis Ltd. has income from continuing operations of $270,000 for the year ended December 31, 2005. It also has the following items (before considering income taxes): (1) an extraordinary fire loss of $60,000, (2) a gain of $40,000 from the discontinuance of an identifiable business segment, which includes a $110,000 gain from the operation of the segment and a $70,000 loss on its disposal, and (3) a cumulative change in accounting principle that resulted in a $30,000 increase in the prior years' amortization. Assume all items are subject to a 40% income tax rate.

Prepare irregular items portion of income statement.
(SO 6) AP

Instructions

(a) Prepare Davis's income statement for the year ended December 31, 2005, beginning with "Income from continuing operations."
(b) Indicate the statement presentation of any items not included in (a).

Problems: Set A

Prepare horizontal analysis and comment.
(SO 2, 6) AN

P18–1A **Nortel Networks Corporation** experienced rapid growth in the 1990s, as did most technology-based companies, followed by rapid declines in the 2000s after the market collapsed. The following selected information is available for the three most recent years of this maker of telecommunication products:

NORTEL NETWORKS CORPORATION
Income Statement
Year Ended December 31
(in U.S. millions)

	2002	2001	2000
Revenues	$10,560	$ 17,511	$27,948
Cost of revenues	6,953	14,167	15,114
Gross profit	3,607	3,344	12,834
Operating expenses	7,670	30,903	14,652
Net loss from continuing operations before income taxes	(4,063)	(27,559)	(1,818)
Income tax recovery (expense)	478	3,252	(1,177)
Net loss from continuing operations	(3,585)	(24,307)	(2,995)
Net loss from discontinued operations	0	(2,995)	(475)
Net loss	$ (3,585)	$(27,302)	$ (3,470)

NORTEL NETWORKS CORPORATION
Balance Sheet (partial)
December 31
(in U.S. millions)

	2002	2001	2000
Current assets	$ 8,476	$11,762	$16,530
Total assets	15,971	21,137	42,180
Current liabilities	6,982	9,457	9,058
Total liabilities	14,011	16,313	13,071
Common shares	35,696	34,975	31,835
Deficit	33,736	30,151	2,726

Instructions

(a) Prepare a horizontal analysis of Nortel.
(b) What components found in Nortel's balance sheet and income statement have been the primary drivers of the company's deterioration?
(c) How has Nortel mostly been financing its operations?

Prepare vertical analysis, calculate profitability ratios, and comment on profitability.
(SO 3, 4) AN

P18–2A Comparative statement data for Chen Inc. and Couric Ltd., two competitors, appear below. All balance sheet data are as at December 31.

	Chen Inc.		Couric Ltd.	
	2005	2004	2005	2004
Net sales	$1,849,035		$539,038	
Cost of goods sold	1,080,490		338,006	
Operating expenses	502,275		79,000	
Interest expense	6,800		1,252	
Income tax expense	103,800		48,300	
Current assets	325,975	$312,410	83,336	$ 79,467
Noncurrent assets	651,115	500,000	214,010	125,812
Current liabilities	66,325	75,815	35,348	30,281
Noncurrent liabilities	108,500	90,000	29,620	25,000
Common shares	500,000	500,000	120,000	120,000
Retained earnings	302,265	146,595	112,478	29,998

Instructions

(a) Prepare a vertical analysis of the 2005 income statement data for Chen and Couric.

(b) Calculate the gross profit margin, profit margin, return on assets, asset turnover, and return on equity ratios for both companies.

(c) Comment on the relative profitability of the companies.

P18–3A The comparative statements of Johnson Ltd. are presented below.

Calculate ratios.
(SO 4) AP

JOHNSON LTD.
Income Statement
Year Ended December 31

	2005	2004
Net sales	$1,918,500	$1,750,500
Cost of goods sold	1,005,500	996,000
Gross profit	913,000	754,500
Operating expenses (including $60,000 and $50,000, respectively, of amortization expense)	506,000	479,000
Income from operations	407,000	275,500
Interest expense	28,000	19,000
Income before income tax	379,000	256,500
Income tax expense	113,700	77,000
Net income	$ 265,300	$ 179,500

JOHNSON LTD
Balance Sheet
December 31

Assets	2005	2004
Current assets		
Cash	$ 60,100	$ 64,200
Temporary investments	54,000	50,000
Accounts receivable	107,800	102,800
Inventory	143,000	115,500
Total current assets	364,900	332,500
Property, plant, and equipment	625,300	520,300
Total assets	$990,200	$852,800

Liabilities and Shareholders' Equity		
Current liabilities		
Accounts payable	$170,000	$145,400
Income tax payable	43,500	42,000
Total current liabilities	213,500	187,400
Bonds payable	66,000	200,000
Total liabilities	279,500	387,400
Shareholders' equity		
Common shares, 56,000 and 60,000 issued, respectively	280,000	300,000
Retained earnings	430,700	165,400
Total shareholders' equity	710,700	465,400
Total liabilities and shareholders' equity	$990,200	$852,800

Additional information:

1. All sales were on account.
2. On July 1, 2005, 4,000 shares were reacquired and cancelled.
3. Cash provided by operating activities was $280,000.
4 Net capital expenditures during the year were $165,000.

Instructions

Calculate the following ratios for 2005:

(a) Current ratio   (i) Return on assets
(b) Inventory turnover   (j) Return on equity
(c) Days sales in inventory   (k) Earnings per share
(d) Receivables turnover   (l) EBITDA
(e) Collection period   (m) Debt to total assets
(f) Gross profit margin   (n) Interest coverage
(g) Profit margin   (o) Free cash flow
(h) Asset turnover

Calculate ratios and comment.
(SO 4) AN

P18–4A Condensed balance sheet and income statement data for Pitka Corporation appear below:

PITKA CORPORATION
Balance Sheet
December 31

Assets	2005	2004	2003
Cash	$ 25,000	$ 20,000	$ 18,000
Accounts receivable	50,000	45,000	48,000
Merchandise inventory	90,000	85,000	64,000
Investments	55,000	70,000	45,000
Property, plant, and equipment	500,000	370,000	258,000
	$720,000	$590,000	$433,000
Liabilities and Shareholders' Equity			
Current liabilities	$ 90,000	$ 75,000	$ 30,000
Long-term debt	170,000	85,000	20,000
Common shares	325,000	325,000	300,000
Retained earnings	135,000	105,000	83,000
	$720,000	$590,000	$433,000

PITKA CORPORATION
Income Statement
Year Ended December 31

	2005	2004
Sales	$740,000	$700,000
Less: Sales returns and allowances	40,000	50,000
Net sales	700,000	650,000
Cost of goods sold	420,000	400,000
Gross profit	280,000	250,000
Operating expenses	236,000	218,000
Income before income tax	44,000	32,000
Income tax expense	11,000	8,000
Net income	$ 33,000	$ 24,000

Additional information:

1. The market prices of Pitka's common shares were $4, $5, and $8 for 2003, 2004, and 2005, respectively.
2. All dividends were paid in cash. (*Hint*: Analyse retained earnings to calculate dividends.)
3. On July 1, 2004, 5,000 common shares were issued, bringing the total number of shares to 35,000.

Instructions

(a) Calculate the following ratios for 2004 and 2005:

1. Profit margin   5. Price-earnings
2. Gross profit margin   6. Payout
3. Asset turnover   7. Debt to total assets
4. Earnings per share   8. Current ratio

(b) Based on the ratios calculated, briefly discuss the improvement or lack of improvement in the financial position and operating results for Pitka Corporation from 2004 to 2005.

P18–5A Financial information for Click and Clack Ltd. is presented below:

Calculate ratios and comment.
(SO 4) AN

CLICK AND CLACK LTD.
Balance Sheet
December 31

Assets	2005	2004
Cash	$ 70,000	$ 65,000
Temporary investments	45,000	40,000
Accounts receivable	94,000	90,000
Inventories	230,000	125,000
Prepaid expenses	25,000	23,000
Land, buildings, and equipment	390,000	305,000
Total assets	$854,000	$648,000
Liabilities and Shareholders' Equity		
Notes payable	$170,000	$100,000
Accounts payable	45,000	42,000
Accrued liabilities	40,000	40,000
Bonds payable, due 2008	250,000	150,000
Common shares, 20,000 issued	200,000	200,000
Retained earnings	149,000	116,000
Total liabilities and shareholders' equity	$854,000	$648,000

CLICK AND CLACK LTD.
Income Statement
Year Ended December 31

	2005	2004
Sales	$900,000	$840,000
Cost of goods sold	620,000	575,000
Gross profit	280,000	265,000
Operating expenses (including amortization expense of $15,000 and $11,000, respectively, for each year)	194,000	180,000
Income before income tax	86,000	85,000
Income tax expense	30,000	30,000
Net income	$ 56,000	$ 55,000

Additional information:

1. Inventory at the beginning of 2004 was $115,000.
2. Accounts receivable at the beginning of 2004 were $88,000, net of an allowance for doubtful accounts of $3,000.
3. Total assets at the beginning of 2004 were $630,000.
4. Total shareholders' equity at the beginning of 2004 was $287,000.
5. All sales were on account.

Instructions

Using ratios, indicate the changes in Click and Clack's liquidity, profitability, and solvency from 2004 to 2005. (*Note*: Not all ratios can be calculated.)

Calculate and analyse
ratios for two companies.
(SO 4, 6) AN

P18–6A U.S. retailer **Best Buy Co., Inc.** owns Future Shop Ltd., which is Canada's largest consumer electronics retailer. Ontario-based **InterTAN, Inc.** also sells consumer electronics, through Radio Shack and Rogers AT&T stores in Canada. Selected financial data of these two close competitors are presented here (in U.S. millions) for a recent year:

	Best Buy	InterTAN
	Income Statement	
Sales	$20,946.0	$403.0
Cost of sales	15,710.0	239.3
Gross profit	5,236.0	163.7
Operating expenses	4,226.0	144.1
Income from operations	1,010.0	19.6
Other revenue (expense)	4.0	(2.8)
Income before income tax	1,014.0	16.8
Income tax expense	392.0	8.5
Net income	$ 622.0	$ 8.3
	Balance Sheet	
Current assets	$4,867.0	$127.0
Noncurrent assets	2,796.0	39.3
Total assets	$7,663.0	$166.3
Current liabilities	$3,793.0	$ 50.7
Noncurrent liabilities	1,140.0	18.1
Total liabilities	4,933.0	68.8
Shareholders' equity	2,730.0	97.5
Total liabilities and shareholders' equity	$7,663.0	$166.3
	Other Data	
Average accounts receivable	$ 279.5	$ 14.6
Average inventories	2,152.0	86.8
Average total assets	7,519.0	155.7
Average total shareholders' equity	2,625.5	93.0
Net cash provided by operating activities	667.0	5.7

Instructions

(a) For each company, calculate the following ratios. Industry averages are provided in parentheses following each ratio, where available.

1. Current ratio (1.7:1)
2. Receivables turnover (25.9 times)
3. Collection period (14 days)
4. Inventory turnover (5.1 times)
5. Days sales in inventory (72 days)
6. Debt to total assets (n/a)

7. Profit margin (1.6%)
8. Asset turnover (2.4 times)
9. Return on assets (4.0%)
10. Return on equity (8.9%)
11. Gross profit margin (29.5%)

(b) Compare the liquidity, solvency, and profitability of the two companies.

(c) Would your interpretation in (b) change if you learned that Best Buy reported a US$441 million loss from discontinued operations (net of tax)? This loss reduced the US$622 million income from continuing operations actually reported on Best Buy's income statement.

Determine impact of
transactions on ratios.
(SO 4) AN

P18–7A The following ratios are available for Yami Corporation:

Current ratio	1.5:1	Profit margin	10%
Inventory turnover	10 times	Debt to total assets	40%
Asset turnover	2 times		

Instructions

(a) Indicate whether each of the above ratios would increase, decrease, or remain unchanged as a result of each of the following independent transactions:
1. Yami pays an account payable.
2. Yami collects an account receivable.
3. Yami repays a long-term note payable (ignore the impact of this transaction on interest).

4. Yami sells merchandise for cash at a profit.

5. Yami buys equipment for cash (ignore the impact of this transaction on amortization).

(b) Would your answers to any of the above change if the current ratio were 0.5:1 instead of 1.5:1?

P18–8A The following ratios are available for fast-food competitors **McDonald's Corporation** and **Wendy's International, Inc.** for fiscal 2002:

Analyse ratios.
(SO 4) AN

	McDonald's	Wendy's	Industry
Liquidity			
Current ratio	0.7:1	0.9:1	0.7:1
Receivables turnover	17.7 times	28.4 times	30.7 times
Inventory turnover	60.9 times	52.3 times	30.1 times
Solvency			
Debt to total assets	49.2%	32.0%	44.8%
Interest coverage	5.4 times	9.3 times	6.3 times
Profitability			
Gross profit margin	57.0%	29.3%	38.9%
Profit margin	6.4%	8.0%	5.4%
Return on equity	9.6%	15.1%	14.6%
Return on assets	4.1%	8.2%	6.3%
Asset turnover	0.7 times	1.2 times	1.2 times
Payout ratio	31.2%	9.5%	10.6%
Earnings per share	$0.77	$1.89	$1.04
Price-earnings ratio	20.9 times	14.3 times	n/a

Instructions

(a) Which company is more liquid? Explain.

(b) Which company is more solvent? Explain.

(c) Which company is more profitable? Explain.

(d) Which company do investors favour? Is your answer consistent with your findings in (a) to (c)?

P18–9A Nextec Corp. has been in business for five years. Nextec has plans to create a new software package that will allow users with limited computer knowledge to easily navigate the Internet by using their television sets and a control box that plugs into the cable jack.

Analyse ratios and make loan decision.
(SO 4) AN

You are the loan officer at a Canadian chartered bank. The manager has asked you to analyse Nextec's financial statements and recommend whether or not the bank should lend Nextec additional funds for the project, based on its historical financial statements. Comparative financial statements follow:

NEXTEC CORP.
Balance Sheet
March 31

Assets	2005	2004
Cash	$ 45,000	
Accounts receivable	535,000	$470,000
Inventory	150,000	140,000
Prepaid expenses	5,000	10,000
Patents	38,000	0
Total assets	$773,000	$620,000
Liabilities and Shareholders' Equity		
Bank overdraft		$ 20,000
Accounts payable	$ 50,200	60,000
Current portion of long-term debt	60,000	50,000
Long-term debt	184,000	160,000
Common shares	100,000	100,000
Retained earnings	378,800	230,000
Total liabilities and shareholders' equity	$773,000	$620,000

NEXTEC CORP.
Income Statement
Year Ended March 31

	2005	2004
Sales (all on credit)	$1,600,000	$1,400,000
Cost of goods sold	900,000	800,000
Gross profit	700,000	600,000
Operating expenses		
Salaries	370,000	340,000
Office	20,000	20,000
Rent	40,000	40,000
Interest	20,000	30,000
Amortization	2,000	
	452,000	430,000
Income before income tax	248,000	170,000
Income tax (40%)	99,200	68,000
Net income	$ 148,800	$ 102,000

Selected comparative ratios and industry averages follow:

	2005	2004	2005 Industry Average
Current ratio	6.7:1	4.8:1	3.0:1
Average collection period	115 days	123 days	60 days
Inventory turnover	6.2 times	5.7 times	5 times
Return on equity	37%	31%	30%
Debt to total assets	38%	47%	40%
Interest coverage	13.4 times	6.7 times	10.9 times

Instructions

(a) Indicate whether the 2005 ratios presented above are favourable or unfavourable compared to the industry average.

(b) Based on a comparison of Nextec's ratios to the industry average, identify *one* significant area that Nextec must improve and what it should do to improve it.

(c) The President of Nextec estimates that the company needs $1 million to ensure the new software project's success. Based on the ratios given and the financial statements presented, determine whether or not you would lend $1 million to Nextec. Explain your decision.

(d) Identify one additional thing Nextec could do (other than borrow) to raise the money it needs.

(e) In addition to the financial statements of Nextec Corp., list two other non-financial factors that should be considered when evaluating this company.

Prepare income statement with irregular items. (SO 6) AP

P18–10A The ledger of Hyperchip Corporation at November 30, 2005, contains the following summary data:

Net sales	$1,500,000	Other revenues	$40,000
Cost of goods sold	800,000	Other expenses	30,000
Operating expenses	240,000		

Your analysis reveals the following additional information that is not included in the above data:

1. The entire ceramics division was discontinued on August 31. The loss from operations for this division before income tax was $150,000. The ceramics division was sold at a pre-tax gain of $70,000.

2. On July 12, a transport truck crashed into one of the company's plants. This resulted in an extraordinary loss of $80,000 before income tax.

3. During the year, Hyperchip changed its amortization method from straight-line to declining-balance. The cumulative effect of the change on prior years' net income was a decrease of $30,000 before income tax. (Assume that amortization under the new method is correctly included in the ledger data for the current year.)

4. The income tax rate on all items is 30%.

Instructions

Prepare an income statement for the year ended November 30, 2005.

Problems: Set B

P18–1B Over the past few years, the airline industry has faced a number of significant challenges. The economic slowdown of 2001, the terrorist attacks of September 11, 2001, the growth of low-cost competition, high oil prices, and the war in Iraq have all contributed to the decline in fortunes that **Air Canada** and several other airlines face today. This decline continued through 2003, and on April 1, 2003, Air Canada filed for bankruptcy protection.

Prepare horizontal analysis and comment. (SO 2) AN

The following selected financial information (in millions) for the most recent five-year period is available for Air Canada:

	2002	2001	2000	1999	1998
Operating revenues	$ 9,826	$ 9,611	$9,296	$6,443	$5,898
Operating expenses	10,049	10,321	9,213	6,028	5,802
Interest expense	221	275	210	154	174
Income tax expense (recovery)	384	330	(45)	121	(34)
Net income (loss)	$ (828)	$(1,315)	$ (82)	$ 140	$ (44)

	2002	2001	2000	1999	1998
Current assets	$ 1,771	$2,235	$2,229	$1,258	$1,092
Total assets	7,416	8,744	9,732	6,705	6,422
Current liabilities	2,592	2,869	3,560	1,405	1,279
Total liabilities	9,704	10,204	9,416	5,980	4,965
Share capital	992	992	992	990	1,305
Retained earnings (deficit)	(3,280)	(2,452)	(676)	(265)	152

Instructions

(a) Prepare a horizontal analysis of Air Canada.
(b) What components found in Air Canada's balance sheet and income statement have been the primary drivers of the airline's decline?
(c) How has Air Canada mostly been financing its operations?

P18–2B Comparative statement data for Breau Ltd. and Shields Ltd., two competitors, appear below. All balance sheet data are as at December 31.

Prepare vertical analysis, calculate profitability ratios, and comment on profitability. (SO 3, 4) AN

	Breau Ltd.		Shields Ltd.	
	2005	2004	2005	2004
Net sales	$350,000		$1,400,000	
Cost of goods sold	180,000		720,000	
Operating expenses	51,000		272,000	
Interest expense	3,000		10,000	
Income tax expense	29,000		100,000	
Current assets	130,000	$110,000	700,000	$650,000
Property, plant, and equipment	405,000	270,000	1,000,000	750,000
Current liabilities	60,000	52,000	250,000	275,000
Long-term liabilities	50,000	68,000	200,000	150,000
Common shares	288,000	210,000	677,000	700,000
Retained earnings	137,000	50,000	573,000	275,000

Instructions

(a) Prepare a vertical analysis of the 2005 income statement data for Breau and Shields.
(b) Calculate the gross profit margin, profit margin, return on assets, asset turnover, and return on equity ratios for both companies.
(c) Comment on the relative profitability of these companies.
(d) Identify two main reasons for the difference in profitability.

Calculate ratios.
(SO 4) AP

P18–3B The comparative statements of Rosen Inc. are presented here:

ROSEN INC.
Income Statement
Year Ended December 31

	2005	2004
Net sales	$780,000	$624,000
Cost of goods sold	440,000	405,600
Gross profit	340,000	218,400
Operating expenses (including amortization expense of $46,000 and $45,000, respectively)	143,880	149,760
Income from operations	196,120	68,640
Interest expense	9,920	7,200
Income before income tax	186,200	61,440
Income tax expense	46,550	24,000
Net income	$139,650	$ 37,440

ROSEN INC.
Balance Sheet
December 31

Assets	2005	2004
Current assets		
Cash	$ 23,100	$ 21,600
Temporary investments	34,800	33,000
Accounts receivable (net)	106,200	93,800
Inventory	122,400	64,000
Total current assets	286,500	212,400
Property, plant, and equipment	465,300	459,600
Total assets	$751,800	$672,000
Liabilities and Shareholders' Equity		
Current liabilities		
Accounts payable	$200,850	$132,000
Income tax payable	15,300	24,000
Total current liabilities	216,150	156,000
Bonds payable	0	120,000
Total liabilities	216,150	276,000
Shareholders' equity		
Common shares (15,000 issued)	150,000	150,000
Retained earnings	385,650	246,000
Total shareholders' equity	535,650	396,000
Total liabilities and shareholders' equity	$751,800	$672,000

Additional information:

1. All sales were on account.
2. Cash provided by operating activities was $36,000.
3. Net capital expenditures during the year were $51,700.

Instructions

Calculate the following ratios for 2005:

(a) Current ratio
(b) Inventory turnover
(c) Days sales in inventory
(d) Receivables turnover
(e) Collection period
(f) Gross profit margin
(g) Profit margin
(h) Asset turnover

(i) Return on assets
(j) Return on equity
(k) Earnings per share
(l) EBITDA
(m) Debt to total assets
(n) Interest coverage
(o) Free cash flow

P18–4B Condensed balance sheet and income statement data for Colinas Corporation appear below:

Calculate ratios and comment.
(SO 4) AN

COLINAS CORPORATION
Balance Sheet
December 31

Assets	2005	2004	2003
Cash	$ 40,000	$ 24,000	$ 20,000
Accounts receivable	73,000	45,000	48,000
Inventory	80,000	75,000	62,000
Investments	90,000	70,000	50,000
Property, plant, and equipment	650,000	400,000	360,000
	$933,000	$614,000	$540,000

Liabilities and Shareholders' Equity			
Current liabilities	$ 98,000	$ 75,000	$ 70,000
Long-term debt	250,000	75,000	65,000
Common shares	400,000	340,000	300,000
Retained earnings	185,000	124,000	105,000
	$933,000	$614,000	$540,000

COLINAS CORPORATION
Income Statement
Year Ended December 31

	2005	2004
Sales	$800,000	$750,000
Less: Sales returns and allowances	40,000	50,000
Net sales	760,000	700,000
Cost of goods sold	420,000	400,000
Gross profit	340,000	300,000
Operating expenses (including $45,000 and $40,000, respectively, of amortization expense)	184,000	228,000
Interest expense	10,000	9,000
Income before income tax	146,000	63,000
Income tax expense	65,700	28,350
Net income	$ 80,300	$ 34,650

Additional information:

1. All dividends were paid in cash.
2. There were 30,000 common shares on December 31, 2003; 34,000 on December 31, 2004; and 40,000 on December 31, 2005.
3. The market prices of Colinas' common shares were $10 and $8 for 2004 and 2005, respectively.

Instructions

(a) Calculate the following ratios for 2004 and 2005:

1. Profit margin	5. Price-earnings
2. Gross profit margin	6. Payout
3. Asset turnover	7. Debt to total assets
4. Earnings per share	8. Current ratio

(b) Based on the ratios calculated, briefly discuss the changes in financial position and operating results of Colinas Corporation from 2004 to 2005.

Calculate ratios and
comment.
(SO 4) AN

P18–5B Financial information for Star Track Ltd. is presented here:

STAR TRACK LTD.
Balance Sheet
December 31

Assets	2005	2004
Cash	$ 50,000	$ 42,000
Temporary investments	80,000	100,000
Accounts receivable	100,000	87,000
Inventories	440,000	400,000
Prepaid expenses	25,000	31,000
Land	75,000	75,000
Building and equipment (net)	570,000	500,000
Total assets	$1,340,000	$1,235,000
Liabilities and Shareholders' Equity		
Notes payable	$ 125,000	$ 125,000
Accounts payable	160,000	140,000
Accrued liabilities	50,000	50,000
Bonds payable, due 2009	200,000	200,000
Common shares (100,000 issued)	500,000	500,000
Retained earnings	305,000	220,000
Total liabilities and shareholders' equity	$1,340,000	$1,235,000

STAR TRACK LTD.
Income Statement
Year Ended December 31

	2005	2004
Sales	$1,000,000	$940,000
Cost of goods sold	650,000	635,000
Gross profit	350,000	305,000
Operating expenses	235,000	215,000
Income before income taxes	115,000	90,000
Income tax expense	28,750	22,500
Net income	$ 86,250	$ 67,500

Additional information:

1. Inventory at the beginning of 2004 was $350,000.
2. Receivables at the beginning of 2004 were $80,000.
3. Total assets at the beginning of 2004 were $1,175,000.
4. Current liabilities at the beginning of 2004 were $300,000.
5. Total shareholders' equity at the beginning of 2004 was $740,000.
6. All sales were on account.
7. Cash provided by operating activities was $80,000 in 2005 and $65,000 in 2004.

Instructions

Using ratios, indicate the changes in Star Track's liquidity, profitability, and solvency from 2004 to 2005. (*Note*: Not all ratios can be calculated.)

Calculate and analyse
ratios for two companies.
(SO 4) AN

P18–6B **Inco Limited** and **Falconbridge Limited** are two of the world's leading producers of nickel and other metals and minerals. Selected financial data of these two close competitors are presented here (in U.S. and CDN millions, respectively) for a recent year:

	Inco	Falconbridge
	Income Statement	
Net sales	$ 2,161	$2,394
Cost of sales and operating expenses	1,513	1,869
Interest expense	50	88
Other expenses	2,718	389
Income (loss) before income taxes	(2,120)	48
Income and mining tax recovery	639	25
Net income (loss)	$(1,481)	$ 73
Income (loss) per share	$ (8.27)	$ 0.34
	Balance Sheet	
Current assets		
Cash and cash equivalents	$1,087	$ 260
Accounts receivable	251	312
Inventories	576	448
Other current assets	73	0
Total current assets	1,987	1,050
Property, plant, and equipment	6,345	3,955
Other assets	208	199
Total assets	$8,540	$5,204
Current liabilities	$ 930	$ 424
Long-term liabilities	3,805	2,494
Total liabilities	4,735	2,918
Shareholders' equity	3,805	2,286
Total liabilities and shareholders' equity	$8,540	$5,204
	Other Data	
Average accounts receivable	$ 264	$ 301
Average inventories	538	454
Average total assets	9,064	5,136
Average total shareholders' equity	4,550	2,283
Dividends	26	83

Instructions

(a) Calculate liquidity, solvency, and profitability ratios, as appropriate, for each company.
(b) Compare Inco's liquidity, solvency, and profitability to those of Falconbridge and of the industry. Selected industry averages are available for the following ratios:

Current ratio	1.2:1	Profit margin	1.6%
Receivables turnover	8.3 times	Return on assets	0.8%
Inventory turnover	4.9 times	Earnings per share	$0.13
Debt to total assets	40.1%	Return on equity	2.3%
Interest coverage	2.0 times	Asset turnover	0.6 times

P18–7B The following ratios and measures are available for Hubei Corporation:

Determine impact of transactions on ratios. (SO 4) AN

Receivables turnover	10 times
Profit margin	10%
Earnings per share	$2
Debt to total assets	40%
Free cash flow	$25,000

Instructions

(a) Indicate whether each of the above would increase, decrease, or remain unchanged by each of the following independent transactions:

    1. Hubei issues common shares.
    2. Hubei collects an account receivable.
    3. Hubei issues a mortgage note payable.
    4. Hubei sells equipment at a loss.
    5. Hubei's share price increases from $10 per share to $12 per share.

(b) Would your answers to any of the above change if the profit margin were negative and the earnings per share were a loss per share?

Analyse ratios.
(SO 4) AN

P18–8B The following ratios are available for tool-makers **The Black & Decker Corporation** and **Snap-on Incorporated** for fiscal 2002:

	Black & Decker	Snap-on	Industry
Liquidity			
Current ratio	1.5:1	1.9:1	2.1:1
Receivables turnover	6.1 times	3.6 times	5.1 times
Inventory turnover	3.8 times	2.9 times	3.1 times
Solvency			
Debt to total assets	67.5%	30.1%	35.9%
Interest coverage	4.6 times	6.6 times	6.1 times
Profitability			
Gross profit margin	37.5%	48.2%	37.9%
Profit margin	5.2%	4.9%	4.8%
Return on equity	38.3%	12.4%	12.0%
Return on assets	5.6%	5.2%	4.8%
Asset turnover	1.1 times	1.1 times	1.0 times
Payout ratio	16.9%	55.1%	34.5%
Earnings per share	$2.84	$1.76	$1.39
Price-earnings ratio	15.1 times	16.0 times	n/a

Instructions

(a) Which company is more liquid? Explain.
(b) Which company is more solvent? Explain.
(c) Which company is more profitable? Explain.
(d) Which company do investors favour? Is your answer consistent with your findings in (a) to (c)?

Analyse ratios.
(SO 4) AN

P18–9B Selected ratios for two companies operating in the beverage industry follow in alphabetical order. Industry ratios, where available, have also been included.

Ratio	Refresh Corp.	Taste.Com	Industry
Asset turnover	1.0 times	1.0 times	0.9 times
Current ratio	0.6:1.0	1.1:1.0	0.8:1.0
Debt to total assets	56%	72%	n/a
Earnings per share	$0.98	$1.37	$1.08
Gross profit margin	73.8%	60.0%	57.7%
Inventory turnover	5.8 times	9.9 times	8.3 times
Price-earnings	50.3 times	24.3 times	32.2 times
Profit margin	12.3%	11.2%	8.1%
Receivables turnover	11.4 times	9.8 times	9.3 times
Return on assets	11.2%	9.3%	7.2%
Return on equity	25.7%	29.8%	26.4%
Interest coverage	15.3 times	7.9 times	5.3 times

Instructions

Answer the following questions, referring to appropriate ratios to justify your answer:

(a) Which company appears to be the most liquid? Explain.

(b) As a potential investor, are you concerned with the debt levels of either company? Why or why not?

(c) Which company is the most profitable? Explain.

(d) One should always be cautious in interpreting ratios. Identify any two facts that you should keep in mind about the limitations of ratio analysis as you interpret the ratios in this question.

P18–10B The ledger of Zurich Corporation at December 31, 2005, contains the following summary data:

Prepare income statement with irregular items. (SO 6) AP

Net sales	$1,700,000
Cost of goods sold	1,100,000
Operating expenses	260,000
Other revenues	20,000
Other expenses	28,000

Your analysis reveals the following additional information that is not included in the above data:

1. The entire Personal Communication Devices division was discontinued on August 31. The gain from operations for the division before income taxes was $20,000. The Personal Communication Devices division was sold at a loss of $70,000 before income tax.
2. On May 15, company property was expropriated for a highway. The settlement resulted in an extraordinary gain of $100,000 before income tax.
3. During the year, Zurich changed its amortization method from double declining-balance to straight-line. The cumulative effect of the change on prior years' net income was an increase of $60,000 before tax. Amortization under the new method is correctly included in the ledger for the current year.
4. The income tax rate on all items is 30%.
5. The retained earnings balance at the beginning of the year was $340,000.
6. Dividends declared during the year totalled $25,000.
7. There were 100,000 common shares.

Instructions

Prepare an income statement for the year ended December 31, 2005.

Continuing Cookie Chronicle

(Note: This is a continuation of the Cookie Chronicle from Chapters 1 through 17.)

The comparative balance sheet of Cookie & Coffee Creations Ltd. at October 31, 2007, for the years 2007 and 2006, and the income statements for the years ended October 31, 2006 and 2007, are presented below:

COOKIE & COFFEE CREATIONS LTD.
Balance Sheet
October 31

Assets	2007	2006
Cash	$ 34,324	$13,050
Accounts receivable	3,250	2,710
Inventory	7,897	7,450
Prepaids	6,300	6,050
Equipment	96,500	75,500
Accumulated amortization	(25,200)	(9,100)
Total assets	$123,071	$95,660

Liabilities and Shareholders' Equity	2007	2006
Accounts payable	$ 3,650	$ 2,450
Income taxes payable	10,251	11,200
Dividends payable	28,000	25,000
Salaries payable	2,250	1,280
Interest payable	188	0
Note payable—current portion	3,000	0
Note payable—long-term portion	4,500	0
Preferred shares, $6 cumulative, 3,000 and 2,500 shares issued, respectively	15,000	12,500
Common shares, 23,180 shares issued	23,180	23,180
Contributed capital—reacquisition of shares	250	250
Retained earnings	32,802	19,800
Total liabilities and shareholders' equity	$123,071	$95,660

COOKIE & COFFEE CREATIONS LTD.
Income Statement
Year Ended October 31

	2007	2006
Sales	$485,625	$462,500
Cost of goods sold	222,694	208,125
Gross profit	262,931	254,375
Operating expenses		
Amortization expense	17,600	9,100
Salaries and wages expense	147,979	146,350
Other operating expenses	43,186	42,925
Total operating expenses	208,765	198,375
Income from operations	54,166	56,000
Other expenses		
Interest expense	413	0
Loss on sale of computer equipment	2,500	0
Total other expenses	2,913	0
Income before income tax	51,253	56,000
Income tax expense	10,251	11,200
Net income	$ 41,002	$ 44,800

Additional information:

Natalie and Curtis are thinking about borrowing an additional $20,000 to buy more kitchen equipment. The loan would be repaid over a four-year period. The terms of the loan provide for equal semi-annual instalment payments of $2,500 on May 1 and November 1 of each year, plus interest of 5% on the outstanding balance.

Instructions:

(a) Calculate the following ratios for 2006 and 2007:
    1. Current ratio
    2. Debt to total assets
    3. Gross profit margin
    4. Profit margin
    5. Return on assets (Total assets at November 1, 2005, were $33,180.)
    6. Return on common shareholders' equity (Total common shareholders' equity at November 1, 2005, was $23,180.)
    7. Payout ratio
    8. EBITDA
(b) Prepare a horizontal analysis of the income statement for Cookie & Coffee Creations Ltd., using 2006 as a base year.
(c) Prepare a vertical analysis of the income statement for Cookie & Coffee Creations Ltd. for 2007 and 2006.
(d) Comment on your findings from parts (a) to (c).

(e) What impact would borrowing an additional $20,000 to buy more equipment have on each of the ratios in (a) above, assuming that no changes are expected on the income statement and balance sheet. Comment on your findings.

(f) What would justify a decision by Cookie & Coffee Creations Ltd. to buy the additional equipment? What alternatives are there instead of bank financing?

B R O A D E N I N G   Y O U R   P E R S P E C T I V E

Financial Reporting and Analysis

 Practice Tools

Financial Reporting Problem

BYP18–1 You are considering investing in **The Forzani Group Ltd.'s** common (class A) shares. Before doing so, you decide to analyse the company further, using Forzani's financial statements presented in Appendix A of this textbook.

Instructions

(a) Prepare a two-year vertical analysis of the balance sheet and income statement. Comment on the significance of any trends you observe.

(b) For 2003, calculate (1) the current ratio and (2) the receivables turnover. What is your assessment of Forzani's liquidity?

(c) For 2003, calculate these ratios: (1) debt to total assets, (2) interest coverage, and (3) free cash flow. What is your assessment of Forzani's solvency?

(d) For 2003, calculate these ratios: (1) gross profit margin, (2) profit margin, (3) asset turnover, (4) return on assets, and (5) return on equity. What is your assessment of Forzani's profitability?

(e) What information not included in the financial statements may also be useful to you in making a decision about Forzani?

Interpreting Financial Statements

BYP18–2 **Canadian National Railway Company (CN)** is the only railroad in North America to cross the continent from east to west and north to south. **The Burlington Northern Santa Fe Corporation (BNSF)**, through its subsidiary The Burlington Northern and Santa Fe Railway Company, operates another of North America's largest railways in two provinces and 28 states. At one time, CN planned to merge with BNSF, but a U.S. moratorium on rail mergers was subsequently introduced. The following data were taken from the December 31, 2002, financial statements of each company:

	CN (in CDN millions)		BNSF (in U.S. millions)	
	2002	2001	2002	2001
Cash and cash equivalents	$ 25	$ 53	$ 28	$ 26
Accounts receivable	722	645	141	172
Total current assets	1,163	1,164	791	723
Total assets	18,924	18,788	25,767	24,721
Total current liabilities	2,134	1,638	2,091	2,161
Total liabilities	12,297	12,427	17,835	16,872
Total shareholders' equity	6,627	6,034	7,932	7,849
Revenues	6,110		8,979	
Operating expenses	4,994		7,323	
Interest expense	353		428	
Income tax expense	268		456	
Net income	571		760	
Cash provided by operating activities	1,173		2,106	
Capital expenditures	571		1,358	
Dividends	179		183	

Instructions

Answer the following questions. Where available, industry averages are shown in parentheses next to each ratio.

(a) Calculate the following liquidity ratios for 2002 and discuss the relative liquidity of the two companies and of the railroad industry:

    1. Current ratio (0.7:1)   3. Collection period (28 days)

    2. Receivables turnover (13.0 times)

(b) Calculate the following solvency ratios for 2002 and discuss the relative solvency of the two companies and of the railroad industry:

    1. Debt to total assets (46.8%)   3. Free cash flow (n/a)

    2. Interest coverage (3.3 times)

(c) Calculate the following profitability ratios for 2002 and discuss the relative profitability of the two companies and of the railroad industry:

    1. Asset turnover (0.4 times)   3. Return on assets (2.9%)

    2. Profit margin (8.1%)   4. Return on equity (8.8%)

(d) What factors might contribute to the differences that you found?

Accounting on the Web

BYP18–3 Besides earnings per share, the price-earnings ratio (PE) is a popular analysis tool used to form an opinion as to whether a share is a good buy. This case will review several Canadian corporations to evaluate their PEs.

Instructions

Specific requirements of this Internet case can be found on the Weygandt website.

Critical Thinking

Collaborative Learning Activity

BYP18–4 You are a loan officer for a local bank. Ted Boucier, president of Boucier Corporation, has just left your office. His company is interested in a five-year loan for expansion purposes. The borrowed funds would be used to purchase new equipment. As evidence of the company's creditworthiness, Boucier provided you with the following facts:

	2006	2005
Current ratio	1.8:1	1.2:1
Receivables turnover	12 times	10 times
Net income	Up 32%	Down 8%
EBITDA	$100,000	$30,000
Earnings per share	$2.00	$1.50

Ted Boucier is a very insistent (some would say pushy) man. When you told him that you would need additional information before making your decision, he acted offended and said, "What more could you possibly want to know?" You responded that, at a minimum, you would need audited financial statements.

Instructions

(a) Explain why you would want the financial statements to be audited.
(b) Discuss the implications of the ratios provided for the lending decision you are to make. That is, does the information present a favourable picture? Are these ratios relevant to the decision?
(c) List other ratios that you would want to calculate for this company, and explain why you would use each.
(d) What are the limitations of ratio analysis for credit and investing decisions?

Communication Activity

BYP18–5 You are a new member of the board of directors of Shifty Inc. You are preparing for your first meeting of the audit committee and want to reassure yourself about the quality of the company's earnings.

Instructions

Write a list of questions that you should raise at the audit committee meeting in order to satisfy any concerns you may have about Shifty's earnings quality.

Ethics Case

BYP18–6 Sabra Surkis, president of Surkis Industries, wishes to issue a press release to improve her company's image and share price, which has been gradually falling. As controller, you have been asked to provide a list of financial ratios along with some other operating statistics relative to Surkis Industries' first quarter operations.

Two days after you provide the ratios and data requested, Carol Dunn, the public relations director of Surkis, asks you to prove the accuracy of the financial and operating data contained in the press release written by the president and edited by Carol. In the news release, the president highlights the sales increase of 25% over last year's first quarter and the positive change in the current ratio from 1.5:1 last year to 3:1 this year. She also emphasizes that production was up 50% over the prior year's first quarter.

You note that the release contains only positive or improved ratios, and none of the negative or weakened ratios. For instance, there is no mention that the debt to total assets ratio has increased from 35% to 55%. Nor was it mentioned that inventories are up 89%. There was also no indication that the reported income for the quarter would have been a loss had the estimated lives of Surkis' machinery not been increased by 30%.

Instructions

(a) Who are the stakeholders in this situation?
(b) Is there anything unethical in president Surkis' actions?
(c) Should you as controller remain silent? Does Carol have any responsibility?

Answers to Self-Study Questions
1. b   2. d   3. c   4. c   5. b   6. b   7. b   8. b   9. d   10. d

Answer to Forzani Review It Question 4
Forzani did not report any discontinued operations or extraordinary items in fiscal 2003. It did separately report an unusual gain on the sale of investments, but this is not an extraordinary item because management was involved in the decision to sell.

 Remember to go back to the Navigator Box at the beginning of the chapter to check off your completed work.

appendix A
Specimen Financial Statements:

The Forzani Group Ltd.

www.forzanigroup.com

In this appendix we illustrate current financial reporting with a comprehensive set of corporate financial statements that are prepared in accordance with generally accepted accounting principles. We are grateful for permission to use the actual financial statements of The Forzani Group Ltd.—Canada's largest sporting goods retailer. Forzani's financial statement package features a statement of management's responsibilities for financial reporting, auditors' report, balance sheet, combined statement of operations (or income statement as we know it) and retained earnings, cash flow statement, and notes to the financial statements.

We encourage students to use these financial statements in conjunction with relevant material in the textbook, and to solve the Review It questions in the Before You Go On section within the chapter and the Financial Reporting Problem in the Broadening Your Perspective section of the end-of-chapter material.

Annual reports, including the financial statements, are reviewed in detail on the interactive Student Navigator CD that accompanies this textbook.

**Annual Report
Walkthrough**

A FOCUSED DIRECTION

MANAGEMENT'S RESPONSIBILITIES FOR FINANCIAL REPORTING

The Annual Report, including the consolidated financial statements, is the responsibility of the management of the Company. The consolidated financial statements were prepared by management in accordance with generally accepted accounting principles. The significant accounting policies used are described in Note 1 to the consolidated financial statements. The integrity of the information presented in the financial statements, including estimates and judgments relating to matters not concluded by year-end, is the responsibility of management. Financial information presented elsewhere in this Annual Report has been prepared by management and is consistent with the information in the consolidated financial statements.

Management is responsible for the development and maintenance of systems of internal accounting and administrative controls. Such systems are designed to provide reasonable assurance that the financial information is accurate, relevant and reliable, and that the Company's assets are appropriately accounted for and adequately safeguarded. The Board of Directors is responsible for ensuring that management fulfills its responsibilities for final approval of the annual consolidated financial statements. The Board appoints an Audit Committee consisting of three directors, none of whom is an officer or employee of the Company or its subsidiaries. The Audit Committee meets at least four times each year to discharge its responsibilities under a written mandate from the Board of Directors. The Audit Committee meets with management and with the independent auditors to satisfy itself that they are properly discharging their responsibilities, reviews the consolidated financial statements and the Auditors' Report, and examines other auditing, accounting and financial reporting matters. The consolidated financial statements have been reviewed by the Audit Committee and approved by the Board of Directors of The Forzani Group Ltd. The consolidated financial statements have been examined by the shareholders' auditors, Deloitte & Touche, LLP, Chartered Accountants. The Auditors' Report outlines the nature of their examination and their opinion on the consolidated financial statements of the Company. The independent auditors have full and unrestricted access to the Audit Committee, with and without management present.

Bob Sartor, C.A.
Chief Executive Officer

Bill Gregson, C.A.
President & Chief Operating Officer

AUDITORS' REPORT

TO THE SHAREHOLDERS OF THE FORZANI GROUP LTD.

We have audited the consolidated balance sheets of **The Forzani Group Ltd.** as at February 2, 2003 and January 27, 2002 and the consolidated statements of operations and retained earnings and cash flows for the years then ended. These consolidated financial statements are the responsibility of the Company's management. Our responsibility is to express an opinion on these consolidated financial statements based on our audits.

We conducted our audits in accordance with Canadian generally accepted auditing standards. Those standards require that we plan and perform an audit to obtain reasonable assurance whether the financial statements are free of material misstatement. An audit includes examining, on a test basis, evidence supporting the amounts and disclosures in the financial statements. An audit also includes assessing the accounting principles used and significant estimates made by management, as well as evaluating the overall financial statement presentation.

In our opinion, these consolidated financial statements present fairly, in all material respects, the financial position of the Company as at February 2, 2003 and January 27, 2002 and the results of its operations and its cash flows for the years then ended in accordance with Canadian generally accepted accounting principles.

Calgary, Alberta
March 7, 2003

Deloitte & Touche LLP

Chartered Accountants

37

A FOCUSED DIRECTION

CONSOLIDATED BALANCE SHEETS

(in thousands)

(audited)

As at	February 2, 2003	January 27, 2002
ASSETS		
Current		
Cash	$ 523	$ 494
Accounts receivable	38,275	35,988
Inventory	268,519	229,270
Prepaid and other expenses	11,123	4,481
	318,440	270,233
Capital assets (Note 3)	142,236	120,525
Goodwill and other intangibles (Note 4)	38,684	37,394
Other assets (Note 5)	7,452	8,112
	$506,812	$ 436,264
LIABILITIES		
Current		
Indebtedness under revolving credit facility (Note 6)	$ 4,204	$ 17,094
Accounts payable and accrued liabilities	209,873	188,995
Current portion of long-term debt	3,638	14,032
	217,715	220,121
Long-term debt (Note 7)	32,062	35,454
Deferred lease inducements	52,251	46,623
Future income tax liability (Note 10)	1,061	2,021
	303,089	304,219
SHAREHOLDERS' EQUITY		
Share capital (Note 9)	124,866	83,719
Retained earnings	78,857	48,326
	203,723	132,045
	$506,812	$ 436,264

On behalf of the Board:

Roman Doroniuk, C.A.

John M. Forzani

CONSOLIDATED STATEMENTS OF OPERATIONS AND RETAINED EARNINGS
(in thousands, except share data)
(audited, except where otherwise noted)

	For the 53 weeks ended February 2, 2003	For the 52 weeks ended January 27, 2002
Corporate and Franchise Retail Sales (unaudited – Note 12)	$ 1,053,449	$ 876,434
Revenue		
Corporate	$ 715,003	$ 579,196
Franchise	208,792	179,061
	923,795	758,257
Cost of sales	603,326	497,758
Gross margin	320,469	260,499
Operating and administrative expenses		
Store operating	177,252	142,788
General and administrative	60,230	55,215
	237,482	190,003
Operating earnings before undernoted items	82,987	62,496
Amortization	29,624	22,574
Interest	4,354	4,901
Gain on sale of investments (Note 13)	(1,454)	-
	32,524	27,475
Earnings before income taxes	50,463	35,021
Provision for (recovery of) income taxes (Note 10)		
Current	22,133	6,434
Future	(2,201)	7,958
	19,932	14,392
Net earnings	30,531	20,629
Retained earnings, opening	48,326	27,697
Retained earnings, closing	$ 78,857	$ 48,326
Earnings per share	$ 1.01	$ 0.76
Diluted earnings per share	$ 0.96	$ 0.74
Total number of common shares outstanding	30,787,179	27,622,447
Weighted average number of common shares outstanding	30,082,408	27,085,234

A FOCUSED DIRECTION

CONSOLIDATED STATEMENTS OF CASH FLOWS

(in thousands)
(audited)

	For the 53 weeks ended February 2, 2003	For the 52 weeks ended January 27, 2002
Cash provided by (used in) operating activities		
Net earnings	$30,531	$ 20,629
Items not involving cash		
Amortization	29,624	22,574
Amortization of finance charges	571	181
Amortization of deferred lease inducements	(8,767)	(6,394)
Gain on sale of investment	(1,445)	-
Future income tax expense	(2,201)	7,958
Cash flow from operations (Note 9 (c))	48,313	44,948
Changes in non-cash elements of working capital (Note 8)	(27,300)	(24,161)
	21,013	20,787
Cash provided by (used in) financing activities		
Proceeds from issuance of share capital	40,416	1,311
Principal repayment of long-term debt	(13,786)	(2,683)
(Decrease) increase in revolving credit facility	(12,890)	17,094
Proceeds from deferred lease inducements	14,395	11,559
	28,135	27,281
Cash provided by (used in) investing activities		
Addition of capital assets	(50,085)	(40,791)
Addition of other assets	(1,186)	(1,710)
Acquisition of wholly owned subsidiary, net of cash acquired (Note 14)	-	(18,518)
Sale of investments	1,690	-
Disposal of capital assets	276	347
Disposal of other assets	186	68
	(49,119)	(60,604)
Increase (decrease) in cash	29	(12,536)
Net cash position, opening	494	13,030
Net cash position, closing	$ 523	$ 494

Supplementary cash flow information (Note 8)

NOTES TO CONSOLIDATED FINANCIAL STATEMENTS (Tabular amounts in thousands, except share data)

1. Nature of Operations

The Forzani Group Ltd. "FGL" or "the Company" is Canada's largest sporting goods retailer. FGL currently operates 215 corporate stores under the banners: Sport Chek, Sport Mart, Coast Mountain Sports, and Forzani's. The Company is also the franchisor of 161 stores under the banners: Sports Experts, Intersport, R'n'R, Econosports and Atmosphere. FGL operates two websites, dedicated to the Canadian online sporting goods market, at www.sportchek.ca and www.sportmart.ca.

2. Significant Accounting Policies

The consolidated financial statements have been prepared by management in accordance with Canadian generally accepted accounting principles. The financial statements have, in management's opinion, been prepared within reasonable limits of materiality and within the framework of the accounting policies summarized below:

(a)   Organization

The consolidated financial statements include the accounts of The Forzani Group Ltd. and its subsidiaries, all of which are wholly owned.

(b)   Inventory

Inventory is valued at the lower of laid-down cost and net realizable value. Laid-down cost is determined using the weighted average cost method and includes invoice cost, duties, freight, and distribution costs. Net realizable value is defined as the expected selling price.

Volume rebates and other supplier discounts are included in income when earned.

(c)   Capital assets

Capital assets are recorded at cost and are amortized using the following methods and rates:

- Building - 4% declining-balance basis
- Building on leased land - 20 years straight-line basis
- Furniture, fixtures, equipment and automotive - straight-line basis over 3-5 years
- Leasehold improvements - straight-line basis over the lesser of the length of the lease and estimated useful life of the improvements, not exceeding 10 years

(d)   Goodwill and other intangibles

Goodwill represents the excess of the purchase price over the fair market value of the identifiable net assets acquired. Goodwill and other intangible assets, with indefinite lives, are not amortized, but tested for impairment at least annually, at year end, and, if required, asset values reduced accordingly.

The method used to assess impairment is a review of the profitability of the assets acquired.

Non-competition agreement costs are being amortized, on a straight-line basis, over the five-year life of the agreements.

(e)   Other assets (see Note 5)

Other assets include financing costs, system and interactive development costs, long-term receivables, and an investment in a wholesale distribution company.

Interactive development costs relate to the development of the sportchek.ca interactive web site, designed as a part of the Company's multi-channel retailing and branding strategy. These costs are being amortized over five years following the commencement of the web site's operations in June, 2001.

Financing costs represent fees incurred in establishing the Company's revolving credit facility. These costs are being amortized over the term of the facility.

System development costs relate to the implementation of software. Upon activation, costs are amortized over the estimated useful lives of the systems.

Long-term receivables are carried at cost less a valuation allowance.

A FOCUSED DIRECTION

The investment in shares of a wholesale distribution company is carried at cost and periodically reviewed for impairment. The method used to assess impairment is a review of the operation's profitability.

(f)   Deferred lease inducements
Deferred lease inducements represent cash and non-cash benefits that the Company has received from landlords pursuant to store lease agreements. These lease inducements are amortized against rent expense over the term of the lease, not exceeding 10 years.

(g)   Revenue recognition
Revenue includes sales to customers through corporate stores operated by the Company and sales to, and service fees from, franchise stores. Sales to customers through corporate stores operated by the Company are recognized at the point of sale, net of an estimated allowance for sales returns. Sales of merchandise to franchise stores are recognized at the time of shipment. Royalties and administration fees are recognized when earned, in accordance with the terms of the franchise agreements.

(h)   Store opening expenses
Operating costs incurred prior to the opening of new stores are expensed as incurred.

(i)   Fiscal year
The Company's fiscal year follows the retail calendar. The fiscal years for the consolidated financial statements presented are the 53-week period ended February 2, 2003 and the 52-week period ended January 27, 2002.

(j)   Foreign currency translation
Foreign currency accounts are translated to Canadian dollars as follows:

At the transaction date, each asset, liability, revenue or expense is translated into Canadian dollars by the use of the exchange rate in effect at that date. At the year-end date, monetary assets and liabilities are translated into Canadian dollars by using the exchange rate in effect at that date and the resulting foreign exchange gains and losses are included in income in the current period. The amendments to Foreign Currency Translation, of the Canadian Institute of Chartered Accountants, "CICA", Handbook Section 1650, applicable January 1, 2002, did not have an impact on the Company's operations.

(k)   Financial instruments (see Notes 7 and 16)
Accounts receivable, accounts payable and accrued liabilities, long-term debt and derivative transactions, constitute financial instruments. The Company also, in the normal course of business, enters into leases in respect of real estate and certain point-of-sale equipment.

The Company enters into forward contracts and options, with financial institutions, as hedges of other financial transactions and not for speculative purposes. The Company's policies do not allow leveraged transactions and are designed to minimize foreign currency risk. The Company's policies require all hedges to be linked with specific liabilities on the balance sheet and to be assessed, both at inception, and on an ongoing basis, as to their effectiveness in offsetting changes in the fair values or cash flows of the hedged liabilities.

(l)   Measurement uncertainty
The amounts recorded for amortization of capital assets, the provision for shrinkage and obsolescence of inventory are based on estimates. By their nature, these estimates are subject to measurement uncertainty and the impact on the consolidated financial statements of future periods could be material.

(m)   Stock Option Plan
The Company has a stock option plan as described in Note 9 (d). No compensation expense is recognized when stock options are issued to employees. Any consideration paid by employees on the exercise of stock options is credited to share capital.

(n)   Income taxes (see Note 10)
The Company follows the liability method under which future income taxes and obligations are determined based on differences between the financial reporting and tax basis of assets and liabilities, measured using tax rates substantively enacted at the balance sheet date.

FORZANI ANNUAL REPORT F2003

(o) **Employee Profit Sharing Plan (see Note 9(e))**

The Company has an Employee Profit Sharing Plan that causes an amount no less than 1%, and no greater than 5%, of consolidated earnings before income taxes, to be paid to a Trustee for the purchase of shares of the Company. These shares are distributed to participating employees on a predetermined basis, upon retirement from the Company. Compensation expense is recognized when such contributions are made.

(p) **Comparative Figures**

Certain 2002 comparative figures have been reclassified to conform with the current year's presentation.

3. Capital Assets

	2003 Cost	2003 Accumulated Amortization	2003 Net Book Value	2002 Cost	2002 Accumulated Amortization	2002 Net Book Value
Land	$ 638	$ -	$ 638	$ 638	$ -	$ 638
Buildings	6,280	1,637	4,643	6,036	1,406	4,630
Building on leased land	3,159	1,186	1,973	3,159	1,029	2,130
Furniture, fixtures, equipment and automotive	97,117	52,438	44,679	74,330	39,778	34,552
Leasehold Improvements	145,150	54,847	90,303	119,079	40,504	78,575
	$ 252,344	$ 110,108	$ 142,236	$ 203,242	$ 82,717	$ 120,525

4. Goodwill and Other Intangible Assets

	2003	2002
Goodwill	$21,319	$19,438
Trademarks/Tradenames	16,702	16,702
Non-competition agreements	3,000	3,000
	41,021	39,140
Less accumulated amortization	2,337	1,746
	$38,684	$37,394

During the prior fiscal year, the Company adopted new CICA standards on "Goodwill and Other Intangible Assets". Under the new accounting standards, goodwill and other intangible assets with indefinite lives are no longer amortized, but are tested for impairment at least annually. At year end, there was no impairment of goodwill and other intangible assets. Prior to the January 29, 2002 adoption of CICA Handbook requirements for goodwill and other intangible assets, the Company amortized pre-existing trademarks over ten years and pre-existing goodwill over five years, each on a straight-line basis.

In accordance with the transitional provisions of the new standards, CICA 3062, the following is a summary of the fiscal 2002 comparable 52-week period, net earnings and earnings per share, had the new standards been applied retroactively to January 29, 2001.

	For the 52-week Period ended 27-Jan-02 (previously reported)	For the 52-week Period ended 27-Jan-02 (restated)
Earnings before income taxes	$35,021	$35,021
Amortization of goodwill	-	552
Earnings before income taxes	$35,021	$35,573
Provision for income taxes	14,392	14,619
Net earnings	$20,629	$20,954
Earnings per share	$0.76	
Earnings per share adjusted		$0.77

A FOCUSED DIRECTION

5.   Other Assets

	2003	2002
Interactive development	$2,649	$2,649
Deferred financing charges	2,124	1,397
System development	1,471	1,121
	6,244	5,167
Less accumulated amortization	2,246	960
	3,998	4,207
Long-term receivables	950	1,005
Investment in shares of a wholesale distribution company	2,504	2,900
	$7,452	$8,112

6.   Indebtedness

The Company has a $140 million credit facility with General Electric Capital Canada Inc. (G.E.) and National Bank of Canada, comprised of a $115 million revolving loan and a $25 million term loan repayable at maturity on December 20, 2003. Under the terms of the credit agreement, the interest rate payable on both the revolving and term loans is based on the Company's financial performance as determined by its interest coverage ratio. As at February 2, 2003, the interest rate paid was 4.5%. The facility is secured by general security agreements against all existing and future acquired assets of the Company. As at February 2, 2003, the Company is in compliance with all covenants.

Subsequent to the fiscal year end, on February 3, 2003, the Company extended its existing credit agreement to February 3, 2006. This agreement with G.E. was amended to: assign a 21.43% pro rata share of the revolving credit facility and term loan to each of National Bank of Canada and The Royal Bank of Canada and; grant an increase of the maximum revolving credit commitment to $150 million via the exercising of a single, irreversible option.

7.   Long-term Debt

	2003	2002
G.E. term loan (see Note 6)	$25,000	$25,000
Vendor take-back re: Sport Mart acquisition, with interest rates from prime plus 1% to prime plus 2% (see Note 14)	7,039	15,000
Various long-term debts, with interest rates from prime plus 1.5% to prime plus 2%	-	5,490
Mortgages, with monthly blended payments of $52,611, including interest at rates from approximately 7% to 10%, compounded semi-annually, supported by land and buildings, renewable July 1, 2004 and August 1, 2005.	3,631	3,966
Security Deposits	30	30
	35,700	49,486
Less current portion	3,638	14,032
	$32,062	$35,454

Principal payments on the above mortgages due in the next five years, assuming the mortgages continue to be renewed on similar terms, are as follows:

2004	$370
2005	$404
2006	$296
2007	$169
2008	$182

Based on estimated interest rates currently available to the Company for mortgages with similar terms and maturities, the fair value of the mortgages at February 2, 2003 amounted to approximately $3,600,000 (2002 - $3,966,000). Interest costs incurred for the 53-week period ended February 2, 2003 on long-term debt amounted to $2,330,983 (2002 - $2,312,906). The fair value of the other long-term debt components above, approximates book value.

FORZANI ANNUAL REPORT F2003

8. Supplementary Cash Flow Information

	2003	2002
Changes in non-cash elements of working capital		
Accounts receivable	$ (2,287)	$ (3,044)
Inventory	(39,249)	(50,130)
Prepaid and other expenses	(6,642)	942
Accounts payable	20,878	28,071
	$(27,300)	$(24,161)
Cash interest paid	$ 5,195	$ 5,190
Cash taxes paid	$ 14,897	$ 790

9. Share Capital

(a)   Authorized

An unlimited number of Class A shares

An unlimited number of Preferred shares, issuable in series

(b)   Issued

Class A shares

	Number	Consideration
Balance, January 28, 2001	26,918,448	$ 02,408
Shares issued upon employees exercising stock options	703,999	1,311
Balance, January 27, 2002	27,622,447	83,719
Shares issued upon employees exercising stock options	664,732	2,817
Shares issued March 26, 2002 upon public stock offer		
(net of issuance costs and related future income tax)	2,500,000	38,330
	30,787,179	$124,866

(c)   Earnings and Cash Flow Per Share [1]

	2003	2002
Earnings Per Share		
Basic	$1.01	$0.76
Diluted	$0.96	$0.74
Cash Flow Per Share		
Basic	$1.61	$1.66
Diluted	$1.53	$1.61
Weighted average number of common shares outstanding		
Basic	30,082,408	27,085,234
Diluted	31,678,044	27,944,114
Common shares outstanding		
Basic	30,787,179	27,622,447
Diluted	32,382,815	28,481,327

Diluted calculations assume that options under the stock option plan have been exercised at the later of the beginning of the year or date of issuance, and that the funds derived therefrom would have been used to repurchase shares at the average market value of the Company's stock, 2003 - $19.55 (2002 - $8.33).

(1) Cash flow per share is a not a recognized measure under Canadian generally accepted accounting principles. Cash flow per share is defined to be cash flow from operations before non-cash changes in working capital divided by the weighted average shares outstanding. Management believes that cash flow per share is a key measure, as it demonstrates the Company's ability to generate cash flow necessary to fund future growth.

(d)   Stock Option Plan

The Company has granted stock options to directors, officers and employees to purchase 2,437,968 Class A shares at prices between $3.00 and $22.06 per share. These options expire on dates between March 31, 2003 and June 5, 2007.

A summary of the status of the Company's stock option plan as of February 2, 2003 and January 27, 2002, and any changes during the year ending on those dates is presented in the following table:

Stock Options	2003 Shares	2003 Weighted Average Exercise Price	2002 Shares	2002 Weighted Average Exercise Price
Outstanding, beginning of year	1,997,700	$4.84	2,109,233	$3.13
Granted	1,105,000	$8.88	595,800	$7.37
Exercised	664,732	$4.24	703,999	$1.86
Forfeited	-	-	3,334	$3.81
Outstanding, end of year	2,437,968	$6.81	1,997,700	$4.84
Options exercisable at year end	1,103,482		935,247	

The following table summarizes information about stock options outstanding at February 2, 2003:

Range of Exercise Prices	Options Outstanding Number Outstanding	Options Outstanding Weighted Average Remaining Contractual Life	Options Outstanding Weighted Average Exercise Price	Options Exercisable Number of Shares Exercisable	Options Exercisable Weighted Average Exercise Price
$3.00 - $3.90	1,162,000	0.9 years	$3.25	682,000	$3.40
$4.16 - $4.26	393,501	1.3 years	$4.23	193,500	$4.20
$6.18 - $14.65	697,467	3.8 years	$11.21	227,982	$11.36
$16.49 - $22.06	185,000	4.2 years	$18.00	-	-
	2,437,968			1,103,482	

The Company does not recognize an expense in the financial statements, for share options granted to employees and directors, when issued at market value.

Effective January 1, 2002 , Canadian generally accepted accounting principles require disclosure of the impact on net earnings, using the fair-value method, for stock options issued on or after January 1, 2002. If the fair-value method had been used, the effect on the Company's net earnings and earnings per share, for the 53-week period ended February 2, 2003, would have been as follows, if the expense had been realized based on the number of stock options granted in the period (the pro forma amounts):

	For the 53-week period ended February 2, 2003
Net earnings - as reported	$30,531
- pro forma	$30,201
Earnings per share - as reported	$1.01
- pro forma	$1.00
Diluted earnings per share - as reported	$0.96
- pro forma	$0.95

(e)   **Employee Profit Sharing Plan**

Under the terms of the Employee Profit Sharing Plan the Company has accrued $1,000,000 for the purchase of shares, in trust, for distribution to participating employees.

10. Income Taxes

The components of the future income tax asset (liability) amount as at February 2, 2003 and January 27, 2002, are as follows:

	2003	2002
Current assets	$ (4,610)	$ (3,567)
Capital and other assets	(14,776)	(14,733)
Tax benefit of share issuance costs	556	-
Deferred lease inducements	17,769	16,279
Future income tax liability	$ (1,061)	$ (2,021)

A reconciliation of income taxes at the combined statutory federal and provincial tax rate to the actual income tax rate is as follows:

	2003		2002	
Federal and provincial income taxes	$19,222	38.10%	$ 13,856	39.60%
Increase (decrease) resulting from:				
Effect of substantively enacted tax rate changes	451	0.90%	48	0.10%
Permanent differences	(60)	(0.10)%	317	0.90%
Other, net	319	0.60%	171	0.50%
Provision for income taxes	$19,932	39.50%	$ 14,392	41.10%

Federal Part I.3 tax and provincial capital tax expense in the amount of $960,000 (2002 - $790,000) is included in operating expenses.

11. Commitments

(a) The Company is committed, at February 2, 2003, to minimum payments under long-term real property leases for the next five years as follows:

	Gross
2004	$55,251
2005	$51,638
2006	$50,165
2007	$47,827
2008	$47,005

In addition, the Company may be obligated to pay percentage rent under certain of the leases.

(b) As at February 2, 2003, the Company has open letters of credit for purchases of inventory of approximately $3,031,000 (2002 - $3,735,000).

The Company has entered into long-term lease agreements for the rental of data processing hardware and software equipment. The leases, expiring at various dates until 2007, call for minimum lease payments of, $3,799,413 in 2004, $2,456,400 in 2005, $1,793,500 in 2006, and $218,700 in 2007.

12. Corporate and Franchise Retail Sales

Total corporate and franchise retail sales have been shown on the Consolidated Statements of Operations and Retained Earnings to indicate the size of the Company's total retail sales level (on an unaudited basis). Only revenue from corporately owned stores, wholesale sales to, and fees from, franchisees are included in the Consolidated Statements of Operations and Retained Earnings.

13. Sale of Investment

During the year, the Company sold its investment in a wholesale distribution operation. The Company held 668,668 common and 334,334 series C preferred shares, which were valued at $2,899,800. The Company received consideration of $1,690,100 and 234,771 shares in a publicly traded wholesale distribution company, resulting in a pre-tax gain of $1,445,000. Subsequent to the initial transaction, 13,400 shares of the 234,771 received were sold, for a gain of $9,000, resulting in an overall pre-tax gain on sale of investments, of $1,454,000.

14.   Acquisition

Effective August 1, 2001, the Company acquired all of the outstanding shares of Sport Mart Inc. This acquisition has been accounted for using the purchase method and accordingly the consolidated financial statements include the results of operations since the date of acquisition.

The purchase of all of the outstanding common; class B and preference shares, 9,891,267; 368 and 17,761,718 shares respectively, was made for a consideration of $35 million, consisting of $20 million cash and a vendor take-back loan of $15 million payable as to $8.5 million on August 1, 2002, $3.0 million on August 1, 2003 and $3.5 million on August 1, 2006. The loan is secured by a general security agreement and bears interest at rates of prime plus 2% on the first and second installments and prime plus 1% on the final installment. The assigned fair values of the underlying assets and liabilities acquired by the Company, as at August 1, 2001, are summarized as follows:

Current assets	$ 24,939
Capital assets	8,704
Trademarks/trade names	16,443
Goodwill	17,938
Non-competition agreements	3,000
Total assets acquired	$ 71,024
Current liabilities	$(24,060)
Long-term liabilities	(8,710)
Future income tax liability	(3,254)
Total liabilities assumed	(36,024)
Total consideration	$ 35,000

15.   Contingencies

(a)   As part of its operations, the Company has entered into agreements with certain franchisees to buy back inventory in the event that the franchisees' bank realizes on related security. The maximum exposure to the Company is limited to the lesser of 75% of the book value of inventory or the franchisees' bank indebtedness. As at February 2, 2003, the maximum exposure was $25,874,232 (2002 - $20,320,000).

(b)   Claims and suits have been brought against the Company in the ordinary course of business. In the opinion of management, all such claims and suits are adequately covered by insurance, or if not so covered, the results are not expected to materially affect the Company's financial position. Any costs to the Company arising from these claims and suits will be charged to earnings in the year in which they occur.

16.   Financial Instruments

The carrying value of the Company's accounts receivable and accounts payable and accrued liabilities approximates, based on available information, fair value as at February 2, 2003.

The Company is exposed to credit risk on its accounts receivable from franchisees. The accounts receivable are net of applicable allowance for doubtful accounts, which are established based on the specific credit risks associated with individual franchisees and other relevant information. Concentration of credit risk with respect to receivables is limited, due to the large number of franchisees.

The Company purchases a portion of its inventory from foreign vendors with payment terms in non-Canadian dollars. To manage the foreign exchange risk associated with these purchases, the Company hedges its exposure to foreign currency by purchasing foreign exchange options and forward contracts to fix exchange rates and protect planned margins. The Company has the following derivative instruments outstanding at February 2, 2003 and January 27, 2002:

FORZANI ANNUAL REPORT F2003

	Notional amounts maturing in			
	Less than 1 year	Over 1 year	**2003 total**	2002 total
Foreign exchange contracts ($CAD)				
United States dollar contracts	**12,712**	-	**12,712**	10,958
EURO contracts	**367**	-	**367**	1,812
Swiss Franc contracts	-	-	-	8
Total	**13,079**	-	**13,079**	12,778

As at February 2, 2003, these instruments had unrealized losses of $0.2 million (2002 - $0.1 million gain).

The Company is exposed to interest risk on its credit facility and the term loan. Interest rate risk reflects the sensitivity of the Company's financial condition to movements in interest rates. For fiscal year 2003, a +/-1% change in interest rates would change interest expense by +/- $292 (2002 +/- $421).

17.   Segmented Financial Information

The Company operates principally in two business segments: corporately-owned and operated retail stores and as franchisor of retail stores. Identifiable assets, depreciation and amortization, interest expense and capital expenditures are not disclosed by segment as they are substantially corporate in nature.

	2003	2002
Revenues:		
Corporate	**$ 715,003**	$ 579,196
Franchise	**208,792**	179,061
	923,795	758,257
Operating Profit:		
Corporate	**87,201**	65,426
Franchise	**16,163**	12,396
	103,364	77,822
Non-segment specific administrative expenses	**20,377**	15,320
Amortization	**29,624**	22,574
Interest expense	**4,354**	4,901
Gain on sale of investments	**(1,454)**	-
	52,901	42,801
Earnings before income taxes	**50,463**	35,021
Income tax expense	**19,932**	14,392
Net Earnings	**$ 30,531**	$ 20,629

18.   Related Party Transaction

The Company has advanced $320,567 (2002-$398,750) to an officer for housing purchase assistance. The advance is being repaid over a four-year term commencing on January 28, 2002 and bears interest at bank prime rate.

Company Index

A cumulative index appears at the end of each Part.

Subject Index

A cumulative index appears at the end of each Part.

Photo Credits